African American Writers
and Classical Tradition

African American Writers and Classical Tradition

WILLIAM W. COOK & JAMES TATUM

The University of Chicago Press | Chicago and London

WILLIAM W. COOK is professor emeritus of English and African and African American studies at Dartmouth.
JAMES TATUM is professor emeritus of classics at Dartmouth.

The University of Chicago Press, Chicago 60637
The University of Chicago Press, Ltd., London
© 2010 by The University of Chicago
All rights reserved. Published 2010
Printed in the United States of America

18 17 16 15 14 13 12 11 10   1 2 3 4 5

ISBN-13: 978-0-226-78996-5 (cloth)
ISBN-10: 0-226-78996-9 (cloth)

Library of Congress Cataloging-in-Publication Data

Cook, William W. (William Wilburt)
    African American writers and classical tradition / William W. Cook and James Tatum.
        p. cm.
    Includes bibliographical references and index.
    ISBN-13: 978-0-226-78996-5 (cloth : alk. paper)
    ISBN-10: 0-226-78996-9 (cloth : alk. paper) 1. American literature—African American authors—History and criticism. 2. American literature—Classical influences. I. Tatum, James. II. Title.
    PS153.N5C665 2010
    810.9'896073—dc22

                                                    2009034995

⊗ The paper used in this publication meets the minimum requirements of the American National Standard for Information Sciences—Permanence of Paper for Printed Library Materials, ANSI Z39.48–1992.

To the memory of Louise Cook Jacobs
1931–1993
beloved sister and friend

Contents

There can be no doubt that in art no small portion of our task lies in imitation, since, although invention came first and is all-important, it is expedient to imitate whatever has been invented with success. And it is a universal rule of life that we should wish to copy what we approve in others. It is for this reason that children copy the shapes of letters that they may learn to write, and that musicians take the voices of their teachers, painters the works of their predecessors, and farmers the principles of agriculture which have been proved in practice, as models for their imitation. In fact, we may note that the elementary study of every branch of learning is directed by reference to some definite standard that is placed before the learner. We must, in fact, either be like or unlike those who have proved their excellence.

Quintilian

Introduction

One of the earliest reviews of African American writers and classical tradition appeared in 1784 in Thomas Jefferson's *Notes on the State of Virginia*. It was not favorable: "Religion, indeed, has produced a Phyllis Wheatley; but it could not produce a poet. The compositions published under her name are below the dignity of criticism." That such poetry was intimately related to Greek and Latin literature needed no explanation in 1784, since classical myths and poetry played a central role in every educated person's life in colonial America, including Jefferson's. In plainer English, he means that Wheatley's work isn't worth judging, period. The reviewer walks out of the theater, he doesn't file a review. Jefferson figures importantly in Henry Louis Gates's recent book about the fate of Phillis Wheatley's work from her own day to the present. His reaction to the upstart Wheatley was also prophetic of a more general response of Americans and Western Europeans to the very notion that African Americans could or would engage with classical literature.

This book traces the interaction between African American writers and the literature of ancient Greece and Rome, from Phillis Wheatley and her *Poems on Various Subjects, Religious and Moral* (1773) to Rita Dove's book of sonnets, *Mother Love* (1995). A basic theme throughout is the changing American reception of Greek and Latin literature, especially as it was inflected by American racial politics and the accessibility of classical learning and literature to African Americans in the times of slavery and slavery's aftermath.

What classics and the classical could mean also changed, depending on what was available through translations and the educational system of the day. At every moment the constraints on freedom and individual dignity were fundamental in determining who was able to write, and when, and where.

This is also the most recent of several collaborative projects we have engaged in, each of them to be echoed in one way or another in the pages that follow. We began with the translation (by Tatum) and performance (directed by Cook) of Plautine comedies at Dartmouth. In retrospect our then untenured gaze seems to have been drawn to such plays as *Truculentus* (*The Savage Slave*) and *Casina* (*The Battered Bride*) by their constrained subversiveness. They were originally created as entertainment for the slave-owning society of ancient Rome by the actor and playwright Plautus, who enjoyed a social standing little different from the slave-playwrights that animate his comedies. Amateur pianism and African American poetry and its tradition of combined readings and musical performances provided another kind of collaboration. Originally conceived as "Black Talk/Black Tunes," this combo paired folk poetry like "Staggolee," the toast "Titanic," the dozens of "Signifying Monkey," and poets and writers as diverse as Paul Laurence Dunbar, Vachel Lindsay, Sarah Fabio, Langston Hughes, and Gwendolyn Brooks with the rags of Scott Joplin, Artie Matthews, James Scott, Joseph Lamb, and Eubie Blake. We performed this show in a number of venues beyond academe, with Cook's voice and Tatum's piano, at churches and social clubs (often sponsored by Don Evans), at an awards ceremony at Joe Papp's Public Theater in New York, and in a jazz club in New Hope, Pennsylvania, where to our surprise we were the entr'acte for a drag show, "The Male Misstique."

Our project's more immediate origins lie in a course we put together in the early 1990s and taught a number of times thereafter, at Dartmouth as well as at Princeton and Drew Universities (taught by Tatum mostly, with crucial visits by Cook). We learned that to follow these poets and writers in their use of the classical is to put ourselves in Heraclitus's stream. We shall never step into the same story twice.

Here is an example of what we mean. To the extent that any person stolen into slavery could be said to have luck, Phillis Wheatley had it in being sold to the enlightened family of John and Susanna Wheatley, in Boston, as a young girl directly off the French slaver *Phillis*. Starting with not much more than her given names, an amalgam of the name of her slave ship and the family that bought her, she learned to write heroic couplets in the style of Alexander Pope on religious as well as classical themes, and by the age of twenty had published her first book of poetry. The slave that history knows as Frederick Douglass, by contrast, was not even supposed to learn to read and write, still less to learn classical rhetoric. He tells us how he did both in his 1845 *Narrative*, by a canny combination of unobtrusive learning on the sly from little white boys his age, and by acquiring a copy of *The Columbian Orator*, Caleb Bingham's 1797 handbook designed to teach rhetoric to the young citizens of the new American republic.

The contrast between Wheatley and Douglass underscores our point, that it would be a mistake to think there was some single notion of Greco-Roman classics informing African American writers. Whereas Wheatley was invited to read and imitate not only Pope and Milton, but classical poets like Horace, Vergil, and Ovid, Douglass was not a classicist at all and never aspired to be identified with a tradition of learning that would come to seem increasingly arcane in the popular culture of his day. Nonetheless he quickly learned how to construct periodic sentences that would equal those of any Roman or English orator, through what educational theorists have identified as deutero- or secondary learning. Aiming to become an effective orator and writer by studying and memorizing the many exemplary speeches and dialogues of the *Orator*, he acquired what classically trained orators regarded as essential skills for anyone engaged in public life in the complementary arts of rhetoric and dialectic. Douglass uses none of this learned terminology in talking about his self-education (nor had Bingham), yet his absorption of these quintessentially classical arts was profound and far-reaching in its consequences.

The learning of Greek and Latin was a basic part of American secondary and collegiate education until after the beginnings of the twentieth century. African American scholars who could gain an education in the free North, and more rarely in the slave-owning South, also learned Greek and Latin where they could. The most sustained African American engagement with classics as it was then preached and practiced came after the Civil War and Reconstruction, up to the 1920s. W. E. B. Du Bois learned his classics at Fisk University, then switched to the new international discipline of sociology after he studied at Harvard and later at Berlin. He makes frequent use of his classical learning in his earlier works, above all in *The Souls of Black Folk*. The older professional classicist William Sanders Scarborough had grown up in slavery and earned his MA from Oberlin. An important and representative figure in African American education and political life, Scarborough was a founding member of the Modern Language Association and one of the first black members of the American Philological Association (APA), where he made his debut with a scholarly paper in 1884 at its meeting at Dartmouth.

As Horace might put it, nothing is happy in every respect—not least the kind of learning that enables one to allude to Horace. At the same time that Scarborough and Du Bois were arguing so strenuously for the advantages of classical learning and literature, there appeared a number of works by prominent African American writers and poets who did not engage so profoundly with Greece and Rome. Famous mythical figures and their tragedies would be invoked, only to have their potential effectiveness and the power of such texts as the *Oedipus* or the *Medea* dissipated in clouds of gentility and timid learning; tales of incest turn out not to be about incest after all; family murders become lapses in good taste. Classicists and people wanting the respectability of knowing about them in white America also engaged in the same kind of careful, discreet learning, so it is no surprise that some of the most educationally privileged African Americans, having gained the right to liberal education and the social and intellectual status it could confer, proceeded to embrace gentility just as eagerly. Here are familiar figures whose best work—or at least what they are best remembered for—lay elsewhere, such as Jessie Fauset, Countee Cullen, and even Du Bois himself, in an economic treatise cast into the form of a long romance, *The Quest of the Silver Fleece*.

In the second half of the book (chapters 5 through 8) the story becomes more complex, because we find writers who begin to blend classical and African American folktale and African myth into single works. While Ralph Ellison's landmark novel *Invisible Man* (1951) works in explicit dialogue with Greek myth and poetry, some novels of Toni Morrison, such as *Song of Solomon* (1977) and *Beloved* (1987), consistently downplay these classical connections in ways ably discussed by Patrice Rankine in his recent *Ulysses in Black* (2006). La Vinia Delois Jennings argues in *Toni Morrison and the Idea of Africa* (2009) even more strongly for Morrison's engagement with African myth and ritual. By contrast, the younger Rita Dove has created explicitly classically themed works across several genres: novel (*Through the Ivory Gate*, 1992), drama (*The Darker Face of the Earth*, 1994; final revised version, 2000) and an homage and response to Rilke's *Sonnets to Orpheus*, the sonnet cycle *Mother Love* (1995).

There are also some less well-known writers who deserve to be better known, not only because of their classical connections but also because of the sheer quality in how they use them. Melvin B. Tolson, whom we stylize as the Pindar of Harlem, is the most important of all these later figures, though he has strong competition from Fran Ross, a contemporary of Richard Pryor and Bill Cosby whose 1974 satiric novel *Oreo* recounts the adventures of a female Theseus in a journey from the Peloponnese of Philadelphia to the Athens of New York City's Upper West Side.

Given these riches, we have necessarily had to be selective. Our last chapter is devoted to Dove, whose work is among the most substantial treatments of classical themes in contemporary poetry. Since each chapter begins with a summary about where it is going and what it aims to say, we will not rehearse further what readers will find for themselves. African American writers' engagement with Greek and Roman antiquity remains as much as ever a work in progress.

We are grateful to students, colleagues and friends whose calls and response over the years have added much to the argument this book seeks to make: Don Evans, Ishmael Reed, Shelley Haley, Betye Saar, David Dorsey, Michele Valerie Ronnick, Catharine Stimpson, Amy Richlin, Andrew Feldherr, Kwame Anthony Appiah, Robert Kaster, Valerie Smith, Noliwe Rooks, Joy Connolly, Costanze Güthenke, Helene Foley, Deborah Roberts, Myra Jehlen, Marilyn Young, Margaret Williamson, Roberta Stewart, Rose MacLean, Hans Hansen, Cirri Nottage, Kristina Guild, Jon Schroeder, Lee Reitelman, Johanna Edge, Froma Zeitlin, Charles Rowan Beye, Mary DeForest, Susan Ford Wiltshire, Shane Butler, William Noble, and residents at the Rockefeller Foundation's center at Bellagio in the fall of 2006. The librarians of Baker-Berry Library at Dartmouth and Firestone Library at Princeton were unfailingly helpful at every stage, as were their colleagues in the New York Public Library and its Schomburg Center for the Study of Black Culture. Costanze Güthenke, Michele Ronnick, Bob Kaster, and Jane Taylor read a draft with exceptional care and offered many helpful suggestions.

Dartmouth has supported our research and teaching on this subject from first to last. We are particularly grateful to our editor Susan Bielstein for her encouragement and wise counsel, as well as her sagacity in choosing Chicago's anonymous readers. They were so helpful, and their threshold of pain so high, that they came to seem as much this book's hidden collaborators as its referees. Carol Saller provided expert copyediting and was appropriately subversive where necessary.

Along the way sympathetic friends have asked how we planned to divide our work. We still don't know. At this point we are too far advanced to put asunder what was long ago joined together. If some division of labor is desired, however, imagine that this time Tatum provides the words, while Cook supplies the music.

The Leisure Moments of
Phillis Wheatley

The following Poems were written originally for the Amusement of
the Author, as they were the Products of her leisure Moments.
Poems on Various Subjects, Religious and Moral

The poet history knows as Phillis Wheatley was born about 1753 in Western Africa, in today's Gambia or Ghana. Her first name came to her from
the French slave ship *Phillis* that brought her as a young girl to Boston in
1761. As usual with American slaves her surname was given her by John and
Susanna Wheatley, who bought her for domestic service. A few tantalizing references here and there in her poetry possibly refer to a childhood
in Africa, but the world she actually wrote about was the English colonial
city of Boston and its political and religious connections to London and
her English patrons. She was taught to read by John and Susanna's daughter, Mary, and her range of learning quickly expanded beyond ABCs. With
her first published poem in 1765 and a widely admired funeral elegy for the
evangelist George Whitefield in 1770, she proved to be a precocious student of the Bible and the neoclassical poetry of Milton, Dryden, and Alexander Pope, as well as of Pope's translation of Homer and Dryden's Vergil.
In the authenticating preface to *Poems on Various Subjects* John Wheatley
reports that she was learning Latin. How much Latin she learned and how
widely she read is a matter for speculation. As is often the case with poets,
a scholar's expertise in the language did not prove to be of much moment.

She lived in a time when detailed commentaries and literal prose translations as well as poetic imitations were available for all the major classical
poets. With the support of Whitefield's English patron Selina Hastings,
the Countess of Huntingdon, Wheatley published her first book of poems
in London in 1773. *Poems on Various Subjects, Religious and Moral* gathered
new and previously published poems and opened with "To Maecenas," a
bold imitation of the famous opening poem of Horace's *Odes*. With the
coming of the American Revolution she shifted her political allegiance in
the poem "To His Excellency George Washington," and some correspondence between them is preserved. These proved to be the high points of
her artistic life. Within a few years after her return from London both Susanna and John Wheatley were dead, and she was free in fact if not by formal emancipation to marry the freed black slave John Peters, in 1778. She
hoped to publish a second volume of poetry but never found the sponsors
for it. Phillis was not able to make a living on her own; nor was her husband. They had three children and all of them died, with Phillis Wheatley
Peters herself dying with her youngest child in December 1784. She was
buried in an unmarked grave in Boston.

Wheatley's remark in the preface to her volume about her leisure moments is notable in two ways. Leisure is not something a slave should have.
It is not appropriate or even allowable for such an economic entity to consider that she has such a thing as leisure at her disposal. More to the point
of our reading of this neoclassical poet, the leisure time that literature
requires recalls a familiar Roman scenario for the philosophical and literary pursuits of *liberi*, free people. When a slave in Plautus's comedies talks
about his *otium*, his "free time," he is making a joke. Wheatley's "leisure" is
the Latin *otium*, which could mean something pejorative, such as idleness,
but when used in connection with poetry it has a positive sense: freedom
from work, freedom to enjoy the fruits of a liberal education devoted to
cultural pursuits like philosophy and the writing of poetry.

In this opening chapter we focus on three poems that show Wheatley's
neoclassical poetics at its most accomplished, as well as some evidence
for the way she refined and revised her work from earlier drafts to the
final published version: the signature opening poem "To Maecenas," modeled after Horace's first *Ode* to Maecenas and Vergil's first *Eclogue*; her Miltonic treatment of the David and Goliath story from the Bible, "Goliath
of Gath," which incidentally has a number of suggestive parallels with the
boasting contests of the early West African epic *Sundiata*; and "Niobe in
Distress for Her Children Slain by Apollo," a free imitation of Ovid also
inspired by Richard Wilson's painting of the slaying of Niobe's children.

Wheatley's "Niobe" transforms Ovid's story in the *Metamorphoses* into a miniature epic by an adroit appropriation of the opening of Pope's 1725 translation of the *Iliad*. The Wrath of Achilles and the pains thousandfold it brought upon the Achaeans become the story of the Wrath of Apollo that destroys Niobe and her children.

The texture of this first chapter is much shaped by the particular art it describes, the versifying of a young provincial poet of great promise, possibly even genius. Her poetry demands that we learn to think with her and, for the space of this chapter at least, read poetry like her, and that is no simple thing. The conventions of eighteenth-century English prosody can be as remote and unfamiliar to present-day readers as the most difficult contemporary poetry. As in the next chapter's discussion of the complexities of Frederick Douglass's periodic style, we believe nothing less detailed could do justice to their art.

The Color Black

> Is not a Patron, my Lord, one who looks with unconcern on a Man struggling for Life in the water and when he has reached ground encumbers him with help?
>
> Samuel Johnson to Lord Chesterfield, 1755

The first African American to publish a book of poetry with classical themes worked under severe limitations. It was widely believed that people of African descent could not read poetry or understand art, let alone create them. Thomas Jefferson conceded that blacks could deliver themselves of spontaneous bursts of emotion, but he did not believe they were capable of the intellect and concentration that great art requires. Phillis Wheatley had her defenders then and later, but Jefferson's passing comment remains the single most quoted passage in Wheatley criticism, simply because it was Jefferson who wrote it. Many of the poems in *Poems on Various Subjects, Moral and Religious* in fact confirm his comment about the sincerity of her religion. Her verse is nothing if not devout, and many of her poems celebrate Christian themes. We would expect nothing less of a beginner schooled in Puritan classicism, with models like Milton and his sublime blend of the classical and the biblical.[1] Her best poems suggest a precocious talent for a twenty-year-old. Skill in versifying religious subjects was expected of a Christian poet. Engagement with classical myth and literature was every bit as important for her art as the Bible, but even then she could expect many of her readers to read something like her imitation of Ovid in "Niobe in Distress" strictly as a neoclassical moral narrative which employed a classic mainly as a pretext to teach Christian values like humility and obedience to God.

After Jefferson, the less religion counted in critical estimations of her poetry, the less Wheatley's standing even as a Christian. For much of the nineteenth century and nearly all of the twentieth, her reputation was not enhanced by her piety. To incredulous readers during the civil rights era and later she came to seem more and more a poet who had actually embraced slavery. The question of color and race was at the center of much negative criticism of Wheatley, not least because she seemed to deal with it so clearly in her poetry.

The most frequently anthologized—and certainly the most maligned— of her poems are two that seem to refer directly to race. "On Being Brought from Africa" is a tribute for God's grace in bringing her from Africa to America and the Christian's faith ("'Twas Mercy brought me from my *Pagan* land") and "To the University of Cambridge" (Harvard), where she speaks as an "Ethiope" determined to give moral instruction to the university's young students.

The problem with all this modern outrage at Wheatley's betrayal of the race is that her verbal signifiers for race did not center on the word "black" in its current sense. She limited her use of racial labels to those found in the Bible. The most frequent such markers in her poetry are "Ethiopian" and its variants and "African" in a variety of forms. She uses "black" not so much to refer to race, but as a sign of a depraved spiritual condition. Negative moral connotations of the word "black" are documented well into the nineteenth century, as in the work of Frédéric Portal and Paillot de Montabert. In his 1837 book on color symbolism in art, Portal observes:

> Symbol of evil and falsity, black is not a color, but rather the negation of all nuances and what they represent. Thus red represents divine love, but united to black it represents infernal love, egotism, hatred and all the passions of degraded man. Symbolic of error, of nothingness . . . black is the negation of light, it has been attributed to the author of all evil and falsity.[2]

Wheatley rejects the argument of many of her contemporaries that Africans were soulless, that redemption was not intended to include them. "On Being Brought" places this argument in the mouth of seemingly nameless others.

Some view our sable race with scornful eye,
"Their colour is a diabolic die."

And then she answers them. Her fellow Christians are responsible for this confusion about the color black.

Remember, *Christians*, *Negros*, black as *Cain*,
May be refin'd, and join th'angelic train.

Wheatley wrote this poem in the midst of fierce contemporary arguments over the wisdom of preaching to slaves and converting them. Many of the opposition voices questioned the possibility that Africans even had souls. She does more than celebrate the boundlessness of God's mercy in this short lyric; she also clearly places herself on the positive side of the argument when she notes that her formerly benighted soul now understands its true nature. Rather than a poem apologizing for her African origins, these lines in "On Being Brought" are a confident rebuke to one of the major racist beliefs born of slavery. It is an example of the doctrine of the Fortunate Fall, which argues that what seems the most tragic experience may be transformed into a glorious triumph of redemption.

What a pre-Christian (pagan) imagination might perceive as tragedy is nothing substantial to a Christian's way of thinking. The end of life is not the end of the story, and mortality takes on a different meaning when the certainty of an afterlife beckons. The salvation of the soul, not the end of life itself, is of paramount concern. Unless Wheatley's religion is kept in mind, her verse is easily misread as temporizing, when in fact it was conceived as something that could not be measured by the notions of this world alone.

We can see the same moral and religious scruples in "To the University of Cambridge in New England," which reveals Wheatley as a participant in what Sacvan Bercovitch terms the American jeremiad, a sermon form characterized by an unshakeable optimism.[3] Wheatley's poetry and especially her elegies are most often marked not by lamentation but by joyful resolutions. Movement in the poems almost always favors elevation both physical and spiritual. This is the voice through which Wheatley frequently speaks. Her scolding tone in her address to the Harvard students is the voice of a preacher delivering a sermon, a persona frequently donned by Wheatley. Her Afric muse is a bringer of light and the knowledge of light. As her first stanza demonstrates, her soul's journey has been the familiar Christian's progress from darkness to light.

While an intrinsic ardor prompts to write,
The muses promise to assist my pen;
'Twas not long since I left my native shore
The land of errors, and *Egyptian* gloom:
Father of mercy, 'twas thy gracious hand
Brought me in safety from those dark abodes.

That darkness is specifically "Egyptian" suggests a parallel between that progress and the experience of the Exodus of Israel out of Egypt. The second stanza reminds the students of their experience of light, both the light of earthly knowledge, where astronomy is conflated with heavenly wisdom, and the light of the redeemer. The jeremiad occupies the closing stanza and is firmly in grasp of the truth with its series of imperative statements that close the poem.

Let sin, that baneful evil to the soul,
By you be shunn'd, nor once remit your guard;
Suppress the deadly serpent in its egg.
Ye blooming plants of human race divine,
An *Ethiop* tells you 'tis your greatest foe;
Its transient sweetness turns to endless pain,
And in immense perdition sinks the soul.

Her address to Harvard's future clergymen began in the sublime imagery of astronomy and Jesus; the poet, true to her mission as an eighteenth-century Jeremiah, closes with the counterfate toward which her listeners may be tending. Once again the horror of having been kidnapped into slavery becomes a kind of Fortunate Fall; out of that tragedy has come the superior knowledge of religion and the freedom which she now has also brings the assurance of Christian redemption. Even when she is concerned with a specifically classical theme Wheatley's poetry is never far from a firm linkage with Christian doctrine and the Bible. Her syncretistic readings of scripture and classics always trace connections between both.

Modern anthologists were not interested in this kind of stuff.[4] Until Henry Louis Gates, Jr., and Nellie Y. MacKay's 2003 Norton collection of African American literature, most of them ignored Wheatley's classical poems altogether and had little good to say about much of the rest.

Wheatley herself provides a better introduction to the real scope of her work with "To Maecenas," the opening poem of her volume.[5] It is at once a gracious tribute to a patron and a sophisticated exercise in neoclassical

poetics. While the elaborate prefatory testimonials of prominent Bosto-
nians like John Wheatley and others are certain to be flipped past quickly
by most of her readers today, they were essential for the publication of
Poems on Various Subjects in 1773.[6] We should not flip past them too quickly.
"To Maecenas" is an implicit response to those very authenticating documents. It establishes Wheatley's own voice even as it confirms the claims
those documents make for her art.

Wheatley as Neoclassicist: "To Maecenas"

Mneme in our nocturnal visions pours
The ample treasure of her secret stores;
Swift from above she wings her silent flight
Through Phoebe's realms, fair regent of the night;
And, in her pomp of images display'd,
To the high-raptur'd poet gives her aid,
Through the unbounded regions of the mind,
Diffused light celestial and refin'd.

(Phillis Wheatley, "To Recollection" [*Mneme*])

"To Maecenas" is a free imitation in fifty-five lines of the thirty-six
Latin lines of Horace's ode to his patron, which begins *Maecenas atavis edite regibus* (Maecenas, descendent of kings of old) and turns from praise of
him to a declaration of Horace's ambitious vocation as a poet. Wheatley
opens with a similarly direct address to her own Maecenas (1–6) but departs quickly from Horace's example to range through the classical canon
of great poems whose power she also wants to recall: first to Homer's *Iliad* (7–20), then Maro's (Vergil's) *Aeneid* (21–26). But this is no epic poem,
nor is she fit to sing of her Maecenas in the company of such epic poets
(27–36). She then makes a surprising move, away from the Augustans Horace and Vergil, to Terence "of *Afric*'s sable race" (37–42). He lived a century
before them and was famous for his elegant comedies, but in Wheatley's
poem, he is invoked as her African predecessor poet. She ends by praising
her Maecenas, whose protection she prays to enjoy as long as London's
Thames and all attendant nature endures (43–55).[7]

"To Maecenas" is the most recent poem of the volume, written after
all the rest of *Poems on Various Subjects* had been composed, and those poems themselves are not arranged in a chronological order of composition,
but with some attention to variation of tone and type. It is a *recusatio*, or

confession of an inability to equal one's predecessors, in its claims that
Homer, Horace, and Vergil are not enabling texts for Wheatley, that she is
unworthy to be in their company.

> But I less happy, cannot raise the song,
> The fault'ring music dies upon my tongue. (35–36)

It is poetic convention which she at once invokes even as she claims she
cannot speak through it, and is no more to be taken literally than is Horace's warning in *Odes* 4.2, to would-be rivals of Pindar, not to imitate Pindar. This confession of inability is an artfully created low point that makes
Terence's appearance as her true inspiration at the center of the poem all
the more effective. Lines 1 to 36 record the silencing power of a tradition
in which she found precedents for her poetic efforts; hence the silence.
Then she introduces Terence, the poet and ancestor who will release her
tongue from its "fault'ring" and her mind from "grov'ling." The language of
the poem shifts with this evocation. She speaks of inspiration, grace, virtues, and best of all, the laurel crown of the poet, which will amusingly not
be awarded by the Muse, as Horace and any other classical poet's crown of
leaves would be, but an honor the poet takes for herself.

> While blooming wreaths around thy temples spread,
> I'll snatch a laurel from thine honour'd head,
> While you indulgent smile upon the deed. (45–47)

The triple rhyme underscores the wit of this variation on a familiar theme.
The closing stanza of the poem attests not only to her place as poet but
also to the permanence of that place.

> As long as *Thames* in streams majestic flows,
> Or *Naiads* in their oozy beds repose,
> While *Phoebus* reigns above the starry train,
> While bright *Aurora* purples o'er the main,
> So long, great Sir, the muse thy praise shall sing,
> So long thy praise shall make *Parnassus* ring.

Maecenas links Wheatley to a great line of poets. This is a far cry from
the humility and silence of the opening stanzas of the poem. She has, in
this signature poem, snatched not only the poet's laurel but also her own
definition of self as artist.

Wheatley lived within what the American cultural historian Caroline Winterer terms "The World of Words" in colonial American classicism.[8] For a poet who would write on a classical subject, reading and using classical literature then as now usually entailed a mishmash of translations, commentaries, and other aids, all fortified when desirable by detailed scrutiny of the original. Great English translators like Dryden and Pope tell us explicitly how they did this, and we can assume that Wheatley followed the same path. Attention to detail in prosody and word choice was always expected. Her opening lines demonstrate knowledge of the original Latin, clear grasp of both individual poems and the larger generic traditions they represented, and an understanding of how first words in a classical text serve to define the poem to follow.

> MAECENAS, you, beneath the myrtle shade,
> Read o'er what poets sung, and shepherds play'd.

Maecenas famously begins Horace's poem, from antiquity to the present a name synonymous with exalted literary patronage.

> Maecenas atavis edite regibus,
> o et praesidium et dulce decus meum.

> Maecenas descended from ancient kings, O you who are both the stronghold and sweet ornament of my life.

Wheatley's contemporary the English poet Christopher Smart published an iambic tetrameter version in 1767, capturing much of Horace's line by giving it two shorter lines of his own.

> MAECENAS, of a race renown'd,
> Whose royal ancestors were crown'd;
> O patron of my wealth and praise,
> And pride and pleasure of my days!

Wheatley immediately complicates the Horatian allusion by introducing the pastoral world of Vergil's first *Eclogue*. Because of the exact placement imitating Vergil's second word "you" (*tu*), a poem to Maecenas seems to be veering away from dedicatory lyric to the pastoral world of the *Eclogues*.

> Tityre, tu patulae recubans sub tegmine fagi
> silvestrem tenui musam meditaris avena.

Tityrus, here you loll, your slim reed-pipe serenading
The woodland spirit beneath a spread of sheltering beech.

(C. Day Lewis)

Wheatley's opening marks her shift from the *Ode* to the *Eclogue* by following exactly the poets' Latin words in their original order.[9]

Horace: *Maecenas* [atavis . . .]
Vergil: [Tityre,] *tu* . . .
Wheatley: MAECENAS, you . . .

And there is more to this blending of voices than a fusion of poetic
forms. The *Eclogues* were composed in the years in which Octavian, the
adopted son and heir of Julius Caesar, was rising to power, and before the
turning point in the demise of the Roman Republic, the defeat of Antony
and Cleopatra at the sea battle of Actium in 31 BCE.[10] *Eclogue* 1 begins
with a dialogue between two shepherds with names that suggest they have
stepped out of Vergil's own Greek model, Theocritus's *Idylls*, but it is soon
evident that they are also living in the middle 30s of the Roman Republic,
after the defeat of Sextus Pompey in the year 36.[11] This marked the end of
the civil war between Octavian and his supporters and the factions that
had assassinated Julius Caesar. Meliboeus first speaks, and his voice establishes a profound difference between his fate and that of Tityrus.[12]

Tityre, tu patulae recubans sub tegmine fagi
silvestrem tenui Musam meditaris avena;
nos patriae finis et dulcia linquimus arva.
nos patriam fugimus; tu, Tityre, lentus in umbra
formosam resonare doces Amaryllida silvas. (*Eclogue* 1.1–5)

Tityrus, you, reclining under the protection of a spreading beech, woo the
pastoral muse on slender pipe. We are leaving the bounds of our fatherland and our sweet fields. We are exiled from our fatherland. You, Tityrus,
at ease in the shade, teach the woods to resound "beautiful Amaryllis."
(Michael Putnam trans.)[13]

For all its evocation of the pastoral ease and happiness that Tityrus enjoys,
Meliboeus inhabits a world of loss and exile. Throughout the poem, he
draws one contrast after another between his fate and the prosperity of
Tityrus. He knows only devastation and plunder; Tityrus, only happiness.

What Tityrus has found at Rome is *libertas*, "freedom," as loaded a word in Roman politics as in Wheatley's day. Ostensibly it is freedom from the fair Galatea, who stole Tityrus's freedom from him until he later learned to love Amaryllis. But the older Tityrus went to Rome to be freed from his bondage to Galatea; nowhere else but there could he be freed from the slavery (*servitium*) of love. And there the young Octavian, who is never named, freed him from a lover's slavery. *Libertas* was a slogan appropriated by Octavian's Caesarian party, not too subtly implying that his enemies were opposed to it.

The contrast between the fortunate Tityrus and the hapless Meliboeus could not be clearer. Where one has the blessings of living under "the Youth of Heav'ly Birth" (Dryden), Octavian, the other can only look forward to exile and slavery at the ends of the earth. Meliboeus must become an exile working the fields owned by another, the very essence of chattel slavery, and that fate is nothing to sing about—literally: "No songs shall I sing" (*carmina nulla canam*, 77). Wheatley builds on Vergil's contrast of freedom and servitude, only now it is not the difference between Tityrus and Meliboeus but between the happy state of Maecenas and her own situation.

> But here I sit, and mourn a grov'ling mind
> That fain would mount, and ride upon the wind. (29–30)
> ... I less happy, cannot raise the song,
> The fault'ring music dies upon my tongue. (35–36)

The contrast between the *libertas* of Tityrus and the *servitium* of Meliboeus underlies "To Maecenas" as surely as the public meanings of these words underlie the far-from-innocent talk of the older and younger shepherds in Vergil. At once a figure from Vergilian pastoral and Horatian lyric, Wheatley's Maecenas is credited with the same level of feeling and inspiration as the poets.

> Their noble strains your equal genius shares
> In softer language, and diviner airs. (5–6)

This Maecenas is an artistic soul fully alive to what the poet has created. These lines are about the power of sympathy, and "softer language" and "diviner airs" suggest a feminine rather than masculine sympathy.[14] Something like a feminization of heroic male classicism is also suggested by Wheatley's praise of the power of Homer's art.

When gentler strains demand thy graceful song,
The length'ning line moves languishing along. (15–16)[15]

Her account of the *Iliad* is notable for the episode she chooses to use. It
is not the rage poem of Achilles she invokes—the heroic, epic theme that
plays a major role in "Niobe in Distress"—but rather Patroclus' tears at
the opening of book 16, a passage that was also one of Alexander Pope's
favorites.[16]

When great *Patroclus* courts *Achilles'* aid,
The grateful tribute of my tears is paid;
Prone on the shore he feels the pangs of love,
And stern *Pelides'* tend'rest passions move. (17–20)

The *Aeneid* is passed over in a more cursory fashion. In contrast to her
deep reading of the Patroclus scene, Wheatley's reference to Vergil and
the *Aeneid* in lines 21–30 is about the very idea of the other great epic poet
of classical antiquity, rather than about any salient detail of his work: "O
could I rival thine and *Virgil's* page." An exercise in *recusatio*, that wist-
ful desire to write something grand combined with a confession that one
can't do it, is what the Horatian critic Gregson Davis terms a "generic disavowal." Far from excluding epic, the mere mention of Vergil suggests a
competence to undertake the themes of the most ambitious of all classical
forms. This is as far from a literal confession of inability as it can be.[17] It is
akin to the familiar rhetorical figure of preterition (*praeteritio*), where an
orator passes over something, pretending not to mention it, then mentions it, thereby giving the idea even more prominence than if he had
merely said it without this disingenuous prelude.[18] At first it seems as if
Wheatley aspired to be an epic poet:

Soon the same beauties should my mind adorn,
And the same ardors in my soul should burn;
Then should my song in bolder notes arise,
And all my numbers pleasingly surprize;
But here I sit, and mourn a grov'ling mind
That fain would mount, and ride upon the wind. (25–30)

But as is common in the traditions of *recusatio*, the invocation of Homer
and Vergil ("O could I rival thine and *Virgil's* page") leads to a collapse, and
it amounts to nothing more than the lyric poet's convention of professing

inability to attempt an epic poet's task. A "grov'ling mind" strikes an oddly discordant note in a poem so devoted to the transcendent and the inspiring. This clash is quite deliberate. Wheatley has more in mind than the generic disavowal she had learned from Horace. Slavery had been a reality for him, because his own father was a *libertus* or freedman, but it was distant now, chiefly a humble origin to have risen above. For Roman descendents of ex-slaves, something like an American concept of upward social mobility was possible. Most importantly, ancient slavery was not organized according to the color of one's skin.[19] Nothing comparable exists for the younger, more vulnerable Horatian and Vergilian voice of "To Maecenas."

> But I less happy, cannot raise the song,
> The fault'ring music dies upon my tongue. (35–36)

These lines carry Davis's idea of generic disavowal one step further. They are a confession of an inability to sing at all. How can a poet remain a poet if she falls silent? Wheatley finally leads us to what makes not only grand things like epic, but even poetry itself, impossible: her status as an African.

> The happier *Terence** all the choir inspir'd,
> His soul replenish'd, and his bosom fir'd;
> But say, ye *Muses*, why this partial grace,
> To one alone of *Afric's* sable race;
> From age to age transmitting thus his name
> With the first glory in the rolls of fame? (37–42)

Terence's name is starred with an author's note at the bottom of the page: "*He was *African* by birth."

Terence's six comedies made him a favorite with Latin teachers who had to worry about the moral education of their pupils; with the possible exception of *The Eunuch*, they are far more respectable than most of the surviving ones by his livelier predecessor Plautus. Even then, Terence was only read as a school text in Wheatley's day, never performed in Puritan New England.[20] It was not so much his genteel comedies as his biography that drew Wheatley to him. A contemporary *Life of Terence* (the 1768 edition of George Colman's translation of the comedies) available to Wheatley in Boston offers obvious parallels with her own history.

> Publius Terentius Afer was born at Carthage, and was a slave of Terentius
> Lucanus, a Roman Senator; who, perceiving him to have an excellent

understanding and a great deal of wit, not only bestowed on him a liberal
education, but gave him his freedom in the very early part of his life.

. . . Our Poet was beloved and much esteemed by noblemen of the first
rank in the Roman Commonwealth; and lived in a state of great intimacy
with Scipio Africanus, and C. Laelius, to whom the beauty of his person
also is supposed to have recommended him.[21]

A common history as African slaves rescued from slavery by their patrons
links Wheatley to Terence. Both also gained new identities by being given
their masters' family names (Terentius, Wheatley), thereby losing altogether the African ones to which they were born. Both won the opportunity to learn to read and write by masters who recognized their "excellent
understanding and great wit" and gave them the kind of education suitable
for free people, not slaves. For both, a liberal education was not the elit-
ist entitlement it now seems, because both came from a world of slavery
that defined what a liberal education means in its original sense: a privilege
proper to free persons, *liberi*, by definition an education forbidden to slaves.

The despair underlying what might be expected to be a triumphant
poem is all the deeper when we recall the finale of the three books of Horace's *Odes* in which the poet essentially says, "I told you I would do it." *Odes*
3.30 (*Exegi monumentum aere perennius*, "I have raised a monument more
lasting than bronze") is set in the same meter as the opening ode of book 1,
Maecenas atavis edite regibus, and is the poet's claim of immortality through
the monument of his verse, a conceit widely known and imitated by Ovid,
Shakespeare, and many others. Horace ends the original "Maecenas" of
Odes 1.1 by asking for the muse Polyhymnia's favor. In his version Christopher Smart renders that ending this way:

If not Euterpe, heavenly gay,
Forbid her pleasant pipes to play,
Nor Polyhymnia disdain
A lesson in the Lesbian strain,
That, thro' Maecenas, I may pass
'Mongst writers of the Lyric class,
My muse her laurell'd head shall rear,
And top the zenith of her sphere.

Then at the end of *Odes* 3.30, as Horace commands Polyhymnia's sister
Melpomene to accept the honors he's won for her and wreathe his brow

with Apollo's crown, Smart is closer to Horace's sense and more intelligible than in *Maecenas atavis*.

> Assume, Melpomene, that pride
> Which is to real worth ally'd;
> And in good-will descending down,
> With Delphic bays my temples crown.

As we have seen, Wheatley reverses everything that Horace creates to establish a separate identity from his patron.

> While blooming wreaths around thy temples spread,
> I'll snatch a laurel from thine honour'd head,
> While you indulgent smile upon the deed. (45–47)

Her Maecenas wears the laurel crown that she will snatch from his head—more exactly, one leaf of it. What's more, her Maecenas will smile upon this little theft, with its witty conceit of laurel-snatching that turns upside down the cliché of bestowing a victor's crown of laurels on a poet. One leaf will do just fine.

But it's not all smiles. Unlike Horace, this poet needs her Maecenas as much at the end of her poem as she does at its beginning. There is no escape from mortal constraints into the immortality that art can confer. There is a learned play on the central image of Horace's *Odes* 3.30, which ties the future of his monument to the endurance of Rome itself.

> As long as priest and silent maid
> Shall to the Capitol parade;
> Where Aufidus in rapture goes,
> And where poor Daunus scarcely flows,
> Once rural king—I shall be thought
> The prince of Roman bards, that brought
> To Italy th'Aeolian airs,
> Advanc'd from want to great affairs.[22]
>
> (*Odes* 3.30.13–20, Smart trans.)

Wheatley pointedly does not follow Horace into expressing any pride in her provincial origins; there isn't a hint of the muddy Charles or Boston, but rather the capital of the Countess of Huntingdon. Horace's Rome

becomes London, and his Tiber, the Thames, the tidal river and capital
city of the British imperial world.

> As long as *Thames* in streams majestic flows,
> Or *Naiads* in their oozy beds repose,
> While *Phoebus* reigns above the starry train,
> While bright *Aurora* purples o'er the main,
> So long, great Sir, the muse thy praise shall sing,
> So long thy praise shall make *Parnassus* ring. (48–53)

Given the importance of the sun's rising and setting in several of the poems
to follow (ones Wheatley had already written), she may have been inclined
to measure the future praise of her Maecenas by Phoebus and Aurora as an
allusion to a motif that will appear again. These two particular gods also
offer a way of claiming an immortality coextensive with the heavens themselves. The hybrid waters and water deities of an English river (Thames)
and classical water nymphs (Naiads) also tie Maecenas to a natural world
that may last as long as the symbols of *Roma aeterna* that Horace invokes in
the Capitoline Hill and the Vestal and the priest (*pontifex*).

There has been some speculation about the exact identity of the
"great Sir" being addressed here. Men in Boston like John Wheatley who
thought they were Wheatley's Maecenas could feel flattered and imagine
themselves the "great Sir" being addressed here, but Vincent Carretta is
probably right in thinking that the Countess of Huntingdon, if she fancied
herself to be a Maecenas, might have been amused by the ambiguity of
"great Sir."[23] In any case, the last and most arresting of Wheatley's transformations of Horace is her concluding couplet:

> Then grant, *Maecenas*, thy paternal rays,
> Hear me propitious, and defend my lays. (54–55)

Maecenas is asked to grant "paternal rays" (presumably like Apollo), and
this amounts to nothing less than to continue to serve as a patron to the
poet. (The words "paternal" and "patron" are linked in their common Latin
root for "father," *pater*.) To be kindly disposed and to defend the poet's
lays is the greatest possible departure from the independent life, verging
ever more clearly toward literary immortality, which Horace claims for his
poetry at the end of the *Odes*. Wheatley ends with Horace's beginning, as
much in need as ever of a patron, no doubt because she had no illusions as

to what her fate would be if the Maecenas who supported her disappeared. "To Maecenas" is at once a consummately Horatian poem, and in a disturbing way, not at all like the triumphant, confident opening and closing poems of the *Odes*.

What this implies about the future of her work is as prescient in its own way as Horace's claim for immortality. The poet who wrote "To Maecenas" would not have been surprised at the appearance as far away as the year 2003 of a book entitled *The Trials of Phillis Wheatley*; she was then as much in need of defenders of her lays as ever, whether they were the critic Henry Louis Gates or her Penguin editor Vincent Carretta.[24] Playing under the sunny skies of Horace's ode, at the same time evoking Vergil's eclogue, "To Maecenas" carries within it a bitterness and darkness that reflect the world for which it was made.

For everything really did depend on the protection of Wheatley's Maecenas, to a degree unparalleled in Horace's experience. Notices of her funeral appeared in the Boston newspapers of December 1784, but for the circumstances of her death we have to rely on the memoir of the great grandniece of Susanna Wheatley, Margaretta Matilda Odell of Jamaica Plains, Massachusetts. Odell does not disguise her abolitionist sympathies in telling the family's story of Wheatley's life. W. E. B. Du Bois would later use her account of the last days of Wheatley in an extended allegory of African American literature in the eighteenth and nineteenth centuries, originally entitled "The Vision of Phillis the Blessed: An Allegory of African American Culture."[25] Skilled polemicist that he was, Du Bois knew perfectly well there was nothing blessed about Odell's account of the end of Phillis Wheatley.

At length a relative of her lamented mistress heard of her illness, and sought her out. She was also visited by several other members of that family. They found her in a situation of extreme misery. Two of her children were dead, and the third was sick unto death. She was herself suffering for want of attention, for many comforts, and that greatest of all comforts in sickness — cleanliness. She was reduced to a condition too loathsome to describe. . . . It is painful to dwell upon the closing scene. In a filthy apartment, in an obscure part of the metropolis, lay the dying mother, and the wasting child. The woman who had stood honored and respected in the presence of the wise and good of that country which was hers by adoption, or rather compulsion, who had graced the ancient halls of Old England, and rolled about in the splendid equipages of the proud nobles of Britain, was now numbering the last hours of life in a state of the most abject misery, surrounded by all the emblems of squalid poverty![26]

With the foresight that is often typical of poets, she may have grasped the possibility of these later events as well in her imagination as we now do, in history.

While "To Maecenas" sets a high standard for neoclassical verse in the way it moves quite beyond the themes of the classical models it evokes, the rest of *Poems on Various Subjects* rarely rises to the same level. Wheatley submitted her book for publication at the precocious age of no more than twenty, with juvenilia like "To the University of Cambridge" and "On Being Brought from Africa to America" side by side with more substantial poems like "Goliath" and her most ambitious poem of all, "Niobe in Distress." In these last two she achieves something that approaches the artistry of "To Maecenas."

Saepe stilum vertas: Wheatley and the Art of Revision

> However minute the employment may appear, of analysing lines into syllables, and whatever ridicule may be incurred by a solemn deliberation upon accents and pauses, it is certain that without this petty knowledge no man can be a poet; and that from the proper disposition of single sounds results that harmony that adds force to reason, and gives grace to sublimity; that shackles attention, and governs passions.
>
> Samuel Johnson, *The Rambler* 2.195 (Saturday, January 19, 1751)

We have made many claims about the accomplished verse of "To Maecenas." It is well to realize that Wheatley's best poetry wasn't achieved easily, that there is good evidence for this, and that she went through drafts in a tradition that classicizing poets knew, which reaches straight back through Pope to Horace and others of the original Augustan Age. As Johnson's comment in the *Rambler* suggests, how she learned to perfect her verse—or at least make it better—can be as interesting to us now as the final version. We have a number of Wheatley's drafts for poems, some published and others not. Alexander Pope has lots to say about the right and the wrong way to compose verse, just as Horace had before him. And if the Romans did not give aspiring poets earlier drafts to learn from, they did tell them quite plainly why such revision was necessary, and even how to go about it. In his translation of the *Satires* published in 1764, the

Reverend Philip Francis renders Horace's precept with a familiar reference to the pen-and-ink culture's blotting paper.[27]

> Would you a Reader's just Esteem engage?
> Frequent correct with Care the blotted Page;
> Nor strive the Wonder of the Crowd to raise,
> But the few better Judges learn to please.

In his recent version the American Charles Passage has yet another way of conveying Horace's image.

> Do not neglect your eraser if works are to merit a second
> Reading, and never mind trying to work for the crowd's admiration;
> Rather, rejoice to be read by the few.
>
> (Horace, *Satires* 1.10.72–74)

"Do not neglect your eraser" for *saepe stilum vertas* is something a modern pencil user could understand, but more literally, Horace is saying "reverse your stylus often," with the sense not so much not to neglect your eraser, as to use it *a lot*. Romans wrote on wax tablets with a pointed stylus that had a flat paddle on the end instead of a modern pencil's eraser; to blot out something written in the wax, one simply reversed the stylus and smoothed it out. From his earliest published poetry (ca. 35 BCE), and certainly from his first three books of *Odes* published in 23, Horace became a poet for everyday use in the schoolroom, not least as the most quoted of ancient authorities on the fine and necessary art of revision.

Pope gives Wheatley and anyone else who would follow him an amusing guide to bad taste, bad prosody, and bad criticism in the *Essay on Criticism*, through a catalogue of errors calculated to make any aspiring poet wince.[28] Mindless adherence to rules and a fondness for clichés are just a few of many ways to bathos.

> These *Equal Syllables* alone require,
> Tho' oft the Ear the *open Vowels* tire,
> While *Expletives* their feeble Aid *do* join,
> And ten low Words oft creep in one dull Line,
> While they ring round the same *unvary'd Chimes*,
> With sure Returns of still *expected Rhymes*.
> Where-e'er you find *the cooling Western Breeze*,
> In the next Line, it *whispers thro' the Trees*;

If *Chrystal Streams with pleasing Murmurs creep*,
The Reader's threaten'd (not in vain) with *Sleep*.

(*An Essay on Criticism*, 344–53)

Pope's *Essay* follows the example of Horace's literary epistle to the father and son Gnaeus and Lucius Calpurnius Piso now commonly known as the *Ars Poetica*.[29]

As a poet who wrote both in the lyric meters of the *Odes* and *Epodes* and in the hexameters of the *Satires* and *Epistles*, Horace commanded a wide range of styles, and much of that variety offered an encouraging model for neoclassical poets. Wheatley develops a similar range of neoclassical verse forms in her own volume, with a variety of poetic genres that corresponds to the variety of the subjects they treat. And if her preference for the heroic couplet over most other forms led her to write mainly in that measure, she could do so because it had the elasticity to enable a poet like Pope to write in one and the same verses a true epic (his translation of the *Iliad*), satiric and mock epics (*The Rape of the Lock, The Dunciad*), and theoretical and philosophical essays in the style of Horace's *Epistles* (the *Essay on Criticism*, the *Essay on Man*).

With the examples of Horace, Dryden, and Pope before her, a talented poet like Wheatley would well understand that even as she turned out good lines, they were nonetheless often perfectible. The existence of both variant and published versions of some of her poems shows her working to perfect the heroic couplet, to change single words to conform to current usage, and especially to speak to nature, as the neoclassical poets defined that term. The ultimate goal is to make one's work seem the product of a spontaneous talent, effortlessly produced.

Modern critical assessments of her revisions vary. She certainly revised, but in the opinion of Robert Kuncio, for example, she didn't revise enough.[30] Reviewing five manuscripts for poems found in Philadelphia, he cites Julian Mason's introduction to his 1966 edition of *The Poems of Phillis Wheatley*, where it is claimed that Wheatley was a "spontaneous not a laborious poet."

The examples of the improvements of which she was capable and the poor quality of some of the extant poems for which there is no evidence of rewriting lead one to retain the conviction that she probably did not revise all of her poems, certainly did not revise most of them much, and obviously should have revised more.[31]

Kuncio offers the manuscript poems as evidence of Wheatley's spontaneity; his view was repeated by others. Muktar Ali Isani, in "Phillis Wheatley and the Elegiac Mode," demonstrates a rather different method of composition and editing. His Wheatley does more than blindly adhere to the strict classicism of Pope or to the conventions of the Puritan elegy. He argues that though the poems "appear to be composed with rapidity and sometimes even in haste, they are generally the result of careful planning and thoughtful revision."[32]

In considering the choices Wheatley makes when she edits, special attention must be paid to still another aspect of neoclassical poetry, what M. A. Richmond in *Bid the Vassal Soar* describes as the "rigid boundaries" that "defined the thoughts and emotions that inhabited her poetic world."[33] Richmond specifically names that definition as "the decasyllabic line in the heroic couplet . . . the ornate diction of neoclassicism and the ritualistic obeisances it prescribed." The problem, as Richmond sees it, is Wheatley's too-close adherence to neoclassical poetics.

But what better example of the heroic couplet could Wheatley have followed than Alexander Pope's? In editing *The Waste Land*, Ezra Pound canceled the heroic couplets in T. S. Eliot's draft, not because he disliked neoclassical poetics, but because Eliot had failed to match the excellence of his presumed target: "Pope has done this so well that you cannot do better; and if you mean this as a burlesque, you had better suppress it; for you cannot parody Pope unless you can write better verse than Pope—and you can't."[34]

Wheatley had learned that neoclassical poetry offered a number of well-identified poetic forms or genres. It was also quite clear as to how language was to be used in such poetry. Since she selected poems for her first book to demonstrate her control of the recognized genres of her day, she necessarily revised to bring her language up to the highest possible standard. For the neoclassical poet editing was not just a question of grammatical correctness. As Gregory Tillotson explains, just as "nature" had a specific meaning unrelated to actual natural phenomena, so too "correctness" was defined in special terms:

> The poet must discover the balked intentions of nature and so vicariously free her. He must allow nature freedom to become Nature. He will do this by removing all the accidentals, by seeking the common ground in the mind of all men (or of all men who can be thought of as having minds) and by erecting his poem on that.[35]

The aim was to create Pope's ideal of "What oft was thought, but ne'er so well expressed" (*Essay on Criticism*, 290). For him, diction is more concerned with the words appropriate to design and subject matter than "any anthology of correct words. Appropriateness was a cardinal virtue for Pope in life as well as literature."[36]

> Expression is the dress of thought, and still
> Appears more decent, as more suitable. . . .
> For diff'rent styles with diff'rent subjects sort.
> As several garbs with country, town and court.
>
> (*Essay on Criticism*, 318)

Appropriate diction in this Latinate manner leads to compression of the number of words and, Pope would argue, greater precision. Good taste also requires the avoidance of too many "low" (sc. Anglo-Saxon) words such as "birds," "fish," and "sheep," choices often made as much for precision as for euphony.

Observing Wheatley edit from the samples we possess can offer clear evidence of how much of the poetics of Pope she had internalized and how clearly she worked toward his model. A particular number of genres, correction of language, and a definition of nature that excluded the sentimental and the unnaturally individual or unique were the goals toward which she was striving. When she revises she's more apt to trim or compress than to expand. Almost every line of a poem can be improved by more concentrated diction or by tightening the rhythm of a couplet. In an earlier draft of "To the University of Cambridge" she wrote:

> Its transient sweetness turns to endless pain
> And brings eternal ruin on the soul.

The clumsy rhythm of "ruin on the soul" is replaced by the iambic "immense" for "eternal," while the Latinate, Miltonic "perdition" gives greater sonority to the closing line in the published 1773 version.

> Its transient sweetness turns to endless pain
> And in immense perdition sinks the soul.

The alliteration of "sinks the soul" has something of the effect of a hammer. The caesura after the word "perdition" and the sibilant sounds that follow slow down the line. This is the way to end a poem with power.

Paul Fussell recommends that we think of English Augustan Age poems as being put together the way a building is constructed: clear architectural design and close-fitting joins are what we should expect to see, and hear. Most importantly, their materials were often found somewhere outside the singular consciousness of the maker. The materials are found sometimes in nature and sometimes in other poems of the same kind. One either quarries the building material or borrows it from structures already built, a construction which is stylistically less an expression of its maker's personality than an embodied average of public ideas about what such a building should be.

For many readers today the ideal of a fixed principle of versification may seem an unacceptable constraint. But Pope's and Wheatley's concentration on this form was in fact liberating, as Fussell explains in a comment on Samuel Johnson's praise of revision and prosody quoted at the beginning of this section.

Johnson would simply not have understood a technique of versification which drew the prosodic structure of each poem from the nature of the matter of that particular poetic occasion; to Johnson, as to most of the conservative metrical theorists, it was the poet's duty to settle his prosodic principles early, to triumph by an effort of the will over his adolescent taste for irregularity and inequality in rhythmical effects, and to apply his fixed prosodic principles to whatever subject-matter might present itself: it was the nature and the office of the subject-matter to yield, not the prosody.[37]

Wheatley's apologies that appear in even her best poems, as in her reference to herself in "Niobe in Distress" as the "last and meanest of the rhyming train" or the "grov'ling mind" of "To Maecenas," are an acknowledgment that she is following an aesthetic and moral example that Johnson recommends. The classical norm of her poetry is harmonious with her subjects, which are religious and moral. She would no more wish to turn out a badly written line of verse than she would wish to break the laws of the religion she espoused.

This search for perfection and regularity even before choosing a subject both expresses the poet's regularity as a religious and moral authority, and sets a standard for anyone who would read her poetry. It may be no more than the theme of "subjects moral and religious" in her volume's title that Thomas Jefferson alludes to in *Notes on the State of Virginia*. Wheatley was long dead before that book was widely available, but his back-handed compliment about her work as a testament to the power of religion might in fact have meant as much to her as any aesthetic appreciation. As Fussell observes, in the eighteenth century good verse making bespoke good morals and religious principles.

> Prosodic regularity forces the ordering of the perceiver's mind so that it may be in a condition to receive the ordered moral matter of the poem, just as, in ethics and religion, a conscious regularizing of principles and even of daily habits is the necessary condition for the growth of piety. The regularizing, whether prosodic or ethical, serves an attention-calling function; it hammers into the consciousness of the perceiver the recognition that a formal process is at work, a process comprising certain elements of ceremony, self-awareness, artifice, and control. The moral office of all poetry, the ethical function of a regularistic prosody, and the concept of regularity and fixity of ethical habits and religious commitment are thus seen to be indissolubly fused.[38]

What this means in practice is that as we follow Wheatley's revisions of her lines from one draft to another, we can see her engaged in not simply a struggle for technical mastery—though that process is obviously what engages her attention—but a struggle to make sure that the form of the poem will reach the level where the prosody is unassailable. Then the moral and religious instruction of the poem would be unassailable as well. It matters as much that the line be as good as possible, as that its ideas be well conceived.

A Biblical Epic Theme: "Goliath of Gath"

The importance of the Bible to most slaves cannot be overestimated and is forcefully borne out by Wheatley's inclusion of "Goliath of Gath," the longest poem in her volume. It tells of the confrontation between Goliath and the boy David, with the underdog as victor. Both black and white Americans achieved literacy through Bible study, but they did not read the same Bible. The sharpest contrasts can be found in their typological readings of the myth of the Promised Land in scripture. While the Europeans' journey to America typologically reenacted the flight of the Jews from bondage in Egypt and their entry into Canaan, the black spirituals completely reversed this typology. For their singers, coming to America more closely parallels the entry of Israel into a new bondage, where America becomes Egypt, not the Promised Land. Hope for freedom from bondage lies somewhere in the future for the black singers of such spirituals as "Go Down, Moses" and "Canaan Land."

> God did say to Moses one day,
> Say, Moses, go to Egypt Land,
> And tell him to let my people go
> Canaan Land is the land for me,
> And let God's saints come in.[39]

This imprecation would later appear in the fiery oratory of the Bostonian Maria Stewart (1803–1879), the first American-born woman to break the prohibition against women as public speakers as well as the first black woman orator and abolitionist.

> America, America, foul and indelible is thy stain! Dark and dismal is the cloud that hangs over thee, for thy cruel wrongs and injuries to the fallen sons of Africa. . . . You may kill, tyrannize and oppress as much as you choose, until our cry shall come up before the throne of God; for I am firmly persuaded, that he will not suffer you to quell the proud, fearless and undaunted spirits of the African forever; for in his own time, he is able to plead our cause against you, and to pour out upon you the ten plagues of Egypt.[40]

Black and white Christians agreed that they were inheritors of the new covenant but disagreed as to whether the inheritance was a reality or a promise for the future. As Albert Raboteau observes, "Slaves were distrustful of the white folks' interpretation of the Scriptures and wanted to be able to search them for themselves."[41] In doing so they developed a list of favored texts, of which one of the most popular was the triumph of the boy David over Goliath.

> Little David, play on your harp
> Hallelu' Hallelu'
> Little David, play on your harp
> Hallelujah
> Little David was a shepherd boy
> He killed Goliath and shouted for joy.

"Goliath of Gath" creates a syncretism of the Christian and the classical by using an episode in the Bible but telling it in the style of the Puritans' great epic, *Paradise Lost*. Wheatley's invocation strikes an unusual note. While she depicts the avenging Christ "in the dread image of the pow'r of war," she calls on "martial pow'rs" and the nine muses.

> Ye martial pow'rs, and all ye tuneful nine,
> Inspire my song, and aid my high design.
> The dreadful scenes and toils of war I write,
> The ardent warriors, and the fields of fight:
> You best remember, and you best can sing
> The acts of heroes to the vocal string:
> Resume the lays with which your sacred lyre,
> Did then the poet and the sage inspire. (1–8)

This is the only warlike invocation in her surviving poetry, appropriately enough, since "Goliath" is her only poem concerned with traditional epic themes of war and battle. She converts the biblical incident and language into a miniature epic, with typical variations in the name of the presiding deity: "heav'ns monarch" in line 136, "Jehovah's awful hand" in 240. The "thunder and storm monarch" of lines 141–42 must be Jehovah, but he sounds like Jove, and the "judge of all the gods" in line 126 sounds distinctly Homeric and pagan. Periphrastic naming of Goliath ("Philistia's son") and David ("Jesse's youngest hope") echoes both Homeric and neoclassical verse.

The visit from an admonitory angel is one of Wheatley's original contributions to the story in I Samuel. Here she fleshes out character by the lofty rhetoric and fierce animosity of the antagonists. Such flights of pride and defiance have strong parallels in the "flyting" or poetical invective practiced in contests of ritual abuse by Scottish bards, Homeric heroes, and other figures in traditional oral cultures.[42] These exchanges constitute what the West African historian D. T. Niane's informant calls "the War of Mouths" in the Malian historical epic *Sundiata*.[43] Like the taunts of the boxing champion Muhammad Ali they are meant to dampen an opponent's spirit, heighten his awe of the boaster, and convince him of certain defeat. Such exchanges also fire up the pride and rage of the speakers. In the *Sundiata*, two kings meet on the field, but their first confrontation is verbal, not physical.

> "Behave yourself little boy, or you will burn your foot, for I am the red hot cinder. But me, I am the rain that extinguishes the cinder; I am the boisterous torrent that will carry you off."

"I am the mighty silk cotton tree that looks from on high on the
top of other trees."
"And I, I am the strangling creeper that climbs to the top of the forest
giant."
. . . Thus Sundiata and Soumaoro spoke together. After the war of
mouths, swords had to decide the issue.[44]

The power of Wheatley's scene lies in its ability to define the proud
and unbending nature of Goliath with a minimum of description. His
character lies in the words he speaks and in his defiance and arrogance.
His challenge could be delivered by one of the Greek or Trojan heroes of
Pope's *Iliad*:

Your armies I defy, your force despise,
By far inferior in Philistia's eyes:
Produce a man, and let us try the fight,
Decide the contest, and the victor's right. (37–40)

Goliath also sounds like Satan in book 4 of *Paradise Lost*, whose pride leads
him to defy God's "proud limitary cherub," the Archangel Gabriel. Not
even a vaguely Olympian sign of doom from heaven dissuades him, so
confident is he of his power. While Satan does eventually flee the battle,
the results of which are so clearly prophesied, Goliath, in his determination, refuses to believe the "radiant cherub" who descends with an order
to cease and desist.

Goliath, well thou know'st thou hast defy'd
Yon Hebrew armies, and their God deny'd:
Rebellious wretch! Audacious worm! Forbear,
Nor tempt the vengeance of their God too far.
Them, who with his omnipotence contend,
No eye shall pity, and no arm defend. (118–23)

The syntax recalls Milton's characteristic inversion of phrase and clauses,
with English words made to imitate Latin word order and grammar.
The echo of Gabriel and Satan's encounter in Milton and the "War of
Mouths" exchange from the *Sundiata* highlight the characters' relationship to right and goodness, their pride, and the consequences of their defiance. Wheatley's compressed narrative style imitates Milton, who in turn
was imitating Vergil, so that a sentence like "When David answered the

King thus" is reduced to "When David thus," and "Then Jesse's youngest hope" [sc. spoke].[45] And there are careful turns to Latinate English redolent of the style of *Paradise Lost*, as in the prophecy of Goliath's ultimate fate: "Beasts shall be your animated tomb" (161)—"animated" in its Latin sense, "filled with life," an ingenious way of saying he will reside not in a mausoleum but in the stomach of the living beasts who will devour his flesh. More familiar words like "demand" in lines 146–47 appear in a sense now obsolete in English.

> Now David comes; the fatal stones demand
> His left, the staff engag'd his better hand.

The word has shifted to a meaning somewhat akin to "request," with authority and legal right. Yet the Latin sense of the word enriches the image when we consider its meanings, "to give in charge," "entrust," "commit." Similarly, after Goliath's death in battle, his severed head is "depending" from David's hand (212). We retain something of the Latin meaning in the word "pendant, " or "dependant," but "dangling" or "hanging" would be the choice in modern usage. Wheatley may be recalling the end of book 2 of *Paradise Lost,* where Satan gets his first view of the world.

> And fast by hanging in a golden chain
> This pendant world, in bigness as a star
> Of smallest magnitude close by the moon. (11.1051–53)

Milton gives us a modern reading of pendant as in "subordinate" (i.e., the world is subordinate to the will of God), pendant as in "hanging down from," and pendant, as in "like a jewel" on a golden chain. The same clusters of meaning can be read into Wheatley's addition of the Latin derivative for "blood-stained" in her use of "th'ensanguined plain" (173). Latinate English is not decoration but a recovery of associations still alive the educated English of Wheatley's day.

Wheatley's retelling of the David and Goliath story is equally inventive in its reshaping and adding to the original biblical version of their combat. She introduces a warning angel for the heedless Goliath in order to conform to those Greek and Roman narratives in which divine beings come to earth to warn, praise, or assist invariably heedless mortals. She borrows the song of the women from 1 Samuel 8 to celebrate David's victory. By lifting this song of triumph from its original setting and placing it at a different place in her narrative she achieves the beauty of the bond between David

and Saul but avoids the nasty sequel of Saul's jealousy and his growing re-
sentment of David. Her narrative closes with Saul's gratitude and love. She
has no interest in his growing madness or his later plots against David.

> And now aloud th'illustrious victor said,
> "Where are your boastings now your champion's dead?"
> Scarce had he spoke, when the Philistines fled:
> But fled in vain: the conqu'ror swift pursu'd:
> What scenes of slaughter! and what seas of blood!
> There Saul thy thousands grasp'd th'impurpled sand
> In pangs of death the conquest of thine hand;
> And David there were thy ten thousands laid:
> Thus Israel's damsels musically play'd. (188–96)

The triumph of David over Goliath becomes a Christian moral lesson set
to Miltonic and Popean English. As a young poet's work goes, this is not a
bad exercise. It ends without a hint of either the eventual rivalry of David
and Saul and Saul's death, nor is this the story of a classical hero's death,
like Hector's in the *Iliad*. Goliath was deaf to divine decrees and there is no
room for anything but satisfaction at this justly deserved downfall.

An Imitation of Ovid: "Niobe in Distress"

> To state it fairly; imitation of an author is the most advantageous way for a
> translator to show himself, but the greatest wrong which can be done to the
> memory and reputation of the dead.
>
> John Dryden, preface to *Ovid's Epistles* (1680)

Wheatley's "Niobe" belongs to the third and last of Dryden's categories
of translation. After the word-by-word and line-by-line "metaphrase" and
the freer treatment of "paraphrase" comes "imitation," "where the translator (if now he has not lost that name) assumes the liberty, not only to vary
from the words and sense, but to forsake them both as he sees occasion;
and taking only some general hints from the original, to run division on
the groundwork (sc., to rearrange the order or structure), as he pleases."[46]
Wheatley's "Niobe" is all that Dryden describes, and more. The full title
signals the complexity of what she attempts in this version of the Niobe
myth. It is a poem that comes both from reading words and from looking
at images: "NIOBE in Distress for her children slain by APOLLO, from

Ovid's Metamorphoses, Book VI. and from a view of the Painting of Mr. *Richard Wilson.*"[47]

The story of the mother whose pride in her children led her to insult Latona the mother of Apollo was well known from Ovid's *Metamorphoses.* Ovid's tale is embedded in a series of myths in book 6 centered on Thebes. It is preceded by the story of the contest between Arachne and Minerva, and the link between that tale and this one (always a device of great wit and variety for Ovid) is that Niobe had known Arachne, and also knew the outcome of her contest with Minerva, yet did not learn the ostensible moral of Arachne's punishment: *cedere caelitibus verbisque minoribus uti* (6.151, "Give way to the gods and do not boast"; or, in George Sandys's version, "Yet slights that home example: still rebells / Against the Gods; and with proud language swels").

Like many of Ovid's imitators, Wheatley does not so much translate him as transform the poet of transformations. By linking Wilson's image with Ovid's words she turns his story into a narrative that is at once an *ekphrasis* or literary description of Wilson's painting and a narrative that is dominated by the frozen image of Niobe in distress for her children slain by Apollo. She uses the moment frozen in time in Wilson's painting to recast Ovid's story, making changes to the moral of Ovid's original version in a way that would be familiar to colonial American readers of George Sandys's translation of 1632.[48] In Wheatley, Niobe's offence against the gods is acknowledged, but barely. The beauty of her children and her pride in them remain, and for that pride—for which now read "sin" in the Christian imagination—she is punished. The emphasis on her suffering moves to the center of Wheatley's poem, just as it does in Wilson's painting.

"Niobe in Distress" exemplifies the cyclical flow from image to words and back to image that Leonard Barkan has argued is the particular quality of ekphrasis in an Ovidian context: "A form of art where image automatically lures one to verbal translation and ekphrastic deception automatically turns one toward image: this cyclical flow . . . involved the constant transformation from life to art, from picture to words."[49] Furthermore, Wheatley could have learned about what Barkan terms "unions between picture and word" from the illustrations that were popular in translations of the classics in the seventeenth and eighteenth centuries. Their importance was obvious enough for George Sandys's edition of 1632 to be signaled in the title: *Ovid's* Metamorphosis *[sic]: Englished, Mythologized, and Represented in Figures.*

The engraving Sandys places at the beginning of book 6 shows how the Niobe story could be used to impose a kind of visual unity on the diversity of the tales of Arachne and Minerva, Apollo and Marsyas, Latona and the Lycian peasants turned into frogs, and even the most horrific story of all, Tereus's rape of his sister-in-law Philomela and the revenge of Philomela and her sister Procne on Tereus, through the butchery and cooking of Procne and Tereus's son Itys.

As such Theban tales go, Niobe's is comparatively respectable. In Sandys's engraving the gods Apollo and Diana are at the top and the Niobids at the bottom, both framing the entire sequence of stories, always with a quite pointed reference to details in them: Arachne and Minerva are signaled by not only the spider and her web, but also the boxwood shuttle with which Minerva strikes Arachne; Marsyas is tied to a tree, Apollo stripping off his flesh; Latona with her infant children Apollo and Diana, and the Lycian peasants who insult her, are splashing around in the water and turning into frogs. Niobe is surrounded by her children at different moments: sons and daughters already dead, sons and daughters fleeing and not yet struck. Prominent in the left foreground and framing Niobe in the center is her firstborn son Ismenus on his horse, the arrow of Apollo bearing down on him; on the right, the brothers Phaedimus and Tantalus are wrestling, with Diana high above, aiming the single arrow that will transfix them both.

As we have already observed in "To Maecenas," the classical texts available to Wheatley were in general far more solicitous of their readers' needs than our comparatively austere modern counterparts. In Sandys's volume alone she would have found all the education she needed to enter directly into the theory and practice of ekphrastic art, as exemplified by the illustrations to each book of the *Metamorphoses*. As Sandys observes in the preface to his reader:

And for thy farther delight I have contracted the substance of every Booke into as many Figures (by the hand of a rare Workman, and as rarely performed, if our judgments may be led by theirs, who are Masters among us in that Faculty) since there is betweene Poetry and Picture so great a congruitie; the one called by *Simonide*s a speaking Picture, and the other a silent Poesie: Both Daughters of the Imagination, both busied in the imitation of Nature, or transcending it for the better with equall liberty: the one being borne in the beginning of the World; and the other soone after, as appears by the Hieroglyphicall Figures on the Aegyptian Obelisques, which were long before the invention of Letters: the one feasting the Eare, and the other the Eye, the noblest of the sences, by which the Understanding is only informed, and the mind sincerely delighted: and as the rarest

peeces in Poets are the descriptions of Pictures, so the Painter expresseth
the Poet with equall Felicite; representing not onely the actions of men,
but making their Passions and Affections speake in their faces; in so much
as he renders the lively Image of their Minds as well as of their Bodies;
the end of the one and the other being to mingle Delights with Profit. To
this I was the rather induced, that so excellent a Poem might with the like
Solemnity be entertained by us, as it hath beene among other Nations:
rendered in so many languages, illustrated by Comments, and embellished
with Figures; withall, that I may not prove lesse gratefull to my Autor, by
whose Muse I may modestly hope to be rescued from Oblivion.[50]

Wheatley is not a translator in the strict sense of Dryden's creator of a
metaphrase, nor is she like Sandys, whose rendering of Ovid into rhyming
couplets is at once as faithful as possible to Ovid's Latin, yet a poem in its
own right in English—in Dryden's term, a paraphrase. Her imitation of
Ovid uses Wilson's painting to establish a theme altogether different from
the sequence Ovid gives. It is a simplified, concentrated short narrative of
Niobe's loss and grief.

An epic poem in miniature, like Catullus's Poem 64 on the wedding of
Peleus and Thetis, "Niobe" is far more compelling than "Goliath of Gath."[51]

APOLLO'S Wrath to man the dreadful spring
Of ills innum'rous, tuneful goddess, sing!
Thou who did'st first th'ideal pencil give,
And taught'st the painter in his works to live,
Inspire with glowing energy of thought,   5
What Wilson painted, and what Ovid wrote.
Muse! lend thy aid, nor let me sue in vain,
Tho' last and meanest of the rhyming train!
O guide my pen in lofty strains to show
The Phrygian queen, all beautiful in woe.   10

And if Wilson's image of Niobe gives Wheatley her concentration on an
epic theme, the opening of Alexander Pope's translation of the *Iliad* supplies its language and even most of the scaffolding on which her words
appear.

ACHILLES' Wrath, to Greece the direful spring
Of woes unnumber'd, heav'nly goddess, sing!

That wrath which hurl'd to Pluto's gloomy reign
The souls of mighty chiefs untimely slain;
Whose limbs unbury'd on the naked shore
Devouring dogs and hungry vultures tore.
Such was the sov'reign doom, and such the will of Jove.

                                    (*Iliad* 1.1–7, Pope trans.)

She opens "Niobe" with a proem that begins by echoing much of the opening couplets of Pope's *Iliad*, through exact imitation of phrasing and synonyms. In this and the following passage we print in bold type the few words she actually changes.

ACHILLES' Wrath, to **Greece** the direful spring
Of woes unnumber'd, **heav'nly** goddess, sing! (Pope)

APOLLO'S Wrath to **man** the dreadful spring
Of ills innum'rous, **tuneful** goddess, sing! (Wheatley)

The imitation is so close, both in the choice of words and their position in the line, that it would more than qualify Wheatley for a charge of plagiarism in the present academic and legal environment, where guardians of intellectual property rights are obsessed with art's protection and profitability. For a novice neoclassical bard like Wheatley, it all means nothing more than that she is displaying her knowledge of the most relevant poem by the most relevant poet. And truthfully she departs quite quickly from this close imitation as soon as the poem she wants us to know is clearly established. The hybridity—Ovidian tale, but Pope's Homeric versification—is similar to what we observed at the beginning of "To Maecenas."

Virtually the only real change in going from Pope to Wheatley is from Achilles to Apollo as the agent of disaster, but it is significant. The story of Niobe is turned into the story of the wrath of Apollo, which is imminent from the very beginning of "Niobe in Distress" and thus marks a radical change from Ovid's Apollo. For Ovid there is no hint of divine, epic wrath in this tale from the *Metamorphoses*, but simply a son so impatient to avenge the slight to his mother that he doesn't even let her finish her rather lengthy complaint.

Lo I, your mother, proud in you alone;
(Excepting *Juno*, second unto none)

Am question'd if a Goddesse: and must loose,
If you assist not, all religious dews.
Nor is this all: that curst *Tantalian* Seede
Adds foule reproaches to her impious deed,
She dares her children before you prefer;
And calls me childlesse: may it light on her!
Whose wicked words her father's tongue declare.
About to second her report with prayer;
Peace, *Phoebus* said, complaint too long delayes
Conceiv'd revenge: the same vext *Phoebe* sayes.

(Metamorphoses 6.204–15, Sandys trans.)

Sandys captures beautifully Apollo's terse language: "*Desine!*" *Phoebus ait* (6.215); in modern parlance, "'Shut up,'" or possibly "'Stop it,' Apollo said." The wrath of Apollo is immanent in the *Iliad*, from the moment the poet asks how Agamemnon and Achilles first came to battle with each other, and precedes the wrath of Achilles that will be cosmic in its devastation.

Declare, O Muse! in what ill-fated Hour
Sprung the fierce Strife, from what offended Pow'r?
Latona's Son a dire Contagion spread,
And heap'd the Camp with Mountains of the Dead;
The King of Men his Rev'rend Priest defy'd,
And, for the King's Offence, the People dy'd.

(Iliad 1.10–15, Pope trans.)

Only when Chryseis has been returned to her father Chryses and the Greeks have propitiated Apollo with sacrifice does their affliction end. Achilles tells Priam the story of Niobe at the end of the *Iliad* when he has come to ransom Hector's body to encourage Priam to eat. He is not the first or the last parent to lose a child.

Such Griefs, O King! have other Parents known;
Remember theirs, and mitigate thy own.

(Iliad 24.780–81, Pope trans.)

In this sense we could say that the wrath of Apollo frames the entire story of the wrath of Achilles, from start to finish. At the beginning it comes as an unseen, devastating plague on the Greeks whose cause Achilles dedicates himself to discovering. The cause of the plague is Agamemnon and his offence to Apollo's priest Chryses. In discovering Apollo's role, Achilles also uncovers Agamemnon's role; the god's intervention leads to Achilles' intervention, which leads to the quarrel with Agamemnon and all its devastating consequences. At the end, Apollo is equally important, but this time the avenging god who punishes Niobe for her offence against his mother Latona is part of Achilles' consciousness. He knows the story and uses it to persuade Priam to eat and live.

> So was her Pride chastiz'd by Wrath divine,
> Who match'd her own with bright Latona's Line;
> But two the Goddess, twelve the Queen enjoy'd;
> Those boasted twelve th'avenging two destroy'd.
>
> (*Iliad* 24.763–66, Pope trans.)

As is often noted about the final book of the *Iliad*, there are many polarities in both characters and events that offer positive examples to balance the negative examples with which the poem opens: in book 1, a father comes as suppliant to reclaim his living daughter from a tyrannical king's spoils of war, and in book 24 another father comes to claim the body of his dead son from his bitterest enemy. For Achilles in the *Iliad*, Apollo thus plays a critical role, first in a negative way as a god who brings about present devastation, which in turn brings on Achilles' quarrel with Agamemnon and all its consequences; then in a distant, past story of his punishment of a mortal mother's pride, which Achilles employs in a positive way, not to mitigate the devastation Niobe suffered, but to see the consequences of Apollo's wrath there as leading to the example that even one who has suffered as much as Priam has suffered did not refuse to eat and sustain life in mourning.

> But now the peaceful Hours of sacred Night
> Demand Refection, and to Rest invite:
> Nor thou O Father! thus consum'd with Woe,
> The common Cares that nourish Life, foregoe.
> Not thus did *Niobe*, of Form divine,
> A Parent once, whose Sorrows equal'd thine:
> Six youthful Sons, as many blooming Maids
> In one sad Day beheld the *Stygian* Shades;
> These by *Apollo*'s silver Bow were slain,
> Those, *Cynthia*'s Arrows stretch'd upon the Plain.
>
> (*Iliad* 24.753–62, Pope trans.)

Achilles comes to understand not only the overwhelming power of gods like Apollo, but also what human suffering is and how mortals must learn to cope with it. "Niobe in Distress" captures this essential insight in Homer and appropriates it to Wheatley's rewriting of Ovid. Her tactic is plain enough. If an Iliadic theme were to be made from the story of Niobe, what could be better than Apollo's wrath for its organizing theme?

Ovid characterizes the hybris of Niobe quite directly, and gives much more space to her obnoxious comments, including her anger at the Theban women for daring to honor Latona rather than herself.[52] As Ovid observes, Niobe is beautiful, but not as pretty as she could be: *et, quantum ira sinit, formosa* (6.167), "and, as much as her wrath allows, she's lovely." Part of Niobe's paradoxical character is that she cares more for the glory her children confer on her than she cares for the children themselves. So what if some of them were knocked off? With seven sons and seven daughters she would end up with plenty, and that would still be more than the measly two that Latona has. Wheatley turns the Ovidian Niobe's boasting into something slightly more tasteful.

> Round me what a large progeny is spread!
> No frowns of fortune has my soul to dread.
> What if indignant she decrease my train
> More than *Latona*'s number will remain. (81–84)

Ovid's Niobe by contrast has an unconscious at work that tempts fate even more than she knows. It is Niobe herself who imagines what could happen to her glorious progeny. Her only error is that she assumes there would be some limit to their loss. She is willing to imagine losing a few, but presumes they are so numerous they couldn't all be slain. As she insultingly says of Apollo and Diana's mother, Latona had just two children, and that's only one-seventh the number *she* has. She sounds like a Theban Mother Hubbard, who has so many children she doesn't know what to do: no worries, no matter what Fortune brings. By comparison Latona is practically childless (6.196–207).

It is a wonderfully Ovidian setup: Niobe is asking for it, and Wheatley doesn't ignore the passage; she simply transfers it out of the mouth of Niobe and into her narrative proper and makes it part of an encomium of Niobe's children, before the priestess Manto and the Theban women come to worship Latona ("Niobe," 37–52) and before Niobe's grotesque outburst.

Seven sprightly sons the royal bed adorn,
Seven daughters beauteous as the op'ning morn,
As when *Aurora* fills the ravish'd sight,
And decks the orient realms with rosy light
From their bright eyes the living splendors play,
Nor can beholders bear the flashing ray. (23–28)

The Aurora simile likens the appearance of the children to dawn's light in a dazzling image that resembles other references to dawn in her poetry; it may resonate with Wheatley's own dawn as a child in Africa before she was stolen away into slavery. She manages to be notably more sympathetic to Niobe than Sandys is here:

> *Niobe* in times past had knowne *Arachne*, yet could not be admonished by her example, but exceed her in insolency; proud of her high parentage, and of her husband *Amphion*; both descending from *Jupiter*. . . . *Niobe* glories besides in her beauty, her riches, her dependency, but especially in her children; exalting her self above the reach of fortune, or degree of a mortall, affects divine honours; enraged at those which were given to an other. Her anger transports her beyond decency, and eclipseth her beauty: whose intemperancy distorts the sweetnesse of the aspect, extends the veines, discolours the blood, and darts those flames from the eyes which love never kindled. The prescribed remedy for this evill is a glasse, wherein they may see how they change themselves into *Gorgons*, and take an affright from their shaddowes. For women who are enamoured on their pretious beauties, had rather have their soules deformed then their faces.[53]

Instead, imitating an epic poet's occasional direct address to sympathetic characters such as Patroclus in *Iliad* 16, or to the "fortunate pair" Nisus and Euryalus in *Aeneid* 9 — a paradoxical moment, because the "fortunate pair" has just been apprehended and slain — Wheatley addresses Niobe directly.

Wherever, *Niobe*, thou turn'st thine eyes,
New beauties kindle, and new joys arise.
But thou had'st far the happier mother prov'd,
If this fair offspring had been less belov'd.
What if their charms exceed *Aurora*'s teint,

No words could tell them, and no pencil paint,
Thy love too vehement hastens to destroy
Each blooming maid, and each celestial boy. (29–36)

The glance back at Aurora of the simile adds still more resonance to the allusive dawn theme. All of this is quite gentle in Wheatley compared to the bombast of Niobe in Ovid. As for Wheatley's gods, they acquire a distinctive suggestion of masters who are provoked to anger because they are facing a rebellion. Latona says,

Niobe sprung from Tantalus inspires
Each Theban bosom with rebellious fires;
No reason her imperious temper quells,
But all her father in her tongue rebels. (95–98)

Apollo picks up on his mother's theme of Niobe as the inciter of a rebellion, and unlike the terse one line of Ovid's Apollo, this one comes from a post–*Paradise Lost* pantheon, where pride is a sin to be punished and rebellion something to be quashed.

Cease thy complaints, mine be the task assign'd
To punish pride, and scourge the rebel mind. (103–4)

The idea of a rebellion had obvious resonance for Wheatley's world, both in the rebellion of Satan against God and in the rebellion of slaves against their masters, and of course neither is present in Ovid's original version.
    Once Niobe has been set up as a more sympathetic figure, the sequel follows Ovid exactly. The seven sons are slain and Niobe, though crushed, is incapable of refraining from boasting that she still has seven children left.

Be sated cruel *Goddess*! with my woe;
If I've offended, let these streaming eyes,
And let this sev'nfold funeral suffice:
Ah! take this wretched life you deign'd to save,
With them I too am carried to the grave.
Rejoice triumphant, my victorious foe,
But show the cause from whence your triumphs flow?
Tho' I unhappy mourn these children slain,
Yet greater numbers to my lot remain. (180–88)

Niobe has asked for it again, with the fatal result following as soon as she has finished speaking. The slaying of the seven sons in both Ovid and Wheatley is a long and carefully varied slaughter, reminiscent of the variation one sees in Homeric battle scenes, with no two youths dying the same way (109–60). The first six daughters are dispatched more quickly (195–206), so that only one is left for Niobe to shield. And here again Wheatley follows Ovid closely.

> One only daughter lives, and she the least;
> The queen close clasp'd the daughter to her breast:
> "Ye heav'nly powers, ah spare me one," she cry'd,
> "Ah! spare me one," the vocal hills reply'd:
> In vain she begs, the Fates her suit deny,
> In her embrace she sees her daughter die. (207–12)

The concluding couplet corresponds exactly to what Wheatley's title promises. Nonetheless Wheatley's volume rounds out the story with the obligatory metamorphosis of Niobe into stone.

> *The queen of all her family bereft,
> without or husband, son, or daughter left,
> Grew stupid at the shock. The passing air
> Made no impression on her stiff'ning hair.
> The blood forsook her face: amidst the flood
> Pour'd from her cheeks, quite fix'd her eye-balls stood.
> Her tongue, her palate both obdurate grew,
> Her curdled veins no longer motion knew,
> The use of neck, and arms, and feet was gone,
> And ev'n her bowels hard'ned into stone:
> A marble statue now the queen appears,
> But from the marble steal the silent tears. (213–24)

But these lines are not by Phillis Wheatley. We can only speculate about who supplied them, and why. An author's starred note in Wheatley's first edition says "*This Verse to the End is the Work of another Hand."

Whoever's hand it was has much in common with Sandys's moralizing approach. Noting Niobe's descent from Tantalus and other notorious criminals of mythology, he reads her ancestry allegorically, and her fate as an example to us (Christians) all.

Niobe is said to be the daughter of *Tantalus*, and *Taygeta* one of the *Pleiades*,
or rather of *Euryanassa*, that is, of Avarice and Riches, which ingender
pride in hearts of Mortalls: from whence proceeds the contempt both of
God and man, and an insolent forgetfulnesse of humane instability: when
such not seldome from the height of Glory are reduced by the divine vengeance to be the spectacles of calamity, and subject to their pitty whom
they formerly despised, who neither having the virtue to make use of, nor
the courage to support their afflictions; are aptly fained to be turned into
stone, as besotted and stupified with immoderate sorrow.[54]

We suspect a reader with the mindset of a Sandys had a hand in cobbling
together this ending to "Niobe in Distress," perhaps one for whom Niobe's
transformation would exercise fascination and more than a little satisfaction at her punishment. Perhaps it was Phillis's teacher Mary Wheatley,
or Mary's mother Susanna. Whoever it was, some literal mind realized
that all of Ovid's story wasn't there, especially its concluding metamorphosis. With the metamorphosis omitted, the ending might have seemed
too abrupt, and, ending with Niobe's grief, too sympathetic. We can only
imagine what kind of argument was ended with the inclusion of these ex-
tra lines and the explanatory note that they were not by the author. Poets
know what to leave out, and metamorphosis was no more Phillis Wheatley's theme than it had been Richard Wilson's.

Because Wheatley saw Wilson and read Ovid as a slave hoping soon
to be an ex-slave, "Niobe in Distress" is about something more than the
wrath of Apollo. Loss is Wheatley's theme, just as it is Wilson's. And because of the typological thinking of a Christian poet, a myth about Niobe bespeaks not just loss of a general kind, but a mother's loss of her
children—and not just any mother's loss, but a slave mother's loss. Niobe
suffers what every mother of nearly every slave would know who made it
through the Middle Passage to America, and what the mothers of all those
who didn't also knew. Recall that the poet we know as "Phillis Wheatley"
has a pseudonym even more contrived than "H.D." She was neither the
French slave ship *Phillis*, nor the property of the family Wheatley. She
was herself a child of Niobe, a Niobid. For to be taken into slavery from
West Africa and never to return is to be as forever lost to your mother as
any son or daughter of Niobe. What must she have thought as she sailed
back and forth across the Atlantic, between Boston and London, instead
of south, to West Africa? She experienced at first hand the kind of trian-
gulation of personal history that would become foundational for Anglo-
American black Atlantic studies at the end of the twentieth century and

the beginning of the twenty-first, a new field in the history of the African diaspora where Derek Walcott and C. L. R. James would figure so importantly.[55] We find a contemporary sequel to this kind of thinking and to this level of art in Toni Morrison's *Beloved* and Rita Dove's *Mother Love*. One of the earliest encounters of African Americans with classical literature turns on the story of a mother's loss of her child, as do some of the latest.[56]

Two

Frederick Douglass and
The Columbian Orator

I am well aware that there are certain writers who would absolutely bar all study of artistic structure and contend that language as it chances to present itself in the rough is more natural and even more manly. If by this they mean that only that is natural which originated with nature and has never received any subsequent cultivation, there is an end to the whole art of oratory.

Quintilian, *The Education of the Orator* 9.4.3

Frederick Augustus Washington Bailey was born in 1818 into the squalor of rural slavery in Talbot County, Maryland, on the Eastern Shore of Chesapeake Bay. His father was an unnamed white man and his mother, Harriet Bailey, a slave owned by Aaron Anthony. A public speaker of legendary presence and power, Douglass would become one of the most important and widely known advocates for the abolition of slavery in his age, and after the Civil War, a tireless defender of the rights of all African Americans. We know more about his life than the lives of most slaves through his three autobiographies: *The Narrative of the Life of Frederick Douglass, American Slave* (1845), the expanded and more detailed version of the same story, *My Bondage and My Freedom* (1855), and *The Life and Times of Frederick Douglass*, which he published in 1881 and revised for a new edition in 1892. At the age of seven Frederick was sent to Thomas Auld's brother Hugh and his wife Sophie in Baltimore, where he managed to begin a largely surreptitious self-education. Mrs. Auld taught him his ABCs, but as soon as Mr. Auld learned of it he forbade further instruction, rightly fearing that literacy would have fatal consequences for any slave's usefulness and loyalty. Frederick then began to copy the lessons of the little white boys he played with and learned to read and write by writing in the spaces left in a white child's copy book. It was during his time in Baltimore that he was able to buy a copy of Caleb Bingham's *Columbian Orator*, an anthology of exemplary rhetoric and set pieces of dialectic that by his own account played a crucial role in his education as a speaker and writer.

Baltimore was no paradise, but far preferable to the Eastern Shore, where he was made to return when Mr. Anthony died. Frederick was sent back to work for Thomas Auld, but proved so unmanageable that Auld turned him over to Edward Covey, a brute who specialized in breaking the spirit of rebellious slaves. After many savage beatings and a foiled attempted escape he was again sent to Hugh and Sophie Auld and eventually was able to develop a marketable skill as a caulker in the Baltimore shipyards. He finally escaped from slavery by the underground railroad and made his way to New York City. New York proved too dangerous to stay in long, both because of the racial prejudice that abounded in its immigrant populations and because of the many bounty hunters engaged in the lucrative business of returning runaway slaves to slavery. He moved to New Bedford and found Massachusetts a far more congenial place to live and work.

By this point Douglass tells us he had dropped his two middle names, kept his given name Frederick, and chosen his own surname from the heroic Scottish character Douglass in Sir Walter Scott's *Lady of the Lake*. He became a constant reader of William Lloyd Garrison's abolitionist paper the *Liberator* and attended meetings of the American Anti-Slave Society at Nantucket in 1841. From that time onward he was one of the central figures in the Northern abolitionist fight against slavery. It was dangerous work, and he was soon sent to England, where he could lecture and write more safely for the abolitionist cause. His new friends and supporters there finally raised 150 pounds sterling and purchased his freedom so that he could return to the United States as a legally free man. He moved to Rochester, New York, began serving as a conductor for the underground railroad there, and published the first of several newspapers he would found, the *North Star*, named for the guiding star that showed escaping slaves the way north to freedom. During the Civil War he served in the all-black 54th Massachusetts Regiment and came to know Abraham Lincoln, an admiring reader of his work. After the war and Reconstruction he served in various administrative posts in Washington, D.C.; he was U.S. marshall for the District of Columbia, living in Anacostia in the southeastern quadrant of the city. He was well known to successive Republican administrations and was consul general to Haiti from 1888 to 1891. In 1884, two years after his first wife Anna died, Douglass married his white secretary Helen Pitts, an editor, feminist, and advocate of women's rights whose own skills strongly complemented Douglass's political and intellectual powers. After his death in 1895, Helen worked hard to establish a memorial and foundation in Douglass's memory. When she died in 1903 she was buried beside him in Rochester, New York.

Douglass became an orator and a writer of prose as accomplished as anyone schooled in classics, his published prose the equal of any educated person's. He had no chance to study Greek or Latin formally, but by working through Caleb Bingham's *Columbian Orator* he acquired what the anthropologist Gregory Bateson and his followers term "deutero-learning." Students focusing on one task learn something more than they expected to learn; they might not even at first be aware what else it is they acquire. In service to the democratic ideals of the new American Republic, Bingham's 1797 *Orator* removed every trace of the forbidding technical terminology of classical rhetoric, offering one example after another of the cadenced, periodic prose of British, American, and occasionally classical historians and orators in translation for the young American student to study, memorize, and imitate. What all this amounted to was the Greek rhetorician's *progymnasmata* or preliminary exercises, the essential grounding for anyone who wanted to learn how to be an orator.

Equally important was the *Orator*'s carefully composed first lessons in dialectic. Douglass studied the dialogues provided by Bingham's colleague Edward Everett, particularly the "Dialogue between a Master and a Slave." Here too philosophical terms like "elenchus" and "syllogism" never appear, but the *Orator* taught him by example how to cross-examine an opponent's argument and expose the logical fallacies and self-contradictions that slavery's defenders invariably relied on.

This chapter traces first Douglass's learning of rhetorical tropes through imitation, then his turn away from such highly wrought language as he evolved into a more assured speaker using the plainer style that became the norm of American political discourse from the Jackson era onward. He learned colometry—the measurement of subsections of a sentence, and a technical term neither the *Orator* nor he ever employs—through imitation and practice. This largely forgotten technique developed by ancient rhetoricians and their followers teaches how to measure sentence structure, rhythm, and word placement with great precision. We show our readers how an orator so trained could produce periodic prose in which the number of words, syllables, and word accents were carefully calculated to achieve a desired effect. Douglass attained an eloquence Cicero and Quintilian would have recognized, even as he argued for a cause that many American followers of those ancient Romans would never have countenanced. His education from the *Orator* would stay with him to the end of his career, when he had to oppose the rising danger of Jim Crow and other practices that would undo much that had been won in the struggle before the Civil War and its aftermath.

Douglass and the Dominant Discourse of His Day

In Alice Walker's 1982 neo–slave narrative *The Color Purple*, the character Celie, writing to her sister, comments on attempts to teach her how to "speak proper," as Geneva Smitherman puts it—that is, how to speak standard English.[1] Her attitude toward the privileged discourse of her day marks the distance between a narrative with its twentieth-century sensibilities and those of the same kind of narrative in Douglass's time.

> Darlene trying to teach me how to talk. She say us not so hot. A dead
> country giveaway. You say us where most folks say we, she say, and peoples
> think you dumb. . . .she say I feel more happier talking like she talk. . . .
> Every time I say something the way I say it, she correct me until I say it
> some other way. Pretty soon it feel like I can't think. My mind run up on a
> thought, git confuse, run back and sort of lay down.[2]

She comments sarcastically on the primers she is given to study and concludes: "Look to me only a fool would want you to talk in a way that feel peculiar to your mind." Although Walker may share with her nineteenth-century predecessors a master narrative in a common plot arrangement, her character's dismissive attitude to educated speech in the time of slavery would not make sense to Olaudah Equiano (1745–97), Frederick Douglass, Harriet Jacobs (1813–97), or the woman preacher and spiritual leader Zilpha Elaw (born 1790). For them, literacy in the most privileged modes of culture was considered the highest possible prize. A frequently cited passage in *The Interesting Life of Olaudah Equiano, or Gustavus Vassa, the African* (1789) provides a model of the common figure in many of the slave narratives, what Henry L. Gates, Jr., calls the "trope of the talking book."[3]

I had often seen my master and Dick employed in reading; and I had a great curiosity to talk to the books, as I thought they did; and so to learn how all things had a beginning. For that purpose I have often taken up a book, and talked to it, and then put my ears to it, when alone, in hopes it would answer me; and I have been very much concerned when I found it remaining silent.[4]

Fredric Jameson terms these kinds of stories "allegorical master narratives," narratives that "reflect a fundamental dimension about our collective thinking and our collective fantasies about history and reality."[5] To study rhetoric is to learn how to talk and to write in a way that may at first feel peculiar to your mind.

Even more than Equiano's narrative, Douglass's became an initiating story, the allegorical master narrative for later African American texts as varied as *Black Boy, The Street, Invisible Man, The Color Purple*, and *Beloved*. All these works are neo–slave narratives that reproduce the pattern he devised. In addition, in its manipulation of language and its rhetorical strategies, his narrative illustrates the symbiotic relationship between literacy and liberation in African American literature. It also demonstrates the range of verbal strategies by which an African American voice both inserts itself in the dominant discourse of the culture and, at the same time, seizes primacy over and priority to that discourse. Finally, the *Narrative of the Life of Frederick Douglass, an American Slave* takes us into the language traditions of nineteenth-century America prior to the shift in learned as well as popular speech which occurred in the decades following the Civil War. As one of Douglass's recent biographers, William S. McFeely, puts it:

> In the public mind, oratory was not just a demonstration of great learning, though it was sometimes that, nor was it simply entertainment, though it was decidedly that as well, and people listened for hours; oratory was power . . . a force more impressive even than the biblical power of the word that Frederick had been told about in church.[6]

Thus we find Ralph Waldo Emerson's testimony to the preeminent position held by orators and oratory in his journals.

> Go and hear a great orator to see how presentable truth and right are, and presentable as common facts. . . . A true orator will instantly show that states and kingdoms of the world, all senators, lawyers, and rich men are caterpillars, webs and caterpillars when seen in the light. . . .

The eloquent man is he who is . . . inwardly desperately drunk with his
matter (a certain belief). . . . The possession by the subject of his mind is
so entire that it ensures an order of greatest force. . . . This mind is con-
templating a whole, and inflamed with the contemplation of the whole.[7]

In Emerson's terms, Douglass's writing and speaking became "the first
of a first"—that is, the model on which subsequent narratives would be
composed. And it even influenced the manner in which they would be
received. This is not to deny the priority of Equiano's narrative (1789),
or Briton Hammon's *A Narrative of the Uncommon Sufferings . . . of Briton
Hammon, A Negro Man* (1760); rather, the sales and reputation of Douglass's *Narrative* and its influence on both the criticism and the structure of
future slave narratives as well as neo–slave narratives made it the generic
exemplar. And the chief reason for Douglass's preeminence was the power
of his oratory and the rhetorical sophistication that sets his story apart
from all the others.

As the prime example of Gates's talking book, Douglass's *Narrative* is
concerned specifically with oratory and the character of the orator. He approached *The Columbian Orator* with a clear goal in mind: he wanted to learn
to read, to understand why things are as they are just as Equiano earlier had
desired the same of the "talking book" he encountered. And it is significant
that the book Equiano spoke of was the Bible, while Douglass's book is a
secular text. The conversion narratives (and Equiano's narrative is in part a
conversion narrative) swept away defenses of slavery and black oppression
based on a belief that blacks were not redeemable; they cleared the way for
the slave narratives to perform a secular, political task. Thus while Douglass details his progress in learning to read and to write, he deals with much
more than the primary learning that was the goal of a struggle for literacy.

> I used to spend the time in writing in the spaces left in master Thomas'
> copybook, copying what he had written. I continued to do this until I
> could write a hand very similar to that of Master Thomas. Thus after a
> long, tedious effort for years, I finally succeeded in learning how to write.[8]

He opens the next chapter demonstrating the final result of his early steps
toward literacy. He has learned not only to read and to write but also the
distance between his own condition and that of other human beings slave
and free. He wanted to learn to write in order to "have the occasion to
write my own pass"—in short, what Mr. Auld most feared and Douglass
most desired.

His reading and writing soon went beyond the primary goals with which he approached those skills. Reading "gave tongue to interesting thoughts of my own soul, which had frequently flashed through my mind, and died away for want of utterance." It "enabled me to utter my thoughts, and to meet the arguments brought forward to sustain slavery," and led him to "abhor and detest my enslavers" and led to a desire for freedom that he could not resist or avoid.

Another effect of literacy on young Douglass went well beyond his original aim of learning how to write passes for slaves seeking to escape to freedom. It was a deutero- or secondary kind of learning, an unforeseen consequence of his wanting to learn to read and write.

By studying the examples of classical oratory which constitute the bulk of *The Columbian Orator* Douglass learned from his imitation of those models not only how to reason and to argue but also how to structure his ideas and his argument according to clear patterns widely used in American public discourse in the decades leading up to the Civil War. His *Narrative* not only argues for abolition by giving an account of his life; it also demonstrates through his mastery of classical rhetoric and oratory his own worth as a literate human being. Along with the content of his models, he took in the rhetorical and oratorical strategies so carefully selected by Bingham. He gained control of the very kind of speech that admitted no place for a black voice—recall Jefferson's dismissal of Wheatley's poetry—and inscribed there just such a voice. In this he repeats in the secular realm that task which his predecessors, the authors of the conversion narratives, had accomplished in the sacred realm.

All this was very much what Bingham had hoped his *Orator* would make possible. It was the purpose he announced in his title: *The Columbian Orator: Containing a Variety of Original and Selected Pieces; Together with Rules; Calculated to Improve Youth and Others in the Ornamental and Useful Art of Eloquence.* The epigraph of the title page includes a quotation from the French rhetorician Charles Rollin: "Cato cultivated eloquence, as a necessary means for defending the rights of the people, and for enforcing good counsels." The point is to teach the eloquence which is central to freedom, and to do so by example and imitation.[9]

Douglass's sympathetic contemporaries cherished the lofty figures we find in the 1845 *Narrative*, its precise diction and arrangement of the sublime; all these things were part of an art that could be learned. The *Narrative* gave the readers of his day not only the image of a black man transformed by literacy, but the self-portrait of a superior black man possessing great thoughts and noble feelings, empowered by learning. In his final chapter, he confesses that the greatest achievement of his life up to that point was oratory: "I spoke but a few moments when I felt a degree of freedom, and said what I desired with considerable ease."[10]

How Words Count

> The period is designed precisely to provoke a pause that is not so much an-ticipatory as it is reflective, while the listener rehearses what this sentence's long embrace has contained.
>
> Shane Butler, "Cicero's Capita" (2009)

Until some years after the First World War, education of any kind in America was rarely separated from religious instruction. By his own account, an important first step in turning Frederick Douglass into the orator and writer he came to be was similar to what Olaudah Equiano and others had reported before him. Douglass began to learn by hearing his mistress Mrs. Sophie Auld read from the Bible.

> The frequent hearing of my mistress reading the Bible—for she often read aloud when her husband was absent—soon awakened my curiosity in respect to this *mystery* of reading, and roused in me the desire to learn. Having no fear of my kind mistress before my eyes (she had then given me no reason to fear) I frankly asked her to teach me to read; and without hesitation, the dear woman began the task, and very soon, by her assis-tance, I was master of the alphabet, and could spell words of three or four letters.[11]

The pious act of reading from the Bible would have seemed unexception-able, though in fact it is telling that Douglass says Mrs. Auld would do so only when her husband was not around to hear. Any kind of reading would present a problem for slave owners, in particular any part of the Old or New Testaments that spoke to the poor in spirit and downtrodden of the earth.

The Bible could be used only with the greatest selectivity. The pro-slavery minister Charles Colcock Jones (1804–1863) instructed ministers and others in how to preach and teach slaves. Jones advised the slave and plantation missionaries in many publications as to the best passages or texts to use and even how to conduct Bible study classes for slaves.[12] His goal was to prove that conversion to Christianity would make them more obedient and contented, and for that purpose he cites passages from St. Paul's Epistles for slave missionaries, such as 1 Timothy 6:1 ("Let as many servants as are under the yoke count their own masters worthy of all honour, that the name of God and his doctrine be not blasphemed") and Ephesians 6:5–7 ("Servants, be obedient to them that are your masters according to the flesh with fear and trembling, in singleness of your heart, as unto Christ; not with eye service, as men-pleasers; but as the servants of Christ, doing the will of God from the heart").[13]

But under no circumstances should one teach slaves to read. Like any teacher, Mrs. Auld was proud of her pupil's progress, and, like any proper slave owner, her husband Hugh Auld was aghast. Douglass illustrates this by offering a garland of direct quotations from Mr. Auld with his own ironic voiceover.

Mr. Auld promptly forbade the continuance of her instruction; telling her, in the first place, that the thing itself was unlawful; that it was also unsafe, and could only lead to mischief. To use his own words, further, he said, "if you give a nigger an inch, he will take an ell"; "he should know nothing but the will of his master, and learn to obey it." "Learning would spoil the best nigger in the world"; "if you teach that nigger"—speaking of myself— "how to read the bible, there will be no keeping him"; "it would forever unfit him for the duties of a slave"; and "as to himself, learning would do him no good, but probably, a great deal of harm—making him disconsolate and unhappy." "If you learn him how to read, he'll want to know how to write; and, this accomplished, he'll be running away with himself." Such was the tenor of Master Hugh's oracular exposition of the true philosophy of training a human chattel; and it must be confessed that he very clearly comprehended the nature and the requirements of the relation of master and slave. His discourse was the first decidedly anti-slavery lecture to which it had been my lot to listen.[14]

In American slavery's characteristic inversion of the Bible—in this instance, the tasting of the fruit of the Tree of Knowledge is now prohibited not by God but by a slave owner—Douglass learns precisely what his master did not want him to learn, simply by taking to heart what his master said.

"Very well," thought I; "knowledge unfits a child to be a slave." I instinctively assented to the proposition; and from that moment I understood the direct pathway from slavery to freedom.[15]

Mrs. Auld eventually loses her struggle against thinking like a slave owner and turns against Frederick. She is a portrait of a woman whose moral character is slowly but surely corrupted by the necessary role a slave owner must play: "Nature has done almost nothing to prepare men and women to be either slaves or slaveholders. Nothing but rigid training, long persisted in, can perfect the character of the one or the other."[16] Soon she is turned into a harpy by her role ("I have had her rush at me, with the utmost fury, and snatch from my hand such newspaper or book, with something of the wrath and consternation which a traitor might be supposed to feel on being discovered in a plot by some dangerous spy").[17] But the damage was done—or as Mr. Auld would put it, his wife had given Frederick an "inch" and "no ordinary precaution could prevent [him] from taking the ell." Douglass's solution to the problem was to get his white boyhood friends to give him lessons in reading. In the course of his time with them, he found that children his own age never defended slavery, but saw him as someone like themselves, who deserved to be as free as they were. In the meantime, Douglass managed to steal knowledge for himself as effectively as Phillis Wheatley seized her laurel crown from Maecenas. In Douglass's case, there was neither indulgence nor smiles at the same feat.

This is why Hugh Auld had to put a stop to young Frederick Bailey's ABCs. At the very least slaves would learn only to be unhappier with their fate. They would find out what the wider world beyond American slavery was like, and inevitably become discontent. More dangerously, any slave who could read and write would have a powerful instrument for escaping to freedom. And this was in fact Douglass's first goal in achieving literacy: he wanted to be able to forge documents that could be used by runaway slaves. He sums up the differences between himself and his master in a memorable passage from his 1845 *Narrative*:

> What he most dreaded, that I most desired. What he most loved, that I most hated. That which to him was a great evil, to be carefully shunned, was to me a great good, to be diligently sought; and the argument which he so warmly urged, against my learning to read, only served to inspire me with a desire and determination to learn. In learning to read, I owe almost as much to the bitter opposition of my master, as to the kindly aid of my mistress. I acknowledge the benefit of both.

The contradictions of slavery create a passage of contradictions. The balanced antitheses of the sentence complement the opposition between master and mistress and master and slave.[18] Classic periodic style of this order requires attention to minute details that readers or listeners may not catch unless they are willing to stop and take a sentence apart, much the same way it was written, word by word. Either by calculation or more likely through an instinctive art that came through much practice, Douglass had learned how to count words and syllables as well as word accents. Each "limb" or "member" (Greek *kôlon*, Latin *membrum*) of a well-written periodic sentence is set in an elaborate balancing act with others in its number of words, syllables, and rhythms.[19] In the following representation of Douglass's paragraph, accent marks bring out the full range of patterns and deliberate variation.[20] In keeping with classical rhetorical practice, the numbers represent syllables accented as counted from the *end* of each member. The trick is to achieve variation even as a recognizable pattern is set; what you want to avoid is establishing a predictable pattern. Thus the first four members each consists of four words, but of varying rhythm in their *clausula*, or closing rhythm. In marking the rhythm, the syllables stressed are numbered by counting *backward* from the last syllable.

Whát he most dreáded,	5–2
thát I most desíred.	5–1
Whát he most lóved,	4–1
thát I most háted.	5–2

This short first sentence is followed by longer, more complex one, also divided into members of roughly the same length as the first.

That which to him was a gréat évil,	3–2
to be cárefully shúnned,	4–1
was to me a gréat goód,	2–1
to be díligently soúght;	5–1
and the argument which he so wármly úrged,	3–1
against my leárning to réad,	4–1
only sérved to inspíre me	5–2
with a desire and determinátion to leárn.	4–1

This sentence in turn is followed by a shorter one, again in four members:

In léarning to réad,	4–1
I owe álmost as múch	4–1
to the bitter opposítion of my máster,	6–2
as to the kindly aíd of my místress.	5–2

The paradox of owing almost as much to bitter opposition as to kindly aid is neatly rounded out by the shortest sentence of all, consisting of but a single member.

I acknowledge the bénefit of bóth.   5–1

This terse sentence concludes the long train of thought and longer sentences, abruptly, with an alliterative phrase ("benefit of both") that blends the master and mistress's conflict into this paradoxical benefit: thanks to them, Douglass not only learned how to read but also grasped what was at stake as he did so.

These and other schemas we will inflict on our readers in this chapter may seem too elaborate for words, but nothing less can bring out a crucial point about the formation of the future orator and writer who became Frederick Douglass.[21] At an early age, probably by his midtwenties, he had learned some of the most characteristic techniques of classical rhetoric, particularly the periodic style in which the phrases and clauses of a sentence could be analyzed and created with the greatest precision by a number of stylistic devices that succeed most when they don't call attention to themselves, but simply seem to make whoever is speaking, and what he or she is saying, all the more impressive.

This should not be a surprise. Rhythm is an essential skill in the mesmerizing arts of a public speaker, and American public and intellectual life in the first half of the nineteenth century was in some respects not so different from classical Greece and Rome, where effective use of the spoken word in public settings was by far the most important means of communication.[22] By a combination of revision and constant practice, both in writing and in listening to others, as well as speaking, he was able to make a selected passage come to life in a way altogether more contrived and calculated than ordinary patterns of speech.

Such ornate passages in the *Narrative* are rare; it tends more to the plain and direct approach of a personal statement, save when the author wants to emphasize a particular point. This passage is a summing up of an extended account of how Douglass's master and mistress were at once opposed to and in favor of his learning, and out of their opposition he creates a mimetic style of oppositions, antitheses in both ideas and word placement. It is a deliberate turn to an ornate, obviously calculated style of speaking and writing that Cicero or Quintilian's modern students would easily recognize. He returns to this kind of writing only at points where an elevated oratorical style is most appropriate, above all in the celebrated account of what he imagined to be the final days of his grandmother in slavery.

It is also fair to say that this is the work of a tyro who has only recently learned the tricks of a classical orator's trade. In his later style Douglass was notably less given to this kind of showy rhetoric, both because of his maturing sense of style and because such elaborate prose would soon be going out of favor in American political speech.

What is most striking about Douglass's precocious achievement is that he did not have to immerse himself in classical authors to learn it. While he would have read a few passages from Cicero, Tacitus, and others in translation, he learned classical figures of thought and language entirely through the English of European and American orators who themselves had been trained in Latin and the classics. In the same way that Shakespeare has been credited with a mastery of Plutarch's *Lives* through North's translation—itself a translation of Amyot's French version of the original Greek—Douglass was able to acquire the essentials of classical rhetorical theory and practice entirely through translation. Unlike Phillis Wheatley, who as a poet in her time was necessarily a neoclassicist following Pope, Milton, and Dryden, Douglass was not a classicist in any sense of the word, because his source for learning classical rhetoric, Bingham's *Orator*, had already carefully removed every trace of the elaborate kind of analysis and terminology invented by the Greeks and their Roman successors. Go back a generation or two before, and Douglass would not have been so lucky; then rhetorical treatises and handbooks, like that of the Parisian scholar and pedagogue Charles Rollin, were replete with classical learning and exhaustive analytical exercises, and in French. At Dartmouth Caleb Bingham himself had read and learned from Rollin in the original. Furthermore, by the time he published his *Narrative* in 1845, Douglass had already served for some years as a minister in the North and would have had considerable experience with the cadences of the Bible as a reliable source for public eloquence. But it is *The Columbian Orator* that he credits with his education, above all else.

Besides his 1845 *Narrative*, the other early Douglass work that reflects much study of classical rhetoric and oratory is his novella published a few years later, "The Heroic Slave." Thanks to Bingham's book, he learned what ancient rhetoricians were most concerned their students know: how to read one's audiences and how then to project a character and a style of delivery that would be appropriate for any occasion, with the aim, always, of being persuasive. The first experience he had of this kind of power lay in the ministry, but it did not long detain him.

The Limitations of Christian Ministry

In her book on oratory and power in early America, Sandra Gustafson explains how generations of Europeans used a common language to create a sense of national identity.

> "Founding documents"; "one voice, one vote"; "sign your John Hancock"; "vox populi, vox dei": American identity derives important features from the symbolism of spoken and written language. Lacking the common ethnicity, often marked by a distinctive language that provided each European state with a sense of nationhood, Americans made the forms of language carry much of the burden of national union.[23]

For a writer and orator like Douglass, determined to fracture this same national union that legitimized and protected human chattel slavery, the obvious course lay in driving a wedge between those same forms of language that carried the burden of national union, exposing wherever possible the hypocrisy and illogic of those contrived denials that white Americans North and South called "compromises." He did not come to this perception immediately, however. He began his career in oratory as an ordained minister in the African Methodist Episcopal Zion church, and in that tradition we would expect him to write a conversion narrative, one strictly religious in aims and intended audiences. The religious language in the *Narrative* appears to link it to earlier conversion narratives, where the aim was to prove that the Negro had a soul and could be called to preach God's word. This had to be made clear before Douglass's secular work could be done. In fact he produced a political and social jeremiad whose attack on the uses of Christianity in American slavery suggests an activist who had completely evolved away from anything connected to organized American religion, whether for whites or blacks. His appendix to the 1845 *Narrative* begins apologetically, with Douglass worrying that his fierce comments on Christian support of slavery might be construed as the argument of an enemy of religion. Far from it, he declares; he means it "strictly to apply to the slaveholding religion of this land, and with no possible reference to Christianity proper."[24]

For, between the Christianity of this land, and the Christianity of Christ, I recognize the widest possible difference—so wide, that to receive the one as good, pure, and holy, is of necessity to reject the other as bad, corrupt and wicked.[25]

This is disingenuous and Douglass's sympathetic contemporaries knew it. John Greenleaf Whittier's 1836 poem "Clerical Oppressors" had already made the point, and Douglass quotes it to round out his own.

Just God! and these are they,
    Who minister at thine altar, God of right!
Men who their hands, with prayer and blessing, lay
    On Israel's ark of light.
What! preach, and kidnap men?
    Give thanks, and rob thy own afflicted poor?[26]

Christian sermons are always events where one waits for the relevant scripture to be brought to bear on whatever subject is in question; in this instance, Douglass confirms his and Whittier's claims immediately with a close paraphrase of Jesus's condemnation of the scribes and Pharisees for their hypocrisy in Matthew 23.14–28: outwardly they appear holy and righteous, but within they are filled with hypocrisy and iniquity. Abolitionist orators frequently turned to this passage to indict Christian apologists for slavery.[27]

Dark and terrible as is this picture, I hold it to be strictly true of the overwhelming mass of professed Christians in America. They strain at a gnat, and swallow a camel. Could anything be more true of our churches? They would be shocked at the proposition of fellowshipping a *sheep*-stealer; and at the same time they hug to their communion a *man*-stealer, and brand me with being an infidel, if I find fault with them for it. They attend with Pharisaical strictness to the outward forms of religion, and at the same time neglect the weightier matters of the law, judgment, mercy, and faith.[28]

Douglass concludes his refutation of the charge of being antireligious by producing a parody of a popular Southern hymn, "Heavenly Union" (though he doesn't give the title), which he professes to have been written by a Northern Methodist preacher visiting down South. Douglass achieved early fame through his parodies of Southern sermons, and this exercise is very much in that spirit. The now-forgotten slave owner's hymn "Heavenly Union" does not fare well when juxtaposed with Jeremiah 5:9: "Shall I not visit for these things? saith the Lord. Shall not my soul be avenged on such a nation as this?"[29] This is the very passage with which he closes the lengthy periodic sentences describing the death of his grandmother, which we will turn to shortly.

Come, saints and sinners, hear me tell
The wonders of Emmanuel,

Who saved me from a burning hell,
And brought my soul with Christ to dwell,
And gave me heav'nly union.

When Jesus saw me from on high,

Beheld my soul in ruin lie,

He looked on me with pitying eye,
And said to me as He passed by,

With God you have no union.

"Oh God, have mercy," then said I,
And looked this way and that to fly;
It grieved me sore that I must die;
I strove salvation then to buy,

But still I had no union.

But when depressed and lost in sin,

My dear Redeemer took me in,
And with His blood He washed me clean,
And Oh what seasons I have seen,
Since first I felt this union!

Come, saints and sinners, hear me tell
How pious priests whip Jack and Nell,
And women buy and children sell,
And preach all sinners down to hell,

And sing of heavenly union.

They'll bleat and baa, dona like goats,
Gorge down black sheep, and strain at notes,
Array their backs in fine black coats,
And seize their negroes by their throats,
And choke, for heavenly union.

They'll church you if you sip a dram,
And damn you if you steal a lamb;
Yet rob old Tony, Doll, and Sam,
Of human rights, and bread and ham;
Kidnapper's heavenly union.

They'll loudly talk of Christ's reward,
And bind his image with a cord,
And scold, and swing the lash abhorred,
And sell their brother in the Lord
To handcuffed heavenly union.[30]

The appendix's defense against the charge of impiety actually deepens Douglass's assault on Christian hypocrisy. In the end, we have the impression that this apologia for offending the religious reader is actually part of Douglass's larger design to displace the authenticating documents that Garrison and Wendell Phillips had supplied to certify his narrative by the weight of their names. Less eloquent here in the appendix, because somewhat diffuse, Douglass nevertheless manages to add yet one more layer of authority to a book that has moved us far beyond scripture and American religion generally.

> Sincerely and earnestly hoping that this little book may do something toward throwing light on the American slave system, and hastening the glad day of deliverance to the millions of my brethren in bonds—faithfully relying upon the power of truth, love, and justice, for success in my humble efforts—and solemnly pledging myself anew to the sacred cause,—I subscribe myself,
>
> FREDERICK DOUGLASS
> Lynn, Mass., April 28, 1845.[31]

The echoes of the conclusion of the Declaration of Independence are as palpable as the uppercase signature; its names were subscribed "And for the support of this Declaration, with a firm reliance on the protection of divine Providence, we mutually pledge to each other our Lives, our Fortunes, and our Sacred Honor." The slave who wrote his own life story signs off with an abolitionist's John Hancock. The appendix, in short, suggests, as abolitionist rhetoric often did, that those who oppose slavery were continuing the work of the American Revolution—*not* the Constitution, in which, for the time being, the Peculiar Institution was inscribed and sanctioned.

Douglass's text at first looks and even sounds like a conversion narrative, but it is not religious in any deep sense. Whereas the conversion narratives record movement from a condition of sin to (in most instances) a call to preach, Douglass records his leaving behind the clerical life and moving into the secular and political battles over slavery. Writers of most of the conversion narratives gained literacy by miraculous means. But that literacy was limited to a literacy of the Bible, which was the sole gateway to redemption. Douglass was determined to fight and resist dehumanizing slavery and was impatient with divine-dependent, turn-the-other-cheek Christianity.

Frederick Douglass's Poor Old Grandmother

The *locus classicus* for Douglass's engagement with classical rhetoric is a
florid passage on the fate of his grandmother, which, when printed as a
straightforward prose text, may seem tediously prolix. This is because it
needs to be heard in order to be read. He starts this sequence with one
sentence in plain style, "She had served my old master faithfully from
youth to old age," then follows with its opposite, a periodic sequence in
more elaborate form.

> She had been the source of all his wealth; she had peopled his plantation
> with slaves; she had become a great-grandmother in his service. She had
> rocked him in infancy, attended him in childhood, served him through life
> and at his death wiped from his icy brow the cold death-sweat, and closed
> his eyes forever.

The members are constructed so that there are audible parallels in words,
and at the same time each is written with careful attention to variation. As
the historian of rhetoric Morris W. Croll advises, we should think of these
elements not only as syntactic or logical units but also as psychological
and rhythmical constructions.[32] A schema like the one we employed earlier
shows how this passage is put together. Remember that one counts backward from the end of each member; 2 is second syllable from the end, 4 is
fourth from the end, and so on.

She had béen	the sóurce	of áll his weálth;	7–5–3–1
she had peópled	his plantátion	with sláves;	7–4–1
she had becóme	a great-grándmother	in his sérvice.	10–7–2
She had rócked	him	in ínfancy,	6–3
atténded	him	in chíldhood,	6–2
sérved	him	through lífe	4–1
and	at	his deáth	1
wíped	from	his ícy brów	6–3–1
		the cóld deáth-sweát,	3–2–1
	and	clósed his éyes foréver.	6–4–2

He closes the passage with anaphora, or repeated words, and a *tricôlon*,
or triad of phrases, creating a figure Greek rhetoricians termed a *klimax*
or "ladder" effect, where the words of the first member of the triad are

repeated with an ever-increasing number of syllables and correspondingly more powerful effect:

If my poor grandmother now lives, she lives to suffer in utter loneliness; she lives to remember and mourn over the loss of children, the loss of grandchildren, and the loss of great-grandchildren.

This can be schematized as:

If my poór grándmother now líves,	6–5–1
she líves to súffer in útter lóneliness;	10–8–5–3
she líves to remémber and moúrn	7–4–1
over	
the lóss of chíldren,	4–2
the lóss of grándchildren [*tricôlon*, *klimax*],	5–3
the lóss of greát-grandchildren.	6–4

Like an aria in an opera, this is a set piece that imposes narrative stasis; the flow of events stops and the writer expatiates upon a particular emotional moment. All three levels of eloquence that Cicero defines can be seen here: the high, the medium, and the low or simple diction.[33]

It is not surprising that Douglass learned how to write obsessively triple-phrased sentences like these, since a series of variations on the tricolon is what the first extract he read in *The Columbian Orator* amounts to. "An Oration on Eloquence, Pronounced at Harvard University, on Commencement Day, 1794" by graduating senior Joseph Perkins has the same calculations as the above passage of Douglass's but, as it were, in shorthand. We will dispense with syllable counting in this example, but mark the word accent.

The	éxcellence,
	utílity,
and	impórtance of éloquence;
	its órigin,
	prógress,
and	présent státe;
and its	supérior claím
to the	partícular atténtion
of	Colúmbia's freé-born sóns,

will exercise for a few moments
the patience of this   léarned,
                                  políte,
                   and   respécted assémbly.
       Speech and reason are the   cháracterístics,
                          the   glóry,
                          and   háppiness of mán.[34]

And so Perkins goes, much the same as his careful reader Douglass would. It is safe to say that both of them have got the tricolon down pretty well. Quintilian would probably say, altogether too well:

> With regard to genuine figure, I would briefly add that, while, suitably placed, they are a real ornament to style, they become perfectly fatuous when sought after overmuch. There are some who pay no consideration to the weight of their matter or the force of their thoughts and think themselves supreme artists, if only they succeed in forcing even the emptiest of words into figurative form, with the result that they are never tired of stringing figures together, despite the fact that it is as ridiculous to hunt for figures without referent to the matter as it is to discuss dress and gesture without reference to the body. But even perfectly correct figures must not be packed too closely together. (9.3.100–101)[35]

In Perkins's and Douglass's plethora of tricolons we have just what Quintilian warns against. The same vices can be heard in public discourse today, where a fondness for anaphora and the three-fold effect of the tricolon are easily mistaken for eloquence.

In less than ten years Douglass seems to have come to the same conclusion about the lament for his poor old grandmother, because he took some care to distance the entire set piece from the main text of his much revised and amplified 1855 autobiography, *My Bondage and My Freedom*: "Ten years ago, while speaking of the state of things in our family, after the events just named, I used this language."[36] Then he quotes the entire passage verbatim, but in a smaller type font, and passes on without a single further comment. In his autobiography *The Life and Times of Frederick Douglass*, published in 1893, the entire episode of the wicked Aulds, his grandmother, and her fate is elided. It seems that her pitiful story had been a fantasy of Douglass's own invention, the sort of thing that could have happened and, for all he knew, did happen. Inconveniently, it didn't. When he met his former master Thomas Auld after the Civil War, he learned that, far from being abandoned to die alone in a hovel, his grandmother had been well cared for by the Aulds until her dying day. Auld was much aggrieved that Douglass had so misrepresented his family's sincere charity and care. He changed the story in his successive memoirs, but never revised the first version of his memoir. As he informed Thomas Auld when they met, even though what he had written and published was not true, the account of his grandmother's pitiful fate was too useful for abolitionist polemic to be corrected.

Quintilian's comment in the epigraph to this chapter makes an important point for those of us today, living in what Kenneth Cmiel terms a postrhetorical age. Except for those who teach speech—the present American incarnation of ancient rhetoric as a living art, as opposed to its historical study—many now imagine it is possible to be an effective orator without such formal study. Also implicit in Quintilian's remarks here is the notion that many have, that rhetorical training was something more typical of earlier stages of a career than later. But it is an art that we are speaking of, and though we concentrate on its earlier stages in Douglass's public speaking and writing, it is one that would stay with him throughout his life. There is a continuity in oratorical style from the 1845 *Narrative*— though not in the 1855 or 1893 autobiographies, whose styles change radically—to the public speaking of his middle and late career.

An evolution beyond any strictly classical model from ancient Greece or Rome was also implicit in the design of *The Columbian Orator* itself. Like Rollin's, Bingham's examples gave a wide selection from contemporary or near-contemporary orators, preachers, philosophers, and divines; a modern classicist's strict-constructionist sense of "classics" as confined solely to Greco-Roman antiquity was alien to his enterprise. What was more to the point were the distinctions to be drawn between elaborate, highly wrought periodic style and the plain, direct language that eschewed figures of speech and thought, as well as elaborate colometric design. As Rollin and Bingham show through numerous examples, one could find both extremes of oratory already in classical antiquity, ranging from the laconicism of Cato, to the military concision of Caesar, to the grandiloquence of Cicero's orations. Classically trained rhetoricians wouldn't mind French critic Sainte-Beuve's commonplace "The style is the man," so long as one realizes that these varied styles are each of them born of a carefully studied eloquence that aims to create a desired image of that man. They would consider it naïve to assume that what an orator says is an expression of some genuine inner self.

In telling this story in his 1855 autobiography, Douglass was undoubtedly influenced by the growing American taste for what Kenneth Cmiel terms the *sermo humilis* of "Saxon Eloquence."[37] But when occasion demanded it, he could revert to the more elaborate style he first learned from *The Columbian Orator*. John F. Kennedy's elaborate inaugural address of 1961 with its intricate Gorgianic figures ("Let us not negotiate out of fear, but let us not fear to negotiate," etc.) and the plain speaking of that American Cato Harry Truman ("If you want a friend in Washington, get a dog") are on a continuum of recognizable rhetorical styles. So too is Martin Luther King's passionate and carefully calculated "I Have a Dream" speech at the March on Washington in 1963.

The Columbian Orator as Bible

By its very nature as a handbook, then, *The Columbian Orator* could be a student's bible, a single, self-sufficient volume. This is what Douglass made of it, and, given the increasing tendency of the American government to accommodate slavery, he was lucky to have it.[38] One could say the same of Cicero's *On the Orator* (*De Oratore*) and Quintilian's *Education of the Orator* (*Institutio Oratoria*): they were just one book, too. But what books! Between their covers they contain everything needed to move from a beginner's stage to higher skills in the art of rhetoric. The historian of rhetoric George Kennedy has remarked that Quintilian's book alone requires a course of study that would take as many years to complete as an undergraduate or even graduate degree in a modern subject.[39]

Douglass surely had plenty of experience listening to ministers' sermons. But it is not preachers, storytellers, or camp meetings that he credits with his education as an orator. It is his reading of Bingham's *Columbian Orator* that was decisive. He changed his life story in many ways over the nearly fifty years he spent living it and writing it—so much so that Lewis Hyde uses these changing self-fashionings to read Douglass's narratives as the traces of a trickster at work.[40] But there is one story he never wavered in telling, which was how important Bingham's book had been to him. By 1893's *Life and Times* he has a more pious tone than in 1845, even inclined to see God's guiding hand at work. His fervor for the *Orator* is stronger than ever.

> Here indeed was a noble acquisition. If I had ever wavered under the
> consideration that the Almighty, in some way, had ordained slavery and
> willed my enslavement for His own glory, I wavered no longer. I had now
> penetrated to the secret of all slavery and of all oppression, and had ascer-
> tained their true foundation to be in the pride, the power and the avarice
> of man. With a book in my hand so redolent of the principles of liberty,
> and with a perception of my own human nature and of the facts of my past

and present experience, I was equal to contest with the religious advocates of slavery, whether white or black; for blindness in this matter was not confined to the white people. I have met, at the south, many good, religious colored people who were under the delusion that God required them to submit to slavery and to wear their chains with meekness and humility. I could entertain no such nonsense as this, and I quite lost my patience when I found a colored man weak enough to believe such stuff.[41]

In other words, what Douglass got from the *Orator* was explicitly not what preachers and camp meetings had to offer. A preacher's cooptation by pro-slavery Christians was always a possibility, and part of the problem. Nearly fifty years later his outrage at the way Christianity and the Almighty had been used to defend slavery had not faded from view.

Douglass evolved beyond what he started with in the *Orator*. Almost as if he had heard Quintilian's warning about the danger of overusing trite rhythmical figures, ten years later he employs art to conceal art, and turns his early account of learning his ABCs with Mr. and Mrs. Auld into one of studied simplicity. In the 1855 autobiography the antitheses are still there, but handled now with much greater sophistication.

> *He* wanted me to be *a slave*; I had already voted against that on the home plantation of Col. Lloyd. That which he most loved I most hated; and the very determination which he expressed to keep me in ignorance, only rendered me the more resolute in seeking intelligence. In learning to read, therefore, I am not sure that I do not owe quite as much to the opposition of my master, as to the kindly assistance of my amiable mistress. I acknowledge the benefit rendered me by the one, and by the other; believing, that but for my mistress, I might have grown up in ignorance.[42]

Douglass breaks up the balanced periodic style to make the sentences less elaborate and self-conscious. Italics replace word placement and other earmarks of colometric schemes, overt antitheses are cut down to just one brief example, so that what began as a tour de force in antithetical periodic prose turns into a more circumstantial and personal comment. The actual experience of a slave's desires and his master's fears is stated plainly, because 1845's Douglass and his fascination with rhetorical figures has disappeared by 1855. "I am not sure that I do not owe quite as much" and "believing, that but for my mistress, I might have grown up in ignorance" replace the more assured confidence of "I owe almost as much to the bitter opposition of my master, as to the kindly aid of my mistress" with a more tentative, humbler incertitude. The irony of the concluding "I acknowledge the benefit of both" is thereby retained, but not the anger. The reflective tone suggests a more mature speaker, in whom we think we see more of the character of the man and less of the calculations of the orator. This effect is of course entirely calculated.

As we saw, Douglass had vilified his former master and Hugh Auld in his 1845 autobiography, only to learn later that what he had written in fact proved not to be true.[43] But he was not seeking to be a dispassionate historian in his writing, as his "Letter to His Old Master" published along with *My Bondage and My Freedom* attests. There is still plenty of fire.

> I intend to make use of you as a weapon with which to assail the system of slavery—as a means of concentrating public attention on the system, and deepening the horror of trafficking in the souls and bodies of men. I shall make use of you as a means of exposing the character of the American church and clergy—and as a means of bringing this guilty nation, with yourself, to repentance. In doing this, I entertain no malice toward you personally. There is no roof under which you would be more safe than mine, and there is nothing in my house which you might need for your comfort, which I would not readily grant. Indeed, I should esteem it a privilege to set you an example as to how mankind ought to treat each other.
>
> I am your fellow man, but not your slave.[44]

Ten years later Douglass was still Bingham's pupil. The arresting conclusion to his letter to Hugh Auld's brother Thomas comes directly from the antitheses that abound in *The Columbian Orator*'s "Dialogue between a Master and a Slave," as the slave cross-examines his master's use of such words as "rascal," "slave," "power," "right," "gratitude," "humane," "liberty," and any other term a slave owner can think of to defend his practice.

> *Master.* Suppose I were to restore you to your liberty, would you reckon that a favor?
>
> *Slave.* The greatest; for although it would only be undoing a wrong, I know too well how few among mankind are capable of sacrificing interest to justice, not to prize the exertion when it is made.
>
> *Master.* I do it, then; be free.
>
> *Slave.* Now I am indeed your servant, though not your slave.[45]

What Douglass picked up from *The Columbian Orator* was the dialectician's strategy of always being one step ahead of an interlocutor. In this kind of conversation, which is more than a simple exchange of opinion, the Socratic trick is to keep pushing the other speaker off any comfortable resting point, constantly revealing the inadequacy of every attempt to come to rest content with a half-understood idea.[46]

A Self-Portrait of Douglass the Orator

> To be an orator was to be a certain kind of person. It implied an ethos, a character that pervaded one's whole self. This ethos was ideally embodied in the cultivated gentleman and was purchased through a liberal education, which Quintilian, Cicero and others after them stressed was necessary for the orator.
>
> Kenneth Cmiel, *Democratic Eloquence*

With the notable exception of Marcus Tullius Cicero, few of the great orators in history have cared to tell us at any length what it was that made them so great. But it is a legitimate question for others to ask. How did great orators perceive their rhetorical skills and the effect of their eloquence on those who heard them? Frederick Douglass's only work of fiction "The Heroic Slave" supplies an answer that no one who is concerned with rhetoric and its possibilities should miss.[47] It introduces us to a narrator who hears and judges the protagonist not on meeting or seeing him, but simply by hearing him and being won over by his eloquence. For Douglass, in this story at least, mastery of oratory becomes what Cicero and every other preceptor in classical rhetoric hoped to convey: more than a sign of educational achievement, eloquent speech is a mark of superior moral character. When the eponymous Mr. Listwell finally sees that the disembodied voice of the man he has heard so well belongs to a Negro and a slave, he is converted as dramatically and suddenly to his cause as if he had been listening to a passionate evangelist's conversion narrative.

> The speech ... rang through the chambers of his soul and vibrated through his entire frame. Here indeed is a man, thought he, of rare endowments,—a child of God,—guilty of no crime but the color of his skin,—hiding away from the face of humanity, and pouring out his thoughts and feelings, his hopes and resolutions to the lonely woods. ...
> From this hour I am an abolitionist. I've seen enough and heard enough, and I shall go to my home in Ohio resolved to atone for my past

indifference to this ill-starred race, by making such exertions as I shall be able to do, for the speedy emancipation of every slave in the land.[48]

Frederick Douglass published "The Heroic Slave" in 1853, eight years after the first edition of the *Narrative of the Life of Frederick Douglass, an American Slave*. The heroic slave of the title is an actual figure from history, Madison Washington, the slave who led the mutiny on the slave ship *Creole* in October 1841.[49] The *Creole* was bound from Hampton Roads, Virginia, to New Orleans with a cargo of 135 slaves, and eleven days into the voyage was standing off the British Bahamas. Washington and eighteen other slaves led a successful revolt at night that completely surprised the small crew and took control of the ship with only a few casualties, principally the death of one slave owner, John Hewel, and a few other wounded. They compelled the captain to steer the brig into Nassau harbor and threw themselves on the mercy of the British government. After some hesitations and an abortive attempt by proslavery Americans to seize back the *Creole*, the combination of British justice (England having outlawed slavery in the West Indies by the Abolition of Slavery Act of 1833) and the black population of Nassau eventually brought about the complete freedom of all the slaves on the ship. The slave mutiny of the *Creole* was a celebrated case in its day, coming only two years after the slave rebellion on the Spanish slaver *Amistad* in 1836, when the slave mutineers killed the ship's captain and crew; they were eventually recaptured by the Americans, and their case wound up before the United States Supreme Court in 1841, where they were successfully defended by former President John Quincy Adams.[50]

Douglass gives the story of the *Creole* in the last section of "The Heroic Slave" as retold by the first mate of the ship. Tom Grant offers an eyewitness account to "a company of *ocean birds*" (sailors) he met some time later in New Orleans. Grant himself is "a trim, compact, manly looking person," an appearance corresponding to the personal character he reveals in telling his story. In spite of himself, he came to admire the ex-slave Madison Washington for his superior qualities. For Washington proved to be formidable in both his cunning and his courage. The experience of meeting Washington transformed him, Grant swears; he will never set foot again on a slave ship. All throughout his narrative he has to contend with a devil's advocate named Jack Williams, "a regular old salt" who gives voice to all the racism and hatred of the Southern slaveholders, outraged at the idea that black slaves could be capable of anything so daring as the *Creole* rebellion, and contemptuous of Grant and anyone else who would think otherwise. But Grant stands his ground. He was compelled by his own observations to change his mind about slaves, above all by the intelligence and the eloquence of Madison Washington.

> Mr. Williams speaks of "ignorant negroes," and, as a general rule, they are ignorant; but had he been on board the *Creole* as I was, he would have seen cause to admit that there are exceptions to this general rule. The leader of the mutiny in question was just as shrewd a fellow as ever I met in my life, and was as well fitted to lead in a dangerous enterprise as any one white man in ten thousand. The name of this man, strange to say, (ominous of greatness,) was MADISON WASHINGTON [caps original]. In the short time he had been on board, he had secured the confidence of every officer. The Negroes fairly worshipped him. His manner and bearing were such, that no one could suspect him of a murderous purpose. The only feeling with which we regarded him was, that he was a powerful, good-disposed negro. He seldom spake to any one, and when he did speak, it was with the utmost propriety. His words were well chosen, and his pronunciation equal to that of any schoolmaster. It was a mystery to us *where* he got his knowledge of language; but as little was said to him, none of us knew the extent of his intelligence and ability till it was too late. It seems he brought three files with him on board, and must have gone to work upon his fetters the first night out; and he must have worked well at that; for on the day of the rising, he got the irons *off eighteen* besides himself.[51]

In this way the slave named Madison Washington reverses the common and unsubtle irony of a slave's naming, whereby classical names like Pompey or Caesar were employed in *antiphrasis*, as the Greek rhetoricians put it, "by contradiction" naming someone with a stature or quality the opposite of what their actual status is. He becomes a genuine embodiment of both a founding father of the Constitution of the United States and its first great general and president as well.

"The Heroic Slave" has wider implications beyond what it reveals about Douglass's view of himself and his presentation to the world. It also runs completely counter to a characteristic myth of American exceptionalism, a view of the world in which the United States is God's New Israel and its citizens are its chosen people. People from diverse lands, diverse faiths, and diverse identities embrace a common identity, invent a common history, and project a common destiny. There are sacred sites in this myth, as in the book of Exodus, and there are sacred texts, the documents of the Revolution and the republican tradition of the Constitution. All of these views of American identity are reinforced by the literature and art of America.

"The Heroic Slave" begins with a prologue that might be termed "Frederick Douglass's *Notes on the State of Virginia*," a laudatory opening whose immediate predecessors could be found in any number of contemporary commemorations. It also sounds a theme as ancient as the encomium, the prose poem that is a tribute to the memory of a great man and seeks to preserve his memory.[52] The State of Virginia itself starts at the pinnacle of its glory but quickly descends from that eminence, the ironic intent made clear by a sentimental epigraph. The well-worn myth of Virginia the Mother of Presidents is brought forth only to lead to the real memory that is to be preserved: not Madison or Washington's, but the memory of one who took their names and put them to very different use.

> Yet not all the great ones of the Old Dominion have, by the fact of their birth-place, escaped undeserved obscurity. By some strange neglect, *one* of the truest, manliest, and bravest of her children,—one who, in after years, will, I think, command the pen of genius to set his merits forth, holds now no higher place in the records of that grand old Commonwealth than is held by a horse or an ox. Let those account for it who can, but there stands the fact, that a man who loved liberty as well as did Patrick Henry—who deserved it as much as Thomas Jefferson,—and who fought for it with a valor as high, an arm as strong, and against odds as great, as he who led all the armies of the American colonies through the great war for freedom and independence, lives now only in the chattel records of his native State.[53]

As is often the case with abolitionist rhetoric, Revolutionary oratory that had won Americans their liberty serves equally well for gaining slaves their liberty too. As Douglass himself had observed in the *Narrative* some eight years before,

> In coming to a fixed determination to run away, we did more than Patrick Henry, when he resolved upon liberty or death. With us it was a doubtful liberty at most, and almost certain death if we failed. For my part, I should prefer death to hopeless bondage.[54]

All the traits of the classicizing orator Douglass are here in the language of the narrator and Madison Washington: the studied interruptions of normal sentence structure by parenthetical comments to emphasize a chosen

word ("have, by the fact of their birth-place, escaped"); the kind of stut-
tering, inverted word order that Oxbridge academics use so effectively to
trap the unwary into thinking they aren't confident about what they are
saying (the plain style of "I think he's one who will command the pen of genius in after years" turning into the more artful, and artificial, "one who, in
after years, will, I think, command the pen of genius"); and that first trick
of self-conscious writing that we always find beginners using, the tricolon
or trios of words ("truest, manliest, bravest") and its more elaborate form
of whole clauses that grow progressively longer, leading to the *klimax* of

> a man who loved liberty as well as did Patrick Henry—who deserved it as
> much as Thomas Jefferson,—and who fought for it with a valor as high, an
> arm as strong, and against odds as great, as he who led all the armies of the
> American colonies through the great war for freedom and independence.

Washington's name is not there, deliberately, both for the arresting effect
of completing the triad begun by "Patrick Henry" and "Thomas Jefferson"
with a fulsome characterization, and for the real purpose behind this invocation of these icons of the American Revolution. Douglass turns the
eloquent and ironic name "Washington," which would signify the opposite
of what it means in a slave, into a name of literal fact. And then he catches
the self-contradiction and inhumanity of slavery by reducing this reborn
Washington to the level of beasts: "no higher place . . . than is held by a
horse or an ox."

This characterization also identifies Madison Washington with one
other figure in American history, Frederick Douglass himself.

> I have no authentic knowledge of my age, never having seen any authen-
> tic record containing it. By far the larger part of the slaves know as little
> of their ages as horses know of theirs, and it is the wish of most masters
> within my knowledge to keep their slaves thus ignorant.[55]

As Gates observes in his discussion of what he terms "a profoundly relational type of thinking" in the *Narrative*, Douglass "brings together two
terms in special relationships suggested by some quality that they share;
then by opposing two seemingly unrelated elements, such as the sheep,
cattle, or horses on the plantation and the specimen of life known as
slave, Douglass's language is made to signify the presence and absence of
some quality—in this case, humanity."[56] And as often happens with writers who shift from their usual work to a new kind of writing, Douglass

recycles what he had already written about himself into this fictional narrative. What the similar characterizations of Washington and Douglass signify is that the Heroic Slave is at once reminiscent of a figure of history, and a recognizable version of Douglass himself. This has important consequences for our reading of the story, which we can see is Douglass's fictional account of his own life, with all the distance needed for an analytical and detached view that goes even further than what autobiography would offer.

At the same time, Douglass goes out of his way to emphasize how elusive Madison Washington will be: "brought to view only by a few transient incidents." Three similes in the grandiloquent epic style create a slave who is a barely visible epic hero.

> Like a guiding star on a stormy night, he is seen through the parted clouds and the howling tempests; or, like the gray peak of a menacing rock on a perilous coast, he is seen by the quivering flash of angry lightning, and he again disappears covered with mystery.
>
> But alas! he is still enveloped in darkness, and we return from the pursuit like a wearied and disheartened mother, (after a tedious and unsuccessful search for a lost child,) who returns weighed down with disappointment and sorrow. Speaking of marks, traces, possibles, and probabilities, we come before our reader.[57]

These similes are not subtle, each emphasizing in a sentimental way the visible invisibility of this hero. He is like the guiding star, later identified in Washington's own words quite explicitly with the North Star, the name of Douglass's first newspaper and the guiding star for flight to Canada; also, a mountain peak glimpsed through lightning. And the narrator himself is like a mother bereft and unsuccessful in finding her vanished child. But the story that follows is distinguished by its turn away from this emphasis on the visible and invisible, to the acoustic. "We come before our readers" is the mark of an orator or lecturer coming to the stage. The first appearance of Madison Washington bears out the similes, for we first hear him rather than see him.

The Northern traveler in Virginia later identified as "Mr. Listwell" continues to live up to his name. Madison Washington gradually comes into acoustic focus, the sheer sounds of his voice marked by "rich and mellow accents" even before Listwell creeps close enough to make out what he is saying.

What, then, is life to me? it is aimless and worthless, and worse than worthless. Those birds, perched on yon swinging boughs, in friendly conclave, sounding forth their merry notes in seeming worship of the rising sun, though liable to the sportsman's fowling-piece, are still my superiors. They *live free*, though they may die slaves. They fly where they list by day, and retire in freedom at night. But what is freedom to me, or I to it? I am a *slave*,—born a slave, an abject slave,—even before I made part of this breathing world, the scourge was platted for my back; the fetters were forged for my limbs.[58]

Whoever is speaking, he has an excellent grasp of the rhetorical figure of the apostrophe. Douglass had already used it in his apostrophe to the ships in the *Narrative*.

You are loosed from your moorings, and are free; I am fast in my chains, and am a slave! You move merrily before the gentle gale, and I sadly before the bloody whip! You are freedom's swift-winged angels, that fly round the world; I am confined in bands of iron! O that I were free! O, that I were on one of your gallant decks, and under your protecting wing! Alas! betwixt me and you, the turbid waters roll. Go on, go on. O that I could also go! Could I but swim! If I could fly! O, why was I born a man, of whom to make a brute! The glad ship is gone; she hides in the dim distance. I am left in the hottest hell of unending slavery.[59]

Douglass then appeals to the Christian god for help, as one might expect ("O God, save me! God, deliver me! Let me be free!"), but for Douglass, as for Madison Washington, God helps those who help themselves. He concludes his apostrophe to the ships by turning to his own salvation at his own hands:

It cannot be that I shall live and die a slave. I will take to the water. This very bay shall yet bear me into freedom. The steamboats steered in a North-East course from North Point. I will do the same; and when I get to the head of the bay, I will turn my canoe adrift, and walk straight through Delaware into Pennsylvania.[60]

In exactly the same way, the voice that Mr. Listwell hears in "The Heroic Slave" rises above this desperation and resolves to be free in a peroration that blends calculated structure and variation into a passionate resolution.

He frames it with the abstract ideal of "liberty" and closes with "*I shall be free.*"

> *Liberty* I will have, or die in the attempt to gain it. This working that others may live in idleness! This cringing submission to insolence and curses! This living under the constant dread and apprehension of being sold and transferred, like a mere brute, is *too* much for me. I will stand it no longer. What others have done, I will do. These trusty legs, or these sinewy arms shall place me among the free. Tom escaped; so can I. The North Star will not be less kind to me than to him. I will follow it. I will at least make the trial. I have nothing to lose. If I am caught, I shall only be a slave. If I am shot, I shall only lose a life which is a burden and a curse. If I get clear, (as something tells me I shall,) liberty, the inalienable birth-right of every man, precious and priceless, will be mine. My resolution is fixed. *I shall be free.*[61]

The eloquence is indistinguishable from the narrating voice of "The Heroic Slave" or, for that matter, from the eloquence of Douglass himself. And it is the voice alone that Mr. Listwell hears. He gains his entire impression of the noble character and power of the speaker from his words, more particularly, his *voice*: its choice of words, their arrangement, their delivery, all combined into a morally persuasive portrait of the character of the man who utters them, where passionate delivery is only one factor in explaining his rhetorical power.

This scene dramatizes an ancient doctrine about the relationship between a native ability and the role education and art can play in developing it. By this reckoning, ancient rhetoric and the arts it offers are fine things to gain, but above all, as Cicero, Quintilian, and others point out, individual talent is the *sine qua non* of great literature. It is what creates the effect Longinus describes in *On the Sublime*, a work that was readily available in Bingham's day, in Rollin's original French or in English translation.[62]

Listwell finally raises his head and sees at last the man whose character he has already learned through his soliloquy. Now he looks on silently, at the silent orator, and the body and the deportment of Madison Washington bear out what the style has already proclaimed is the man.

> Madison was of manly form. Tall, symmetrical, round, and strong. In his movements he seemed to combine, with the strength of the lion, a lion's elasticity. His torn sleeves disclosed arms like polished iron. His face was "black, but comely." His eye, lit with emotion, kept guard under a brow as dark and as glossy as the raven's wing. His whole appearance betokened

Herculean strength; yet there was nothing savage or forbidding in his aspect. A child might play in his arms, or dance on his shoulders. A giant's strength, but not a giant's heart was in him. His broad mouth and nose spoke only of good nature and kindness. But his voice, that unfailing index of the soul, though full and melodious, had that in it which could terrify as well as charm. He was just the man you would choose when hardships were to be endured, or danger to be encountered—intelligent and brave. He had the head to conceive, and the hand to execute. In a word, he was one to be sought as a friend, but to be dreaded as an enemy.[63]

Tall, symmetrical, round, strong: Madison Washington is aestheticized, as if he were himself an embodiment of oratory. Herculean strength is an apt comparison—even though Hercules is commonly celebrated more for his great strength and endurance than his eloquence. Mr. Listwell is even more provocative when he muses that Madison Washington's face was "black, but comely." In chapter 1, verse 5, of the Song of Solomon, the bride is speaking to the daughters of Jerusalem and her bridegroom: "I am black but comely, O ye daughters of Jerusalem, as the tents of Kedar, as the curtains of Solomon." There is an erotic charge to all this that is hard to miss. More to the point, the following verse, which Douglass does not cite, but which he could expect his readers to know, suggests the whole episode is a kind of Song of Solomon to abolitionist America: "Look not upon me, because I am black, because the sun hath looked upon me: my mother's children were angry with me; they made me the keeper of the vineyards; but mine own vineyard have I not kept."

Douglass has reprised in his own telling what it is like to hear and see Frederick Douglass speaking. If the primacy of the slave's word resonates with biblical as well as classical overtones, the first sight of Madison Washington in person recreates the impression Douglass himself made on William Lloyd Garrison at Nantucket in 1841.

There stood one, in physical proportion and stature commanding and exact—in intellect richly endowed—in natural eloquence a prodigy—in soul manifestly "created but a little lower than the angels"—yet a slave, ay, a fugitive slave,—trembling for his safety, hardly daring to believe that on the American soil, a single white person could be found who would befriend him at all hazards, for the love of God and humanity! Capable of high attainments as an intellectual and moral being—needing nothing but a comparatively small amount of cultivation to make him an ornament to society and a blessing to his race—by the law of the land, by the voice of

the people, by the terms of the slave code, he was only a piece of property,
a beast of burden, a chattel personal, nevertheless![64]

This kind of astonishment was to be characteristic of Douglass's public
performances throughout his long career. No matter how much we gain
from reading his words, their original delivery was an experience that witness after witness declared was inimitable.[65] Douglass may not have been
much of a novelist, but he had an excellent grasp of the effect he could
create through the force of his voice and presence.

The 1852 Fourth of July Oration and Douglass's Maturing Style

Naturally Douglass's style and political views changed over the course of
a fifty-year career in public speaking, writing, and activism. We can see
the way he modified his use of rhetorical figures by tracing his treatment
of his grandmother's story through the narratives of 1845, 1855, and 1893.
At all times he was famous for the slow and quiet start of his orations that
eventually led to a ringing and elaborately crafted peroration. First, "The
Southern Style of Preaching to Slaves: An Address Delivered in Boston,
Massachusetts, on 18 January 1842."

> But what a mockery of His religion is preached at the South! I have been
> called upon to describe the style in which it is set forth. And I find our
> ministers there learn to do it at the northern colleges. I used to know they
> went away somewhere I did not know where, and came back ministers; and
> this is the way they would preach. They would take a text—say this:—"Do
> unto others as you would have others do unto you." And this is the way
> they would apply it. They would explain it to mean, "slaveholders, do unto
> *slaveholders* what you would have them do unto you":—and then looking
> impudently up to the slaves' gallery, (for they have a place set apart for us,
> though it is said they have no prejudice, just as is done here in the northern
> churches; looking up high to the poor colored drivers and the rest, and
> spreading his hands gracefully abroad, he says, (*mimicking*,) "And you too,
> my friends, have souls of infinite value—souls that will live through endless
> happiness or misery in eternity. Oh, *labor diligently* to make your calling
> and election sure. Oh, receive into your souls these words of the holy
> apostle—"Servants, be obedient unto your masters." (*Shouts of laughter and
> applause.*) Oh, consider the wonderful goodness of God! Look at your hard,

horny hands, your strong muscular frames, and see how mercifully he has adapted you to the duties you are to fulfill! (*continued laughter and applause*) while to your masters, who have slender frames and long delicate fingers, he has given brilliant intellects, that they may do the *thinking*, while you do the *working.*" (*Shouts of applause.*) It has been said here at the North, that the slaves have the gospel preached to them. But you will see what sort of a gospel it is:—a gospel which, more than chains, or whips, or thumb-screws, gives perpetuity to this horrible system.[66]

William Andrews observes that Douglass, through "sophistication in marshalling figurative language along with literary allusions and a ready supply of examples from American and European history helped to establish a reputation for oratorical genius."[67]

No other work of Douglass better confirms Andrew's statement than his speech "What to the Slave Is the Fourth of July?," an epideictic (display) oration he delivered ten years after "The Southern Style of Preaching to Slaves," on July 5, 1852, in Rochester, New York. This speech Andrews further classifies as an "outstanding example of his mature style" and "the most famous antislavery speech Douglass ever gave."[68] The occasion for this speech was the July 5th celebration held by many abolitionist groups and by blacks in those cities in which they represented a sizable portion of the population. The function of such gathering was to comment on the irony of the celebration of liberty and freedom for all by a nation of slaves and slaveholders.

Douglass's oration owed a great deal of its success not only to his brilliant delivery but also to his careful attention to the patterns laid down for classical oratory. A review of the speech will demonstrate this if we keep in mind the way in which he moves in sequence from the *exordium* or opening section in which the orator assumes a nonthreatening, noncombative relationship with the audience, commenting on his powers as too feeble for such a distinguished gathering and occasion. He then moves to the *narratio* to offer background in history or the situation that is his subject. In the *explicatio* he defines both the terms of his argument and the important issues that define his topic. The *partitio* provides the issues he is about to prove: his thesis. This thesis is further developed in the *confirmatio* in which he offers proof and support for that thesis, and the *refutatio* in which he answers opposing arguments. He closes with the *peroratio* or conclusion, which includes a call to action. This last Douglass was exceptionally adept at employing with great power and success. Audiences who heard his speech opposing the acceptance by the Scottish church of churches in the slaveholding South rose from their seats to shout repeatedly to Douglass's repeated words, "Send back the money."

Not always noted, however, is Douglass's use of maxims to create a ground of shared belief and to punctuate some of his most powerful periods, such as "Oppression makes a wise man mad," "That which is human cannot be divine," and "Where all is plain, there is nothing to be argued."[69] They grow more radical and aggressive as the speech progresses: "For revolting barbarity and shameless hypocrisy, America reigns without a rival."[70] A second aspect of the richness of this oration is Douglass's metaphors that link in striking ways his subject to the known experience of his listeners.

> Great streams are not easily turned from channels, worn deep in the course of ages. They may sometimes rise in quiet stately majesty, and inundate the land, refreshing and fertilizing the earth with their mysterious properties. They may also rise in wrath and fury and bear away, on their waves, the accumulated wealth of years of toil and hardship. They, however gradually flow back to the same old channel, and flow on as serenely as ever. But, while the river may not be turned aside, it may dry up and leave and leave nothing behind but the withered branch, and the unsightly rock, to howl in the abyss-sweeping wind, the sad tale of departed glory. As with rivers, so with nations.[71]

It is clear that doom is possible, that America, as a result of its sins and wrongs, can, in spite of its noble beginnings, become the land of "departed glory." The power of this extended metaphor is due in no small part to Douglass's handling of anaphora (the repetition of "They"), the arrangement of sentences in order to lead to the simple maxim which closes the sequence.

> From the round top of your ship of state, dark and threatening clouds may be seen. Heavy billows, like mountains in the distance, disclose to the leeward huge forms of flinty rock! That bolt drawn, that chain broken, and all is lost. Cling to this day—cling to it, and to its principles with the grasp of a storm-tossed mariner to a spar at midnight.[72]

In this metaphor Douglass elaborates on his earlier statement that "the Declaration of Independence is the ring-bolt to the chain of your Nation's destiny." Absent the ring-bolt (Douglass's experience of ships proved the importance of such a crucial connecting device), safety for the storm-tossed mariner is not at all assured. The ring-bolt is a vital connection. Not only the world of ships but other experiences qualify him for his role as an American Jeremiah: "I was born amid such sights and scenes. To me the American slave trade is a terrible reality."[73] This statement closes his description of a slave auction in which he moves from audible images to visual images as he constructs yet another nearly flawless anaphora. He orders his audience to "hear" in the opening and moves to a series of commands to "see." But Douglass saves his energies for an extended peroration calling his audience to action. He uses antithesis in each member of the figure to reveal the hypocrisy of America. Structurally it is tied together by anaphora (the repeated words are printed bold here to bring out the patterns), and it is not quite as abandoned in style as it may at first seem. Each of the sections is designed to be dispatched in long phrases, as marked by the commas. Ancient rhetoricians saw clear connections between song and oratory, in ways most of us now do not, but Douglass clearly did. In a simpler way than our earlier colometric analysis, we mark here the basic structure of these in bold type.

You boast of your love of liberty and your superior civilization, and your pure Christianity, **while** the whole political power of the nation, as embodied in the two great political parties, is solemnly pledged to support and perpetuate the enslavement of three millions of your countrymen.

You hurl your anathemas at the crowned headed tyrants of Russia and Austria, and pride yourselves on your democratic institutions, **while you yourselves** consent to be the mere tools and body-guards of the tyrants of Virginia and Carolina.

You invite to your shores fugitives of oppression from abroad, honor them with banquets, greet them with ovations, cheer them, toast them, salute them, protect them, and pour out your money to them like water; the fugitives from your land, **you** advertise, hunt, arrest, shoot and kill.

You glory in your refinement and your universal education; **yet** you maintain a system as barbarous and dreadful as ever stained the character of a nation—a system begun in avarice, supported in pride, and perpetuated in cruelty.

You shed tears over fallen Hungary, and make the sad story of her wrongs the theme of your poets, statesmen and orators, till your gallant sons are ready to fly to arms to vindicate her cause against her oppressors; **but** in regard to the ten thousand wrongs of the American slave, **you** would enforce the strictest silence, and would hail him as an enemy of the nation who dares to make those wrongs the subject of public discourse!

You are all on fire at mention of liberty for France or for Ireland; **but** are as cold as an iceberg to the thought of liberty for the enslaved of America.

You discourse eloquently on the dignity of labor; **yet**, you sustain a system which, in its very essence, casts a stigma upon labor.

You can bare your bosom to the storm of British artillery, to throw off a threepenny tax on tea; **and yet** wring the last hard-earned farthing from the grasp of the black laborers of your country.

You profess to believe that, "of one blood God made all nations of men to dwell on the face of all the earth" and hath commanded all men, everywhere to love one another; **yet you** notoriously hate (and glory in your hatred) all men whose skins are not colored like your own.

You declare, before the world, and are understood by the world to declare, that **you** "hold these truths to be self evident, that all men are created equal, and are endowed by their Creator with certain inalienable rights, and that among these are life, liberty, and the pursuit of happiness"; **and yet, you** hold securely in a bondage, which according to your own Thomas Jefferson, "is worse than ages of that which our fathers rose in rebellion to oppose," a seventh part of the inhabitants of your country.[74]

Douglass could by this point pack his own work with as much learning and citations as any orator in Caleb Bingham. His speech is replete with citations from the Bible (Isaiah, Jeremiah, Psalms), *Macbeth*, Longfellow, Whittier, and those favorite scriptures among black abolitionists—Psalm 68 and Matthew 23. And to what purpose was such a display of learning?

At a time like this, scorching irony, not convincing argument is needed! O, had I the ability, and could I reach the nation's ear, I would, to-day, pour out a stream of biting ridicule, blasting reproach, withering sarcasm, and stern rebuke. For it is not light that is needed, but fire; it is not the gentle shower, but thunder. We need the storm, the whirlwind, and the earthquake.[75]

"What to the Negro Is the Fourth of July?" is the rhetorical equivalent of a Beethoven symphony at full volume.

In one of his last public addresses more than forty years later Douglass had lost none of the fire of his youth, even when praising the greatest man he had ever known, in "Abraham Lincoln, the Great Man of Our Century, an Address Delivered in Brooklyn, New York, on 13 February 1893."

Gentlemen—I beg to remind you at the outset that reminiscences are generally tedious. I hope you may find mine an exception to the general rule, though I fear the contrary, for speakers are often more interesting and eloquent about what they do not know than about what they do know. (*Applause.*) It is impossible for me, and, perhaps, for anybody else, to say anything new about Abraham Lincoln. (*Applause.*) He is in the minds and hearts of all of us. We know him and know of him, as we know of no other great man of our century. (*Applause.*)

I had the good fortune to know Abraham Lincoln personally and peculiarly. I knew him, not on the side visible to the free, rich and powerful, but on the side which he presented to the unfortunate, defenseless, the oppressed and the enslaved. (*Applause.*) It is something to know how a man will deport himself to his admitted equals, but more to know how he will bear himself to those who are recognized as his inferior. (*Applause.*) It is this knowledge of Mr. Lincoln upon which I depend for any interest, value or significance of my story to you this evening.

Of course, and on general principles, it is a great thing for any man of what ever condition to know a great man. For a truly great man is rebuke to pride and selfishness in the strong, and a source of strength to the weak and unfortunate. The memory of such a great man is ennobling to men already noble, and we shall all feel better for reviving and keeping alive the memory of such a man tonight. (*Applause.*)[76]

For his peroration Douglass tells of attending a reception at the White House after being present and hearing Lincoln's second inaugural in March 1865. The policemen guarding the doors refused to let him in, until Douglass managed to get word to the president, "Tell Mr. Lincoln that Frederick Douglass is at the door and is refused admission." He then entered, to the astonishment of the police and others.

But as soon as President Lincoln saw me I was relieved of all embarrassment. In a loud voice, so that all could hear, and looking toward me, he said, "And here comes my friend, Frederick Douglass!" (*Good! Good!*) I had some trouble in getting through the crowd of elegantly dressed people to Mr. Lincoln.

When I did succeed, and shook hands with him, he detained me and said, "Douglass, I saw you in the crowd to-day, listening to my inaugural address. How did you like it?" I replied, "Mr. Lincoln, I must not stop to talk now. Thousands are here, wishing to shake your hand." But he said, "You must stop. There is no man in the United States whose opinion

I value more than yours. How did you like it?" (*Applause*) I said, "Mr. Lincoln, it was a sacred effort," and passed on, amid some smiles, much astonishment and some frowns. And this was the last time that I heard the voice and saw the face and form of honest Abraham Lincoln.

In this memoir Douglass has come full circle in his view of Lincoln. For much of Lincoln's first presidency he was disappointed by what he saw as Lincoln's equivocation and temporizing about the abolition of slavery. The Emancipation Proclamation at the beginning of 1863 marked a new turn, as Douglass came to appreciate more clearly the difference between being an activist for one cause and people and a president responsible for the fate of an entire nation in a civil war.[77]

Douglass's last major public address, "Lessons of the Hour: An Address Delivered in Washington, D.C., on 9 January 1894," exhibits a continuing mastery of the orator's precept that Cicero and Quintilian always advised their students to pay the most attention to: the opening and closing of an oration.

> Friends and fellow citizens: No man should come before an audience such as the one by whose presence I am now honored, without a noble object and a fixed and earnest purpose. I think that, in whatever else I may be deficient, I have the qualifications indicated, to speak to you this evening. I am here to speak for, and to defend, so far as I can do so within the bounds of truth, a long-suffering people, and one just now subject to much misrepresentation and persecution. Charges are at this time preferred against them, more damaging and distressing than any which they have been called upon to meet since their emancipation.

The cultivation of the audience's favor and the high seriousness of purpose are standard themes to sound in an *exordium*. The peroration is worked out in a similarly skillful way. After the blunt, brief command, "Put away your race prejudice," Douglass builds one long sentence to lead to his final words, "Your Republic will stand and flourish forever."

> Put away your race prejudice. Banish the idea that one class must rule over another. Recognize the fact that the rights of the humblest citizen are as worthy of protection as are those of the highest, and your problem will be solved; and, whatever may be in store for it in the future, whether prosperity, or adversity; whether it shall have foes without, or foes within, whether there shall be peace, or war, based upon the eternal principles of

truth, justice and humanity, and with no class having any cause of complaint or grievance, your Republic will stand and flourish forever.

Invisible Man Dreams of Frederick Douglass

Frederick Douglass commanded an art which would come to seem alien and old-fashioned as the art of rhetoric receded from public view in the century after his death. But his example was always there to inspire later orators, not least the young narrator of Ralph Ellison's 1951 novel, *Invisible Man*, even though Douglass's mastery of the periodic style and his orator's spatial conception of a word's placement in a speech would be skills lost to many of his would-be followers. A schematization of the *membra* of part of the last sentence in "Lessons of the Hour" might go as follows:

Whatever may be in store for it in the future
    whether   prosperity
       or   adversity
    whether it   shall have   foes without
       or   foes within
    whether there   shall be   peace
       or   war
                          based upon the eternal principles
                          of   truth
                                   justice
    and   humanity
    and   with no class having any cause   of complaint
                                         or grievance
your Republic will stand and flourish forever.

Just as a trained actor knows the "beats" or points for pause and emphasis in delivering a line on stage, some understanding of how words are placed and sentences constructed is a necessary if such complex language is to be delivered effectively to an audience. Nothing remotely like this kind of art lies within Invisible Man's ken. For him, Frederick Douglass represents not so much a life story to be imitated, or an orator's art to be learned, as the embodiment of a successful career.

One way to track the evolution of Ellison's narrator is to watch his growing power as a public speaker, as he seeks to persuade his audiences with an increasingly bitter eloquence he cannot control. To begin with, white racists in the South reward Invisible Man's earliest effort at oratory for following the politics and at moments for even quoting verbatim from Booker T. Washington's Atlanta Exposition speech of 1895. To trace the long arc of Invisible Man's evolution from that tyro's first effort to his final speech at the martyred Tod Clifton's funeral in Harlem is to follow what might be termed the Diseducation of the Orator, one created through brutal social realities rather than the schoolroom, finally leading to a nihilistic finale in which Invisible Man renounces public speech and street activism altogether.[78]

At one point, after a successful debut for a Marxist front organization, the Brotherhood, Ellison's narrator is in an expansive, self-satisfied mood. Inspired by a picture of Frederick Douglass in the party headquarters of the Brotherhood, he imagines he is well on the way to achieving what Douglass had achieved. He thinks he has discovered the power oratory can confer on those who know how to use it.

> For now I had begun to believe, despite all the talk of science around me, that there was a magic in spoken words. Sometimes I sat watching the watery play of light upon Douglass's portrait, thinking how magical it was he had talked his way from slavery to a government ministry, and so swiftly. Perhaps, I thought, something of the kind is happening to me. Douglass came north to escape and find work in the shipyards; a big fellow in a sailor's suit who, like me, had taken another name. What had his true name been? Whatever it was, it was as *Douglass* that he became himself, defined himself. And not as a boat-wright as he'd expected, but as an orator. Perhaps the sense of magic lay in the unexpected transformations. "You start Saul, and end up Paul," my grandfather had often said. "When you're a youngun, you Saul, but let life whup your head a bit and you starts to trying to be Paul—though you still Saul around on the side."[79]

Though the narrator thinks he has grasped a fundamental point about what the spoken word can achieve, anyone who knows even a minimum about oratory or Douglass's career will realize that Invisible Man has not half understood Douglass's achievement. Innocent as he is, untutored about what Douglass actually accomplished and how he did it, the narrator mistakes the effects of oratory for its cause, thinking there is "magic" in spoken words. That perception is fine for an orator's audience, but Quintilian and Cicero would want their orators to be more knowing about what it is they are actually doing. In most respects Ellison's Invisible Man is merely lucky in the times and places he speaks; he falls into situations where an orator is needed, so he gets up and starts talking. One senses he could no more reliably reproduce the same success on other occasions than he could explain how it was he came to say what he did. And if he is a gifted orator by instinct, it is significant that as an orator he ends his story by going into a kind of Dantesque hibernation where writing, not speaking or organizing, is the next necessary stage.

Invisible Man's grasp of Douglass in history is just as illusory. Douglass may have talked his way "from slavery to a government ministry," but only over the course of forty years. The comical simplemindedness of the hero at this point is entirely characteristic of Ellison's novel, not least in the way Invisible Man conceives of Douglass as a modern careerist. Invisible Man the character invents himself as an orator every time he speaks, but as an orator he is a paradigm of instability, from first to last not just responsive to the audiences he appears before, but entirely shaped by them.

The pity of it is how distant Ellison's narrator is from the great orator and verbal magician he so envies. Douglass is an ideal who appears to him through a "watery play of light," and that shimmering mirage is all too accurate about what Invisible Man cannot understand. For him, at midtwentieth century, Frederick Douglass and the age of oratory are nothing but a mirage. Thirty years after *Invisible Man*, Alice Walker would create a character in *The Color Purple* who is as ignorant of rhetoric and the uses of language as Invisible Man, but without a trace of Ellison's knowing irony.

Three
The Making of the Talented Tenth

Mr. Booker T. Washington has as helpers the son of a Negro senator, trained in Greek and the humanities, and graduated at Harvard; the son of a Negro congressman and lawyer, trained in Latin and mathematics, and graduated at Oberlin; he has as his wife, a woman who read Vergil and Homer in the same class room with me; he has as college chaplain, a classical graduate of Atlanta University. . . . And yet one of the effects of Mr. Washington's propaganda has been to throw doubt upon the expediency of such training for Negroes, as these persons have had.

W. E. B. Du Bois, *The Talented Tenth* (1903)

The study of classics was a basic part of American secondary and collegiate education until well into the twentieth century, when the rise of academic professionalism and the pressure for marketable vocational training led more and more students and their families away from liberal education. Before the Civil War, African American scholars who could gain an education in the free North, and more rarely in the slave-owning South, learned Greek and Latin wherever they could. For a long time their premier Northern college for liberal learning was Oberlin. In the years following the Civil War more African American women as well as men studied classics there than at any other institution. Their most sustained engagement with classics as it was then practiced came through Reconstruction and up to the 1920s, in close parallel to a comparable prosperity in American classics generally. This chapter focuses on two of the great leaders in the fight for liberal education: the most famous African American for several generations in his long life, the sociologist W. E. B. Du Bois (1868–1963); the other, the classicist William Sanders Scarborough (1852–1926), president of Wilberforce University in Ohio and a prominent figure in African American higher education. Lost to history until recently, Scarborough has become known once again through the indefatigable research of the classicist Michele Valerie Ronnick.[1]

Born and raised in Great Barrington, Massachusetts, William Edward Burghardt Du Bois studied classics in high school and at Fisk University, from which he graduated at the age of twenty in 1888.[2] He transferred to Harvard and graduated in 1890, but by then he had switched to the new international discipline of sociology; after several years of study in Berlin, he took his PhD in the subject at Harvard in 1895. He makes frequent use of his classical learning in his earlier works, above all in *The Souls of Black Folk* (1904), in which he first defined one of the major themes that he would return to throughout a long career of writing and political activism.

> The problem of the twentieth century is the problem of the color-line—
> the relation of the darker to the lighter races of men in Asia and Africa,
> in America, and the islands of the sea. It was a phase of this problem that
> caused the Civil War; and however much they who marched South and
> North in 1861 may have fixed on the technical points of union and local
> autonomy as a shibboleth, all nevertheless knew, as we know, that the
> question of Negro slavery was the real cause of the conflict.[3]

The fourteen chapters of *Souls* are a carefully composed series of connected essays on the whole range of African American culture, history, and political life at the beginning of the twentieth century: Booker T. Washington, "sorrow songs" (which Du Bois argues more accurately describes what is being sung about than the religious term "spiritual"), the role African Americans should play in commerce and industry, Atlanta University—where Du Bois taught for many years—and Alexander Crummell (1819–1898), an educator, abolitionist, and advocate of Pan-Africanism (the connection that linked all people of African birth or descent). Each chapter has a double epigraph: first a quotation from a wide range of world poetry, such as James Russell Lowell, Byron, Schiller (in German), Whittier, Fitzgerald's *Omar Khayyam*, Shakespeare, the wedding song from Wagner's "Lohengrin," and the Song of Solomon. Each poetic text is then matched with a staff of music from one of the sorrow songs, but the notes only, no text. Each poem and song is always suggestive of its chapter's subject. For the elegiac chapter 12 on Crummell, for example, Du Bois matches lines from Tennyson's *Idylls of the King* on the passing of Arthur with the sorrow song "Swing Low, Sweet Chariot." *The Souls of Black Folk* is poetic in design and prophetic in tone throughout.[4] Here his classical education served Du Bois well, more felicitously than it would in his 1911 novel *The Quest of the Silver Fleece*.

The older William Sanders Scarborough was born in Macon, Georgia, under slavery and like Frederick Douglass had to gain much of his education surreptitiously. After the Civil War he completed his education in high school and studied classics at Atlanta University, which had been founded in 1865 for the education of freed slaves. He then moved to Oberlin, where he received his BA in 1875. Scarborough completed his studies just as the institution of the German research university and its seminars was being brought to the United States by the Confederate veteran Basil Lanneau Gildersleeve and other German-trained scholars like William Dwight Whitney, first at the newly founded Johns Hopkins University, then at Harvard, Yale, the University of Michigan, and other centers of learning.[5] But Scarborough was more than able to enter professional American classics through his publications and conference papers—when he was allowed to participate, that is. The cities and universities of the former Confederacy usually contrived to deny him a bed to stay in or even a place on the meeting's program, not least the northernmost of the Southern universities, Princeton. Whitney in particular became a close friend of Scarborough and an early and ardent champion.

His first major publication was an elementary Greek textbook, *First Lessons in Greek* (1881). At one stroke it offered a convincing refutation of John C. Calhoun's notorious pronouncement of 1833: no black man was capable of learning such a challenging subject as Greek grammar, and if any such person did, he allowed that he would admit that blacks were the intellectual equals of whites and deserving of an equal education. Scarborough's textbook made him a leading figure in African American education from the time it appeared. He eventually became a professor and then president of Wilberforce University in Ohio and was a prolific essayist and advocate for the role that classical literature could play in improving the lives of students in all walks of life. He lived long enough to see the waning of the educational ideals that he and Du Bois argued should be available for African Americans. In this respect his fate was no different from that of most other classicists, whose role in American education also steadily contracted from the 1920s onward.

Of different generations, the older Scarborough and younger Du Bois both realized that the actual number of students who were ready for a liberal education of this kind might be smaller than Du Bois's alliterative phrase "The Talented Tenth" proclaimed. This did not deter them from arguing that an educated elite was indispensable for the future of the race. Their educational philosophy brought them into direct conflict with Scarborough's contemporary and fellow ex-slave Booker T. Washington (1856–1915). Washington's advocacy of accommodationism, epitomized by his Atlanta Exposition speech of 1895, was still well known and worth quoting—more exactly, parroting—as late as Ralph Ellison's *Invisible Man* (1951). While Du Bois attacked Washington's argument head-on in a polemical chapter of *The Souls of Black Folk*, Scarborough managed to maintain a more diplomatic relationship with the canny politician and friend of American presidents known not always affectionately as the Wizard of Tuskegee.

Matthew Arnold Hears Mary Church Terrell Read Greek

You may think you are doing little, but it is something worthwhile to have proved Calhoun's statement false, and by your philological success alone you have lifted us all out of the ditch where he proposed we should always lie.

                    Richard T. Greener, letter to William S. Scarborough

Du Bois's biographer David Levering Lewis observes that the actual number of African Americans who could match Du Bois's fortunate experience of being well born and educated in the liberal North was not great, but that those who did fit something like his profile could be thought of as members of the Talented Tenth: "A far more accurate characterization would have been the Talented Hundredth."[6] Scarborough's career shows that even those who were not so fortunate could obtain that ideal as well. A college or university course in Greek and Latin was already the education of choice for some of the most gifted women of color in late nineteenth- and early twentieth-century America, well before the appearance of *The Souls of Black Folk*. Like much else in the history of African Americans and the reception of classical literature and learning, this achievement was for a long time unreported and its extent not recognized until recently.[7] If more young African Americans received a thorough humanistic education in classics than would do so later in the twentieth century, the same was true of their white American counterparts.

Jessie Fauset (1882–1962) was a Phi Beta Kappa graduate of Cornell and an accomplished classicist who was awarded an honors degree in Latin and Greek and went on to earn a master's in French from the University of Pennsylvania. Like many classics-trained students in her day she did not continue her studies as a teacher or professional scholar in the subject. After some years of distinguished editorial work at Du Bois's the *Crisis*, where she was the leading literary critic and supporter of many of the important poets and writers in her generation, she made her living for the rest of her life as a teacher of French at the high-school level and did her own writing as time permitted. In addition to the challenge of overcoming racist stereotypes Fauset had the equally daunting obstacle that educated women of color faced: the firmly entrenched male belief that women should not be too highly educated, and that they would likely become unfit for women's proper work if they were. Fauset herself did not make much of this form of prejudice.

For that, we have Mary Church Terrell (1863–1954), who did. In her 1940 memoir, *A Colored Woman in a White World*, Fauset's contemporary states concisely the problem that women of color faced.

> This is the story of a colored woman living in a white world. It cannot possibly be like a story written by a white woman. A white woman has only one obstacle to overcome—that of sex. I have two—both sex and race. I belong to the only group in this country which has two such huge obstacles to surmount. Colored men have only one—that of race.[8]

Terrell gives a vivid account of what it was like for a woman to study Greek and Latin. She was very good at classics, yet she almost didn't get a chance to read them or anything else.

> To tell the truth, I came very near not being on this mundane sphere at all. In a fit of despondency my dear mother tried to end her life a few months before I was born. By a miracle she was saved, and I finally arrived on scheduled time none the worse for the prenatal experience which might have proved decidedly disagreeable, if not fatal, to my future.[9]

After this near miss, her life turned out as happily as anyone could expect. When she studied at Oberlin (1880–1884), she decided that she wanted to do the classical course rather than the literary course. The literary course was judged to be appropriate for women; it lasted only three years, and those who completed it received a certificate instead of the BA degree. Classics required five years and was notably more demanding—it implied a drive for intellectual preeminence that would be unseemly for a proper young woman. Her friends tried to discourage her from taking it.

> They pointed out that Greek was hard; that it was unnecessary, if not positively unwomanly, for girls to study that "old, dead language" anyhow; that during the two extra years required to complete it I would miss a lot of fun which I could enjoy outside of college walls. And, worst of all, it might ruin my chances of getting a husband, since men were notoriously shy of women who knew too much. "Where," inquired some of my friends sarcastically, "will you find a colored man who has studied Greek?" They argued I wouldn't be happy if I knew more than my husband, and they warned that trying to find a man in our group who knew Greek would be like hunting for a needle in a haystack.[10]

As is often the case with bright students, a particular teacher played a crucial role in shaping Terrell's love of classics, as well as her persistence. He seems to have fit the stereotype of the distracted professor very well.

> The Greek professor in college was also one of my favorites. He looked like an ascetic, tall and straight and thin. I usually sat on the front seat in his class and drank in every word he said. I took much more Greek than the curriculum required, both because I enjoyed the Grecian authors and because I was fond of my teacher.[11]

In the course of recollecting her studies at Oberlin, Terrell provides us with one of the great moments in the long-playing comedy of Europeans colliding with American culture and higher education, though in this context it is a comedy with a familiar, bitter twist.

> One day Matthew Arnold, the English writer, visited our class and Professor Frost asked me both to read the Greek and then to translate. After leaving the class Mr. Arnold referred to the young lady who read the passage of Greek so well. Thinking it would interest the Englishman, Professor Frost told him I was of African descent. Thereupon Mr. Arnold expressed the greatest surprise imaginable, because, he said, he thought the tongue of the African was so thick he could not be taught to pronounce the Greek correctly.[12]

Arnold's ethnology was not as consciously vicious as that of the Yale graduate John C. Calhoun's, but the idea of using the classics as an index into the civilizing potential of people of color was substantially the same in the 1880s as it had been in 1833. In this instance, Arnold was not reacting to what he saw—Terrell was light-skinned—but simply to the racial category he heard. The mere phrase "of African descent" was all he needed.

Terrell's encounter with the famous Victorian critic is important in appreciating what even those African American writers who knew Greek and Latin had to contend with. The path some followed was either to suppress details of their education as they took up their careers, or to use it in ways that would not offend or attract undue attention. Overt classicism in a black writer still wouldn't register in 1940, nor had it outside of the academy where Scarborough had worked, nor often even for as well-known a writer as W. E. B. Du Bois. As Terrell herself remarks, if she had been attending Oberlin in the year she published her memoir, she might not have been so free from the race prejudice as she had been fifty-six years before, at the time she was her Greek professor's star pupil.[13] It would not be until 1974 that the first African American classicist would win the American Philological Association's Goodwin Award of Merit for the best book published by a member in that year, Prof. Frank M. Snowden of Howard University, for his book *Blacks in Antiquity*.[14] The opportunities open to African Americans for writing and publishing around the turn of the century were few and this may have denied us more writers and poets than just Mary Terrell. She was an accomplished classical scholar but went on to become an advocate of civil rights and women's rights. She wanted to try a career as a professional writer, but in her full life of political work and raising a family she never found the time to do so.[15] Her encounter with Matthew Arnold shows what was at stake in Scarborough's and Du Bois's struggles to bring the ideals of liberal education to African Americans. The very idea of such an education was resisted, not only by whites, but by the famous founder of the Tuskegee Institute. Even when someone went ahead and studied classics, like Mary Church Terrell, her accomplishment would be greeted by puzzlement and curiosity. As any classicist can tell you, "Classics? What can you do with that?" remains a familiar refrain today.

Scarborough's Philological Humanism

"It seems to me," said Booker T.
"It shows a mighty lot of cheek

To study chemistry and Greek
When Mister Charley needs a hand
To hoe the cotton on his land,
And when Miss Ann looks for a cook
Why stick your nose inside a book?"

"I don't agree," said W.E.B.
"If I should have the drive to seek
Knowledge of chemistry or Greek,
I'll do it. Charles or Miss can look
Another place for hand or cook.
Some men rejoice in skill of hand,
And some in cultivating land,
But there are others who maintain
The right to cultivate the brain."

Dudley Randall, *Booker T. and W.E.B.*

Scarborough and Du Bois crossed paths several times, none of them happy ones for either man. After he finished his degree at Oberlin in 1875 the dark-skinned Scarborough applied for a position at the recently founded Atlanta University, but was told that the board did not believe the time was yet right for a colored person to join the faculty there.[16] After taking his PhD at Harvard in 1895, W. E. B. Du Bois went to his first teaching appointment as a professor of Greek and Latin at Wilberforce University. He was replacing Horace Talbert, who had replaced Scarborough after he had been maneuvered out of his position in 1891 by the machinations of the influential bishop B. W. Arnett and other members of the board presiding over the university.[17] In his autobiography Scarborough is discreetly obscure about the reasons; perhaps they resented his independence and intellectual distinction.

Du Bois's engagement with Wilberforce was even more unsatisfactory. After teaching Greek and Latin for two years, he resigned in 1896 in disgust at the provincialism and hypocritical piety that he believed distorted the university's mission. When the lighter-skinned and more credentialed Du Bois later applied to Atlanta University, he was offered a position immediately. In the meantime Scarborough's standing was high in African American academic life and the American Philological Association; he eventually returned in triumph as a professor and head of the Classical Department and also as vice president of the university. He was appointed to the presidency of Wilberforce in 1908 to the wide acclaim of American academic leaders and politicians, ranging from Booker T. Washington, who offered characteristically foxy congratulations ("I think you are the right man in the right place and we feel proud of your appointment"), to the Republican candidate for president that year, William Howard Taft ("I am delighted to congratulate you and Wilberforce on your election to the Presidency").[18]

To learn to use the classics as part of one's intellectual armament was a great advantage, but to actually live the life of a classicist and write about the classics was to marginalize oneself, as surely as all other professional classicists were increasingly marginalized. For within classics there was a shift as well, from being a field of general education and general culture and humane criticism, to the professionalization of academic language and an increasing disinclination of the leading scholars in the field to concern themselves with the broader public.[19] In the words of Booker T. Washington's Atlanta Exposition speech, Scarborough was destined to cast down his particular bucket where he was, which was in the academic life of the liberal arts college. There he championed offerings in liberal arts in addition to the "industrial" education advocated by Washington at Tuskegee. Washington's strategy was designed to pose no threat to the educated white class that ruled the relatively uneducated majority of white Southerners. He voiced reservations about blacks studying Greek to the end of his life.[20]

For Scarborough, classics was as much a means to culture as a career based on the German model of scientific, professional scholarship. And he sought an even broader audience than many professors of classics. He was a prolific writer, teaching and publishing on both Greek and Latin literature, not least because he could read German, the indispensable language for the international discipline that classics had become. His range extended far beyond professionalism, to essays on blacks in the military, public speeches, journalism, and introductions to books on such topics as African Methodism in the South, Frederick Douglass's speeches, and the teachings of Jesus; reviews of books on the history of black churches in the United States; biographical essays on Richard Greener, a classicist and law professor, the first black graduate of Harvard College (1870) as well as the first African American to join the American Philological Association (1876); two major European writers and poets of black ancestry (Alexandre Dumas and Pushkin), as well as presidents Theodore Roosevelt and Warren G. Harding; travel narratives, the education of blacks, general philology, political essays, and Negro farm life.[21] He did his best to keep up with the state of the question in philological studies, but as he notes after quoting a letter in which the classicist Charles Forster Smith provided him with exact citations from a number of recent publications, even as late as 1922 he found it difficult at Wilberforce to get to the research materials he needed.[22] For him, the distinction now customarily drawn between research and popular writing did not really exist. Classical philology was synonymous with literature, and literature was the basis of a liberal education.[23]

For Scarborough, classics was obviously the heart of literary education, and literature is what he conceived himself as writing, whether it was conference papers, published articles and essays, even his *First Lessons in Greek: Adapted to the Greek Grammar of Goodwin and Hadley and Designed as an Introduction to Xenophon's "Anabasis" and Similar Greek*.[24] *First Lessons* is the work of an experienced teacher ("The use of a blackboard cannot be too highly recommended. In my own classes I have found its daily use indispensable"). He did not create his own Greek grammar but keyed the progressive chapters of *First Lessons* to the paradigms and rules of standard Greek grammars available at the time by Goodwin and others. His model was Elisha Jones's recently published *First Lessons in Latin . . . Prepared as an Introduction to Caesar's Commentaries on the Gallic War* (1878). This military initiation into Greek and Roman literature was partly due to the seeming simplicity and directness of both Xenophon and Caesar (both are more artful than they seem, and Caesar, who wrote his *Commentaries* with an eye to their reception in the turmoil of Roman Republican politics, is at many points more than a little disingenuous), but just as much to a conviction that boys (for it was usually boys) would be interested in learning Greek and Latin by reading about the great generals and wars of antiquity. Scarborough focuses on written exercise and silent reading, still a common way classical languages are taught, rather than the total-immersion technique developed by modern language teachers. As the students learn their vocabulary and their paradigms and grammar, they are asked to translate into Greek such morally improving phrases and sentences as

Among the tents of the well-disposed generals.
The beautiful villages are full of corn.
Good girls love their parents.
Wine is not agreeable.
The general was in the very (*express by superlative*) beautiful park of Cyrus.
Do not admire the bad boys.

The further Scarborough's beginners go, the more complicated their grammatical and moral lives become. In keeping with a nation that was raised on McGuffey's readers, good morals are never far from the grammarian's mind. Even then, Xenophon's *Anabasis*, with its exotic world of an army of mercenary Greeks invading the Persian Empire under the command of Cyrus the Younger, supplied vivid sentences for translation into Greek.

The boy who is standing by (*what preposition?*) the sea is very bad.
There are five goats in the park.
The Greeks were braver than the barbarians.
They say that not even if you should be willing would you be able.

Scarborough's only other book, the expanded text of a paper first given at the APA in 1886 and published in that same year, is *The Birds of Aristophanes: A Theory of Interpretation* (1886). *The Birds* is a comic fantasy about the creation of an Athenian utopia in Cloud Cuckoo Land (*Nephelokokkygia*), a idealized world that comes to seem more and more like the real Athenian world supposedly left behind. His publication on one of Aristophanes' greatest plays displays learning and a command of languages ancient and modern. And in addition to saying whatever he has to say about ancient Greek comedy, he is also saying something even more important about himself. Scarborough proves himself as an African American classicist in a way that is even more compelling than his textbook for beginner's Greek. As any German philologist would, he frames his own interpretation by situating his reading in relation to his predecessors.

It has been asserted by some that there is no ground whatever for supposing that Aristophanes did not share fully the sanguine hopes of the vast majority of his countrymen in regard to the success of the Sicilian expedition; that the whole play contains not a word of warning; that no hint of impending misfortune troubles the exuberant gaiety of his play. I see strong reasons ... in favor of a theory that Aristophanes was *not* in full sympathy with the ambitious schemes of his countrymen, and especially this wild undertaking against Sicily [sc. the Athenians' Sicilian expedition during the Peloponnesian War in 416 BCE that ended in the total annihilation of their forces]. His extreme conservatism; his vigorous opposition to innovations and conquests; his longing after the good old days of the old democracy; his intense hatred to any notions not strictly in keeping with what was styled the old Attic *purity, dignity, and simplicity,* are all conclusive proof that he would not be in sympathy with such a movement, though he might deem it unwise to oppose it openly as all Athens seemed stirred up over it.
    While the position taken by Süvern and his followers is in the main a strong one, yet there are some points advanced by him that might be questioned with propriety.[25]

This kind of circumspection was not the style of Gildersleeve or another doyen of nineteenth- and early twentieth-century philology, A. E. Housman, feared for the witty nastiness of his reviews of the work of scholars long dead as well as living. What mattered more for Scarborough was that he was making himself a participant in the international conversation that classical philology had become. To have reservations about Süvern and his followers means, among other things, that you know the state of the question in German. He concludes by observing that Aristophanes was far too subtle to make such criticisms of Athenian politics or people overtly, which is one of the reasons why the German Süvern misread the play.

In order to get to this conclusion Scarborough moves carefully through a survey not only of relevant scholarship, but of classical literature generally; in this he proceeds just as many in classics still do, where doxography—Greek for proving you have done your homework—is the required entry ticket for a serious scholarly contribution. He writes the way classicists did then and many still do; proof is made by citation and the extensive quotation of testimonia. Four scholars publishing in English are quoted extensively, as are many others. Scarborough quotes both scholarly Latin by the German classicist Wilhelm Dindorf and an entire page of the Roman historian Cornelius Nepos's life of Alcibiades, as well as Greek, and above all, German. None of it is translated.

On three consecutive pages a slender ribbon of Scarborough's comments runs along the top over long notes set in a smaller type font, with direct, unmediated, and uncommented-on German from "Ueber Aristophanes *Vögel* von Herrn Süvern."[26] To show that one could read and aptly quote long swatches of Greek, French, Latin, and German, whether rightly or wrongly interpreted, was an indisputable sign of belonging to the international world of classical learning.

By printing pages and pages of untranslated German, Latin, French, and Greek that he had read, and by assessing and criticizing what he does quote, Scarborough demonstrates that *he* reads these languages and that he assumes his readers can, too; nowhere does he offer to translate what he quotes. Not merely the fact of writing on a classical Greek text but the way he does it as a scholar of Greek automatically signals that he is an authority in his chosen field. And so he would be, to all but the very small audience of classicists who could read German, Latin, Greek, and French as fluently as he does. *Aristophanes' Birds* thus advances him to a level beyond the elementary Greek text, gratifying though that was.[27] This may be the reason why for only the second time in his life he went to the trouble and the expense of publishing a work on his own. It was a good career move.

Scarborough also had a go at the kind of bloodless scholarly language that was coming into vogue. He knew that the man of letters and the orator were being replaced in the academy by disciplinary specialists and their professional discourse.[28] Strange as it may seem, as a scholarly communication, his abstract for his first paper to the APA is nothing out of the ordinary. "The Theory and Function of the Thematic Vowel in the Greek Verb" is appropriately stilted, a kind of prose he was later rarely guilty of writing.

After remarking upon the agglutinative character and complexity in structure of the Greek verb, the writer defined "thematic vowel," and gave illustrations from the Greek, Latin, and Sanskrit. Explanations of the phonetic changes of the vowel, peculiar to each of the languages, were offered. The theories of Bopp, Pott, and Curtius as to the nature of these languages were passed in review and briefly discussed. Cases of apparent omission in several Greek Verbs were presented, and the explanation of omission by syncopation was condemned. The conclusion was drawn that the vowel is an important element in the make-up of the verb for euphonic purposes; that its especial function is to facilitate pronunciation, and that in force it is conjunctive, serving to unite or connect the termination with the verbal base.[29]

This is abstract in a literal sense, squeezing the life out of what it is talking about. The relentless impersonal passives are probably due to a neophyte's desire to appear as professional as possible. It is the kind of writing that the New York Times ridiculed in its report of the 1885 meeting of the American Philological Association at New Haven, in a satirical article "The Philologists."[30] But this too was confirmation that Scarborough was what he claimed to be.

It is important to stress this issue of self-authentication, because even by this early point in their careers Du Bois and Scarborough were living on different planets, simply because Du Bois had actually completed the Germanic degree of PhD at Harvard after working with the leading graduate faculties in both the United States and Germany.[31] Accomplished as Scarborough was, thanks to his Oberlin MA, as a young scholar he did not have the opportunity for the advanced schooling required to attain Du Bois's level of scholarship. Du Bois published his first book The Suppression of the African Slave Trade in 1896; it was his revised Harvard dissertation and the inaugural volume in Harvard's series of books in sociology.

Apart from his professional career as both scholar and academic administrator, Scarborough was to serve for a brief time near the end of his life in Washington during the Harding administration, an appointment gained from having known Harding personally and from having worked steadily for the Republican party in Ohio politics over the years. This job yielded a monograph on farmers and land tenure in Virginia, but it was largely the work of subordinates rather than Scarborough himself. He did publish a number of articles in the journal *Current History* on migration, city life, and the credit system's harm to African Americans.[32]

Scarborough believed his greatest achievement was as a teacher. He inspired several generations of Wilberforce youth and was warmly remembered by them. In the conclusion to his memoirs, "Looking Forward and Backward," he is quite clear about what teaching meant to him.

> If I could be said to have had a hobby it was "Youth." I loved youth and it loved me. My heart never grew old and I could enter into its pleasures with hearty zest, either as host or guest. I have had a rare pleasure in instructing young people. It has been a delight to aid their fresh open minds to discover the beauties of the Greek and Latin tongues and literature, and I gave all possible of myself to the task. Their companionship has been an inspiration to me, and I learned from them as they learned from me. Yes, I can truly say I lived with my students, as they clustered about me in classroom, in dormitory, and in my home. I recall for them here the many pleasant hours when they were gathered under our roof or on our lawn for an evening or afternoon of jollity, and I can see in memory the long line passing at ten o'clock down the stairway and through the long hall, a happy throng, grasping our hands with an appreciative word as they said goodbye—each made happier by bearing away from the large basket at the door an apple, an orange, a huge popcorn ball as they left us, an uplifted company to live on higher planes and eagerly look forward to another gathering. How well I knew their higher education was being added to by this contact with ourselves, our books, pictures, and games.[33]

Like many dedicated teachers in college and university life, Scarborough had some reason to wonder whether his dedication was an achievement that would prove to be as evanescent as the passing generations of young students he served—even whether it had been a dedication rightly made. As the Latin tag has it, *Verba volant, scripta manent*, Words uttered fly away, only what's written endures—though not even that is guaranteed, as we have seen. But this is to miss why people become teachers in the first place. If one's achievement *qua* teacher has no longer life than the memories of his or her students, that is nothing any sensible teacher is going to worry about. One might as well fret over the unlikelihood of personal immortality. Proud as they may be of all their books and articles, few published scholars in the long run fare any better.

Scarborough admired the African American Richard T. Greener (1844–1922) above all other scholars he had known, even though Greener had not been able to make a career for himself as a teacher in classics, a profession for which he had been well trained. His mentor wrote to him on several occasions, Scarborough says, and he cherished what Greener had written to him.

You have demanded without ceasing nothing less than opportunity for the highest intellectual development of the race and you have inspired our young men and women to reach out for it not only by your enthusiastic classroom work to which all testify wherever met, but by your own philological studies and literary achievements that have given you place, prestige, and influence that the race may well bless you for.[34]

It says something about Scarborough's clear sense of where he stood in the history of his race and his times that he was able to include this testimony in his memoir, along with his gratitude for a career in teaching the young. And there also remains his dispatch of the spectre of John C. Calhoun. Properly understood, *First Lessons in Greek* deserves to be remembered as one of the signal achievements of African American literature and culture.

W. E. B. Du Bois and the Eloquence of Cicero

Twice in his life, Du Bois tells us, he turned to Cicero's oration *Pro Archia Poeta* (*For the Poet Archias*). The first time was when he was a young teacher working in the back country of Tennessee during a summer vacation from Fisk University; the second came many years later, when he was a father over fifty years old attempting to advise his headstrong daughter Yolande about her course of study. *Pro Archia* was a talisman for Du Bois of the virtues of a classical and liberal arts education because it was a standard text for intermediate Latin students—one of the few that was not concerned with the dispassionate subjugation of Caesar's Gaul or that other favorite of high-school teachers if not their students, Cicero's orations against the iniquitous conspirator Catiline.

In what follows we shall make much of what seems little, for Du Bois's references to Cicero's famous speech are brief and in passing. But they are worth pausing over because they reveal much of the reason why the very rhetorical tradition and humanistic learning that had mattered so much to Douglass and Wheatley could become as hidden to the rising generations as the Mysteries of Demeter at Eleusis.

Cicero delivered his speech for Archias in the year 62 BCE after his famous previous year as consul, in which he successfully defeated and discredited the conspiracy of Lucius Sergius Catiline to take over the Roman Republic. The *Pro Archia* has always been a potent text to invoke, both for its place in literary culture and for its politics.[35] The year we know as 63 BCE had been a perilous one for Cicero, but perhaps also his finest hour, for it was only in that year that he realized perfectly a lifelong ambition to integrate completely his literary and oratorical talents into the role of a major player in Roman political life. In later stages of the dynastic conflicts that finally destroyed the substance of the Roman Republic and left only its scaffolding to mask the autocratic rule that replaced it, the genuine power players were Pompey and Caesar, and, after their deaths, Marc Antony and Caesar's adopted heir, Octavian, who eventually became Augustus Caesar a few years after Antony and his paramour Cleopatra were dispatched.

At every later stage in his career Cicero was not nearly as engaged in political decisions as he would have liked to be. He was an uncertain partisan, first for Pompey and the Republic, then reconciled in some degree to Caesar after his victory over the Pompeians, Cato the Younger, and others who had opposed Caesar and Caesarism. After the assassination of Caesar in 44 BCE, Cicero ran afoul of Marc Antony, and in a series of brilliant invectives (the *Philippics*, modeled after the orations Demosthenes of Athens had delivered against the rising power of Philip of Macedon), most of which were written and published rather than actually delivered, he fixed Antony's reputation forever after and signed his own death warrant. He was proscribed by the Second Triumvirate of Lepidus, Octavian, and Antony and executed in 43 BCE.[36]

The ostensible purpose of the *Pro Archia* was to defend the Greek poet Archias, who was resident in Rome and probably involved in partisan politics on the side of Pompeians like his patron family the Luculli, and especially to refute the charge that Archias was not a Roman citizen, which under the Lex Papia would have led to his expulsion. But Cicero actually signals in his opening sentence that his real theme is a defense of the man who taught him poetry and the cultivation of literary taste, Aulus Licinius, the Roman name of the Greek Archias. This opening *exordium* is incidentally one of the excerpts Douglass would have read in translation in the *Columbian Orator*.

> Whatever talent I possess, judges — and I realize its limitations — whatever may be my oratorical experience — and I do not deny that my practice to date has been not inconsiderable — whatever knowledge of the theoretical side of my profession I may have derived from a devoted literary apprenticeship — and I admit that at no period of my life has the acquisition of such knowledge been repellent to me — to any advantage that may be derived from all these my friend Aulus Licinius has a pre-eminent claim, which belongs to him almost by his own right.

Cicero closes his refutation of the few flimsy charges against Archias not very long after he has begun to speak (*Pro Archia* 11), and the balance of the oration is given over to a continuation of his praise of his teacher Archias, which expands into a panegyric on what literature contributes to the good life. Readers looking for a purely forensic argument naturally would consider all of this a digression from the point, but as the opening sentence suggests, Cicero has something like this personal defense of Archias in mind from the very beginning. Roman governing classes were notoriously suspicious of Greek culture, and Cicero goes out of his way to reassure them of the dignity and the merit of literary culture: Even if we Romans happen to be without much taste for literature or any ability in writing it, that's no cause to criticize it. Scipio Africanus, the conqueror of Hannibal, is said to have put up a marble statue in honor of the poet Ennius, but Ennius more than returned the favor in the panegyric he produced that honored both the Scipios and the Roman people.

At the point Cicero is speaking, the poets Catullus and Lucretius were alive; Cicero himself turns up in one of the epigrams of Catullus, as does Julius Caesar. The generation that came to be thought of as the golden age of classical Latin literature, Vergil, Horace, Livy, the elegiac poets Propertius, Tibullus, and Ovid, were to come soon. It was still possible for Cicero to play off what in modern terms would be termed a cultural inferiority complex that the Romans are sometimes thought to have had about their standing in relation to the Greeks. In fact, it was all more of a rhetorical ploy, if not indeed a cliché, that Romans had been playing around with since the comedies of Plautus. "Translation" is after all a Roman word for a characteristically Roman cultural activity: running off with somebody else's language, or literature, or even the images of their gods. This does not mean that Roman cultural insecurity wasn't still a good card to play in front of a jury, especially if it could be linked to what Romans were best at—conquering other people.

> For if anyone thinks that the glory won by the writing of Greek verse is naturally less than that accorded to the poet who writes in Latin, he is entirely wrong. Greek literature is read in nearly every nation under heaven, while the vogue of Latin is confined to its own boundaries, and they are, we must grant, narrow. Seeing, therefore, that the activities of our race know no barrier save the limits of the round earth, we ought to be ambitious that wherever our arms have penetrated there also our fame and glory should extend; for the reason that literature exalts the nation whose high deeds it sings, and at the same time there can be no doubt that those who stake their lives to fight in honor's cause find therein a lofty incentive to period and endeavor. (23)

This testimony leads into one the most frequently cited passages from the *Pro Archia*, the story of Alexander the Great's visit to the tomb of Achilles near the site of Troy. "Fortunate youth!" exclaimed Alexander, "to have found in Homer a herald of your valor!" (24). Cicero is good at drawing the obvious moral.

> Well might he so exclaim, for had the *Iliad* never existed, the same mound which covered Achilles' bones would also have overwhelmed his memory.

This testimony to the power of song accords well with what Homer's poetry tells us, even with Achilles' own words in the poem.

Cicero uses the defense of Archias as an occasion to offer a display speech in which the law and politics of the case become a pretext for a defense not only of Greek literature for Romans, but also of Roman literature, of which Marcus Tullius Cicero—more exactly, his epochal consulship of the previous year—will be the culmination. All men as Cicero's audience understands them are drawn along in life by their *studio laudis*, by their eagerness for praise (26). Why not admit as much? Why shouldn't Rome cherish and protect a poet whom the Muses inspire? Cicero decides he must say something about all this to the jury, which at this point begins to sound more like a jury in a trial imagined by W. S. Gilbert than one governed by Roman law.

The measures which I, jointly with you, undertook in my consulship for the safety of this city, the lives of our citizens, and the republic, have been taken by my client as the subject of a poem which he has begun; he read this to me, and the work struck me as at once so forcible and so interesting, that I encouraged him to complete it. For magnanimity [or courage: *virtus*, the same quality that Achilles and other heroes possess] looks for no other recognition of its toils and dangers save praise and glory; once rob it of that, gentlemen, and in this brief and transitory pilgrimage of life what further incentive have we to high endeavor? If the soul were haunted by no presage of futurity, if the scope of her imaginings were bounded by the limits set to human existence, surely never then would she break herself by bitter toil, rack herself by sleepless solicitude, or struggle so often for very life itself. But deep in every noble heart dwells a power which plies night and day the goad [*stimulus*, as in a riding whip] and bids us see to it that the remembrance of our names should not pass away with life, but should endure coeval with all the ages of the future. (28–29)

John Dugan suggests that the ultimate rhetorical strategy of the *Pro Archia* is to fuse literary culture and politics with Archias the poet and Cicero his defender, so that they become inextricable, and the ensemble, overwhelmingly persuasive.[37]

The *Pro Archia* acquired a life of its own in later history, enacting over and over again what Cicero asserts at the beginning of his speech.[38]

Indeed all the arts which have any bearing upon the common life of human beings [*humanitas*] have a certain kind of common bond and are bound together in a mutual relationship. (2)

Little wonder that *Pro Archia Poeta* became a favored text in arguments for the humanities, even though there are a number of ironies in using it as an argument in favor of making literature a necessary part of human life.

Perhaps the most salient is that while the oration may have won Archias his case, it did not win what Cicero wanted even more, a poem immortalizing his momentous consulship. It is not even clear that a second Homer could have saved him from the consequences of his year as consul in 63. His greatest glory was in some ways also one of his greatest disasters. He would be prosecuted and exiled for a time some years later by enemies who did not recall his consulship with as much admiration as he did. Against this personal and political failure must be set the eloquence of the *Pro Archia*, which became the text that inspired Quintilian, Petrarch, teachers of classics and humanists in all ages, and not least Du Bois. Between what *Pro Archia Poeta* did not accomplish, and what it did, one sees the limitations of relying on any tradition, no matter how constructed.[39]

In her comprehensive survey of classical influences in *The Souls of Black Folk*, Carrie Cowherd argues that the most intriguing classical reference of all is to Cicero's *Pro Archia*.[40] We might say more generally that the Roman and American audiences of Cicero and Du Bois had more than a little in common: a deep suspicion of what actually happens in a liberal education—that is, education devoted to the cultivation of the self, rather than an education aimed at learning practical and marketable skills—and even more, a skepticism about anyone who is attempting to persuade us that such an education is a necessary one.

In chapter 4 of *The Souls of Black Folk*, "Of the Meaning of Progress," Du Bois recounts his first, idealistic efforts to be a teacher and leader of his people. The *Pro Archia* was much in his thoughts. He begins "Of the Meaning of Progress" with an epigraph from Schiller's 1801 tragedy on Joan of Arc, *The Maiden of Orleans*, and the passage quoted in German warns us to send out spirits (*Geister*) to do the most difficult work: "the immortal, the pure ones, the ones who are unsentimental [*die nicht fühlen*; literally, "Those who feel nothing"], the ones who do not weep."[41] The Sorrow Song that is quoted is "My Way's Cloudy." The youths Du Bois encounters seem almost a living, walking embodiment of Aristotle's eloquent opening sentence in the *Metaphysics*: "All human beings by nature desire to know."

> First came Josie and her brothers and sisters. The longing to know, to be a student in the great school at Nashville, hovered like a star above this child-woman amid her work and worry, and she studied doggedly. . . . There they sat, nearly thirty of them, on the rough benches, their faces shading from a pale cream to a deep brown, the little feet bare and swinging, the eyes full of expectation, with here and there a twinkle of mischief, and the hands grasping Webster's blue-back spelling book. I loved my school, and the fine faith the children had in the wisdom of their teacher was truly marvelous.[42]

The children and grownups he wanted to teach never wavered in their desire to learn, as Du Bois observes. But they were not in control of their lives; economic realities were, and so were their families. The classes dwindled until Du Bois had to go back to them and start all over again.

> When the Lawrences stopped, I knew that the doubts of the old folks about book-learning had conquered again, and so, toiling up the hill, and getting as far into the cabin as possible, I put Cicero "Pro Archia Poeta" into the simplest English with local applications, and usually convinced them—for a week or so.[43]

His pupils never had any doubt about book-learning at all. He had the satisfaction of opening their eyes to the larger world beyond, through reading and the first steps of education.

> The mass of those to whom slavery was a dim recollection of childhood found the world a puzzling thing: it asked little of them, and they answered with little, and yet it ridiculed their offering. Such a paradox they could not understand, and therefore sank into listless indifference, or shiftlessness, or reckless bravado. There were, however, some—such as Josie, Jim and Ben—to whom War, Hell, and Slavery were but childhood tales, whose young appetites had been whetted to an edge by school and story and half-awakened thought. Ill could they be content, born without and beyond the World. And their weak wings beat against their barriers—barriers of caste, of youth, of life; at last, in dangerous moments, against everything that opposed even a whim.[44]

The outcome of this experiment in liberal education was sad. When Du Bois returned ten years later to the Tennessee country where he had spent two summers, he found everything he knew obliterated: Josie long dead, with some material prosperity here and there where there had been none before. But in the main it was as if his efforts at his school had never been.

> My journey was done, and behind me lay hill and dale, and Life and Death. How shall man measure Progress there where the dark-faced Josie lies? How many heartfuls of sorrow shall balance a bushel of wheat? How hard a thing is life to the lowly, and yet how human and real! And all this life and love and strife and failure,—is it the twilight of nightfall or the flush of some faint-dawning day?
>   Thus sadly musing, I rode to Nashville in the Jim Crow car.[45]

"Of the Meaning of Progress" is one of the most moving chapters in a book that has many.

When Du Bois turned for the second time to the *Pro Archia*, it was for his own daughter's sake. "So the Girl Marries" was published in the *Crisis* in June 1928 following the huge society wedding of his daughter Yolande to the famous young poet Countee Cullen. This was the grandest wedding in Harlem up to that date, and perhaps none since has come close to it, because its extravagance and expense were exceeded only by the bride and groom's mutual folly.[46] The misalliance of Yolande Du Bois and Countee Cullen was due in part to Cullen's uncertain and undefined status as what today would be termed a gay man (the term and the ease with which it is now used did not exist then), and just as much to the independent mind and taste of Du Bois's daughter.

Yolande did not take to a liberal education, though her father had tried, first with some success, by sending her to school in England. His argument was not helped by the dramatic difference between English education and the Brooklyn high school she moved to when the family settled her back in New York. One subject after another didn't work.

> Then came Latin. The English teacher talked Latin and his class at Bedale's romped with Caesar through a living Gallia. The American teacher in the Brooklyn Girl's High did not even talk English and regarded Latin as a crossword puzzle with three inches of daily solution. "Decline Stella!"; "Conjugate Amo"; "What is the subject of 'Gallia est omnis divisa—'" "Nonsense," said the Girl (which was quite true,) "I've dropped Latin!"
>
> "But the colleges haven't," I moaned. "Why college?" countered the Girl.
>
> Why indeed? I tried Cicero "Pro Archia Poeta." The girl was cold. Then I pleaded for my own spiritual integrity: "I have told 12 millions to go to college—what will they say if you don't go?" The Girl admitted that that was reasonable but she said she was considering marriage and really thought she knew about all that schools could teach effectively. I, too, was reasonable and most considerate, despite the fact that I was internally aghast.[47]

This account of Du Bois's second failure with Cicero seems crafted to illustrate the familiar dictum about an event in history happening the first time as tragedy and the second time as farce. "The Girl" a.k.a. Yolande may have been a spoiled child, but what impresses us even more is her father's notion that a teenager would be moved to do the right thing by hearing about Cicero's *Oratio pro Archia Poeta*.

Of the Uses of Atalanta

All art is propaganda and ever must be, despite the wailing of the purists.
I stand in utter shamelessness and say that whatever art I have for writing
has been used always for propaganda for gaining the right of black folk to
love and enjoy. I do not care a damn for any art that is not used for propaganda. But I do care when propaganda is confined to one side while the
other is stripped and silent.

W. E. B. Du Bois, "Criteria of Negro Art" (1926)

This view of the political uses of art in his "Criteria" of 1926 came over
twenty years after the publication of what proved to be Du Bois's most
famous work, but it is an accurate guide to what his intentions were when
he wrote *Souls of Black Folk*. He published *Souls* in his thirty-fifth year, half-
way through his biblically allotted three score and ten. He was even then,
perhaps especially then, a propagandist because he used myth and poetry
to educate all his readers, black and white; specifically, to sweep away, if
not what he called "the Veil" hiding American blacks and whites from one
another, then at least the delusion and ignorance that made the separation and invisibility of blacks possible. For this purpose the most powerful
weapon he had was the profession he had the deepest training in, sociology, as it was practiced in its first generation of scholars trained in Berlin
and Harvard. In a sense, by using it, but in earlier stages, he reenacts his
movement beyond the fundamental humanistic education he had received
at Great Barrington, Massachusetts, and Fisk, and his most sustained use
of classical material comes in the fifth chapter of *The Souls of Black Folk*,
"Of the Wings of Atalanta." The arresting title introduces a figurative
reading of the story of Atalanta that is originally narrated by Orpheus in
the tenth book of Ovid's *Metamorphoses*.

The goggle-eyed youth Hippomenes sees the lovely maiden Atalanta
fly by on a winged course that leaves all the young men pursuing her far
behind (*Metamorphoses* 10.587); she goes as straight in her flight as a Scythian's arrow (10.588, Scythians being famous for both their speed and their
skill at shooting arrows at their pursuers). Her very speed in the race adds
to her beauty: the wind of her swift course blows back the winged heels
of her feet, yet another metaphor suggesting that she actually flew on the
winged heels (*talaria*) of the god Mercury or the hero Perseus (10.591).[48]
For the chapter's epigraph Du Bois chose John Greenleaf Whittier's poem
of 1869, "Howard at Atlanta," about the establishment of the Freedmen's
Bureau after the war.

Of the black boy of Atlanta!
  But half was spoken;
The slave's chains and the master's
  Alike are broken;
The one curse of the races
  Held both in tether;
They are rising—all are rising—
  The black and white together.

Whittier was right to see the slave and the master as enchained alike by slavery, but this chapter like many others in *Souls* is not so optimistic. Thirty years later the black is in grave danger of not rising together with the white. The Sorrow Song cited at the opening of chapter 5 is "The Rocks and Mountains."

The essay begins with by making "Atlanta" and "Atalanta" into homonyms and leads to an allegorical reading of the story of Atlanta, the capital of black America, as an incarnation of all the aspirations Du Bois has for the best education possible for Negro youth.

Perhaps Atlanta was not christened for the winged maiden of dull Boeotia; you know the tale,—how swarthy Atalanta, tall and wild, would marry only him who out-raced her; and how the wily Hippomenes laid three apples of gold in the way. She fled like a shadow, paused, startled over the first apple, but even as he stretched his hand, fled again; hovered over the second, then slipping from his hot grasp, flew over river, vale, and hill; but as she lingered over the third, his arms fell round her, and looking on each other, the blazing passion of their love profaned the sanctuary of Love, and they were cursed. If Atlanta be not named Atalanta, she ought to have been.[49]

Du Bois the experienced lecturer is in evidence in this transition into the main part of the essay ("You know the tale"), a graceful way of telling a story that the majority of his readers may in fact not know. The ancient Athenian prejudice against its northern neighbor Boeotia as the homeland of yokels and fools is adroitly made to sound like the state of Georgia. At the same time Du Bois is far from trying to be an exact reporter of Ovid. His swarthy Atalanta has been running in the Georgia sunshine, "swarthy" suggesting a beautiful woman of color.

Ovid describes Atalanta's beauty in an altogether different way. His Orpheus (who turned to the love of boys in his grief for some consolation after losing Eurydice a second time to the underworld) tells a story that is told by the goddess Venus to her lover the beautiful Adonis, of an Atalanta whose ivory-snow complexion (*eburnea*) was made blushing red with the boyish heat (*puellari candore*) of exercise. This sexually ambivalent detail is so attractive that the teller of the tale—not Ovid, but Ovid's character Orpheus thinking of boys, or Orpheus's own character Venus looking at Adonis, take your pick—employs a simile from luxurious Roman life to capture the sight. Atalanta's beautiful colors were like the purple awnings one sees in the atrium of a well-appointed house; as the sun shines, a purple light filters down onto the white marble below.[50]

> All her young, fair body
> is flushed with rose, just as a purple awning
> within a marble hall will lend white walls
> a darker hint, a veil, a shadowed tint. (10.595–96; Mandelbaum, 350)[51]

There is thus plenty of reason to agree with Cowherd that Du Bois's treatment of this well-known mythological race came from reading Ovid's story, not just a summary of it in a popular source like *Bulfinch's Mythology*.[52] It was a careful reading that enabled him to transform the story of Atalanta into something distinctly un-Ovidian, closer to the spirit of the United States in 1903 than anything Greek or Roman.

Du Bois begins the chapter with a fulsome evocation of Atlanta that sounds as if it were written for a chamber of commerce.

> South of the North, yet north of the South, lies the city of a Hundred Hills, peering out from the shadows of the past into the promise of the future. I have seen her in the morning, when the first flush of day had half-roused her; she lay gray and still on the crimson soil of Georgia; then the blue smoke began to curl from her chimneys, the tinkle of bell and scream of whistle broke the silence, the rattle and roar of busy life slowly gathered and swelled, until the seething whirl of the city seemed a strange thing in a sleepy land.[53]

The rhetoric of American boosterism is so perfectly captured and so pleasing that we might not suspect at first that this is a setup. The flowery "crimson soil of Georgia" will become "the dull red hideousness of Georgia" at the end of the next chapter, "Of the Training of Black Men."[54] Rome herself had only seven hills, but Atlanta—she has a hundred. The aftermath of Sherman's siege and the destruction of the city in 1864 is characterized from the beginning as a spiritual devastation, one in which both ex-masters and freed slaves share.

> It is a hard thing to live haunted by the ghost of an untrue dream; to see the wide vision of empire fade into real ashes and dirt; to feel the pangs of the conquered, and yet know that with all the Bad that fell on one black day, something was vanquished that deserved to live, something killed that in justice had not dared to die; to know that with the Right that triumphed, triumphed something of Wrong, something sordid and mean, something less than the broadest and best. All this is bitter hard; and many a man and city and people have found in it excuse for sulking, and brooding, and listless waiting.[55]

"Of the Wings of Atalanta" is in fact not a simple recital of an exemplary myth as a text for a sermon, but a dialectical story that constantly progresses by turning back on itself, contradicting what was said before. This passage, for example, effectively nullifies the hopeful epigraph from Whittier with which it begins. Atlanta in its present moral and material condition leads into yet another encomium of the city, even more extravagant, now resuming the mythical timelessness of Ovid's story.

> Atlanta, Queen of the cotton kingdom; Atlanta, Gateway to the Land of the Sun; Atlanta, the new Lachesis, spinner of web and woof for the world. So the city crowned her hundred hills with factories, and stored her shops with cunning handiwork, and stretched long iron ways to greet the busy Mercury in his coming. And the Nation talked of her striving.[56]

The threefold repetition of Atlanta leads in the last phrase to a surprising turn of phrase. Lachesis is the second of the three Fates, Clotho, Lachesis, and Atropos; it is her task is to assign us our lot, the destiny that Clotho actually spins and Atropos cuts. She stands in for all three as the spinner of the fabric of the world—that is, of the destiny of the world. The full irony of Du Bois's combination of civic bombast and classical learning will not become clear until the end of the chapter.

For all his education, Du Bois wears it lightly in *The Souls of Black Folk*, and his representation of the myth is far-reaching. If he had read Ovid in Latin—and there seems to be plenty of evidence that he had—his recollection of the *Metamorphoses* was also guided by the standards of taste and decorum of Christian American secondary and collegiate education in the 1870s and 1880s. This was a myth whose story of the race of Atalanta and

Hippomenes could be safely hung as a picture in schoolrooms or printed in Latin textbooks. The tale of Atalanta and Hippomenes was a favorite Ovidian fable to give to young students of Latin, for whom it was a wholesome story of boys and girls on the playing fields of Boeotia. In Ovid the story appears in one of the more unsettling ensembles of stories in a poem filled with many such ensembles.

Carefully not mentioning the name of Atalanta until she is already under way, Venus begins "Perhaps you have heard of a certain woman who beat the fastest men in contest," teasingly naming Atalanta by indirection.[57] Venus allows that she is not used to the rigors of the hunter's chase, so she settles back in a grassy nook under a poplar, lays her head on Adonis's breast, and tells the story of a certain maiden who was terrified by a prophecy that she would not follow a god's advice and be lost. Atalanta attempts to live unwed and sets some harsh terms: any man who catches her in a race will win her, but if he does not, he will die.[58] This is the maiden Hippomenes falls in love with. Venus hears his prayer for help and supplies him with three golden apples. Each apple he throws slows down Atalanta for a moment, but it is the last one that finally does the trick.[59] Venus suddenly realizes that her telling of the story is taking longer than the race itself, she says, so she abruptly stops. Hippomenes wins the race and Atalanta, and then promptly forgets all about his debt to Venus.

For this, she tells Adonis, Venus has her revenge. She fires up Hippomenes with such desire for Atalanta that he can't wait for a proper bed but drags her into the nearest cave to have her. Unfortunately the cave he selects is a space sacred to Cybele the Mother goddess, and as punishment for this defilement Cybele turns both Atalanta and Hippomenes into lions. This is why Adonis should avoid lions whenever he hunts. He does avoid them, scrupulously, but Venus neglects to tell him to watch out also for wild boars, and he doesn't. So one kills him.

This is the matrix of lust, thwarted desire, and absurdity out of which the improving myth in "Of the Wings of Atalanta" comes. Throughout the chapter Du Bois switches back and forth between Atlanta the city and Atalanta the allegorical figure, so that the identities of both become inseparable. The sinister cave and Cybele disappear, to be replaced by a "Temple of Love." Du Bois does not follow Ovid's way with the story and hints not too indirectly that virginal Atalanta prostitutes herself by her lust for gold. Sanctimonious paganism is blended with Christian terminology—neither of which Du Bois believes in for a minute—to warn Atlanta away from wealth.

Atalanta is not the first or the last maiden whom greed of gold has led
to defile the temple of Love; and not maids alone, but men in the race of
life, sink from the high and generous ideals of youth to the gambler's code
of the Bourse; and in all our Nation's striving is not the Gospel of Work
befouled by the Gospel of Pay? So common is this that one-half think it
normal; so unquestioned, that we almost fear to question if the end of racing is not gold, if the aim of man is not rightly to be rich. And if this is the
fault of America, how dire a danger lies before a new land and a new city,
lest Atlanta, stooping for mere gold, shall find that gold accursed!

It was no maiden's idle whim that started this hard racing; a fearful
wilderness lay about the feet of that city after the War. . . . How fleet must
Atalanta be if she will not be tempted by gold to profane the Sanctuary![60]

The three golden apples have been blended into the purest of all symbols
of greed, arousing an appetite that feeds so easily into sexual desire that it
is impossible to tell whether this latter-day serpent tempting Eve is a rapist or a capitalist. Probably he is both.

Du Bois's sermon from classical mythology on all these evils is very
much in the spirit of his contemporary Frank Norris, whose *McTeague*
(1899) and *The Octopus* (1901) detail the destruction of American character
by wealth, unchecked industrialization, and the spread of the railroads.
Both Du Bois and Norris are responding to the argument of Andrew Carnegie for the legitimacy of the massive fortunes that were being made in the
late nineteenth century. In "The Gospel of Wealth" (1899) Carnegie maintained that such Midas-like accumulations were actually in the public interest, because they brought a material prosperity that all could benefit
from. Provided those who had the new money realized their responsibilities to society and shared what they had with others less fortunate, there
was nothing to fear from capitalism's success. Carnegie was an enthusiastic supporter of the inheritance tax.

The problem of our age is the administration of wealth, so that the ties of
brotherhood may still bind together the rich and poor in harmonious relationship. The conditions of human life have not only been changed, but
revolutionized, within the past few hundred years. In former days there
was little difference between the dwelling, dress, food, and environment
of the chief and those of his retainers. . . . The contrast between the palace
of the millionaire and the cottage of the laborer with us today measures
the change which has come with civilization.

This change, however, is not to be deplored, but welcomed as highly beneficial. It is well, nay, essential for the progress of the race, that the houses of some should be homes for all that is highest and best in literature and the arts, and for all the refinements of civilization, rather than that none should be so. Much better this great irregularity than universal squalor. Without wealth there can be no Maecenas. The "good old times" were not good old times. Neither master nor servant was as well situated then as today.[61]

The problem with Carnegie's argument was not its ideals but its optimism about human nature. While he endowed libraries in his name across the United States and built the most famous concert hall of the nation, other millionaires were happily engaged in an uncontrolled exploitation of labor and the mineral wealth of the country that would be slowed only by the introduction of antitrust legislation beginning in the administrations of Theodore Roosevelt and Woodrow Wilson, with future reforms that would not be fully realized until the Great Depression and the first administration of Franklin Roosevelt, in the 1930s—and then undone again in the 1980s and 1990s and early twenty-first century.

Du Bois's hortatory mode in *The Souls of Black Folk* is not due to his naïveté about the likelihood that he will not be heard. With the founding of the NAACP and his journal the *Crisis* he would keep up his arguments and his exhortations for several generations to come. Du Bois would not concede the hopelessness of racial justice and fair government for all in America until the 1960s, when he moved with his last wife to Ghana. He died on the eve of the 1963 March on Washington, when Martin Luther King and others acknowledged his contribution to that event and to the struggle for civil rights that was about to enter its legislative heyday with the administration of Lyndon Johnson.

It is of little moment that Du Bois recalls details in Ovid's account only when he wants to. He has a great deal more on his mind than any literalist notion of fidelity to a text even begins to suggest. Atalanta consulted a god, and the oracle gave her the paradoxical response that she shouldn't marry but wouldn't be able to avoid doing so, and would thereby lose her maidenhood anyway. For Du Bois, the association of prophecy and god is enough, because he wants to contrast this god ignored with the other gods circulating around Atlanta.

The Sanctuary of our fathers has, to be sure, few Gods,—some sneer, "all too few." There is the thrifty Mercury of New England, Pluto of the

North, and Ceres of the West; and there, too, is the half-forgotten Apollo of the South, under whose aegis the maiden ran, — and as she ran she forgot him, even as there in Boeotia Venus was forgot.[62]

Atalanta as Atlanta has forgotten the genteel Southern gentleman with all his romantic grace, courtliness, and knightly ways, and stooped to pick up the apples of gold, things that men "busier and sharper, thriftier and more unscrupulous" throw in her way. Du Bois then moves the classical myth even further into his own world, both by personal reference to his New England boyhood in Great Barrington, Massachusetts, and by invocation of that omnipresent barrier that *The Souls of Black Folk* is always bringing us back to, the Veil that flutters between Black Folk and the world. All Southerners are in danger, but most especially Black Folk.

> Golden apples are beautiful — I remember the lawless days of boyhood, when orchards in crimson and gold tempted me over fence and field — and, too, the merchant who has dethroned the planter is no despicable *parvenu*. . . . Yet the warning is needed lest the wily Hippomenes tempt Atalanta to thinking that golden apples are the goal of racing, and not mere incidents by the way.
>
> Atlanta must not lead the South to dream of material prosperity as the touchstone of all success; already the fatal might of this idea is beginning to spread; it is replacing the finer type of Southerner with vulgar money-getters; it is burying the sweeter beauties of Southern life beneath pretence and ostentation.
>
> . . . Not only is this true in the world which Atlanta typifies, but it is threatening to be true of a world beneath and beyond that world, — the Black World beyond the Veil. To-day it makes little difference to Atlanta, to the South, what the Negro thinks or wills. . . . Hither has the temptation of Hippomenes penetrated; already in this smaller world, which now indirectly and anon directly must influence the larger for good or ill, the habit is forming of interpreting the world in dollars.[63]

The transformation of Atalanta into the embodiment of the future of black youth, in fact, their very souls, is complete. She is the ideals of the race, what the Preacher and the Teacher once embodied, but ideals that may not withstand the lure of gold.

> Here stands this young Atalanta, girding herself for the race that must be run; and if her eyes be still toward the hills and sky as in the days of old,

then we may look for noble running; but what if some ruthless or wily
or even thoughtless Hippomenes lay golden apples before her? . . . Must
this, and that fair flower of Freedom which, despite the jeers of latter-day
striplings, sprung from our fathers' blood, must that too degenerate into a
dusty quest of gold, — into lawless lust with Hippomenes?[64]

Alliterative monstrosities like "lawless lust" are just the kind of thing Sinclair Lewis's hero would learn to employ so well in his 1927 novel about evan-
gelical hucksterism, *Elmer Gantry*. Du Bois does not invoke classical myth
and Christian morality because he believes in them, but because he wants
to exploit them. It is a measure of his commitment to what he would later
identify as propaganda that he has no concern that this extended rhetorical
question culminating in the "lawless lust of Hippomenes" moves far from
pagan mythology and close to revivalist polemic. This impassioned rant
rounds out Du Bois's extended parable about Atlanta and Atalanta, an allegorization that is ultimately no more classical in spirit than it is Christian in
morality. He then modulates to an encomium of Atlanta University and the
need for more universities like it, better than those, candidly, that are universities only in name. Wilberforce could well have been at the top of his list.
    "Of the Wings of Atalanta" enters its final movement when Du Bois at
last decodes his arresting title.

The need of the South is knowledge and culture, — not in dainty limited
quantity, as before the war, but in broad busy abundance in the world of
work; and until she has this, not all the Apples of the Hesperides, be they
golden and bejeweled, can save her from the curse of the Boeotian lovers.
    The Wings of Atalanta are the coming universities of the South. They
alone can bear the maiden past the temptation of golden fruit. They will
not guide her flying feet away from the cotton and gold; for—ah, thoughtful Hippomenes!—do not the apples lie in the very Way of Life? But they
will guide her over and beyond them, and leave her kneeling in the Sanctuary of Truth and Freedom and broad Humanity, virgin and undefiled.[65]

This is a delightful heap of mythological apples.[66] Hercules' labor after the
apples of the Hesperides is rather different from the apples of Venus and
her Boeotian businessman Hippomenes—but by this point mythological consistency is not what concerns Du Bois. Moral purity and intellectual integrity are cast as a spiritual virginity too easily lost. His "Way of
Life" doesn't lead to salvation, but to a temple where political virtues are
maintained.

This is not myth the way Ovid tells it, or even Bulfinch. Atalanta and Hippomenes have become characters in a sociological allegory about the dangers of succumbing to the lure of Mammon. Du Bois would little care about a Latin teacher's reaction to his story. What really inspires him is the homonym he makes of "Atlanta" with "Atalanta"; from that point he lets the story take him where his political purposes lead him. His allegorization of classical myth ends with one of the more improbable commands in American literature:

> When night falls on the City of a Hundred Hills, a wind gathers itself from the seas and comes murmuring westward. And at its bidding, the smoke of the drowsy factories sweeps down upon the mighty city and covers it like a pall, while yonder at the University the stars twinkle above Stone Hall. And they say that yon gray mist is the tunic of Atalanta pausing over her golden apples. Fly, my maiden, fly, for yonder comes Hippomenes![67]

It is a finale at once urgent and, in this final exhortation, a little ridiculous—a truly mythical sports story. To Du Bois's great delight, George Schuyler would later write a wonderful send-up of Du Bois himself as well as this kind of moralizing grandiloquence in his portrait of Dr. Shakespeare Agamemnon Beard in *Black No More*.[68] In fact Du Bois was being no more cavalier with the myth of Atalanta than actual American capitalists were. The robber baron Jay Gould (1836–1892) had a private Texas & Pacific Railroad car which he traveled in about the country in his unceasing depredations. The car's name was "Atalanta."[69]

Four

Genteel Classicism

Owing to the circumstance that this knowledge of the classics has become part of the elementary requirements in our system of education, the ability to use and to understand certain of the dead languages of southern Europe is not only gratifying to the person who finds occasion to parade his accomplishments in this respect, but the evidence of such knowledge serves at the same time to recommend any savant to his audience, both lay and learned. It is currently expected that a certain number of years shall have been spent in acquiring this substantially useless information, and its absence creates a presumption of hasty and precarious learning, as well as of a vulgar practicality that is equally obnoxious to the conventional standards of sound scholarship and intellectual force.

Thorstein Veblen, *The Theory of the Leisure Class* (1899)

Around the year 1900 economics and social evolution made strange bedfellows of Booker T. Washington and Thorstein Veblen. At the same time, and for different reasons and different audiences, both drew attention to a certain level of impracticality in the study of classics. Washington had a clear grasp of what was needed in order for African Americans to be employed, and famously made it clear that he thought Greek was a waste of time for any black person who wanted to make a living. Du Bois and Scarborough fought back with all they had against such views of humane learning, views typical of a respectable segment of the United States even to the present day. For his part, Veblen was writing what has come to seem more and more the work of a satirist, one masquerading at the time as a social critic and economist in his *Theory of the Leisure Class*. His comments about the essential uselessness of classical education cannot be taken literally, since he acquired the very kind of classical education he lampoons. At another point in the *Theory* he can be found quoting learnedly from Horace's *Carmen Saeculare*, without reference to where the lines occur in Horace's poetry, and without translating them. Veblen expects readers of *The Theory of the Leisure Class* to be able to recognize his allusions to Horace at sight—or at least to know enough to keep quiet if they don't.[1]

The reason we should consider the phenomenon of genteel classicism in African American literature is that such humane learning does not invariably lead to success. It can play a decisive role in any person's life, as Wheatley, Douglass, Scarborough, and countless others show. And then it may not at all. Knowing the varied legacies of Greece and Rome does not always lead to enduring literary achievement; in some cases it seems to guarantee there is none. From the later nineteenth century onward we can find African Americans invoking classical myth and learning for the sake of social respectability, just like Veblen's leisure class. Occasionally there is a hint of scandal—the danger of incest, class exploitation, larceny, murder of family members—but finally nothing that would shock a proper audience of any kind.

We will consider the mixed results of writing fiction on classical themes in W. E. B. Du Bois and his friend and colleague Jessie Fauset, then go on to trace the same problem in Countee Cullen, one of the most admired African American poets in the first half of the twentieth century—although many who wrote about him wished he had been better than he was. Cullen wrote some enduring poems, but also seems to have spent much of his career invoking classical models, only to flee from them in what struck even his sympathetic contemporaries as some kind of failure of nerve, or talent, or both.

Of the Quest of the Silver Fleece

For it does not belong to the art of weaving to make fleeces, but to use them, and also to know what sort of fleece is good and suitable or bad and unsuitable. (Aristotle, *Politics* 1258 a)

W. E. B. Du Bois seems to have cared only to play around with the adventure of the voyage of the *Argo* rather than make anything serious of it. He had already put this myth to work in the eighth chapter of *The Souls of Black Folk*, "Of the Quest of the Golden Fleece." One of the wonders of *Souls* is how constantly the voice of each chapter changes from what went before. By the time Du Bois reaches chapter 8 he no longer speaks with the fervor that marks "Of the Wings of Atalanta," but in an easy conversational style—talking about a myth now, not reliving it.

> Have you ever seen a cotton-field white with the harvest,—its golden fleece hovering above the black earth like a silvery cloud edged with dark green, its bold white signals waving like the foam of billows from Carolina to Texas across that Black and human Sea? (456)

Cotton transforms the Black Belt that was the human subject of the preceding chapter into a human Black Sea across which the *Argo* sails in the quest for the golden fleece. No sooner has metaphor piled on metaphor and simile on simile than Du Bois turns from all that fancy talk to a more analytical, detached reflection, making the metaphor, showing off his knowledge of Greek by using the Latin form of the Greek *chrysomallos* ("golden fleece") as if it were a proper name.

> I have sometimes half suspected that here the winged ram Chrysomallus left that Fleece after which Jason and his Argonauts went vaguely wandering into the shadowy East three thousand years ago; and certainly one might frame a pretty and not far-fetched analogy of witchery and dragon's teeth, and blood and armed men, between the ancient and the modern Quest of the Golden Fleece in the Black Sea. (Ibid.)

In contrast to "The Wings of Atalanta," which gives away the allegorical game relatively late in its telling, Du Bois now merely alludes coolly to Greek mythology, making an allegory of contemporary Southern economic life.[2]

> And now the golden fleece is found; not only found, but, in its birthplace, woven. For the hum of the cotton-mills is the newest and most significant thing in the New South today. All through the Carolinas and Georgia, away down to Mexico, rise these gaunt red buildings, bare and homely, and

yet so busy and noisy withal that they scarce seem to belong to the slow
and sleepy land. Perhaps they sprang from dragons' teeth. So the Cotton
Kingdom still lives; the world still bows beneath her sceptre. Even the
markets that once defied the *parvenu* have crept one by one across the
seas, and then slowly and reluctantly, but surely, have started toward the
Black Belt. (456–57)

The move from mythologizing to more analytical language is done with a
sure hand, down to such precise touches as turning "Golden Fleece" into
the lowercase "golden fleece." *The Souls of Black Folk* is the work of a writer
who knows how he wants to use classical myth, and it is not so much for
a literary as for a rhetorical, even propagandistic use. When Du Bois returned to this same kind of didactic mythmaking as the basis for a long
novel, the results would be less compelling.

The *Quest of the Silver Fleece* was published in 1911 to generally favorable reviews, if disappointing sales. In *Dusk of Dawn* (1920) Du Bois refers
back to *The Quest* modestly; he was just taking a stab at writing fiction. "It
was really an economic study of some merit."[3] He himself realized that
the novel had been an economist's treatise masquerading as a romance.[4]
Du Bois wanted his readers to see the voyage of the *Argo* and the Golden
Fleece as a heroic adventure that could be related to economic theory, and
that was at least a laudable social and economic goal.

The problem emerged in the writing. Du Bois was a genius as a political thinker and activist, but not as a novelist or a poet. Barrett Wendell had been his English professor at Harvard, for whom he had written
guilelessly, enthusiastically, "I believe foolishly perhaps, but sincerely, that
I have something to say to the world, and I have taken English 12 in order
to say it well." He picked the wrong mentor. Arnold Rampersad speculates
that the publication in 1900 of Wendell's influential *Literary History of
America* set back the cause of American literary criticism and scholarship
by some years.

> With little formal reading in literature himself, Du Bois was being trained
> in the appreciation of letters by a charismatic figure disdainful of the
> problems of a struggling national literature, of the vitality of folk expres-
> sion, or of the experimentation in forms and themes by which literature
> revitalizes itself. This reactionary approach left its mark on Du Bois.
> As editor of *The Crisis* . . . he played a major role in the Harlem Renais-
> sance, but his inability to develop a taste for the progressive in art, or an

appreciation of the earthier forms of expression, contributed to his failure to respond to the variety of black art. He was not deeply read in poetry, fiction, or literary criticism. His formal training was in other fields, and his informal reading was not nearly enough.[5]

Perhaps because Du Bois sensed his limitations in literary culture, even more probably because it was so obviously relevant to the economic history of any period, he returned to the same kind of didactic mythologizing he had used to create the fictional world of *The Quest of the Silver Fleece*. The technique of the novel reminds one of sharply drawn characters in the work of naturalist novels like Frank Norris's *The Pit* (1903) or Upton Sinclair's *The Jungle* (1906).[6] But the love story of the two most important characters Blessed ("Bles") Alwyn and a Medea-like swamp woman named Zora is at the center of the fiction, and for this Du Bois knew how to write only in a way neither Norris nor Sinclair could abide, the sentimental style of contemporary romances.[7]

David Levering Lewis points to last-minute editorial correspondence with Du Bois's publishers that led him to exchange his original title's golden fleece for silver.[8] The novelist David Graham Phillips had published a popular romance in 1903 whose title led Du Bois's publishers to fear an overlap in marketing: *Golden Fleece: The American Adventures of a Fortune Hunting Earl*. While economics and social justice were Du Bois's overriding concern in the novel, the fictional style he worked in to create his hero Bles and heroine Zora was rooted in Phillips's kind of sentiment. The redemptive power of Zora's love is what ultimately pulls Bles up to her level of educated enlightenment; it is the first instance in his fiction of Du Bois's lifelong support for the feminist cause.[9] But *The Quest* ends as conventionally as any contemporary romance, with hairpin turns of plot and cliff-hangers right to the finish line.

His voice was slow and firm:
   "Emma? But I don't love Emma. I love—some one else."
   Her heart bounded and again was still. It was that Washington girl then.
   She answered dully, groping for words, for she was tired:
"Who is it?"
   "The best woman in all the world, Zora."
   "And is"—she struggled at the word madly—"is she pure?"
   "She is more pure than snow."

"Then you must marry her, Bles."

"I am not worthy of her," he answered, sinking before her.

Then at last illumination dawned upon her blindness. She stood very still and lifted up her eyes. The swamp was living, vibrant, tremulous. There where the first long note of night lay shot with burning crimson, burst in sudden radiance the wide beauty of the moon. There pulsed a glory in the air. Her little hands groped and wandered over his close-curled hair, and she sobbed, deep-voiced:

"Will you—marry me, Bles?" (433–34)

And then the author of *The Souls of Black Folk* draws aside his fictional veil—not *the* Veil—and speaks *in propria persona* just as he had in 1904 in *The Souls of Black Folk*.[10]

L'ENVOI

Lend me thine ears, O God the Reader, whose Fathers aforetime sent mine down into the land of Egypt, into this House of Bondage. Lay not these words aside for a moment's phantasy, but lift up thine eyes upon the Horror in this land;—the maiming and mocking and murdering of my people, and the prisonment of their souls. Let my people go, O Infinite One, lest the world shudder at

THE END. (434)

Du Bois borrowed heavily from his earlier work to write this romantic story. The last-minute switch from a golden to a silver fleece was not felicitous, but it is prophetic about what awaits Du Bois's readers who persist to the end. Rampersad was the first critic to describe what awaits those who do.

The "silver fleece" of the title is the way of labor, love and beauty in life. Zora is the most conspicuous pilgrim in a search that all men must make. The epic breadth is sustained in two principal ways: first, by using charged language to describe Zora's search; and second, by exploiting the physical dimensions of the cotton industry so that it provides a world-wide setting for a story that is at first provincial.[11]

To these generalized epic qualities we can add some more specific ways that Du Bois adapted and transformed elements of the myth of the Golden Fleece.

A boy and girl appear who are not named but seen first as types. They are a young, black Everyman and Everywoman. The boy hears music in the darkness and draws near a cabin, where a door suddenly opens.

Amid this mighty halo, as on clouds of flame, a girl was dancing. She was black, and lithe, and tall, and willowy. Her garments twined and flew around the delicate moulding of her dark, young, half-naked limbs. A heavy mass of hair clung motionless to her wide forehead. Her arms twirled and flickered, and body and soul seemed quivering and whirring in the poetry of her motion.

As she danced she sang. He heard her voice as before, fluttering like a bird's in the full sweetness of her utter music. It was no tune or melody, it was just formless, boundless music. The boy forgot himself and all the world besides. (14–15)

Recall that Medea was the daughter of Aeëtes, who was the son of Helios and the brother of the enchantress Circe. The nameless girl who appears to the boy in a fiery vision suggests something just as remote: the primitive, the barbaric (non-Greek, precivilized), she performs a ritual dance and song that are bewitching and, as it were, preclassical (formless, boundless). She promises the boy more dreams in the swamp that lies beyond. The girl seems to be assuming the role of Medea, an African cousin of the Greek offspring of Helios. It turns out that she is in fact not a witch, but the daughter of one, whose "deep, harsh tones" the boy hears before he sees an apparition that actually is a witch.

This overheated atmosphere changes radically in the next chapter when the boy enters Miss Sarah Smith's school. Suddenly there are words for everything, even Latin words.

"You mean you can pay what we ask?"
"Why, yes. Ain't that all?"
"No. The rest is gathered from the crumbs of Dives' table."
Then he saw the twinkle in her eyes. She laid her hand gently upon his shoulder. (25)

The boy Bles doesn't know how to say "Rich man" in Latin, but is encouraged to reveal his own allegorizing name, "Blessed Alwyn." We have entered into a familiar web of words and from this point will never leave it, because Miss Smith is offering the kind of liberal education that

Scarborough and Du Bois advocated. When the Northerner Mary Taylor
tells her brother she wants to leave for Alabama to teach in Miss Smith's
school, he dismisses her with a contemptuous wave of the hand.

> "You ought to know, John, if I teach Negroes I'll scarcely see much of
> people in my own class."
> "Nonsense! Butt in. Show off. Give 'em your Greek—and study Cotton.
> At any rate, I say go." (27)

Later, when the dangers of educating Negroes have yet to dawn on Mary
Taylor's brother John, Du Bois puts the argument of his pedagogical enemy Booker T. Washington into the mouth of the Alabaman Harry Cress-
well when he confronts John Taylor in his New York office.[12]

> "Why, are you daft? See here! American cotton-spinning is built on cheap
> niggers. Educating, or rather trying to educate niggers, will make them
> restless and discontented—that is, scarce and dear as workers. Don't you
> see you're planning to cut off your noses? This Smith School, particularly,
> has nearly ruined our plantation. It's stuck almost in our front yard; you
> are planning to put our plough-hands all to studying Greek, and at the
> same time to corner the cotton crop—rot!" (160)

The guilty party here is Miss Smith, the kind of New England schoolmarm
whose dedicated teaching in the South after the Civil War Du Bois had
praised in *The Souls of Black Folk*. She is one of the few admirable persons in
the entire novel, white or black.[13] In a tense conversation with her cynical
benefactor, the Northern socialite Mrs. Vanderpool, she also appears to be
a constant reader of W. E. B. Du Bois.

> "I—hope I'm not too blunt; I hope I make myself clear. You know, statis-
> tics show—"
> "Drat statistics!" Miss Smith had flashed impatiently. "These are folks."
> Mrs. Vanderpool smiled indulgently. "To be sure," she murmured, "but
> what sort of folks?"
> "God's sort."
> "Oh, well—" (23–24)

Everyone in the novel comes to life as a walking, talking character shaped
by Du Bois's earlier work. The transformation of the classical myth of the
Golden Fleece into Du Bois's Silver Fleece emerges in Miss Mary Taylor's

classroom. Bles knows everything about cotton, and Miss Taylor knows nothing about it; she thinks it grows on vines, like grapes. Bles is pleased to give her a graphic account of the many stages involved in the raising of cotton, from the sowing to the picking. Du Bois also enlists him to make sure that the novel's text harmonizes with the novel's new title.

> She bent wondering over the pale plants. The poetry of the thing began to sing within her, awakening her unpoetic imagination, and she murmured:
> "The Golden Fleece—it's the Silver Fleece!"
> "What's that?" he asked.
> "Have you never heard of the Golden Fleece, Bles?"
> "No, ma'am," he said eagerly; then glancing up toward the Cresswell fields, he saw two white men watching them. He grasped his hoe and started briskly to work. (31–32)

The otherwise prosaic Mary Taylor now realizes that the present day's Golden Fleece is cotton. She also discovers on her own initiative one of Du Bois's most well-known words from *The Souls of Black Folk*, the Veil.

> She started thinking of cotton—but at once she pulled herself back to the other aspect. Always before she had been veiled from these folk: who had put the veil there? Had she herself hung it before her soul, or had they hidden timidly behind its other side? Or was it simply a brute fact, regardless of both of them? (32)

Later she makes good on her promise to teach Bles and tells him the story of Jason and the Argonauts, but is puzzled when he seems less than thrilled to hear the story, which he regards as anything but heroic.

> "All yon is Jason's."
> "What?" she asked, puzzled.
> He pointed with one sweep of his long arm to the quivering mass of green-gold foliage that swept from swamp to horizon.
> "All yon golden fleece is Jason's now," he repeated.
> "I thought it was—Cresswell's," she said.
> "That's what I mean."
> She suddenly understood that the story had sunk deeply.
> "I am glad to hear you say that," she said methodically, "for Jason was a brave adventurer—"
> "I thought he was a thief."

"Oh, well—those were other times."

"The Cresswells are thieves now."

"Bles, I am ashamed to hear you talk so of your neighbors simply because they are white."

But Bles continued.

"This is the Black Sea," he said, pointing to the dull cabins that crouched here and there upon the earth, with the dark twinkling of their black folk darting out to see the strangers ride by. (35–36)

Bles has become as adept at drawing the parallel between ancient myth and modern example as the writer who created him, and he's already surpassed his teacher Miss Taylor. Myths have their own logic, though; just because you start interpreting everything allegorically doesn't mean you'll be any better off.

"He's going to Elspeth's," he said.

"Who is he?"

"We just call him Old Pappy—he's a preacher, and some folks say a conjure man, too."

"And who is Elspeth?"

"She lives in the swamp—she's a kind of witch, I reckon, like—like—"

"Like Medea?"

"Yes—only—I don't know—" and he grew thoughtful. (37–38)

Mythological parallels are not as easy to handle as Bles imagined.

Zora finally finds what is at stake in what Rampersad identifies as the moral of *The Quest of the Silver Fleece*, in the words of a preacher whose sermon finally articulates what it is that Zora's emancipation from Elspeth and her liberal education both prepared her for.

Only in a whole world of selves, infinite, endless, eternal world on worlds of selves—only in their vast good is true salvation. The good of others is our true good; work for others; not for *your* salvation, but the salvation of the world. (294–95)[14]

This preacher's moral applies as much to Du Bois as it does to Zora. As an ex-Medea she identifies completely with this call to duty. The voices of the preacher and the author's concluding *Envoi* summoning us to a higher calling are, not surprisingly, one and the same voice.

Given Tragedy, We'll Take Romance

There actually is such a thing as Greek Tragedy even in these days. We were
almost swamped with it. But the wave missed us. (*The Chinaberry Tree*)

Jessie Fauset (1882–1961) remains an important figure among early twentieth-century African American intellectuals.[15] She was present for the
explosion of creativity in the Harlem Renaissance which was fueled by
the Great Migration of Southern blacks to the North that peaked in the
first two decades of the century. Fauset published four novels, with *The
Chinaberry Tree* appearing in 1931, roughly fifty years after the young Mary
Church Terrell surprised Matthew Arnold with her command of Greek.
She enlisted the popular novelist Zona Gale to write an introduction.[16]
Susan Tomlinson observes that Gale's obliging introduction is a peculiarly
twentieth-century version of that enduring stamp of approval from earlier stages of African American literature, the authenticating document.[17]
Like all such authenticators, Gale had good intentions. She was a popular
and successful writer herself and must have thought she was doing Fauset a
favor, yet, as Tomlinson shows, by inviting the reader to look on the novel
as a window into the unfamiliar world of respectable black bourgeois life,
she makes *The Chinaberry Tree* sound more like a sociological study than a
work of fiction.

> It seems strange to affirm, — as news for many, — that there is in America
> a great group of Negroes of education and substance who are living lives
> of quiet interests and pursuits, quite unconnected with white folk save as
> these are casually met. That these men and women carry on their lives,
> educate their children, and fill their times with interests social, domestic,
> and philanthropic as if there were not white people in America, save those
> who serve them in shops and in traffic.[18]

The spell of Du Bois's *Souls of Black Folk* may account for much of the
abiding association of even fictional accounts of African American lives
with social scientific models. As for Fauset's career, Deborah E. Mc-
Dowell observes that even as well-known and accomplished a journalist
as she was — a close friend of Du Bois and the literary editor of the *Crisis*
for many years — she was nonetheless in the double bind that any gifted
African American writer and artist had to struggle with. At the time she
was publishing her novels, African Americans were regularly portrayed in

fiction as "uninhibited, primitive exotics"; even Gale saw what Fauset was foregoing by choosing to write about the men and women of the black urban middle class to which she belonged, rather than the more fashionable underclass.[19]

This very choice of characters lends a surreal quality to the story. Fauset was able to inflect it with a classical reference that could be expected to add even more grace to this story of the fate of some of the Talented Tenth. The theme of incest surfaces in the novel, which might lead us to suspect another version of the *Oedipus*.[20] Unlike Rita Dove's *Darker Face of the Earth*, which genuinely does deal with mother-and-son incest, what is discovered in *Chinaberry Tree* is more like something from Greek New Comedy, or Roman comedy or Shakespeare, where a brother and sister find out one another's true identity in the nick of time so that incest is avoided. Fauset's young character Melissa turns out to be as naïve and as misinformed as a believable character can be. Yet Fauset had to be careful how she introduced anything as lofty as Greek tragedy and its themes into a work aimed at a wide readership expecting a genteel woman's novel of manners.[21]

One of the things Fauset was doing was working out a complication of the familiar Tragic Mulatto plot, and she wanted to extend its fiction about the suppression of family ties and the discovery of miscegenation to embrace themes seemingly explored only in ancient Greek tragedy.[22] As Rita Dove would later point out, miscegenation and the suppression of family ties had in fact already been worked out repeatedly in actual African American family history. The budding love affair of Melissa and Malory Forten ends suddenly when first he and then she discover that they have different black mothers but the same white father. Even Fauset's sympathetic critics have read their fate as an unfortunate distraction from the main event, the love story of Laurentine and her long-suffering suitor Stephen Denleigh. As Mary Jane Lupton puts it in her article "Bad Blood in Jersey,"

> The incest motif, while it adds a special horror to the plot and while it further amplifies the Greek tragic patterns of the novel, ultimately detracts from the realistic treatment of women and race which otherwise dominates the book. I would agree with Hiroko Sato's judgment that "if there is anything to blame in this novel, it is this artificial subplot of incestuous love—obviously influenced by Greek tragedies."[23]

Joseph Feeney also notes the many cultural differences that distance Fauset's characters from ancient drama: ancient religious beliefs, the notion of fate or family curses, and the like are all quite different from a book that

"remains at heart a domestic novel."[24] We can agree with Lupton and Feeney that the potentially tragic motif of incest doesn't work very well for
Fauset, but the reason it doesn't is that she was working not with a tragic
motif, but with one more familiar from comic plots involving a brother
and sister related by one parent or another.

This is why it is not possible to trace any explicit textual echo or allusion between Fauset's novel and Sophocles, though Melissa *sounds* as if she
had read something like the *Oedipus* at school. This vague memory gets her
nowhere trying to figure out what is wrong with Malory. It is telling that
what she does recall is not anything as imposing as Sophocles, but merely
the iconic images of Greek masks for tragedy and comedy.

> Her tired mind refusing to cope any longer with such an unsolvable
> problem switched involuntarily to a discussion which they had had in
> her English class on the ancient Greek drama. She had meant to read
> up on the subject but she had been too tired. However, Miss Scarlett,
> her teacher, had been as always very clear and precise in presenting the
> details. She could remember, she thought, almost every word of it, in case
> an examination was sprung. What had intrigued her attention most had
> been the pictures which Miss Scarlett had shown of the masks of Trag-
> edy and Comedy. After they had gone the round of the class Melissa had
> secured them again and pored over them in an agony of fascination, fear,
> and repulsion.

Nor is she an admiring student when it comes to such classical icons.

> She hated the sightless eyes, the horrid, gaping mouths, the snaky hair.
> Even the plane of the cheeks and the moulding of the lips seemed to carry
> a suggestion, in both masks, of a mad, deliberate cruelty. In particular she
> was at once magnetized and repelled by the hint of laughter in the Comic
> Mask. If anyone were ever to look at her with that vacant, leering grin,
> that promise of heartless mirth. . . . "I'd scream out loud," she told herself
> cowering under her warm covers. (183–84)

Greek tragedy has so little substance for her, and she is so sheltered from
the world she lives in, that finally Malory must spell out for her what their
tragedy actually is. The family name, after all, is "Strange."

> "Your mother . . . with that rotten Strange blood in her . . . she was never
> married to any man named Paul; she—was my father's mistress, his

woman . . . and you're his child and my—my sister!" He raised his tortured
eyes, he strained frantic arms toward the blazing, pitiless sky. "Oh God,
how could you do it? You knew I loved her . . . You knew I wanted her . . .
and she's my sister!

"Your mother was my mother's best friend—and she betrayed her. She
ate my mother's bread . . . and slept with my father; my father went off
with her and came home to die and told my mother . . . You're bad, bad, all
of you!" (331)

Malory Forten plunges back onto the road and disappears from the novel,
never to be seen again. He and Melissa never even come close to consummating their passions. Thank goodness.

The threat of sibling incest is usually displaced in just this way in ancient
New Comedy and especially the gothic fiction with which *The Chinaberry
Tree* has such affinity.[25] Fauset writes the great mystery of Malory Forten
into the heart of her novel, and Melissa turns out to have been visited by
prophetic dreams, such as running after an obscure, shuffling figure on a
country road; that dream turns into reality in the shape of Malory when
she comes upon him and finally hears the truth from his own lips. Fauset presents this teasingly, first simply saying that Melissa "dreamed the
dream" (182), then describing it in more detail (218–19), and finally letting
Melissa discover its prophetic truth when she meets Malory for the last
time (329–30). With this many textbook Aristotelian recognition scenes
going on, no wonder Stephen Denleigh draws the proper conclusion. The
wave of Greek tragedy really did miss them.

In fact neither Denleigh nor anyone else in the novel has been anywhere near a Greek tragedy. They are at the end of a romance where love
finally conquers every obstacle and all are wed and live happily forever after. Even the ill-fated Melissa turns out not to be cursed after all. In addition to avoiding consummating her love with Malory or being murdered
by a relative, she has a perfectly good backup suitor in the stolid farmer
Asshur, who is devoted to her. He seems hardly able to restrain himself at
his unexpected triumph.

In his veins his blood ran hot and thick. His thoughts were inchoate; he
was the triumphant male. Boyishly, crudely, he pictured the rapture of his
marriage . . . There would be Melissa, home, children . . . he would order
their well-being. He would work for them, protect them, love them, *have*
them . . . he stretched strong, sinewy arms well above his head. . . . He
could have broken into a dance all rhythm and joy. (340)

Perhaps understandably, Laurentine and Melissa are not as cheerful as their future husbands, who are clueless about the fate they all avoided. Still, subdued as they both are—"so different," Fauset adds thoughtfully—their fate is bright enough to suggest "everywhere about them the immanence of God. . . . The Chinaberry Tree became a temple" (341). Only Malory really found out what a Greek tragedy was like, and he was dispatched from the novel as soon as his immediate usefulness to both Melissa and the plot was exhausted.

What Fauset handles with more confidence than tragic plots is her depiction of an American know-nothing type like the manly Denleigh. There are continual hints that Malory comes from etiolated stock and would be a prime candidate for the kind of disastrous parentage that is eventually discovered. Denleigh passes by one day and finds Malory scanning Vergil's *Aeneid* with Melissa.

> A harmless enough diversion, he decided, for a boy and girl. The lad whom he didn't recognize had a nice open face he noticed—there was something a little feminine, womanish about it, he thought, as though it might break under strain. (171)

There is something faintly degenerate and unsettling about a man's reading Vergil in Latin. It is not a subtle foreshadowing, but it does confirm our impression of the manliness of Laurentine's future husband.

> He could not think of a single possibility which might mar Laurentine's and his own serenity, he assured himself,—and flicked away as one might an insect his tiny insistent wonder as to why it upset him, frightened him a little to see Melissa, so confidently, so matter-of-factly at ease in the company of Malory Forten. (200)

As Denleigh's and other characters' forebodings about Malory mount, we realize we are in the company of people turning a member of their community into a scapegoat. In ancient Greek culture the *pharmakos*, whether an actual person or simply a made-up figure of one, could be of considerable use for a community. As Jean-Pierre Vernant observes of the original model in Greek society:

> He is the double of the king, but in reverse, like those carnival rulers crowned for the duration of a festival, when order is set upside down, social hierarchies reversed: sexual prohibitions are lifted, theft becomes

legal, the slaves take their masters' place. . . . But when the festival is
over, the counter-king is expelled or put to death, taking with him all the
disorder which he incarnates and of which the community is purged at
one blow.[26]

Earlier, in *The Anatomy of Criticism*, Northrop Frye had identified the *pharmakos* figure as a phenomenon in literary criticism, as opposed to the historical figure that Vernant describes.[27]

He is neither innocent nor guilty. He is innocent in the sense that what
happens to him is far greater than anything he has done provokes, like the
mountaineer whose shout brings down an avalanche. He is guilty in the
sense that he is a member of a guilty society . . . or living in a world where
such injustices are an inescapable part of existence.[28]

This is Malory's situation. As much as anyone else in the novel, he is guilty
only in the sense that he is living in a guilty society, Frye's "world where
such injustices are an inescapable part of existence."

Since *The Chinaberry Tree* is at heart not tragedy at all, but melodrama,
Melissa has the grace to simply faint and fall on the ground when she
learns her true identity. To keep things in tragic Greek perspective, we
might recall that women who make momentous discoveries at comparable
moments in Sophocles or Euripides tend to leave the stage and commit
suicide.[29] Only Malory has to take the guilt of the crime of incest that he
and his sister were in danger of committing, but never consummated. The
most tasteful touch of all is that this scapegoat expels himself. Malory is
the one character in the novel washed away by a wave of Greek tragedy,
not his half-sister Melissa or anyone else in *The Chinaberry Tree*. So far as
they are concerned, incest has made a near miss.

The threat or even the suspicion of incest can be a useful thing for a
novelist. As James Twitchell observes, the evocation of brother and sister
incest between Quentin and Caddy Compton in Faulkner's *The Sound and
the Fury* "seems more in the service of narrative demands, of character development, of consciousness itself, than in unfolding social concerns or
generating shocks."[30] The women Laurentine and Melissa come to the end
as numbed but wiser women. The contrast between them and their lovers
is egregious, and between their men and Malory, even more so. Although
Asshur and Denleigh have Malory to thank for their sudden good fortune,
Fauset makes it clear that neither man is ever likely to realize as much.[31]
Ignorance of tragedy is bliss.

The New Negro as Endymion

I am for sleeping and forgetting
　All that has gone before;
I am for lying still and letting
　Who will beat at my door;
I would my life's cold sun were setting
　To rise for me no more.

Countee Cullen, "Requiescam"

In his comprehensive study of Countee Cullen's engagement with classical themes, David Dorsey quotes the poem "Icarian Wings" which the high-school junior Cullen published in his yearbook *The Clintonian 1921* in New York.[32] He did not include this juvenile exercise of an eighteen-year-old in *Color* or later volumes, but "Icarian Wings" is worth knowing both because it seemed to promise a genuine poetic talent that would mature into something more substantial, and because it reveals a penchant for twisted allusion to classical myths that Cullen would sustain throughout his artistic life.

At dusk when drowsy zephyrs blow,
My soul goes clad like Icarus
To genie lands of summer snow;
Rejuvenated impetus
For laggard limbs is there; the lamp
Of far Cathay, my passive slave,
Works mighty change in court and camp,
And none my ire have strength to brave.

When silver rifts disturb the night,
And herald light's diurnal reign,
My airy oars my pleas requite
With disobedience; in vain
Cajoleries and arts; once more
My lot to don the drab dull husk
You know; my golden wings I store
And wait the halcyon time of dusk.[33]

As Dorsey observes, "Icarian Wings" is an odd treatment of Daedalus and Icarus. The soul of Cullen's poet is clad "like Icarus," whose winged flight is a byword in classical and neoclassical poetry for the danger of trusting in art (or technology) too much. Ovid tells the story of Daedalus and Icarus in *Metamorphoses* 8.183–235, which ends with Daedalus's poignant discovery of his son's death, the unhappy father who is now no longer a father (8.231–233). The story was popular reading for high-school Latin texts because of its relatively straightforward language, and not least because it was retold almost verbatim in Thomas Bulfinch's popular handbook of mythology first published in 1855.[34]

The Icarian flight of Cullen's poem effectively negates a moral that the story of Daedalus and Icarus is often thought to point to. The fall of an impetuous boy who soars too near the sun and destroys the very wings that lift him up is a figurative comment on the dangers and ironies of technological and artistic invention. From Homer onward the artist Daedalus (the Greek *daidalos* means "adorner," "artificer") is an engineer and craftsman as well as an artist, much like his divine counterpart Hephaestus, the blacksmith of the gods.[35] The escape and flight of Daedalus and Icarus are at once a marvel of art's power and a parable about exceeding mortal limitations. "Icarian Wings" carries the poet's soul on a night flight, not as thrilling as the course that Daedalus and Icarus followed, but a lot safer. The poet's soul is still a boy's soul. Like Icarus he would soar in the sunshine, here rendered in exceedingly Latinate language as "light's diurnal reign." Cullen employs Latinate English and inverted sentence structure à la Milton, with flowery results that don't entirely make sense ("My airy oars my pleas requite / With disobedience"). "Icarian Wings" is a poetic flight about entirely the opposite of what it proclaims. Wings that have veto power over the youth who would be Icarus are not Icarian at all. They are judicious, a sign of prudence and restraint. The dissociation between artistic imagination and its instruments is striking. This Icarus will take no risks in the sunshine; only the nighttime will do.

While not too much should be made of an early poem which the poet himself never intended to reappear after 1921, we have read "Icarian Wings" here because it shows at the beginning of Cullen's career a persona that often appears in much of the poetry to come.[36] The Let-Me-Die epilogue "Requiescam" that concludes his first volume of verse published six years later strikes the same tone of resignation and withdrawal. In person Cullen was regarded as a witty and engaging man, not at all like the solemn voice of these and similar poems, such as "The Black Christ."[37] He was drawn to the poetry of John Keats above all others, and to Keats's poem *Endymion* most of all.

In his *Beauties of Mythology* Bulfinch offers a Keatsian reading of the Endymion myth that Cullen's high-school teachers may also have imparted to him.

The story of Endymion has a peculiar charm from the human meaning which it so thinly veils. We see in Endymion the young poet, his fancy and his heart seeking in vain for that which can satisfy them, finding his favorite hour in the quiet moonlight, and nursing there beneath the beams of the bright and silent witness the melancholy and the ardor which consumes him. The story suggests aspiring and poetic love, a life spent more in dreams than in reality, and an early and welcome death.[38]

Cullen died at a relatively early age, not as young as his idol Keats, but even by then the particularly reclusive quality of his work was clear to some critics. "A critic once called Keats a 'lost strayed Elizabethan,'" wrote Helen Wolfert in the magazine *PM* on the occasion of Cullen's death (May 10, 1947). "'Far more so Cullen may be called a lost Keats, for he was lost not only out of his age, but to himself and to us. Not even at the beginning did Cullen allow himself, without self-chastisement, to be what he was, a true poet." Cullen's sonnet "To Endymion" (written in Rome in August 1926 after a visit to the grave of Keats) is an answer to the epitaph on Keats's gravestone: "This grave contains all that was mortal of a young English poet who, on his deathbed, in the bitterness of his heart at the malicious power of his enemies, desired these words to be engraven on his tombstone, 'Here lies one whose name was writ in water.'"

> High as the star of that last poignant cry
> Death could not stifle in the wasted frame,
> You know at length the bright immortal lie
> Time gives to those detractors of your name,
> And see, from where you and Diana ride,
> Your humble epitaph—how misapplied![39]

The conflation of Keats and his character Endymion is nothing more than what Keats himself suggests, but the whole point of Endymion's myth is his eternal sleep. An eternal life of riding with Diana (or the Moon) across the sky is not a compelling variation of the myth, but as feeble a reversal of the story as the discreet epithet "misapplied." If consistency in inverting myths is a virtue, Cullen is at least consistent.

This consistency had major consequences for Cullen's career as a poet, most of them unfavorable. To make a great Romantic like Keats the center of one's poetry in the 1920s was to withdraw from where poetry was being made as surely as Endymion withdrew from the world. Writing in 1947 after Cullen's death, Harvey Curtis Webster thought he was "an able and perplexed intelligence, and a sensitive and confused heart."

> Cullen was singularly unaware of what was going on in the world of poetry. In the age of Pound and Eliot he tortured syntax and used words like "aught" and "albeit." He nowhere shows the sign of studying any modern poets other than Millay, Wylie, and Housman. Perhaps because of his failure to absorb the technical discoveries of his contemporaries he was singularly unselfcritical and could allow such monstrosities as "Dear Friends and Gentle Hearts" to be printed. Certainly his failure to study carefully what other poets did is in part responsible for his never developing a style peculiarly his own. Even the good poems in *On These I Stand* could have been written by any other talented craftsman, they bear no stylistic signature.[40]

Yet Cullen was celebrated as a prime exemplar of Du Bois's Talented Tenth and could do no wrong so far as black America was concerned. And that, as Webster astutely observed in 1947, was possibly what blocked his development as a poet.

> One of Cullen's great misfortunes must have been that he was usually commended by both Negroes and whites for extra-poetic reasons. He was praised by Negroes because he was a Negro of distinction, by whites because they feared dispraise might be called prejudice. Consequently, Cullen's poetry was never severely and sympathetically criticized while he was able to benefit from it.[41]

If Cullen's admirers in the black community, like Du Bois and most of Harlem, would not acknowledge it, contemporary critics like Webster and Wolfort did sense some disabling life experiences behind the ineptitude, and perhaps even knew more of them than they would publish. Cullen's early years remained a mystery to others throughout his life: growing up in an orphanage, adoption by the prominent minister Rev. Frederick Asbury Cullen, a devotion to Reverend Cullen that was often an object of ridicule by his male contemporaries—all these things must have affected the poet in ways that were not to be articulated fully until Levering Lewis's portrait of him in *When Harlem Was in Vogue* (1981), Alden Reimonenq's work on Cullen's "Uranianism" (1993), and A. B. Christa Schwarz's essay on Cullen as a gay poet *avant la lettre* (2003).[42]

Throughout his career Cullen turned to classical myth to make central points in a poem, but he never seems to have thought his way through to the pith of the story. The effect of such allusive art should be to raise the particular experience to a broader sphere, suggesting something as timeless and recurrent as the ancient myths themselves—at the least, an ironic negation of the myth. In fact his invocations of the monsters, heroes, and heroines of mythology nearly always blunts this effect, because no sooner are they invoked than their relevance is called into question. We are left with the suspicion that Cullen wants us to know that he knows myth, but once we know that, he then wants us to know that he won't let it mean what we would suppose it means. The opening poem of his anthology *On These I Stand* is the sonnet "Yet Do I Marvel," perhaps his most cited poem because of its concluding couplet,

> Yet do I marvel at this curious thing:
> To make a poet black, and bid him sing![43]

The humor in this sardonic poem couldn't be better; its sarcastic profession of faith in God ("I doubt not God is good, well-meaning, kind") makes him sound like a white benefactor, its wide-ranging question, If God is good, how can suffering be in the world? a familiar indictment of an all-caring deity who is evidently not all-knowing. Speaking in inverted Miltonic English, the poet "doubts not" that God could

> Make plain the reason tortured Tantalus
> Is baited by the fickle fruit, declare
> If merely brute caprice dooms Sisyphus
> To struggle up a never-ending stair.

Abiding frustration is all too characteristic of this poet whom God makes black and bids to sing. Poems become puzzles, not because of depth but because of ineptitude.

"One Day We Played a Game (I Deep in Love)" is dedicated to Yolande Du Bois ("Yolande: Her Poem"). In its original publication in the collection *Copper Sun* (1927), it was faced with an illustration by Cullen's brother Charles, in the style of Aubrey Beardsley.[44] The illustration (Cullen termed them "decorations") "Deep in Love" depicts two lovers whose black identity is minimized. The game in question is one in which Yolande would name a famous male lover of myth or history and Countee would reply with the male's female partner. Yolande's appearance and conduct are arresting.

> Crouched Sphinx-like in the grass, you hugged your knees,
> And called me "Abelard"; I, "Heloise."

So are Cullen's ellipses. For "I" we understand "And I called you Heloise." Here the poet is thinking of the Sphinx simply as one who poses riddles, though the image of Yolande as "crouched Sphinx-like in the grass" is unsettling, suggesting as it does the hybrid monster with the head of a woman and the body of a lion who crouches before the pyramids at Giza. But the Sphinx is also the creature with a woman's head and breasts on a lion's body that slew any man who could not answer her riddle, the riddle that Oedipus solved.

The not entirely flattering, feline associations return a few lines later: "'Tristan,' you purred to me . . . I laughed, 'Isolde.'" Both the poet and Yolande only mention lovers famous for the disastrous consequences of their love: Heloise and Abelard, Pelléas and Mélisande, Ninus and Semiramis, Guinevere and Lancelot, and finally the two who started everyone down the same garden path, Adam and Eve. At this point the game suddenly takes a by now familiar Miltonic turn. There is a Latinate participial construction ("with ardor purposing to leave") and a recollection of the last word Satan utters in *Paradise Lost* (10.502–3). There Milton's ingenious sibilants in Satan's last line, "What remains, ye Gods, But up and enter now into full bliss" are now glossed with the rhyming word Milton counted on his readers knowing but not hearing, "hiss." (In Milton's next line Satan and his followers are transformed into serpents.)

> And round with ardor purposing to leave
> Upon your mouth a lasting, seal of Bliss.
> But midway of our kissing came a hiss
> Above us in the apple tree; a sweet
> Red apple rolled between us at our feet.
> And looking up we saw with glide and dip,
> Cold supple coils among the branches slip.
> "Eve! Eve!" I cried, "Beware." Too late. You bit
> Half of the fruit away . . . The rest of it
> I took, assuring you with misty eyes,
> "Fare each as each, we lose no Paradise."

But they do lose Paradise in this learned poem. The poet turns misty-eyed at the end, moved presumably by his own self-sacrifice. (It is notable that it is not Yolande who does so.) The gnomic conclusion "Fare each as each, we lose no Paradise" recalls the end of *Paradise Lost* where Adam and Eve's status is defined precisely as their faring "each as each," instead of faring with God, "with wandr'ring steps and slow, Through Eden took their solitary way" (*Paradise Lost*, 12.645–49). "One Day We Played a Game" is a Miltonic poem through and through, which may be one way of appreciating how distant Cullen was from the contemporary world of twentieth-century poetry.

At an autobiographical level we might speculate that such poems came to Cullen because he was never really interested in creating poetry about women, still less so, poetry about loving them.[45] Every time he comes to the task his sense of mythology seems warped by an inability to recognize the implications of what he is saying. In the unfortunate sonnet "What I am saying now was said before"—a flatfooted way of saying you grasp a tradition—he imagines some future poet saying the same thing he is saying, and turning, like Cullen, to look at his pencil ("our sword") and page ("our shield"), as both of them, like Perseus, try to confront by averted gaze "Her columned throat and every blandishment." The face of Medusa is of course what sits on top of her columned throat, and in the sonnet "Medusa," though warned in suitably archaic language ("Ware! Those eyes are basilisk's she gazes through, And those are snakes you take for strands of hair!"), the poet knowingly and willingly looks directly at Medusa.

> Though blind, yet on these arid balls engraved
> I know it was a lovely face I braved.[46]

After some initial consternation, we realize that these "arid balls" are the blind eyeballs of a poet transformed into stone by gazing on Medusa. In short, she's done her work once again. In a facing sonnet across the page from "Medusa" ("I have not loved you in the noblest way") Cullen again alludes to Greek myth to emphasize his vulnerability.

> What hurts my heart hurts deep and to the grain;
> My mother never dipped me in the Styx,
> And who would find me weak and vulnerable
> Need never aim his arrow at my heel.

That is, "I am even more fragile than you think I am." The story of Achilles' being dipped in the Styx by his mother Thetis has to do with the one

vulnerable spot left on the otherwise invulnerable body of the hero. This
poet is so vulnerable that an arrow anywhere will do the trick.

An Opportunity Missed: Cullen's Black Medea

One of the most shameful practices of European man is his disregard for
members of the various snow-White races. Only by depicting the wife as
a Negro was I able to make the Medea-Jason marital problem clear to its
fullest extent.

Hans Henry Jahn, "On *Medea*" (1963)

When Cullen turned to an adaptation of Euripides' *Medea* his handicaps
both as a poet writing about love and as an observer of other human beings
brought him face-to-face with a classical text that excels on both counts.
Medea has long been one of the most performed of all Greek tragedies.
It was the inspiration for a notable imitation by the German poet and
thinker Hans Henry Jahn, who had the brilliant idea of conveying ancient
Greek prejudice against women and barbarians by making the Medea of
his 1926 play a black woman.[47] If he had been able to see his version produced with the black actress Rose McClendon, along with a white Jason,
Countee Cullen might well have achieved much more than we can now
glean from the unperformed script of *Medea*.[48] But McClendon died suddenly and unexpectedly in 1936. As it was, when Cullen published his version, along with some other poems, he found some appreciative critics like
the reviewer for the *Nation*, who praised him for at least not continuing
the ghastly Swinburnian style that English translators of Greek tragedy
then tended to perpetrate.

By one with the sense of the integrities of language, few drearier experiences can be imagined than reading a Greek play in one of the current
academic translations, or sitting through a performance of the same translation in a commencement week program. The translator's first concern
seems to be to sound like the Bible or Shakespeare; his actual achievement, in most instances, is to give a poor imitation of a ham poet in the
eighteenth century. Even when, as in the case of Prof. Gilbert Murray, the
translator has literary gifts, he usually conceals the dramatic qualities of
the play by using stilted, archaic language. What Cullen renders as, "There
you have reason to be sad,"A. S. Way renders as "Sooth, Lady, reason was
that thou shouldst grieve"; Gilbert Murray, "Woman, thou has indeed

much cause for grief"; A. T. Murray, "In sooth, good reason, woman, hast thou for thy grief." Where Oxford dons have so often failed, an American Negro writer has succeeded.[49]

Where Cullen was not so successful was in his attempts to elide large portions of detail in the text, particularly famous lines that have as much resonance now with modern feminism as in the culture that invented the concept of the barbarian (*barbaros*).[50] In Medea's entrance speech to the sympathetic chorus of Corinthian women, she says:

> You don't know how difficult it can be for a stranger in a foreign land. One is so easily misunderstood.[51]

Compare this with his immediate predecessors, the flowery A. S. Way, or the more talented John Jay Chapman's version, and we can see that Cullen really is better.

> For justice dwells not in the eyes of man,
> who, ere he hath discerned his neighbor's heart,
> hates him at sight, albeit no wise wronged.[52]

> For justice lives not in the eyes of men—
> who hate before they look—though nothing wronged.[53]

At the same time, Cullen's lines obscure both the question of justice in the treatment of men, and the way men can be misjudged simply by their appearance. You would have thought that he would have seized on this common human failing of judging by appearance, but it is consonant with his practice elsewhere to blunt almost any specific political point in the ancient play—or one that might be construed as political. All Medea seems to be talking about is the awkward social situation a foreigner may encounter abroad. She sounds as helpless as Cullen's males, and even says so.

> I loved Jason with my whole heart and he has left me. What am I to do? We women are so helpless. . . . But a man is free to come and go.[54]

This leads into one of the most famous lines of *Medea*, and Cullen's way of dealing with it is symptomatic.

It is part of Medea's rhetorical strategy in Euripides to make her situation and that of the Corinthian women seem similar, all the better to win them to her side. She suffers, she wants to convey to them, not as a barbarian, but simply as a woman; she wants to dispel the image of being a foreigner, and an exotic one at that, by being in the same sisterhood as the women of Corinth. Cullen was not pretending to offer a translation, only a version, but he still had plenty of opportunities to get Euripides right. For example, even A. S. Way's version of 1929 gets the basic point across.

> But we, say they, live an unperiled life
> At home, while they do battle with the spear—
> Unreasoning fools! twice would I under shield
> Stand, rather than bear childbirth-peril once.[55]

Cullen's Medea instead says this:

> And if they fail us we are better off in our grave. They imagine, just because . . . Forgive me; I didn't mean to bore you with my troubles.[56]

As the critic for the *Nation* in 1935 observed, in what is otherwise a quite positive review, this is a significant omission, since it elides Medea's identity as both a woman and a mother.[57] With Medea now playing the role of the perfect hostess—temporarily, to be sure, for in the end she does get her revenge—Cullen's other innovations seem equally ill-conceived.[58] Creon is made as down-to-earth as a ward politician, which well might work in a fully realized character, but not with undeliverable clichés like "I'm not one for beating about the bush, Medea"; "I must think of my own flesh and blood. Charity begins at home."[59]

As the accomplished translator of Greek and Latin poetry Dudley Fitts observed in a review of *On These I Stand* when it appeared in 1947, this mediocre work was not only Cullen's loss.

> Mr. Cullen wrote like all of one's poets of the traditional orders; but faintly, but in what dilution! "Yea, I have put thee from me utterly, / And they who plead thy cause do plead in vain." Precisely, and to what else can this venerable gesture lead but to what in fact it *does* lead: "God, thou hast Christ, they say, at thy right hand; close by thy left Michael is straight and leal," and so on, pre-Raphaelite and fake and wholly dead, down to the Yellow-Book pseudoblasphemy of the close: "Criest Thou never, Lord, above their song: 'But Lucifer was tall, his wings were long?'" The answer to that is, No; He does not.

Yet the true pity of it is that men like Cullen—sincere—and not a po-
seur, can never see the cheapness of it. For their poetry is a special ritual
with its old liturgical language and its beautiful tropes, and even when
their attention engages actual fighting life, as Mr. Cullen's so often did,
they are hampered by their holy-day cope.[60]

Deprived of Rose McClendon's potentially crucial collaboration, Cullen's additions to the script of a prologue and epilogue serve to make the
play Fitts reviewed longer, but not better, by extending its reach into the
mythical before-time of Jason and Medea's first meeting and falling in
love, and by ending the play with an extended scene set in Athens twenty
years later.

The epilogue discovers Medea and the aged Aegeus living in Athens with
the young man Aegeus assumes is his son, borne by Medea in exchange for
the refuge he gave her after she murdered her children and fled Corinth,
as in the end of Euripides' play. As Patrice Rankine observes, Cullen decided to turn his *Medea* into a Shakespearean revenge tragedy.[61] But Cullen
outdoes even Shakespeare's and Seneca's raising of the level of violence in
his version of the play. Seneca had Medea kill one child, then when Jason
appears, kill the other one in front of him to make him suffer more. What
Cullen contrives doesn't leave a single Greek column standing.

First he has an older Jason appear and assume that the child named Pandion is the son of the now aged Aegeus and Medea. To punish them for the
loss of his own children, Jason cuts young Pandion's throat in revenge, only
to learn from Medea that he, Jason, was really the father of the child, not
Aegeus. When Medea had to find refuge in Athens with Aegeus how else
could she be sure, she explains, that she would be able to provide him with
a son? She was already pregnant with Jason's child. All that she had to do
was bear it and her compact with Aegeus would be fulfilled. Jason is aghast
with remorse and stabs himself, following his son into death.

Then Aegeus interposes: if only he hadn't lost his sight about that time,
surely he would have been able to see the features of Jason and not himself
in Pandion's face? To be sure, counters Medea, with a mixture of reluctance and forthrightness. When the time drew near for her to have the
child, however, she administered Aegeus a poison that robbed him of his
sight.

> *Medea*: I knew too well if you but looked upon the child, he would be
> known for what he was, the very breath and like of Jason. How

could it have been otherwise? Then you too should have driven me
forth from Athens, with stones, as a strumpet is driven.
Aegeus: It needs not the casting of stones to proclaim the strumpet.[62]

She then hands Aegeus the dagger that Jason had used on Pandion and
himself, and bids him kill her, but Aegeus instead turns it on himself and
with a single blow falls dead.

Only Medea is left standing—strictly speaking, she should be, according to mythology. But Cullen was never interested in mythological correctness. With a final exclamation to the gods, she pulls out a small vial
of poison, drinks it, saying, "It is fire for a moment, but the ashes will be
cold," and with the stage direction "She tosses her head and writhes," she
dies.[63] The Chorus intones a traditional exit song that is somewhat closer
to ancient example than these startling events.

Immortal Zeus controls the fate of man, decrees him love or grief; our
days the echo of his will resound in fury or pass in nothingness away.[64]

If Cullen's translation were performed, it would be perhaps apparent—
more than it can be in a dry mythological recital such as this—that what
he really has in mind is not a revision of the Medea myth or the Euripides
play, but rather a plot resolution of the kind that works so well—or at least
so predictably—in melodrama and parodies of melodrama by Gilbert and
Sullivan, Oscar Wilde, and Joe Orton.

For all its exotic associations and the prestige that comes with almost
any attempt at recreating ancient Greek tragedy for a modern audience,
Cullen's amplified *Medea* comes to an ending not all that different from
the cheerful finale of Fauset's and Du Bois's romances. The difference is
that everybody dies, as they frequently do in the work of this unhappy and
uncertain poet.

The invocation of classical myths and literature may confer the kind of
prestige Veblen describes, but as he well knew, this learning in itself is not
the stuff from which great or even interesting writing comes. There are
just as many examples of such shallow classicism in contemporary white
American writers and poets. Edwin Arlington Robinson's much-antholo-
gized poem from 1917, "Cassandra," is a harangue about the evils of the day
in which actual reference to the myth of Cassandra and her representation
in Greek literature stays on the surface of things in a similar way.

I heard one who said: "Verily,
What word have I for children here?
Your Dollar is your only Word,
The wrath of it your only fear."

Robinson simply ventriloquizes the idea of a Cassandra, with no reference whatever to the complicated tale of divine love and its mortal frustration that lies behind the story of the young Trojan priestess who was given the gift of prophecy by Apollo and then, when she reneged on her promise to give herself to him, awarded the additional gift that no one would believe anything she said. What Robinson will not or cannot do is go more deeply into the substance of the myth he seeks to use.

"Think you to tread forever down
The merciless old verities?
And are you never to have eyes
To see the world for what it is?

"Are you to pay for what you have
With all you are?"—No other word
We caught, but with a laughing crowd
Moved on. None heeded, and few heard.

In this poem, as in Du Bois's and Fauset's fiction, classical allusion and mythological figure and tale stand side by side with the modern figure and its voice, and the connection is no deeper than the mention of a name. In the same way Cullen's Greek and Roman myths are but sad mirror images for the poet himself. With an American poet as famous as Robinson indulging in inverted word order ("Think you to tread"), archaic, biblical language ("verily"), and what seems to be a simpleminded veneration of classical tradition ("merciless old verities"), why couldn't the young Countee Cullen do the same?

The contrast with a later poet who does go deeper than all this is instructive. When Rita Dove quotes from Milton's *Paradise Lost* for the epigraph to the seventh and final section of her sonnet cycle *Mother Love*, she engages at once with her own poetic journey through the squalid realities of modern Sicily, and with her predecessors in poetry. Her reference relates her poem not only to the ancient Sicily of the Homeric *Hymn to Demeter*, which is in constant play throughout the sonnets of *Mother Love*, but also to the first vision that Satan gains of Paradise in book 4 of Milton's epic poem.

> Not that fair field
> Of Enna, where Proserpine gath'ring flow'rs
> Herself a fairer Flow'r by Gloomy Dis
> Was gather'd, which cost Ceres all that pain
> To seek her through the world.

That is, paradise is far more beautiful than the infernal garden that Dis (Hades) created to lure Persephone to her doom. Dove fuses a mother's loss of her daughter, today, with the Christian poet's reminder of the Homeric *Hymn*, in a return to the biblical scene of the Garden of Eden, and loss of paradise and the beginnings of all our woe. In this simple way the allusions to the *Hymn to Demeter* and *Paradise Lost* reflect a complexity in both thought and art that is beyond the ken of those who practice genteel classicism.

five

Invisible Odyssey

Somewhere beneath the load of the emotion-freezing ice which my life had conditioned my brain to produce, a spot of black anger glowed and threw off a hot red light of such intensity that had Lord Kelvin known of its existence, he would have had to revise his measurements.

Invisible Man

As a man hides a brand beneath the dark embers in an outlying farm, a man who has no neighbors, and so saves a seed of fire, that he may not have to kindle it from some other source, so Odysseus covered himself with leaves.

Odyssey 5.488–91 (Fitzgerald trans.)

Ralph Waldo Ellison's father gave him his first two names when he was born in Oklahoma City in 1914 because he wanted his son to become a poet or philosopher, so from the very beginning of his life Ellison had to learn to contend with the destiny that portentous naming threatens to bestow. He discarded part of the hand his parents had dealt him by dropping "Waldo" altogether, but writing *Invisible Man* provided the best revenge. He created a young "Mr. Emerson" who is not the kind of Ralph Waldo his father had in mind. This one tries to seduce Ellison's gullible young hero, who is so obtuse he is only vaguely troubled and never quite realizes what this Mr. Emerson has in mind.

In high school and then at Tuskegee Institute young Ralph studied music, both the trombone and the piano, and music, especially jazz music, came to be a central part of his creative life as a writer. He left Tuskegee after his third year and moved to New York to make money to finish his degree. He never did, but lived and worked in New York for most of the rest of his life. He became a close friend of the artist Romare Bearden and found an important champion of his work in Richard Wright, who urged him to turn to the writing of fiction. His own experience with significant names and the destinies they seem to promise may have created a certain affinity for Homer's Odysseus. The great hero's name also is eloquent, promising much pain to himself and others.

Ellison's original vocation of music, and jazz in particular, remained with him all his life. It gave him a way of thinking about writing and storytelling that makes his way of writing a novel often resemble Homer's way of storytelling, long before the actual techniques of ancient oral verse-making were widely known outside of classical scholarship. A reader of *Invisible Man* (1952) will profit as much from knowing, listening to, and thinking about jazz as from knowing any of the many poets and writers who figure in its telling, including Homer.[1] At several points in this chapter we shall bring out some of the musical designs that Ellison often employs in telling his story.

Ellison later wrote that he thought long and hard about epics, mock epics, the picaresque, all such traditions brought vividly to life in the earlier part of the twentieth century by the Odyssean James Joyce and *Ulysses*. *Invisible Man* opens with a prologue, its narrator hidden beneath the streets of New York and withdrawn from the world above. He tells his life story up to the moment he entered his subterranean lair, from the time he was at a Negro college in the South. The college is reminiscent of Booker T. Washington's Tuskegee, Ellison's alma mater. His hero is expelled from the college because of a mishap he commits in driving an important trustee about the countryside. Armed with letters of introduction from the college's president Bledsoe, he goes to New York and finds himself turned down time after time, because the letter he carries is actually one that urges its recipients not to hire him under any circumstances. After finally getting a job in a paint factory, he is nearly killed in an accident there, recovers, and eventually connects with the Brotherhood in New York. He turns out to be a public speaker of some talent. The Brotherhood is run by doctrinaire dialectical materialists—the word "Communist" is never mentioned—and for much of the rest of the novel Invisible Man tries to do their bidding. Eventually he sees their true purpose, which has nothing to do with working for the people of Harlem, and strikes out on his own in the city as it erupts in riots reminiscent of the Harlem riots of 1943. The story comes full circle in an epilogue, with Invisible Man once again in his underground lair, resolved to turn from speech making and political activism to writing.

Invisible Man is an amusingly awkward book to write about because it is narrated by a character who never reveals his name. Ellison's most recent biographer, Arnold Rampersad, has found a way around the problem by referring to him simply as "Invisible."[2] The central figure at work throughout the novel is invisibility, the inability of the white race to see the black race, and the corresponding sense in black people in the United States of having no name, no identity—in short, their invisibility.

Ellison's narrator and Homer's Odysseus both know desperate moments in their stories, moments that each will survive. This is what the two epigraphs to this chapter are about, each of them marking a low point in each story. In chapter 12 of Invisible Man, freshly out of the hospital and aware at last of the treachery of his college president's letters of introduction to various offices in New York, Invisible begins the intellectual and spiritual thaw that the spot of black anger with its hot red light signifies. He moves away from white, which symbolizes his obliviousness to the lie of the white-dominated world he believed in at his beautiful college in the South, with all its white buildings, and later his abbreviated stint mixing white paint in the Liberty Paint factory in New York. By this chapter he is moving into Harlem and the black world of the Brotherhood, and beyond that, to the red world of the fires of the Harlem riots. Black and red become the dominant colors as Invisible Man enters its second half, and at the end of chapter 12 Ellison echoes Homer's simile about the dark embers with their seed of fire, lines at the end of Odyssey book 5 that capture the potential which remains with Odysseus to surmount his present circumstances.

Barely surviving Poseidon's wrecking of his raft, nearly drowning, only to escape with his patron goddess Athena pointing the way, the exhausted Odysseus is cast up on the shore of the island of the Phaeacians; from that nadir in his wanderings he will go forward, first to King Alcinous's cordial reception in Phaeacia, and from there at last home to Ithaca. Homer's embers simile is not the only such turning point in the Odyssey—the poem, like its hero, is constantly turning and twisting in unexpected ways—but it captures marvelously the hidden fire that remains within him even when he seems at his lowest point. Patrice Rankine has shown in Ulysses in Black how an Odyssean voice is to be heard from beginning to end of *Invisible Man*, often at the same level of mystery and suggestiveness with which the novel ends: "Who knows but that, on the lower frequencies, I speak for you?"[3] No reader of *Invisible Man* can listen to it for long before realizing that this Homeric tune is playing in counterpoint with many other voices.

Invisible Man turned out to be the only novel Ralph Ellison would publish. In a long career after it won the National Book Award, he put together several important collections of literary and cultural criticism: *Shadow and Act* (1964) and *Going to the Territory* (1986).[4] But he never succeeded in completing a projected second novel, provisionally entitled *Juneteenth*. (June 19, 1865, known in Texas as "Juneteenth," was the day the news finally reached Texas that the Civil War had ended and slavery had been abolished.) This failure to follow up such a stunning debut was a matter of much regret to many of Ellison's critics and readers. In another way, the decision to write what Herman Melville termed "a mighty book, on a mighty theme" led to a work that absorbed much of his life. *Invisible Man* required so many years of revisions and editing that itself came to be like an epic: a performance that it is impossible to imagine repeated.[5] Most epic poets write one epic poem, not many; the Homer of the *Odyssey*, whoever he was, is different in many ways from the poet of the *Iliad*, even though both poems have a common idiom and intimately related techniques of oral composition. Ellison was also much influenced in his project by Lord Raglan's 1936 book *The Hero*, which argued for an archetypal hero who could pull every other kind of hero into a single character.[6] He spent years writing thousands of pages for *Juneteenth*, but it never came together in his lifetime.

After his death in 1994 a version of *Juneteenth* was compiled, and in 1999 it was published by Ellison's literary executor, John Callahan. For those who are interested in the abundant classical references in Ellison's many drafts, Patrice Rankine offers a reading of this composite novel that traces many thematic links between *Invisible Man* and the fragmentary *Juneteenth*.[7] We have nothing further to add to his admirable discussion, both because *Juneteenth* is as much his literary executor's creation as Ellison's, and because we find the published version of *Juneteenth* in no way comparable to *Invisible Man* as a work of literature.

The Odyssean Voice of *Invisible Man*

It is a peculiar sensation, this double-consciousness, this sense of always looking at one's self through the eyes of others, of measuring one's soul by the tape of a world that looks on in amused contempt and pity. One ever feels his two-ness,—and American, a Negro; two souls, two thoughts, two unreconciled strivings; two warring ideals in one dark body, whose dogged strength alone keeps it from being torn asunder. (W. E. B. Du Bois, *The Souls of Black Folk*)

Homer's *Odyssey* is the epic of a man who is *polutropos*, constantly shifting and changing shape and direction, elusive in both his person and his versatile ways of dealing with others. The poet's way of telling his story is itself polytropic, constantly shifting focus back and forth in the first half of the poem, whose constantly surprising narrative and design became as perennial a model for later imitation as the comparatively simpler, straight-line story of the *Iliad*. Out of the *Iliad*, Aristotle observes, one could make one tragedy, but out of the *Odyssey*, many; in later antiquity after Aristotle it wasn't only many tragedies that would appear. The *Odyssey* was the major inspiration for Greek inventors of romance, and its wandering ways were picked up again by the ancients' successors in the early modern period, in the picaresque tradition. An Odyssean tale and Homer's way of telling it are both much in play in Ralph Ellison's *Invisible Man*, usually in ways that are as fleeting and deeply embedded as the fire hidden within Odysseus and Invisible Man.

In his prologue to the story, Ellison's narrator tells us it all began twenty years ago, the same length of time Odysseus was away from Ithaca, first for the ten years of the Trojan War, then for the ten years of his voyage back. Of all the *nostoi* or journeys home Odysseus's was by far the hardest and the longest. The one that Invisible Man the narrator embarks on will eventually make of him a black Odysseus, but unlike Leopold Bloom, who comes home to Molly in the final chapter of Joyce's *Ulysses*, this Odyssean narrator will end where he begins, in a coal cellar hidden deep beneath the streets of New York City. And at first he is no Odysseus at all: in his time at a black college in the South, and for the first part of his life in New York, he's living through a version of the *Telemachy*, Telemachus's story. In the opening four books of the *Odyssey*, Odysseus himself does not appear. His son Telemachus is the central figure, with no sign of a father until we discover him in book 5, languishing under the smothering hospitality of the divine sea nymph Calypso. To begin with, Invisible is just as callow and as much in danger from the schemes and traps of older and cleverer enemies as Telemachus, who must contend with his mother Penelope's suitors. But Telemachus is also lucky to have the guidance and protection of Athena disguised in the original role of Mentor. Invisible Man is not so lucky, since nearly every mentor he meets proves to be treacherous in the end. The difference is that Ellison's gullible Telemachus eventually matures into an Odysseus. It is as if Joyce's Stephen Dedalus and Leopold Bloom were to meld into a single figure at the end of *Ulysses*.

What happens to Invisible Man in the course of his story leads him finally to the simple truth, "that I am nobody but myself." This is but one of many playful allusions to Odysseus's encounter with the Cyclops Polyphemus and the trick of naming himself "Nobody" (Greek *outis*) to throw the blinded one-eyed giant off the scent. More overt is a reference like the opening of chapter 11, when the unconscious narrator comes to in a cold, rigid chair in the hospital and sees "a man looking at me out of a bright third eye that glowed from the center of his forehead"—a doctor, he finally realizes. We can see a Cyclops in this white world, and eventually so does Invisible Man. In an altercation in chapter 22 with the leaders of the Brotherhood, a Communist front organization that Invisible gets involved with in New York, the Odyssean connection finally becomes explicit, and in a startling way. In the middle of a vehement argument a glass eye suddenly falls out of the face of Jack, the leader of the Brotherhood, and into a glass of water on the table, "an eye staring fixedly at me as from the dark waters of a well," he says. Jack tries to get Invisible Man's attention again: "He stopped, squinting at me with Cyclopean irritation." The voice here is no longer the voice of a Telemachus, but that of a trickster as capable as Brer Rabbit or Odysseus himself. Growing up fast, Invisible Man effectively turns aside the attempt of Jack and others to pull him back into the unquestioning obedience the Brotherhood demands.

Rankine offers a persuasive reading of Ellison's novel that makes these Cyclopean moments a central trope for reading *Invisible Man* by focusing on the folkloric quality of the drunken, blinded ogre, whom he identifies as a pervasive theme in Ellison's representation of what is monstrous in American society. This motif is made manifest not only in the Cyclopean episodes mentioned here, he argues, but also in the battle royal of the first chapter of the novel, where Invisible Man and other black youths are forced to box with one another blindfolded. Rankine also uses epigraphs from the *Odyssey* and *Invisible Man* to bring out the parallels between the Cyclops Polyphemus at his most ferocious and Invisible Man's grandfather, on his deathbed.

> His hands reached out, seized two of them [my men], and smashed
> Them to the ground like puppies. Their brains spattered out and

Oozed into the dirt. He tore them limb from limb to make his
Supper, gulping them down like a mountain lion, leaving nothing
    behind—guts, flesh, or marrowy bones.
                                    (*Odyssey* 9, Stanley Lombardo trans.)

On his deathbed [the narrator's grandfather] called my father to him
and said, "Son, after I'm gone I want you to keep up the good fight. I
never told you, but our life is a war and I have been a traitor all my born
days, a spy in the enemy's country ever since I give up my gun back in the
Reconstruction. Live with your head in the lion's mouth. I want you to
overcome 'em with yeses, undermine 'em with grins, agree 'em to death
and destruction, let 'em swoller you till they vomit or burst wide open."
(Ellison, *Invisible Man*, 16)

The most salient parallel is the injunction "let 'em swoller you till they
vomit or burst wide open," which is exactly what Polyphemus does when
Odysseus plies him with wine and he falls back in a drunken stupor.

Even as he spoke, he reeled and tumbled backward,
his great head lolling to one side: and sleep
took him like any creature. Drunk, hiccupping,
he dribbled streams of liquor and bits of men. (*Odyssey* 9, Fitzgerald trans.)

In other words, the grandfather counsels his son and his eavesdropping
grandson to stuff the Cyclopes of America just the way Odysseus's men
did in the *Odyssey*. (Like Invisible himself, neither father nor grandfather
nor mother is given a name, a sure sign that invisibility runs in the family.)
Rankine finds much support for this framework for reading the theme of
Odysseus and the Cyclops in Ellison's later essay "Change the Joke and Slip
the Yoke," in which he sees a link between Invisible Man's grandfather and
Odysseus.

I knew the trickster Ulysses just as early as I knew the wily rabbit of Negro American lore, and I could easily imagine myself a pint-sized Ulysses
but hardly a rabbit, no matter how human and resourceful or Negro.[8]

This parallel is at its most explicit earlier in the essay, where Ellison is re-
plying to his friend Stanley Edgar Hyman's suggestion that he was working
with Jungian archetypes in *Invisible Man*.

So intense is Hyman's search for archetypal forms that he doesn't see that narrator's grandfather in Invisible Man is no more involved in a "darky" act than was Ulysses in Polyphemus' cave. Nor is he so much a "smart-man-playing-dumb" as a weak man who knows the nature of his oppressor's weakness. There is a good deal of spite in the old man, as there comes to be in his grandson, and the strategy he advises is a kind of jujitsu of the spirit, a denial and rejection through agreement.[9]

At the same time, Ellison's relation to his literary predecessors was wide-ranging. Explicit Odyssean references like the Brotherhood leader Jack losing his glass eye and "squinting at me with Cyclopean irritation" (chapter 22, 474) are as rare as they are provocative. From the very beginning of the novel to its end, Ellison often seems to point almost anywhere but to the *Odyssey*.

The two epigraphs of the novel come from Herman Melville's *Benito Cereno* and Eliot's *The Family Reunion*, not Homer, and Dante's *Inferno* figures importantly in the prologue, as does the music of Louis Armstrong.[10] Furthermore, our never-named narrator Invisible opens the story with a close paraphrase of another nameless narrator, that of Dostoevsky's *Notes from Underground*. And as if that weren't enough, it was noted only many years later by Houston Baker that James Weldon Johnson had already exploited the potential for this deliberate suppression of a narrator's identity in his 1912 novel *Autobiography of an Ex-Coloured Man*, with a storyteller who teases us with hints but never tells us his name.[11] (Following Rampersad, we might call Johnson's hero "Ex-.") Both Johnson's and Ellison's device of never naming narrators builds on Du Bois's concept of the Veil that makes white and black Americans invisible to one another.

Given these and many other signals, it is reasonable to say that Ellison went to some lengths to cover his Odyssean tracks in *Invisible Man*. Nothing surprising in that: Odysseus himself is forever covering his tracks as well. Ellison's later comments in "Change the Joke and Slip the Yoke" are another matter, and Rankine's reading through that later essay brings Ellison's retrospective view of his work to bear in a most productive way, one which we hope the following comments will complement.[12] In what follows we shall focus on the trope of the *Odyssey*'s invisibility in the novel, the way it is worked out both in relation to the *Odyssey* and to many other, later texts that at points seem to us to be just as present.

For example, an early publication (presently chapter 1 of the novel) and some later sections dropped from the final draft but later published separately will show how Ellison used Homer as a hidden model for the narrative we read as told by the Invisible Man. For ultimately *Invisible Man* proves to end in a total inversion of the *Odyssey*'s patterns of disguise, recognition, lying, and recognition. This odyssey never reveals the name of its hero, he never reaches an Ithaca, and while he meets plenty of Sirens, he has no Penelope to return to. What Ellison creates instead is a deliberately incomplete odyssey, as suddenly suspended in its way as the *Odyssey* itself ends, in midframe of an exciting shot.[13] Reference to a discarded draft of an episode of the novel tends to support this reading. (It was later published separately as "Out of the Hospital and Into the Bar," and has many aspects that Ellison decided would not fit well into his final draft.)

We will end with a more speculative argument of the kind urged by E. M. Forster in *Aspects of the Novel* (1956), with an imaginary conversation between Ellison's 1951 novel and Richard Wright's 1940 *Native Son*. We don't propose anything as fashionable as a discussion of the influence of a novel published in 1951 on one published in 1940. We shall simply suggest that Wright's *Native Son* stands in much the same relation to Ellison's *Invisible Man* as the *Iliad* does to the *Odyssey*: a tragic story of annihilation and loss, followed by the twists and turns of a survivor's story.

The Polyphony of *Invisible Man*

> When I started writing, I knew that in both *The Waste Land* and *Ulysses* ancient myth and ritual were used to give form and significance to the material; but it took me a few years to realize that the myths and rites which we find functioning in our everyday lives could be used in the same way. (Ralph Ellison, *The Art of Fiction: An Interview* [1955])

So the *Odyssey* is just one of many such voices. The challenge in tracing a classical thread through the labyrinth of Ellison's particular brand of modernism is to beware of insisting on any single one that will confine us to one path. The best way to read Ellison is to think in jazz, following Invisible Man's reverie about Louis Armstrong's upbeat performance of Andy Razaf's mournful song "What Did I Do to Be So Black and Blue?" For him Armstrong "made poetry out of being invisible" (8).[14] Invisible says he often listens to "Black and Blue" while enjoying his favorite dessert of vanilla ice cream and sloe gin. This is also a great example of Ellison's way with synesthesia, for the colors black, white, and red will be heard and seen throughout the novel. Here, in the prologue, one of them (the black man) is eating the other two (white vanilla ice cream covered with red sloe gin). To reread the novel is to learn how these colors recur again and again, never in a random way.

Then there are echoes of Henri Bergson's *Creative Evolution* (1907) and its argument for a more subjective and individual sense of time, as opposed to our customary chronological thinking about history. And there are references to T. S. Eliot's *Four Quartets* (1943), shimmering not so quietly behind the prologue speaker's abrupt transition into chapter 1: "But that's getting too far ahead of the story, almost to the end, although the end is in the beginning and lies far ahead." Lawrence Patrick Jackson's research into the revisions and editing process of *Invisible Man* at Random House suggests to us that these famous lines from Eliot may have also been something of an authorial in-joke between Ellison and his editors, since they asked him to split the long, original text of the prologue of the novel in two and put much of it into an epilogue instead. Originally, the end of *Invisible Man* was quite literally in its beginning.[15]

The most salient of all Ellison's voices is the opening sentence, "I am an invisible man," a riff on the opening of Dostoevsky's *Notes from Underground*, "I am a sick man." In this polyphony the *Odyssey* has an important place, even though it seems at first not to be invoked at all. For if not naming yourself or your hero is Dostoevsky's game with the narrative voice in *Notes from Underground*, this is also true of Homer's way of revealing Odysseus in the *Odyssey*.

Ellison seems to have developed an epic as well as a musical conception of his novel at an early stage.[16] He has a spatial, architectural conception of his story's evolution. Just as Vergil is said in an ancient life of the poet to have sketched out the entire plot of the *Aeneid* in twelve books and worked now on this book, now on that, depending on where the muse inspired him to go, Ellison worked in much the same way. There is nothing startling in this. Anyone writing a book of almost any kind has to think such architectural thoughts at some point. More immediate models for this kind of creative thinking and writing would be Joyce's *Ulysses*, and especially Dante's *Commedia*, where concern for structure and numerological significance is raised to a high art. Ellison himself speaks of how important "transitions" were between these points in his overall design of *Invisible Man*. This seems to presuppose larger sections already completed or in clear enough shape to be ready for fitting into a larger pattern. He later said that not finding the right transitions was one the chief problems he encountered in completing a second novel after *Invisible Man*. There are doubling characters, themes, and motifs throughout, conceived in a schematic way and often across wide distances in his text. They are never simply repetitions of a leitmotif, but appear as variations on a theme at recurring points, with ever-changing significance. Most of the time the doublings link characters and events that are opposed to one another, creating a polarity of opposites.

Not only literary predecessors inspire this. Doubles and polarities would also reflect an American world marked by the opposition of the black and white races, of the kind that Mark Twain created in his most disturbing work, *Pudd'nhead Wilson*, or in African American Tragic Mulatto fiction generally. Beyond the American scene, this technique reflects a pattern of oppositional thinking which can be traced from ancient to contemporary cultures; pairs of likes and opposites are a familiar way for societies to organize themselves, and for individuals to conceive of one another. Leon Forrest describes how Ellison's careful plotting of the design of individual chapters often turns on the polar distance his hero traverses from a chapter's beginning to its end.[17] Chapter 2 seems to open simply ("It was a beautiful college," 34), then close with equal simplicity, as the hero eagerly accelerates the car to get the trustee Mr. Norton to a bar after he has heard the farmer Trueblood's at turns harrowing and hilarious story of incest (70).

In retrospect the beginning of chapter 2, "It was a beautiful college," comes to seem the most sardonic of opening lines, for this beautiful college is more a pedagogical plantation than a university, with a president named Bledsoe who functions like an overseer to keep his students veiled from any education that would open their eyes to the reality of their Booker T. Washington paradise. After the white trustee Mr. Norton has been knocked out cold at the Golden Day bar and revived with a stiff drink, Invisible drives him back in silence (97). The ominous tone at the end of the previous chapter deepens unmistakably. Forrest is concerned to bring out the Dostoevskian quality of the story.

> Ellison's arrangement of characters and themes in confrontational moments forms a constant source of instruction, as we see how these apparently oppositional forces are really quite closely connected. This device recalls anthropologist Claude Lévi-Strauss's concept of *thesis, counterthesis, synthesis*. And it is related to Dostoevski's uses of *doubling* and of character. One way of looking at doubling is to see it as a blending of opposites — characters who stand in sharp opposition to each other and yet have much in common. (268–69)

Among the confrontational moments he also cites are those involving the doctrinaire Hambro of the Brotherhood, the stern pedagogue who seeks to lead Invisible into the correct ways of thinking that Jack desires, and the blind minister Homer A. Barbee, recalling the blind singer Demodocus whose songs so enchant Odysseus; this bard bamboozles the youth of Bledsoe's college with the thrilling story of their college's founder, lulling them into a specious nostalgia as he does so. Or the bluesman Peter Wheatstraw and his song "She's got feet like a monkey, Legs like a frog—Lawd, Lawd!" (173), who at first is a total cipher to Invisible Man; and in the same chapter the young Mr. Emerson mentioned above, the homosexual son of a father whose tyranny he cannot escape but only see more clearly, thanks to being able to afford wealthy New Yorkers' fashionable cult of psychoanalysis. Emerson's veiled proposition of playing Huck to Invisible's Jim is a siren song highly reminiscent of Leslie Fiedler's famous 1948 essay in *Partisan Review* on homosocial bonding in American literature, "Come Back to the Raft Ag'in, Huck Honey."[18]

At least young Emerson does Invisible the favor of finally revealing the truth about the letters from Dr. Bledsoe, with their lethal charge to string along the bearer to infinity: "I beg of you, sir, to help him continue in the direction of that promise which, like the horizon, recedes ever brightly and distantly beyond the hopeful traveler" (191). So when Invisible hears someone whistling "O well they picked poor Robin clean" when he is riding home on the bus from Emerson's office, deluded by Bledsoe no more, the song he hums is a dirge that corresponds to Peter Wheatstraw's earlier blues—only now at least our hero realizes that he is the poor Robin of the song (193).

As Forrest observes, though they never meet and are never associated explicitly, "the homosexual at the top and the bluesman at the bottom are also linked; for both are existential outlaws in our society, yet at the same time both are high priests from the peripheral underground, warning the hero of hidden reality."[19] As he realizes what has been done to him, Ellison's youth pulls together his memory of his dream of his grandfather's letter, "Keep this Nigger Boy running," Bledsoe's letter that he has just read, and the dirge for poor Robin, all three blended into a single, bitter refrain.

"My dear Mr. Emerson," I said aloud. "The Robin bearing this letter is a former student. Please hope him to death, and keep him running. Your most humble and obedient servant, A. H. Bledsoe."

Sure, that's the way it was, I thought, a short, concise verbal *coup de grace*, straight to the nape of the neck. And Emerson would write in reply? Sure: "Dear Bled, have met Robin and shaved tail. Signed, Emerson." (194)

With the fatal letters from Bledsoe as his introduction to New York, the unsuspecting Invisible Man replays the story of the hero Bellerophon, who was falsely accused by the wife of King Proteus of attempted rape. In the earliest version of the myth in Homer, Proteus does not kill Bellerophon, but sends him off with tokens, "murderous signs" (*sêmata lugra*), which are instructions to whoever receives him to do Proteus's killing for him (*Iliad* 6.156–97). Invisible Man himself—or more accurately, his unconscious, in a dream—recycles Bledsoe's wicked trick so that it is no longer a serious story of deception and betrayal, but a mock-epic kind of joke.[20]

There is at least one further classical resonance in Invisible's discovery of Bledsoe's murderous signs. William S. Scarborough delivered a paper, "Bellerophon's Letters, *Iliad* VI.168 ff.," at the 1891 meeting of the American Philological Association, arguing that the Greek word "signs" (*sêmata*) actually did mean "letters," and that Homer knew the art of writing and may even have used it "as circumstances demanded."[21] This is a question repeatedly posed and answered in different ways in Homeric studies, but what is significant about it is not so much Scarborough's conclusion, reasonable enough, as that he, an ex-slave, wrote on such a topic at all. There is a parallel between African Americans' winning the right to literacy and the freedom it can bring, and the murderous power that language also offers. Scarborough may have been drawn to the story of Bellerophon's letters because of the way it dramatizes the power that language can have over people, whether for good or ill, and whether spoken or written. The eloquence that Frederick Douglass discovered and learned how to wield could be turned against him as surely as those letters of Bellerophon. Language and literacy can have good uses and bad, and at the same moment. No one knows this better than a man who has been a slave—or now, a grandchild of slaves.

In a similar way this opposition of Dostoevskian doublings can organize our reading of complementary characterizations throughout the novel into pairs of seemingly opposite characters: the wealthy white, Northern benefactor and trustee, Mr. Norton, versus the poor, uneducated black farmer Jim Trueblood. Trueblood is willing to give a recital of committing incest with his daughter in great detail—has in fact been retained by the white community over the objections of the black community specifically for this purpose.[22] His tale and living example have a horrifying fascination for Mr. Norton, who had earlier told Invisible Man of his "pleasant fate" (39)—a phrase that in retrospect soon becomes even more fatuous than it sounds at first hearing—of supporting the college and its president Dr. Bledsoe. More revealingly, and in pathetic detail, Mr. Norton had already told Invisible of the love of *his* life, a daughter who died while the two of them were on a trip in Europe.

> She was a being more rare, more beautiful, purer, more perfect and more delicate than the wildest dream of a poet. I could never believe her to be my own flesh and blood. Her beauty was a well-spring of purest water-of-life, and to look upon her was to drink and drink and drink again. . . . She was rare, a perfect creation, a work of purest art. A delicate flower that bloomed in the liquid light of the moon. (42)

Norton's grotesque eroticism recalls Edgar Allan Poe at his best—or worst—in "Annabel Lee."

> I was a child, and she was a child,
> In this kingdom by the sea,
> But we loved with a love that was more than love,
> I and my Annabel Lee,
> With a love that the winged seraphs in heaven
> Coveted her and me.

The collision of a black man who seems to have nothing to hide and a white man whose secrets are apparent to us if not Ellison's narrator makes for comedy of a high order.

As is often the case until the later chapters of the novel, Invisible scarcely seems to notice what is unfolding in front of him. For his part, the farmer Trueblood cannot fathom Norton's neurotic fascination.

> "You did and are unharmed!" he shouted, his blue eyes blazing into the black face with something like envy and indignation. Trueblood looked helplessly at me. I looked away. I understood no more than he.
> "You have looked upon chaos and are not destroyed!"
> "No suh! I feels all right."
> "You do? You feel no inner turmoil, no need to cast out the offending eye?"
> "*Suh?*"
> "Answer me!"
> "I'm all right, suh," Trueblood said uneasily. "My eyes is all right too. And when I feels po'ly in my gut I takes a little soda and it goes away." (51)

So much for Lot's daughters and other psychoanalytic worries.[23]

What is striking about Ellison's writing here and elsewhere is the way he manages to combine Invisible Man's acute description of what he's seeing, with an apparently total incomprehension of what it signifies at the time ("his blue eyes blazing . . . with something like envy and indignation . . . Trueblood looked helplessly at me. I looked away. I understood no more than he"). He could be following the example of any number of novelists in creating what later narratology would term the *focalizers* of a narrative (characters who tell a story through their own subjective perceptions at that time); less technically, this scene is also a great example of Lord Raglan's argument about the inability of "most people" to present a truly objective account of the past. For most people this may be so, but for a novelist like Ellison it would not at all be the case.[24]

For his part, Norton, a white man oblivious to reality in his own way, tries to play out this sharecropper's story as if it came from the pages of Freud and Sophocles. Trueblood knows none of this, nor need he. Ghastly as his story is, he is the only one of the three actually in touch with reality. His seemingly easy survival of incest is not just the mark of a depraved man—his pregnant daughter is visible proof of that—but an indictment of the conditions in which he and his family are forced to live. It's always the local whites who insist he stay put in his place rather than move away, who even pay him handsomely to tell his awful tale, which they clearly take as confirmation of the worst fantasies racist Americans could conceive about black men.

> And I cain't stop—although I got a feelin' somethin' is wrong. I git loose from the woman now and I'm runnin' for the clock. At first I couldn't get the door wide open, it had some kinda crinkly stuff like steel wool on the facing. But I gits it open and gits inside and it's hot and dark in there. I goes up a dark tunnel, up near where the machinery is making all that noise and heat. It's like the power plant they got up to the school. It's burnin' hot and as iffen the house was caught on fire, and I starts to runnin', tryin' to git out. I runs and runs till I should be tired but ain't tired but feelin' more rested as I runs, and runnin' so good it's like flyin' and I'm flyin' and sailin' and floatin' right up over the town. Only I'm still in the *tunnel*. (58–59)

So Trueblood slogs on and on, through bursting lights and rising lakes of water, until at last this inspired parody of pornography and psychoanalytic symbolism climaxes with Trueblood's emergence "in the cool daylight again." Trueblood's matter-of-fact survival of what Mr. Norton imagines

would be an annihilating violation of the incest taboo is a vivid juxtapo-
sition of characters who are in one sense total opposites, yet in another
closely linked. Trueblood did what Norton appears to have wanted to do,
though we can never be sure that he actually did it. Trueblood has indeed
looked on chaos and lived, and not only because he seems not to understand Norton's use of the fancy Greek word "chaos."

Norton gives Trueblood a substantial tip for reciting his story, which
for Norton and any other white racist would appear to be a purely pornographic account of an act of father-daughter incest. Norton's earlier rhap-
sodies to Invisible Man about his own dead daughter make it plain that he
has not been a disinterested audience, nor is he thinking about such things
for the first time. The apparently matter-of-fact acceptance of incest is a
sure sign, as Patrice Rankine points out, that a story of incest among black
people is of no great moment to the white men who pay Trueblood to tell
it again and again, because the only thing they really fear from blacks is
miscegenation.

> Trueblood more than suggests that he has committed incest with his own
> daughter, yet the truth of the matter is that, within American society, his
> actual transgression would be less of a violation than if he had slept with
> a white woman. . . . Trueblood's dream suggests that either he sublimates
> the fear of incest as miscegenation, or his awareness of Norton's lily-white
> worldview informs the details of his story. In either case, Trueblood's
> narrative succeeds in providing his audience—both Invisible Man and
> Norton—with images that reinforce its own fears and desires. Proof of his
> success is that Norton rewards him and has no problem.[25]

Our point is not to gainsay Forrest's Dostoevskian reading, but simply to
observe that this thinking in polarities and opposites appears all over the
place in literature—not least in ancient Greece.

The opening of the *Odyssey* is a tour de force in the art of setting out
these kinds of oppositions in both character and theme.[26] Within fewer
than a hundred lines Homer establishes a pattern of negative and positive paradigms that will work through all the way to the end of the poem.
Agamemnon, murdered by his own wife and her lover Aegisthus, is a negative foil for Odysseus, everything that a returning warrior should hope not
to find at home. Frozen in time at the moment of his death, his shade in the
world of the dead cannot stop complaining about the perfidy of women.[27]
Until he has tested Penelope and slain all the suitors, Odysseus cannot be

sure that he won't have a homecoming like Agamemnon's. Even after he has slain all Penelope's suitors, he is easy prey to her testing lie about the conjugal bed he built for them; for an instant, until she tearfully confesses she had to be wary, it seems she might have become a Helen or Clytemnestra after all. Although she is never named as anything but Agamemnon's wife in the *Odyssey*, Clytemnestra serves as a demonic doppelganger to Penelope, not only committing adultery like her sister Helen but murdering her husband in his bath in the bargain. Finally, in the first speech of the poem, Zeus himself tells the story of Orestes, the avenger of his father's murder and the slayer of Clytemnestra's lover Aegisthus. Orestes becomes if not a negative paradigm for Telemachus, at least an ominous one: Odysseus's son could conceivably be forced into playing the same role if his mother Penelope gave way to the suitors and if they succeeded in killing Odysseus upon his return. Much of Telemachus's growing up in the *Odyssey* consists in maturing enough to face that possibility. In the event, he comes to a happier ending than Orestes, not because of his own efforts, but because his mother and father are not Clytemnestra and Agamemnon.

Beyond these polarities, the *Odyssey* is as cagey about the name and identity of its hero as Ellison is with his. Homer seems to start the poem by nodding. To judge from its title, it's supposed to be about Odysseus, yet there Zeus is in the first speech of the poem complaining about Aegisthus and the sad news of the house of Atreus. Athena has to remind her all-knowing father that he's launched into the wrong story. That's all very well about Aegisthus, he got what was coming to him, she briskly observes. What about Odysseus?

> My child, what strange remarks you let escape you.
> Could I forget that kingly man, Odysseus? (1.86–87, Fitzgerald trans.)

That is to say, "Of course I know this is the beginning of the *Odyssey*." Now that Odysseus's story is underway, it does not matter in the least that Odysseus himself will not appear until the fifth book. After this opening we would expect nothing less. And it is in this setting that Homer employs that marvelous simile of the glowing coal hidden among the embers of an old fire.

Invisible Man is a novel whose grand architectural design, like the *Odyssey*'s, suggests an artist of seemingly infinite polytropic ability. Ellison is an Odyssean writer, like the poet of the Odyssey himself: *andra moi ennepe, mousa, polutropon*, "Tell me of the man, Muse, of many twists and turns."

Riffs

One of the standard procedures of literary criticism is to juxtapose texts by different authors in order to bring out the particular qualities and relative merits of each. In jazz the constant network of cross-performances means that that task is implicit and inherent in the accumulating catalogue of the music. The performance of a given player simultaneously answers certain questions (about musicians he is playing with or who have come before, about his relation to the developing tradition) and raises other questions (about what he himself is doing, about his own worth, about the form he's working in); the musicians he works with and who come after him provide provisional answers but these answers are questions—about the worth of *these* musicians, *their* relation to tradition. In an elaborate critical kind of circular breathing, the form is always simultaneously explaining and questioning itself.

Geoff Dyer, *But Beautiful: A Book about Jazz* (1991)

Verbal music is what makes this Odyssean voice and others blend seamlessly into the novel's language. Ellison brings his musician's ear to the writing. *Invisible Man* needs to be read with a sense of *tempo rubato*, "stolen time" or flexible expressivity, in contrast to a simultaneously steady beat, a performance as natural to the performance of Chopin as it is to Louis Armstrong. Ellison admired this quality and was able to translate it into an off-beat rhythm, carefully avoiding the regular and predictable. So does his hero.

> Invisibility, let me explain, gives one a slightly different sense of time, you're never quite on the beat. Sometimes you're ahead and sometimes behind. Instead of the swift and imperceptible flowing of time, you are aware of its nodes, those points where time stands still or from which it leaps ahead. And you slip into the breaks and look around. That's what you hear vaguely in Louis' music. (8)

In his essay "Living with Music," Ellison tells us that when he resolved to become a writer he tried to put away all thoughts and practice of performing music.[28] Having given up the trumpet and piano for the typewriter, he gradually found himself drawn back into listening to music with more and more passion, and with a increasing dedication to high fidelity that eventually swamped the small New York apartment he and his wife lived in with speakers, amplifiers, and an ever larger record collection. When he recalled the actual writing of *Invisible Man*, he brought all parts of his life

and experiences together. As he observes in his introduction to the thirti-
eth-anniversary edition, the writer of the novel had not so much evolved
from jazz musician and other roles in his previous life, as retained all of
those skills. He had an improvisatory, jazzy approach to the writing which
shaped the prologue in particular.

> The Prologue was written afterwards, really—in terms of a shift in the hero's
> point of view. I wanted to throw the reader off balance—make him accept
> certain non-naturalistic effects. It was really a memoir written underground,
> and I wanted a foreshadowing through which I hoped the reader would view
> the actions which took place in the main body of the book.[29]

In this musical sense the prologue of the novel can be likened to the effect
of the proem (*prooimion*) or introductory song which opens the *Odyssey*.
Homer takes twenty-one lines to get to the actual name of the "man" (*andra*), the first word of the first line. The clues begin to accumulate, and by
the end of this tease we take as much delight in the disguise and postpone-
ment of Odysseus's name and identity as we will at any point in the story
that follows. This is a poem whose plot is as much about the suppression
of Odysseus's name as it is about its revelation.[30]

Compared to Joyce's *Ulysses*, Ellison's story will end in an upside-down
Ithaca even more distant from Homer than the Odyssean reunion and non-
reunion of Molly and Leopold Bloom. New York and Harlem stand above
Invisible Man's underground lair. And that cellar itself, with its sophisticated electronics and phonograph, sounds suspiciously like the Ellisons'
old New York apartment, the "audio booby trap" described in the article
"Living with Music" that Ellison published in *High Fidelity* in 1955.[31] Most
tellingly, Invisible Man ends his story by becoming a writer, not an orator.

He also encourages us to trace another literary thread along with
Homer and Dostoevsky, as Robert J. Butler argues. Dante's *Inferno* has
many parallels with the overall design for *Invisible Man*.[32] This is compelling especially because Ellison later explained how he had divided his work
into three parts. His divisions are not as symmetrical as Dante's, though
there are flashes of a kind of numerological play reminiscent of the elaborate structure and terza rima of the *Divine Comedy*. When Invisible Man
says that there are "exactly 1,369 lights" that he's wired in his hole in the
basement (7), the number 369 is at once alluding to the 369th Regiment,
the "Harlem Hellfighters" who won many awards and medals for their ferocity and bravery in World War I, and also playing with multiples of three
(3, 6, 9) that the *Divine Comedy*'s tripartite structure and terza rima entail.

In his later essay "The Art of Fiction" he is quite explicit about these kinds of calculations in the writing of the novel.

> The symbols and their connections were known to me. I began it with a chart of the three-part division. It was a conceptual frame with most of the ideas and some incidents indicated. The three parts represent the narrator's movement from, using Kenneth Burke's terms, purpose to passion to perception. These three major sections are built up of smaller units of three which mark the course of the action and which depend for their development upon what I hoped was a consistent and developing motivation. However, you'll note that the maximum insight on the hero's part isn't reached until the final section. After all, it's a novel about innocence and human error, a struggle through illusion to reality. Each section begins with a sheet of paper; each piece of paper is exchanged for another and contains a definition of his identity, or the social role he is to play as defined for him by others. But all say essentially the same thing, "Keep this nigger boy running." Before he could have some voice in his own destiny he had to discard these old identities and illusions; his enlightenment couldn't come until then. Once he recognizes the hole of darkness into which these papers put him, he has to burn them. That's the plan and the intention; whether I achieved this is something else.[33]

Like every literary allusion in Ellison, what starts out as Saul converts to Paul, a plausible new connection or model, and then ends up maybe being only Saul after all, a transformation imperfectly made. Dante and the *Commedia* are invoked, only to recede as the novel progresses. *Invisible Man* begins and ends in what seems an infernal or at least underground realm, with no *Purgatorio* or *Paradiso* in sight.[34] Dante is like Dostoevsky, Homer, and every other voice evoked, each a melodic line that can be heard distinctly on its own, or in counterpoint with others. When the prologue speaks of hearing each melodic line of music, this applies as well to the authorial voice we can hear.

> So under the spell of the reefer I discovered a new analytical way of listening to music. The unheard sounds came through, and each melodic line existed of itself, stood out clearly from all the rest, said its piece, and waited patiently for the other voices to speak. (8–9)

Marijuana's well-known effect of altering ordinary perceptions of both time and space, bending both of them, slowing them down, stretching them out, enables Invisible Man to separate the voices of jazz, rendering the polyphony we hear in recordings of music by Louis Armstrong or many jazz musicians' favorite classical composer Bach into an analyzed monody, complex voices broken down into single voices. From this, the prologue suddenly shifts to the voice of the pilgrim Dante, with the *Inferno*'s beginning, "I found myself in a dark wood," so that Invisible Man experiences both time and space as if they were music. In fact, they are music as Ellison creates it.

> That night I found myself hearing not only in time, but in space as well. I not only entered the music but descended, like Dante, into its depths. *And beneath the swiftness of the hot tempo there was a slower tempo and a cave and I entered it and looked around and heard an old woman singing a spiritual as full of Weltschmerz as flamenco, and beneath that lay a still lower level on which I saw a beautiful girl the color of ivory pleading in a voice like my mother's as she stood before a group of slave owners who bid for her naked body, and below that I found a lower level and a more rapid tempo and I heard someone shout:*
> *"Brothers and sisters, my text this morning is the 'Blackness of Blackness.'"*
> (9, italics original)

Riffs, musical variations on a themes, are what we look for in the prologue of *Invisible Man* and the rest of the novel, a collection of individual voices whose ensemble is greater than any single one of its parts.

So to conceive of the opening of the novel as jazz being played is not a figurative exercise. It may be the easiest way to understand what Ellison is doing. In two relatively brief sentences there are refrains of Dostoevsky's opening sentence in *Notes from Underground*, the closing sentence of Richard Wright's 1940 essay "How 'Bigger' Was Born," and an allusion to a Hollywood movie based on H. G. Wells's 1897 novella *The Invisible Man*.

> I am an invisible man. No, I am not a spook like those who haunted Edgar Allan Poe, nor am I one of your Hollywood-movie ectoplasms. (3)

It is not easy to single out one melody when there are so many in play.[35] To spell out perhaps the least familiar: as Frederick Griffiths has pointed out, this mention of Edgar Allen Poe plays a riff on the harmonious ending of Wright's "How Bigger Was Born":

> We do have in the Negro the embodiment of a past tragic enough to appease the spiritual hunger of even a James; and we have in the oppression of the Negro a shadow athwart our national life dense and heavy enough

to satisfy even the gloomy broodings of a Hawthorne. And if Poe were alive, he would not have to invent horror; horror would invent him.[36]

The "Hollywood-movie ectoplasm" refers to Claude Rains's performance in James Whale's 1933 movie *The Invisible Man*, made from the Wells story. But the leading voice turns out to be the first one we hear, playing off the opening of Dostoevsky's *Notes from Underground*. As his recent translator Michael Katz notes, the opening three sentences of *Notes* constitute a trio of carefully varied and balanced short sentences.

> I am a sick man.
> I am a spiteful man.
> I am an unattractive man.[37]

If we take this triadic idea—not a farfetched notion, given what Ellison later would write about his work—the novel's prologue appears to be a series of expanding riffs on that opening theme, correcting it, enlarging it, comparing it to something else. The punctuation and the grammar of the sentences form just one structure, and the ideas unfolding across them and through them are another, like the multiple voices in a jazz ensemble. Not just the opening sentence, but the entire opening paragraph of *Invisible Man* riffs on these opening three sentences of *Notes from Underground*, each section composed of three statements that grow longer and longer, as the successive parts of the triad are marked off by natural beats in the reading.

> I am an invisible man.
>   No, I am not a spook like those who haunted Edgar Allan Poe, nor am I one of your Hollywood-movie ectoplasms.
>   I am a man of substance, of flesh and bone, fiber and liquids—and I might even be said to possess a mind.
>   I am invisible, understand, simply because people refuse to see me. Like the bodiless heads you see sometimes in circus sideshows, it is as though I have been surrounded by mirrors of hard, distorting glass. When they approach me they see only my surroundings, themselves, or figments of their imagination—indeed everything and anything except me.

"I am invisible, understand, simply because people refuse to see me" is roughly the center of the paragraph, restating the opening theme and glossing it, leading into the third riff, which is the longest of all, the most elaborate with its figurative comparison and the same idea as "I am an invisible man," given its most elaborate variation in "they see only my surroundings, themselves, or figments of their imagination," with the correction "indeed everything and anything except me." The paragraph opens with "I" the subject and closes with "me" the object, and like any good jazz theme even its statement of the theme is already a significant variation of that theme, so that the relation of this performance to that theme is at once recognizable and off and running with its own new melody.

Thereafter Ellison exercises considerable care to link the identity of his never-named, momentarily Dostoevskian hero with the way the identity of Odysseus is established in the *Odyssey*. There significant names abound, none more than the name of Odysseus, and here we can see Ellison's jazz technique of the near miss, a development expanding beyond the deliberate inversion of classical models of the kind Joyce canonized in *Ulysses*.

Invisible Man's grandfather is never named, but he plays a critical role in his grandson's story and is the avatar of Autolycus, the grandfather of Odysseus.[38] Chapter 1 begins with a clear evocation of the twenty years of war and wandering that Odysseus experienced.

> It goes a long way back, some twenty years. . . . It took me a long time and much painful boomeranging of my expectations to achieve a realization everyone else appears to have been born with: That I am nobody but myself. But first I had to discover that I am an invisible man! (15)

It took ten years for the Greeks to capture Troy and ten more years for Odysseus to make it back to Ithaca.[39] Going a long way back, some twenty years, suggests an Odyssean voyage of some kind. The only other reference to the passing of time leads to an equally significant date.

> And yet I am no freak of nature, nor of history. I was in the cards, other things having been equal (or unequal) eighty-five years ago. I am not ashamed of my grandparents for having been slaves. I am only ashamed of myself for having at one time been ashamed. About eighty-five years ago they were told that they were free, united with others of our country in everything pertaining to the common good, and, in everything social, separate like the fingers of the hand. (15)

The end of the Civil War and the total emancipation of slaves in 1865 would date the present time to about 1950, the year Ellison completed his novel, finally published after substantial revisions and editing in 1952.

"United . . . in everything pertaining to the common good, and, in everything social, separate like the fingers of the hand" quotes directly from
Booker T. Washington's 1895 Atlanta Exposition address, the high-water
mark for accommodationism in African American political life, and here
echoed in a context that turns Washington's rhetoric back against itself.

> And they believed it. They exulted in it. They stayed in their place,
> worked hard, and brought up my father to do the same. (15–16)

By contrast, Invisible Man's grandfather, who had actually lived in slavery, never believed in Washington's ideal at all. He turns out to be the
crucial member of Invisible's family, even when Invisible is stuck in the
role of a Telemachus who can't seem to grow up and doesn't realize it for
a long time.

> He was an odd old guy, my grandfather, and I am told I take after him. It
> was he who caused the trouble. (16)

Whatever the names of grandfather and grandson may be, we would expect they would be like many names in the United States, where given
names and surnames are also thought to have such predictive powers.[40]
They would have originally signaled something about the character or
social standing of the person, as well as being a way of identifying them
individually.[41] What Ellison takes from Homer is a special bond between
grandfather and grandson, now in this world each equally nameless, but
with the role each plays quite clear. In the *Odyssey* the names of Autolycus
and Odysseus have a semantic meaning that Homer gives it to Autolycus
himself to explain.

   At the crucial moment in book 19 when the nurse Eurycleia suddenly
sees a scar on the thigh of the disguised Odysseus and realizes his identity,
Homer takes us back to the moment in the past when this visible sign
was acquired.[42] There turns out to be a link between that present sign and
the hitherto invisible sign of the disguised Odysseus's name. Although we
learn about the boar hunt on which he acquired it, the real purpose of the
so-called "digression" on the scar of Odysseus is to tell us how he acquired
his name, and what it means, and in this his grandfather Lone Wolf, as
suggested by the compound *auto-* ("self") and *lykos* ("wolf") was the key
player. When Autolycus came to Ithaca to visit his daughter Anticleia and
son-in-law Laertes, the nurse Eurycleia put their infant son in his lap and
asked Autolycus to name him.

My son-in-law, my daughter, call the boy
by the name I tell you. Well you know, my hand
has been against the world of men and women;
odium and distrust I've won. Odysseus
should be his given name. (19.477–81, Fitzgerald trans.)

A more literal translation by the classicist Jenny Strauss Clay glosses the eponymous "Odysseus" by quoting the Greek.

My son-in-law and daughter, give the name I say:
for I come here a curse (*odyssamenos*) to many
men and women all over the much-nurturing earth;
therefore let his name appropriately be *Odysseus*. (19.406–9)[43]

Fitzgerald conveys beautifully the *odyssamenos-Odysseus* pun by his ingenious combination of two words that sound like homonyms of the Greek, *od*ium and *dis*trust.[44] If that sounds corny to our ears, so does the original. Ellison carries the notion of the *onoma eponumon* or "appropriate name" of a troublemaker directly forward into the words Invisible Man has for his grandfather, that "odd old guy" he is said to take after. "The one who caused the trouble" is a close paraphrase of what Autolycus says about himself and his grandson's name. After his triumph of winning a scholarship, Invisible Man seems ready to face anything, even his grandfather's picture.

I even felt safe from grandfather, whose deathbed curse usually spoiled my triumphs. I stood beneath his photograph with my brief case in hand and smiled triumphantly into his stolid black peasant's face. It was a face that fascinated me. The eyes seemed to follow everywhere I went. (32–33)

The "curse" referred to here is actually the old man's confession of the kind of life he had led, which is a life neither Invisible Man nor anyone else in his family thinks is one respectable people should now live. Grandfather warned them they had better wake up and follow his advice.

Son, after I'm gone I want you to keep up the good fight. I never told you, but our life is a war and I have been a traitor all my born days, a spy in the enemy's country ever since I give up my gun back in the Reconstruction. Live with your head in the lion's mouth. I want you to overcome 'em with yeses, undermine 'em with grins, agree 'em to death and destruction, let 'em swoller you till they vomit or bust wide open. (16)

At a lower frequency—which, for the inverted world of this novel, is the place where higher wisdom is to be found—Invisible Man's grandfather has handed down an identity for his grandson as vivid as the name Autolycus supplied.[45] The problem is that it may take a long time for this particular child to realize the identity his grandfather bestowed.

> That night I dreamed I was at a circus with him and that he refused to laugh at the clowns no matter what they did. Then later he told me to open my brief case and read what was inside and I did, finding an official envelope stamped with the state seal; and inside the envelope I found another and another, endlessly, and I thought I would fall of weariness. "Them's years," he said. "Now open that one." And I did and in it I found an engraved document containing a short message in letters of gold. "Read it," my grandfather said. "Out loud!"
> "To Whom It May Concern," I intoned. "Keep This Nigger-Boy Running." I awoke with the old man's laughter ringing in my ears. It was a dream I was to remember and dream again for many years after. But at that time I had no insight into its meaning. First I had to attend college. (33)

Like all children, Invisible Man has to grow into an understanding of what his grandfather was saying to him. He never seems to have understood anything his grandfather said at the time.

> "You start Saul, and end up Paul," my grandfather had often said. "When you're a youngun, you Saul, but let life whup your head a bit and you starts to trying to be Paul—though you still Sauls around on the side." (381)

At that point in the story Invisible fondly believes he has become something of a Saul on the road to Damascus, converted into Paul by his experience. This will not prove to be the case. His grandfather's words are wiser than he knows.

Out of the Hospital, Under the Bar—and More from the *Odyssey*

Another way to appreciate how carefully Ellison measured his evocation of the *Odyssey* can be seen in the revisions he made of earlier drafts of the novel. Unlike the labyrinthine twists and turns we have been following, where it makes sense not to exaggerate a classical voice at the expense of other ones, we have here good evidence of his concern in revising to evoke one of the most famous episodes in Homer, the adventure of Odysseus and his companions in the cave of the Cyclops Polyphemus.

Ten years after the publication of *Invisible Man* Ralph Ellison allowed an episode that he had omitted from his prize-winning novel to be printed for the first time in an anthology of new work by African American writers edited by Herbert Hill.[46] "Out of the Hospital and Under the Bar" is a substantial fragment of fiction—forty-five pages, from a novel whose final version runs to 580 pages—and if it was not new to Ellison himself, it would have been of considerable interest to anyone else looking for something more along the same lines of *Invisible Man*.[47] In this episode the nurse Mary, "a woman of the folk," succeeds in freeing Invisible Man from the psychiatric machine he woke up to after losing consciousness in the explosion at the Liberty Paint factory in Brooklyn. After he finally succeeds in escaping from that contraption and the hospital, Ellison's narrator makes his way via subterranean passages to the cellar of a bar and, eventually, to freedom, through a manhole cover on a city street. Ellison says that considerations of space led him to reconceive this part of his novel and omit the story, and that he was pleased to see Mary's exploits into print: "She deserved more space in the novel and would, I think, have made it a better book. . . . Reading it now, almost ten years after it was put aside, I have the feeling that it stands on its own if only as one of those pieces of writing which consists mainly of one damned thing after another sheerly happening" (245).

The story does not quite stand on its own, since it is obviously an episode in a larger work, but Ellison was right to have it published, because in other respects it is a hilarious send-up of a romance's rescue of a young hero from the clutches of wicked men, all carried off by a resourceful older woman who is equally unimpressed by the authority of medical doctors and the intelligence of Ellison's hero.

"What's supposed to be wrong with you?"

"I don't remember, but I'm all right now."

"What you mean you don't remember? You in there, ain't you? Now when *I* was in the hospital I had a tumor. They damn near took out all my works—all but the important ones, that is," she added coyly. "So don't come telling me you don't remember." (247)

Mary is so positive that her patient is lying when he says he can't remember that she's on the point of leaving him to his fate, so in desperation Invisible Man is forced to make up a long story of an encounter with a white man that jumps from one made-up incident to the next, under Mary's prodding. Invisible hopes she will be discreet enough not to have him spell out what the "white man" was trying to get from him by pressing a twenty-dollar bill into his hand.

> "And he said, 'Look at me, black boy, what kind of man am I?'"
> "What kinda man he was?" she said, frowning.
> "Yes. And I . . ."
> "And what you tell him?"
> "I said, 'You're a white man, sir,' and his eyes got bright and he started laughing and said, 'That's right, but what *other* kind of man am I?'
> "I didn't know. So I had to tell him I didn't know. And that made him angry.
> "He said, 'Don't play dumb, boy. You nigger boys always try to play dumb!'" (254)

Invisible Man finally rises to the challenge and provides Mary with a satisfying story that she can believe because she now understands why any decent young man would be ashamed to tell it. Even as a storyteller Invisible Man is not so much original as desperately improvising whatever he thinks it will take to get Mary not to abandon him. It is hard to say who is leading whom more here, the storyteller or his audience.

> "That's when I did it."
> "Did what, boy?"
> "I didn't know what else to do. He kept coming up on me and I tried to tell him not to do it, but he kept on coming and I decided to run past him, and he said, 'You want to be smart? You can have this microscope, too. I won't be needing it any more.' And by then he had rolled the money into a little wad like a spit-ball, rolling it slowly between his fingers. He said, 'It won't take but a minute,' and then he reached out and touched me and I swung the bottle at him and ran . . ."
> "You hit him, boy?"
> "I think so . . ."
> "You kill him? You think you killed him?" she asked excitedly.
> "I ran, I've been running ever since."
> "You run a long ways, didn't you, son?"
> "Yes," I said.
> "And hopped them freight trains and everything."
> "I don't want to talk about it," I said. "I've got to get out of here. Can't you see why I have to get out?"

"Yeah," she said, looking at me with dead seriousness. "I see it now. You
probably killed him, or hurt him bad, and they looking for you. . . . I tell
you what, it's too late to do anything right now 'cause it's time for me to go
and that nurse'll be coming in here . . ."

"You can't help me?"

"Yeah, but not tonight. You stay here like nothing happen until I get
back tomorrow and I'll help you git outa here."

"But they might transfer me," I protested.

"No they won't. They don't aim to do that till next week. You just have
to be patient awhile. Besides, you oughta told me the truth when I first
ask you." (256–57)

"Out of the Hospital and Under the Bar" is so good that we may regret
that Ellison did not feel free to let his comic imagination continue with
more chapters along this line. It subjects both Invisible Man and everyone
he meets to a level of absurdity that is notably wilder and less controlled
than most of the novel Ellison finally published. Here, when Invisible Man
escapes his infernal machine and then the hospital, he never finds the time
to get clothes for himself and has to flee from one set of pursuers to another, stark naked. It is a scene we cannot imagine either Dostoevsky's
Underground Man or Ellison's imitation of him in the prologue playing.
Invisible's emergence from the sewer is, as they say, classic:

For a second the cap tittered upon my head, making a wavering crack
through which I could see the glint of street lights. Then it clanged to the
side and I pushed it away and seemed to shoot through the hole, moving
so furiously that I stumbled and sprawled on the walk, my head striking
the pavement, dazing me. Then from above there came a sound like thunder and a woman yelled, "Lord, God, what in the world is this?"

I rolled, looking into the faces of two women dressed in white.

"Police! A naked man, a naked . . . !" the woman screamed. "Police!"

"Oh no! No!" called a woman who crouched against a building front.
"Not *naked*! Is he, Sis Spencer? Let's us be sure 'fore we call the cops.
Wait'll I change my glasses." (282–83)

There are other reasons beyond its length and stylistic brio that might
have led Ellison to replace what became "Out of the Hospital and Under the Bar" with chapter 11 and the opening of chapter 12 as eventually
published.[48] If he had kept this mad scramble through the bowels of the
hospital to a bar's coal bin and out a manhole cover onto the streets of

Harlem, he would have had a doublet with the scene in chapter 25, where Invisible Man falls down a manhole to escape from looters in the Harlem riots. More to the point, he would also have collapsed the imagery of the extended, partly literal and partly figurative, *Notes from Underground* prologue and epilogue; Invisible Man would have enjoyed a parodic encounter with a Dantesque underworld that would strike readers as anything but sinister. Possibly Ellison developed his opening and closing Dostoevskian scenes out of this episode, since he tells us that he wrote the prologue and epilogue last.

What is significant for the novel as we have it is what Ellison wrote in place of this wildly inventive comic romance. In revision he makes a much more explicit gesture to the *Odyssey*, one any reader of Homer would be sure to pick up on.[49] Thus revision is important not only for its own sake—and we might join Ellison in regretting that there is not more of this version of Mary and the kind of humor she brings with her—but for what it reveals to us about Ellison's Odyssean conception of his narrator's story. As always, what he substituted is not a simple, unmediated replay of Homer. As Robert List observes in his study of the connections between James Joyce's fiction and Ellison's:

> Too many critics have attempted to "plug in" the plots of the *Odyssey* or the *Aeneid* into *Ulysses* and *Invisible Man*. An unacknowledged critical confusion has often resulted.
>
> A critical dead end results . . . if exact parallels are sought between classical source material and the myth-syncopated works of Joyce and Ellison. Rather, we need to keep time with the many comic near-misses, the literary dissonances that result from the juxtapositions. . . . The parallels are close, but they are also strained. They begin to crack apart, miss the story-teller's beat, as if the narrators or the narrative voices of *A Portrait*, *Ulysses*, or *Invisible Man* were so many exhausted Tiresias figures with memory lapses.[50]

List's parallels that "begin to crack apart" and his sense of the storyteller's beat describe what happens when traditional tunes (myths, stories, prior texts) are played with like the way a jazz musician can play with straight music—Louis Armstrong's way with Andy Razaf's "What Did I Do to Be So Black and Blue?" If we take Ellison seriously as a performer but especially an informed critic of jazz, why shouldn't he treat Homer or Joyce the way Armstrong treats Razaf? Ellison's revision entailed anything but exact parallels; a comic near miss is exactly the right spirit to look for in this

invisible odyssey. This very invisibility comes from Ellison's understanding of the character of the *Odyssey* itself. It almost looks as if it is not going
to live up to its name, since Odysseus himself does not appear until book
5 of twenty-four books. The first word of the *Odyssey* ("man," *andra*) is as
opaque as the first word of the *Iliad*, the semidivine "rage" or "wrath" of
Achilles (*mênin*), is explicit.

It is worth rehearsing this familiar comparison of the opening lines of
Homer's two very different poems, because the same kind of "near miss"
technique—summoning up remembrance of texts past, only to issue forth
in confusing and deliberately unfaithful memories—was dear to the heart
of *any* poet or writer who knew the *Odyssey*, not only modernists like Joyce
and Ellison; for example, Milton (the "one greater Man" of *Paradise Lost*'s
proem) and Vergil (*arma virumque*). Replacing the opening lines of "Out
of the Hospital" ("When I awakened she stood looking down. Her newly
straightened hair gleamed glossily in the intense light, her blue uniform
freshly ironed and stiffly starched. Seeing me awake she shook her head
and grinned. I tensed, expecting a trick"; 246), Ellison begins chapter 11
with a fine example of one of List's near misses: "I was sitting in a cold,
white rigid chair and a man was looking at me out of a bright third eye that
glowed from the center of his forehead" (231). Invisible Man is not really in
charge of what he is seeing, but simply reporting it now. And perhaps the
right term for this passage isn't so much near miss as in-joke. The "bright
third eye that glowed from the center of his forehead" is a deadpan reference to the Cyclops Polyphemus in the ninth book of the *Odyssey*, who
is there described as having only one eye. In the iconography of this Odyssean creature he is sometimes represented as having a third eye in the
middle of his forehead. As so often, Invisible himself is not aware of what
he's telling us ("A thin voice with a mirror on the end of it . . ."; 231).

Ellison has transformed the cave of Polyphemus in which Odysseus and
his men were trapped into a modern hospital room equipped with an electric shock machine wielded by psychiatrists and researchers. As doctors
from Hippocrates onward have always been wont to do, they discuss the
pros and cons of their experiment openly, quite oblivious to the possibility
that their subject can hear them. They also sound like Homeric gods chat-
ting about what fools these mortals be, or Polyphemus taunting Odysseus
("I'll do you a great favor and eat *you* last of all").

I listened with growing uneasiness to the conversation fuzzing away to a
whisper. Their simplest words seemed to refer to something else, as did
many of the notions that unfurled through my head. I wasn't sure whether

they were talking about me or someone else. Some of it sounded like a
discussion of history . . .

"The machine will produce the results of a prefrontal lobotomy without
the negative effects of the knife," the voice said. "You see, instead of sever-
ing the prefrontal lobe, a single lobe, that is, we apply pressure in the proper
degrees to the major centers of nerve control—our concept is Gestalt—and
the result is as complete a change of personality as you'll find in your famous
fairy-tale cases of criminals transformed into amiable fellows after all that
bloody business of a brain operation. And what's more," the voice went on
triumphantly, "the patient is both physically and neurally whole."

"But what of his psychology?"

"Absolutely of no importance!" the voice said. "The patient will live
as he has to live, and with absolute integrity. Who could ask more? He'll
experience no major conflict of motives, and what is even better, society
will suffer no traumata on his account." (236)

Reading this dispassionate exchange makes us long for the straightforward, carnivorous ways of Polyphemus in his parallel cave.

Neither reply nor pity came from him,
but in one stride he clutched at my companions
and caught two in his hands like squirming puppies
to beat their brains out, spattering the floor.
Then he dismembered them and made his meal,
gaping and crunching like a mountain lion—
everything: innards, flesh, and marrow bones.
We cried aloud, lifting our hands to Zeus,
powerless, looking on at this, appalled;
but Kyklops went on filling up his belly
with manflesh and great gulps of whey,
then lay down like a mast among his sheep. (*Odyssey* 9.316–27, Fitzgerald
trans.)

Ellison's transformation of the Polyphemus scene is a near miss only if
we expected a level of literalism in working with classical themes that no
good imitator of Homer has ever been interested in. It is a metamorphosis
of the fabulous monster and his Greek victims into the calm, scientific
procedures of physicians and researchers of modern medicine, with a not-
too-subtle implication that the Cyclops Polyphemus has been reincar-
nated in the modern American MD. The complete change of personality

that the machine promises will create a patient who is at once "physically and neurally whole" and at the same time someone who will experience "no major conflict of motives," society around him suffering "no traumata on his account." The language is pseudoscientific, affecting to be professional and detached but actually euphemistic about the destruction of a person's identity. The latent criminal thinking of these medical scientists is betrayed by their effortless glide into the all-too-familiar language of the age of lynch mobs and Jim Crow.

> There was a pause. A pen scratched upon paper. Then, "Why not castration, doctor?" a voice asked waggishly, causing me to start, a pain tearing through me.
> "There goes your love of blood again," the first voice laughed. "What's that definition of a surgeon, 'A butcher with a bad conscience?'"
> They laughed. (237)

From this it is only a short step to trying more current in another round of electric shocks. What the white scientists are engaged in is controlled experimentation with a machine that approximates the favored means of execution in the United States by midtwentieth century, the electric chair. What we witness is a disintegration of identity, as Invisible Man's fear, anger, and indignation are momentarily obliterated.

> I heard them move away; a chair scraped. The machine droned, and I knew definitely that they were discussing me and steeled myself for the shocks, but was blasted nevertheless. The pulse came swift and staccato, increasing gradually until I fairly danced between the nodes. My teeth chattered. I closed my eyes and bit my lips to smother my screams. Warm blood filled my mouth. Between my lids I saw a circle of hands and faces, dazzling with light. Some were scribbling upon charts.
>
> "Look, he's dancing," someone called.
> "No, really?"
> An oily face looked in. "They really do have rhythm, don't they? Get hot, boy! Get hot!" it said with a laugh.
> And suddenly my bewilderment suspended and I wanted to be angry, murderously angry. But somehow the pulse of current smashing through my body prevented me. Something had been disconnected. For though I had seldom used my capacities for anger and indignation, I had no doubt that I possessed them; and, like a man who knows that he must fight,

whether angry or not, when called a son of a bitch, I tried to *imagine* myself angry—only to discover a deeper sense of remoteness. I was beyond anger. I was only bewildered. And those above seemed to sense it. There was no avoiding the shock and I rolled with the agitated tide, out into the blackness. (237–38)

What was in an earlier draft a routine and unexceptional hospital stay turns into a brilliant variation on the Odysseus and Polyphemus theme, where the identities of monster and human are confused, the integrity of American science and medicine compromised by the indifference and sadism of those who practice it.

This is one Cyclops's cave that Ellison's Odysseus will not escape on his own (as he does with Mary's aid in "Out of the Hospital"). This is an Odyssean dilemma, but he has no Odyssean trick to play. There is no chance of getting these Cyclopes drunk with wine, even less chance of drilling that single eye in the forehead out with the red-hot tip of a sharpened stake, or of hiding under the blinded giant's sheep as a way of escaping from his cave. What Ellison's radical change in character and plot then leads to is an even more dazzling variation on one of Odysseus's most ingenious tricks.

> "Kyklops,
> you ask my honorable name? Remember
> the gift you promised me, and I shall tell you.
> My name is Nohbdy: mother, father, and friends,
> everyone calls me Nohbdy." And he said,
> "Nohbdy's my meat, then, after I eat his friends.
> Others come first. There's a noble gift, now." (9.393–99, Fitzgerald trans.)

Odysseus's lying ruse of the name "Nobody" that the credulous Polyphemus believes comes alive once again in the hospital and its shock-therapy ward. Fitzgerald's syncopated "Nohbdy" recreates (without footnotes) the wordplay Odysseus achieves by using the Greek pronoun *outis* ("no man") as if it were a proper name, which would be signaled by a change in pitch accent, from the acute to the circumflex (*oútis, Oûtis*).[51] So when Polyphemus is blinded and crying out for help from his fellow Cyclopes, and he says "no man" has helped him, they naturally assume he means "NoMan" and shout in reply:

> Sure no man's driving off your flock? No man [*mê tis*]
> has tricked you, ruined you? (9.440–41, Fitzgerald trans.)

Each of their lines begins *ê mé tis*, a way of saying, as Fitzgerald renders the change from one form of the negative (*ou*) to the other (*me*), "surely no one . . ." He also has Polyphemus say "Nohbdy" three times rather than just once, to make sure we get the joke: "Nohbdy (*Oûtis*), Nohbdy's tricked me, Nohbdy's ruined me!" (9.443). And the other Cyclopes reply, using their pronoun *mé tis*, so that their words and Polyphemus's word *Oûtis* cross each other in mutual incomprehension:

> "Ah well, if nobody has played you foul
> there in your lonely bed, we are no use in pain
> given by great Zeus. Let it be your father,
> Poseidon Lord, to whom you pray." So saying
> they trailed away. (9.447–51)

Since at this point in the *Odyssey* (books 9–12) Odysseus is telling his host Alcinous and the Phaeacian court a story about his own wit and resourcefulness, he does not hesitate to pay himself a compliment, in the course of which he introduces yet another word play on "nobody."

> And I was filled with laughter
> to see how like a charm the name deceived them. (9.451–52, Fitzgerald
> trans.)

"How like a charm" is Fitzgerald's way of rendering *mêtis*; Robert Fagles is more literal and instead of making a joke, he explains it.

> They lumbered off, but laughter filled my heart
> to think how nobody's name—my great cunning stroke—
> had duped them one and all. (9.461–63, Fagles trans.)[52]

Mêtis is "cunning," "wit," the attribute that is most distinctive about the hero who is *polytropos*, the man of many twists and turns, much traveled, versatile—all qualities much esteemed in ancient Greek culture and the African and African American worlds of Eshu-Elegbara and the Signifying Monkey.[53]

Ellison did not have Fitzgerald to work with (he is still regarded as one of the best of contemporary *Odyssey* translators in English), but even the literal 1919 Loeb version isn't too bad for this famous joke ("NoMan" vs. "no man"). It all begins when a man dressed in black (a psychiatrist, we assume) scribbles something on a card and holds it up:

WHAT IS YOUR NAME? A tremor shook me; it was as though he had suddenly given a name to, had organized the vagueness that drifted through my head, and I was overcome with swift shame. I realized that I no longer knew my own name. (239)

This is a complete inversion of what happens in the *Odyssey*. There Odysseus and his audience know his identity, here the cyclopean characters already know the name and are just trying to find out if their patient can remember it. Repeated attempts to get Invisible Man to remember all fail.

WHAT . . . IS . . . YOUR . . . NAME?

WHO . . . ARE . . . YOU?

WHAT IS YOUR MOTHER'S NAME?

Invisible Man's wit comes back to him before his name or speech can, triggered by the doctor's oblivious use of a phrase impossible to utter in African America without suggesting an insult.

WHO WAS YOUR MOTHER? I looked at him, feeling a quick dislike and thinking, half in amusement, I don't play the dozens. And how's *your* old lady today? (241)

A new man writes out a question that fills him with amazement.

WHO WAS BUCKEYE THE RABBIT?

Somehow the memory of his childhood singing and dancing comes back to him.

Buckeye the Rabbit
Shake it, shake it
Buckeye the Rabbit
Break it, break it. . . .
      Yes, I could not bring myself to admit it, it was too ridiculous—and somehow too dangerous. It was annoying that he had hit upon an old identity and I shook my head, seeing him purse his lips and eye me sharply.
      BOY, WHO WAS BRER RABBIT? He was your mother's back-door man, I thought. Anyone knew they were one and the same: "Buckeye" when you were very young and hid yourself behind wide innocent eyes; "Brer," when you were older. (242)

Nothing seems to work, but if Ellison's hero hits rock bottom for the doctors, he gives encouraging signs of not having forgotten his heritage after all. For the moment, though, since he doesn't know who he is, he can't help himself out of the prison he's caught in.

> Whoever else I was, I was no Samson. I had no desire to destroy myself even if it destroyed the machine; I wanted freedom, not destruction. It was exhausting, for no matter what the scheme I conceived, there was one constant flaw—myself. There was no getting around it. I could no more escape than I could think of my identity. Perhaps, I thought, the two things are involved with each other. When I discover who I am, I'll be free. (243)

Finally Invisible is declared cured and is reminded of his name when the director of the hospital mentions it to him.

> "What is your name? Oh here, I have it," he said, studying the chart. And it was as though someone inside of me tried to tell him to be silent, but already he had called my name and I heard myself say, "Oh!" as a pain stabbed through my head and I shot to my feet and looked wildly around me and sat down and got up and down again very fast, remembering. I don't know why I did it, but suddenly I saw him looking at me intently, and I stayed down this time. (245–46)

Hearing his name and learning who he is does lead Invisible Man to freedom from the hospital. But the identity that has been returned to him is not at all the same as Odysseus's final revelation of his identity to the blinded Polyphemus as he sails away. Invisible Man's personality and individuality remain as much a mystery to us as before, because we suspect that even if we knew what else to call him besides the only name we have for him, nothing but an echo of Ellison's title, we would know him no better than before. This is a complication that turns the game of naming and not naming in another direction, at once like and not like Homer's practice in the *Odyssey*—or Dostoevsky's *Notes from Underground*.

Ralph Ellison's *Iliad*

I respected Wright's work and I knew him, but this is not to say that he "influenced" me as significantly as you assume. Consult the text! I *sought out* Wright because I had read Eliot, Pound, Gertrude Stein and Hemingway, and as early as 1940 Wright viewed me as a potential rival, partially, it is true, because he feared I would allow myself to be used against him by political manipulators who were not Negro and who envied and hated him. But perhaps you will understand when I say he did not influence me if I point out that while one can do nothing about choosing one's relatives, one can, as artist, choose one's "ancestors." Wright was, in this sense, a "relative"; Hemingway an "ancestor." Langston Hughes, whose work I knew in grade school and whom I knew before I knew Wright, was a "relative"; Eliot, whom I was to meet only many years later, and Malraux and Dostoyevsky and Faulkner, were "ancestors"—if you please or don't please!

Ralph Ellison, "The World and the Jug" (1964)

Richard Wright died in 1960 at the age of fifty-two. In 1963 the critic Irving Howe published an essay "Black Boys and Native Sons" that responded to James Baldwin's 1949 essay "Everybody's Protest Novel," which had criticized a tradition Baldwin saw in American literature running from *Uncle Tom's Cabin* to Richard Wright's *Native Son*.[54] Baldwin saw Wright fitting into a tradition that purportedly represented the Negro as a victim of society and a potent sexual being, stereotypes that served more to reinforce the status of Negroes in American racist society than to change that status. Howe excused Baldwin's critique in a condescending way, likening it to the usual oedipal father-killing that one would expect from a young writer trying to establish his own reputation. He took Baldwin to task for not continuing in the line of writing that Wright had followed, simply because it made no sense politically for him to do anything else.

If it is true, as Baldwin said in "Everybody's Protest Novel," that "literature and sociology are not one and the same," it is equally true that such statements hardly begin to cope with the problem of how a writer's own experience affects his desire to represent human affairs in a work of fiction. Baldwin's formula evades, through rhetorical sweep, the genuinely difficult issue of the relationship between social experience and literature.

Yet in *Notes of a Native Son*, the book in which his remark appears, Baldwin could also say: "One writes out of one thing only—one's own experience." What, then, was the experience of a man with a black skin, what *could* it be in this country? How could a Negro put pen to paper, how could he so much as think or breathe, without some impulsion to protest, be it harsh or mild, political or private, released or buried? The "sociology" of his existence formed a constant pressure on his literary work, and not merely in the way that might be true for any writer, but with a pain and ferocity that nothing could remove.[55]

Howe saw Wright's fiction (and perforce Baldwin's and Ellison's, if they will do what they ought to do) as being doubly determined, first by the inescapable sociological facts of life in America, and second by the naturalistic tradition exemplified by Theodore Dreiser's *An American Tragedy*. Howe wants to read Ellison by these relevant contexts, and even by his contemporaries, so that Ellison fails to follow Wright's example because he wrote a novel like his Jewish American contemporary Saul Bellow. He singles out one sentence in particular in "Everybody's Protest Novel" as a sign that Baldwin unwittingly marked himself as a writer more typical of midcentury American politics than he realized: "Our burden, our life; we need not battle for it; we need only to do what is infinitely more difficult—that is, accept it.[56] While the major target of Howe's essay was Baldwin's critique of Wright, he also believed that Ellison furthered the line of argument which "Everybody's Protest Novel" had begun.

Howe grudgingly concedes in passing that *Invisible Man* is the only novel thus far published that is equal to *Native Son*. Even so, neither Baldwin nor Ellison did his filial duty when they chose not to follow in Wright's footsteps.

Ellison's response to Howe came quickly in the essay "The World and the Jug," which was published in two parts in late 1963 and early 1964.[57] Throughout it he maintains a much lighter touch than Howe and takes special delight in skewering him with the implication that what the Jewish New York intellectual Howe was actually engaged in was a renewal of the parable in Genesis 9 of Ham, the dishonored son of Noah who was regularly made into the ancestor of the black race because he had seen his father naked and been cursed for it.

In his myth Howe takes the roles of both Shem and Japheth, trying mightily (his face turned backward so as not to see what it is he's veiling) to cover the old man's bare belly, and then becoming Wright's voice from beyond the grave by uttering the curses which Wright was too ironic or too proud to have uttered himself, at least in print. In response to Baldwin and Ellison, Wright would have said (I virtually quote the words he used in talking to me during the summer of 1958) that only through struggle could men with black skins, and for that matter, all the oppressed of the world, achieve their humility [*sic*: Howe's essay says "humanity"]. It was a lesson,

said Wright, with a touch of bitterness yet not without kindness, that the
younger writers would have to learn in their own way and their own time.
All that has happened since bears him out.

What, coming eighteen years after *Native Son* and thirteen years after
World War II, does this rather limp cliché mean? Nor is it clear what is
meant by the last sentence—or is it that today Baldwin has come to out-
Wrighting Richard?[58]

Ellison goes to considerable length to explain patiently how he was able
to write *Invisible Man* without any of the oedipal drama Howe imagines is
crucial to the development of a Negro novelist. He is also good at making
clear the limitations of Howe's mode of criticism; by following sociological categories he produces a kind of criticism whose analytical and scientific results could have been predicted even before a particular work of art
was produced—or afterward, read.

"If such young novelists as Baldwin and Ralph Ellison were able to move
beyond Wright's harsh naturalism toward more supple modes of fiction,
that was only possible because Wright had been there first, courageous
enough to release the full weight of his anger."

It is not for me to judge Wright's courage, but I must ask just why it
was possible for me to write as I write "only" because Wright released
his anger? Can't I be allowed to release my own? What does Howe know
of my acquaintance with violence, or the shape of my courage or the
intensity of my anger? I suggest that my credentials are at least as valid as
Wright's, even though he began writing long before I did, and it is possible
that I have lived through and committed even more violence than he.
Howe must wait for an autobiography to tell us what a Negro is, yet few
wish, even in a joke, to be one. But if you would tell me who I am, at least
take the trouble to discover what I have been.[59]

Wright was no spiritual father of Ellison, and he never claimed to be.
What Ellison points to instead are the writers he mentions in the quotation that begins this section. He makes a fine distinction between the relatives one is born with and the ancestors whom one chooses to follow. It is
in this sense that we can point to an ancestor not of Ellison himself, but of
the novel he created.

For there is a further implication about the Odyssean identity we
have been tracing in *Invisible Man*. Ellison was perfectly correct to resist
Howe's attempt to turn him into a disobedient "son" of Richard Wright,

and to point to the complicated literary and artistic genealogy that he insists was his by choice rather than something assigned by social identity. At the same time, by the very act of creating an Odyssean narrative, he raises the interesting possibility of whether there might be an Iliadic work corresponding to *Invisible Man*; namely, Richard Wright's *Native Son*.[60]

We know enough about the creation of Wright's novel to be certain that he was in no sense either consciously or unconsciously engaged in writing an *Iliad*. On the contrary, we have a good deal of evidence of the careful sociological and historical research he did on juvenile offenders incarcerated in Chicago. He wrote *Native Son* from anything but a classical or mythological perspective.[61]

What Wright created out of his research and experience in Chicago nonetheless gained the concentration of a tragedy whose protagonist lives up to the novelist's claim for him: the son of America, born there and shaped there into the fugitive killer he becomes. *Native Son*'s focus on the fear and rage of Bigger Thomas, with all their consequences, is so concentrated, it deals so directly with the grim realities of living as a Negro in the ghettoized Northern cities after the Great Migration, and its pace is so tightly constructed, that it is very much the opposite of the kind of narrative Ellison would create. Whereas Invisible Man's family is a hazy conception at best, only a grandfather and no one else, as detached from the world he moves in as Odysseus is until he reaches home, Bigger Thomas is completely bound up in his family in a way that parallels the family relationships of Achilles.

The most compelling parallels come in the first book of *Native Son*, "Fear." This emotional state and its attendant counterstate, rage, may be compared with the emotional states of Achilles in the *Iliad* and his relationships with others like Agamemnon, the first target of his irrepressible rage. If we compare the genealogy of Bigger Thomas and Achilles, with their powerful mothers and absent fathers, we can see a genealogy of two fractured families.

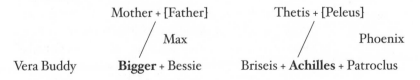

With their self-esteem and conception of themselves reliant more on interaction with peers than with family groups, much of the work that a Greek or African American father does to mold a son's identity is missing, and the interaction between mother and son, correspondingly more intense. Putting Achilles on the shrink's couch alongside Bigger, we can see how the combination of a hovering mother and an absent father could complicate their lives in particularly nasty ways. Homer's godlike, mortal hero has more than a little affinity with Wright's Bigger Thomas.

It adds much to the power of Homer's portrait of Thetis that she behaves in ways that resonate with what a mortal mother could be expected to do. Both Bigger's mother and Achilles' immortal mother Thetis see clearly the danger their sons are in and their probable doom if they persist. For Achilles, it is a matter of destiny; for Bigger, a matter of probability. Father substitutes like Bigger's defense attorney Max and Achilles' old tutor Phoenix are more palliative than substantial substitutes for their fathers. Both Bigger and Achilles are the bane of even their friends' existence; their progressive isolation renders concubines like Bessie and Briseis mere status symbols for whom they feel no real love at all, and they manage to destroy even those who counted as more to them than their family members did, Bigger brutally murdering Bessie, Achilles in effect sending Patroclus out to do his fighting—and dying—for him. Faced with this likely outcome, their mothers are unable to do anything but remind them of the truth of their existence and their destiny.

> She left Vera on the bed and turned a pair of cold eyes upon Bigger . . .
> "Bigger, honest, you the most no-countest man I ever seen in all my life!"
> "You done told me that a thousand times," he said, not looking round.
> "Well, I'm telling you agin! And mark my word, some of these days you going to set down and *cry*. Some of these days you going to wish you had made something out of yourself, instead of just a tramp. But it'll be too late then."
> "Stop prophesying about me," he said.
> "I prophesy much as I please! And if you don't like it, you can get out. We can get along without you. We can live in one room just like we living now, even with you gone," she said.
> "Aw, for Chrissakes!" he said, his voice filled with nervous irritation.
> "You'll regret how you living some day," she went on. "If you don't stop running with that gang of yours and do right you'll end up where you never thought you would. You think I don't know what you boys is doing, but I do. And the gallows is at the end of the road you traveling, boy. Just remember that." (*Native Son*, 9)

It is not so much a literary affiliation that brings the contemporary black mother and her renegade teenage son together with the divine goddess and her son, as a cultural, even biological, similarity of a mother grieving for a child she knows she is already lost.

> Thetis answered him then letting the tears fall: "Ah me,
> my child. Your birth was bitterness. Why did I raise you?
> If only you could sit by your ships untroubled, not weeping,
> since indeed your lifetime is to be short, of no length.
> Now it has befallen that your life must be brief and bitter
> beyond all men's. To a bad destiny I bore you in my chambers. (*Iliad*
>   1:413–18, Lattimore trans.)

Both Bigger and Achilles are incapable of changing in any way, for both are too far into their alienation and rage to do anything else; this does not mean that they cannot take in what they hear and know themselves. Bigger sees a destined violent end looming with greater and greater clarity and inevitability as his day advances toward the time for his appointment for an interview with the Daltons. Bigger's intuition about his fate grows increasingly stronger.

> "Every time I think about it I feel like somebody's poking a red-hot iron down my throat. Goddammit, look! We live here and they live there. We black and they white. They got things and we ain't. They do things and we can't. It's just like living in Jail. Half the time I feel like I'm on the outside of the world peeping in through a knothole in the fence . . ."
>   "Aw, ain't no use feeling that way about it. It don't help none," Gus said.
>   "You know one thing?" Bigger said.
>   "What?"
>   "Sometimes I feel like something awful's going to happen to me." Bigger spoke with a tinge of bitter pride in his voice.
>   "What you mean?" Gus asked, looking at him quickly. There was fear in Gus's eyes.
>   "I don't know. I just feel that way. Every time I get to thinking about me being black and they being white, me being here and they being there, I feel something awful's going to happen to me . . ." (*Native Son*, 21)

Achilles has equal clarity about his destiny because of the foreknowledge of his mother Thetis. We know as much from what she says to him, and from what she says to Zeus when she asks him to intervene in the war to punish the Greeks for the dishonor Achilles suffered at the hands of Agamemnon.

> Mother tells me,
> the immortal goddess Thetis with her glistening feet,
> that two fates bear me on to the day of death.
> If I hold out here and I lay siege to Troy,
> my journey home is gone, but my glory never dies.
> If I voyage back to the fatherland I love,
> my pride, my glory dies . . .
> true, but the life that's left me will be long.
> The stroke of death will not come on me quickly. (*Iliad* 9.497–505, Fagles
>   trans.)

So far the role of mothers and sons in the family drama seems plausible.

Mênin, the opening word of the *Iliad* that English customarily translates as "anger" and more lately "rage" (the more exalted "wrath" worked fine for Alexander Pope but is now archaic for contemporary ears), has a much broader semantic range than any single word we can use to translate it. The Homeric linguist Leonard Muellner devotes a entire book to the word, pointing out that it extends to the cosmic status of the gods and to the most far-reaching implications for social order.[62] The theme of the opening book of *Native Son* is not "rage" or "anger," however we wish to relate such modern social-specific concepts of the emotions to a far different and in ways quite alien concept of Homer's word *mênis* ("anger," "rage" as experienced and worked out by immortal gods and Achilles). It is "Fear." But Wright is being analytical about the psychology of violence; fear and dread are the antecedent emotions of a rage to destroy and to kill, because what we hate and rage against is very often what we most fear.

The opening scene of *Native Son* shows how intimately connected fear and rage are. "*Brrrrrriiiiiiiiiiiiiiiiinng!*" The opening word of *Native Son* is as much a concentrated expression of the narrative that will unfold as the *Iliad*'s "anger," *mênin*, in the ring of an alarm clock, which Arnold Rampersad uses to introduce an essay on Wright's novel: "The sound of the alarm that opens *Native Son* was Richard Wright's urgent call in 1940 to America to awaken from its self-induced slumber about the reality of race relations in the nation."[63] The alarm clock starts a narrative that is scrupulously calibrated to the hours of the long day that will end with the killing of Mary Dalton and the beheading and burning of her body in the furnace of her parents' house. The fear of Bigger's mother and sister gradually becomes visible: the huge black rat that squeals and leaps at Bigger's trouser leg and snags it in his teeth. Both human beings and rat are suffused with fear and a murderous rage, the commonplace murderousness of a cornered rat becomes literal fact, and it is hard to say who is more scared, or more filled with the desire to kill, the man or the animal. The cornered black rat acts out the role that Bigger himself will play by the end of book 1. It is a battle as deadly as any duel of warriors on a battlefield. Both Bigger and the rat show their teeth.

"Goddamn!" Bigger whispered fiercely, whirling and kicking out his leg with all the strength of his body. The force of his movement shook the rat loose and it sailed through the air and struck a wall. Instantly, it rolled over and leaped again. Bigger dodged and the rat landed against a table leg. With clenched teeth, Bigger held the skillet; he was afraid to hurl it, fearing that he might miss. The rat squeaked and turned and ran in a narrow circle, looking for a place to hide; it leaped again past Bigger and scurried on dry rasping feet to one side of the box and then to the other, searching for the hole. Then it turned and reared upon its hind legs.

"Hit 'im, Bigger," Buddy shouted.

"Kill 'im!" the woman screamed.

The rat's belly pulsed with fear. Bigger advanced a step and the rat emitted a long thin song of defiance, its black beady eyes glittering, its tiny forefeet pawing the air restlessly. Bigger swung the skillet; it skidded over the floor, missing the rat, and clattered to a stop against a wall.

"Goddamn!"

The rat leaped. Bigger sprang to one side. The rat stopped under a chair and let out a furious screak. Bigger moved slowly backward toward the door.

"Gimme that skillet, Buddy," he asked quietly, not taking his eyes from the rat.

Buddy extended his hand. Bigger caught the skillet and lifted it high in the air. The rat scuttled across the floor and stopped again at the box and searched quickly for the hole; then it reared once more and bared long yellow fangs, piping shrilly, belly quivering.

Bigger aimed and let the skillet fly with a heavy grunt. There was a shattering of wood as the box caved in. The woman screamed and held her face in her hands. Bigger tiptoed forward and peered.

"I got 'im," he muttered, his clinched teeth bared in a smile. "By God, I got 'im."

He kicked the splintered box out of the way and the flat black body of
the rat lay exposed, its two long yellow tusks showing distinctly. Bigger
took a shoe and pounded the rat's head, crushing it, cursing hysterically:
"You sonofa*bitch*!" (*Native Son*, 6–7)

Degrading as it is, the Battle Royal in the opening chapter of *Invisible
Man* is a violence of a different order: an arena sport staged for drunken
white men who act as if they were gods or heroes watching games in the
Iliad or the *Odyssey*, as blindfolded black youths box and make a blood
sport of it. It is brutal, but stops short of being a battle to the death, as
Bigger's fight is. Bigger triumphs over the rat and destroys his enemy. It is
a battle that his mother and sister watch in horror, and his brother joins
in. The rat prefigures what is going to happen to Bigger himself, in the
eyes of the white world and its conception of any black man as a potential
animal, criminal, in instinct as feral and deadly as the rat, and something
that needs to be exterminated ruthlessly. The three books of *Native Son*
are the alliterative "Fear," "Flight," and "Fate," and Bigger's battle, which is
anything but royal, is fully anticipated in the opening tableau of the novel.
The titles of each of *Native Son*'s three books are an invitation to think
analytically about the particular human drama that unfolds.[64]

In that spirit, we can see that the battle to the death between Bigger
Thomas and the black rat is a literalization of one of the commonest ways
we have of conceiving of anger and violence, through figurative language.
In so many words, Bigger is fighting and destroying a creature which is
a symbolic anticipation of what he will become in the eyes of the white
world: a cornered rat, the native son born and bred by white American
racism. Wright created Bigger out of his researches into teenage prisoners
and a sociological study of the records of criminal violence in Chicago,
and his characteristically ferocious literary device could be glossed by the
work of professional psychologists and sociologists' studies of emotions.
In their project on the cognitive model of anger in American English, for
example, the psychologists George Lakoff and Zoltán Kövecses much
later argued that there is a logic of emotions in which we can detect complex conceptual structures organizing our thinking about anger, and that
much of this thinking is figurative.[65]

It is a very widespread metaphor in Western culture . . . PASSIONS ARE
BEASTS INSIDE A PERSON [capitalization original]. According to this
metaphor, there is a part of each person that is a wild animal. Civilized
people are supposed to keep that part of them private, that is, they are

supposed to keep the animal inside them. In the metaphor, loss of control is equivalent to the animal getting loose. And the behavior of a person who has lost control is the behavior of a wild animal. There are versions of this metaphor for the various passions—desire, anger, and so forth. In the case of anger, the beast presents a danger to other people.[66]

Such is one recent notion, how animalistic qualities are attributed to people who commit violence in a rage.

This conception of a human being as an animal is what American racist society, its newspapers and its police and politicians and prosecutors, all conceive Bigger Thomas to be. But he emphatically does not turn into a beast the way Achilles and Homeric heroes do. When they kill, they are in a rage to do it and take great pleasure in it. For example, Achilles killing Asteropaeus, who vainly tries to wrench Achilles' spear out of a river bank:

Three times he tried to wrench it free, tugging madly,
thrice gave up the struggle—the fourth with all his might
he fought to bend Aeacides' [sc. Achilles'] shaft and break it off
but before it budged the hero was all over him,
slashing out his life, slitting his belly open—
a scooping slice at the navel and all his bowels
spilled out on the ground, darkness swirled his eyes
as he gasped his breath away. And trampling his chest
Achilles tore his gear off, glorying over him now:
"Lie there with the dead! Punishing work, you see,
to fight the sons of invincible Cronus' son,
even sprung from a river as you are!" (*Iliad* 21.199–210, Fagles trans.)

Bigger can take this kind of delight in violence, as in his total humiliation of his friend Gus in a pool hall.

His face softened a bit and the hard glint in his bloodshot eyes died. But he still knelt with the open knife. Then he stood.

"Get up!" he said.

"Please, Bigger!"

"You want me to slice you?"

He stooped again and placed the knife at Gus's throat. Gus did not move and his large black eyes looked pleadingly. Bigger was not satisfied; he felt his muscles tightening again.

"Get up! I ain't going to ask you no more!"

Slowly, Gus stood. Bigger held the open blade an inch from Gus's lips.

"Lick it," Bigger said, his body tingling with elation.

Gus's eyes filled with tears.

"Lick it, I said! You think I'm playing?"

Gus looked round the room without moving his head, just rolling his eyes in a mute appeal for help. But no one moved. Bigger's left fist was slowly lifting to strike. Gus's lips moved toward the knife; he stuck out his tongue and touched the blade. Gus's lips quivered and tears streamed down his cheeks. (38–39)

But when it comes to the actual killing of Mary Dalton and Bessie, Bigger is no cornered rat at all, but a man consumed by fear. There is no anger in either scene. The murder of Bessie in book 2 has more calculation and is drawn out longer, the worst thing about it being Bigger's realization that he cannot afford to risk a gunshot and that he will have to bash her head in with a brick, in the dark. It is not rage, but book 2's Fate that seems to be driving him—a cornered rat, perhaps, but one with a conscience.

He was rigid; not moving. This was the way it *had* to be. Then he took a deep breath and his hand gripped the brick and shot upward and paused a second and then plunged downward through the darkness to the accompaniment of a deep short grunt from his chest and landed with a thud. Yes! There was a dull gasp of surprise, then a moan. No, that must not be! He lifted the brick again and again, until in falling it struck a sodden mass that gave softly but tautly to each landing blow. Soon he seemed to be striking a wet wad of cotton, of some damp substance whose only life was the jarring of the brick's impact. (237)

The fear of being caught and the necessity of murder work a transformation in Bigger Thomas that he will not be able to begin to articulate until the end of the novel, in his last meeting with his lawyer Max. But at this point it becomes clear how fear is the basis of anger and violence, and we begin to learn how they are deeply related to his sense of self and an identity that brought him such misery.

So close had danger and death come that he could not feel that it was he who had undergone it all. And yet, out of it all, over and above all that had happened, impalpable but real, there remained to him a queer sense of power. *He* had done this. *He* had brought all this about. In all of his life these two murders were the most meaningful things that had ever happened to him. He was living, truly and deeply, no matter what others might think, looking at him with their blind eyes. Never had he had the chance to live out the consequences of his actions; never had his will been so free as in this night and day of fear and murder and flight. (239)

Just as we can see the beginnings of the *Odyssey*, the survivor's poem, in the tragedy of victims of Achilles' anger and the deaths of Patroclus, Hector, and Achilles himself, so can we see the seeds of what would become Ralph Ellison's Odyssean answer to the blindness of the Daltons, who pretend there is no distinction between black and white, and the wider Daltonism of racist America.[67]

Irving Howe's complaint about Baldwin's and particularly Ellison's failure to continue in the mode of *Native Son* thus makes no more sense for *Invisible Man* than it would to object that the *Odyssey* does not continue the *Iliad* as an *Iliad*. Howe could not see what readers of the *Iliad* have had to confront since the Greeks themselves: like the *Iliad*, *Native Son* is a story that cannot be repeated; it comes to its end as surely as Priam and Troy and Achilles soon will. In an obvious mythological sense the *Odyssey* continues the *Iliad*, in that it picks up the story of what happens after Troy is gone, but its poetic vision is profoundly different—as different, say, as the difference between tragedy and comedy, of which the *Iliad* and *Odyssey* are sometimes taken to be the prototypes. As Invisible Man observes at the end of the epilogue,

> Even hibernations can be overdone, come to think of it. Perhaps that's my greatest social crime, I've overstayed my hibernation, since there's a possibility that even an invisible man has a socially responsible role to play. (*Invisible Man*, 581)

Stripped of delusions, this is a survivor's voice, the words of a man ready to continue. The contrast between this and the discoveries of Bigger Thomas is extreme.

> He had killed twice, but in a true sense it was not the first time he had ever killed. He had killed many times before, but only during the last two days had this impulse assumed the form of actual killing. Blind anger had come often and he had either gone behind his curtain or wall, or had quarreled and fought. And yet, whether in running away or in fighting, he had felt the need of the clean satisfaction of facing this thing in all its fullness,

of fighting it out in the wind and sunlight, in front of those whose hate for him was so unfathomably deep that, after they had shunted him off into a corner of the city to rot and die, they could turn to him, as Mary had that night in the car, and say: "I'd like to know how your people live." (*Native Son*, 240)

At the end of book 3 ("Fate"), Bigger will finally manage to articulate what he has learned and gained from the murders of Mary and Bessie and his own approaching execution. In their final moments together, his lawyer Max has tried all the platitudes at his command, including direct reminders to Bigger that he is going to die and to adjust himself to what is unavoidable, to have confidence that his life has its meaning in the larger realm of politics, which has a higher significance than any individual life. These consoling words are platitudinous and meaningless to Bigger. He finally moves beyond anything Max can think of think to say, and what he says is terrifying.

> "I didn't want to kill!" Bigger shouted. "But what I killed for, I *am*! It must've been pretty deep in me to make me kill! I must have felt it awful hard to murder . . ."
> Max lifted his hand to touch Bigger, but did not.
> "No, no; no . . . Bigger, not that . . ." Max pleaded despairingly.
> "What I killed for must've been good!" Bigger's voice was full of frenzied anguish. "It must have been good! When a man kills, it's for something . . . I didn't know I was really alive in this world until I felt things hard enough to kill for 'em. . . . It's the truth, Mr. Max. I can say it now, 'cause I'm going to die. I know what I'm saying real good and I know how it sounds. But I'm all right. I feel all right when I look at it that way."
> Max's eyes were full of terror. Several times his body moved nervously, as though he were about to go to Bigger; but he stood still.
> "I'm all right, Mr. Max. Just go and tell Ma I was all right and not to worry none, see? Tell her I was all right and wasn't crying none . . ." (429)

"But what I killed for, I *am*": this is the essential meaning of the words that Wright chose for his title: grown and raised in this soil, and the child of everyone of that soil. Bigger knows himself precisely, and no one else, not Max or his mother, can face it.[68]

In this way *Native Son* can be read as an African American *Iliad* to Ralph Ellison's *Odyssey*. There can be comic moments at any turn in *Invisible Man*, as there never can be in *Native Son*; for example, when invisible man is buying buttered yams from a yam seller in Harlem.

> "Sho, that way you can get the most out of 'em. Yessuh," he said, handing over the yams, "I can see you one of these old-fashioned yam eaters."
> "They're my birthmark," I said. "I yam what I am." (*Invisible Man*, 266)

If the cartoon hero Popeye the Sailor Man seems an incongruous allusion, it is no more bizarre a reference than the one Odysseus uses to preface one of his many elaborate lies in the *Odyssey,* by echoing verbatim the famous words Achilles had spoken to Odysseus himself in book 9 of the *Iliad*, when Achilles rejects the first and most devious of Agamemnon's ambassadors with the back of his rhetorical hand.

> I hate that man like the very Gates of Death
> who says one thing but hides another in his heart. (*Iliad* 9.378–79, Fagles
>   trans.)

The poet crafting the *Odyssey* into shape has a fine sense of humor and might expect the more intelligent and sophisticated members of his audience to pick up on the allusion. Or maybe Odysseus himself just thinks it would be a great line to recycle for the audience he's telling the story to. In any case, when Achilles' shade appears to Odysseus from the world of the dead, he entertains no such fondness for the glorious death in battle which has brought him fame, even though he characteristically hopes for just as much for his son Neoptolemus.

> Let me hear no smooth talk
> of death from you, Odysseus, light of councils.
> Better, I say, to break sod as a farm hand
> for some poor country man, on iron rations,
> than lord it over all the exhausted dead.
> Tell me, what news of the prince my son: did he
> come after me to make a name in battle
> or could it be he did not? (*Odyssey* 9:577–84, Fitzgerald trans.)

The world of the *Iliad* is as dead to this new world of the *Odyssey* as Achilles himself, and the same might be said of Richard Wright's *Native Son* and its hero Bigger Thomas in relation to *Invisible Man*. Ellison's achievement was not to write an answer to Wright's novel, but rather to create a novel that is impossible to read without thinking of *Native Son* as its great predecessor text. We see the same thing in the *Odyssey*, the survivor's poem and sequel to the *Iliad*. Such authorial conversations should not be mistaken for something as trivial as rivalry.

The Pindar of Harlem

Seeing how a Pindaric ode makes sense from beginning to end is the
hardest thing for a modern reader. Nothing in a Pindaric ode seems
to conform to our notions of logic or of what to expect.

Frank J. Nisetich, *Pindar's Victory Songs*

Melvin Beaunorus Tolson was born in Moberly, Missouri, in 1898 and attended high school in Kansas City, graduating in 1919. He began college at
Fisk University in Nashville but transferred to Lincoln University in Pennsylvania, where he received his degree in 1924. He moved that same year to
the faculty of Wiley College in Marshall, Texas, taking up an appointment
as professor of literature, and was soon celebrated for his brilliant teaching and witty mind. He was a trade unionist and much engaged in political life in deeply segregated East Texas. Among his most famous students
was James Farmer, the future civil rights activist and ally of Dr. Martin
Luther King. He won a Rockefeller Foundation fellowship to study for
his MA at Columbia University and in the course of the academic year
1930–1931 did much of the research for his thesis on the Harlem Renaissance, many of whose well-known figures he also got to know. Tolson was
in no particular hurry to finish the thesis, since it always provided a good
excuse to get back to New York, but he finally did so in 1941 because Wiley
was under review for accreditation and the college's president thought it
would look better to have some faculty with advanced degrees. As it was,

Tolson's thesis was the first and for a long time the only historical and critical account of that renaissance. (*The Harlem Group of Negro Writers* was not
published until 2001, by the Greenwood Press.) As Tolson's own career attests, the Harlem Renaissance was not confined to Harlem.

A follower of the charismatic Greek-Armenian mystic G. I. Gurdjieff,
Tolson brought that guru's gospel of spiritual awareness and vitality to the
classroom as well as to his coaching of the college's award-winning debating team. He later wrote a column, "Caviar and Cabbage," for the African
American national newspaper *Washington Tribune* based in Washington,
D.C. In 1935 his Wiley team defeated the University of Southern California in a national competition. This great achievement of Tolson and his
students, as well as a sharp portrait of what it was like to be a highly educated and politically aware African American in segregationist East Texas,
was made into a movie in 2007. *The Great Debaters* was directed by Denzel
Washington, with Washington himself playing Melvin B. Tolson, and while
the film is a slightly romanticized version of history—the great victory is
won over Harvard instead of USC—it does bring out a side of Tolson's life
that this focus on his poetry does not.

The Lincoln University connection worked very well for Tolson throughout his later career. Langston Hughes studied there and became a life-long
friend, and it was through another classmate who became president of the
university and through Lincoln's historic ties with Liberia that Tolson was
appointed poet laureate of Liberia in 1947. In that same year he moved to
Langston University in Oklahoma, where he remained for the rest of his
career, being elected three times mayor of the town. Among his students
there was Nathan Hare, the future founder of the journal the *Black Scholar*
and one of the major figures in the development of ethnic studies during
the civil rights revolution of the 1960s and afterward. Tolson's *Libretto for
the Republic of Liberia* finally appeared in 1953, to great critical acclaim. He
spent much of the rest of his life working on the odes of the *Harlem Gallery*,
and received awards from the White House and from Tuskegee, where he
was appointed Avalon Professor for two years. He published the first book
of the *Gallery* in 1965, as accomplished as the poetry of the *Libretto*, but on
a vaster scale. He died of cancer in 1966 in the middle of his appointment
at Tuskegee, leaving what might have become one of the monumental projects of twentieth-century American poetry unfinished.

For Tolson as poet, the classical parallels are hard to miss. We see him
as the Pindar of Harlem because of his evolution as a poet and critic, because of the circumstances in which he produced his greatest poetry, and
because of the enviable reputation his mature work quickly earned for its

prodigious learning and baffling obscurity. Expert scholars of Pindar have conducted long and vigorous debate on whether his difficulty was intentional or a consequence of his writing in an archaic age which frustrates as much as it fascinates classicists trying to understand it. Some think he did not aspire to be difficult, that it was his later readers and commentators who made him so. Others argue that he demands hard work of anyone who would understand him. His contemporaries thought well enough of him to pay him well for his work, from one end of the Greek-speaking Mediterranean world to the other.

We know far more about Tolson's motives than we can even guess about those of an ancient poet such as Pindar. Being difficult was a reputation Tolson coveted, and not for difficulty as an end in itself. Having begun his career by following much the same path as Countee Cullen and other genteel poets, he had gone on to follow the example of Edgar Lee Masters's *Spoon River Anthology*, substituting African American people and places for Masters's Illinois village people. Then, beginning with his appointment as poet laureate of Liberia to commemorate the centennial of the republic and the ensuing *Libretto for the Republic of Liberia*, in all his later poetry he strove to bring African American literature a new voice by creating verse that was as learned and challenging as anything the American modernists Hart Crane and William Carlos Williams had achieved. His only miscalculation was in his timing: he was approximately one generation too late, publishing his last and greatest work, book 1 of the *Harlem Gallery*, in the same year as the second Fisk University conference and the advent of the Black Arts Movement. It was not a time for learned poets writing in a formalist tradition. One of many admirable things about Tolson is that he realized all this as well as any of his critics did, and then went right ahead, continuing on the increasingly unfashionable course he had chosen.

Sometimes it takes a poet to understand what another poet is doing. Twenty years later Rita Dove would publish a reassessment of *Harlem Gallery* that would mark the beginning of critics' efforts to move his readers beyond the baffled reception that greeted Tolson's last book of poems when it first appeared.

In this chapter we will offer a fairly complete reading of Tolson's complex but manageable *Libretto for the Republic of Liberia* and a briefer look at the last two of the twenty-four odes of *Harlem Gallery*. We originally planned to discuss a dauntingly difficult autobiographical poem published in 1952, "The Man from Halicarnassus." It offers a parallel between Tolson and the historian Herodotus who lived at the margins of a Hellenic civilization.[1] But the effort to explicate it far outweighs the artistic merit of the poem itself. It is so jammed with recondite allusions that their decoding becomes the true theme of "The Man from Halicarnassus," not Herodotus, or even Tolson himself.[2]

Pindar, Tolson, and the Lure of Difficult Poetry

> Sometimes a work of art is bitter crystalline alkaloid
> to be doled out
> at intervals, between the laugh and flout
> of an Admirable Doctor; but, if taken too much
> at a time, it delivers the cocainizing punch
> of a Jack Dempsey nonesuch.
>
> *Harlem Gallery*, "Omega"

Prepared correctly by an expert cook, one of the great delicacies of Japanese cuisine is the puffer fish, fugu (*Fugu rubripes*). With the slightest slip of the chef's knife, however, fugu is also the deadliest thing one can eat. The poison tetrodotoxin in its liver, skin, and other organs is deadlier than cyanide, capable of paralyzing the muscles while the victim stays fully conscious until he or she eventually dies of asphyxiation. Unlucky gourmands have been dispatched slowly and agonizingly, just by ingesting a small piece of improperly prepared puffer fish. The same toxic shock is a familiar characteristic of many first encounters with difficult modernist poets like Eliot and Pound. Yet it was an old recipe the modernists were reviving. Difficult as such poets may be, few have attained the level of exegetical toxicity for which Pindar of Thebes has been famous since antiquity.

To conceive of Melvin Tolson as the Pindar of Harlem is thus not an entirely auspicious claim. Save that he writes in English a good deal of the time—not often enough, in the estimation of his friend Langston Hughes, who found the extensive quotations from many foreign languages, ancient as well as modern, a serious obstacle to understanding—Tolson delighted in being a poetic puffer fish.[3] He can have much the same effect on his readers that Pindar has often had on his. The German classicist Franz Dornseiff described that peculiar effect of what can happen when people start trying to read Pindar in his 1921 book *Pindars Stil*. Even today, most readers feel helpless when they first confront a Pindaric ode, either in translation or the original Greek.[4]

Shock and incomprehension, even total paralysis: these have been common reactions to Pindar since his recovery in the Renaissance, and to date much the same reception has greeted Tolson's last and greatest work. Like Sarah Fabio when confronted with Tolson's *Libretto* or *Harlem Gallery*, many critics of Pindar threw their hands up at him and didn't engage with his poetry at all.[5] When they did, the results were not always positive. Until the critical edition of the German philologist Augustus Boeckh (*Pindari Opera Quae Supersunt*) the poetic form of Pindar's odes and their highly complex systems of strophe, antistrophe, and epode were also not well understood. Pindar seemed to have written the freest of free verse two millennia before its official invention. As the Pindarist David C. Young observes, he was for this and many other reasons widely misunderstood until Boeckh's edition appeared.[6]

Pre-Boeckh Pindar in the earlier modern era was a poet entirely different from the Pindar even later classical antiquity knew. Dryden knew only to employ irregular stanzas for his "Song for St. Cecilia's Day" and "Alexander's Feast" in order to achieve a Pindaric style. As John Hamilton has argued, this misapprehension of Pindar's wild and woolly ways was fostered particularly by Horace's ode "Pindarum quisquis studet aemulari" ("Whoever strives to rival Pindar," *Odes* 4.2), especially its hyperbolic claim that Pindar was "transported in meters free from rules" (*numerisque fertur lege solutis*, lines 11 and 12).[7] As Hamilton observes of the ode, "Not only does it provide a fundamental metaphorical codification of Pindaric genius, but also, and more importantly, it presents many, if not all, of the problems peculiar to the Pindaric tradition. Indeed, the history of Pindar's poetic reception in the West consists of little more than an ever-renewed, ever-reinterpreted use of this single poem."[8]

It is thus worth pausing to gain some sense of how fraught with peril the Pindaric calling could be. The first English poet to compose Pindaric odes was Abraham Cowley (1618–1667), and his incomprehension of Pindar's metrical virtuosity inspired a whole generation of less gifted imitators to try their hand at this ancient form. In his *Lives of the English Poets* (1779–1781) Samuel Johnson found that Cowley and his followers had much to answer for.

> This lax and lawless versification so much concealed the deficiencies
> of the barren, and flattered the laziness of the idle, that it immediately
> overspread our books of poetry; all the boys and girls caught the pleasing
> fashion, and they that could do nothing else could write like Pindar.[9]

Johnson was so fundamentally unsympathetic to the whole enterprise of ambitious, deliberately difficult praise poetry that he found even more fault with Thomas Gray (1716–1771), even though Gray himself could read Pindar in Greek and provided extensive learned notes to his Pindaric ode, "The Progress of Poesy."

> Awake, Aeolian lyre, awake
> And give to rapture all thy trembling strings.
> From Helicon's harmonious springs
> A thousand rills their mazy progress take:
> The laughing flowers, that round them blow,
> Drink life and fragrance as they flow.

If he had lived, Tolson might well have provided notes for his *Gallery* in the same way he already had for the *Libretto*. In their concern not to leave their audiences in the dark, Gray and Tolson are surely kindred spirits, for Gray was no more merely parading his learning than Tolson was. An imperfectly educated critic had assumed that "Aeolian lyre" at the opening of "The Progress of Poesy" referred to Aeolus the wind god rather than the Aeolian mode of Greek music. In his accompanying note for the above opening stanza Gray accordingly felt compelled to cite three different odes of Pindar (*Olympian* 1, *Pythian* 2, and *Nemean* 3) that lay behind his verse, and in a note to line 3 he makes it clear that he is adapting what he understood as Pindar's characteristic poetics to English measures.

> The subject and simile, as usual with Pindar, are united. The various sources of poetry, which gives life and lustre to all it touches, are here described; its quiet majestic progress enriching every subject (otherwise dry and barren) with a pomp of diction and luxuriant harmony of numbers; and its more rapid and irresistible course, when swollen and hurried away by the conflict of tumultuous passions.

The mediating voice of Horace is unmistakable in Gray's note, particularly the second strophe of *Pindarum quisquis studet aemulari*:

> Monte decurrens velut amnis, imbres
> quem super notas aluere ripas,
> fervet immensusque ruit profundo
>   Pindarus ore. (*Odes* 4.2.5–8)

> From the mount descending like a river, which
> the rain has fed over the well-known limits,

he boils and boundless crashes at the mouth
profound, Pindar.[10]

Yet what Johnson criticizes in Gray's odes is identifiably the characteristic
qualities of Pindar that the poet labored so hard to acquire.

> To select a singular event, and swell it to a giant's bulk by fabulous append-
> ages of spectres and predictions, has little difficulty, for he that forsakes
> the probable may always find the marvelous. And it has little use; we are
> affected only as we believe; we are improved only as we find something to
> be imitated or declined. I do not see that The Bard promotes any truth,
> moral or political . . .
> These odes are marked by glittering accumulations of ungraceful
> ornaments; they strike, rather than please; the images are magnified by af-
> fectation; the language is laboured into harshness. The mind of the writer
> seems to work with unnatural violence. Double, double, toil and trouble.
> He has a kind of strutting dignity, and is tall by walking on tiptoe. His art
> and his struggle are too visible, and there is too little appearance of ease
> and nature.[11]

As the later eighteenth- and nineteenth-century Pindaric ode in English
literature evolved into its own English literary tradition (as surveyed by
its historian Paul Fry), its creators gained ever greater confidence and had
less need of apologetics to counter the kind of criticisms Johnson raised.[12]
   As it happens, Tolson could read the right language, so far as the fruits
of Pindaric scholarship in his own day were concerned, in the elegant English of one of the great American classicists of the nineteenth and early
twentieth centuries, one already mentioned in this book, Basil Lanneau
Gildersleeve. In his commentary and Richmond Lattimore's later translation of Pindar we can gain a good sense of how much Pindar was accessible
to Tolson and his generation. It is an open question how closely Tolson
worked with any classicists' accounts of Pindar, since the Pindaric tradition in English, German, and other languages flourished without the need
of their guidance. But many of the same critical and theoretical problems
surface throughout the whole history of Pindar reception, and knowing
something of what the classicists did with such a challenging poet will at
least be consoling and encouraging to those who want to know more about
the poet we have dared to call the Pindar of Harlem.
   Until well into the twentieth century, Pindaric scholarship was almost
exclusively a German business.[13] But the best of all Pindar commentaries

in the late nineteenth century and for much of the first half of the twentieth was published in1890 by the German-trained classicist Gildersleeve
of Johns Hopkins University, and in him Pindar found one of his most
perceptive and sympathetic critics.[14] Recall that in the course of his long
life (1831–1924), the Southerner Gildersleeve fought in the Civil War as an
officer in the Confederate army, went to Göttingen for his PhD, and was
instrumental in the establishment of the first university in America modeled on the German research university.[15] He made no attempt to divide
his scholarly and political lives. As a veteran of the losing side in a civil
war, Gildersleeve could be sympathetic with Pindar, who, as a citizen of
Thebes, one of the Greek cities that "Medized" (i.e., allied itself with the
invading Persians, or Medes), wound up for a time on the wrong side of history. For many Greeks, starting with the Athenians, Pindar's and Thebes's
Medizing constituted a betrayal of democratic ideals not easily forgiven.[16]
But in Gildersleeve's judicious opinion, Thebes's temporary alliance with
Greece's enemies was quite compatible with the ardent Panhellenism that
is manifest throughout the *Odes*.[17] He provides an eloquent argument for
the way poetry such as Pindar's victory odes transcends its particular occasion and the confines of what may at first seem a highly specialized form.
To show that the victory ode is not a narrow art, Gildersleeve resorts to
figurative language as often as Pindar himself. It is not at all the accepted
style of today's classical commentaries, but Gildersleeve was able to be an
exacting philologist and explicator of Pindar's difficult Greek and at the
same time respond to his poetry, as poetry. In his general introduction he
characterizes the Pindaric ode, not by a catalogue or summary, but by swift
images and figurative fancy. The genre of epinician or victory poetry is no
barrier at all to grasping Pindar's greatness.

> There is scope enough for the highest work, as high as the brazen heaven
> not to be climbed of men, deep as the hell in which "yon people" bear
> toil and anguish not be looked at with mortal eye, broad as the family, the
> house, the race, mankind. And yet the poetry of Pindar does not lose it-
> self in generalities. He compares his song to a bee that hastes from flower
> to flower, but the bee has a hive. He compares his song to a ship, but the
> ship has a freight and a port. His song does not fly on and on like a bird
> of passage. Its flight is the flight of an eagle, to which it has so often been
> likened, circling the heavens, it is true, stirring the ether, but there is a
> point on which the eye is bent, a mark, as he says, at which the arrow is
> aimed.[18]

As both pedagogue and commentator Gildersleeve compares very well with Richmond Lattimore and his 1947 translation of Pindar—even though the passage of not much more than fifty years of American classicism makes them seem to inhabit different planets.

Lattimore was a gifted poet as well as a superb Hellenist (his 1951 translation of the *Iliad* set the standard for American classics translations for several generations of students and is still widely used today), but in the intervening years the more austere approach of British classicism as well as German philology was also leading classicists and translators away from the abundance of Gildersleeve to a less florid style. Lattimore's translation of *Olympian* 1 is comparably austere, so exact and word-for-word that it can help beginners in Pindar construe his Greek.

> Best of all things is water; but gold, like a gleaming fire
> by night, outshines all pride of wealth beside.
> But, my heart, would you chant the glory of games,
> look never beyond the sun
> by day for any star shining brighter through the deserted air,
> nor any contest than Olympia greater to sing.

This was the matrix of Pindar that Tolson had available to him as he worked on the *Gallery* and other poems up to its publication in 1965: a great commentary, and a new translation by one of the best translators of Greek in America. And it amounts to only a fraction of what Tolson pours into the Pindaric odes of the *Gallery*.

In her essay on Tolson's art in his last work, Rita Dove explains that Tolson's baroque surface in fact closely mirrors black street speech. His form and his difficulty may be recognizably Pindaric, as we argue, but his language is entirely his own.

> Tolson's virtuoso use of folk talk and street jive was forgotten whenever the reader stumbled across more "literary" allusions like "a mute swan not at Coole." In the controversy over racial loyalties and author's intent, nobody bothered to read *Harlem Gallery* on its own terms. The poem—and the story it tries to tell—got lost in the crossfire.[19]

In a further departure from all the strands we know of the various Pindaric traditions—which in any case are often far removed from the poetry of Pindar himself—Tolson peoples the *Gallery* with several characters whose stories as artists get told in the course of it, so that it reads at once as a set of lyric odes and a portrait of the lives of those who people the *Gallery*. Indeed *Harlem Gallery* can be read simply as a recognizable variation, or recollection, of traditions firmly rooted in African and African American oral traditions, as Dove explains, above all of toasts such as Shine and Staggolee. As for classical connections, she cites Geneva Smitherman's comment on this tradition in her 1977 book *Toastin' and Signifyin'*, where she draws a parallel to Greek and Roman epic poetry.

> Toasts represent a form of black verbal art requiring memory and linguistic fluency from the narrators. Akin to grand epics in the Greco Roman style, the movement of the Toast is episodic, lengthy and detailed. Since the overall structure is lengthy and episodic, there is both room and necessity for individual rhetorical embellishments and fresh imaginative imagery. . . . The material is simply an extension of black folk narrative in the oral tradition.[20]

Harlem Gallery pushes to the limits the potential of classical hybridity, but in its sheer difficulty, in its paralyzing and intricate art, it is Pindar that Tolson comes the closest to being, an identification that as we shall see is not the easiest role for a poet to play.

The Odes of the *Libretto for the Republic of Liberia*

> Hired to celebrate a particular victory for a specific patron, Pindar nonetheless devised a poetics that exceeded and therefore freed him from the given occasion. According to the popular representations of the day, he was a poet who barely kept to the matter for which he was engaged. Following nothing but his own genius, he allowed his verse to go wherever it willed, indifferent to the expectations of his benefactors.
>
> John T. Hamilton, *Soliciting Darkness*

In this reading of the *Libretto* we shall trace some important connections between Tolson and the traditions of the English Pindaric ode. Occasionally we will suggest some parallels with the poetry of Pindar himself, even when the likelihood is not great that Tolson would have taken much account of his verse as it was commonly known in the 1940s and 1950s.

More than any classical model, anyone coming to Tolson for the first time should keep the sight and sound of the odes of the *Libretto* and the

Gallery uppermost in mind. This reflects our experience, at least, that aesthetic experience should always be the first thing to seek in even the most difficult poetry—perhaps nowhere more so than there. There is a performative and social dimension to even the most difficult art which argues against the idea that it only can be grasped by first engaging in elaborate study, explication, or theoretical preparation. The civic choreography of public dance is as central to traditional African ritual and celebration as it was to the *choreia* of ancient Greece, and in various new forms it continues in communities throughout the African diaspora. Pindar is undoubtedly a difficult, challenging poet, but it's wise to keep in mind that he enjoyed widespread fame and employment throughout the Greek world, however difficult he now may be. Alban Berg makes the same point about his astoundingly complex 1925 opera *Wozzeck*: you could study the score and its intricacies, but what he recommended above all was that his audiences put all that learning aside and simply watch and listen to *Wozzeck* as a piece of theater and opera like any other.

In the conventions of modern printing, by contrast, the visual dimension of poetic song is expressed not by choreography but by the shape of a printed, silent stanza—literally the Italian for a "stopping place" or "room" created by four or more lines that structure a poem. With its strophes and antistrophes Greek choral lyric actually has more in common with African dance than it has with our modern printed page; *strophê* (literally "turn") and *antistrophê* ("counterturn") describe verse conceived as movement through time and space. One of the consequences of trusting in performance is that what seem to be problematic or even incomprehensible sections of the *Libretto* such as "Ti" or "Do" may not loom so large in a performative context as they do in the modern convention of silent reading and critical commentary.[21] A recitation of the *Libretto* takes from forty-five minutes to as much as an hour, depending on the reader, the space, and the audience. This does not allow for time to flip back and forth to Tolson's extensive endnotes, and footnotes would seem by definition unperformable. In fact Tolson's are often extremely amusing and, like Eliot's notes to *The Waste Land*, frequently a spoof of scholarly display—unless you attempt to take them all seriously. As the *Libretto*'s earliest reviews suggest, then they can be anything but amusing.[22] Some years ago Deborah Warner and Fiona Shaw made an effective theater piece of one of the important models for the *Libretto*, T. S. Eliot's *Waste Land*, and Shaw's performance worked quite well without footnotes.

In the first edition of 1953 the *Libretto* runs to twenty-nine pages of text, followed by sixteen pages of dense endnotes.[23] In them Tolson quotes or

cites over 230 literary, historical, sociological, political, religious, and scientific authors or works. Like Eliot, he sometimes raises a point, or even
makes jokes that take us far beyond the clarification we are schooled to look
for in a commentary. All of this appears to have been integral to the *Libretto*
from the start.[24] Not a few serve to obscure something we thought we had
understood, and Tolson doesn't hesitate to add references that would have
been more at home in his newspaper column "Caviar and Cabbage" than
in a volume of poetry.[25] Luckily for his readers, Tolson was a witty man and
did not compartmentalize his life and art in such a tidy fashion.

"Do"

> *Liberia?*
> No micro-footnote in a bunioned book
>   Homed by a pedant
>   With a gelded look.

It is hard to convey all that Tolson may be expressing in this italicized
opening question. At the very least the tone seems incredulous. The Great
Seal of Liberia bears the motto "The Love of Liberty Brought Us Here,"
but much of the history of the country has been of an ideal never attained.
Tolson begins the *Libretto* with just this cognitive dissonance, as if this African "Freedom's Land" were a contradiction in terms. Many of the books
about Liberia have the same dissonance Tolson hears in the very name of
Liberia, as in John-Peter Pham's 2004 book that traces the history of the
country and its ideals from its founding to the present day: *Liberia: Portrait
of a Failed State*. Liberia did not live up to its name, and Tolson's vehement
opening reflects this history.

Tolson received his commission in 1947 as part of the commemoration
of the centennial of Liberia's independence in 1847. His connections to
Lincoln University and its president helped him win this honor. More recently famous as the custodial institution of the Barnes Foundation and
its great collection of French painting, Lincoln traces its origins back to
Jehudi Ashmun and the American Colonization Society during the administration of president James Monroe; hence Liberia's capital named in his
honor, Monrovia. Tolson's entire engagement with Liberia took place under the presidency of William V. S. Tubman (1895–1971). Tubman's grandparents Sylvia and William Shadrach Tubman came from Georgia as the
freed slaves of Richard Tubman, and it was from these Americo-Liberian

ancestors that his position in the ruling elite of Liberia was secured. Tubman and his regime were improbable patrons for anyone's art, least of all
such an irreverent writer and poet as Tolson. It is likely neither Tubman
nor his advisors read a word of Tolson before they appointed him. Tubman ruled longer than any other leader of Liberia, serving in the office
of president from 1944 until his death in 1971. He expanded the rights of
the native peoples of the country, permitting some to join the Americo-
Liberian elite in government, and one of his most notable achievements
was extending suffrage to women at the beginning of his term.

But the achievements of Tubman were counterbalanced by his corruption of the Liberian Constitution, which had been closely modeled on the
American Constitution and then morphed over the years into an instrument for elite authoritarian rule. At barely 2 percent of the total population, this ruling class was a tiny minority compared to the ratio between
slave-owning whites and slaves in the American South at the time of the
Civil War. As a member of the Liberian Supreme Court in 1935, Tubman
proposed an amendment to limit the term of a president to one term of
eight years, without possibility of a consecutive second term; this sounds
liberal, but in fact he was just planning ahead. Four years after he became
president, he proposed an amendment which was passed in 1949, with all
the twists and contradictions of language needed to serve the ambition
of one man. No president was supposed to be elected to a second term,
the amendment said, then thoughtfully continued by spelling out what
the government of Liberia should do, if a first-term president *were* elected
for a second term after all.[26] An effective state security service guaranteed
that most political and intellectual opposition to Tubman's hegemony
would be thwarted. Perhaps it was just as well that the poet laureate for
Liberia was ensconced thousands of miles away at Langston University in
Oklahoma, since as an anti-Tubman biographer Tuan Wreh observes, "Intellectuals, the critically inclined, and a large body of the educated elite of
ethnic background were systematically excluded from his government."[27]
But perhaps Tolson would have been in no danger anyway. As if guided by
the spirit of Pindar himself, Tolson would create a poetic tribute to Liberia so sophisticated, and so demanding, that it outstripped the abilities
of most contemporary critics and readers in America, to say nothing of
what Tubman and his censors were used to in their monitoring of Liberia's
intellectual elite.

Considering the political and historical problems involved in celebrat-
ing Liberian independence, there are then good reasons for the incredulous opening "*Liberia?*" But there is an even deeper reason in the tradition

of English Pindaric odes for this kind of surprising opening. Tolson's *"Liberia?"* is a twist characteristic of the Pindaric tradition that effectively shoves aside all these political traps. As Paul Fry points out, most such odes up to the time of Keats "have a steady negative pull that alternately releases and retards the sublimation of flight."[28] While we have to keep clear the distinction between Pindar and the long tradition that developed in modern Europe invoking his name, this is one aspect of his art that he shares with his successors. Pindar brings a dialectical imagination to his victory odes, often beginning by questioning his theme, even for some time seeming to turn away from it. The most famous of all his opening lines, the first of the *Olympian Odes*, begins with an enigmatic move whose full significance will not be grasped until the ode's ending. Hieron of Syracuse is celebrated for his victory in the race for a single horse (476 BCE), and to celebrate this event and athlete Pindar begins with water and fire.

> Water is preeminent and gold, like a fire   *Turn 1*
>   burning in the night, outshines
> all possessions that magnify men's pride.
>   But if, my soul, you yearn
>   to celebrate great games,
>   look no further
>   for another star
> shining through the deserted ether
> brighter than the sun, or for a contest
> mightier than Olympia—
>   where the song
> has taken its coronal
> design of glory, plaited
> in the minds of poets
>   as they come, calling on Zeus' name,
>   to the rich radiant hall of Hieron
> who wields the scepter of justice in Sicily,   *Counterturn 1*
>   reaping the prime of every distinction. (Nisetich trans.)

The opening releases the song into an upward flight and makes the first appearance of Hieron's name all the more impressive for being in such company of "the best." At the same time, this opening poses a question about Hieron that will require elaboration if the transition from water and gold to great games and their victors is to be fully understood. A hierarchy of value has been established, and it remains to be seen how Hieron and his victory will fit into it, even if the poet's soul yearns to celebrate them. The opening lines establish an opposition of similarity and dissimilarity, as Hamilton observes.[29]

We can observe the same kind of process in the English Pindaric tradition. A negative pull follows the opening of Wordsworth's *Intimations Ode* (1802–1804), which begins with an upward soaring toward recollections of what existed before our birth, then is quickly pulled down by present reality.

> There was a time when meadow, grove and stream,
> The earth, and every common sight,
>   To me did seem
> Apparalled in celestial light,
>   The glory and the freshness of a dream.   5
> It is not now as it hath been of yore;—
>   Turn wheresoe'er I may,
>   By night or day,
> The things which I have seen I now can see no more.

"It is not now as it hath been of yore" marks a sharp turn from the idealized time in which the ode begins. Conversely, the opening of Coleridge's *Dejection: An Ode* (1802) seems to promise nothing but a negative pull, beginning with a jaunty epigraph of the *Ballad of Sir Patrick Spence*, then going rapidly downhill from there.

> Late, late yestreen I saw the new Moon,
> With the old Moon in her arms;
> And I fear, I fear, my Master dear!
> We shall have a deadly storm.

What is tranquil and pleasant now will soon grow as stormy as that song. Coleridge's first word is as arresting as Tolson's "*Liberia?*"

> Well! If the Bard was weather-wise, who made
>   The grand old ballad of Sir Patrick Spence,
>   This night, so tranquil now, will not go hence
> Unrous'd by winds, that ply a busier trade
> Than those which mould yon clouds in lazy flakes,   5
> Or the dull sobbing draft, that moans and rakes

Upon the strings of this Aeolian lute,
Which better far were mute.

Dejection literally casts down every impulse that would rise above it:

For lo! the New-moon winter-bright!
And overspread with phantom-light!   10
(With swimming phantom-light o'erspread
But rimm'd and circled by a silver thread)
I see the old Moon in her lap, foretelling
The coming on of rain and squally blast.

As an accomplished teacher of English literature, Tolson well knew these classic examples of the Pindaric tradition. Closer to his own time he had the example of the modernists whose work the *Libretto* emulates, even though Pound in particular took great glee in ridiculing Pindar.

Perhaps because of Pindar-haters like Pound—who as usual has some affinities with a poet he ridicules—most of Tolson's twentieth-century American predecessors in the ode seem to have preferred to avoid the antique word "ode" itself. And "ode" does seem a trifle fusty for the likes of Hart Crane—at least he avoided it—though not the Southern Fugitive Poet Allen Tate, whose "Ode for the Confederate Dead" eventually found its answer in Robert Lowell's "For the Union Dead." But Crane's greatest work *The Bridge* is self-consciously within the English and American Pindaric tradition. In a letter written to his friend Gorham Munson in 1923, while he was working on *The Bridge*, Crane conceives of poetry and music as intimately connected arts. And if he was not willing to use the classical term for Pindar's poetic form, he was quite ready to become the next Pindar himself.

The modern artist needs gigantic assimilative capacities, emotion,—and the greatest of all—vision. . . . Potentially I feel myself quite fit to become a suitable Pindar for the dawn of the machine age, so called.[30]

In a similar manner Tolson called his centennial odes the *Libretto*, and recreated Pindaric song even as he avoided what might be termed the O-word.

The extent to which Tolson was not merely showing his credentials as someone working in the modernist tradition but also establishing his own distinctive voice apart from it was not fully appreciated at the time. Twelve years after the publication of the *Libretto* his friend Karl Shapiro wrote an enthusiastic introduction to book 1 of *Harlem Gallery* and began by acknowledging how little known Tolson was to his contemporaries: "Allen Tate paid homage to him in an introduction to the *Libretto for the Republic of Liberia*, in an essay which for a time was more famous or at least more quoted than the poem."[31] Tate had indeed been complimentary, even though he regarded the final ode of the *Libretto* as more successful rhetoric than poetry. Tolson may have found this last comment amusing. Accomplished debating coach that he was, he loved rhetoric and saw its teaching and learning as a central element in black American language. Tate's comments are otherwise generous.

> For there is a great gift for language, a profound historical sense, and a first-rate intelligence at work in this poem from first to last. On the first page I received a shock, in that region where bored skepticism awaits the new manuscript from a poet not clearly identified, when I saw Liberia invoked as
> ... the quicksilver sparrow that slips
> The eagle's claw!
> From that passage to the end I read the poem with increasing attention and admiration.[32]

Drawn to the arresting image of the sparrow escaping a predatory claw, Tate doesn't bother to give the entire sentence in which it occurs. He thereby elides the vehemence and anger with which the *Libretto for the Republic of Liberia* actually begins.

> *Liberia?*
> No micro-footnote in a bunioned book
>   Homed by a pedant
>   With a gelded look:
>   You are   5
> The ladder of survival dawn men saw
> in the quicksilver sparrow that slips
>   The eagle's claw!

The first of Tolson's extensive endnotes to the *Libretto* at line 7 says that it is inspired by a passage from Dryden's play *All for Love*, a scene that carries with it more than just a felicitous image.

>   ... upon my eagle's wings
> I bore this wren, till I was tired of soaring,
> and now he mounts above me.

All for Love or *The World Well Lost* (1678) is the story of Antony and Cleopatra, a knowing and at times radical revision of Shakespeare's *Antony and Cleopatra*. Where Shakespeare's play ranges over great distances in time and space, with a cast of over thirty, Dryden compresses the same story into a neoclassical five-act tragedy with only a third the number of actors, observing the neoclassicist's unities of time, place, and action. Everything in *All for Love* takes place in one climactic day at the Temple of Isis in Alexandria. No doubt Tate and any still functioning modernist police who cared about bringing this kind of erudition to contemporary poetry would approve of such graceful adaptation, but the allusion actually has a sharp political point. In the scene in question Mark Antony's general Ventidius is trying to use flattery to get him to stop fretting about the unworthiness of his rival Octavius, the adopted son of Julius Caesar and the future Augustus.

> *Antony*:   Why should he lord it
> O'er fourscore thousand men, of whom each one
> Is braver than himself?
> *Ventidius*:   You conquered for him.   135
> Philippi knows it; there you shared with him
> That empire which your sword made all your own.
> *Antony*: Fool that I was, upon my eagle's wings
> I bore this wren till I was tired with soaring,
> And now he mounts above me.   140
> Good heav'ns, is this—is this the man who braves me?
> Who bids my age make way, drives me before him
> To the world's ridge, and sweeps me off like rubbish?

Just as the quicksilver sparrow (wren no longer) leaves the conquering eagle of a general far behind, so too does Liberia leave behind the brutish power that got its people where they are. The ladder of survival for dawn men or men of the new, rising age was unknowingly, inadvertently raised to higher than the eagle's station by the eagle himself. Anyone hearing or reading Tolson's poem and Dryden's play will see the implication in this variation of Dryden's Aesopian turn of phrase: America may have helped Liberia be founded, but in doing so it unwittingly delivered Liberia to a greater destiny. In history, Octavius will be the winner, Antony the loser. The same is predicted for the history of tiny Liberia and America.

This razor sharpness behind the pretty image is thus not so different from the sharp and dismissive tone with which the stanza begins. The pun of a "bunioned book" (it is also a "Bunyaned book," as in a *Pilgrim's Prog-ress*) hints at some kind of boring allegorical exercise, and this is not what Liberia will be. Similarly, "homed" (and its quasi homophone "honed," as in "sharpened") means something like "delivered" or "bestowed" in its proper place. The "pedant with a gelded look" is the toughest phrase of all: the scholar-pedant who is responsible for the footnote and the book has a castrated look. Tolson seems to be attacking himself and his work, or at the very least putting a great distance between the Liberia it addresses and the *Libretto* that praises it.[33] "Do" thus begins with an all-out attack on a pedant who annotates poems in books—an Eliot? Tolson himself? The clash of violent and crude language with the elevated tone is characteristic of the modernist aesthetic, so if the *Libretto* is replete with notes it is not because Tolson is apologizing for his poem's obscurity. In the final stanza of "Do" he begins a list of what Liberia may become with the words "No waste land yet." In other words, if you think you are starting another *Waste Land*, you are mistaken.

Another possible target in this gelded pedant is Countee Cullen's "Her-itage," a poem with no footnotes but lots of doubt about the significance of Africa for a twentieth-century African American like Cullen.[34]

> What is Africa to me:
> Copper sun or scarlet sea,
> Jungle star or jungle track,
> Strong bronzed men, or regal black
> Women from whose loins I sprang
> When the birds of Eden sang?

Cullen creates an elegiac lament that the poet's homeland Africa cannot mean as much to him as he could wish. The sad refrain is typical of him.

> One three centuries removed
> From the scenes his fathers loved,
> Spicy grove, cinnamon tree,
> What is Africa to me?

The poet's homeland is distant not so much geographically, as spiritually. He would be there, but he cannot be.

> Africa? A book one thumbs
> Listlessly, till slumber comes.

So Cullen.

Regret is one thing; falling asleep over Africa is another. To a powerful intellect like Tolson's, Cullen's languid ways make "Heritage" an irresistible target.

Africa?

Liberia?

The "pedant with the gelded look" is as fierce as Pound's outrageous mistranslation of Pindar's Greek *tin' andra* (lit., "what man?") into "a tin wreath" (which Tolson will quote in "Beta" in the *Gallery*). Read along with "Heritage," the depressive Cullen is made into a kind of eunuch of African American poetry.

Since the italicized *"Liberia?"* is repeated at the beginning of every stanza, in a reading of the poem (or a hearing), a good reader might want to inflect the single word differently each time. Each repetition of *"Liberia?"* is followed by seven lines, each always consisting of three lines of negatives, balanced by the phrase "You are" in the center of each stanza, followed by three lines of positive declarations about what Liberia is.

Anatomized in this way, "Do" sounds and emerges as a sustained song of both what is and what is not. The Liberia of history dissolves into a Liberia that exists and does not yet exist, or will someday exist, or existed once but no longer. Liberia is *not* a "micro-footnote in a bunioned book," or a "side-show barker's bio-accident," no "haply Black man's X" (sc. Othello's "For haply I am black") on a Magna Charta; no "oil-boiled Barabas," "No pimple on the chin of Africa" or "brass-lipped cicerone of Big Top democracy" (a pawn in the American Cold War circus) or "lamb to tame a lion with a baa"; no "Cobra Pirate of the Question Mark" (sc. the shape of Africa, or perhaps as glossed in a note to line 42, "A ham-bone designed by destiny for the carving-knife of European imperialism"); "No waste land yet." Liberia *is* "the ladder of survival," "the lightning rod of Europe," "Canaan's key," "the rope across the abyss," *"Mehr Licht* ["More light," Goethe's dying words] for the Africa-To-Be"; "the Orient of Colors everywhere," "the oasis of Tahoua," "the salt bar of Harrar" (Artur Rimbaud's destinations in Africa); *"Libertas* flayed and naked by the road to Jericho," "Black Lazarus risen from the White Man's grave," "American genius uncrowned in Europe's charnel house," and finally, the inspiring conclusion:

You are
The iron nerve of lame and halt and blind,
    Liberia and not Liberia,
A moment in the conscience of mankind!

The proverbial "lame and halt and blind" refers to Jesus's words in a Pharisee's house in Luke 14.11–14.

> For whosoever exalteth himself shall be abased; and he that humbleth himself shall be exalted. Then said he also to him that bade him, When thou makest a dinner or a supper, call not thy friends, neither thy kinsmen, nor thy rich neighbours; lest they also bid thee again, and a recompence be made thee. But when thou makest a feast, call the poor, the maimed, the lame, the blind: And thou shalt be blessed; for they cannot recompense thee: for thou shalt be recompensed at the resurrection of the just.

In both an anatomical and a figurative sense (strength), Liberia is the nerve that will draw the poor and unfortunate of the earth to its table; this moment in the conscience of mankind is a geographical location and then no geographical location at all, but an ideal. The dialectic of what Liberia is and is not runs throughout the ode and culminates in the seeming paradox, "You are . . . Liberia and not Liberia, " but what gives this conclusion such an inspiring tone, and what prompted Allen Tate's admiration in the conclusion of the first stanza ("The ladder of survival dawn men saw / in the quicksilver sparrow that slips / The eagle's claw!") has been created by the kind of power of an ode's negative pull that Fry describes. It pulses throughout each of the successive stanzas, and since it is part of a larger design, the poem ends not by completing the diatonic do-re-mi scale but by concluding with a statement that in a single sentence embraces both the enigmatic being and not-being of Liberia, and its true glory.

You are
The iron nerve of lame and halt and blind,
    Liberia and not Liberia,
A moment in the conscience of mankind!

The completion of the octave of "Do" is suspended and the song resumes with "Re," composed in a notably different pattern for both lines and stanza, and the first of a number of challenging quotations of African languages. Even as one tone ends, the *Libretto* glides into the next, with the difference in sound and stanza at once identifiable. Tolson would make the same move into a future when he closes *Harlem Gallery* at the end of its twenty-fourth and last ode, "Omega."

"Re"

In the note to lines 79–80 ("Solomon in all his glory had no Oxford, / Alfred the Great no University of Sankoré"), Tolson cites W. E. B. Du Bois's *The World and Africa* (1946), "a book to which I am deeply indebted for facts." Du Bois's facts appear all over the *Libretto*. He wrote it quickly to get his view of African history out into the postwar world, and frankly acknowledges in his introduction that he is mainly reporting and synthesizing for a general reader what scholars and specialists in African history have already published. His purpose was to educate readers who were just turning from the catastrophic destruction of European and Asian nations at the end of World War II and looking up to Africa for other, older patterns in human history. Du Bois was repeating the kind of intervention he had attempted at the end of the First World War, when he traveled to the Versailles conference in 1919 to gain recognition of the rights of colonialized peoples all over the world to work toward their freedom.

Many of the seemingly arcane allusions and quotations that Tolson makes throughout the *Libretto* were not added to make a difficult modernist poem even harder, but can be traced to this and similar books cited in the notes. A substantial number of the works invoked by the *Libretto* are in fact in the social sciences, history, and anthropology, and they are cited with as much frequency as poets and novelists. Tolson was determined that his work have as much an impact in politics as in literary history, and for this purpose the notes were an indispensable part of the poem. Timbuktu was then a byword for any place unimaginably remote and distant from civilization. For the very reason of its remoteness from usual Western notions of geography Romare Bearden would later transfer Ithaca to Timbuktu in his collages of the *Odyssey*.[35]

Like Bearden, Du Bois and Tolson want us to know that the opposite was once the case. Not only Egyptian civilization but many others besides flourished in Africa long before the Europeans turned to the subjugation and exploitation of them in the process generally termed by its Roman origins, colonization. A map in Du Bois's *The World and Africa* (figure 1) shows "The Political and Cultural Development of Africa: 1325 B.C.–A.D. 1850," where the state of Songhay (1400–1700), the home of Timbuktu, was located.

The organized Songhay state at the height of its power under the black Mohammedan Askia the Great was a remarkable state from any point of view. Its organized administration, its roads and methods of communication, its system of public security, put it abreast of any contemporary European or Asiatic state. It was as large as Europe. The emperor "was obeyed with as much docility on the farthest limits of his empire as in his own palace." Gao, Timbuktu, and Jenne were intellectual centers, and at the University of Sankoré gathered thousands of students of law, literature, grammar, geography, and surgery. A literature began to develop in the sixteenth and seventeenth centuries. The University was in correspondence with the best institutions on the Mediterranean coast.[36]

"Re" turns the facts of *The World and Africa* into poetry:

The Good Gray Bard in Timbuktu chanted:
"*Brow tron lo—eta ne a ne won oh gike!*"

As so often happens in Tolson, wildly unrelated bits of lore and poetry are jammed into the same verse.

This Good Gray Bard is not the American Walt Whitman but his contemporary Tennyson, who won a student prize at Cambridge in 1829 for his poem "Timbuctoo."[37] Tennyson did not publish the poem in his lifetime, but as Tolson observes in a note, his friend Arthur Hallam wrote William Gladstone that it revealed a great poet in the making. In his youth the Good Gray Bard had chanted these lines:

Wide Afric, doth thy Sun
Lighten, they hills enfold a city as fair
As those which starr'd the night o' the elder world?
Or is the rumour of thy Timbuctoo
A dream as frail as those of ancient time?

If this diction seems archaic even for 1829, the sentiment about Timbuktu is up to date and still in current usage. The spirit who can answer this question appears to him:

I am the Spirit,
The permeating life which courseth through
All th' intricate and labyrinthine veins
Of the great vine of Fable, which, outspread
With growth of shadowing leaf and clusters rare,
Reacheth to every corner under heaven,
Deep-rooted in the living soil of truth;
So that men's hopes and fears take refuge in
The fragrance of its complicated glooms,
And cool impleachèd twilights.

Today's readers may be tempted to conclude that Tennyson did well not to include "Timbuctoo" in his published works, but the implication of Tolson's reference is that the official histories of Africa, Timbuktu, and Liberia in particular are all of them no less fantastical than Tennyson's youthful effusion. In any case, "Re" is no homage to Tennyson. Tolson throws him out of his poem, somewhat like a cuckoo taking over another bird's nest. He transforms the Good Gray Bard into a real thing, not the paradigm of Victorian rectitude and family values, and not even Walt Whitman, but a poet of Timbuktu chanting in an African language. According to Tolson's note, what he chants is the opposite of Tennyson's spiritual revelation, more akin to ironic satire than sublime revelation: "The world is too large—that's why we do not hear everything" (58).

The stanzas of "Re" are fourteen lines long, a couplet followed by two six-line stanzas, with each couplet beginning "The Good Gray Bard in Timbuktu chanted," followed by a line in an African language that is never complimentary, or an enigmatic oracular statement in English: "*Wanawake wanazaa ovyo!* ("The women keep having children right and left," 193) *Kazi yenu wazungu!*" ("It's the work of you white men," 73); "Europe is an empty python in hiding grass!" (86). What the Bard tells of in the twelve lines of his song is the true history of Songhay—spelled throughout the *Libretto* by its alternate Songhai—not a European or American confection.

Before Liberia was, Songhai was: before
America set the raw foundling on Africa's   60
Doorstep, before the Genoese diced west,
Burnt warriors and watermen of Songhai
Tore into *bizarreries* the uniforms of Portugal
And sewed an imperial quilt of tribes.

The pinnacle of African civilization was reached in Timbuktu long before
its "discovery" by invaders from the east and north.

> Black Askia's fetish was his people's health: 73
> The world his world, he gave the Bengal light
> Of Books the Inn of Court in Songhai. *Biba mzigo!*   75
> The law of empathy set the market price,
> Scaled the word and deed: the gravel-blind saw
> Deserts give up the ghost to green pastures!

Biba Mzigo!, the note to line 75 informs us, is a repeated phrase meaning
"Lift the loads," "tacked on *ex tempore* to ballads growing out of a diversity of physical and spiritual experiences." There is a constant interplay
between what the verse is saying and what the notes report about it. The
whole notion of a chronological progression in history is upended by this
sweeping view of intellectual history.

> Solomon in all his glory had no Oxford,
> Alfred the Great no University of Sankoré: 80
> Footloose professors, chimney sweeps of the skull,
> From Europe and Asia; youths, souls in one skin,
> Under white scholars like El-Alit, under
> Black humanists like Bugaboo, *Caribou wee!*   84

What Liberia once had in this elliptical language was "footloose professors, chimney sweeps of the skull" and not to be confused, Tolson's note on
line 81 informs us, with the lighthearted vagabonds of the *Carmina Burana*.
Their students were all "souls in one skin," the distinctions of color made
no difference, and as the note to line 84 observes in an extended gloss,
"Among primitives hospitality is a thing poetic—and apostolic. *Jogoo lin-
awika: Karibu wee. 'The rooster crows: Welcome!' Mbuzi wanalia: Karibu
wee. 'The goats bleat: Welcome.'*"

And then the whole edifice of Songhay goes down before the European
python in the hiding grass. *Lia! Lia!* opens and closes the last full stanza
(lines 3–12) of the poem: "Weep! Weep!," and in a note it evokes the refrain
of Cassandra in Aeschylus's *Agamemnon*. At that moment Cassandra sees
not only her death and Agamemnon's, but the earlier murders of Thyestes'
children and his feasting on their flesh. It is all part of the true history of
the House of Atreus, and the Chorus of Argive elders cannot or will not

acknowledge it easily. Tolson's Good Gray Bard is another Cassandra, and like her delivers a prophecy that no one may want to believe, which then turns into reality. As in the Cassandra scene, times present, past, and future all blend into a single perception. First the Portuguese, Spanish, and Saracen conquerors, then *Dieu seul est grand!* (92), a Christian sentiment uttered at the funeral of Louis XIV, and then Songhay has returned to the deserted, remote place and its capital Timbuktu.

> And now the hyenas whine among the barren bones   93
> Of the seventeen sun sultans of Songhai,
> And hooded cobras, hoodless mambas, hiss   95
> In the gold caverns of Falémé and Bambuk,
> And puff adders, hook scorpions, whisper
> In the weedy corridors of Sankoré. *Lia! Lia!*

The ode concludes by breaking off the stanza of fourteen lines after the beginning couplet, and the Good Gray Bard vanishes with a riddling line.

> The Good Gray Bard chants no longer in Timbuktu:
> "The maggots fat on yeas and nays of nut empires!"   100

Nuts are a major source of wealth in Africa, a point underscored in the note to line 100, where a poem from a newspaper of May 1948 reports that "The sun of Empire will not set while Empire nuts abound."

"Mi"

The fourteen-line stanza pattern of "Re" gives way to a simpler ode of six quatrains on the history of the American Colonization Society in 1816. This story is of far briefer compass than the Good Gray Bard's song of Timbuktu. The ACS's program to save the new republic from the economic and political consequences of American slavery by expatriating freed slaves and free blacks back to Africa seemed to offer a way out of one of the many increasingly obvious American dilemmas about slavery and its consequences. When the society was founded, the numbers of blacks had grown from nearly 60,000 in the 1790 census to over 186,000 by 1810.[38] Their presence north as well as south was an embarrassment even to slavery's apologists, since it exposed the absurdity of their "natural" argument for judging inferiority by a person's color. Even to sympathetic abolitionists their growing presence was worrisome. What were Americans going to do to accommodate all these free people of color?

Tolson's take on the famous and not-so-famous names in American history reflects the mixed motives of those who began working for the repatriation of freed slaves one generation after the Revolution and two generations before the Civil War.

> Before the bells of Yankee capital
> Tolled for the feudal glory of the South
> And Frederick Douglass's Vesuvian mouth
> Erupted amens crushing Copperheads . . .

Organizing under president James Monroe, who would provide the name for the capital of the new nation, a wide range of Protestant clergymen and politicians put together a winning formula that combined high morals and sound business sense to solve the problem of what to do with freed slaves. The answer was emigration to the east, to Africa—a reversal of the westering mythology of American exceptionalism. Before the Civil War, a lot of optimism lay behind this project. As Ralph Randolph Gurley, the biographer of the young American minister Jehudi Ashmun (1794–1828), who did much to stabilize the new republic in Africa in the 1820s, tells the story, its founders had high expectations.[39] This history is reflected in the names today of the Ashmun Institute as well as of Lincoln University.

In the event, this ideal republic was not to be realized. In the *Libretto*, the story unfolds in one long sentence that piles one quatrain upon another. Robert Finley is "Jehovah's Damsels," God's version of the reforming Athenian archon who furthered the liberation of Athens after Solon by serving longer in office than he was entitled to. Finley swoops like a bird of prey down to "To pinion Henry, the shuttlecock": Henry Clay is more flatteringly known to American history textbooks as "The Great Compromiser" for the deals he cut in the Missouri Compromise of 1820 and the Compromise of 1850, the latter of which may have delayed the coming of civil war by some years, but not incidentally perpetuated slavery in the South. Here Clay is pinioned as a moral lightweight, all cork and feathers, flying back and forth from one racket to another in nineteenth-century America's game of badminton over slavery. Bushrod Washington, the nephew and heir of the first president, supported the American Colonization Society and won over Francis Scott Key (author of the lines—but not the tune, originally a drinking song—of "The Star-Spangled Banner") to the cause of founding Liberia.

And Bushrod Washington: his magnet Yea
Drew Lawyer Key, the hymnist primed to match   110
A frigate's guns.
These and other worthies "eagled"
The gospel for the wren Republic in
Supreme Court Chambers. That decision's cash
And credit bought a balm for conscience, verve
Black Pilgrim Fathers to Cape Measured,
Where sun and fever, brute and vulture, spelled
The idioms of their faith in white bones.

But neither the ACS nor Americans of the twentieth century had a "linguist of the Braille of prophecy" to tell them what would happen in the future, when Liberia would be of real use to America.

No linguist of the Braille of prophecy ventured:
The rubber from Liberia shall arm
Free peoples and her airport hinterlands
Let loose the winging grapes of wrath
Upon the Desert Fox's cocaine nietzcheans
A goose-step from the Gateway of the East!

The Firestone Rubber Company and the landing fields of Liberia for trans-Atlantic flights would play a crucial role in World War II in the repulse of Rommel and the Nazis in their attempt to take Egypt and the Suez Canal. This was what Liberia actually accomplished for America in the long run.

"Fa"

The theme of Liberia's 1947 celebration of its centennial was "West Africa in a World of Peace," and it was this theme that Tolson's commissioned poem was expected to honor.[40] "Fa" is built around the italicized refrain "*in the interlude of peace*," whose peaceful melody is constantly at war with the feral imagery in each quatrain: gorged boa constrictor ("A fabulous mosaic log . . . eyeless, yet with eyes"), a raptor bird ("The beaked and pouched assassin"), and the most striking image of all, the tiger.

The tawny typhoon striped with black   135
torpors in grasses tan:

a doomsday cross, his paws uprear
the leveled skull of a man. . . .
in the interlude of peace.

The briefest of the odes, "Fa" expresses the distinctive poetics of the *Libretto* in its most concentrated form. It redefines the anniversary and the culmination of history that Liberia celebrates as an "interlude," and as if that were not disdainful enough to what those who commission commemorative poetry might expect, the agents of history are removed altogether and only the animals of the natural world are the agents. Human beings make their appearance only as a gnawed skull held aloft between the paws of the animal that has eaten them.

"Fa" continues the diminuendo that starts with "Re" and is itself an interlude in the otherwise pervasive poetics of obscurity so characteristic of the *Libretto*. Tolson himself regarded it as the only ode that could be given to any reader without notes of any kind, because it's the only ode that requires no learning in poetry or history to be grasped. But in the Pindaric tradition, in whatever era we conceive of it, it is always wise to beware of taking simplicity at face value. "Fa" is as "natural" as the world of nature that it contains, and in that sense is a highly wrought poem that is not natural in any respect. Its studied refrain is a rebuke of centennial thinking and all that comes with it; its violent images of killing and consuming prey are vivid and concrete, and they clash repeatedly with the Latinate words "interlude" and "peace." Both "peace" and "interlude" are concepts not simply ironized, but rendered meaningless by the contrast with the continuing life of predators and prey that is the world of nature's verdict on the Roman and more generally European tendency to mark out an era and call it peace.

"Sol"

In the diatonic scale *sol* is the dominant, as G is the dominant of the note C (*do*) in the C-major scale. If we conceive of the "interlude of peace" harmonically, "Sol" marks the turning point in the *Libretto*, the first of the three tones that will lead us at once upward in scale and backward in tone, to the longest ode of all. Jon Woodson argues that the tarot plays an important role in the *Libretto*, and the fifth card is the Hierophant; the tone of "Sol" is hierophantic in a literal sense, with African griots' proverbs occupying its center.[41] It is composed in tercets that typically seem to be

leading up to a symmetrical close of thirty tercets, only they stop just before that symmetry is realized. Of the twenty-nine tercets, fourteen are
devoted to the proverbs of the griots, eleven to Elijah Johnson's survival
of the passage back to Liberia, and his struggle to defend the first settle-
ments makes of him a kind of Jonah of Liberia's history.

> Elijah Johnson, his *Tygers heart*
> In the whale's belly, flenses midnight:
> "How long? How long? How long?"   156

To reach Johnson as the Jonah scraping out the blubber of the Middle Passage, Tolson blends white and black Pilgrims' crossings of the Atlantic, so
that the blacks hear the refrain "shule, agrah" ("Move, my heart," according to the note, "a refrain from an old Gaelic ballad").

> This is the horned American
> Dilemma: yet, this too, O Christ,
> This too, O Christ, will pass!   145

An American Dilemma is the title of Gunnar Myrdal's 1944 study of race relations in America, as Tolson dutifully notes on line 143. Myrdal describes
American racism in such a way that he seems to have studied a country not
all that different from the divided nation up to the Civil War.[42]

But this is more than an allusion to Myrdal's famous book; recall the
griots' proverb "A stinkbug should not peddle perfume." Tolson creates a
conflict in his notes that extends the point in a line well beyond the poetry,
by referring to Herbert Aptheker's 1946 response to Myrdal.[43] Aptheker's
polemic underlies the design of "Sol" and is the ideological framework for
the extensive quotation of griot proverbs at the heart of the ode. In many
ways the voice of Aptheker and the voice of the griots are one and the
same. Both subject foolish and pernicious wisdom to a devastating scrutiny. As Aptheker says, it is not just that anyone with a half a brain would
object to being termed a "problem." Myrdal seemed to be genuinely unaware that his research was actually supporting the American status quo
rather than providing an instrument for changing it.

> The class bias of Myrdal is so insistent that he does not refrain from
> making it explicit by pointing out that his position—that of a liberal re-
> former—is functionally useful, if not vital, to the maintenance of the basic

status quo. He asserts that it is "urgent . . . from a conservative point of view *to begin allowing the higher strata of the Negro population to participate in the political process as soon as possible, and to push the movement down gradually*" (518–19, italics original). This he rationalizes by slander again, asserting that the masses are "less intelligent . . . and most likely to constitute the corrupt" voters. But he warns that "political conservatives, who have been successful for any length of time, have always foreseen impending changes and have put through the needed reforms themselves in time. *By following this tactic they have been able to guard fundamental conservative interests even in the framing of reforms. They have thereby also succeeded in slowing them up; changes have not overwhelmed them as avalanches. They have kept the control and preserved a basis for the retention of their political power.*" (My emphasis — H. A.) Is it not amusing — and revealing — how, when the distinguished doctor recommends action he relaxes his grip upon his philosophical idealism?[44]

To Aptheker's disgust, Myrdal actually rediscovers some of the conciliatory tactics that proslavery antiabolitionists in the nineteenth century had proposed. Myrdal thought it a shame, Aptheker records, that the Southern slave-owners were not reimbursed for the loss of their property; compare Czar Alexander II of Russia, Aptheker says, who reimbursed the landowners of Russia following the emancipation of the serfs in 1861.[45]

Never have explanatory footnotes concealed more polemic than Tolson's notes to the *Libretto*. The "American Dilemma" is a devil's dilemma, infernal because it poses the wrong kinds of questions and comes up with the wrong kinds of answers for both African and American history.[46] Aptheker's critique is essential for understanding this and much else in the *Libretto*, since it is the ideology of Myrdal and other allegedly scientific observers of the American scene that has done so much harm. In a response to Myrdal's above-it-all, ex cathedra tones, Aptheker's polemic is ad hominem and unsparing in its scrutiny of Sweden's neutrality with Nazi Germany in World War II.

Elijah Johnson's voyage eastward to freedom and his struggle to protect the fledgling colony of Liberia recapitulate the Middle Passage, the horror whose timeless presence impinges on any later event.

This is the Middle Passage: here
Gehenna hatchways vomit up   150
The debits of pounds of flesh.

This is the Middle Passage: here
The sharks wax fattest and the stench
Goads God to hold His nose!

In *The World and Africa* Du Bois had cited Eugene Guernier's notorious
dictum that Africa alone of all the continents had no history. In a note
to line 170 Tolson says that "the scope of native cultural is vertical—not
horizontal," by which he means that the griots' proverbs that follow speak
to every time, before them as well as after them, and not simply to a single
historical moment. By this reckoning Guernier's notion is rendered meaningless, a literal piece of parroting.

He hears the skulls plowed under cry:
"*Griots*, the quick owe the quick and dead.
A man owes man to man!"
"Seule de tous les continents," the parrots   170
chatter, "l'Afrique n'a pas d'histoire!"

The first response of the griots to this bit of colonializing wisdom
makes reference to Liberia's most coveted product, so far as the Firestone
Rubber Company was concerned. Elijah Johnson hears their wisdom and
functions as a medium between their world and ours.[47]

"Africa is a rubber ball;   173
the harder you dash it to the ground,
the higher it will rise."

The griots' proverbs are the musical center of the poem.[48] The proverbs
that follow are sometimes confined to a single line, as in the one on Kipling
(194), but just as often they enjamb both lines and stanzas. They are wise
sayings about the limits of all things.

"A camel on its knees solicits   185
The ass's load. Potbellies cook
no meals for empty maws.

"When skins are dry the flies go home.
Repentance is a peacock's tail.
The cock is yolk and feed.   190

"Three steps put man one step ahead.
The rich man's weights are not the poor
man's scales. To each his coole."

Toward the end of the proverbs the vertical wisdom of the griots is en-
jambed into the contemporary postwar world of Myrdal, Aptheker, and
"the American Dilemma" as the stanzas blend one into another.

"It is the grass that suffers when   206
two elephants fight. The white man solves
between white sheets his black
problem. Where would the rich cream be
without skim milk? The eye can cross   210
the river in a flood.
Law is a rotten tree; black man, rest
thy weight elsewhere, or like the goat
outrun the white man's stink!"

The griots' wisdom is vertical rather than horizontal because it applies as
much to Elijah Johnson in the 1820s as it does to the Liberia and the United
States of the 1940s and 1950s, before the momentous Supreme Court decision of *Brown vs. Board of Education* in 1954. Noah Johnson has found his
home at last, as Liberian and biblical history blend into one story in the
stanza that ends "Sol."

And every ark awaits its raven,
Its vesper dove with an olive-leaf,   225
Its rainbow over Ararat.

Coming to rest on its own version of Mount Ararat, the voyage of
Elijah Johnson in this ode gives way to another voyager, with different
results.

"La"

The opening of Crane's poem "The Dance" in section 2 of *The Bridge* is
recalled at the beginning of this short ode that leads into the last two,
which are the longest.

The swift red flesh, a winter king—
Who squired the glacier woman down the sky? (Crane, *The Bridge*)

Glaciers had shouldered down
The cis-Saharan snows,
Shoved antelope and lion
Past *Uaz-Orîet* floes. (Tolson, *Libretto*)

The shorter quatrains of iambic trimeter move briskly over the continent of Africa, but cover an even wider scope in time. The ode begins in such a "vertical" fashion that it skips from the cultural history of "Sol" to geological time, with an ice age extending down into Africa, demarcated by the ancient Egyptian Uaz-Orîet (Mediterranean) waters. Where Crane could see the nobility of primitive times, however, Tolson sees the future colonial nations as nothing but bestial cavemen, and infernal cavemen at that.[49]

Leopard, elephant, ape,   231
Rhinoceros and giraffe
Jostled in odysseys
To Africa: siamang laugh
And curse impaled the frost   235
As Northmen brandished paws
And shambled Europe-ward,
Gnashing Cerberean jaws.

The account of Jehudi Ashmun in "La" corresponds to the sixth tarot card of the Lovers, with an iconography suggesting in Arthur Waite's account of the "Doctrine Behind the Veil": "Youth, virginity, innocence and love before it is contaminated by gross material desire. This is in all simplicity the card of human love, here exhibited as part of the way, the truth and the life. It replaces, by recourse to first principles, the old card of marriage . . . and the later follies which depicted man between vice and virtue."[50]

After *netami lennowak* [the first men]
A white man spined with dreams   240
Came to cudgel parrot scholars
And slay philistine schemes.

As he often does, Tolson annotates a line with a reference whose implications extend far beyond whatever he quotes. In this instance we may wonder how apt the reference is. At line 240 he cites Vergil's *Aeneid*, 4.625: "Exoriare aliquis!" This phrase is near the end of Dido's speech cursing Aeneas and all his descendents for his seduction and abandonment of her. The "someone" (*aliquis*) she hopes will arise is Hannibal, the deadliest foe of Rome, who functions equally well as a Semitic hero (for Freud) and an African hero (for Tolson).[51]

"The Prophet Jehudi Ashmun" (245) loses his wife early on in the process of settling Liberia, so the marriage that he discovers is of a higher kind.

> When the black bat's ultima smote
> His mate in the yoke, he felt
> The seven swords' *pis aller*
> Twist in his heart at the hilt.   250
> He said: "My Negro kinsmen,
> America is my mother,
> Liberia is my wife,
> And Africa is my brother."

This praise of Ashmun is as close as Tolson ever comes in the *Libretto* to doing what is customarily thought to be the chief duty of a poet commissioned to write an ode, but he does it in a long note to "Prophet Jehudi Ashmun" (line 245), which is the one point in the *Libretto* where the connections between Tolson, his alma mater Lincoln University, and Liberia are made clear. Whether or not President Tubman and other Liberians appreciated the note, Tolson clearly aimed to please his friend President Horace Mann Bond of Lincoln University. Here he speaks like a loyal alumnus of Lincoln rather than an Eliotic annotator.

> Lincoln University, the oldest Negro institution of its kind in the world, was founded as Ashmun Institute. The memory of the white pilgrim survives in old Ashmun Hall and in the Greek and Latin inscriptions cut in stones sacred to Lincoln men. The annual Lincoln-Liberian dinner is traditional, and two of the graduates have been ministers to Liberia.

The intertwined stories of Lincoln University, Liberia, and Tolson are clearly set out in this brief excursion into praise poetry at its most transparent. This ode and all the ones preceding it are but prelude to the final two odes, which together are twice as long and far more irregular in form than the poems that precede them.

"Ti"

"Ti" and "Do" comprise two-thirds of the entire *Libretto*, and both question whether any contribution to Liberia, Ashmun's or anyone else's, can
withstand the destructive cycles of world history that most recently had
brought humanity the first uses of the atomic bomb. For the Republic of
Liberia to transcend its particular history and offer any enduring myth or
poetry for any other people, the poet needs to move out of the particular-
ity of history altogether. This is a huge ambition, and it accounts for what
may at first seem a bizarre imbalance in the proportions of the odes.[52] The
stanzas in "Ti" vary enormously in length, from six to as many as thirty-six
lines, each one's ending marked by the Hebrew word *Selah*, the musical no-
tation found in the poetic books of the Hebrew bible, especially Psalms,
where *Selah* means "shift the mode," marking the end of one performance
style and a turn to another.[53] Tolson published an earlier version of "Ti" in
Poetry in 1950, together with Allen Tate's preface, and it is this publication
that William Carlos Williams celebrates in the second section of book 4 of
Paterson.[54] It is not just a reference, but an adaptation of the characteristic
tone of the ode, especially its polyphony of language. At the same time,
Williams does not miss the veiled condescension of Tate's preface.

> —and to Tolson and to his ode
> and to Liberia and to Allen Tate
> (Give him credit)
> and to the South generally
>   *Selah*!

> —and to 100 years of it—splits
> off the radium, the Gamma rays
> will eat their bastard bones out who
> are opposed
>   *Selah*!

> *Pobres bastardos, misquierdos*
>   *Pobrecitos*
>   *Ay! que pobres*

> —yuh wanna be killed with your
> face in the dirt and a son-of-a-bitch
> of a Guardia Civil giving you the

coup de (dis)grace
right in the puss?
Selah! Selah!

Credit! I hope you have a long credit
and a dirty one
Selah!

Williams follows his Spanish stanza with a translation of the murder of
Lorca by the Guardia Civil in 1936 into American vernacular. The credit he
gives Tolson and (Give him credit) Tate is part of the larger theme of credit,
which is "credit" in more than one sense. But the refrain from Psalms also
marks a blending of biblical psalmody with the English Pindaric ode's tradition of irregular stanzas. The opening stanza of "Ti" is the briefest of all
and establishes the praise pattern.

> O Calendar of the Century,   255
> red-letter the Republic's birth!
>   O Hallelujah,
>   Oh, let no *Miserere*
>   venom the spinal cord of Afric earth!
>   *Selah!*   260

Williams echoes Tolson's echo of the Psalms' *Selah*, which marks a break
in the song. Thus David praises the Lord for his marvelous works in Psalm
9:19–20 and ends by telling of his punishment of the wicked.

> Arise, O Lord; let no man prevail: let the heathen be judged in thy sight.
> Put them in fear, O Lord: that the nations may know themselves to be but
> men. Selah.

The distinctive poetics of "Ti" plays in a similar fashion with a mythical
and historical dread that keeps pressing forward into the present celebration. The words of the ode flow into one another in an acrostic of "barb
and" (barbarian) and "Arab" and other figures that mirror the poetry's fusion of points in geography commonly thought to be as separate as epochs
in history.

> Man's culture in barb and Arab lies: 286
>   The Jordan flows into the Tiber;

> the Yangtze into the Thames,
> the Ganges into the Mississippi, the Niger
> into the Seine.   290

A typical passage, this captures as well as any the spirit guiding the final
two odes of the *Libretto*. As so often in modernist verse and particularly in
this poem, "Ti" delights in juxtaposing reference and imitations of high
classical art with learning so arcane not even the author can reveal where
it came from. The repression (as we would call it) of the past crimes of the
House of Atreus is one of the great revelations of the choral odes of the
Agamemnon, and Tolson adapts their characteristic imagery to lead into a
peculiar version of the Sphinx's riddle to Oedipus, with yet another acrostic play with the archaic verb "cark" ("load," "burden") and "crack," which
then spirals into a cosmic vision that runs well beyond Greek myth and
thought, to an exuberant play on words ("enmesh," "ethos"; "masôreth,"
"pillars," and "flesh") and a confusion of sociology with liturgy ("intone the
Mass of the class as the requiem of the mass").

> Elders of Agâ's House, keening
>   at the Eagle's feast, cringing
> before the Red Slayer, shrinking
> from the blood on Hubris' pall—   300
> carked by cracks of myriad curbs,
> hitherto, against the Wailing Wall
>   of Ch'in, the blind men cried:
>   All cultures crawl
>   walk hard
>   fall,
>   flout
>   under classes under
>   *Lout*,
>   enmesh in ethos, in *masôreth*, the poet's flesh,   310
> intone the Mass of the class as the requiem of the mass . . .

In many ways "Ti" is Tolson's most overt reference to Eliot's *Waste Land*,
chiefly with an aim to developing mysteries that Eliot did not pretend to
solve. About "the Wailing Wall of Ch'in," the note to line 303 says, "I came
across these words somewhere: 'The Ch'in emperor built the Great Wall
to keep out Mongolian enemies from the north and burned the books of
China to destroy intellectual enemies from within,'" a clear play on Eliot's

style in his note on *Waste Land*, line 199, "I do not know the origin of the ballad from which these lines are taken: it was reported to me from Sydney, Australia." Stanza 5 refers back directly to Eliot's use of the tarot in *The Waste Land*, and specifically to the fortune-teller Madame Sosostris's puzzled line, "I do not find The Hanged Man" (54–55). It builds the tarot into the poem in such a way that the twelfth arcanum, the Hanged Man, is "the black flower T" that awaits any prophet. He will be like the Hanged Man, suspended upside down from a tau cross, with one leg crossed under another to form a fylfot or swastika-like cross. As an explicator of the tarot, Waite, the one Tolson would have known, veils more than he reveals: "It is a card of profound significance, but all the significance is veiled. . . . It has been called falsely a card of martyrdom, a card of prudence, a card of the Great Work, a card of duty; but we may exhaust all published interpretations and find only vanity."[55]

> Behind the curtain, aeon after aeon,   337
>   he who doubts the white book's colophon
>   is Truth's, if not Laodicean, wears
>   the black flower T of doomed Laocoön.   340

Tolson's aim is to go beyond the fate of a Laocoön, who was punished by the gods simply because he revealed the doom of a civilization. Tolson will not be a poet laureate devoured for telling the hidden truths. "Ti" is a historical wasteland, more accurately, the wasteland that the *Libretto* teaches history will lead to; thereby Tolson seems to want us to think we are reaching the limits of Eliot's great poem, then seeing beyond it, to the resolution to come in the *Libretto*'s concluding "Do." The way he does this at the conclusion of the last stanza (an asymmetrical number of stanzas, naturally) is to pose his two favorite ways of analyzing the vertical and horizontal conception of history and time. Either way leads to ruin.

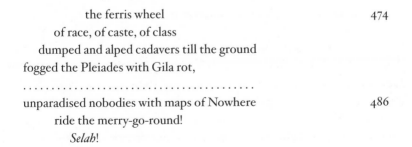

>   the ferris wheel   474
>   of race, of caste, of class
>   dumped and alped cadavers till the ground
>   fogged the Pleiades with Gila rot,
> . . . .
> unparadised nobodies with maps of Nowhere   486
>   ride the merry-go-round!
>   *Selah!*

"Do"

And what a conclusion it is. At first reading, the first of the three sections of this ode seems gibberish. It is by far the most deliberately difficult part of the *Libretto*, as we have seen a polyglot collage of references and quotations of arcane information from all kinds of sources jammed together into eleven long-lined sestets that not even Tolson's most assiduous critics can yet fully explain. As Woodson observes, however, this excessive difficulty is itself neither unconscious nor without design; the first part of the final ode (lines 489–554) is difficult precisely because Tolson wants to deflect all but the most dedicated readers.[56] He follows the same strategy in the equally obscure verses of "The Man from Halicarnassus." What does it mean then to become an initiate in this final ode?

In the interest of brevity for this short run, the ultimate answer may lurk in the tarot and our decoding of it, as Woodson suggests. But Tolson's whole aim is to lose the reader in a maze of allusions and references, not least in the notes that purport to explain or otherwise answer questions we might have. What predominates above all else in the eleven strophes is the imagery and even the sounds of Dante's *Inferno*. The concluding ode that will lead the *Libretto*'s audiences as well as the Republic of Liberia onto the highest ground begins at the lowest point imaginable in Western and particularly Christian imagination, the infernal landscape of the bottom of hell, where every orifice but the mouth becomes the main instrument of communication, the vagina as well as the anus. The language comes from drought-stricken Brazil and a Japanese officer's diary in Norman Mailer's *The Naked and the Dead*.

> a *pelaygeya* in *as seccas* the old she-fox today
> eyes dead letters mouth a hole in a privy   490
>   *taschunt* a corpse's in a mud-walled troy of *jaguncos*
> (*naze naze desu ka servant de dakar*) (*el grito de yara*)
>   cackles among the garbage cans of mummy truths
>   o frontier saints bring out your dead.

The old she-fox's language is language stretched to the breaking point, as Williams observes, and her infernal language is itself inspired by that of Plutus in Dante's *Inferno*.[57] She echoes both the famous gateway to hell ("per me si va nella città dolente," 500) as well as Plutus's meaningless cry "aleppe" (554), and throughout her section Tolson drops all punctuation and capitalization. The appearance of gibberish is, as Williams also observes, actually an elegant illusion that Tolson creates to beguile the incurious, the lazy, or anyone else who is not willing to invest the labor in rising to his poem's challenge. The appearance of lack of control is simply that, an appearance. What Tolson creates is an infernalization à la Dante of the attempt to communicate final coherence and meaning. This apocalyptic ending awaits anyone who would bestow something like Pindar's version of immortality on his patrons and their victorious athletes, and it will always recur, just like the infernal language of Dante's hell. Unlike Dante, or for that matter Eliot, Tolson has no salvation to offer that would lift either humanity or Liberia out of this endlessly recurring cycle.

All of the old she-fox's stanzas build up to an unexpected resolution within the ode "Do," as if it were itself creating another ode entirely. In fact all it is actually doing is evolving the most complex of all the systems of the odes of the *Libretto*, toward the single stanza that breaks with the first section and poses the essential question: What then is the future of Liberia if it is a future not just of the Republic, but of humanity generally? It is a series of rhetorical questions, each asking with considerable precision about notorious moments in the history of Africa, from ancient Egypt to the desecration of the tomb of the Mahdi who had defeated General Gordon, and then on to Napoleon, and further.

> Tomorrow ... O ... Tomorrow, 555
> Where is the glory of the *mestizo* Pharaoh?
>   The Mahdi's tomb of the foul deed?
> Black Clitus of the fatal verse and Hamlet's arras?
>   The cesspool of the reef of gold?
>   *Der schwarze Teufel*, Napoleon's savior? 560
>   The Black Virgin of Creation's Hell Hole?
> Tomorrow ... O ... Tomorrow,
>   Where is the Jugurtha the dark Iago?

The answer to the question posed by the most difficult of all poetry in the *Libretto* comes in the concluding section to "Do" (575–770), which is, if not quite as Williams maintains, the least difficult part of the entire poem, a conclusion notably more lucid and direct than anything that has come before in "Do."[58] Tate found this concluding section section more successful as rhetoric than poetry, by which we take it he means that the presentation of the ideas of a great future seem to come across simply as prose rather than poetry.

But the verse in this last section of *Do* is not prose at all. It consists of enormously long lines of verse—out-Pindaring Pindar, we might say—which read and sound as "poetic" as anything we have heard earlier in the poem. Tolson regarded the appearance of poetry on a page as important as its sound and sense, which taken all together he termed "The Trinity of Parnassus." In the first of twenty-six highly irregular stanzas, each of the lines introduced by recurring refrains ("The Futurafrique," and later by "The United Nations Limited," "The Bula Matadi," "*Le Premier des Noirs*," and finally "The Parliament of African Peoples") is an inversion of the refrain "*Selah!*" in *Ti* as well as a final glance back to the opening ode's refrain of "*Liberia?*" Unlike those, each of the recurring lines builds solidly on recognizable points in the future as well as the present of Liberia. It is a vision of both that is singularly unclouded by the delusions that fill the first, infernal section of the ode. Furthermore, each time the refrain appears, it introduces what is formally a single line of verse. It may look like a paragraph of prose, but it actually is (and should be read as) a single, long line. These are the longest lines of all in the poem, dwarfing any measure that has come before.

> The Futurafrique, the *chef d'oeuvre* of Liberian   575
>   Motos slips through the traffic
>   swirl of axial Parsifal-Feirefíz
>   Square, slithers past the golden
>   statues of the half-brothers as
>   brothers, with *cest prace* . . . ["all honor to labor"]

This is all to be read and understood as a single line, with a pause indicated by the ellipsis that appears at the end. The ode concludes not with Liberia's transcendence, but the transcendence of Liberia by a larger entity, the Parliament of African Peoples. It is at once a triumph and something that an ordinary reckoning of triumph would be baffled by: abolition of all the things that have conspired to make every nation and people transitory. Except that in Tolson's poetry this destiny is avoided.

> The Parliament of African Peoples signets forever
>   the *Recessional of Europe* and
>   trumpets the abolition of itself:
>   and no nation uses *Felis leo* or
>   *Aquila heliaca* as the emblem of   760
>   *blut und boden*; and the hyenas

> whine no more among the bar-
> ren bones of the seventeen sun-
> set sultans of Songhai; and the
> deserts that gave up the ghost
> to green pastures chant in the
> ears and teeth of the Dog, in
> the Rosh Hashana of the Afric
> calends: "*Honi soit qui mal y*
> *pense!*" 770

The desert restored to green pastures has the lighthearted last word, which is also the motto of the Order of the Garter: "Shame to anyone who thinks ill of it!" Tolson's final ode ends with a cultural fusion that is one of his hallmarks; for example, at the beginning of "The Man from Halicarnassus," the absurdly obscure poem we refuse to explicate, he cries out, "O Togas of the Yeas on Ares Hill." What this means is something like "O those wearing Roman togas on the Areopagus who voted 'Yes' in the high court for civil and criminal cases in ancient Athens." Here he is in much better form; with "the Rosh Hashana of the Afric calends," he conflates the Jewish new year and the first of the month in the Roman calendar. And he thereby has recreated for all time the glories of Timbuktu that "Re" had seen as irrecoverably lost in the past—and with much the same images.

> And now the hyenas whine among the barren bones
> Of the seventeen sun sultans of Songhai,
> And hooded cobras, hoodless mambas, hiss
> In the gold caverns of Falémé and Bambuk,
> And puff adders, hook scorpions, whisper
> In the weedy corridors of Sankoré. *Lia! Lia!*

More prosaically we might say that the end of "Do" is simply referring to January 1 in the year of a new era. But the finale to Tolson's first book of Pindaric odes is anything but prosaic.

A Pindaric Reading of *Harlem Gallery*: "Psi" and "Omega"

The *Gallery* is Tolson's greatest work and of a length and complexity that permit us merely to sample what is there. Rita Dove's 1985 essay remains the best introduction to it. What we offer here is a reading of some cardinal passages near the end of the poem.

Readers of the *Gallery* should realize how venerable, even ancient, a predicament Tolson faced. Like Pindar, he seemed destined for a paradigmatic untimeliness. He discovered high modernism at the point when it was on the wane, just as he cultivated the white racist critic and poet Allen Tate without any illusions about the Confederate loyalist he was dealing with, yet with the hope (largely justified) that Tate's prestige might do his own work some good. All this happened at the very moment when both the brand of modernism that Tate represented and the larger tradition of Eliot and Pound were rapidly becoming passé. Karl Shapiro was more sympathetic to Tolson's genius than either Tate or William Carlos Williams, and he correctly focused on the distinctive grandeur and scale of the *Gallery* rather than the circumstances in which it was produced.

> Like so many great works of poetry it is a comic poem. It is funny, witty, humoristic, slapstick, crude, cruel, bitter, and hilarious. The baroque surface of the poem modifies none of this. The *Harlem Gallery* is as if improvised by one of the great architects of modern poetry. It may be that this work, like other works of its quality in the past, will turn out to be not only an end in itself but the door to poetry that everyone has been looking for.[59]

For "baroque" we could also say "Pindaric." Like Pindar's odes, Tolson's version of this ancient form invites the endless work of commentary and rereading, to a degree without parallel in African American literature published before or since. Considering the scale of just book 1, we cannot easily imagine what the magnitude of the completed five books of the *Gallery* could have been like—at the very least, a work surpassing Crane's *The Bridge*, possibly more on the scale of Williams' *Patterson*, or even Pound's *Cantos*. As it is, each of its twenty-four Greek-lettered odes develops a distinctive character that calls for separate commentary as well as the kind of synthesizing critical views that Tolson's critics and biographers have provided.[60] For this purpose Raymond Nelson's notes in the 1999 edition mark a good beginning. At more than one point he admirably confesses he has no idea what to make of something Tolson is saying.[61]

The irony of Tolson's untimely conversion to modernism thus has deeper roots than modernism, something he himself might have found amusing. Whatever he strove to be, he succeeded in becoming more like Pindar in his reception than any other modern American author. At the end of his influential survey of Pindar criticism David Young complains that one of the problems with Pindaric scholarship has been the disinclination of Pindar's commentators and critics to take note of one another's work. This is not a venial sin for classicists working in the Germanic tradition of classical philology; professional classicists are not supposed to write monologues, nor should they labor under the illusion of having no connection with their predecessors.[62] We could put Young's point in a more positive way: it is essential not simply to follow Michael Bérubé, Robert Farnsworth, and other specialists in Tolson, but to insist that a comparativist like John Hamilton is also needed for a reading of Tolson. For all the differences of poets and fields, we have to do with essentially the same modern audiences and their response to difficult poetry, so that what Hamilton writes about Pindar applies just as well to Tolson. Both the ancient and the modern poet are essentially out of date, out of step. As Hamilton puts it, "Either the poems can no longer deal with the world or the world can no longer deal with the poems."[63] Craig Werner articulates something similar in his work on the Afro-modernist aesthetic of *Harlem Gallery*.[64]

The further that modernism and the Black Arts movement of the 1960s and 1970s recede in time, however, the less important Tolson's seeming apostasy from his contemporary world becomes, the more obvious it seems that difficult poetry like the *Gallery* can be made timely by focusing on individual odes in their entirety rather than on a synoptic commentary that ranges over all these wildly varied creations.

As he comes to the end of his tour of the *Gallery* in two of the longer odes, the Curator addresses first "Black Boy" and then "White Boy" in "Psi." For Tolson's first readers these are names that would resonate first of all with Richard Wright's 1945 autobiography *Black Boy*; more abstractly, they are also specimens of what Nelson identifies as *Homo Aethiopicus* and *Homo Americanus*, dialectically opposed types that the Curator first addresses separately, and then in "Omega" takes together, speaking directly to both of them, "Black Boy, White Boy" and "White Boy, Black Boy."[65] Taken together, the two final odes of book 1 of the *Gallery* are the Curator's demolition of the ever-gathering threat of racism and the whole conception of "the Negro." As Woodson puts it, "Psi" is "a dance of the seven veils of the intellect," the angriest moment in the *Gallery*, where first the Curator and then Dr. Nkomo attack the whole concept of race, which they see as an invention of depraved minds.[66] With his blond hair, blue eyes, and white skin, the Curator is a living and speaking contradiction of racism, because he looks "white" and is "black" by definition.

White Boy,
as regards the ethnic origin
of Black Boy and me,
the *What* in Socrates' "*Tò ti?*"
is for the musk-ox habitat of anthropologists;
but there is another question,
dangerous as a moutaba tick,
secreted in the house
of every Anglo-Saxon sophist and hick:

Who is a Negro?

(I am White in deah ole Norfolk.)
Who is White?
(I am Negro in little old New York). ("Psi," Nelson edition, 350)

Tolson's indictment owes something perhaps to the satire of George Schuyler's 1931 novel *Black No More*, but, even more, Woodson argues, to Oswald Spengler's arresting images of the evanescence of the concept of "race" in *The Decline of the West* (1918).[67] Here is Spengler's characteristically vivid refutation of the allegedly "scientific" anthropology of his day, with its classifications of human beings into races.

> What are the hall-marks for our sense, and above all for our eye, by which we recognize and distinguish races? . . . Think of one of those mass-graves of the War in northern France, in which we *know* that men of all races, white and coloured, peasants and townsmen, youths and men lie together. If the future had no collateral evidence as to their nature, it would certainly not be enlightened by anthropological research. In other words, immense dramas of race can pass over a land without the investigator of its grave-skeletons obtaining the least hint of the fact. It is the *living* body that carries nine-tenths of the expression—not the articulation of the parts, but their articulate motions; not the bone of the face, but its mien. And, for that matter, how much potentially interpretable race-expression is actually observed even by the keenest-sensed contemporary? How much we *fail* to see and hear! What is it for which—unlike many species of beasts—we lack a sense-organ?[68]

Tolson's Curator is imbued with a Spenglerian contempt for the division of human beings back and forth across the color line. In this respect the

Curator's visible contradiction of theories of race and racism, which is also a dialectical contradiction, is very much a part of the world of Ralph Ellison's *Invisible Man*. The same strand continues in "Psi":

> Since my mongrelization is invisible
> and my Negroness a state of mind conjured up
> by Stereotypus, I am a chameleon
> on *that* side of the Mason-Dixon
> *that* a white man's conscience
> is not on.

The Curator then launches into a typical Tolson wordplay of "whiteness" as a sign of purity, with its Latinate associations of whiteness in the sense of "candor" (literally, a dazzling whiteness, a brilliance, and then a "stainlessness" or purity of character) and especially "candidate" (literally, "clothed in white," as in wearing a white toga that signals a Roman as "pure" and thus fit for office).

> My skin is as white
> as a Roman's toga when he sought an office on the sly,
> my hair is as blond
> as Xanthein;
> my eyes are as blue
> as the hawk's-eye.

The conjunction of whiteness with the venality of a Roman politician reduces the connection between white and purity to absurdity, and nothing else about the Curator can be gauged by what is supposedly seen. His blond hair is actually "xanthein" (or possibly "xanthin"; both of them derived from the Greek *xanthos*, "yellow"), the compound that gives yellow flowers their color, while his blue eyes are, impossibly, "as blue as the hawk's-eye," which is perhaps the name of a semiprecious quartz stone or an actual hawk. The Curator's "Negroness" is actually a way of exposing the hypocrisy of his fellow Curators—which could suggest, for example, the critics or poets who profess to speak about "the Negro race" and believe they are its friends for doing so.

> At the Olympian powwow of curators,
> when I revealed my Negroness,
> my peers became shocked like virgins in a house
> where satyrs tattooed on female thighs heralds of success.

This is the heart of the ferocious dialectical examination of race in "Psi."
For its beginning, Tolson sensed that either his Curator or he himself was
nearer the end of life than the beginning, so when he begins "Psi" with
his first of many vocatives, a somber tone is set that never leaves until
"Omega" opens with "White Boy, Black Boy."

> Black Boy,
> let me get up from the white man's Table of Fifty Sounds
> in the kitchen; let me gather the crumbs and cracklings
> of this autobio-fragment,
> before the curtain with the skull and bones descends. ("Psi," Nelson
> edition, 342)

The Table of Fifty Sounds is the roughly identifiable fifty phonemes in the
English language, a language which the Curator perforce has to use but
about whose power to shape his thinking in spite of the cultural damage
the white man's language can do to him he has no illusions.[69] The power
of that language can be seen by Tolson's recurrence to Myrdal's *American
Dilemma*, a book and an argument from which, as we've seen, he vigorously
dissents.

> Black Boy,
> you stand before your heritage,
> naked and agape;
> cheated like a mockingbird
> pecking at a Zeuxian grape,
> pressed like an awl to do
> duty as a screw-
> driver, you
> ask the American Dilemma in you:
> "If the trying plane
> of Demos fail,
> what will the trowel
> of Uncle Tom avail?"

Black Boy is seduced by the appearance of things, like the birds that pecked
at a painting of Zeuxis which was so realistic that it seemed to be actual
fruit rather than art. His questions are all wrong, addressing "the American Dilemma," which Herbert Aptheker and Tolson have already shown us
is no dilemma at all for African Americans. Accommodationism isn't the

answer. Dr. Nkomo intervenes in the Curator's long cross-examination of Black Boy and White Boy with some of the most beautiful poetry in this ode, by inverting William Blake's famous Tyger poem to argue that Nature's design of the African—not the "Negro"—is superior evolution.

> In spite of the pig in the python's coils,
> in spite of Blake's lamb in the jaws of the tiger,
> Nature is kind, even in the raw: she toils
> . . . aeons and aeons and aeons . . .
> gives the African a fleecy canopy
> to protect the seven faculties of the brain
> from the burning convex lens of the sun;
> she foils
> whiteness
> (without disdain)
> to bless the African
> (as Herodotus marvels)
> with the birthright of a burnt skin for work or fun;
> she roils
> the Aryan
> (as his eye and ear repose)
> to give the African an accommodation nose
> that cools the drying-up air;
> she entangles the epidermis in broils
> that keep the African's body free from lice-infested hair.
> As man to man,
> the Logos is
> Nature is on the square
> with the African.
> If a black man circles the rim
> of the Great White World, he will find
> (even if Adamness has made him half blind)
> the bitter waters of Marah *and*
> the fresh fountains of Elim. ("Psi," Nelson edition, 346)

The Logos or word of creation and existence is direct and fair: Nature has treated the African fairly. The African cannot be harmed by the sun the way the Aryan can, and the African body is far better adapted to its environment. Nature has done well with the African, he is the noblest and most admirable kind of human being—a sentiment Nkomo shares with the Man from Halicarnassus, Herodotus—and even if he is born into sin and depravity, so that his Adamness makes him half blind, he will enjoy the same blessings as the children of Israel, who found the bitter waters of Marah made sweet and the oasis of Elim in their wanderings in the wilderness.[70] But the threat of annihilation still hangs over the African. This is the century of Buchenwald and ethnic genocide, and the Holocaust of European Jewry may anticipate some similar atrocity by white people in the future. It is a warning expressed through jazz.

> White Boy,
> *Buchenwald* is a melismatic song
> whose single syllable is sung to blues notes
> to dark wayfarers who listen for the gong
> at the crack of doom along
> . . . that Lonesome Road . . .
> before they travel on. ("Psi," Nelson edition, 354)

And if the Curator himself does not believe in the doctrine of original sin (hence his self-identification as a Pelagian) that does not mean that he has been able to rid himself of the fear that Nature will turn on him as Blake's Tyger after all.

> A Pelagian with the *raison d'être* of a Negro,
> I cannot say I have outwitted dread,
> for I am conscious of the noiseless tread
> of the Yazoo tiger's ball-like pads behind me
> in the dark
> as I trudge ahead,
> up and up . . . that Lonesome Road . . . up and up.

As the folksong goes, "Look down, look down that lonesome road before you travel on," and as he does so, the Curator foresees that African Americans may yet be devoured by the white world, no matter how clearly they see through the delusions of race.

> In the Strait of Octoroon,
> off black Scylla,
> after the typhoon Phobos, out of the Stereotypus Sea,
> had rived her hull and sail to a T,

the *Défineznegro* sank the rock
and disappeared in the abyss
(*Vanitas vanitatum!*)
of white Charybdis.

The landscapes of the *Odyssey*, particular the settings for Odysseus's fantastic tales of his adventure, are all turned into markers of racism, fear, and a destruction of the good ship "Define the Negro" (*Défineznegro*) in a whirlpool of a white Charybdis, which also recalls the way Ulysses and his men are overwhelmed at the end of canto 26 in Dante's *Inferno*. This ending is the nadir of the Curator's catechism of the White Boy and the Black Boy, yet he immediately turns the sinking *Défineznegro* around and concludes the *Gallery* triumphantly with a celebration of the redemptive power of art.

Since the difference of white and black is nothing but a delusion, the Curator combines his two addressees into one in what is an innovative turn to the traditional object of praise, the victorious athlete, the hero— in the Pindarist Elroy Bundy's term, the *laudandus*, the one to be praised. Now there are two to be praised, who are at the same time one and the same human being, as the hendiadys, or expression of one idea through saying two, declares at the opening of "Omega."

White Boy,
Black Boy,
you have played blackjack with Tyche,
you have shot craps with Hap;
yet, things-as-they-are in the ghetto
have sported you for a sap.
Sometimes,
a guy born in a house with the graffito
of doom lucks upon the know-how of a raccoon
that gnaws off its leg to escape from a trap.
Now, the difference between
you and me
is the little matter of
a Harvard Ph. D.
You may have a better brain—
but no Nestor taught you how
to get rid of
its ball and chain. ("Omega," Nelson edition, 355)

The Boys have played the game with Tyche or Fortune, and they may have been lucky, but they haven't learned that they might have to gnaw off a leg to escape from where they are. Education, even in the style made famous by W. E. B. Du Bois, will do nothing whatever to free them from their situation unless they have a wise counselor, a Nestor, to free them from the very constraints that their superior education confers.

The thing that saves the Curator's bacon is the same thing that saves Pindar's: the art of his poetry is all that can be opposed to the exceedingly clear-eyed survey of the world that the first book of the *Gallery* has provided. Is this art difficult? Is it hard to grasp even after repeated attempts? Of course it is, but no more so than the world whose magnificence and intricacy we would never dream of being able to fully comprehend. At no other place in the *Gallery* does Tolson come closer than he does here to suggesting that the Curator is speaking as much of Tolson's own work, the *Gallery*, as he is of art in general.

> White Boy,
> Black Boy,
> freedom is the oxygen
> of the studio and gallery.
> What if a *chef-d'oeuvre* is esoteric?
> The cavernous By Room, with its unassignable variety
> of ego-dwarfing
> stalactites and stalagmites,
> makes my veins and arteries vibrate faster
> as I study its magnificence and intricacy.
> Is it amiss or odd
> if the apes of God
> take a cue from their Master? ("Omega," Nelson edition, 359)

The baffled reception of the *Gallery* would have come as no surprise to Tolson. He even has advice for his dedicated readers, making the same kind of distinction that Pindar makes between his audiences of those who understand, and those who do not.

> Do not scholars tear their beards—vex
> their disciples over the Palestinian and Byzantine
> punctuation of the Masoretic texts? ("Omega," Nelson edition, 359)

The Curator confesses that he himself has never had what it takes to be an artist, but he does not deserve to be read too literally.

I confess without regret
in this omega of my education:
I no longer have the force of a gilbert,
nor have I ever had the levitation
to sustain a work of art.
I have only pilgrimed
to the cross street
(a godsend in God's acre)
where
curator and creator
meet—
friend yoked to friend at the candle end. ("Omega," Nelson edition, 360)

The finale of book 1 of the *Gallery* is perhaps the most salient example of Tolson's use of the visual in his Trinity from Parnassus. "Curator" and "creator" derive from completely unrelated Latin roots, but as they cross here, they are made to seem to have more in common. It is a crossing and an intersection that we see as much in the mind's eye as on the page. In the cross street to which the Curator has pilgrimed, small changes in one can yield the other. Both are active agents, inseparably bound together as critical and creative minds always are. We might imagine that crossing as something like this:

Book 1 of the *Gallery* was not designed to be the poet's last words or the end of his works, but merely the grand first book of a much larger structure.

Our public may possess in Art
a Mantegna figure's arctic rigidity;
yet—I hazard—yet,
this allegro of the Harlem Gallery
is not a chippy fire,
for here, in focus, are paintings that chronicle

a people's New World odyssey
from chattel to Esquire! ("Omega," Nelson edition, 363)

Tolson ends with this promise to African Americans that their New World odyssey is a cause for hope, even optimism. It is all the more poignant that he did not live to see his most ambitious work through to its own conclusions.

Seven

It Is Impossible Not to Write Satire

If a state can prescribe, as a rule of civil conduct, that whites and blacks shall not travel as passengers in the same railroad coach, why may it not so regulate the use of the streets of its cities and towns as to compel white citizens to keep on one side of a street, and black citizens to keep on the other? Why may it not, upon like grounds, punish whites and blacks who ride together in streetcars or in open vehicles on a public road or street? Why may it not require sheriffs to assign whites to one side of a courtroom, and blacks to the other? And why may it not also prohibit the commingling of the two races in the galleries of legislative halls or in public assemblages convened for the consideration of the political questions of the day? Further, if this statute of Louisiana is consistent with the personal liberty of citizens, why may not the state require the separation in railroad coaches of native and naturalized citizens of the United States, or of Protestants and Roman Catholics?

In my opinion, the judgment this day rendered will, in time, prove to be quite as pernicious as the decision made by this tribunal in the Dred Scott Case.

Justice John Marshall Harlan,
Dissenting in *Plessy vs. Ferguson* (1896)

At the beginning of the second century Quintilian could with some justice claim that satire was altogether a Roman thing. After the first of many catalogues of vices of imperial Rome, his contemporary Juvenal summed up a satirist's impulse in the celebrated line *Difficile est saturam non scribere*. "Impossible," rather than the namby-pamby English derivative "difficult," is an appropriate word to describe what African American satirists confront: a patent illogic and lack of social justice in White America that would make even the excesses of Juvenal's Rome seem tame. There is a strong current of outrageous humor and satire running through African American literature, some of it written in knowing imitation of classical models, much of it not. But the point is that writers and poets with strong roots in African and African American culture were inspired by much the same societal conditions that can make writing satire impossible to resist for writers with comic gifts at any time and place, whether it be in imperial Rome or contemporary America. All that needs to happen is that they somehow be able to get away with writing it, and that we then are able to read it, or hear it, or watch it.

If a particular classical literary form could be said to characterize much of African American satire, it would be Menippean.* In a revaluation of the history and concept of a particular form of satire attributed to the Syrian Greek Menippus of Gadara (third century BCE), Howard Weinbrot argues that we should focus not on purely formal questions but rather on what provokes the urge to write this kind of work in the first place.

> Menippean satire is a form that uses at least two other genres, languages, cultures, or changes of voice to oppose a dangerous, false, or specious and threatening orthodoxy. In different exemplars, the satire may use either of two tones: the severe, in which the threatened angry satirist fails and becomes angrier still, or the muted, in which the angry satirist offers a partial antidote to the poison he knows remains. . . . Though norms may be overtly or covertly present, the text's dominant thrust is to resist or protest events in a dangerous world, however much the protest may fail.[1]

Even then it is more the philosophical (or political, social) affinities that are of interest, rather than strict questions of literary form. About that Weinbrot is rigorously restrictive.[2] Without the kind of opposition to "a dangerous, false, or specious and threatening orthodoxy," purely formal similarities (such as one of Menippean satire's standard definitions, that it

---

* When we mentioned this to a distinguished colleague not familiar with this learned term, he took us to be saying "Men a-peein'." *Se non è vero, è ben trovato.* This inspired misperception is just what the Menippean satirist does to his victims—pee all over them.

is a mixture of prose and verse) too easily include the bland, the apolitical, and the inoffensive with a kind of satire that is never anything less than the antithesis to that kind of political unconscious.

Another reason not to be so focused on Rome in thinking about satire, in spite of the Roman word, is that another Syrian Greek, Lucian of Samosata, was a prolific writer whose works largely survive, and which were a satiric model later as popular as any Roman's. His type of fantastic mythological travesty is the model for Erasmus's *Praise of Folly*, and his spoof of ancient ethnography and travel histories the *True History* inspired the scenario for Swift's *Gulliver's Travels*.

Satire so conceived is not the exclusive property of literature. The Dred Scott case of 1857 allowing the capture and return of escaped slaves in free states and the *Plessy vs. Ferguson* decision that institutionalized the segregationist doctrine of separate and equal in 1896 both provided benchmarks for satirists with a strong sense of outrage and an eye for the absurd. Even the judicial language of the Supreme Court explaining those decisions invited parody from the moment they appeared. In his courageous dissent from *Plessy vs. Ferguson*, which he correctly predicted would be as great a calamity as *Dred Scott*, Justice Harlan had no recourse but to ridicule the majority's arguments. Faced with the absurdity of segregationist thinking, even a Supreme Court justice found it impossible not to write satire.[3]

If it has been impossible not to write satire in African America, it is often equally difficult to mark out a separate and equal category of purely satirical writing. Melvin Tolson and Frederick Douglass have a great sense of humor that can surface at any point, with great effect, as have Ralph Ellison and Rita Dove. For the broadest perspective, readers should go to works like Mel Watkins's *On the Real Side*, which chronicles African American humor from both Africa and African American slave society into the contemporary world of comedians and satirists such as Richard Pryor, Spike Lee, and Chris Rock. In this chapter we will confine ourselves to three novels by writers who happily for the rest of us had to write satire: George S. Schuyler's *Black No More* (1931), Ishmael Reed's *The Last Days of Louisiana Red*, and Fran Ross's *Oreo*, both published in 1974.

The Metamorphoses of Black-No-More™

In a long career in journalism George S. Schuyler published just two novels, and both in the same year. Because of its thoroughly realized, savage fantasy, the enduring one has thus far proved to be the first: *Black No More*,

written in 1930 and published in 1931. Schuyler's extensive travels and research throughout southern as well as northern black communities some
years before gave him plenty of material to work with in the writing of
his first novel. He was similarly well equipped to write *Slaves Today* by a
three-month fact-finding expedition later in 1931 to Liberia. He wrote and
published that at a prodigiously fast pace in the same year after returning
from his trip. Even though it is a tragic romance in which the young man
Zo and his wife Pameta both die, pitifully, David Jackson, the archvillain
responsible for so much suffering, is gratifyingly hacked to death by Zo's
machete before Jackson's guard can gun Zo down. Then the business of
Liberia resumes the same course, unchanged. This second novel has many
affinities with the satire of *Black No More*. *Slaves Today* is a *Tendenzroman*,
a novel with a purpose.[4] Schuyler's avowed purpose is to expose to the entire world, especially the still flourishing European and American imperial
world, the wickedness and injustice of modern slavery visited by Liberians
on Liberians themselves.

As Melvin Tolson would also later show (*"Liberia?"*), the ironies of the
name "Liberia" are as unsubtle as the satire of *Black No More*. "Freedom's
Land," the very nation that was founded as a refuge for people from Africa
who had been enslaved in America, had itself become a despotic society,
for all practical purposes a slave society in the modern world not greatly
different from the slave society of nineteenth-century America.

Even though he published two successful novels in a single year, Schuyler was not at heart a novelist. It was a remarkable achievement, but the
very speed with which he dispatched them, their many formal similarities, and their explicit didacticism all suggest that he was not particularly
interested in exploring anyone's idea of the art of the novel. He was using
fiction for the same purpose he had in writing for newspapers and journals and weekly magazines: to expose and attack human folly and injustice, vices that he early had concluded both black and white people were
equally capable of perpetrating. He found his great model for this kind of
journalism in the work and the person of H. L. Mencken.

Schuyler's professional life was one fight after another, but for most of
it he tells us that it was comparatively happy. In 1928 he married the beautiful and sophisticated Josephine Cogdell, the daughter of a Texas banker
and rancher in Fort Worth, and settled down to live the rest of his life
with her in Harlem. Their daughter Philippa was a child prodigy and grew
up to become a composer and successful classical pianist and journalist,
performing in Africa and Asia as well as New York. In the cultural history of her times Philippa Schuyler's meteoric career took on a different

aspect for African Americans living outside the tight orbit of Harlem and New York City musical life. As if James Weldon Johnson's *Autobiography of an Ex-Coloured Man* had never been published—or her father's *Black No More*—Philippa became a racial and cultural paradigm. Born of a white mother and black father, her achievements were constantly brought to the attention of African American schoolchildren whose teachers were always looking for inspiring examples of what the race could achieve when it pushed light-skinned children to the fore. In spite of an ever growing body of criticism and satire ranging from Johnson and Schuyler himself to later kindred writers like Ishmael Reed, it never seems to have dawned on those who looked up to near-white pianists playing classical European music how limited these ideals would be to children or adults who might be equally talented, but who were darker and not capable of passing as near-white.[5]

Philippa came to a tragic end when she was killed at the age of thirty-five in a helicopter crash in 1967 in Da Nang Bay during the American Vietnam War. Besides performing for ambassador Henry Cabot Lodge and the American forces in Vietnam and rescuing Vietnamese orphans from the combat zone, she was by then a foreign correspondent for William Loeb's ultraconservative *Manchester (N.H.) Union Leader*.[6] This family tragedy fell on Schuyler and his wife only a year after he published his memoir, *Black and Conservative* (1966).[7] By then he was far removed from the liberal consensus politics of midcentury America, especially from African American mainstream literature and the civil rights movement. At the end of his career he was chiefly a regular columnist for the *Manchester Union Leader*, a journal famous then and later for finding a communist or socialist lurking inside every liberal politician.

Black No More opens a few years in the future, on New Year's Eve of 1933. Max Disher is a coffee-brown young man who has "Negroid features of a slightly satanic cast" (3) who goes looking for a new girlfriend, preferably white. As his sidekick Bunny Brown observes, "Every gal he's seen him with looked like an ofay." So when a party of white people enter with a "tall, slim, titian-haired girl who had seemingly stepped from heaven or the front cover of a magazine" (5) Disher's fate is sealed. He falls for her at once, even though he realizes she's from the South. As he puts it, "I can tell a cracker a block away. I wasn't born and raised in Atlanta, Georgia, for nothin', you know. Just listen to her voice" (6). After helping the white men in her party score some bootleg liquor, Max works up his courage to go ask the blond beauty to dance.

"No," she said icily, "I never dance with niggers!" Then turning to her friend, she remarked: "Can you beat the nerve of these darkies?" She made a little disdainful grimace with her mouth, shrugged daintily and dismissed the unpleasant incident. (8)

Disher is appropriately dashed, but not for long. He becomes obsessed with the girl from Atlanta. He falls asleep and

dreamed of dancing with her, dining with her, motoring with her, sitting beside her on a golden throne while millions of manacled white slaves prostrated themselves before him. Then there was a nightmare of grim, gray men with shotguns, baying hounds, a heap of gasoline-soaked faggots and a screeching, fanatical mob. (9)

Max's self-hatred is as palpable as his craving for white women. And at that moment in his life, like a deus ex machina or a genie out of a bottle, the *New York Times* reports the news of the biologist Dr. Junius Crookman's invention of process than can change a black man into a white man in just three days. As is common in satire ancient and modern, many of Schuyler's characters have significant names, some as finely tuned as his contemporary Evelyn Waugh's Candide-like hero Pennyfeather of *Decline and Fall* (1928). Crookman's Black-No-More, Inc., markets a process that exploits the fantasies of African Americans who would rather be white than colored, even though the cost of it is to endure a process in a machine that puts its patients through an ordeal akin to the electric chair (18). At the end of it all the exhausted Disher, drained of all color, is reborn Black-No-More and emerges an early and enthusiastic convert. White, blond, and jubilant, he rushes off at once to try out his new self on astonished friends and acquaintances in Harlem. Only the beautician Mrs. Sisseretta Blandish, owner of the "swellest hair-straightening parlor in Harlem," sees through the apparent solution of turning white: "Well, she sighed, "I suppose you're going down town to live, now. I always said niggers didn't really have any race pride" (28).

Mrs. Sisseretta Blandish has got it exactly right. A metamorphosis always brings some form of punishment with it down the line. *Black No More* is basically a satire that turns on the fulfillment of wishes and the realization of fears. Everyone gets what he or she most wants to have, and the consequences are dire.

With this astonishing metamorphosis and a compulsion that comes straight from racist white American as well as African American fantasies,

Schuyler's novel is off and running with a relentless logic that does not stop, from the dedication page to the last sentence of the novel. From the perspective of earlier literature it now reads as a continuation of knowing send-ups of fictional explorations, movements, and demolitions of the color line: the tradition of the Tragic Mulatta, romances of passing, and episodes of hair-straightening, from Twain's *Pudd'nhead Wilson* through the one-drop racism of *Plessy vs. Ferguson* to Johnson's *Ex-Coloured Man*. These themes would have a long life beyond *Black No More*. Forty years later Malcolm X could write a harrowing account of what was involved in "conking" his African hair with a lye compound to straighten it and render the color "white"; from that moment onward he was long known as "Red" because of conking.[8]

In Schuyler the familiar ironies and reversals that come from being granted what you most desire by the gods are supplied by the twentieth century's most revered gods, scientists. To step up in class as well as race, the transformed Max Disher enhances his new self by posing as an anthropologist and changing his first name to "Matthew" and moving from what sounds too working-class ("One who makes or serves dishes") to the more conventional "Fisher." The transformation is as magical as anything in Ovid or Apuleius, and just as problematic. It might even be that Matthew imagines his old self as hidden within his new white body as surely as the letters of "Max Disher" lurk within "Matthew Fisher." Only at the end of the story do we come to appreciate how prophetic his dream of white slaves and lynching parties is, or how truthful Mrs. Blandish's comment on race pride will prove to be.

In a sense Schuyler's *Black No More* does nothing more than obey American laws and customs, and then, following the logic of what race and color in America in the 1920s and 1930s required, it breaks every one of them. One of the most serious consequences of landmark cases such as *Plessy vs. Ferguson* was the way they brought about a complete polarization of the white and black races in America.[9] Thanks to the logic of the "one-drop" theory, black American writers were compelled to think they all had one thing in common: a separation from white America through their identity as a group associated by perceived color and race, if not artistic affinities. As a journalist and investigative reporter Schuyler departed from this orthodoxy in a number of ways, most memorably in his dissenting 1926 essay in the *Nation*, "The Negro Art Hokum." In his critique of ethnicity's role in the arts Schuyler argued that there was no such thing as an art that was uniquely black, as opposed to white art; both of them were inspired as much by a common European tradition as the English language they shared. His polemic was circulated in advance of its publication because of its rare dissenting view among the artists and thinkers of the Harlem Renaissance. With an advance copy of Schuyler's piece, and to Schuyler's considerable annoyance, owing to some delay of his own work's appearance, Langston Hughes published his famous reply, "The Negro Artist and the Racial Mountain," in the same issue of the *Nation* in which Schuyler's own essay appeared. Hughes's figurative mountain was not white racism and segregation in twentieth-century America, but the urge in African Americans to be whites themselves.[10] At the same time, he argued for the importance of establishing a Negro art that was uniquely, distinctly different from anything white artists following European traditions could create. Thereafter Schuyler's essay has always been linked with Hughes's "Racial Mountain." His polemic was so extreme that it was not difficult for Hughes's argument to be the more acceptable. What American Negroes then or later would welcome being stereotyped as "merely lamp blacked Anglo-Saxons?" As Jane Kuenz has argued, the range of Schuyler's criticism of Hughes and "the so-called Harlem Renaissance" is liable to be seriously underestimated if his 1926 piece is treated as his last word on the subject. *Black No More* engages with Hughes's argument quite directly in his own version of a Lucianic true history, and his counterargument through fiction is far more developed and compelling. As Kuenz explains, Schuyler regarded Hughes's ideas as naïve and politically dangerous:

> He is particularly disinclined to indulge in racial romanticism of any kind. Though he mocks the end-product, Schuyler's joke is that it is the becoming rather than the being that really renders one "white," that "whiteness" and its corollary "race"—are not physical attributes at all. . . . Their own efforts and desire to be white account for the changes in Schuyler's characters. . . . Wanting to be white is a really white thing to do.[11]

At its best (or worst) moments, *Black No More* reads like Jonathan Swift's *Modest Proposal*, and it works by the same kind of extravagantly rigorous logic: Are the Irish starving? Raise their children to be plump candidates for the kitchen. Do blacks suffer because they are not whites? Turn all of them into whites: end of problem.

In Howard Weinbrot's terms, Schuyler is a Menippean satirist in his most savage mood, "more the isolated cynic than either an amiable humorist or a sedately seated narrator."[12] It is often not so easy to separate the amiable humorist from the savage satirist. We would think twice for example before concluding that Mark Twain was simply amiable in *Huckleberry Finn*. But Weinbrot's distinctions are useful to remind us not to read Schuyler as a purely political creature. Unless handled with the sophistication of a Twain—on this point Mencken was not a good model for Schuyler to follow—such a satirical stance all too easily translates into something far less interesting, less compelling as art. Schuyler played the familiar polarizing role of a curmudgeon opposed to what others perceived to be progressive ideas and reforms. But considered as a writer, he is a more complex figure.

Black No More is the work that Schuyler is now best known for, but in most respects it was an exceptional development in his trajectory as a writer. He was primarily an investigative reporter of considerable energy, a columnist and journalist with a long career from the 1920s to the 1970s. Well into the 1960s he was a reporter and columnist for the *Pittsburgh Courier*, the largest African American newspaper in the first half of the twentieth century.[13] In his later years his anti-Communism and dedication to American conservatism led him to advocate reactionary positions that guaranteed he would be marginalized in the academy and most of African American society. He vigorously defended senator Joseph McCarthy ("a well-intentioned politician"). He even attacked the award of the Nobel Peace Prize to Martin Luther King, Jr.. At the time, this was not as exceptionable as it now seems.[14] And he was a model of good taste compared to Ishmael Reed's burlesque of King in his first novel, *The Free-Lance Pallbearers* (discussed below). The *Courier* rejected Schuyler's piece on King and he saw it published by his friend William Loeb, the publisher of the *Manchester Union Leader*. He never published in the *Courier* again.[15] By the time Ishmael Reed and Steve Cannon interviewed Schuyler in the early 1970s, Reed writes that they were criticized not only for talking to him, but even more, for taking him seriously as a major figure in African American literature.[16] Narrowing conservatism in later life is a familiar story for many who begin their careers in radical dissent from orthodox views.

Schuyler had not begun quite that way. To be sure, he was skeptical and mostly detached from the New York literary and intellectual scene, especially the milieu of the Harlem Renaissance which Alain Locke's 1925 classic *The New Negro* did much to canonize. At the same time, he lived and worked nearly his entire life in the very middle of where everything in black New York happened. Nor did he play footsie with the white crowd downtown. Unlike Ralph Ellison, for example, Schuyler wouldn't have been caught dead in the Century Association or any other establishment that enshrined worship of the book, the arts, or politics. Hence the Montainesque tone of such reflections as this:

Looking back over a lifetime of reading thousands of books, articles, columns, and essays, I would conclude that reading contributes much to one's knowledge but not necessarily to wisdom. The awe in which the lowly poor hold the "intellectuals" is mostly unwarranted. They are more often than not insufferable snobs who preen themselves for the literary one-upmanship that puts them six or eight books ahead of their fellow men. They talk glibly, using phrases culled from the works of others with whom they pretend familiarity and association, although knowing little more about them than the window cleaner or the scrubwoman knows. During my time I have rubbed shoulders with hundreds of the best-known "intellectuals" in America and abroad, conversed with them, read their writings and juggled their theories, and in retrospect it is appalling how downright wrong so many have been and still are. At least the poor whom they chide for not reading more have led nobody astray![17]

Schuyler was never in despair about the future prospects of the Negro in the United States. His daughter showed what could be accomplished, and so did he and his wife Josephine. In sharp dissent from separatists like Marcus Garvey and the later Black Power movement of the 1960s, he didn't claim that the color caste system in the United States was just, only that it was an abiding reality and that it would continue to be so for some time to come. There was simply no point in thinking it could be otherwise.[18]

Uncongenial as he would later be to mainstream African American thought and literature, Schuyler's worldview was much shaped by his experience as an investigative reporter. Sharing Du Bois's contempt for "car-window sociology," he developed a more nuanced view of American political and social history than stay-at-home doctrinaire, political thinkers ever could capture. This came from working for the *Pittsburgh Courier* in a nationwide tour of African American communities in the South as well as the rest of the United States, where he was on assignment from November 1, 1925, to July 4, 1926.[19] In effect he was doing field research on the same order as Frederick Law Olmsted had done sixty years before.[20] He was able to turn that experience to good use when the publisher George Palmer Putnam commissioned him to travel to Liberia and write an exposé of the slave trade that was then flourishing between Liberia and the Spanish plantations on the island of Fernando Po off the cost of Nigeria. The president of Nigeria and most of his government were said to be deeply involved.[21] When Schuyler reached Liberia he found a reality hideously different from the mythical Liberia of American imagination.

Although I had read and heard much of Monrovia, the capital since the "republic" was founded in 1847, I was quite unprepared for the squalor, filth, and degradation I encountered. Compared to it such all-Negro American towns as Boley, Oklahoma, and Mound Bayou, Mississippi, were palatial. Monrovia with its unpaved, rock covered streets, unpainted ramshackle houses, and general slatternly appearance was repugnant and depressing. The swarms of goats helped keep down the weeds but nothing could keep down the odors and the mosquitoes.[22]

Schuyler used the same methods he had followed in 1925–1926 in traveling throughout the South, making extensive notes at the end of every day with his typewriter. Upon his safe return to New York (and seriously ill with malaria), he published a series of articles reporting his investigations in the *New York Evening Post*. When it came to writing the book for Putnam, however, he turned his notes and his experiences in Liberia into a roman à clef with a clear polemical message.[23] He had made a similar connection between the world of fiction and fact in the preface to *Black No More*, completed just a year earlier.[24]

Schuyler maintains in *Black and Conservative* that his earlier experience in the American South taught him not to put much trust in sweeping generalizations about race relations.

> I learned that it was dangerous to generalize; that while the protocol of race relations was everywhere maintained, it was more loose and variable in some places than in others, and in some people more than in others; that people were humans and individuals before they were racial stereotypes. I have since found that this holds true all over the earth. (157)

These twilight memories forty years later are sweetly reasonable, but not at all the kind of stuff that makes for effective satire. Since he is writing a sustained satire, practically all that Schuyler does in *Black No More* is to play with stereotypes, inside both black America and the South, where two of the archvillains of the novel meet a grisly end: the premier genealogist of racist America, Dr. Samuel Buggerie—as in "buggery"—and Arthur Snobbcraft, FFV (First Families of Virginia), president of the Anglo-Saxon Association.

Snobbcraft and Buggerie flee for their lives after the Democratic Party is routed in the national elections in backlash against the transformation of American society by Dr. Crookman's Black-No-More. There are virtually no black people left to discriminate against in the whole country. Without blacks there is a danger that the American underclass will wake up to its own economic exploitation, and that would never do. Following this electoral debacle they escape from the East in a private plane, but unfortunately crashland in Mississippi. The ever-resourceful social scientist Buggerie points out that "real niggers" are scarce now, even in the South, so all they need do to "pass" for black is to color themselves black and no one will realize they are the notorious white scoundrels on the run. Snobbcraft reluctantly agrees, and both men soon have every bit of visible skin covered with black shoe polish: "In five minutes they resembled a brace of mammy singers" (163). The first town they walk into seems to be a veritable Southern Eden.

> Happy Hill, Mississippi, was all aflutter. For some days it had been preparing for the great, open-air revival of the True Faith Christ Lovers' Church. The faithful for miles around were expected to attend the services scheduled for the afternoon of Election Day and which all hoped would last well into the night. (164)

This peaceful evocation of Southern Christianity is overdone, patently setting us up. We quickly learn that Happy Hill has "an inordinately high illiteracy rate and a lynching record beyond reproach."

> The method by which Happy Hill discouraged blackamoors who sought the hospitality of the place was simple: the offending Ethiopian was either hung or shot and then broiled. Across from the general store and post office was a large iron post about five feet high. On it all blacks were burned. Down one side of it was a long line of nicks made with hammer and chisel. Each nick stood for a Negro dispatched. This post was one of the landmarks of the community and was pointed out to visitors with pardonable civic pride by local boosters. (165)

It is into this paradise that Snobbcraft and Buggerie stumble.

The Reverend Alex McPhule is the spiritual leader of Happy Hill and happens to be leading a revival on the very day Snobbcraft and Buggerie arrive. His name is a leitmotif for what follows: "McPhule," as in "fuel," for fire. He and his faithful are looking for a sign from above to help them save the white race from the black menace, and Rev. McPhule improvises magnificently.

> He will send the Sign,
> Oh, He will send the Sign

Loving Little Jesus Christ
He will send the Sign. (171)

And at this moment Buggerie and Snobbcraft in blackface stumble into
town and hear the singing and shouting of Rev. McPhule's service:

"Sounds like a camp meeting," Snobbcraft replied. "Hope it is. We can be
sure those folks will treat us right. One thing about these people down
here, they are real, sincere Christians." (172)

They are indeed. Rev. McPhule and the townspeople (including some ex-
blacks who wisely availed themselves of Black-No-More) chase them down
and are on the point of lynching them when Snobbcraft stops the show:
"We're not niggers," he yelled to the mob. "Take off our clothes and look at
us. See for yourself. My God! Don't lynch white men. We're white the same
as you are" (173). They succeed in freeing themselves for the moment, and
wash off the blackface. But then a newspaper arrives with their pictures in
it, and the news that both men are really niggers who had the Black-No-
More treatment. Snobbcraft and Buggerie are totally confounded, and so
are we, as black is really white, and white is suddenly really black. Schuyler
creates a reductio ad absurdum of both liberal and enlightened views of
color and race, as well as of the concept of race and color as markers of
identity. Abolitionists and civil rights advocates would say to themselves
that what matters is not the appearance of people, but what they really
are inside: color is no index of the soul. Rev. McPhule and his parishioners
couldn't agree more.

   The lynching follows the classic pattern of the practice as so often reported. Both men are stripped, their ears and genitals are cut off, then
they are let loose to run down a road, and are shot down in their flight.
Not yet dead, they are dragged to the iron stake and bound by chains to it:
"Little boys and girls gaily gathered excelsior, scrap paper, twigs and small
branches while their proud parents fetched logs, boxes, kerosene and the
staves from a cider barrel." The dazed men are roused by the flames and
their screams and cries resound: "The crowd whooped with glee and Rev.
McPhule beamed with satisfaction" (175). There are even whitened Negroes present who might have gone to the rescue of the two men, but fear
for their own lives restrains them.

Even so they were looked at rather sharply by some of the Christ Lovers
because they did not appear to be enjoying the spectacle as thoroughly as

the rest. Noticing these questioning glances, the whitened Negroes began to yell and prod the burning bodies with sticks and cast stones at them. This exhibition restored them to favor and banished any suspicion that they might not be one-hundred-per-cent Americans. (176)

In a perfect parallel to the kind of logic that drives Jonathan Swift's *Modest Proposal*, the lynching is completed by a search for skeletal souvenirs, such as forefingers, toes, teeth, or anything else decent enough to take as a memory (176). So much for the villains of the piece.[25]

The inventor of Black-No-More, Dr. Junius Crookman, is not one of them. He is the creator of the engine that drives the plot, the shaman-scientist who creates the possibility of a magical metamorphosis for black America through Black-No-More.[26] Crookman more than lives up to his name, and his invention enables all the other hustlers and con artists like Max Disher a.k.a. Matthew Fisher to flourish in the new all-white world. Among the most engaging is Dr. Shakespeare Agamemnon Beard, the founder of the N.S.E.L. (National Social Equality League, a.k.a. the real National Association for the Advancement of Colored People) and editor of its journal, the *Dilemma* (a.k.a. the *Crisis*): "In limpid prose he told of the sufferings and privations of the downtrodden black workers with whose lives he was totally and thankfully unfamiliar" (65). Shakespeare Agamemnon Beard is, of course, William Edward Burghardt Du Bois. Schuyler has Du Bois's florid rhetoric down to a T in his address to a conference called to deal with Black-No-More's threat to the Negro establishment.

> It were quite unseemly for me who lives such a cloistered life and am spared the bane or benefit of many intimate contacts with those of our struggling race who by sheer courage, tenacity and merit have lifted their heads above the mired mass, to deign to take from a more capable individual the unpleasant task of reviewing the combination of unfortunate circumstances that has brought us together, man to man, within the four walls of the office. (66)

Dr. Beard yields the floor to his "able and cultured secretary and confidant," Dr. Napoleon Wellington Jackson, but not before a peroration that sounds like the finale of an eloquent chapter in *The Souls of Black Folk* gone mad—the conclusion to "Of the Wings of Atalanta," for example.

> Before I gratefully yield the floor to Dr. Jackson, however, I want to tell you that our destiny lies in the stars. Ethiopia's fate is in the balance. The

Goddess of the Nile weeps bitter tears at the feet of the Great Sphinx.
The lowering clouds gather over the Congo and the lightning flashes o'er
Togoland. To your tents, O Israel! The hour is at hand. (67)

But of all the con artists of the novel, Crookman has the most penetrating
intelligence and is the one most reminiscent of Schuyler's own world-weary
public persona. Crookman erases the category of race as a meaningful concept in America, something that Kuenz argues Schuyler himself believed
in.[27] Schuyler conveys the routine, careerist thinking that characterizes his
every move. Crookman is one of those people who can never be excited
by anything.

> He had been monotonously successful but was sensible enough to believe
> that a large part of it was due, like most success, to chance. He saw in his
> great discovery the solution to the most annoying problem in American
> life. Obviously, he reasoned, if there were no Negroes, there could be no
> Negro problem. Without a Negro problem, Americans could concentrate
> their attention on something constructive. Through his efforts and the
> activities of Black-No-More, Incorporated, it would be possible to do
> what agitation, education and legislation had failed to do. He was naively
> surprised that there should be opposition to his work. Like most men with
> a vision, a plan, a program or a remedy, he fondly imagined people to be in-
> telligent enough to accept a good thing when it was offered to them, which
> was conclusive evidence that he knew little about the human race. (35)

There is considerable opposition to begin with, not least among the black
people who will supposedly benefit from his discovery. Later, when the re-
actionaries and racists of the former Confederacy and their sympathizers
all over the country realize that the whitening of American blacks will destroy the system, they try to unite to block the spread of Black-No-More,
but they get nowhere. They are routed at the polls, their leaders Snobbcraft and Buggerie are barbecued, and poetic justice is achieved. Then
Schuyler contrives an abrupt ending, as many satirists have to do. The attack is always more fun than the withdrawal of the spear, so Voltaire lets
Candide cultivate his garden.

At the end of this story, when American blacks are black no more, the
final pages of the novel are introduced by the title "And So On and So On."
At this point Crookman is the surgeon-general of the United States, in the
final days of the victorious President Goosie's administration—possibly
a graceful reference to Herbert Hoover, the president presiding over the

depression that was in full swing when *Black No More* was published—and he publishes a monograph in which he declares that the new Caucasians are in most cases "two to three shades lighter than the old Caucasians, and that approximately one-sixth of the population were in the first group. The old Caucasians had never been really white but rather a pale pink shading down to a sand color and a red" (177). This creates a terrible dilemma for both the ex-black Americans and the white, or more accurately pink, Americans whom they joined. White America actually begins to miss the very blacks it once oppressed and despised. As the song of "America's premier black-faced troubadour" sings (a.k.a. Al Jolson):

Vanishing Mammy, Mammy! Mammy! of Mi—ne,
You've been away, dear, such an awfully long time
You went away, Sweet Mammy! Mammy! one summer night
I can't help thinkin', Mammy, that you went white.
Of course I can't blame you, Mammy! Mammy! dear
Because you had so many troubles, Mammy, to bear.
But the old homestead hasn't been the same
Since I last heard you, Mammy, call my name.
And so I wait, loving Mammy, it seems in vain,
For you to come waddling back home again
Vanishing Mammy! Mammy! Mammy!
I'm waiting for you to come back home again. (115)

It is one thing when Schuyler turns Matthew Fisher's guilt on its head when the lovely blond from Atlanta he saw in the Harlem bar promptly falls in love with the white and blond Matthew and marries him. She then has a baby of color by him and simply assumes that she must be the one who has a black ancestor somewhere in her family tree. It doesn't occur to her that Matthew a.k.a. Max might be responsible. He graciously overlooks her genetic shortcomings. But it's another thing altogether when all the new Caucasians, including Matthew Fisher, realize that they are now *too* white, whiter than a *real* white person ought to be. This has a salutary effect on public morals: "For the first time since 1905, chastity became a virtue" (88).

Crookman's monograph complicates the situation enormously. Whereas before there were only dark suspicions, now there is once again ocular proof of whiteness, and now purity of whiteness is a terrible thing. O for the gift of a single drop of black blood.

The rise of what can only be termed Colorless Prejudice is, of course, deplorable and soon attacked from all sides, not only by President Goosie, but by a man named Karl von Beerde, a thin covering for Carl van Vechten, the Negro's New York friend and patron and author of the offensively entitled novel *Nigger Heaven*. In the same blithe spirit as van Vechten, von Beerde founds "The-Down-With-White-Prejudice-League." His name sounds strangely reminiscent of the black man who once headed the National Social Equality League, Dr. Shakespeare Agamemnon Beard (178). Soon the American enterprising spirit comes alive in business as well as the political sphere. Before they know it, Americans of the upper classes and then all the rest are seeking ways to get darker skin. Naturally, this being America, at first this is an expensive privilege that only those who can afford such things as face powders like *Poudre Nègre, Poudre le Egyptienne*, and *L'Afrique* can enjoy. What is needed is a cheaper and more marketable way of helping people of no color acquire proof of original Caucasianhood, and a Mrs. Sari Blandine comes up with it. Formerly Mrs. Sisseretta Blandish of Harlem, once famed for her hair-straightening, this newly white woman invents a skin stain that is so long-lasting and convincing that her own (stained) daughter receives a proposal of marriage from a young white millionaire (179).

"A white face became startlingly rare. America was definitely, enthusiastically mulatto-minded" (179): Dr. Crookman sees a picture in the Sunday magazine of a crowd of bronzed, brown Americans on the beach at Cannes in their scanty bathing suits. Among them he recognizes many of the hustlers and con artists we get to know in the novel, not least its hero and his wife and child, Matthew and Helen Fisher and little Matthew Crookman Fisher. And so the novel concludes: "Dr. Crookman smiled wearily and passed the section to his wife" (180). Schuyler dedicated his book to a quite particular audience, and we have to read *Black No More* to the end before we grasp what his dedication is actually saying.

> This book is dedicated
> to all Caucasians in the great republic
> who can trace their ancestry
> back ten generations
> and confidently assert that there are no
> Black leaves, twigs, limbs or branches on
> their family trees.

Horace makes much the same point when he asks the reader of his first satire, "Why are you laughing? Change the name and the tale is told about you."[28]

Mastering the Art of Greek Tragedy*

The whole idea is when state magicians fail, unofficial magicians grow stronger. If you want to talk about this time, you have to come up with new myths, like what Jung calls autochthonous myths. That's what I'm trying to do.

Ishmael Reed, "When State Magicians Fail," 1971

A Recipe for Disaster

Ishmael Reed has dedicated much of his work to the creation of myths of history and culture that explicitly demystify the received traditions of the European world and its cultural offspring. He was also an early admirer of the satiric work of George Schuyler.[29] Following the lead of the myth which he presents in *Mumbo Jumbo* (1972), his most thoroughly reasoned novel dealing with an alternative to Eurocentric mythology, he replaces Western high culture with myths and rituals of Africa and the African diaspora.[30] He argues not only for the existence of such roots, but also for their antiquity and for a multicultural alternative to European hegemony. Western history has been a long cultural war between rival systems defining human religious, political, and (most especially) artistic myths of human experience. Linked to this rivalry is a detailed examination of decades of such a rivalry and its roots in religion, aesthetics, and politics. Reed tells the story of this historical struggle by focusing on the 1920s and the cultural upheaval of that decade and the challenge it presents as a result of the artistic explosion of the Harlem Renaissance.

Reed traces his Neo-Hoodoo movement back to a number of challenges to the established ethos through time; moments when it seemed that the challenges to that ethos seemed for a while to emerge triumphant over what he labels the "Atonist," monotheist perversion of culture.[31] All this comes from a research project whose extensiveness Reed takes some pains to convey to his readers. *Mumbo Jumbo* at times reads like a parody of a scholarly monograph. He opens it with a definition of "mumbo jumbo" to explain how far from our standard dictionaries and encyclopedias we are when confronting African and African-derived systems of human experience. He closes it with an extended bibliography to impress on his readers the body of knowledge about which they are assumed to know nothing,

---

* With apologies to Julia Child et al.

or less than nothing. A "monocular vision" of deity determines Americans' limited vision of culture and the god we worship, he says. For the one god of the Atonist path, he substitutes the many gods of African traditions.

More than challenging settled beliefs, Reed's assault calls into question the aesthetic values of his opponents. He upsets received notions of artistic excellence, elevating so-called folk or popular culture to an eminence typically reserved for high culture. Like Toni Morrison, he argues that such cultural products of the folk are dismissed because their creators are not thought capable of true cultural originality. Reed's novels frequently turn into cartoons or the scenarios of B movies. Vaudeville, burlesque, and other popular forms of entertainment are given respectful space, as are the languages of the common people, but he saves his major scorn for the religion that he defines as a negative perversion of African sacred reality. The Jewish and Christian God is one, not multiple like the Loa of Voodoo. From the perspective of the Yoruba Eshu-Elegbara, it is scandalous that nowhere in the Bible does the central deity of the Judeo-Christian tradition laugh. Even more deplorable, he doesn't dance. On the contrary, when King David danced for joy before the Ark of the Covenant, "Michal Saul's daughter looked through a window, and saw King David leaping and dancing before the Lord, and she despised him in her heart" (2 Samuel, 6–14). Dance is central to African modes of worship as well as social interaction, and in African American society being a "wallflower" at community dances is much more than a social faux pas.

Hence Reed invents the "Wallflower Order" for followers of the Atonist or Western, monotheist path. They are responsible for the terrible innovation of the *soloist*. Solo performance is the unnatural enemy of African-based call-and-response patterns of cultural performance, a communal form of musical expression and worship. This African communal ethic carries straight from the church into jazz, where a solo turn is permitted, and the musician always knows how to end a star turn by folding back into the ensemble from which he emerged. "Soloists" like Moses and his modern avatar, a thinly veiled Bob Dylan, are mocked in *Mumbo Jumbo*; ghosts are redefined not as traffic between the world of the living and the dead but as present phenomena to be feared and (one hopes) exorcised. The American system that elevates Emersonian self-reliance, rugged individualism, and severance from the community is anathema to the anti-Atonist. To counter what he derides as the "monomyth" of European traditions, Reed called his new autochthonous myth "Neo-Hoodooism." This belief is "new" because it borrows from African roots but is native to the New World experience.

Reed's first novel, *The Free-Lance Pallbearers* (1967), is a scatological fantasy explicitly reminiscent of Trygaeus and his pet dung beetle in Aristophanes' *Peace* (421–420 BCE). Harry Sam, the leader of the worshipping group, sounds very much like Lyndon B. Johnson. At one point Reed gives an outrageous account of a clandestine recording and public broadcast of a "historic meeting" in the Oval Office, which sounds suspiciously like Martin Luther King's "historic" meetings with presidents Kennedy and Johnson in the early 1960s. A concealed microphone picks up and broadcasts the shrieks and cries of Rev. Éclair Porkchop (Martin Luther King, Jr.) to the throngs gathered outside the White House.

AWWWWW, DO IT TO ME. AWWWWWW. BABY. DO IT TO ME. WHERE DID YOU GET THAT LONG THING? MY MY O LORD, DON'T STOP, DON'T STOP. HELP. PLEASE DON'T STOP. DO IT THIS WAY. DO IT THAT WAY. OOOOOOO MY MY MY YUM YUMMMY OOOO. (*Caps original*)[32]

Kennedy and Johnson are not the only villains in the piece.

To American whites Rutherford B. Hayes may be among the most forgettable of presidents, but not to African Americans. Ulysses S. Grant's successor won the challenged election of 1876 by promising Southerners he would end Reconstruction and remove from the former Confederate states all the Union troops which were there to enforce it. The total collapse of African American participation in civic life followed swiftly, as did the rise of Jim Crow. Four statues of Hayes stand at cardinal points on Harry Sam's Island and each spews out waste from the Great Commode on which Sam has sat for thirty years. The central, Aristophanic image of the novel is shit, ranging from the shit dropping from the Hayes statues to the scholar U. U. Polyglot's research on the Egyptian dung beetle, which he finally mails off to a waiting scholarly world at the end of the novel. The most daring fecal image of all is the construction of Sam's island. It copies the human digestive system in the way excrement passes into the waters surrounding the island, waters that are filled with "deadly Latin roots" which flourish on such fertilizer. The naïve protagonist of this faux *Bildungsroman* does not really know until too late where he is or what a monster Sam is. *Pallbearers* ends not in a revolution against Sam but in the same horror with which it began. There is no counter to Sam and his regime, only new versions of the same.

The reassuring thing about Reed is that he never aims for the moral improvement of his readers. Aggression is all. Typically he creates titles like "Boxing on Paper" and "Writin' Is Fightin'," and boxers like Sugar Ray

Robinson and Mohammad Ali are heroic figures to him. As he observes in
a poem inspired by so-called friends and allies in the contemporary Black
Arts movement,

> If I ever
> If I EVER
> Bring out the
> Best in folks again I
> Want somebody to take me
> Outside and kick me up and
> Down the sidewalk or
> Sit me in the corner with a
> Funnel on my head.

He knows classical myth and literature and frequently refers to them, but
he is incapable of treating them or anything else with reverence. His creative energy and humor rise from the language of black America, where
any Western-educated elite that's around is never there but to be attacked.
This is what happened when Reed turned his deplorable gaze to one of the
most admired works of classical literature, Sophocles' *Antigone*.

How to Cook a Greek Tragedy

> Satirical food tends towards the putrid, disgusting, or taboo, exposing the
> tenuous and often arbitrary divide between what is considered edible and
> what inedible, embodying corruption in the midst of civilization. Food is
> the guts of Roman satire.
>
> Emily Gowers, *The Loaded Table:*
> *Representations of Food in Roman Literature*

"Louisiana Red" is hot pepper sauce, the most famous one being Tabasco
Sauce made and bottled in New Iberia, Louisiana. Only a few drops are
needed to heat up whatever dish it's added to. Anyone who cooks seriously
knows how important it is to use Louisiana Red with care.[33] In sophisticated restaurants like Alice Waters's Chez Panisse in Berkeley it provides
background radiation to dishes, but in such small quantity that most
diners won't realize it's there. In itself, Louisiana Red is not a bad thing.
It is not an evil opposed to something good, such as in the Greek tradition of contesting values; for example, Hesiod's two kinds of Strife (*Eris*),
a Bad Strife and Good Strife, the first one leading to war, the second to

ennobling rivalry and excellence.[34] To understand Louisiana Red, we have to move out of classicists' company and into the kitchen. Add too much Louisiana Red, and your food becomes inedible.

For Reed, the same problem arises in American political life, which he conceives as a cultural recipe gone seriously wrong. There's so much Louisiana Red about that it spoils the distinctive dish produced by the heroic Ed Yellings' Gumbo Works. Louisiana Red becomes a culinary metaphor for the aggressive impulse that gets out of control, as power-crazed businessmen, politicians, and the critics and theorists who serve them debase art and destroy society. *The Last Days of Louisiana Red* (1974) portrays an America overseasoned with aggression and exploitation, and it is antithetical to Reed's own work. As he would later acknowledge, recipes for cooking gumbo are a metaphor for his writing.[35] Literary gumbo is a kind of cuisine Quintilian's Romans would have recognized, as Gowers observes, but the claim that satire is *tota nostra* ("altogether ours," Roman through and through) sounds more like *Cosa Nostra* than a recipe for the way satire actually evolved in either antiquity or more recent times.[36]

In the broad, seemingly chaotic manner typical of much of his fiction, Reed points beyond the internecine struggles of blacks against blacks, to the fundamental, abiding threat of Louisiana Red, and the need for blacks to recognize it and fight against it. The Neo-Hoodoo Papa LaBas (a shaman already introduced in Reed's 1972 *Mumbo Jumbo*; in this novel the voodoo master takes on still other guises) realizes at the end that Louisiana Red, hot pepper sauce, is the great challenge to human happiness and the well-being of society. The same moral applies to families and businesses and governments.

> Had the presence of Solid Gumbo Works meant the complete end of Louisiana Red as Ed wanted? Never, thought LaBas, who subscribed to the viewpoint that man is a savage who does the best he can, and so there will always be Louisiana Red. No, Ed wouldn't go down as the man who ended Louisiana Red, but only one of many people who put it into its last days. But like the tough old swaggering pugnacious vitriolic cuss Louisiana Red was, it would linger on until it was put out of man's mind forever. (175)[37]

The threat of Louisiana Red is the threat of a liquid substance that has undergone a metamorphosis as sinister as anything in Kafka or Ovid. Reed's characters handle it with the same lunatic seriousness with which Sterling Hayden plays General Jack D. Ripper, the madman responsible for the nuclear war unleashed in Stanley Kubrick's 1964 satiric masterpiece, *Dr. Strangelove*.

In the concoction of *Louisiana Red* the entrepreneur Ed Yellings and his family become so many ingredients in a literal recipe for disaster. Ed is the proprietor of a hugely successful New Orleans–based enterprise named the Solid Gumbo Works, and the head of a household that will be destroyed by civil war, with Ed's wife Ruby decamping to Washington, D.C., to play the American political game and his own children neatly dividing into enemies and defenders of Louisiana Red. The four children are ordered symmetrically according to irreconcilable political positions. Wolf Yellings is the oldest and wisest, Sister the hardest worker, Street Yellings the impetuous son who fights first and rarely thinks afterward, and Minnie the youngest, given to argument for the sake of argument, a contrarian who can be counted on only to take the opposite course to what anyone else suggests. The story unfolds in the Bay Area of Northern California, and the consequences are as cosmic as the Theban myths could be for the Athenians. Indeed Reed makes the parallel quite explicit: "Old Doctor Durant, a classics professor, intended Berkeley to be the Athens of the West; that would make Oakland the Thebes" (103). Not long after the time Reed was writing and publishing his novel, Marian Musgrave observed that this story about the efforts of the Louisiana Red Corporation to take control of the world, including anyone like Ed who opposes it, functioned "like a black morality play or a parable of black life in the 1960s and 1970s, when blacks were splintered into many mutually hostile groups, their goals and methods often unsure or contradictory and just as often not inspired by black needs or principles but by borrowed white ones."[38]

George Steiner did not take *The Last Days* into account in his critical and historical study of the reception of Sophocles and the Antigone myth from antiquity to the twentieth century, *Antigones*.

> How can we read, how can we "live" *Antigone* now? What kinds of understanding are possible under the weight of the hermeneutic inheritance, of the sum of preceding commentary and poetic-performative interpretation? . . . Antigones past and present have proved beyond inventory. Already, there are so many gathering in the twilight of tomorrow.[39]

Reed's novel is probably not the kind of twilight gathering Steiner has in mind. Neither the title nor the author would seem to have anything to do with the exalted subject of *Antigones*. Yet *The Last Days of Louisiana Red* gives a sharp twist to that familiar story. Reed had already signaled what he would do with this legendary work of Western art in his poem "Antigone, This Is It," which he published in 1973, the year before *Last Days* appeared.

> Whatever your name, whatever
> Your beef, I read you like I
> Read a book
> You would gut a nursery
> To make the papers, like
> Medea your Poster Queen
> You murder children
> With no father's consent.[40]

Here Reed's animus is stronger than his mythology. It's hard to imagine Medea asking Jason for his *consent* to murder their children. Not surprisingly, "Antigone, This Is It" and *Last Days* made no impact whatever on later feminist theory and criticism about the myth and the play.[41]

In any case, throughout *Last Days* Reed shows a wide knowledge of the later reception of the tragedy *Antigone*, such as Felix Mendelssohn's *Antigone*, op. 55, but he went to some pains to make sure that this would be one book that could not be known by its cover. Adopting his culinary approach, we might say that his way with the Antigone myth is to cover it and Sophocles completely in a recipe that only gradually lets his readers recognize what the main ingredient of this concoction is: nothing less than a revision of the recipe for what was long regarded as one of the most admired and influential of all Greek tragedies.[42] Sophocles and Greek myth are run through a Creole kitchen, just like crawfish or catfish etouffee, smothered (*étouffée*) in a rich sauce of roux, peppers, onions, and other spices.

The recipe for *Antigone* emerges in a characteristically broad treatment of satirical themes; anything can turn up in a Reed novel, including the kitchen sink. He has what Bracht Branham terms an unruly eloquence, like the second-century Greek satirist Lucian, but in the (comparatively) broader and freer environment of racist, imperial America it is an eloquence more rude and more offensive to a wider constituency of readers than any surviving ancient satirist ever seems to have been able to enjoy, even Juvenal.[43] In chapter 4 a character named Chorus appears in Berkeley; a miserable failure in the East, "he had made what one critic called a 'valiant' attempt to restore the Chorus to its rightful role."[44] Thus he appears in the next chapter on a vaudeville stage, and at first there seems to be no connection at all with *Antigone* or anything else classical. But as Reed's novelesque texture shifts to the style of a dramatic script, we learn just how oblique this evocation of *Antigone* will be. Chorus is a thirty-five-year-old stand-up comic with a well-justified inferiority complex.

> In the 1960s I was the stand-up comic who didn't have a nightclub. Now I have all the nightclubs I need, and do you know how I did it? (flicks ashes from his cigar, inhales). Do you know how I fell from protagonist to humiliation, hung around for throwaway parts, kissed the lead's ass to stay in business, and now look at me, so powerful that this morning I closed down the actors' lobby.
>
> What I did was to go back to see where I went wrong. It started with plays like *Antigone*. (27)

Chorus is in the employ of the Louisiana Red Corporation, which is dedicated to spreading its power all over the land, and a follower of the Moochers to boot. Moochers live up to their name: borrowing, never returning, manipulative, they "kill their enemies like the South American insect which kills its foe by squirting it with its own blood. God, do they suffer. 'Look at all of the suffering I'm going through because of you'" (17). So much for Aristotle's dictum that tragedy is an imitation of incidents arousing pity and fear.[45] If suffering can be perceived as a manipulative rhetorical move rather than anything genuine, audiences and interpreters will find it easier to side with Creon than with Antigone. So at least Chorus hopes. One of the effects of classical tragedy and Sophoclean tragedy in particular is the creation of sympathetic vibrations in audiences who witness suffering and take it seriously. It is typical for a satirist to summon up analogies and memories of tragedy, only to render them irrelevant and absurd.

Critical (not tragic) recognition of the complexity of Reed's parodic design thus begins with Chorus. Even then his design is more than a parody of Sophocles. By turning the ancient Greek chorus into an individual actor named Chorus, Reed creates a walking, talking personification of the reception of the *Antigone*, a subject which Steiner would later write about with great depth of philological and historical learning, as indicated by his comments above about the weight of the hermeneutic inheritance and the sum of preceding commentary and poetic-performative interpretation.[46] Steiner constantly directs his argument toward an affective reading of this tradition, as he seeks to understand the perennial fascination *Antigone* and Greek myth in general have had in the West. Among the most touching parts of his book are the closing pages, where he recalls reading Sophocles' Greek as a young student at a lycée in New York during World War II. One of his fellow students left to fight in the French Resistance and died, at probably no more than seventeen years of age.[47]

Chorus is no George Steiner. He embodies received critical opinion about the legend and its interpretation, in a general way, but is no more a dispassionate critic than Sophocles' own chorus of Theban elders had been.[48] He takes Creon's part and sees his way of ruling as necessary and legitimate.

> Antigone comes down through the ages as the epitome of the free spirit against the forces of tyranny. However, some say she went too far. I say she went too far; not only because she opposed a good and just authority, but because she was the beginning of my end. It was in plays like *Antigone* that I, the Chorus, declined until I was cast out, off the scene altogether, but now I'm bouncing back. I say that Antigone got what she deserved. (29)

This is a crazed but recognizable account of the actual history of the Greek chorus. In the fourth century BCE, after the great age of Athenian tragedy ended, choral lyric on the order of *Antigone*'s famous "Ode on Man" quickly became a thing of the past. So apparently did great tragedy at the level of the canonical Aeschylus, Sophocles, and Euripides. But who cares? Not Reed and certainly not Chorus. Thanks to his jealousy and his memories of the original production, Chorus can see Ed Yellings's daughter Minnie only as an incarnation of Antigone herself.[49] He becomes a major player in this new recipe of the Antigone myth. It is clear that Reed would have little sympathy for the basic question Steiner seeks to answer in *Antigones*: "Why the unbroken authority of Greek myths over the imagination of the West?" But Steiner is a widely ranging critic and acknowledges near the end of his book that the fascination with this and other Greek myths is far from universal:

> Because Greek myths encode certain primary biological and social confrontations and self-perceptions in the history of man, they endure as an animate legacy in collective remembrance and recognition. We come home to them as to our psychic roots (but why, then, are they not, strictly speaking, universal and of equal import to *all* cultures, East and West?).[50]

Why indeed not. *The Last Days of Louisiana Red* is Reed's anticipation of the question Steiner would later raise. *Last Days* breaks the authority of Greek myth into little pieces. Its recipe exploits the gap between the exalted reputation of *Antigone* and the present realities of a world to which classical myth has nothing to say. Reed's critical position is well expressed in subsequent collections of essays like *Writin' Is Fightin'*.[51] What he is fightin' here is neither the tradition that Steiner would later explore, nor really the *Antigone* itself, but a Western world that the classic contest between Creon and Antigone does so much to define.

The parallels between the House of Thebes and the House of Yellings are reasonably clear, though naturally Reed takes liberties. Laius, the slain father of Oedipus, is conflated with his son, because Ed Yellings suggests both roles; he is murdered by Amos 'n' Andy, famous white comedians of 1940s and 1950s American radio who played characters in blackface and are now agents of Louisiana Red. Ed's own name is democratized à la americaine, reduced to the nickname (O) Ed (ipus). Ed's wife Ruby is Jocasta, but she's not Greek in any way: a liberated woman who "forgets" the time for her periods and bears him four children—which task completed, she decamps for a political career in Washington. The Yellings children correspond to the four we know from Sophocles: Wolf Yellings is Eteocles, Sister is Ismene, Street is Polynices, and Minnie is Antigone. The family name Yellings probably came about in the first place to give Street Yellings his eloquent name. Street is a clear embodiment of street protestors like H. Rap Brown and other radical types of the sixties and seventies. In similar fashion Minnie supplies the name for all the Moochers, just as Street gives the Yellings their name. Papa LaBas sees Cab Calloway's famous song "Minnie the Moocher" as the key to Minnie's horoscope, which he sings.

> Now here's a story 'bout Minnie the Moocher
> She was a low-down hoochy coocher
> She messed around wid a bloke named Smokey
> She loved him tho' he was a "cokey."

This low-down hoochy coocher plays on the same team as Louisiana Red; in variant lyrics Minnie even has the appropriate color code, where she's called a "red-hot hoochy coocher." To make sure we don't miss the significance of Minnie's name, Reed adds a learned footnote to point out that "hoochy coocher" comes from *Hoochy-Coochy*, "one who practices Voodoo" (*Dictionary of Afro-American Slang*, 34). When a companion of Papa LaBas asks what he needs, it is a translation of the refrain in Calloway's song: "Skid a ma rinky dee, Ho de ho de ho."

In those lines lies the key to Minnie-detection. You see, it has been held that her problems originated from outside of her, suggested in the liberal-social worker lines, "just a good gal but they done her wrong." This means the lines were tempered with. You see, if I can prove that she was no helpless object swept away by forces beyond her control but a dedicated agent of the sphinx's jinx, an acolyte of an ugly cause, if I can interpret her through African Witchcraft, then a lot of people's eyes will be opened and they will be on the lookout for this character posing as a victim of history while all the time she is a cruel jinx with her zombie companion, Smokey. (35)

There was evidently not as much to be done for Minnie's siblings, and Reed lets Wolf and Street shoot each other in a fog and thus replay the Eteocles-Polynices conflict of Aeschylus's *Seven Against Thebes* and its mythical aftermath in the *Antigone*. Sister is dutiful and reasonable, a foil to Minnie just like Antigone's hapless sister Ismene.

Reed does not follow the Sophoclean tragedy to its catastrophe, with the suicides of Antigone, her lover Creon's son, Haemon, and Creon's wife Eurydice. Instead he resorts to an obscure variant of the Antigone myth, known from its use in Euripides' lost *Antigone*, evidently a kind of tragicomedy of some kind in which she bears her lover Haemon a child and is even saved from death at the end, possibly by Teiresias.[52] This is a clever move, since it points out to uncritical admirers of classics who think that a text like the *Antigone* is the Way It Really Was and no other way that Sophocles' drama is as much the result of conscious artistic choices as any other artist's.

After Ed is dispatched, Papa LaBas is drawn into a confrontation with Minnie, which leads Marian Musgrave to identify him as the Creon figure.[53] But as his explication of Calloway's song suggests, Papa LaBas is just as much a Teiresias figure. (Recall that Teiresias is as much a bringer of bad news to Creon in the *Antigone* as he is for Creon's brother-in-law Oedipus in the *Oedipus*.) While he opposes Minnie just as Creon opposes Antigone, LaBas also recognizes that she is part of a world whose operations she doesn't really understand. In LaBas's eyes, she's "a special type of psychic crook we want to find a cure for, but first we have to get her details on file so that we'll be able to spot her whenever she victimizes someone" (34). Unfortunately for Minnie, her old nemesis Chorus catches up with her first, when she and her henchmen Kingfish and Andy skyjack a plane. He shoots her even as he's mistaken for a skyjacker and then shoots himself: "He screamed, 'I'm sick of you cutting into my lines, Bitch!'" (160). Chorus dies as he lived, eternally resentful of Antigone hogging all the good lines.

On her way to New York to be at Minnie's side in the hospital, where she is presumed near death, Sister a.k.a. Ismene begs LaBas to intercede. His disclaimer seems more than a little obscure until we realize it sums up the whole recipe that Reed has concocted.

"I'm not a sociologist, not a classicist. I'm just a trouble-shooter for a
Board of Directors."

"O Pop, you're not all that cold as you make out to be. You have a soft
spot in you. Go and get that girl away from Death. You can do it." (166)

So LaBas goes forth to intercede with Death, who is in the guise of Blue
Coal, a lecherous nightclub owner of the 1920s and 1930s. (There is no
such thing as a linear chronology in this or many other Reed novels.) LaBas
sees but doesn't recognize Chorus, who is at last at peace in this world of
dead myths and moribund tragedies.

> One guest, a young gentleman though mature-looking, impeccably
> dressed in a white tuxedo, hair shampooed, parted down the middle and
> giving off a lustre, was smoking a small cigar. He seemed a little bloodied
> but appeared relaxed, serene even, as if he had gotten something off his
> chest that had been bugging him for many years. (168)

So far as Chorus himself is concerned, this is exactly the ending Antigone-
Minnie deserved.

> You know, people will go through many roundabout ways to get what
> they want. Antigone was that way. Creon had it right when he said that
> Antigone worshipped one god and that was Hades. She was a monothe-
> ist with a twist; she wanted to make it with Death. Creon saw through
> her rhetoric, her passionate appeals, her attempts to impose mob rule on
> Thebes. . . . Why didn't she try to bring Eteocles and Polynices together
> to settle their differences? No, she wanted the whole family dead. She
> wanted them to be the first family of Hades with herself as queen. (87)

But Minnie lives again, if not Antigone, and that is thanks to the intervention of Papa LaBas and African witchcraft. For his part, Chorus is eternally stuck in the ever-renewable past of *Antigone* reception, a past from
which neither he nor any other commentator will ever escape.[54]

Fusion Cooking

> A slave who sat at Habinnas' feet suddenly began to chant the *Aeneid*,
> evidently at his master's request: "Meanwhile Aeneas' fleet traversed the
> main . . ." A more disgusting sound has never assaulted my ears. Not only
> did he barbarize the pitch and rhythm of the verse, he also interlarded lines

from the Atellan farces. For the first time in my life I actually found Vergil revolting.

                            Petronius, *Satyrica* (Branham and Kenney, trans.)

Not all the indigestible ingredients for *Last Days* come from Sophocles' *Antigone*. Max Kasavubu's nightmare is as good an illustration of Reed's tendency to make high art indigestible as any other in the novel. It is an exercise in poetic justice. Kasavubu is a visiting professor from Columbia teaching at Berkeley, but in fact a secret agent for the Louisiana Red Corporation. As his cover for this role he is engaged in writing what is proclaimed to be the definitive critical study of Richard Wright's *Native Son*. The problem for Kasavubu is that he plays his role too well. As the saying goes in academic writing, he is too close to his subject.

> He was a blonde. He lay in the bed, tossing and turning. His room. What was that door? What was that odor? The pungent odor of middle-class perfume making the air misty. He didn't feel right. His hair. What on earth was the matter with his hair? It was long and was covering the pillow. The pillows? They had a flower print and were pink. Pink? He rose in his bed and his breasts jiggled. BREASTS? THE BREASTS?? He looked back into the mirror next to the bed and his mouth made a black hollow hole of horror. "O MY GOD. MY GOD." He was a woman. You know what he said next, don't you reader? He's from New York and so . . . you guessed it! "Kafka. Pure Kafka," he said. (150)

Would that Kasavubu were like Kafka's Gregor Samsa in "The Metamorphosis." Given what ensues, it wouldn't be so bad to be a cockroach. Max finally realizes who he must be when a mysterious dark shadow comes into the room and creeps to the foot of the bed: "A giant colored man—an Olmec-headed giant wearing a chauffeur's cap. Max started to really scream this time" (150–51).

And well he should. This transformation is as frightening as anything in Kafka or Ovid. As an expert writing the definitive book about Richard Wright's *Native Son*, he realizes which part of the novel he's in, and who he is. The giant colored man is none other than Bigger Thomas, and he, Max Kasavubu, has become the lovely and fashionable socialite-socialist Mary Dalton. He knows that as soon as Mary's blind mother Mrs. Dalton comes tap-tapping into the bedroom, Bigger will panic and smother Mary to death with the pillows on her bed to hide his presence. Max's fevered imagination changes roles just in time.

"Please, Ms. Dalton, you will wake the whole house," the figure says. *Look at that white bitch laying there. Sloppy drunk. Probably wants some peter too. That's all they think about anyway. I'll fuck her into a cunt energy crisis she mess with me. That's probably what she wont. Been hittin on me all night. Probably pretending to be drunk. Wonts to see how far I go. I know Jan ain't getting any. One simple dude. Tried to give me that old PROGRESSIVE LABOR line. Who don't know that? Who don't know that old simple ass mutherfucking bullshit? Them mens was working at the Ford plant. Had some good jobs too. Then here comes this Progressive Labor bullshit and them niggers lost they job after it was over. Ha! When is this bitch going to go to sleep?* (151)

The "Ms." is an anachronism, a glimmer of what's left of Kasavubu's 1970s academic mind, and the silent thoughts of Bigger Thomas are similarly contemporary, not the language of Wright's 1940 novel. Max Kasavubu has, as the saying goes, flipped out. When his two accomplices Lisa and T. from the Louisiana Red Corporation try to pull him back to reality, he shoots Feeler and his nightmare becomes waking reality. Lisa, the cleverly disguised Nanny who betrayed Minnie, makes the fatal error of addressing Max by his first name. Recall that "Max" is also the name of Bigger Thomas's lawyer in *Native Son*, and that he never really understands Bigger until the very end, shortly before Bigger's execution for the murder of Mary Dalton.

"Max, let's get out of here. We really must go now."
Max slowly looked up from where he knelt over the corpse. "Who you callin' Max, bitch? I'll whip you into bad health."
"Max, what's the matter with you? Why are you talking that way?"
"I'm gone fix you good. Killing you won't count. Not even the best critics will notice it. I'm going to kill you." He walks toward her. She screams.
"Max! Stop!"
"Max? Who Max? I'm Bigger," Max growls. (156)

Onetime critic Max Kasavubu, undercover agent of Louisiana Red at Berkeley and distinguished scholar of Richard Wright, now goes mad in yet another direction, turning from Mary Dalton into Bigger Thomas, who murders Mary as well as his mistress Bessie. Recall that Max chops up Mary's body and with some difficulty burns it in her family furnace; later he bludgeons his sleeping mistress Bessie with a brick and throws her body down an airshaft. Along with Sophocles' *Antigone*, the horrific murder scenes of *Native Son* are now just one more ingredient in the gumbo that Ishmael Reed concocts to make *The Last Days of Louisiana Red*.

The Heroine with a Thousand Etymologies

Oreo. U.S. slang (depreciative). In African-American usage: an African-American who adopts or identifies with middle-class white culture as opposed to urban African-American culture; a black homosexual man who prefers white men as sexual partners.

Oxford English Dictionary

Once greater *libertas* was at hand, following the civil rights revolution of the 1950s and 1960s, it did not follow that you could play safely with American conceptions of color and race. In 1977 the New York freelance writer Fran Ross traveled to L.A. to try out for the writers' team working for the new *Richard Pryor Show* in production for NCB television. While her satiric novel *Oreo* (1974) plays brilliantly on the edge of one insulting word "oreo," she learned that not even a sophisticated writer and thinker of color could safely use the "troublesome word" that is the subject of Randall Kennedy's encyclopedic study.[55] Pryor had just finished playing a straight dramatic role for Paul Schrader's film *Blue Collar*, and in an effort to make conversation Ross wondered if he'd had any trouble when on location in Detroit. She reminded Pryor that on the *Tonight* show he'd said, "If you see two niggers running in the neighborhood, we're just making a movie." As one of Pryor's biographers Jim Haskins reports,

> Ross recalled, "I was definitely quoting, because, unlike many black people who use the term among intimates with affection, nigger is not a word that I use. Richard said, a touch coldly, 'I said, "two Black men."'"[56]

Ross did not get the job. What Redd Foxx called the "Big N" can still cut both ways, even when black people mean it in a positive sense. In spite of Kennedy's historically informed and optimistic conclusion to his book, "nigger" is still not a word lightly used even in literary criticism, because its effect can never be anticipated, even when said by blacks, to blacks.[57] The Richard Pryor who recoiled at Ross's quotation of his own words was the same performer and comedian of genius who had produced the comedy album *Bicentennial Nigger* just a year before he met Ross. In 1995 he would finally repudiate the use of the word onstage or off, in *Pryor Convictions and Other Life Sentences*.[58]

Ross was not writing at a moment congenial for learned satire. By the early 1970s many political scientists and linguists were committed to the study of black American English and its status in white societies, particularly in cities.[59] If a social and historical matrix for the appearance of *Oreo* were desired, it would include such works as Jim Haskins and Hugh Butts's 1973 study of the psychology of black language, which not only describes such topics as the effect of racist stereotypes and the connections between perceptions of skin color and self-esteem, but also celebrates the very people whose language it analyzes.[60] In a lecture to the African Studies Program at Indiana University in 1970, David Dalby observed white and black interactions in language in both Africa and America, noting that "it has been the Black man who has had to carry the main burden of communication and adjustment between the two races and their cultures. . . . Black people have had to communicate with White, and often with each other, through the medium of 'White' languages or through their own adaptations of these languages. . . . The Black world has hitherto been largely described and interpreted through the eyes of white observers."[61] Even as he addressed the issue of black and white people and languages, however, Dalby wanted his audience at Bloomington to understand that the words "black" and "white" belonged in scare quotes. Both terms are no more than "convenient contrastive labels. . . . The dichotomy which they imply is an over-simplified and conventionalized one, since no such firm dividing line can of course be established within human society, either in respect of race or in respect of language and culture."[62] This crucial point that Dalby raised was notably out of sympathy with the Black Power and Black Arts movements of the 1960s, and it is one Ross entirely agreed with.

Corrective approaches were at hand in disciplines no one would have thought relevant in 1966. The construction of such concepts as "race" and "color" and the degree to which such ideas were historically contingent and capable of being subjected to dispassionate critical scrutiny are not the recent discoveries that theorists sometimes think they are. Historians of languages have known about such things for some time. Ross learned all she needed from the *OED* and from lexicographers and etymologists like C. T. Onions and Eric Partridge. Both Onions and Partridge contribute much to the education of her heroine Oreo.

Readers of *Oreo* need to like dictionaries. Oreo herself usually acts like a classicist, for whom the detection, exposure, and correction of errors in languages ancient or modern is one of life's chief delights.[63] When her mother Louise mentions a neighbor friend who is sick in the hospital, her language requires translation into standard English, as the author warns us, but Louise also attracts the corrections of her daughter.

She paused to think. "I greb-mine take the G bus [I've a great mind to
take the G bus], 'cause it fasta dan dat ol' trolley. I will cenny be glad to see
Lurline on her feet again. Thank de good Lord her sickness not ligament."
"Malignant," Oreo said mechanically.
"Moligment," Louise amended. "Oreo, you in charge. Take care yo'
sweet brother and stay in de back yard." (42)

Oreo is a Theseus from Philadelphia, poised on the brink of still more
adventures to come, but they lie in the future when the novel ends in the
Athens of at least this particular America, New York City. In writing *Oreo*,
Ross may have been inspired by the plot of Jessie Fauset's 1929 romance
Plum Bun, whose heroine Angela Murray also migrates from her origins in
Philadelphia to what she hopes is the freer world of New York. Yet Oreo is
anything but another Angela Murray.[64] Totally capable of dealing with any
challenge, unmoved by her father's Aegeus-like demise, Oreo is as ready as
Theseus to hit back at anyone who dares try to harm her. Like nearly every
page of this novel, the account of her repertory of martial arts has to be
read aloud to savor the philological nuance.

Oreo developed a series of moves that made other methods of self-
defense—jiu-jitsu, karate, kung-fu, judo, aikido, mikado, kikuyu, kendo,
hondo, and shlong—obsolete by incorporating and improving upon their
most effective aspects. With such awesome moves (or, as Oreo termed
them, *blôs*), as the *hed-lok, shu-kik, i-pik, hed-brâc, i-bop, ul-na-brâc, hed-blô,
fut-strîk, han-krus, tum-bloô, nek-brâc, bal-brâc, bak-strîk, but-kik*, the size or
musculature of the opponent was virtually academic. Whether he was big
or small, fat or thin, well-built or spavined, Oreo could, when she was in a
state of extreme concentration known as *hwip-as*, engage any opponent up
to three times her size and weight and whip his natural ass. (55)

Hwip-as recalls the Old English spelling of "what," *hwaet*, in a blend of black
English and etymological precision. Schooled to be physically as well as
mentally heroic, Oreo makes the royal Scottish motto hers, and it becomes
the concluding line of her story: *Nemo me impune lacessit*, roughly, "No one
harms me and gets away with it." She is at the same threshold of heroism
as young Theseus when we last see her. As we will see by some etymological
research of our own, Oreo's adoption of a Scottish motto is not accidental.

For this Theseus, the journey not the goal is what matters. Ross's way
with philology works much like the shticks in Mel Brooks's frequently

tasteless 1974 parody of the American Western, *Blazing Saddles*. We remember not so much the plot of *Oreo*, as its great lines. We often have the sense that an entire scene is set up to clear the way for some outrageous one-liners. In *Blazing Saddles*, when Bart, the new black sheriff (played by Cleavon Little), rides into town, he no sooner takes his place on the welcoming stand than all the Johnsons (the entire town is populated by people named Johnson) pull their guns on him. At the cocking of hammers, Sheriff Bart pulls his gun out and points it at his own head.

> *Bart* [in a low, raspy, Cracker voice]: Hold it! Next man makes a move, the
>   nigger gets it!
> *Olson Johnson*: Hold it, men. He's not bluffing.
> *Dr. Sam Johnson*: Listen to him, men, he's just crazy enough to do it!
> *Bart* [again, in low voice]: Drop it! Or I swear I'll blow this nigger's head
>   all over this town!
> *Bart* [in a high, Steppinfetchit voice]: Oh, lo'dy, lo'dy, he's despit! Do what
>   he sayyyy, do what he sayyyy . . .
> [The Johnsons drop their guns. Bart jams the gun into his neck and drags
>   himself through the crowd and toward the sheriff's office.]
> *Harriett Van Johnson*: Isn't anybody going to help that poor man?
> *Dr. Sam Johnson*: Hush, Harriet, that's a sure way to get him killed!
> *Bart* [higher voice]: Oooh! He'p me, he'p me! Somebody he'p me! He'p
>   me! He'p me! He'p me!
> *Bart* [lower voice]: Shut up!
> [Bart places his hand over his own mouth, drags himself through the door
>   into his office, and slams the door.]
> *Bart* [in normal voice]: Ooh, baby, you are so talented! And they are so
>   DUMB![65]

It is one of Cleavon Little's great scenes and is tasteless enough to be something Richard Pryor would perpetrate.

To succeed, comedians have to love words as much as a word-loving, philological classicist, and they need to be cleverer than anyone else at using them. It is not plots that make comedy routines work, but wit lavished on the smallest details of language, something an audience can grasp instantly. Henny Youngman (1906–1998) was one of the most famous of all stand-up comics for getting maximum mileage out of a minimum of language. He was able to lay down an endless barrage of one-liners on an audience until they were helpless from laughing.

Why do Jewish divorces cost so much? They're worth it.
Why do Jewish men die before their wives? They want to.
Why don't Jews drink? It interferes with their suffering.
A car hit a Jewish man. The paramedic says, "Are you comfortable?"
The man says, "I make a good living."[66]

Youngman's kind of genius for the one-liner and his extreme economy of language abound in *Oreo*. While it is certainly possible to track the way Ross titles each of Oreo's adventures after the exploits of Theseus (Procrustes, Phaea the sow, Sinis the tree-bending sadist) these "labors" are nothing more than suggestive chapter titles that play on the dissimilarity between the present work and the exalted model it invokes. This kind of mythological parody is as old as the seven hills of Rome—the design, for example, of the only complete Menippean satire to survive in Latin literature, Seneca's *Divi Claudii Apocolocyntosis* or *Pumpkinification of Claudius the Clod*. (The spoof title plays on the Greek word for "deification," *apotheosis*.) At his death Claudius is sent in the other direction, to the underworld, where he is judged by Hercules, Augustus, and others of the famous dead and found wanting. Seneca published it safely after Claudius's death, upon the ascension of the new emperor, Seneca's former pupil and soon his own nemesis, Nero.[67]

Oreo's blithe philological games begin with its provocative title and never slacken, for an oreo is an insult before it is a cookie in black America. In the course of the story we find out that "Oreo" is in fact a misapprehension of what the heroine's heroic quest-name was supposed to be. She was christened Christine ("She of Christ") to begin with, which is amusing enough for a girl with an absentee Jewish father, but her name becomes Oreo through faulty oral transmission. Her grandmother Louise has a dream, a bizarre inversion of what is usually a baritone moment in Hollywood Bible movies like *Ben Hur* and *Quo Vadis*, when scripture is intoned and a visit from god is at hand:

Suddenly the clouds parted and a ray of sunshine beamed down right in front of the child. Out of this beam of sunshine came a high-pitched, squeaky voice. "And her name shall be Oriole," squeaked the voice. (39)

Squeaky is good enough for Louise, who goes straight to her dream book, looks up the word "oriole," and sees the number 483. She uses it in the lottery and wins five hundred dollars. She tells the family and the neighbors, and everyone much prefers Oriole to Christine, so her Christian name vanishes. But then the name Oriole becomes Oreo by a process that reduces that Hollywood biblical voice out of a sunbeam to nonsense.

> People had been calling the child various things as she toddled down
> the street after Louise, cursing them under her breath. They called her
> Brown Sugar and Chocolate Drop and Honeybun. But when they looked
> at Christine's rich brown color and her wide smile full of sugar-white baby
> teeth, they said to themselves, "Why, that child does put me in mind of
> an Oreo cookie—side view." And that is how Oreo got her name. Nobody
> knew that Louise was saying "Oriole." (39)

A toddler cursing adults as she stumbles down the street is no ordinary child. All this dithering about the renaming of Christine ought to be serious stuff.

It sure is in Greek mythology. One of its main themes is what is revealed about the character of a hero by his name. The original Greek names *Aias* (the Latin, Ajax) and *Achilleus* (Achilles) are linked with homonyms that say something about their ultimate destinies: Ajax's name recalls a cry of ritual lament, *Ai Ai*, while Achilles suggests one who is a pain (*achos*) to his people (*laos*).[68] For the Greeks these names suggested something central to the character of such a figure: Ajax suffers and commits suicide because his honor as a hero is compromised; Achilles is the hero who brings pain thousandfold to the Achaeans. In the case of Greek Theseus, Plutarch tells us that he was so called because of the circumstances of his birth—or possibly a later encounter with his father Aegeus. "Putting" and "placing" seem to be what "Theseus" is all about.

> When Aethra gave birth to a son, he was at once named *Theseus*, as some
> say, because the tokens for his recognition had been placed (*thesin*) in hid
> ing; but others say that it was afterward at Athens, when Aegeus acknowl
> edged (*themenou*) him as son. (*Life of Theseus*, 3.4)[69]

From this account of all that's going on in the title it is not surprising that what readers usually skip, and publishers call front matter, matters. Ross dedicates her book to the memory of her father Gerald Ross and to her great-aunt Izetta Bass Grayson. Her parents were African Americans from North Carolina and Virginia; her father died in an automobile accident in 1954, twenty years before *Oreo*.[70] This is not the racially mixed genealogy she goes on to create for her heroine.

Ross divides the novel into two parts: "Troezen" and "Meandering." The first is about the education of Oreo, the second about her adventures when she leaves Troezen/Philadelphia and journeys to Athens/New York. As classical allusions go, these references are reasonably obscure and their implications are spelled out in "A Key for Speed Readers, Nonclassicists, Etc." which Ross thoughtfully supplies at the end.[71] Troezen is the city in the Peloponnese from which the great hero Theseus springs, and this latter-day Troezen turns out to be Ross's Philadelphia. The Meander is the famously wandering river of ancient Caria, today the Menderes in western Turkey, and a curious choice of words to describe the peregrinations of the hero "who wants to be another Heracles" (210). To become Heracles-like, Theseus has to pass through a number of adventures that would bear comparison with what Heracles accomplished. There are scholarly genealogies, tables, and diagrams throughout Ross's opening chapter, comparable to—possibly even inspired by—an elegantly illustrated book about Theseus published in 1970 by Anne G. Ward, W. R. Connor, Ruth B. Edwards, and Simon Tidworth, *The Quest for Theseus*.[72]

"Meandering" would be the last term one would think of for an ambitious quest like the one Theseus undertakes. He was nothing if not goal-directed, and he conforms to the universal patterns of the so-called monomyth that the Jungian Joseph Campbell describes in an immensely popular mythology widely read when Ross was writing *Oreo*, *The Hero with a Thousand Faces*.

> The standard path of the mythological adventure of the hero is a magnification of the formula represented in the rites of passage: separation—initiation—return: which might be named the nuclear unit of the monomyth. *A hero ventures forth from the world of common day into a region of supernatural wonder: fabulous forces are there encountered and a decisive victory is won: the hero comes back from this mysterious adventure with the power to bestow boons on his fellow man.* (Italics original)[73]

The nuclear unit in this case starts with Theseus subduing the club-bearer Periphetes at Epidaurus, then moves out of the Peloponnese to Corinth and the pine-tree-bender Sinis, across to Megara and environs, where Theseus conquers the supersow Phaea and Sciron, a bizarre host who compels people to wash his feet and who then kicks them over a cliff into the sea where a huge turtle lurks in wait for them.[74] Finally, Theseus goes past Eleusis and beats Cercyon in a wrestling match and gives Procrustes a dose of his own medicine on his Procrustean Bed. (There's also a bull to subdue at Marathon, to keep up with Heracles' taming of the Cretan Bull, but never mind.) Upon arrival in Athens he is of course cleansed of all blood guilt.[75] One of the considerable delights of part 2 of *Oreo* is how Ross recasts these adventures into bizarre but poetically inspired shapes. Procrustes becomes Sidney, the bullying manager of Krapotkin's shoe store (164–67) who forces all his customers to buy shoes and gloves that don't fit. Oreo successfully gets a size seven and a half rather than the size seven Sidney tries to make her buy, and then she offers him some advice: "You know why business is bad? You give people the wrong sizes." To which he responds, "Please, no lectures. From you I don't need it *oytser*."

> She left in a huff, a snit, and high dudgeon, which many people believe to be automobiles but are actually states of mind. She heard Sidney mumble, "The trouble with shvartzes today is they are beginning to learn about insurance." (167)

Oytser is Hebrew for "treasure," but can also be used ironically in an opposite sense.

Classical allusions to Theseus are just one of the things Ross is murdering. The first chapter's title, "Mishpochech," is the equivalent of a stand-up comedian's transition line "But seriously, folks.". Knowing classical myth helps, but *Oreo* also requires a working knowledge of Yiddish. In Ross's day this was most conveniently supplied by Leo Rosten's *The Joys of Yiddish*. Every bit of Yiddish and Hebrew that appears in *Oreo* can be found in his book. There is quite a lot of it, much of it not nearly as familiar as "cabala" or "kvetch."[76] Rosten often illustrates correct Yiddish usage by jokes and one-liners, all of which make his book a *haimish* (148: "unpretentious, putting on no airs") compendium of Yiddish and Jewish tradition and folklore. Rosten's *shtik* (372: "A studied, contrived or characteristic piece of business employed by an actor or actress; overly used gestures, grimaces, or devices to steal attention") begins with sesquipedalian copy on the other side of the title's colon and it doesn't stop until the last entry *Zohar*, which is then followed by ninety pages of appendixes on Yiddish and Jewish life and learning not previously covered.

> A relaxed lexicon of Yiddish, Hebrew and Yinglish words often encountered in English, plus dozens that ought to be, with serendipitous excursions into Jewish humor, habits, holidays, history, religion, ceremonies, folklore, and cuisine; the whole generously garnished with stories,

anecdotes, epigrams, Talmudic quotations, folk sayings and jokes from the
days of the Bible to those of the beatnik.

Rosten is as useful an introduction to Fran Ross's kind of comedy as he is
to her Yiddish, because he is not simply a lexicographer. A quick consultation shows that *mishpochech*—pronounced *mish-*PAW-*kheh*, to rhyme with
fish loch-eh—is Hebrew for "family" or "clan" (248). Rosten, just like the
editors of the *OED*, also backs up his plain lexicographical information
with an example from contemporary usage.

> The Chase Manhattan Bank's memorable advertising campaign is built
> around the slogan "You have a friend at Chase Manhattan." 'Tis said
> that a sign in the window of the Bank of Israel reads: "But here you have
> *Mishpochech!*"

Oreo is as much a mythological and cultural hybrid as its characters, at
once inspired by *The Joys of Yiddish* as a book like *The Quest for Theseus*.
Hence it is doubly appropriate for Ross to begin with an extensive genealogy of her heroine.

As we have seen, Greek heroes *live* for genealogy, their greatest desire
being nothing more than to prove worthy of their fathers, grandfathers, and
family line in general. So too do Hebrew Bible/Old Testament fathers. In
the introduction to *The Quest for Theseus*, for example, we learn to trace how
Theseus's father Aegeus and mother Aethra joined the family trees of the
Erechthids (children of Erechtheus) and the Pelopids (children of Pelops).[77]

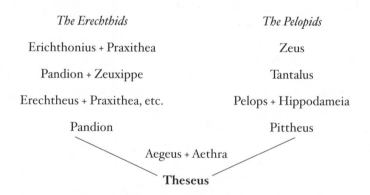

The Erechthids	The Pelopids
Erichthonius + Praxithea	Zeus
Pandion + Zeuxippe	Tantalus
Erechtheus + Praxithea, etc.	Pelops + Hippodameia
Pandion	Pittheus
Aegeus + Aethra	
Theseus	

Oreo's family tree can be built in similar fashion with *Yisroel*, "the people
of Israel" (Rosten, 441), who are prophetically named with the German

Schwartz ("black") on the left and the black (Yiddish *shvartzer*, 377) family of the Clarks on the right. Clark is Scottish in origin, from the Old English *clerec*, "scribe," "scholar," since clergy were the only literate people when the Latin *clericus* (itself from the Greek *klêrikos*) came into the language.[78]

Yisroel	*Blacks*
Jacob Schwartz + Frieda Schwartz	James Clark + Louise Clark

Samuel Schwartz + Helen Clark Schwartz

Christine **(Oreo)**   Moishe (Jimmie C.)

Things get off to a bad start, genealogically, just as they had with Theseus and his family. The news of the marriage of Samuel and Helen causes Oreo's paternal grandmother Frieda to emit a cry "Riboyne Shel O'lem!" and then drop dead of "a racist/my-son-the-bum coronary" (3). There is much learning compressed here, according to Rosten: "Pronounced *ri-*BOY-*neh shel* OY-*lem*, to rhyme with 'Lemoyna shall boil 'em,'" it is Hebrew for "Master of the World," or "Oh, God in heaven! A ringing, rhetorical ejaculation that appeals to God to witness something momentous, like 'Holy Moses!'" (304). Frieda's dying words also remind Rosten of a joke:

> Mr. Abraham, driven to desperation by the endless delayings of the tailor who was making him a pair of trousers, finally cried, "Tailor, in the name of heaven, it has already taken you six *weeks*!"
>
> "So?"
>
> "*So*, you ask? Six weeks for a pair of pants? *Riboyne Shel O'lem*! It took God only six days to create the *universe* . . ."
>
> "*Nu*," shrugged the tailor, "look at it . . ." (304)[79]

As for Oreo's maternal grandfather, the news that his daughter Helen is going to marry "a Jew-boy" and become Helen (Honeychild) Schwartz causes him "to turn to stone, as it were, in his straight-backed chair, his body a rigid half swastika."

"Discounting, of course, head, hands, and feet" (3–4). As Oreo is on the point of leaving home, her grandfather will be freed from his symbolic paralysis. For disabled anti-Semites, half a swastika is better than none.

An equal-opportunity satirist, Ross hits African American phobias as cheerfully as Jewish ones. Publishing at the high tide of the Black Power movement, she provides a chart, "Colors of black people," to pinpoint where all the members of Oreo's extended family belong on the spectrum that runs from white through yellow, light-skinned, dark-skinned to black and all the hues between. Black is the blackest, as a note helpfully explains, because "there is no 'very black.' Only white people use this term. . . . If a black person says, 'John is very black,' he is referring to John's politics, not his skin color" (5). "Christine" was Oreo's original name, after the name of Christ, and a source of much amusement to her father Samuel; in turn he names his black son by Christine's mother Helen "Moishe," thinking it a good joke on a black boy. It scarcely matters, since the boy is soon known as "Jimmie C.," a relatively limited child who is one of the early victims of his sister's wit.

> Whenever they played together, if Oreo thought her brother had said something silly or stupid or sweet, she would make one of her savage "suppose" remarks. . . . Once when they were both doing this, Jimmie C. said, quite seriously, "Let's put our [sc. ear] wax together and make a candle."
>
> Oreo answered, "Suppose you were sliding on a banister and it turned into a razor blade."
>
> Jimmie C. fainted.
>
> Oreo was very sorry when that happened. She did not really want to be mean to her sweet little brother, but sometimes it was a case of simple justice.
>
> When Jimmie C. asked her whether there was such a thing as an emergency semicolon (of course!), she answered, "Suppose you were putting Visine in your eyes and it turned into sulfuric acid."
>
> Jimmie C. fainted.
>
> Oreo resolved to give up her "suppose" game until she found a less deserving person to use it on. (42–43)

Along with an ear attuned to the cruelty essential to humor and such varied sources as Richard Pryor or Greek myth, it is always helpful to have Rosten's book at hand, since many of the more scabrous passages in *Oreo* will remain opaque to goyim who don't know any better. When Oreo's mother Helen and father Samuel part as he heads off Aegeus-like to New York (Athens), he hands Helen a paper with many *farchadat* (*Joys of Yiddish*, 112: "dizzy," "confused," "dopey," "punchy") instructions as well as clues to his daughter's identity and future course in life, just like the sword and sandals that Aegeus leaves in Troezen for little Theseus. When he also expresses the wish to visit from time to time, Helen's only reply is "Later for you, *shmendrick*" (9); that is, "Penis (colloquial; rarely used by men. When used by a female, the intention is to deride by diminutizing)" (*Joy of Yiddish*, 354).

It was the particular genius of Ross to realize what could be accomplished by shifting from contemporary political rhetoric and received opinions to a seemingly more neutral, scientific discourse. By running black English and everything else through her conceptual wringer of lexicography and philological analysis, everything that might be considered sacred or profane in the 1960s and 1970s becomes weirdly distant, defused, impossible to take seriously. The attempt to render black American language in print does not escape Ross's analytical grid. The so-called "eye dialect" of representing black American speech dates back to the nineteenth century and was never conceived as a transcript of actual speech patterns, but was a literary and comic confection from minstrel shows, of white voices mimicking what white Americans thought black speech sounded like. Her grandmother Louise's Southern accent "was as thick as hominy grits" (11); for example, "Taste dis yere tornado Bernice," meaning "Taste this here *tournedos Béarnaise*" (13). Ross solemnly makes short work of yet another touchy subject, how to render actual black speech with dignity rather than parody.

> From time to time, her dialogue will be rendered in ordinary English, which Louise does not speak. To do full justice to her speech would require a ladder of footnotes and glosses, a tic of apostrophes (aphaeresis, hyphaeresis, apocope), and a Louise-ese/English dictionary of phonetic spellings. A compromise has been struck. Since Louise can work miracles of compression through syncope, it is only fair that a few such condensations be shared with the reader. However, the substitution of an apostrophe for every dropped *g*, missing *r*, and absent *t* would be tantamount to *tic douloureux* of movable type. (12)

As she often does, Ross gets to have it both ways through this scientific exposition of African American phonology. She directs our attention to her carefully reasoned act of writing and creating this version of eye-dialect. It's not pandering to racial prejudice, folks, it's just practical science at work.

The love of words, their history as well as their meaning, is central to *Oreo*, not least because it is a novel in which no two people in Oreo's extended family can speak the same language. Somewhat like the Dutch or Scandinavians, she has to become fluent in many languages because no one wants to bother to learn hers. Her often absent, gallivanting mother Helen—as in "of Troy"—may speak and write standard English, but her grandmother Louise expresses herself in difficult black English and exceedingly accomplished menus and cooking. Her brother Jimmie C. lives in his own fantasy world and makes up his own language as he goes. Her absentee father Samuel/Aegeus speaks New Yorkese, and her grandfathers all exhibit the stereotypical Jewish and black speech. Even her dead grandmother plays a role, after the briefest of lines ("Riboyne Shel O'lem!"): dead in paragraph one, "but still, in her own quiet way, a power and a force" (4).

Oreo does not go to school because she is too brilliant for an ordinary American education and because her family is wealthy enough to hire special tutors for her. Her English tutor Professor Lindau teaches her so much from the *OED* and the works of Eric Partridge and C. T. Onions that her mother Louise invents a special dish of partridge and onions in their honor: *Perdrix en poirier à l'oignon* (45). There is a wonderfully obscene account of Oreo and her professor's research into the etymology of the word "cunt"—"or, as Partridge put it, '*c*nt*'"(46). This is inspired by her professor's use of the word "wedge" to describe his girlfriend's sex. Ross is making none of this learning up; at several point she quotes Partridge directly.[80]

In his own quiet way, Eric Partridge was as much an inspiration for Ross's brand of humor as Richard Pryor. He was a famous lexicographer, but at more than one point his donnish humor approaches the level of such unacademic collections as Flaubert's *Dictionary of Accepted Ideas* (*Idées reçues*) or Ambrose Bierce's *The Devil's Dictionary*. In 1941 he published *A Dictionary of Clichés*, in part to try to understand why they are so extensively used: "Their ubiquity is remarkable and rather frightening."[81] With Partridge, Ross could have learned as much about what words to write as about what words to avoid.[82] For his 1958 etymological dictionary, *Origins*, Partridge's discussion of another great taboo word in English may be liberal with asterisks, but it pulls no punches in citations. Partridge is as calmly in command of cursing as he is of etymology.

> f**k, verb hence noun, is a Standard English word classed, because of its associations, as a vulgarism. The derivative expletive F**k (it)!—derivative agent f**ker—and verbal noun and participial adjective f**king, except

when literal (then, they are likewise vulgarisms), belong to low slang. *F**k* shares with *c**t* two distinctions: they are the only two Standard English words excluded from all general and etymological dictionaries since the eighteenth century and the only two Standard English words that, outside of medical and other official or semi-official reports and learned papers, still cannot be printed in full anywhere within the British Commonwealth of Nations.[83]

So much for Dr. Johnson's harmless drudge.

Etymology and stand-up comedy become as one as Oreo becomes skilled in translating her professor's rhizomorphs (weird roots such as fungi have to attach themselves to higher plant life). Professor Lindau tests his pupil's command of etymology by saying, "Mr. Benton is worn out by child–bearing. Of course, his paper was an ill-starred bottle. I don't wonder he threatened to sprinkle himself with sacrificial meal." Oreo replies at once, effortlessly: "You mean that Benton is effete, his paper was a disaster, a fiasco, and he wanted to immolate himself" (47). In the philological enterprise of detecting and exposing error, this is one pupil who quickly surpasses her master.

Once in an adjective-adverb drill, Oreo wrote: "He felt badly." The professor was furious and viciously crossed out the *ly*. He was ashamed of Oreo.

Oreo looked him dead in the eye and said, "I am writing a story about a repentant but recidivous rapist. In the story, this repentant rapist catches his hand in a wringer. Therefore, when he goes out, recidivously, to rape, he feels both bad and badly."

The professor kissed Oreo on both cheeks. (47)

But Oreo's motto is *Nemo me impune lacessit*. Hell hath no fury like a philologist scorned.

Oreo was still angry with him for doubting her, and in her story about the rapist she added such abominations as: "The Empire State Building rises penisly to the sky. As architecture, manurially speaking, it stinks." She felt it appropriate to employ genito-scatological adverbs to express academic vexation.

The professor wept and promised never to cross out her *ly*'s until he was sure of her intentions. (47)

Thus is the education of a hero accomplished.

The tutorials with Professor Lindau were time well spent. Everything we read in part 1, "Troezen," amounts to what we might term the *Oreopaedia* (after Xenophon's fictional account of the education of Cyrus the Great, the *Cyropaedia*). In the chapter entitled "Phaea" (126–37) we are expectant, mythologically, wondering when the supersow Phaea will appear to challenge Theseus on his travels. But it is not until after her visit with a young actor named Scott Scott (a gracious nod to Joseph Heller's characters in *Catch 22*) and his bumbling mother that we actually come to the encounter. As we might expect, it is an adroit blending of classical allusion and Jewish dietary laws that sets back Deuteronomy by many generations.

> As Oreo walked up the street, she saw a pig run squalling out of a doorway, a baker's dozen of pursuers pork-barreling after it. Oreo started running too. As she neared the building from which the pig had made its exit, she saw that it was a pork butcher's. In its attempt at escape, the pig had made a shambles of the shambles. Oreo continued in the pig pursuit. The porker darted across the street. Oreo flung her walking stick at its legs. The cane did a double whirl, tripping up the pig. A taxi turning into Second Avenue screeched on its brakes, but not in time. The cab sideswiped the pig, which tottered a few feet, then fell dead in front of Temple Shaaray Tefila, directly across from the pork store.
>
> Unwittingly, Oreo was the indirect cause of the pig's death, but as she reflected on its porcine demise, she realized that she could take out her list again. That hashed rasher of bacon defiling the temple sidewalk—that surely was "Sow." Yes, that must be so. (137)

One more labor out of the way.

The centerpiece of the chapter "Phaea" however is not about bringing home the Thesean bacon, but rather about Oreo's encounter with another language—more precisely, another language in translation. It is a test she passes brilliantly in her quest to find her father. Scott Scott and his mother Mrs. Scott receive Oreo graciously, give or take a number of smashed dishes and food lost at the hands and feet of Mrs. Scott, who is as clumsy as her son is fleet of foot. It may not dawn on the reader right away what is going on in this encounter.

> A few minutes later, the door opened and a French-accented voice said, "I am arrived." . . .

"Hi, Scott," said Oreo.

The boy threw his arms wide. "What is this that this is that you are so formal? I wish that you me call of my prename."

"Okay. Hi, Scott."[84]

"Well!" said Scott, nodding and rubbing his hands with apache aplomb. "Well, well, well, that goes." He laid his finger aside his nose. "Then, so, in that case, thereupon! How you call you, young girl?"

"I call myself Christine Clark."

"Well, well, well, that goes. Since what hour wait you for me?"

"Since three hours less ten minutes," said Oreo.

"What a damage!" He turned to his mother. "I have need of the tea," he said, speaking the speech trippingly on the tongue as his mother went trippingly into the kitchen. (131–32)

In the course of this interview conducted entirely in French in translation, Oreo learns that she has the wrong Scott Scott. The Scott Scott she is looking for is her father, Samuel Schwartz, who had changed his name for stage purposes. This Scott Scott agrees: "You have reason" (132). Hospitable to a fault, Scott Scott asks his mother to prepare "the outside of the works" (*hors d'oeuvre*) for their guest, and Scott Scott then gets Oreo to help him with his math assignment, a challenge which Oreo passes brilliantly.

> *Q.* Jim has gone to school six times as long as Harry, and in 4 years he will have gone to school twice as long. What grade of motor oil does Jim use?
>
> *A.* The question assumes a knowledge of calculus, thermodynamics, and jacks. It is not fair, and I refuse to answer it.
>
> *Q.* A girl can clean her room in 46 minutes, and her roommate can do the job in 22 minutes. How long will it take them to figure out that they are wasting their time because the house has been condemned?
>
> *A.* Two shakes of Charles Lamb's tale. (134)

We and Oreo finally leave Scott Scott and his mother, but with the greatest reluctance. It seems that he speaks a different language every day, in translation, but with the appropriate foreign accent. Oreo was lucky enough to hit a day when it was *Franglais'* turn at bat. As Mrs. Scott ruefully observes, sometimes it's not so easy to understand her eleven-year-old's accent. She knows many languages, "but for two days the week before, because of her ignorance of Shluh and Kingwana syntax, Scott might as well have been speaking Shluh and Kingwana" (133)—in Shluh- and Kingwana-accented English in translation, of course. Their final parting is flawlessly done.

> "To the to see again," said Scott. He opened the door for Oreo.
> "To God," said Oreo, swinging her walking stick in salute. (137)

Au revoir, Adieu: so our hero's progress goes, from one triumph to the next.

Etymology and lexicography count for more in the exploits of this philological heroine than heroic paradigms. Oreo's choice of mottos, *Nemo me impune lacessit* / *No one harms me with impunity*, is uncommonly appropriate, not just because it speaks to her heroic prowess in physical and intellectual matters, but because of the history of the surname Clark. Oreo lives up to all her names and, incidentally, to the model of Theseus, whose story is evoked only to be shoved aside as irrelevantly dull and boring by comparison. As with Theseus, we begin to suspect that the names and the motto are the actual roots of the whole story, like Achilles Who-Is-a-Pain-to-His-People. Oreo lives up to her etymological identity in a thoroughly satisfying way.

As for Theseus, his example is not completely forgotten, but the roles for women and heroes of the kind that Joseph Campbell celebrates in *The Hero with a Thousand Faces* are utterly confounded.

> Woman, in the picture language of mythology, represents the totality
> of what can be known. The hero is the one who comes to know. As he
> progresses in the slow initiation which is life, the form of the goddess un-
> dergoes for him a series of transfigurations: she can never be greater than
> himself, though she can always promise more than he is yet capable of
> comprehending. She lures, she guides, she bids him burst his fetters. And
> if he can match her import, the two, the knower and the known, will be
> released from every limitation. Woman is the guide to the sublime acme
> of sensuous adventures.[85]

If we were to restate what Ross has created in *Oreo* in terms of the most popular American mythologist of her day, it would be that by following the pattern of Theseus, her heroine Oreo actually combines the two roles Campbell speaks of. She is at once the "all-knowing" female and the male, "the one who comes to know," "the knower and the known." Whether Oreo would countenance anything like Campbell's concept of "the sublime acme of sensuous adventures" is to be doubted. How could a respectable philologist let such lurid diction pass unchallenged? As for

Ross's relation to her African American contemporaries, by passing up the chance to be identified with the Black Arts movement, by not playing the supportive role assigned to black women in some of its more robust male factions, she instead connected herself to the salutary untimeliness that comes from etymology, lexicography, and all those other disciplines that teach us to know the present by studying the past.[86]

Eight
Rita Dove and the Greeks

Finally, Rita Dove. She has engaged as much as any contemporary poet and writer with the myth and literature of ancient Greece, traversing epic, tragedy, lyric poetry, and the Homeric *Hymns*. Classical themes are far from the only kind she has worked with. Perhaps her most widely admired volume of poetry to date is *Thomas and Beulah*, a collection in homage to her maternal grandparents that won the 1987 Pulitzer Prize for Poetry. Born in Akron, Ohio, in 1952, she was a summa cum laude graduate of Miami University in Ohio and later studied in Germany at Tübingen as a Fulbright Fellow, then at the University of Iowa's workshop for writers, where she met and married the German novelist Fred Viebahn (born 1947). Their daughter Aviva Dove-Viebahn was born in 1983. Through abundant criticism and poetry and a distinguished teaching career at Arizona State University and the University of Virginia, Rita Dove has been a leading voice for education as much at the primary and secondary levels as at the university level. She was appointed poet laureate of the United States from 1993 to 1995.

Dove completed two long-meditated and much revised works on classical themes before she published her 1995 book of sonnets *Mother Love*: the novel *Through the Ivory Gate* (the gate in question being Penelope's Gate of False Dreams in the *Odyssey*) and *The Darker Face of the Earth*, an adaptation of Sophocles' *Oedipus* into a plantation setting in South Carolina in the 1820s to 1840s.

This chapter and this book will end with a reading of *Mother Love* and its thirty-five sonnets. Dove's main classical model is the Homeric *Hymn to Demeter*, which is frequently invoked in detail. At the same time, *Mother Love* is an homage to Rainer Maria Rilke's *Sonnets to Orpheus* (1922), so that a mother and daughter's story reliving Demeter and Persephone's myth unfolds in explicit counterpoint to Rilke's already radical reconception of the myth of Orpheus and Eurydice. The world of contemporary African American and European life is an equally vivid presence, as are suggestive portraits of a daughter and a husband that recall in a general way the roles of her own husband and daughter, in much the way the novel *Through the Ivory Gate* with its heroine who is both a musician and performance artist recalls Dove herself. The cycle of sonnets in *Mother Love* ends in a fusion of mythical and modern Sicily, where Hades first burst forth from the earth to carry Persephone away from Demeter and her mother's love.

But we begin with one poem, in Dove's 1989 *Grace Notes*, inspired by an occasion when a classically educated African American poet confronted American classicism as it is sometimes practiced. Here that classicism is embodied in one of the well-known American critics and translators of the second half of the twentieth century, William A. Arrowsmith (1924–1992).

The Flight of an Arrow

Many literary critics and classicists have been drawn to Rita Dove's two-page poem "Arrow." Its subject is a public reading by Arrowsmith that the poet attended with her students. By this poem's account it was an event marked by racist as well as sexist offenses, none of them intentional.[1] Dove would leave Arizona State University for the University of Virginia in 1989. At this late point in his career Arrowsmith had been a prolific essayist, editor, and critic as well as a translator of Petronius's *Satyricon*, Euripides' tragedies (*The Bacchae, Orestes, Alcestis, Cyclops, Hecuba, Heracles*), and Aristophanes' comedies *The Clouds* and *The Birds*. In addition to Eugenio Montale, he translated the poetry of Cesare Pavese, Nietzsche's *Untimely Observations* (*Unzeitgemässe Betrachtungen*, rendered as *Unmodern Observations*), and a book of essays on the films of Michelangelo Antonioni. He had taught at the University of California at Riverside when it opened, then at the University of Texas, where he was instrumental in founding the polemical, antiphilological literary journal *Arion*, then later at Emory, Johns Hopkins, and finally Boston universities. Better known through his translations than most other contemporary classicists, he began as a Rhodes

Scholar from Princeton and returned there for his PhD. But he was never part of the American classical establishment, more a conscious opponent of it from the periphery. He spent his entire, restless career trying at one university after another to reform and redirect the way classicists taught and wrote about literature, sometimes with success, sometime not. You might fondly imagine that a rebellious antiestablishmentarian like Arrowsmith would have been a welcome presence to Rita Dove.

Résumés are not what inspire poetry. Freed from the professional obligation to make sense of whatever a fellow classicist does, Dove creates a lyric that shifts at the end from herself, the teacher's voice of the poem, and from the famous scholar, to her young students, the real target that "Arrow" hits. The paradox of "Arrow" is that something beautiful will emerge from what seems at first a concentrated personal polemic.

It is important to set the stage for reading "Arrow" and keep in mind the collection of poetry where it appears, part 4 of *Grace Notes*, and also that Dove is an accomplished musician as well as a poet. "Grace note" is the common English translation of the Italian *appoggiatura* (from *appoggiare*, "to prop, support"). Grace notes are indicated in a score by a smaller note immediately in front of a regular-sized one, to indicate an auxiliary note that "supports" or otherwise brings out the main tone of a melody. The appoggiatura adds spice, sharpness, accenting its following note, as in the "Janissary" music of rolled chords in the famous *Rondo alla turca* of Mozart's A major Piano Sonata. A more sensational example can be heard in Bernard Hermann's scoring for high-pitched strings that raises a shocking moment in Alfred Hitchcock's 1959 *Psycho* to an even higher pitch when Tony Perkins in Mother's clothing bursts into Janet Leigh's shower in the Bates Motel. Grace notes have a sharp edge to them and offer a felicitous image for lyric poetry, suggesting at once small things, but small things with an unexpected slant, small things that can make sharp bites.

The epigraph for part 4 of *Grace Notes* comes from Claude McKay's 1926 poem "My House" and sounds a leitmotif for what we will hear in "Arrow" and several other poems in this section.

I know the dark delight of being strange,
The penalty of difference in the crowd,
The loneliness of wisdom among fools.

The first poem of the section "Dedication" begins as an homage to Czeslaw Milosz's 1945 poem "Dedication," to all those who did not survive the war as he had.

You whom I could not save
Listen to me.
Try to understand this simple speech as I would be ashamed of another.
I swear, there is in me no wizardry of words.
I speak to you with silence like a cloud or a tree.

Dove's "Dedication" departs knowingly from Milosz, saying what Milosz's
"Dedication" says, by saying the opposite.

Ignore me. This request is knotted—
I'm not ashamed to admit it.
I won't promise anything. I am a magic
that can deafen you like a rainstorm or a well.

In the poem "Ars Poetica," the poet wants to be so small that she will be

a ghost town
on the larger map of wills.
Then you can pencil me in as a hawk:
a traveling x-marks-the-spot.

She then follows with her own version of the Medusa myth—very different
from Countee Cullen's. Dove's Medusa is the mythological creature who
has often served in modern poetry as a figure for a woman poet.[2] Given
Dove's professed love for puzzles and crosswords, Therese Steffen's suggestion seems plausible, that MEDUSA is an anagram of AMUSED and a reference
to Hélène Cixous's 1976 essay "The Laugh of the Medusa" (first published
in 1975 as "Le rire de la méduse").[3] Once freed from the tears they have had
to shed, women will have cause for unceasing laughter, like Medusa freed
from her customary role in classical mythology. All these poems make for a
complementary setting to the critical encounter in "Arrow."

Arrowsmith's still unpublished translation of some of Aristophanes'
Greek into black urban English was unavoidably problematic in America in the 1980s, and any public reading of it at colleges and universities,
even more so.[4] He consistently maintained that this recourse to ethnic
stereotype in his translation of Aristophanes' best surviving comedy—*The
Women of the Thesmophoria* is at least by far his funniest—was not an intentional provocation. As Elizabeth Scharffenberger observes, "his strategy
for translating this character was always wedded to language-based conventions of ethnic representation."[5] He vehemently denied being a racist

or having any intention to appeal to racist sentiments, even as he changed an earlier version of his translation, with parodies of broken "Dutch" (i.e., German) English, into the "urban black speech" Dove describes.[6]

Some years earlier, however, he had had to contend with the same issue when he was editing a series of Aristophanes translations for the University of Michigan Press. Michigan refused to allow the publication of Tim Reynolds's translation of Aristophanes' *Peace* because Reynolds rendered the opening dialogue between two slaves of the Athenian Trygaeus into black slaves on an antebellum plantation, in minstrel dress. The press's intervention enraged Arrowsmith. Since Reynolds's version is rarely cited in discussions of the matter, it may be useful to see what drew the Michigan editors' attention. This is how his version of *Peace* opens.

Liza: ANNUDER SHITCAKE FO' DE BEETLE!
Rastus: Hyar she am.
An' I sho' hopes dat ugly mutha never get no *better'n* dat too.
Liza: Anudder shitcake. He say he want pigshit dis time.
Rastus: Liza, I jes' *gib* him one! He didn' go an' eat dat whole thing already?[7]

Reynolds's loathing for LBJ, the Vietnam War, and oppressive American society evidently outweighed any sense he might have had for the equally contemporary outrages surrounding the civil rights movement. Vietnam completely derailed the Johnson administration's agenda for civil rights. As critics of this and other translations of ancient comedy observe, the context for translation of ethnic humor changes, and it is much harder to carry off than some imagine. The problem is that Reynolds's Liza and Rastus were inappropriate even before they finally appeared in print, several years after Arrowsmith and Michigan parted company.

The challenge dialects pose in translation theory and practice is that any dialect is always going to be specific to a historical context, and if it is rendered in translation by yet *another* dialect, that new one will have its own associations over which the translator can have no control. Neither Reynolds nor Arrowsmith owned black speech, whether rustic or urban, and the appropriation of those languages could never be a neutral act. At the time neither of them could see this problem clearly.

In a 1993 issue of the journal *Arion* dedicated to Arrowsmith after his death, his former colleague, the classicist and fellow translator Douglass Parker, speculated that Arrowsmith may have turned to urban black speech for the Scythian in his own translation out of his "fury" over having his editorial acumen challenged by the Michigan Press.[8] From our own conversations with him in 1982 when we heard him read a sample at Dartmouth, we think it would be a mistake to see the Scythian as Arrowsmith's *only* concern in this translation. More generally he wanted to realize his ideal vision of what a performance of Aristophanes ought to have, which was a great deal more than a translation turned over to a director for production. He insisted that an ancient drama like *The Women of the Thesmophoria* (the literal translation of *Thesmophoriazousae*) be completely realized for a modern audience, without footnotes, and he does this from his elegant title onward: *Euripides Agonistes*, echoing the title of Milton's *Samson Agonistes*. Like a Wagnerian, Arrowsmith in his later years conceived of Greek drama on the modern stage as a *Gesamtkunstwerk*, with music, choreography, stage direction, sets, lighting, costumes, and every other part of the performance as much under a playwright-translator's control as Aristophanes' script. Like many translators of ancient tragedy and comedy, he pointed out that ancient Greek drama was much closer to opera in its complexity than to a modern spoken stage play, and he argued that this musical dimension ought to be translated for modern performance as carefully as Aristophanes' or Euripides' Greek. It is a pity this aspect of his later creative work didn't become better known.

So how could Dove's eminent scholar be racist, when in real life he declared vigorously again and again that he was not? And how could Arrowsmith have imagined that Tim Reynolds's Eliza and Rastus would not be offensive to black people back in the 1960s? Perhaps Dove's poem captures an instance of what Stokely Carmichael termed "institutional racism" in his 1967 book with Charles V. Hamilton, *Black Power*.[9] It is not an individual person's racism but something present in institutions, or cultures, or societies, such as universities, corporations, and other public bodies. Carmichael's phrase was an arresting one and has been one of the lasting contributions of his and Hamilton's 1967 book. Yet his perception was not new. In so many words institutional racism is what Invisible Man confronts in Ralph Ellison's novel, *avant la lettre*.

> That invisibility to which I refer occurs because of a peculiar disposition of the eyes of those with whom I come in contact. A matter of the construction of their *inner* eyes, those eyes with which they look through their physical eyes upon reality. (*Invisible Man*, prologue, 3)

It is enraging to be turned into something invisible. The generally sympathetic critic Helen Vendler—not a classicist, much closer to Arrowsmith's generation than Rita Dove, and a one-time colleague of Arrowsmith's at Boston University—concluded that "Arrow" fails as a poem because it takes no interest in the eminent scholar whom the poem attacks.[10] In our view this stricture sounds like a Christian injunction to turn the other cheek. As a rule neither wounded classicists nor poets pause to reflect thoughtfully on the humanity of those who have just injured them. The voice of the poet in "Arrow" is not interested in such a namby-pamby response, and Invisible explains why.

> You often doubt if you really exist. You wonder whether you aren't simply a phantom in other people's minds. Say, a figure in a nightmare which the sleeper tries with all his strength to destroy. It's when you feel like this that, out of resentment, you begin to bump people back. And, let me confess, you feel that way most of the time. You ache with the need to convince yourself that you do exist in the real world, that you're a part of all the sound and anguish, and you strike out with your fists, you curse and you swear to make them recognize you. And, alas, it's seldom successful. (*Invisible Man*, prologue, 3–4)

Before Dove was born in 1952, Ellison had already described what the encounter in "Arrow" would be like. The poet who speaks there does not beat the eminent scholar within an inch of his life, as Invisible does when he encounters an arrogant blond white man with blue eyes who cannot see him as a fellow human being. She does fight back in the accepted academic way.

> When the moment came I raised my hand,
> phrased my question as I had to: sardonic,
> eminently civil my condemnation
> phrased in the language of fathers—
> felt the room freeze behind me.

The scholar's reply is no surprise at all to the poet, who hears what she expected to hear.

> And the answer came as it had to:
> *humanity—celebrate our differences—*
> *the virility of ethnicity.*

These words have the ring of American professorial authenticity to them. And this isn't a poem just about the teacher.

> My students
> sat there already devising
> their different ways of coping.

They are each of them hit at different times and in different ways by the eminent scholar's reading and they respond in different ways: Dana, by having a migraine right away "to get the poison out," Becky holding off for five hours.

But the real transformation, something that makes "Arrow" more than a piece of invective, is what the poet envisions as a possible future course for Janice, who is earlier described in her red shoes, furiously scribbling that the scholar is an *Arsch Loch*. (Recall that Dove is married to the German novelist Fred Viebahn and fluent in the language.) Janice may dress up as a witch and go to the party for the scholar afterward, Janice of the bright red shoes, or, the poem says at the end, she might do this:

> Janice who will wear red for three days or
> yellow brighter
> than her hair so she can't be
> seen   at all

The invisibility of Janice, the girl in a yellow dress with her yellow hair: the poem visibly disintegrates ever so slightly at the end, with a gap separating "so she can't be / seen" from "at all." Brilliantly—in a literal sense, not the critical cliché—meaning "brightly shining," "lustrous," "glittering," Janice of the yellow hair will possibly wear yellow for three days instead of red, and thereby become as invisible as a blond, white woman, as her teacher was a black invisible to the eminent scholar who could not see her even though she was seated in the audience before him. Nor is Dove simply reacting as a victim of institutional racism. She has as sharp an eye for philological detail as the eminent scholar, who

> "took the bull by the horns,"
> substituting urban black speech for the voice
> of an illiterate cop in Aristophanes' *Thesmophoriazousae*.

There is an extreme shift in register in these three lines. By quoting the eminent scholar ("took the bull by the horns") she juxtaposes the banality of that macho language with the philological and polysyllabic "Aristophanes' *Thesmophoriazousae*," just as she later repeats the clichés of academic

English in the speaker's answer, *"humanity—celebrate our differences—the virility of ethnicity."*

All this is withering enough, but the most arresting thing of all is the poem's title, rhetorically an example of *apocope*, cutting off the last syllable of the name "Arrowsmith": a smith, a metalworker who fashions metal heads for arrows. A play on Freudian castration anxiety is conceivable, but we think it likelier that Dove wants to turn her eminent scholar into the weapon his name declares he makes: arrows. And when we think of men, women, and arrows, we are in a mythological realm where the power of desire is a familiar theme—desire, and its opposite, repulsion.

Think of the first book of the *Metamorphoses*, where Ovid tells of the encounter between the boasting god Apollo and Cupid with his little bow and arrows.

> "O silly youngster,"
> He said, "What are you doing with such weapons?
> Those are for grown-ups!" (1.456–57, Humphries trans.)

But the god of Love has two kinds of arrows in his quiver and uses one on Apollo, and the other on Daphne.

> He drew from his quiver different kinds of arrows,
> One causing love, golden and sharp and gleaming,
> The other blunt, and tipped with lead, and serving
> To drive all love away. (1.468–71)

He shoots the golden one at Apollo and the one tipped with lead at Daphne, a nice act of poetic justice: Apollo chases after Daphne, hopelessly in love, while she flees from him in terror.

Like the radiant Apollo, the eminent scholar of "Arrow" was used to being madly loved by the audiences he hit with his golden arrows, just as all charismatic lecturers like to be. For Arrowsmith was in truth a legendary lecturer of great presence and powerful mind. But in his reading from *Euripides Agonistes* he unwittingly shot the equivalent of Cupid's blunt arrow tipped with lead into the hearts of the poet and her students.

Hard as it may be for white Americans who think they are not racists to comprehend, "Arrow" is a poem about the effects of Carmichael's institutional racism, capturing what it is as surely as in that encounter recalled in the prologue of *Invisible Man*. Furthermore, the poet and her students cannot flee the lecture hall, and that matters. Fixed in their seats, their dilemma is akinetic, the very opposite of Daphne's flight or Invisible Man's assault on the oblivious white man. The poet reiterates the four of them sitting there, as if transfixed:

> And we sat there . . .
> So we sat through the applause . . .
> We sat through it . . .

The revulsion and shock of Dove's "Arrow" are things other Daphnes may understand. Apollos of whatever age or gender, it seems, never.

Through a Gate of False Dreams

In 1993, six years after winning the Pulitzer for *Thomas and Beulah*, Dove published her sole novel to date, *Through the Ivory Gate*. The narrative is associative, moving back and forth in time and fixing on key moments that are linked more by common image and theme than by a chronological progression. It is a musician's and a poet's way of telling a story, beginning with a prologue, an overture announcing themes that will recur throughout the novel. Young Virginia is taken to task by her grandmother for not loving a black doll that she had bought for her, and for her preference for a beautiful white doll with red hair named Penelope. The irony is not subtle, nor could the reference to Homer's *Odyssey* be more explicit. Odysseus's wife Penelope is the one who tells the disguised Odysseus about the Gates of Dreams, one of horn and one of ivory; through the first gate true dreams may come, but through the gate of ivory only false, deluding dreams. Penelope, the white doll, is the young girl's choice, but by the time she is in college in the late sixties and seventies this particular Penelope will take on an entirely different appearance and meaning. The lovely white doll appears to Virginia through the Gate of Ivory, the Gate of False Dreams.

At this point in her life Dove was in her early forties and had moved from Arizona State and Phoenix to the University of Virginia. *Through the Ivory Gate* has some suggestive autobiographical elements, but stops well short of being a roman à clef. There is nothing here about her immediate family, her husband Fred Viebahn and their daughter Aviva, nor of Dove's study in Tübingen. The main character, Virginia King, is a talented young artist in the making, just graduated from college, a gifted cellist and actress, with no prospects of employment in the early 1970s. She returns home to

Akron, Ohio (also Dove's home town), from Phoenix and lands a job teaching children in the local school about puppetry and the creative arts. By the end of the novel, Virginia has decided to leave her African American lover, thinking independent thoughts about returning to a former lover, a white American man, and resolves to move to New York and take the risk of trying for a career in theater. The story stops with a complex nonresolution: Virginia has her grandmother's blessing, but also is moving from a black man to a white man and going away for work as well as for love.

Because people first think more about the covers of books than what is inside them, explicitly classical titles have to be carefully chosen for effective marketing. A substantial demolition of classical paradigms like Reed's *Last Days of Louisiana Red* went unnoticed in Steiner's compendious *Antigones* for this very reason, though if you've read both books you have the feeling that Reed's Hoodooism would not have fit into the tradition Steiner conceived.[11]

One of the best things about Dove's *Through the Ivory Gate* is the rightness of its title. It resonates through the story from start to finish, in a way that compels us to go back to Homer to see its implications.[12] When Odysseus, disguised as an old beggar, tells Penelope that her dream of her husband's imminent return must be true, she gracefully turns his encouragement aside with a self-deprecating remark.

Friend, many and many a dream is mere confusion,
a cobweb of no consequence at all.
Two gates for ghostly dreams there are: one gateway
of honest horn, and one of ivory.
Issuing by the ivory gate are dreams
of glimmering illusion, fantasies,
but those that come through solid polished horn
may be bourne out, if mortals only know them.
I doubt it came by horn, my fearful dream—
too good to be true, that, for my son and me. (*Odyssey* 19.560–69,
        Fitzgerald trans.)

As Fran Ross might say, for the information of nonclassicists, this famous passage is fully glossed for Dove's readers by another character, an alcoholic ex-sixties radical named Parker, who quotes this passage from Fitzgerald's version to Virginia. Somewhat like Dove herself, Virginia tends to be brighter and better educated than almost anyone else in the room, save for a few wise family elders and musicians. In this instance, she is certainly more sober.

> He stopped at the door and turned, his hoarse voice trailing to a whisper as he lifted his arms for the oratory: "Two gates for ghostly dreams there are: one gateway of honest horn, and one of ivory. Issuing by the ivory gate are dreams of glimmering illusion, fantasies, but those that come through solid polished horn may be borne out, if mortals only know them."
>
> "Homer. *The Odyssey*. Right?"

Well, yes, but not for long. Parker shifts to blowsy moralizing that sounds like a bad lecture in a Great Books course, recalling the shadowy figures of the myth of the cave in Plato's *Republic*.

> "Illusion, Virginia. Glimmering illusion. That's all we're doing. We're playing with shadows, pretending they'll come to life with the first rays of the full moon. And we learn to do it so well that other people believe in the shadows. But you know what? To the others the shadows *are* real. Only to us they're not."[13]

A learned allusion and quotation of Homer turns into a Platonist's riff on the Myth of the Cave, and Plato's puppet show becomes as relevant to Virginia's story as Penelope's gate of false dreams.

The Gate of Ivory is a portentous image, one calculated to provoke debate. But the underlying thread that Dove seems to pick up on is that, however false or illusory these dreams may at first seem, in the end they may prove to be as true as true can be. (That is certainly the case for Penelope the Homeric figure, if not Virginia's doll.) Dove had already written a short story that was the basis for one of the important characters in *Through the Ivory Gate*, Virginia's Aunt Carrie, in the last story of her 1985 collection *Fifth Sunday*.[14] There we see and hear Aunt Carrie through the eyes of the narrator first as a child, and then years later, as a fully grown young woman. Carrie recounts a story of brother-and-sister incest that took place long before the young narrator of the short story (and later the heroine of the novel) was born.

There are fatal twists and turns throughout *Ivory Gate*. The child Virginia realizes her mother hates Aunt Carrie, but cannot understand why. She overhears her parents in a bitter argument after her father abruptly moves them away from their home and Aunt Carrie, and it still remains a mystery. She finally learns from Carrie herself about a love letter that

Carrie wrote to her brother, which he secreted in what he thought was the safest of all places, behind the frame of a picture of his mother. His wife discovers the letter by chance, so that Virginia now understands at last why her mother hates Aunt Carrie, and why her father moved their family away from her. Dove carries the device of a hidden letter and its chance discovery into *Through the Ivory Gate*. It is a melodramatic discovery of the truth of a situation that she would improve on when revising her drama *The Darker Face of the Earth*.[15]

In the short story, less so in the novel, Virginia's bond with her aunt is tenuous, their future relationship possible but undeveloped. In the later novel Virginia has a strange dream based on an event in her childhood, when her mother went to meet her father at the train station and brought along both Virginia and Aunt Carrie. Virginia could understand very little of what was going on, though all the adults did: her mother was confronting her father with the evidence of his incestuous liaison with his own sister, years before Virginia's parents had met. This troubling story surfaces in a nightmare whose meaning Virginia cannot unravel (*Through the Ivory Gate*, 211), until she seeks out her Aunt Carrie, tells her about these dimly understood moments in her childhood, and at last hears from Aunt Carrie what had actually happened (235–29).

Malin Pereira offers a psychoanalytic reading of the connections between miscegenation and cultural amalgamation in both this novel and Dove's play *The Darker Face of the Earth*.[16] Pereira's argument for the connections between cultural and sexual mixing and mingling may well explain why it took so long for Dove to get her drama into a performable script, and why she went on to revise it substantially by working closely with directors and actors who performed it.[17]

In a conversation with Therese Steffen, Dove makes it clear that she was striving to find a different way to treat the incest taboo of ancient Greek and modern Western literature.

> One of the things I was trying to do in *Through the Ivory Gate* was to present Aunt Carrie's narrative as a perfectly normal story that just happens to be about incest. What shakes Virginia upon hearing it is that she *isn't* shocked. Incest appears as an almost natural outcome for people who know each other very well.
>
> Even in *The Darker Face of the Earth*, it's not the overwhelming concern. I don't want the audience to think, "Oh no, it's incest," but that it's a shame that Augustus and Amalia can't stay together. In that sense it's similar to what happens in *Through the Ivory Gate*, the emotion that's called

up is not "Horrible—she slept with her brother," but "How sad that this ruined her life." It's a different take on incest, that's true.[18]

Through the Ivory Gate pays intermittent attention to the legendary Gates of Horn and Ivory, implying that the whole story is perhaps nothing but Penelope's and Parker's glimmering illusion, fantasy, and then Virginia's too. But the other theme Dove works out with equal care is the connection between puppetry and human existence. It is not only that Virginia's dream might be an illusion. The lives she and Parker and others are living may also be the shadowy illusions of the kind experienced by the prisoners chained in the famous Myth of the Cave in the *Republic* (7.514a–520a). By going into the outer world of the sun, a prisoner who returned to the shadows and illusions of the cave would see what Parker claims to see, and Virginia as well. Socrates makes the point by his questioning of Glaucon.

> "Now if he recalled the cell where he'd originally lived and what passed for knowledge there and his former fellow prisoners, don't you think he'd feel happy about his own altered circumstances, and sorry for them?"
> "Definitely."
> "Suppose that the prisoners used to assign prestige and credit to one another, in the sense that they rewarded speed at recognizing the shadows as they passed, and the ability to remember which ones normally come earlier and later and at the same time as which other ones, and expertise at using this as a basis for guessing which ones would arrive next. Do you think our former prisoner would covet these honors and would envy the people who had status and power there, or would he much prefer, as Homer describes it, 'being a slave laboring for someone else—someone without property' and would put up with anything at all, in fact, rather than share their beliefs and their life?"
> "Yes, I think he'd go through anything rather than life that way," he said. (*Republic* 7.516c–e, Robin Waterfield trans.)

The reference to Homer quotes the shade of Achilles speaking to Odysseus in the eleventh book of the Odyssey, as he waves aside Odysseus's talk about his glorious deeds and immortal reputation.

> Let me hear no smooth talk
> of death from you, Odysseus, light of councils.
> Better, I say, to break sod as a farm hand

for some poor country man, on iron rations,
than lord it over all the exhausted dead. (*Odyssey* 11.488–92, Fitzgerald
   trans.)

This is the reality of death, and that's what the shadowy show of puppetry
may mean for Virginia as well.

Through the Ivory Gate begins with a prelude (3–10) of emblematic moments out of which the future artist Virginia will come, her first dolls and
puppets. The whole prelude resonates with one of the sociological arguments that helped lead to the Supreme Court's 1954 decision in *Brown v.
Board of Education* to end segregation of the races in public education: the
Clark Doll Test.[19] Childish and understandable in one way, Virginia's preference for Penelope is in another as serious as death.

In a series of experiments and papers the psychologists Kenneth and
Mamie Clark had studied the development of consciousness and racial
identity in young African American children, beginning in the late 1930s
and continuing through the 1940s.[20] When Thurgood Marshall and other
attorneys for the NAACP presented their arguments for the Supreme
Court, social science research came to be one of the most decisive elements in persuading the Court of the pernicious effects of segregation and
racism, and Kenneth Clark's expert testimony about his and his wife's research became the most famous argument from social sciences—and also
the part of the plaintiff's case and the Court's decision that segregationists
immediately attacked, for making law out of social science rather than out
of legal precedent. The Doll Test showed American adults how important
a seemingly trivial toy or plaything could be for the future lives of African
American children.

> The subjects of the Clarks' study were 253 African American children, 134
> of whom were in segregated southern schools while 119 were in integrated
> northern schools. The children were presented with two black dolls and
> two white dolls. Except for color, the dolls were identical in every way. The
> children were asked a series of eight questions concerning the dolls. The
> first four questions were design to reveal racial preference—"Give me a
> doll that you like the best" or "Give me the nice doll." The next three were
> designed to discover racial identification—"Give me the doll that looks
> like a Negro child." The final question, "Give me the doll that looks like
> you," was to reveal self-identification. . . . In the racial preference portion
> of the study, however, the Clarks' results "disturbed" them to such an ex-
> tent that Kenneth later claimed that they delayed publication of the data.

The Clarks wrote that "the majority of these Negro children prefer the *white* doll and reject the colored doll. Two-thirds of the children consistently wanted to play with the white doll and claimed that it was the 'nice' doll. A concomitant percentage rejected the black doll."[21]

The NAACP team argued that the Clarks' Doll Test was compelling evidence that African American children had internalized racism. It was one of the unforeseen consequences of racial discrimination and segregated education.

Highly attuned to the consequences of such social constructions, *Through the Ivory Gate* is nonetheless not simply a transcription of social scientific research into fiction. In a 1996 interview with Mike Hammer and Kristina Daub, Dove says that her novel was actually inspired by a dream she had about a black puppeteer.[22] This dream turns into a pervasive theme of the novel.

The first doll little Virginia sees is a black pickaninny doll, the very image of the racism that a child cannot yet fathom. She next sees "Samba," a vivid doll if there ever was one, "wearing red jacket blue trousers purple shoes with crimson soles and linings and a green umbrella" (5). This is no better, but her grandmother assures her, "I don't care how many dolls they make in this world and how bad you might want them—I ain't going to buy you one until they can do them right" (6). But before they get them right, Aunt Carrie brings Virginia a doll she falls in love with at first sight, "Penelope." And Penelope does more than sound a leitmotiv for the later quotation of Penelope's words from the *Odyssey*. It is a seductive illusion of whiteness: "Penelope with the long red hair and plump good looks of Brenda Starr, Penelope of the creamy skin and dimpling cheeks."

And then comes Virginia's ninth birthday and at last what would be seen at the time as an acceptable design for a child of color, simply because it is for black children, not white: a cheaply made doll with brown skin in a seersucker playsuit, with eyes that do not close, and instead of hair, just molded plastic curls. The political gesture is lost on the child; all she can see is a doll in every way inferior to what she knows and loves in her Penelope. Virginia not only isn't grateful for her grandmother's gift, she finally throws it out the window, to her mother's astonishment, who says to her father, "Your daughter is ashamed of being a Negro. Look what she did to my mother's birthday present. She obviously prefers that fat redhead to her own color" (7). Virginia grows beyond these childish delusions, even as she makes a career as an artist who teaches children to play and imitate human beings with the puppets and doll-like figures that she teaches both them and their parents to make. She becomes a puppeteer in real life, playing roles and teaching the playing of roles, as a profession. She also becomes an accomplished musician, able to learn and perform Bach's six solo suites for cello. She thereby finds her way in life through arts that may seem an illusion, but actually turn out to be a deliverance.

Eventually Virginia's beloved doll Penelope is revealed as nothing but a false dream, a forgettable curiosity, a childish portrait of Dorian Gray. The compromise and moral confusion of the white doll becomes visible in the passage of time and in the decay of neglect, its punctured pinkish white skin discolored to gangrenous black from mildew. By the time Virginia is ready to go off to college Afros have become fashionable, and the doll's once gleaming hair is now appropriately matted and dusty, the stuffing inside rotting through: "Penelope stank. She took the doll to the bathroom and laid her on the scale. She came to four pounds. There was nothing to do but throw her away" (10). This ends the prelude with a theme that carries through to the end of the novel. Then Virginia will come to the point where she will resign her job as an itinerant teacher of puppetry and art and music, and leave her black lover Terry to go off to New York for a risky try at a career in the theater. She even comes to recognize that she had loved a white man before Clayton named Terry.

> Terry was a nice guy. Was she using him? No, it wasn't that vulgar; it was far more complicated and also much simpler. What she felt for Terry was not love, and even love didn't always warrant life-changing sacrifices. She knew: she had loved Clayton. (275)

The novel ends with Virginia poised for a turn away from puppetry and the new life she seems to have chosen.

Penelope's dream that passes through the Gate of Ivory is the deluded dream embodied in Aunt Carrie's gift of the Penelope doll, the doll that Virginia ultimately discards and leaves behind as easily as her Afro leaves behind hair straighteners and curlers. Her dolls and puppets are as problematic for a performer as for her audiences.[23] But if Plato's worry is that such art and illusion appeal to the childlike in people, and are therefore unworthy of them, Virginia is actually teaching and performing for children, and for those who can take pleasure in the delight of children, their parents and such other adults as can be expected to respond with equal delight. Virginia frees the imagination of her pupils and makes them realize that they can act out in art what they already see happening in the world about them. As she explains to their parents at a PTA meeting, children can learn while they play, which is something that adults are not thought to be able to do. She argues that puppetry should be taken as seriously by adults as it demonstrably is by children. This is an argument that actual puppeteers make in America all the time.[24]

Through the Ivory Gate is interspersed throughout with Virginia's practice and performance of music, focusing in particular on the *summa* for cellists, the six unaccompanied suites of Johann Sebastian Bach. There is a steady counterpoint between her musical play and the puppetry that she is assigned to teach and perform with children, and for children. As she explains to the parents and teachers of her pupils,

> Whenever a child pretends that Barbie is about to go on a date with Ken, a small puppet show is taking place. Extend this concept over the course of human history and it becomes logical that the first rock or piece of gnarled wood a cave man used to represent friends or enemies while telling a story was a kind of puppet. So puppets are nearly as old as human beings.
>
> How can a puppet, a lifeless object, show a human being how to portray emotion? A Russian actor by the name of Obrazosov was fascinated with this question. He decided that puppets did not imitate people but that they were instruments for pointing out people's odd characteristics. And with this theory came a startling discovery: puppets did not have to look like real people; they did not even have to act like real people. It was enough that they were symbols of the traits of men. (101–102)

By their very design puppets blend the imaginary and the real. In the second part of *Don Quixote* the Don and Sancho Panza attend a performance of Master Pedro and his puppet show enacting the noble story of the knight Don Gaiferos and his wife Melisendra, whom he frees from captivity among the Moors. Reacting to the puppets' representation of this noble story exactly as a doctrinaire Platonist fears unphilosophical people would, the Don madly takes everything happening on the stage not as a representation of reality, but as reality itself. He leaps amid the puppets and attacks the evil Moors, knocking some over, decapitating others, even coming close to decapitating Master Pedro himself. Only later is it discovered that Master Pedro is actually the scoundrel Ginés de Pasamonte, who showered Don Quixote with stones after the Don had freed him from a chain gang. We are easily taken in by one illusion even as we think we have escaped being taken in by another.[25]

A comparable delusion can be seen near the end of Dove's novel, when Virginia thinks she can walk away from the play of puppetry and life that she has begun with her young pupil Renee, without consequences. "You think you can start something up in one corner, then put it on hold while you go dabble somewhere else," Renee's mother tells her. "When you saw how much she was investing in you, you thought you could stop, just like that. I'm no child psychologist, but one thing I know about kids: what you start, you better finish" (272–73). Inexperienced as she is in the intricate relationship that can develop between a teacher and her young pupils, Virginia had been able to reach even the more reclusive of them and direct their lives to a happier and possibly even better direction through learning about art. She promises to do better by Renee, but that is an outcome we never get to see.

As a piece of fiction *Through the Ivory Gate* is inconclusive, breaking off with the further history of Virginia, her lover Terry, and her student Renee unknown.[26] As Steffen puts it, *Through the Ivory Gate* is not a conventionally plotted piece of fiction, but a series of lyrical vignettes "linked like beads on a string."[27] Virginia's later life journey is no more Dove's real concern here than Aunt Carrie's and her father's incestuous affair before Virginia was born. For the tantalizing thing about this dream that comes through Penelope's Ivory Gate is that in the Homeric Penelope's case what could have been a false dream turns out to be true. The eagle that swoops down and kills Penelope's twenty fat geese in her dream tells her nothing but the truth, however much she may deflect it.

"Be glad," says he, "renowned Ikarios' daughter:
here is no dream but something real as day,
something about to happen. All those geese
were suitors, and the bird was I. See now,
I am no eagle but your lord come back
to bring inglorious death upon them all!" (*Odyssey* 19.546–50, Fitzgerald
    trans.)

In making her heroine Virginia a musician and a puppeteer, Dove combines both the highest kind of art (Bach cello suites) with what is commonly believed to be the humblest, puppetry fit only for children. And for her, as for pupils and adults who understand, there is no such distance between these arts. She understands what Scott Shershow argues for in his book on puppets and popular culture: "The high and the low, the elite and the popular have never been more than each other's shadow, and that appropriation, like culture itself, is always a kind of mirage, an illusion or performance not unlike those more literally histrionic practices in which it so often manifests itself."[28] So far as the artist is concerned, the fictional dream that is not reality and is even illusory is as real and as true as Penelope's dream that *may* have come to her through the Ivory Gate. In the event, it was true for Penelope, and maybe someday it will be for Virginia.

Aristotle and *The Darker Face of the Earth*

In an interview in 2000 with her editor Robert McDowell of the Story Line Press, Rita Dove explained audiences' attraction to Sophocles' *Oedipus*, a curious attraction in some ways, since his fate was set at birth and the audience will already know his fate before the drama begins. She was searching "for a modern analogy, a set of circumstances where the social structure was as rigid and all-powerful as the Greek universe, one against which even the noblest of characters would be powerless," and she found it in slavery, where the power of masters over slaves was as absolute as the power of the gods.[29] Taking the story of Oedipus of Thebes, the son of Laius and Jocasta, who Laius learned was destined to kill his father, Dove transformed the Sophoclean play so that it would encompass both the Greek myth's treatment of the incest taboo and the African American and white American history of slavery, as well as the miscegenation of the two races it regularly led to. The only difference from the usual history, and it will prove to be a crucial one, is that instead of a white master taking his pleasure with a black slave woman, it will be the white mistress, wife of the master of the plantation, who takes a male slave for a lover. The Laius figure becomes the feckless husband, Louis Lafarge, the Jocasta his wife Amalia Jennings Lafarge; Amalia's slave lover Hector becomes the father of Amalia's son, who returns with the name of Augustus Newcastle. Instead of the prophet Teiresias, the conjure woman Scylla becomes the one who knows the true story and warns Augustus of his doom.

Dove's sketch of the initial conception of the drama as it was first conceived in 1979 still describes accurately what the bare outline of the play would eventually be, even in its third edition of 2000, after considerable revisions and productions at the Oregon Shakespeare Festival, the Crossroads Theater in New Brunswick, New Jersey, and various staged readings, especially one directed by Derek Walcott in 1995 at the 92nd St. "Y" in New York.

> A child born of a white plantation mistress and her African lover is sold off but returns twenty years later, unaware of his origins. The open secret of miscegenation would be the key that turns the lock of Fate, and instead

of Tiresias, a conjure woman would prophesy the curse. Pride and rebellious spirit have little chance in the systemic violence of slavery, which brutalizes both slave and master: In a different world, Amalia might have been a woman of independent means and Augustus a poet; instead, both are doomed to be crushed when their emotions run counter to the ruling status quo. The slaves know this and function as a Greek chorus, commenting and warning, all to no avail.[30]

During and after productions and readings Dove went on to make substantial revisions in *The Darker Face of the Earth*, but there was one speech for its hero Augustus that she never changed a word of. This is what gives the play its title: the moment when Augustus imagines his own engendering, at the hands of a white master who visited his slave mother in her cabin. At this point he is telling the story everyone would suppose the truth, but unwittingly, actually telling his own life story to his actual mother Amalia. All the dramatic ironies of the original *Oedipus* are there, magnified, since neither she nor he yet grasps the truth of what happened. We do. Without the benefit of the kind of foreknowledge of myth that a Greek tragedian could count on, it was necessary for Dove to give the background myth to her main drama, which is what she does in an extended prologue set twenty years before this moment, at the time Amalia bore a male child to her slave lover Hector (*Darker Face*: prologue, 17–33).

Augustus' speech is the loveliest lyric of the whole play, even though it tells the unloveliest of stories. Perhaps this is why Dove chose its evocative fourth line for her title.

One soft night in April
when the pear blossoms
cast their pale faces on
the darker face of the earth,
my mother lay sleeping in her cabin.
On that same fine April night
Massa stood up from the porch swing,
stretched as he gazed at the stars
sprinkled across the brow of heaven,
and thought: "I think I'll make me
another bright-eyed pickaninny."
And now that pickaninny,
who started out no more than
the twinkle in his papa's eyes

and the shame between his mama's legs,
is standing in the elegant parlor
of another massa,
entertaining the pretty mistress
with stories of whippings and heartbreak.
(*Darker Face*, 2000, 87)

These are gentle images for the single most enduring mark that American slavery made on whites and blacks alike, the enforced miscegenation repeated millions of times over, that leads directly to the fury of Malcolm X's denunciation in his *Autobiography* of the white master who raped his grandmothers and ancestors long before. In much the same way that she conceived of the recurrent images in the novel *Through the Ivory Gate*, Dove's essential power as a lyric poet enables her to create a dramatic text equally governed by the power of the unforgettable line and image.

She had no interest in following the *Oedipus* of Sophocles to the letter, and most of the changes she did make came from intelligent direction and the necessary practical experience of working with actors performing for audiences. But the interesting outcome of this extended series of productions, readings, and revisions was that her drama did come to be more, not less, like Sophocles' play, and in her opinion and her directors' opinions, a more effective piece of theater.

The most salient change came in the ending. In the first version of 1994 Augustus does not kill Amalia as he was required to do by his fellow conspirators to start their rebellion, and for this he is shot dead immediately after Amalia dies.

> *Augustus*: Stay! (*Augustus clutches Amalia's knees; she stares down at him, tenderly pulling his head against her. Ned and Benjamin rush in, pistols drawn.*)
> *Ned*: Bloody traitor! (*shoots; Amalia falls*)
> *Augustus*: Mother . . . (*Benjamin shoots; Augustus sinks on top of Amalia's body*)
> *Phebe*: Augustus!
> (*She kneels beside him. Ned and Benjamin turn on their heels and leave. The revolting slaves pour in, brandishing sticks and torches.*)
> *Slaves*: We're free! We're free!
> (*Scylla is the last to enter. As Phebe sobs, Scylla takes in the scene, staring at the bodies as she slowly straightens up to her full height. Blackout.*)

In the revised ending Amalia commits suicide, an approximate parallel to Jocasta's last words to Oedipus and her suicide off stage in Sophocles. This change makes her character heroic rather than simply the victim of misfortune. She exercises some will over her destiny, like Jocasta, and does not simply acquiesce to it. Without the religious convention that proscribed actual killing on the ancient Athenian stage, Amalia could die on stage with no need to resort to the ancient tragedians' device of the messenger speech to report the action.

> *Jocasta*: O be persuaded by me, I entreat you: do not do this.
> *Oedipus*: I will not be persuaded to let be the chance of finding out the whole thing clearly.
> *Jocasta*: It is because I wish you well that I give you this counsel—and it's the best counsel.
> *Oedipus*: Then the best counsel vexes me, and has for some while since.
> *Jocasta*:   O Oedipus, God help you! God keep you from the knowledge of who you are!
> *Oedipus*: Here, some one, go and fetch the shepherd for me; and let her find her joy in her rich family!
> *Jocasta*: O Oedipus, unhappy Oedipus! that is all I can call you, and the last thing that I shall ever call you. *Exit.*
>   (Sophocles, *Oedipus the King*, 1064–1073, David Grene trans.)

Because she has a different fate in mind for her Jocasta-like Amalia, Dove picks up on Jocasta's warnings and has Amalia warn him to stop, at an earlier point in her play. It is a warning Augustus ignores, in much the same way as Oedipus dismisses Jocasta's plea. Now Amalia already foresees her own death in saying this.

> *Amalia*: (*Wrenches free to face him; her voice trembling*)
> So you want to know who your mother is?
> You think, if I tell you,
> the sad tale of your life
> will find its storybook ending?
> Well then, this will be my last story—
> and when I have finished,
> you will wish you had never
> stroked my hair or kissed my mouth.
> You will wish you had no eyes to see
> or ears to hear. You will wish
> you had never been born. (2000, 144)

This is as close as Dove comes to a direct echo of Sophocles' lines. For audiences who know both poets, the parallel characters in the *Oedipus* and *The Darker Face of the Earth* become woven into a single fabric, the conjure woman Scylla as an African American voodoo version of Teiresias, for example, or Hector as Laius. Amalia's last words bring all the ominous warnings of the *Oedipus* to the surface, and they are as much an allusion to Oedipus's blindness as to Augustus's own. This brings out the contrast between a Greek hero's collision with his destiny and an African American slave's confrontation with the destiny that slavery made for him in antebellum America. Historically considered, these are utterly different fates. Dove makes them come to signify, dramatically, the same thing. Augustus is our African American Oedipus.

Instead of mopping up the stage by having both Augustus and Amalia shot down, Dove gives Amalia of the revised version the opportunity to exercise a mother's right to help her child, by knowingly killing herself and recalling for the last time her effort to save him when he was born.

> *Phebe*: They'll kill you, Augustus!
> *Augustus*: Time to be free.
> *Amalia*: Poor baby! I thought
> I could keep you from harm—
> and here you are,
> right in harm's way.
> (*Phebe gasps; Amalia stabs herself as Augustus, alerted by Phebe's gasp, jumps up, too late to stop her. The room turns red as the out-buildings go up in flames.*)
> *Augustus*: Amalia! (Catching her as she falls) No . . . (*Calling out in anguish*) Eshu Elewa ogo gbogbo! (2000, 148)

For his part, Augustus is returned to speaking the language of the gods he had very nearly forgot, in the same language his actual father Hector knew, and this is the language of the Yoruba Eshu, the god of the crossroads and the enabler of all connection with divinity that he names. The conspirators burst in, see Amalia's body, and conclude that Augustus accomplished exactly what he was expected to.

> *Slaves*: Selah! We're free! (*The Slaves lift Augustus onto their shoulders. The Slave Woman/Narrator stands at the door, holding a torch, taking in the scene.*)
> *Slaves*: Freedom, freedom, freedom . . .

The "Freedom" chant grows louder and more persistent as the Slaves parade out
of the room, Augustus on their shoulders; Phebe follows them sobbing.
Scylla takes the torch from the Slave Woman/narrator and sets fire to the
window's billowing curtains as she slowly straightens up to her full height.
Blackout. (Ibid., 150)

"Selah! We're free!" is a triumphant delusion, and nothing more. This ironic reversal, with cheering slaves carrying off their hero Augustus, seems a pointed revision of Sophocles, where the self-blinded Oedipus is led off stage as his brother-in-law Creon assumes rule of Thebes. In fact both endings are equally ominous.

In her interview with Therese Steffens, Dove points out that any leader of any slave revolt in antebellum South Carolina could "succeed" in only a limited sense.[31] Augustus is doomed to an eventual death, as every leader of every slave revolt was, up to and including their ardent champion John Brown. In this respect Augustus can be taken as a hero whose story makes him a role model (a rough contemporary American equivalent of "hero") for later African Americans: "I think of Medgar Evers and Emmett Till, Malcolm X, and Martin Luther King, Jr.," Dove adds; "throughout history, heroes get destroyed."[32] Dove also tells us that her twelve-year-old daughter Aviva sat through rehearsals at the first workshop for *Darker Face* and made many helpful suggestions. Perhaps the most helpful of all was her observation on the ending:

"You know, I think he should live. There are worse things than death."
This is a twelve-year-old who really doesn't know what she's saying, but
when she said that I suddenly realized, yeah, that's even worse.[33]

Dove often makes her family actors in her poetic life, even when it entails wisdom from out of the mouths of babes. Aviva was right. It is not necessary to destroy a hero on the tragic stage in order for the drama to drive to an effective conclusion, and as the *Oedipus* shows, there are indeed worse things than death. Augustus's momentary triumph and exit on his followers' shoulders follow the pattern of Oedipus's return to the stage after he has blinded himself with the brooches of Jocasta. Augustus goes off alive and famous, but it is clear he will have a life of nothing but sorrow. The triumph of the redeemed Oedipus, the subject of both Lee Breuer's 1993 musical setting *The Gospel at Colonus* and his model, Sophocles' posthumous *Oedipus at Colonus*, seems like so much wishful thinking, so far as Dove's Oedipus is concerned.

In making *The Darker Face of the Earth* a more stageworthy play, Dove followed the spirit and in some instances even the letter of the most familiar precepts about how a good tragedy can be made. Many critics of Greek tragedy hesitate to use the *Poetics* of Aristotle as a vade mecum for interpreting the plays that survive, since such familiar concepts as the tragic flaw are easily mistaken for a universal key that can unlock all secrets about the ethical conduct of heroes in drama. Aristotle's strictures about the well-made tragic plot seem just plainly wrongheaded for much of surviving tragedy, especially Euripides. But for Aristotle, Sophocles' *Oedipus* emerges as the tragedy par excellence in his *Poetics* because it realizes all the effects that he regards as the most characteristic of tragedy. He praises the *Oedipus* in particular for the way it combines Oedipus's sudden recognition (*anagnorêsis*) of the true story of his life and his real identity, with an equally swift reversal (*peripeteia*) of his fortunes (*Poetics* 10.1452a). In *The Darker Face*, much the same thing happens, as Augustus learns what his mother and lover Amalia has already recognized, that he is the child of Amalia and her former lover and now murdered slave, Hector. Dove never says she or her directors aspired to follow Aristotle, and she was certainly careful to distance her work from too close an imitation of Sophocles, but her revisions all tend to change *The Darker Face of the Earth* in ways that make it conform more, not less, to Aristotle's precepts about what constitutes a well-made tragedy.

Augustus Newcastle is so named after his white benefactor, Captain Newcastle, though he is actually the child of his white mistress Amalia and Hector her slave lover who disappeared into the swamp and will later be slain there by the grown-up young man Augustus. At that moment, like Oedipus at the crossroads with Laius, Augustus cannot know that he is killing his own father. As the protagonist of *Darker Face*, corresponding to Oedipus, he is a hero who has survived countless beatings and shown courage in his defiance of slave owners. Like Oedipus, whose name suggests "swollen foot," Augustus with the imperial Roman name bears the scars of a father's hatred. Just as Oedipus's ankles were pierced and tied together with a thong when he was left exposed on Mt. Cithaeron, so Augustus's presumed father Louis—a name more than hinting at "Laius"—throws his set of spurs into the basket containing the newborn baby that the Doctor carries away. Like the Doctor, Louis knew that he was not the father of the child and hoped the spurs would kill the infant, since the Doctor refused to. They injure Augustus and leave visible scars, later supplemented by the scars from all his beatings as a slave, but Augustus survives, like Oedipus. The details of these visible signs inspired a long digression on Apollo and his son Phaethon that Dove removed in her revisions.

Augustus also plays a role inspired by historical example. He mentions Toussaint L'Ouverture's 1797 revolution in Haiti and Joseph Cinqué's revolt on the slave ship *Amistad* in 1839 as examples of what African American slaves could do. In the times and places the play is set (a prologue in 1820, and then twenty years later), the slave Denmark Vessey planned a massive slave uprising in South Carolina, but he and his fellow conspirators were captured and executed before they got far.

In other respects the fourteen scenes of the first published version of *The Darker Face of the Earth* have much the same structure as the revision, with the cardinal moment of the play coming when Amalia and Augustus become lovers at the end of scene 7. In the revised version, Dove divides the action into two acts, each with eight scenes, and uses the crucial point when Augustus and Amalia become lovers as the critical turn before intermission. But there are many seemingly small changes that in fact add considerably to the dramatic effect of the revised drama.

Their cumulative weight is to shift the characters of Amalia and Augustus to a more dignified level. Compare the end of the 1994 love scene (scene 7) with the more restrained curtain/blackout of the later version. The first is a steamy beginning of their incestuous love, on stage.

Amalia stares at Augustus and puts out a hand. He steps toward her. She slowly clasps his forearm. He takes her hair in his hands and kisses her as the Chorus surges in triumphant song. Blackout. (*Darker Face*, 1994, 77)

The revised ending also employs a blackout, but there is no embrace, and the song of the Chorus is now not triumphant, but a sorrow song—a spiritual.

She touches his cheek; he holds her hand there. They lean towards each other slowly, as the Slaves' sorrow song surges—but before their lips touch, there is a blackout. (*Darker Face*, 2000, 89)

Good taste had nothing to do with this change. It reflects Dove and her later collaborators' decision to make both Amalia and Augustus more dignified, and all the characters, even Amalia's cuckolded husband Louis, less cartoonish.

Language changes along with stage directions. Aristotle advises makers of tragedy to aim for diction that is clear, not mean-spirited or vulgar (*Poetics* 22.1458a17). In the 1994 version of the prologue Louis and Amalia were given lines that brought them closer to David Mamet than to Sophocles.

Amalia: What, Louis—struck dumb?
And after such a show of devotion!
Isn't he a fine strapping boy?
Louis: You bitch!
Amalia: So you can stroll out by the cabins
any fine night you please,
but if I summon a buck
up to the house, I'm a bitch?
(*laughs*)
Well then, I'm a bitch.
(*looking at the baby*)
He certainly is pretty.
No wonder
they have so many of them.
Doctor: This is unnatural (*Darker Face*, 1994, 14–15).

This is jejune stuff and not even an experienced actor would find it easy to deliver. The Doctor's morose "This is unnatural" reads like a laugh line. Neither main character has any dignity here, particularly Amalia; her coarse "bitches" seem to express little more than an inarticulate hatred of Louis, and Amalia is otherwise highly articulate. The dialogue is characteristic of late twentieth-century realistic drama, expressing things in a way that would have been unthinkable in earlier times, but it's a distraction from what is at issue in this exchange. Amalia will see to it that the doctor saves her newborn son, just as Jocasta and kindhearted slaves and shepherds saved Oedipus. In the revised lines all of this static and interference is pared away.

Amalia: What, Louis—struck dumb?
Louis: My God!
Amalia: Isn't he a fine strapping boy?
Louis: Who did this to you?
I'll have him whipped to a pulp—
Amalia: (hissing)
So it's alright [*sic*] for you
to stroll out by the cabins
any fine night you please? Ha—
the Big White Hunter with his scrawny whip!
Louis: That tears it!
Doctor: Quiet! They might hear! (2000, 20–21)

"That tears it!" is not wonderful, but as a replacement for the expletive "Bitch!" it at least gives the actor playing Louis more to work with than inarticulate cursing.

Similarly, in the 1994 version, Amalia goes on rather vividly about her husband Louis's infidelities with slave women. There is a peculiar mixture of self-loathing along with the taunting of Louis.

> *Amalia*: But not even Daddy suspected
> where you would seek your satisfaction.
> As long as you let a slave man
> bring your wife iced drinks
> instead of doing it yourself,
> as long as a black man crawled over
> the perfumed limbs of your wife,
> you thought you had all
> the freedom in the world —
> it was your right
> to pull on those riding boots
> and stalk little slave girls.
> *Louis*: Then I swear I'll kill you —
> *Lunges toward her, the Doctor restrains him.* (1994, 16)

Dove cuts out much of the distracting brutality and thereby gets us to a more developed character in Amalia than the earlier gratuitous invective allows. An added stage direction urges more nuance in the way Amalia's actor should deliver her lines.

> *Amalia*: But not even Daddy
> suspected where you would seek
> your satisfaction.
> It was your right
> to pull on those riding boots
> and stalk little slave girls.
> God knows what you do to them
> in the name of ownership.
> *Depleted from the bravado she has mustered, Amalia bends over the baby so they*
> *won't see her exhaustion. Louis, still sitting in the armchair, grabs the*
> *Doctor by the shirt and pulls him down to his level.*
> *Louis*: Get rid of it! Destroy the bastard! (2000, 21–22).

Like Beethoven's sketchbooks, the revisions a poet makes can teach us a lot about how her work evolves. In this regard it's telling that there is almost no change at all from one version to the next in the character of the conjure woman Scylla. Her name may be Greco-Roman, as are the names of many of the slaves—Phebe, Psyche, Diana, Hector, Alexander, Scipio—but this is as much in keeping with the Southern practice of ironically grand classical names as any eloquent meaning to the name. Scylla plays a central role in both versions, and she has exactly the same action to perform at the end of both versions. When the baby who will grow up to be Augustus is born in the opening scene of the play, Scylla is suddenly possessed by the Voodoo god.

> *Scylla*: Oh! Oh!
> *Others*: What is it, Scylla, What is it?
> *Scylla*: It's out in the world.
> *The Slaves look at her in fear.*
> *Alexander*: Lord have mercy.
> *The Slaves gather around Scylla as she tries to straighten up but cannot.* (*Darker Face of the Earth*, 2000, 19–20)

The actor playing Scylla must go through the entire performance "severely bent over and walking with a limp." The stage direction at the end then reads, "*She slowly straightens up to her full height.*" This should make for an electrifying moment of theater if the audience can be prepared for it: an actress who has played the entire drama in a crouched and contorted posture ends by rising up to her full, commanding height. As Scylla does so, it signifies that her task as one possessed by the Voodoo god is finished. As the deity withdraws from her body and soul, her own posture returns to her. With careful directing and acting the full meaning of Dove's final stage direction should be clear: Scylla, a perfect fusion of the Greek and the African American, at once the Teiresias of *The Darker Face of the Earth* and its *loa*, a divinely inspired being now returning to her human form.

Mother Love

While the maternal bond that mothers have for their daughters is unyielding, daughters do not necessarily reciprocate the same emotional attachment to their mothers. In fact, daughters often find their mothers' love to be stifling and oppressive. Dove reveals that ultimately, either by force or choice, all daughters leave their mothers, and unlike the mythic story do not always return home.

Tracey L. Walters, *African American Literature and the Classicist Tradition*

Intact Form and Violated World

Rita Dove prefaces her 1995 collection of poems *Mother Love* with a tribute to "the intact world" of the sonnet, which she contrasts with the world gone awry in the ancient story of Demeter and Persephone.[34] The formal stability of the sonnet is appropriate for an adaptation of the enduring myth of betrayal and regeneration that the Demeter/Persephone cycle poses, its fourteen lines an ideal form, "since all three—mother-goddess, daughter-consort and poet—are struggling to sing in their chains." This reference to the end of Dylan Thomas's "Fern Hill" underlines the balance the poems will create between mortality and loss and the enduring (or at least surviving) forms that poetry creates.

Oh as I was young and easy in the mercy of his means,
Time held me green and dying
Though I sang in my chains like the sea.

The difference is that it's not now just a contrast between poetry and a young but mortal poet held green and dying, but Dove herself is a mother with a daughter and will perforce flow into a pattern like the mother-daughter plot of Demeter and Persephone. Hence the double dedication of the volume, at once looking back to past mother love and forward to its present and future: "FOR *my mother*, TO *my daughter*."

The sonnets of *Mother Love* will be the proper mode for the verses promised, "and not only in homage and as counterpoint to Rilke's *Sonnets to Orpheus*." The question Dove asks of herself is how far she dares go in the variation of strictly Petrarchan or Shakespearean forms. Rilke's sonnets are revolutionary in the way they rewrite the ancient myth of the poet whose grief for the loss of Eurydice takes him down into the world of the dead. Until Vergil's treatment of the myth at the end of the *Georgics*, Eurydice had hardly any voice of her own in ancient poetry. All of Rilke's *Sonnets* are identical in form, observing the Petrarchan sonnet's structure of an octave with two rhyming sounds and a sestet with two or three rhymes. But they move far beyond the familiar story of the power of art to defy death and create immortality for its subjects.[35] Dove acknowledges the many ways there are to violate the traditional sonnet "in the service of American speech or modern love or whatever."

> I will simply say that I like how the sonnet comforts even while its prim borders (but what a pretty fence!) are stultifying; one is constantly bumping up against Order.

To invoke Rilke's "pretty fences" for homage and counterpoint was a bold move, even more, the choice of the myth of Demeter and Persephone to replace the Orpheus and Eurydice story. In twentieth-century American poetry since Ezra Pound's *Canto* 106 ("And was her daughter like that; / Black as Demeter's gown, / eyes, hair?") and H.D.'s "Demeter," "At Eleusis," and "The Mysteries" it has become one of the central Greek myths for feminist poets.[36] And the epigraphs to each of the seven sections of *Mother Love* range far beyond any single canon: from the Jungian psychologist James Hillman's 1979 book *The Dream and the Underworld* for section 1, to Mother Goose (2), H.D.'s late collection *Hermetic Definition* (3), Jamaica Kincaid's story "The Circling Hand" (4), the Yiddish poet Kadia Molodowsky's "White Night" (5), Muriel Rukeyser's "The Poem as Mask" (6), and, in a telling departure from all that comes before, Lucifer's Lament from the first book of Milton's *Paradise Lost* (7):

> Is this the Region, this the Soil, the Clime
> Said then the lost Arch Angel, this the seat
> That we must change for heav'n, this mournful glow
> For that celestial light? (1.241–45)

So Satan salutes Hell as its new Possessor.

> The mind is its own place, and in itself
> Can make a heav'n of Hell, a Hell of Heav'n. (1.254–55)

As we observed at the end of chapter 4, *Mother Love* ends in Sicily, the site of the Rape of Persephone—lovely, but not to be compared with the Garden of Eden that Satan sees.

> Not that fair field
> Of Enna, where Proserpine gath'ring flow'rs
> Herself a fairer Flow'r by Gloomy Dis

Was gather'd, which cost Ceres all that pain
To seek her through the world. (4.268–72)

The Miltonic allusion is bold enough, but the formal structure of Rilke's
chosen form would be equally daunting.

Walter Arndt's translation of *Sonnets to Orpheus* 2.4 aims to capture exactly the original German's rhyme scheme, and to do this he reorders the
sequence of ideas in Rilke's line to preserve the Petrarchan structure of
octet and sestet. Here is how he turns Rilke's pretty fence of a poem about
the unicorn into English verse.

O dieses is das Tier, das es nicht gibt.
Sie wusstens nicht und habens jeden Falls
—sein Wandeln, seine Haltung, seinen Hals,
bis in des stillen Blickes Licht—geliebt.

Zwar *war* es nicht. Doch weil sie's liebten, ward
ein reines Tier.

Behold, this is the beast that never was.
They, unaware, loved it in any case,
Loved all—its neck, its stance, its ambling pace,
Down to the light of its calm gaze. Because

They loved it though it wasn't, there was bred
The purest creature.[37]

Many of the thirty-five poems that make up *Mother Love* do not conform
to the model of fourteen lines. They are sonnets, but sonnets by stretching
our conception of the form to new limits, formally as radical a change in
the traditional sonnet forms as the changes Dove works out in the myth.

For a poet so obviously aware of Eliot's *Waste Land* (especially in section 3, beginning with "Persephone in Hell"), or Joyce's way with solemn
myths—or for that matter, Aristophanes'—the adaptation and revision of
myth is no more radical than many others who have moved beyond the
modernist aesthetic to expose the inadequacies of patriarchal structures
and practice. Pat Righelato has recently read *Mother Love* as an example
of what T. S. Eliot terms "mythical method . . . the ability to manipulate
a continuous parallel between contemporaneity and antiquity," a volume
whose most direct poetic model is Rilke's *Sonnets to Orpheus* and their
"lyric celebration of the feminine."[38] For Righelato, preoccupation with

gender is at the heart of Dove's version of Eliot's mythic method. A similar
point could be made about the Homeric *Hymn to Demeter*. As Helene Foley
points out, even as the *Hymn* serves a patriarchal agenda (Zeus's reordering
of the cosmos, linking the underworld of Hades with the world of mortals
and Olympus), "Demeter stages a far more decisive resistance on behalf
of herself and her daughter than occurs in any other context in Greek literature."[39] To be sure, stressing the connections between *Mother Love* and
the *Hymn* is to take up but one theme that runs through Dove's poetry, yet
it is far too prominent to do anything less. And it has its analogue in the
remarkably free variations of the sonnet form that Dove creates.

For in addition to the mythical method of returning to the Homeric
Hymn, *Mother Love* makes a complementary move in the shape of the poems themselves. Dove drives the sonnet beyond its prim, picket-fence
form into an explosion of formalist versification. The conception of a
sonnet as a poem of fourteen lines, however else organized, is so often
challenged that the only truly reliable way to understand Dove's poems
as sonnets is to see how they vary the canonical number of fourteen lines,
either by multiples of that number, or by divisions of it, such as the seven
sections into which the entire volume is divided—"mirroring the seven
seeds of the pomegranate" that Hades feeds Persephone to keep her from
leaving the world of the dead.[40]

Insofar as sonnets can be said to be pretty fences—the condescension
lurking in this phrase should alert us not to be too literal-minded about
Dove's prefatory remarks—the form Rilke had employed is as radically
altered as the world of Demeter and Persephone. If there is such a thing as
a sonnet with prim borders, stultifying borders, if it imposes a capital "O"
Order against which the poet is always working, that sonnet exists only
in the imagination of the poet of *Mother Love*. Therese Steffen has well
explained how the myth and the poetics of this volume interact.

> In *Mother Love* Dove uses and recharges the sovereignty of two signifi-
> cant structures: the theme of myth and the form of the sonnet. Both are
> particularly suitable carriers for variety within repetition, and interplay
> of freedom and form. Dove, who otherwise resists and rejects limiting
> demarcations, explicitly welcomes these artistic borders whose inclusions
> and exclusions she renegotiates at will. What renders the rewriting of
> myth so attractive is the absence of a single canonized original.[41]

Our one demurral, predictably enough, is with this last claim, about their
being no single, canonized original. Dove works with a great deal more

than the compendious account of the Demeter myth available in Timothy Gantz's *Early Greek Myth*.[42] As historians and theorists of "the classical" like James Porter have argued repeatedly, what constitutes a "classic" varies greatly from one epoch to the next. No one who engages for long with the reception of classical antiquity today would think of any ancient text as a canonized original.[43]

This view of the changing status of classical text is so familiar today that it is important to stress an irony of history: something like the opposite situation of no canonical text obtained in antiquity, when the Homeric *Hymns* were composed and performed. Much of the later history of the Homeric epics after the introduction of literacy lies precisely in the Greeks' efforts to establish a single, canonized text of the poems. The Athenians of the sixth and fifth centuries BCE fooled around with the record to make sure they came out looking prominent in the *Iliad*, more so than they may have been to Homer's audiences in the eighth century.[44]

It is true that the Demeter and Persephone myth was known and can be found from Hesiod and later Greek poets straight through the Roman imperial era and the fourth-century Latin poet Claudian's *On the Rape of Proserpina* and the fifth-century Greek Nonnos's vast mythological compendium, the *Dionysiaka*.[45] The *Hymn to Demeter* and others were composed to honor and praise the Olympian gods' powers and prerogatives and were in Foley's formulation "sung prayers" that served as *prooimia* ("preludes," literally "fore-songs") to the main event, the recitation of epic poetry. While we know almost nothing for certain about specific ancient audiences and the conditions of performance, the texts we have suggest that these hymns like others and the Homeric epics with which they were associated were composed in a preliterate culture in transition to literacy.[46]

Ironically, yet again for this age so suspicious of canonicity, the canonical *Hymn to Demeter* from early antiquity very nearly did not survive to be any kind of text at all, canonized or otherwise. Our modern critical editions of its text all come from a single mutilated manuscript of the *Hymn* dating from the early fifteenth century CE that was found in a stable in Moscow in 1777. Beginning with Shelley and Mary Wollstonecraft Shelley, by the middle of the nineteenth century the number of poets and writers who drew on it for their own versions of the Persephone and Demeter story was legion. Helene Foley's edition amply documents how accessible the *Hymn* would be to a late twentieth-century poet like Dove, not least because the myth and the *Hymn* were so widely known and imitated.

Cross reading of *Mother Love* and the *Hymn to Demeter* is essential to grasp Dove's achievement. Other, single poems come to seem like glancing blows or passing references to the myth by comparison. This is what Dove means when she calls her work an homage to Rilke, working in counterpoint to his 1922 *Sonnets to Orpheus*. He had created the most far-reaching adaptation of the Orpheus myth since antiquity, and Dove aims to do nothing less with Demeter and Persephone. This is epic-sized ambition, even though it is not an epic poem. It may even be why *Paradise Lost* provides the epigraph for the concluding seventh section. *Mother Love* is no middle flight, so far as Dove is concerned.

The Demeter of *Mother Love*

> It falls to goddesses — to those among them who are mothers — to go far-
> ther, in the myth and the ritual that give them credit for having taken the
> step toward action: from sorrow to wrath, from wrath to secession.
>
> Nicole Loraux, *Mothers in Mourning*

Like the poems that divide her earlier volume *Thomas and Beulah* into Thomas and Beulah halves, Dove's thirty-five sonnets can each be read in two ways, as an individual poem, within each of the seven sections (remembering that the sonnet's fourteen lines is a multiple of seven), and as part of the overall design to which each sonnet and section contributes. This is her most explicit formal homage to Rilke's *Sonnets to Orpheus*, which also permit a multiple and unitary reading.[47] The epigraph to the single sonnet of section 1, "Heroes," comes from the psychologist James Hillman, "One had to choose, and who would choose the horror?" and depicts the casual, unreflecting violence that is the other side of the lovely world of flowers that attracts Persephone. The opening lines of the Homeric *Hymn* at once sing in praise of Demeter and her daughter, and of the wanton power of Zeus, who uses flowers as his instrument of seduction. It is all quite lovely and mouthwatering.

> Demeter I begin to sing, the fair-tressed awesome goddess,
> herself and her slim-ankled daughter whom Aidoneus [Hades]
> seized; Zeus, heavy-thundering and mighty-voiced, gave her,
> without the consent of Demeter of the bright fruit and golden sword,
> as she played with the deep-breasted daughters of Ocean,
> plucking flowers in the lush meadow—roses, crocuses,
> and lovely violets, irises and hyacinth and the narcissus,
> which Earth grew as a snare for the flower-faced maiden
> in order to gratify by Zeus's design the Host-to-Many [Hades],

a flower wondrous and bright, awesome for all to see,
for the immortals above and for mortals below. (1–11, Foley trans.)[48]

Dove's opening sonnet parodies this grand opening. It begins by trivializing the gorgeous array of the flowers that Earth (Gaia) sends forth to snare Persephone, reducing them to the one flower in modern American memory linked with memorial and veterans' days; the bright red poppy was also associated with Demeter specifically. And there is no longer an Olympian Zeus and his cosmos collaborating in this seduction, nor Persephone seduced by the beauty of a flower, but one of the "heroes" of the title.

A flower in a weedy field:
make it a poppy. You pick it.

Picking is the point, not the flower. This is not Sicily of the *Hymn*; the landscape is sparse, with a masculine (or heroic) indifference to whatever is picked. And instead of the slim-ankled daughter of Demeter, all we have is a poor old woman who starts screaming:

You've plucked the last poppy
in her miserable garden, the one
that gave her the strength every morning
to rise!

This leads quickly to more violence that "you" do, with the result that the old woman accidentally falls and goes to the world of the dead. But her way is not Persephone's way. The sonnet is twenty-eight lines long, divided into three-line stanzas, with frequent enjambments, and at its center, the first group of fourteen lines ends and the second begins with no figurative ravishment away into the underworld, but accidental murder.

It's too late for apologies
though you go through the motions, offering
trinkets and a juicy spot in the written history
she wouldn't live to read, anyway.
So you strike her, she hits
her head on a white boulder.

The whole structure of the poem is about counterpoint: counterpoint between lovely Homeric *Hymn* images and hardscrabble reality, between a juicy spot in the written history (like the *Hymn*) and the stark fact of the old woman's death. Dove saves the best line for last, so stark it makes us suspect the three-line stanzas were all arranged not only to lead to it, but to play with the very idea of fourteen-line poems, sonnets, as the poem finishes with two last lines that are just half-lines.

> O why
> Did you pick that idiot flower?
> Because it was the last one
> and you knew
> it was going to die.

Is this a male voice? a collective voice of heroes? a mother's?

The epigraph to section 2 moves us from the high-falutin' culture of Hillman's depth psychology to a Mother Goose poem "Baby, Baby, Naughty Baby," which warns a squealing child to shut up—else Bonaparte will come and eat it up.[49]

> Limb from limb at once he'll tear you,
> Just as pussy tears a mouse.

The twelve poems of part 2 that follow range in voices, constantly shifting even as the extended concept of the sonnet changes: beginning with "Primer," a girl's recalling her torment in grade school and her determination to deal with schoolyard bullies herself, we move to "Party Dress for a First Born," a lovely mother's lyric about the empty thoughts of her infant girl, in recognizably Petrarchan form, with the octet ending à la Demeter and Persephone in the figurative image that recalls the Eleusis cult.

> When I ran to my mother, waiting radiant
> as a cornstalk at the edge of the field,
> nothing else mattered: the world stood still.

Equally vivid, and not at all lovely, is the next simile that turns the sestet to a wholly different direction.

> Tonight men stride like elegant scissors across the lawn
> to the women arrayed there, petals waiting to loosen.
> When I step out, disguised in your blushing skin,

they will nudge each other to get a peek
and I will smile, all the while wishing them dead.

Not flowers, but instruments to cut flowers: the men who clip away. The party dress becomes a disguise, the mother appearing as if her daughter before the men. The sonnet stops, three times in a single line: "Mother's calling. Stand up: it will be our secret."

"Persephone, Falling" returns us directly to that moment in the *Hymn to Demeter* when the earth yawns open and Hades springs forth, replete with formulaic epithets at the end of lines reflecting the *Hymn*'s origins in the traditional oral verse composition.

> The earth with its wide ways yawned
> over the Nysian plain; the lord Host-to-Many rose up on her
> with his immortal horses, the celebrated son of Kronos;
> he snatched the unwilling maid into his golden chariot
> and led her off lamenting. (16–20)

Dove follows the *Hymn* closely here, capturing the delight of Persephone and the suddenness of Hades' attack, as well as a suggestion of the language of an ancient poetic tradition.

> One narcissus among the ordinary beautiful
> flowers, one unlike all the others! She pulled,
> stooped to pull harder—
> when, sprung out of the earth
> on his glittering terrible
> carriage, he claimed his due.

The "glittering terrible carriage" and "his due" show this is no modern rape story but a return to the hymn's myth: Zeus's plan to reorder the cosmos through Persephone's abduction to the realm of his brother god Hades, as well as Zeus's supremely calm distance from any of the pain his plan causes.[50] In the sestet that follows, against this ancient divine scheme that the octet reenacts, Dove juxtaposes a modern mother's daily warning to an inattentive child.

> (Remember: go straight to school.
> This is important, stop fooling around.

Don't answer to strangers. Stick
with your playmates. Keep your eyes down.)

No sooner has the register changed from ancient Greek to the worried modern mom of this aside, than Greek antiquity returns with renewed force.

This is how easily the pit
opens. This is how one foot sinks into the ground.

In "The Search" the boundary between ancient and modern is labile,
present realities and ancient myth exist side by side, simultaneously,
blending the despair of Demeter and Dove's mother as each roams the
world in search of her lost child.

She cast a dark cloak on her shoulders
and sped like a bird over dry land and sea,
searching. No one was willing to tell her the truth,
not one of the gods or mortals;
no bird of omen came to her as truthful messenger. (*Hymn to Demeter*, 42–46)

Blown apart by loss, she let herself go—
wandered the neighborhood hatless, breasts
swinging under a ratty sweater, crusted
mascara blackening her gaze. ("The Search")

Then the neighborhood and contemporary world break back through, just
as Hecate will finally tell Demeter the fate of her daughter.

Sniffed Mrs. Franklin, ruling matron, to the rest:
Serves her right, the old mare.

"Protection" and "The Narcissus Flower" juxtapose mother's and
daughter's voices, the one with a racially inflected turn of phrase that
speaks of hair: white people's hair ("'Good' hair has no body / in this country; like trained ivy, / it hangs and shines") and black people's ("Mine comes
out / in clusters"). It ends with Dove's signature, not even as much as a half
line, with a play on "done" and "gone" that complements the loss ("Are you
really all over with? How done / is gone?"). The narcissus flower becomes
the focal point of the daughter's memory of what happened to her, as if
she had been hit by some nuclear blast, not any fires from hell, because

we know there is no such thing as hellfire in Greek: "the way I could see my own fingers and hear / myself scream as the blossom incinerated." The act of rape is described with a clinical precision, as the fall of Persephone transforms into the inward plunge of the rapist.

> And though nothing could chasten
> the plunge, this man
> adamant as a knife easing into
>
> the humblest crevice, I found myself
> at the center of a calm so pure, it was hate.

The sonnets continue to shift between ancient myth and modern experience, making what is remote, near, and what we think familiar, distant. In "Persephone Abducted" Dove ranges back from the present day to the time of American slavery. The cry of the divine daughter is heard by Demeter and Hecate, but neither of them sees what happens. Only Helios has heard and seen the whole story from start to finish, and he is also aware of Zeus's plan to give Persephone to his brother Hades.[51] Now Persephone's cry becomes the cry of a Southern child.

> She cried out for Mama, who did not
> hear. She left with a wild eye thrown back,
> she left with curses, rage
> that withered her features to a hag's.

But her mother never hears her, because she is the mother who toils all day in the cotton fields.

> She left us singing in the field, oblivious
> to all but the ache of our own bent backs.

The *Hymn*'s divine witnesses are the subject of "Statistic: The Witness," each nameless, each playing the role of Hecate and the Sun.

> No matter where I turn, she is there
> screaming.

In the *Hymn* Helios is the sun god who sees all, knows all, and Demeter begs him to tell her the truth:

> With your rays you look down through the bright air
> on the whole of the earth and the sea.
> Tell me the truth about my child. Have you somewhere
> seen who of gods or mortal men took her
> by force from me against her will and went away? (*Hymn*, 69–73)

It is the simple act of looking that is recalled, and the witness seems to be another young girl. Like Helios, the god who detected the adultery of Aphrodite and Ares when they cheated on Hephaestus, this girl is able to see what she shouldn't see:

> I know I should stop looking, do
> as my mother says—turn my head
> to the wall and tell Jesus—but
> I keep remembering things,
> clearer and smaller: his watch,
> his wrist, the two ashen ovals
> etched on her upturned sandals.

This same young witness is back at the original scene of the crime, not in the present day, but in the mythical time of Hades' rape of Persephone, when the earth opened up in a seductive field of flowers.

> Now I must walk this faithless earth
> which cannot readjust an abyss
> into flowering meadow.

These sonnets are among the most powerful evocations of the language and myth of the Homeric *Hymn*, because the familiar art of imitation becomes one that works both ways, so that the *Hymn* is made a gloss of a story in the present. This blending of poems confounds familiar ways of thinking about past and present, those divisions that we fondly imagine mark off points in time.

Once Demeter has learned all she can from the gods, the truth that Helios confirms, she leaves them and comes down among mortals, to the house of Keleos, the ruler of Eleusis, the future site of the mysteries of Demeter and Persephone. There she takes on the disguise of an old woman past childbearing age and meets the daughters of Keleos on their way to draw water at a well.

Like four goddesses they were in the flower of youth,
Kallidikê, Kleisidikê, fair Dêmô, and Kallithoê,
who was the eldest of them all.
They did not know her—gods are hard for mortals to recognize. (108–11)

Demeter calls herself "Doso" (Greek, literally "Giver") and makes up a Cretan tale of just the kind the disguised Odysseus devises to deceive his loyal swineherd Eumaeus and others in the second half of the *Odyssey*. This parallel with the famously deceitful and resourceful Odysseus would not be lost on the *Hymn*'s original audiences, since epic provides the cultural matrix which makes this and other hymns "Homeric." All of them are later in date of composition than the *Iliad* and *Odyssey*, but each of them tells of the birth of the Olympian gods and the world that comes to be through the justice of Zeus.

The transformed Demeter plausibly claims to have escaped from pirates and to have come from Crete to Eleusis and seeks sanctuary and employment in Keleos's house. Keleos's daughter, the young Kallidikê, brings Demeter a.k.a. Doso to her mother Metaneira, who welcomes what she takes to be another mortal whose suffering she can ease.

We mortals are forced, though it may hurt us, to bear
the gifts of the gods. For the yoke lies on our necks.
But now you have come here, all that's mine will be yours.
Raise this child for me, whom the gods provided
late-born and unexpected, much-prayed for by me. (216–20)

Demeter's visit to Eleusis is the model for a community of different voices that Dove releases in "Grief: The Council," one that ranges from the pedestrian and disinterested to the sincere and loving.

I told her: enough is enough.
Get a hold on yourself, take a lover,
help some other unfortunate child.

This prosy language alternates with glimmering references back to Demeter's determination to abandon the world and let all that grows succumb to blight.

to abdicate
to let the garden go to seed

There are jarring changes in register, switching back and forth between the contemporary and the ancient Greek, such as the contemporary American good business practice of printing pictures of runaway children on milk cartons, followed by the spreading blight from the underworld.

> I thought of those blurred snapshots framed
> on milk cartons, a new pair each week.
> > *soot drifting up from hell*
> > *dusting the kale's*
> > *green tresses, the corn's green sleeve*

Dove's women deliver a stream of clichéd advice, at this point making "Grief: The Council" an homage to John Ashbery's poem "Crazy Weather," which begins

> You are wearing a text. The lines
> Droop to your shoelaces and I shall never want or need
> Any other literature than this poetry of mud
> And ambitious reminiscence of times when it came easily
> Through the then woods and ploughed fields and had
> A simple unconscious dignity we can never hope to
> Approximate now except in narrow ravines nobody
> Will inspect where some late sample of the rare,
> Uninteresting specimen might still be putting out shoots, for all we know.[52]

By the end of "Grief: The Council," Ashbery's voice has been assimilated into its peculiar vernacular just as the Homeric *Hymn* was, and with nothing less than a rare but far from uninteresting specimen putting out its shoots.

> > *the last frail tendril snapped free*
> > *(though the roots still strain toward her)*
> and your basic sunshine pouring through
> the clouds. Ain't this crazy weather?
> Feels like winter coming on.
> > *at last the earth cleared to the sea*
> > *at last composure*

"Grief: The Council" leads directly to the title poem of the volume, "Mother Love," in which we will encounter a hilarious riff on what is for moderns the most bizarre moment in the Homeric *Hymn to*

Demeter—certainly the most magical. The syllabic verses of "Mother Love" turn from Ashbery (born 1927) to a form associated with Marianne Moore (1887–1972), here adapted to the sonnet structure of fourteen lines and divided into two lines of linked syllabic verse which create an expectation of the same number of syllables in a line, but no concern for stress patterns.

> Who can forget the attitude of mothering?
>   Toss me a baby and without bothering
> to blink I'll catch her, sling him on a hip.
>   Any woman knows the remedy for grief
> is being needed.

As Demeter in her disguised self observes,

> Gladly will I embrace the child as you bid me.
> I will raise him, nor do I expect a spell or the Undercutter
> to harm him through the negligence of his nurse. (*Hymn*, 226–28)

But "Mother Love" has a surprise in store for its readers, since it not only recalls Demeter's clever offer to serve as the nurse for Metaneira's last-born son, Demophoön, but takes up what may be the most vivid moment in the *Hymn* after the rape of Persephone. Demeter seeks to make the mortal infant Demophoön into an immortal child, a glorious young god who will take the place of her lost daughter. The scheme makes emotional sense to the extent that we can attribute familiar human emotions to a deity as awesome as Demeter. As Metaneira discovers, however, the anthropomorphic gods are different from you and me.

It all could have gone so well. Under "Doso's" care Demophoön eats no mortal food nor sucks on mother's milk, but is anointed by Demeter with ambrosia, the food of the gods. And he does begin to look like a wonder, growing miraculously fast.

> At night, she would bury him like a brand in the fire's might,
> unknown to his own parents. (239–40)

There has been much speculation about how this scene might reflect the secret rituals of the mystery religion at Eleusis; as Helene Foley observes in her commentary, this combination of divine ambrosia, fire, and Demeter's own divine breath on the child has parallels in the stories of other baby divinities in Greek myth.[53] Metaneira is as much a mother as Demeter is, but she is also mortal, and Demeter's plan goes awry. She doesn't realize it, but spying on "Doso" and her son is akin to the violation of a mystery she should never have witnessed.

> She would have made him ageless and immortal,
> if well-girt Metaneira had not in her folly
> kept watch at night from her fragrant chamber
> and spied. But she shrieked and struck both thighs
> in fear for her child, much misled in her mind,
> and in her grief she spoke winged words.
> "Demophoön, my child, the stranger buries you
> deep in fire, causing me woe and bitter cares." (242–49)

Demeter is enraged at this interruption and snatches Demophoön from the flames:

> "Mortals are ignorant and foolish, unable to foresee
> destiny, the good and the bad coming on them.
> You are incurably misled by your folly.
> Let the god's oath, the implacable water of Styx, be witness,
> I would have made your child immortal and ageless
> forever; I would have given him unfailing honor.
> But now he cannot escape death and the death spirits." (256–62)

She then casts Demophoön to the ground, which may be a reference to the ritual of the Amphidromia (lit., "walking or running around") by which a newborn child is incorporated into a family.[54] Knowing the proposed archaeology of the ritual may make this moment in the *Hymn* less strange to some readers. Dove aims for a different effect.

The voice speaking in "Mother Love" turns out to be Demeter, though with a sense of humor and a taste for the grotesque simile that are very far from the Olympian wit of the *Hymn*'s Demeter. The whole sequence is here, from the quartet of Kallidikê and her sisters, to Metaneira's invitation, to the acceptance of "Doso" as a nurse to young Demophoön, to this Dovish Demeter's decision to put aside her mourning weeds "for the daintier comfort of pity: / I decided to save him." The poem becomes hilariously culinary, so that Demophoön's slow roasting begins to sound like a luau, where meats to be cooked are carefully wrapped and buried in live coals.

Each night
I laid him on the smoldering embers,
sealing his juices in slowly so he might
    be cured to perfection. Oh, I know it
looked damning: at the hearth a muttering crone
    bent over a baby sizzling on a spit
as neat as a Virginia ham. Poor human—
    to scream like that, to make me remember.

The poem recovers a glimmer of maternal sentiment—perhaps—in those
final two lines. But the image of Demophoön sizzling away like a Virginia
ham makes it hard to return to this part of the *Hymn* with a straight face.
What was once a mysterious moment in the *Hymn to Demeter* now reads
like a recipe from yet another authorial cookbook. *Mastering the Art of
Olympian Cooking?*

That poem sets the tone of the final two poems of this most hymnic
section of *Mother Love*, which ends in suburban, modern America, a reductio ad absurdum of Demeter's gifts from the earth: Demeter, the Roman
Ceres, from which cereal comes, now faces the only word in contemporary English that preserves any reference to Demeter, and that through
a Roman not a Greek goddess. "Breakfast of Champions," the trademark
slogan for Wheaties, turns out to be famishing fare.

Arise, it's a brand new morning!
Though I pour myself the recommended bowlful,
stones are what I sprinkle among the chaff.

And the lost daughter Persephone, now a young woman coming home
from a party, is the voice of "Golden Oldie." Like the golden oldies on the
hit parade, this is a tune we've all heard before.

swaying
at the wheel like a blind pianist caught in a tune
meant for more than two hands playing.

This image beautifully captures Persephone's longing for an as yet unknown lover, and with a characteristically knowing figure from music. She
has the tune but cannot see it, and it's a song it takes two to sing.

Baby, where did our love go?—a lament
I greedily took in
without a clue who my lover
might be, or where to start looking.

The mother/daughter romance has shifted to a different register, so that Persephone will be lost the way every daughter is lost to a mother, not by the mother's search, but by the daughter's, for a lover.

Persephone Lost

A simple story, a mother's deepest
dread—that her child could drown
in sweetness.

Mother Love 7: "Her Island"

H.D.'s 1960 collection *Hermetic Definition* reflects what Norman Holmes Pearson terms her Freudian sense "of how to link the tribal myths with the personal dream"; for her, "hermetic definition" is ancient wisdom, which she recovers easily as she moves the way *Mother Love* moves, "through the myths and metaphors of multiple cultures."[55] The epigraph from H.D. comes from the first section of *Hermetic Definition*, "Red Rose and a Beggar," and leads us into "Persephone in Hell" by way of this bleak conclusion (adding the final three lines to the three that Dove quotes).

who can escape life, fever,
the darkness of the abyss?
lost, lost, lost,

the last desperate non-escape,
the reddest rose,
the unalterable law . . .

In a significant twist to the long-standing association of African American expatriates and artists with Paris, the Germanophile Dove uses her critical distance to turn the City of Lights into hell itself. "Persephone in Hell" is divided into seven parts (of course), and presents the American junior year abroad, as seen through the Paris of Baudelaire's *Fleurs du mal* and the unreal city of Eliot's *Waste Land*.

I was not quite twenty when I first went down
into the stone chasms of the City of Lights,
every morning four flights creaking under my rubber soles. (part 1)

By this point in the volume the connections with the Homeric *Hymn*'s plot
and imagery are so firmly established that Dove can keep the connection
vividly before us, even as her young girl threads her way through the quint-
essential challenges of a Parisian street scene ("turn left, cross / the avenue,
dodge poodle shit / and tasking nannies"). The casual sex is all part of that
scene, with only a quirky glance back at Persephone, and not a rape (part 2).

The poems of part 3 draw on earlier poems, echoing the opening lines of
the mother's anxious questions in the earlier "Protection" (*are you having a
good time / are you having a time at all*). We may conceive of these echoes as
musical effects: in counterpoint to Persephone's walk through the bitter
cold of central Paris and its monuments (the Marais, the Centre Pompi-
dou), for example, a similar refrain comes from the earlier "Persephone,
Falling."

> *Mon Dieu*, the wind!
> My head fills with ice.
>   *This is how the pit open*s.

In sections 5 and 6 we meet the voice of the man who will pick up the
daughter.

> I need a divertissement:
> The next one through that gate,
> woman or boy, will get
> the full-court press of my ennui.

Different as they are, they nonetheless are moving together in lines that
will intersect, Dove marking their different voices by typography.

> Soft chatter roaring. French nothings.
> I don't belong here.
>   She doesn't belong, that's certain
>   Leather skirt's slipped
>   a bit: sweet. No gloves? American,
>   because she wears black badly.

They finally come together in their different languages,

> *"Puis-je vous offrir mes services?"*
>
> Sotto voce, his inquiry
> curls down to lick my hand.
> Standard nicety, probably,
> but my French could not stand up
> to meet it.
>
> > *"Or myself, if you are looking"*
> > I whisper this. I'm sure she doesn't understand.
>
> "Pardon me?"
>
> > "Excuse, I thought you were French.
> > You are looking for someone?"

In section 7 of this part of the cycle the sequence ends with what Pereira terms "a duet of loss between mother and daughter, reminiscent of Julia Kristeva's 'Stabat Mater.'"[56] But the actual voice of the mother is at first ambiguous. We might assume it is continuing the man's voice from the previous poem.

if I whispered to the moon

                    I am waiting

if I whispered to the olive

                    you are on the way

which would hear me?

                    I am listening

the garden gone

                    the seed in darkness

the city around me

                    I am waiting

it was cold

                    you rise into my arms

I entered for warmth

                    I part the green sheaths

The fourteen lines (or twenty-eight half lines) of the sonnet can be read vertically as well as horizontally, so that the daughter's thoughts on the left can be read as a continuous stream, as can the mother's on the right. And a mother who speaks of "the seed in the darkness" and parting "the green sheaths" can only be Demeter. The sonnet is a visual representation of the way the poet combines the personal and individual with the archetypal.

Part 4 is overtly psychoanalytic in design. Jamaica Kincaid's story "The Circling Hand" provides an epigraph that shows a mother who inflicts her repetition compulsion on her daughter: "On and on my mother would go. No small part of my life was so unimportant that she hadn't made a note of it, and now she would tell it to me over and over again." The punning "Hades' Pitch" is at once the come-on of a seduction, and an allusion to the dark god of the underworld, black as pitch, "Dark-Haired Hades" in the Homeric *Hymn*'s language. It focuses on the erotics of the foot, the very body part that first sinks into the ground as the earth opens up beneath Persephone, as this junior year abroad version of her succumbs possibly out of "sheer boredom" to his seductive come-on: "*If I could just touch your ankle*, he whispers, *there / on the inside, above the bone.*"

> Her ankle burns where he described it. She sighs
> just as her mother above ground stumbles, is caught
> by the fetlock—bereft in an instant—
> while the Great Man drives home his desire.

The second poem in part 4 is titled by the German psychoanalytic term *Wiederkehr*, "Return" (as in *Wiederkehr des Verdrängten*, "return of the repressed"), and entirely in the voice of the daughter, confessing to herself why she stayed with the man who has seduced her.

> he never asked
> if I would stay. Which is why,
> when the choice appeared,
> I reached for it.

The "return" here is the beginning of a return of the daughter to her mother, from the man who wants her. "Wiring Home" moves from Hades' realm to her mother's company, a dogged flight across a Parisian winter landscape ("Lest the wolves loose their whistles / and shopkeepers inquire, / keep moving"), until she is stopped in her tracks by a reminder of where she came from and what she has lost.

> tales of odyssey and heartbreak
> until, turning a corner, you stand

staring: ambushed
by a window of canaries

bright as a thousand
golden narcissi.

"The Bistro Styx" and a few other poems in *Mother Love* show another daughter after Persephone breaks the ties of dependence, becoming not the Homeric *Hymn*'s lovely flower needing the mother and unable to encounter the world without the fierce protection of the mother's arm, but the daughter Tracey Walters describes, someone more independent, and decidedly less innocent. An earlier poem, "Motherhood" in *Thomas and Beulah,* presents us with a frightening image of the Demeter-like mother as protector. The mother in this instance is described as one who sees nothing but danger for her child. She is on a constant lookout for threats to its welfare. In the last stanza of the poem she sees three men playing with a white wolf.

> She calls
> warning but the wolf breaks free
> and she runs, the rattle
> rolls into the gully, then she's
> there and tossing the baby behind her,
> listening for its cry as she straddles
> the wolf and circles its throat, counting
> until her thumbs push through to the earth.
> white fur seeps red. She is hardly breathing.
> the small wild eyes
> go opaque with confusion and shame, like a child's.[57]

The image is that of one gone mad with the need to protect. It is not clear that the child is in danger, but the mother (Beulah) has imagined the most frightening possible danger for her child. In *Mother Love* the child in "Primer" learns an early lesson in how a protective mother prevents the child from the normal experience of the schoolyard. The short mother and her Cadillac are not a happy sight, but a source of embarrassment and shame.

> Nothing could get me into that car.
> I took the long way home, swore
> I'd show them all. I would grow up. ("Primer," 7)

Reflecting a modern sense of the evolving stages of child psychology, we see more clearly in Dove than in the Homeric *Hymn* the development of a daughter from resentful child to independent adult woman, a development played out in a modern, middle-class society in America and Europe, not the fabulous realms of the Olympian gods. Dove can thus do more to flesh out the character of both Persephone and Hades than the traditional male poet or poets of the Homeric *Hymn* would ever be interested in doing. Thus we see the Persephone figure gaining a modern, independent voice, developing in both sexuality and independence in the second poem of the "Persephone in Hell" sequence in a way that marks the growing independence of Persephone from her mother's world.

> Mother worried. Mother with her frilly ideals
> gave me money to call home every day,
> but she couldn't know what I was feeling;
> I was doing what she didn't need to know . . .
> There was love, of course. Mostly boys:
> A flat-faced engineering student from Missouri,
> a Texan flaunting his teaspoon of Cherokee blood. ("Persephone in Hell,"
>   part 2, p. 25)

That adolescent yearning for love is just as evident in "Golden Oldie" when the daughter remembers the first number-one hit song of the Supremes, "Where Did Our Love Go?" This song of adolescent angst and anticipated future passion was followed by a number of other hits that spoke to young listeners almost always in the childlike voice of Diana Ross. This major crossover group kept young listeners' bosoms throbbing for more than two decades with tunes like "Stop in the Name of Love," "My World Is Empty Without You," "Baby I Need Your Loving," "Back in My Arms Again," "Love Is Like an Itching in My Heart," and "Come See About Me."

> The words were easy, crooned
> by a young girl dying to feel alive, to discover
> a pain majestic enough
> to live by. ("Golden Oldie," 19)

Dove recalls this moment with the slightest touch of humor as she remembers just what the new records coming out of Berry Gordy's Motown Records sounded like. They were everything that overprotective parents feared the most. She describes herself as turning off the air conditioning the better to feel more deeply the sweat and pain of this rebellion against mothers shocked by thoughts they could not believe ever crossed their lovely daughters' minds. This was modern adolescent rebellion.

The full force of that rebellion can be see in part 4 in the long poem "The Bistro Styx" (40–42). When her lovely flower of a daughter enters the restaurant fashionably late, the mother's first thought is "What's this?" She's as far from looking like the colorful flowers of Persephone as can be imagined, appropriately infernal-looking, as if she had just come up from Hades.

> That's when I saw she was dressed in gray
> from a kittenish cashmere skirt and cowl
> down to the graphite signature of her shoes.

The meal that mother and daughter share (or pretend to share) is interesting, for the mother cannot eat with the robust enjoyment of the daughter. In the course of this typically lavish Parisian restaurant meal the daughter might be understood to be mocking her mother and her refusal to enjoy life. We hear what the mother does not say, as well as her responses not only to her daughter's clothing but to the change she sees in the girl who sits across from her and shows no need of her advice and especially not her criticism. The mockery in "Bistro Styx" is that of a woman who is satisfied, happy, and successful, one who toys with her more unfortunate dinner mate, who happens to be her mother. She makes all this clear when she describes her husband and his clothing preferences and her attempt to conform to his clothing choices for herself. She is not complaining; she finds the entire experience amusing. Why, the mother wonders, does she not at least resist his attempts to decide what she should and should not wear? The mother wants to protest:

> Are you content to conduct your life
> as a cliché, and what's worse
> an anachronism, the brooding artist's demimonde?

This unspoken protest is very far removed from the only real question she asks of her daughter. She fears the answer to that question.

"Bistro Styx" is a complex poem in which the mother carries on the real, silent conversation with herself, while conducting another of superficial chitchat with her daughter. The daughter might as well be having her own monologue with herself throughout the meal, preening and commenting on the touristy shop she and her husband run. From her side of the table the mother can only mutter to herself about the artistic ignorance of a man who could talk about things like "Monet's acrylics." The daughter eats, but we do not hear anything about her mother's meal. Dove's imagery reveals a great deal about the daughter's responses, however.

> The Chateaubriand
> arrived on a bone white plate, smug and absolute
> in its fragrant crust, a black plug steaming
> like the heart plucked from the chest of a worthy enemy;
> one touch with her fork sent pink juices streaming.

Then she remembers the question her mother asked. But the wine arrives and she dismisses it with a word or two. The mother can see nothing in her daughter's chatter that would arouse "admiration" in others for the life she leads. The mother's insult is not felt. Besides the dessert has come.

> Fruit
> and cheese appeared, arrayed on leaf-green dishes
> I stuck with café crème.

The daughter has erotic tastes, feasting away on camembert and juicy pears and figs. The images of green plates, vines and sun, bright tufted fields all evoke Demeter's domain—a domain that has been fouled and usurped. The mother makes one last desperate attempt to pierce her daughter's indifference.

> "But are you happy?" Fearing, I whispered it
> quickly. "What? You know, mother"
> she bit into the starry rose of a fig—
> "one really should try the fruit here."

The question strikes her as silly. What is her mother talking about? Her nonanswer answer finally penetrates the mother's consciousness. No amount of railing or seeking revenge on the gods can ever recover what is so clearly lost. Her last words make clear that no recovery is possible. She knows for the first time what her romantic dream of parenthood has become, as the final line of "Bistro Styx" and part 4 acknowledges.

> *I've lost her*, I thought, and called for the bill.

Demeter Wanders the Earth

The Yiddish poet Kadia Molodowsky's "White Night" gives the direction of part 5, and the situation of the Demeter figure who moves into it. What Dove creates is a trip away from the places that have caused her so much grief.

> I'm a difficult passenger, my ship
> is packed with the heavy horns, the shofars of grief.
> Tighten the sails of night as far as you can,
> for the daylight cannot carry me.

This section plays on that part of the *Hymn* that tells of Demeter's withdrawal from the world of the Olympian gods that robbed her of her daughter.

> Then golden-haired Demeter
> remained sitting apart from all the immortals,
> wasting with desire for her deep-girt daughter. (302–4)

The poetry acquires an autobiographical tinge in "Blue Days" and the following poems, weaving a dirty joke into the sonnet (*Why do women have legs?* . . . *I give up; why do they?* As if I weren't one of 'them'"), yet at the same time reminding us of Demeter the goddess who gives men their food.

> Nothing surpasses these
> kernels, taut-to-bursting sweet,
> tiny rows translucent as baby teeth.
> *Remember, you asked for it:*
> *to keep them from tracking slime over the floor.*

The mystery that goes into the hopper here is not so much of Eleusis as the fact of an unchanging misogyny, which Dove then flips over into a matter-of-fact observation in "Nature's Itinerary" about the cycle of fertility. Men make jokes about fertility in order to conceal their fear of it.

> Irene says it's the altitude
> that makes my period late;
> this time, though, it's eluded
> me entirely. I shouldn't worry (I'm medically regulated)
> —but hell, I brought these thirty sanitary pads

all the way from Köln to Mexico, prepared
for more than metaphorical bloodletting among the glad rags
of the Festival Internacional de Poesia.

The poet has crossed all kinds of time zones and faces the amusing fact
that she is at once on time (for the festival in Mexico) and late (for her
period).

The relocation from Germany to Mexico in "Nature's Itinerary" leads,
in "Sonnet in Primary Colors," to an homage to Frida Kahlo ("This is for
the woman with one black wing / perched over her eyes"), and then to
"Demeter Mourning."

Nothing can console me . . .
You can tell me repeatedly
I am unbearable (and I know this):
still, nothing turns the gold to corn,
nothing is sweet to the tooth crushing in.

This poem tracks precisely the repeated attempts of Iris and other Olympian gods to persuade Demeter to return from a self-imposed exile.

Then the father sent in turn all the blessed immortals;
one by one they kept coming and pleading
and offered her many glorious gifts and whatever
honors she might choose among the immortal gods.
Yet not one could bend the mind and thought
of the raging goddess, who harshly spurned their pleas. (*Hymn*, 325–30)

The anger of the goddess Demeter is what then flashes to the fore, in
part 6, and this too follows the drama of the goddess in the *Hymn*. There
Hermes must go down to Hades himself and arrange for Persephone to
come back to her mother. There is no other way to change a situation that
in many respects is a repeat of the pattern of the withdrawal of Achilles
from the Greek armies before Troy.

For Demeter suffers the same thing and the *Hymn* poet uses the same
words as the *Iliad* poet, grief (*achos*) for the loss of a woman (Persephone
here, there Briseis) and a rage (*mênis*) because of this loss. In terms of
Greek culture, the goddess Demeter rises to the same level of rage as the
heroic Achilles, and with the potential for devastations as great as those of
the *Iliad*.[58] Muriel Rukeyser's "The Poem as Mask" is spoken by Orpheus,

who was himself finally torn to pieces by the Maenads (angry, so Ovid says, over his scorn for women after his loss of Eurydice), and who now speaks of making poetry out of fragments.

> There is no mountain, there is no god, there is memory
> of my torn life, myself split open in sleep, the rescued child
> beside me among the doctors, and a word
> of rescue from the great eyes.
> No more masks! No more mythologies!
> Now, for the first time, the god lifts his hand,
> the fragments join in me with their own music.

The obvious way for Dove to create a parallel to the cosmic dimensions of Demeter's wrath is the only way one can go in a modern world where there are no Olympian gods: move beyond the personal to the political, to involvement with everyone else who exists along with us in history.

This is why the first poem of part 6 is "Political," marking a shift from the mythic to the historical realm and the only poem in the entire collection that has a dedication, to Breyten Breytenbach. He was an Afrikaner poet and political dissident who spent seven years in prison.[59]

> There was a man spent seven years in hell's circles—
> no moon or starlight, shadows singing
> their way to slaughter. We give him honorary status.

Yet at the same time the personal comes welling up at the end of the sonnet, and so does Demeter's anger, even as this register has supposedly changed.

> This man did something ill advised, for good reason.
> (I mean he went about it wrong.)
> And paid in shit, the world is shit and shit
> can make us grow. It is becoming the season
> she was taken from us. Our wail starts up
> of its own accord, is mistaken for song.

Demeter is the goddess who makes things grow out of dirt, and shit is what dirt is made of. The rage gets stronger in "Demeter, Waiting," and it is a peculiarly Demeter-like rage, the rage of the earth goddess who causes things to grow.

For mortals she ordained a terrible and brutal year
on the deeply fertile earth. The ground released
no seed, for bright-crowned Demeter kept it buried.
In vain the oxen dragged many curved plows down
the furrows. In vain much white barley fell on the earth. (*Hymn* 305–9)

She is gone again and I will not bear
it, I will drag my grief through a winter
of my own making and refuse
any meadow that recycles itself into
hope. Shit on the cicadas, dry meteor
flash, finicky butterflies! I will wail and thrash
until the whole goddamned golden panorama freezes
over. Then I will sit down to wait for her. Yes. ("Demeter, Waiting")

And then there is a shift back to the political. In "Teotihuacán," Dove
uses a talk by an Indian guide about the cochineal parasites on cactus pads
that the Aztec slaves used to make crimson and orange dyes. This was a
labor-intensive industry, since each female insect had to be carefully cultivated and then removed by hand. The largest city in the pre-Columbian
Americas is a site where their actual slave labor is elided in a wondering
comment about how many cochineals were needed. Combined with a reference to the destructive god from the east (the Spaniards of history pre-
figured in Aztec myth), poets seem oblivious to these things. Or are they?

Plumed serpent who reared his head in the east,
his watery body everywhere: Quetzalcoatl
was a white man, blond hair and tall.
It took millions of these bugs to stain a single wall.
The poets scribble in assorted notebooks. The guide moves on.

Just as politics are reconfigured by this move back and forth from personal
to political, so too can history be. In this case, "History" says, it's in the
mistaken notion that history is something that takes place apart from the
interior life. A woman's experience in having a child seems to contradict
this easy division.

Everything's a metaphor, some wise
guy said, and his woman nodded, wisely.
Why was this such a discovery

to him? Why did history
happen only on the outside?

In "Missing" we return to the voice of the daughter we had heard in
"Bistro Styx," the daughter the mother sees again, just as Demeter sees
Persephone again, and at this point in the hymn and in Dove's poetry her
account of both her abduction and return are significantly different, as
she claims that Hades forced her to eat the fatal pomegranate seeds that
would cause her to have to return to him, but also possibly signaling that
she has acquired an adult role and gained a certain amount of independence from both Hades and her mother.[60]

Persephone seems cheerfully reconciled to having been seized by him
thanks to the scheming of her father Zeus. Most charmingly, in the poetry, the beguiling flowers that had once been an instrument of seduction
are now mingled with the companions whom she names as individuals,
with no notice even that the fatal narcissus that had caused her downfall
(*Hymn*, 7–11) is just one among many. Like the names of the nymphs who
come springing up with Achilles' mother Thetis when she responds to his
cries over the lost Patroclus in *Iliad* 18, the names are both lovely-sounding
and eloquent names, some of them familiar elsewhere in myth (Kalypso,
Styx, Pallas), others meaning "Sweetly Flowing," "Goldie," and the like.[61]

We were all in the beautiful meadow—
Leukippê; Phaino, Elektra; and Ianthê;
Melitê; Iachê; Rhodeia, and Kallirhoê;
Melibosis; Tychê; and flower-faced Okyrhoê;
Khryseis; Ianeira; Akastê; Admetê;
Rhodopê; Plouto; and lovely Kalypso;
Styx; Ourania; and fair Galaxaura; Pallas,
rouser of battles; and Artemis, sender of arrows—
playing and picking lovely flowers with our hands,
soft crocus mixed with irises and hyacinth,
rosebuds and lilies, a marvel to see, and the
narcissus that wide earth bore like a crocus. (417–28)

The prosaic and matter-of-fact language of the poem "Missing," with its
return to the language of American milk cartons, gains even more if we
can see that this glorious mythical song has been reduced to "went out
with the girls."

I am the daughter who went out with the girls
never checked back in and nothing marked my "last
known whereabouts," not a single glistening petal.

With "not a single glistening petal" read "so much for the lovely catalogue
of flowers that Persephone knew."

Now I understand she can ever
die, just as nothing can bring me back—
I am the one who comes and goes;
I am the footfall that hovers.

"Missing" ends in an echo of Morrison's *Beloved*,

Down by the stream in back of 124 her footprints come and go, come and
go. They are so familiar. Should a child, an adult place his feet in them,
they will fit. Take them out and they disappear again as though nobody
ever walked there. (*Beloved*, 275)

Both Dove and Morrison are recalling here the deliberately tacky refrain
of T. S. Eliot's "The Love Song of J. Alfred Prufrock," "In the room the
women come and go / Talking of Michelangelo."

"Demeter's Prayer to Hades" that follows "Missing" asks for just one
thing: "knowledge." It could just as easily be taken as a sardonic parody of
prayer, since the god to whom it is addressed shows not the slightest sign
of learning from any of this.

Now for the first time
I see clearly the trail you planted,
what ground opened to waste,
though you dreamed a wealth
of flowers.

The most telling moment in this concluding poem of section 6 is what it
says about gods and mortals:

There are no curses—only mirrors
held up to the souls of gods and mortals.
And so I give up this fate, too.

Believe in yourself,
go ahead—see where it gets you.

Home to Sicily and the Scene of the Crime

In *Mother Love*'s final section 7, every one of the eleven sonnets becomes
an exercise in connection between one poem and the next, so that the last
line of one sonnet becomes the first line of the next, invariably changed
in meaning. Yet as Righelato observes, while they may look like the most
regular version of sonnets in the collection (varying from thirteen to fif-
teen lines), "the classic formality of the structure plays against but also
echoes, in its circularity, the frustration of the experience conveyed."[62]
They tell a story of a tour the poet (or at least her poetic voice) and her
husband make of the island, starting with Agrigento on the south coast
and its temple of Demeter. The contrast between their enlightened way
of partnering between a man and woman as parents of a child, on the one
hand, and the site of this ancient disruption of maternal and filial ties, on
the other, is expressed in the harshness of the landscape and the violent
changes in mood that come about because of the formal device of starting the next poem with the last line of the preceding poem. Peering at the
litter around an archaeological site, "Let it go: nothing will come of this"
becomes a rejection of the naïveté that leads people to think that a visit
to an archaeological site can possibly recover what has been expressed in
myth and poetry.

> Let it go: nothing will come of this
> textbook rampaging, though we have found, by
> stint and intuition, the chthonic grotto,
> closed for the season behind a chicken-wire gate.

An old man acts as their guide down into the inferno of modern Sicily, in
which the detritus of civilization is carefully explored through the lingua
franca of German and other odds and ends of Romance languages, as he
leads them through sonnets describing a garbage dump and the under-
side of an *autostrada*/expressway. One should have no delusions that Italy
is any more a paradise than America, so far as races are concerned: "His
touch trembles at my arm; / hasn't he seen an American Black / before?"
(69); "The way he stops to smile at me / and pat my arm, I'm surely his
first / Queen of Sheba" (70). In their tour around they finally find the

ultimate expression of ring composition in modern architecture: a race-track set up athwart the whole archaeological site, utterly indifferent to the past.

> We drive the circumference
> with binoculars: no cave, no reeds.
> We drive it twice, first one way, then back,
> to cancel our rage at the human need
> to make a sport of death.

Which leads into a reflection of what is actually happening to the winner of a sports car contest.

> To make a sport of death
> it must be endless: round and round
> till you feel everything you've trained for—
> precision, speed, endurance—reduced to this
> godawful roar, this vale of sound.

This leads into the final poem of 7, via the winner's crowning achievement, which becomes the crown of flowers and sunlight with which *Mother Love* begins.

> Aim for the tape, aim *through* it.
> Then rip the helmet off and poke your head
> through sunlight, into flowers.

> Through sunlight, into flowers
> she walked, and was pulled down.

The end of *Mother Love* returns us to its opening, but it is not simply a signal of the ring composition and return to starting points that we might expect. Going to Sicily teaches us merely that "Where the chariot went under / no one can fathom." Dove's final sonnet "Through sunlight, into flowers" translates all the Greek names of the gods into their primal elements. The Homeric *Hymn* ends as its conventions require with a praise of the uniqueness of its particular deity.[63]

> But come, you goddesses, dwelling in the town of
> fragrant Eleusis, and seagirt Paros, and rocky Antron,

revered Deo, mighty giver of seasons and glorious gifts,
you and your very fair daughter Persephone,
for my song grant gladly a living that warms the heart.
And I shall remember you and a new song as well. (490–95)

Mother Love resolves the break between mother and daughter and the hostility to the husband/rapist the same way the *Hymn* does, with the poet of 7 reconciled to the memories of her past pain and loss, in the company of a loving companion and husband who joins in this voyage into the inferno of modern Sicily.[64]

The finale of *Mother Love* translates these ancient primal powers into elemental terms of nature: Water, Sky, Earth. Malin Pereira argues that this ending marks Dove's achieving a universal through a particular experience, as the African American poet, her German husband, and the Sicilian guide "find a common language that can help guide them toward the archetypal myth."[65] To the extent that *Mother Love* moves between the mythical and ancient text as well as myth and the living present, this must be true. But there is something else happening at the end of this final poem that is perhaps as important as any move between universals and particulars, or recoveries of the archetypal.

Only Earth—wild
mother we can never leave (even now
we've leaned against her, heads bowed
against the heat)—knows
no story's ever finished; it just goes
on, unnoticed in the dark that's all
around us: blazed stones, the ground closed.

With "the ground closed" we return to the intact world with which *Mother Love* begins, a world paradoxically said to be untouched, even as Dove recounts the mythical act that splits it open. "Closed" is the last word for this volume of sonnets with prim borders, pretty fences, and order, and it will be the last word from Dove here as well.

This ending, of this poem and of its book, is no more the last word we shall hear from this poet and future African American writers with their versions of ancient Greece and Rome, than the last word of the poet of the Homeric *Hymn to Demeter* constitutes the last thing we shall hear from him. Only poets and writers are able to close the grounds they open, as surely as Rita Dove opens it in the introduction to *Mother Love* that we now see was ironically entitled "An Intact World."

But I shall remember you and a new song as well.

Chapter One

1. The Christianization of pagan apotheosis (e.g., the transfigured Daphnis in Vergil's fifth *Eclogue*) at the end of *Lycidas* would have particular resonance for a young poet who composed occasional poems on the deaths of notable persons and children, such as "A Funeral Poem on the Death of an Infant of Twelve Months," "On the Death of a Young Gentleman," "On the Death of Mr. George Whitefield," and "To a Clergyman on the Death of His Lady."

> So *Lycidas* sunk low, but mounted high,
> Through the dear might of him that walk'd the waves;
> Where other groves, and other streams along,
> With *Nectar* pure his oozy Lock's he laves,
> And hears the unexpressive nuptiall Song,
> In the blest Kingdoms meek of joy and love.
> There entertain him all the Saints above,
> In solemn troops, and sweet Societies
> That sing, and singing in their glory move,
> And wipe the tears for ever from his eyes. (172–81)

2. Albert Boime, *The Art of Exclusion: Representing Blacks in the Nineteenth Century* (Washington, D.C.: Smithsonian Institution Press, 1990), 2.

3. Sacvan Bercovitch, *The American Jeremiad* (Madison: University of Wisconsin Press, 1978), 7–8: "The European jeremiad, was a lament over the ways of the world. It decried the sins of 'the people'—a community, a nation, a civilization, mankind in general—and warned of God's wrath to follow. . . . This sermon form the puritans brought with them to Massachusetts Bay. But from the start they sounded a different note. Theirs was a peculiar

mission, they explained, for they were a 'peculiar people,' a company of Christians not only called but chosen, and chosen not only for heaven but as instruments of a sacred design. . . . To this end, they revised the message of the jeremiad. Not that they minimized the threat of divine retribution . . . but they qualified it in such a way that turned threat into celebration. In their case, they believed, God's punishments were corrective not destructive." See also David Howard-Pitney, *The African American Jeremiad: Appeals for Justice in America* (Philadelphia: Temple University Press, 2005).

4. In "Phillis Wheatley's Subversion of Classical Style," John Shields argues that "Her sex, her race, her neoclassicism, and her alleged lack of originality—have combined over the years to relegate Wheatley's poetry to marginal status." *Style* 27 (1993) 252–70: 254.

5. "To Maecenas" is what Robert Stepto has described as "an eclectic authenticating document"; *From Behind the Veil: A Study of Afro-American Narrative*, 2nd ed. (Urbana: University of Illinois Press, 1991), 7: "The elaborate authenticating strategy . . . is typical of those found in the first phase or eclectic narrative. The publisher or editor, far more than the former slave, assembles and manipulates the authenticating machinery, and seems to act on the premise that there is a direct correlation between the quantity of documents or texts assembled and the readership's acceptance of the narrative as a whole."

6. In his 1993 essay "Phillis Wheatley's Subversion of Classical Stylistics," John Shields strengthens the reading of "To Maecenas" as a signature poem. Shields argues that "To Maecenas" begins in the pastoral mode, moves to the epic, and then accomplishes its subversive goal by a revelation of her actual attempt not to merely imitate but to subvert the very silencing which she tends to find so overpowering. In this opening poem she works behind the mask to resist control and define her own poetic project. This move restores Wheatley both to the trickster tradition so dominant in African American letters and to the tradition of the pastoral as Annabel Paterson characterizes it—"a dialectical, tensive structure." This pretense that shepherds and maidens singing and at play would have been known to readers in the Renaissance and eighteenth century is a mask for more serious issues. A twentieth-century model would be Robert Frost's "Build Soil: A Political Pastoral."

7. Publius Terentius Afer, or Publius Terence the African (195 or 185-159 BCE), was an ex-slave, but there is no consensus that he was necessarily black, since his cognomen *Afer* refers to the people living on the north coast of the continent and could include the Semitic people of ancient Carthage and environs. The question of Terence's skin color predictably became a point for argument between Martin Bernal, Mary Lefkowitz, and other scholars on either side of the debate over Afrocentrism and classics ignited by the publication of Bernal's *Black Athena: the Afroasiatic Roots of Classical Civilization* (1987–2006); see Mary Lefkowitz, *Not Out of Africa: How Afrocentrism Became an Excuse to Teach Myth as History* (New York: Basic Books, 1996); Kevin J. Wemore's discussion in "Afro(American) centric Classicism" in *Black Dionysus: Greek Tragedy and African American Theatre* (Jefferson, N.C.: McFarland, 2003), 46–61; and Daniel Selden's suggestion that the whole causerie was misconceived: "*Aithiopika* and Ethiopianism," in *Studies in Heliodorus*, ed. Richard Hunter (Cambridge: Cambridge Philological Society, 1998), 182–217, esp. 187–200.

8. Caroline Winterer, *The Culture of Classicism: Ancient Greece and Rome in American Intellectual Life, 1780–1910* (Baltimore: Johns Hopkins University Press, 2002), 29: "Students in the years between the founding of Harvard and the early nineteenth century focused to the exclusion of almost all else upon the grammar of ancient Greek and Latin. Their college days—in class, at least—were spent in a complex liturgy of classical language acquisition that

included parsing, scanning, recitation, and translation. By comparison, history, literature, and antiquities played a minuscule heuristic role." To this world Winterer later opposes the "worlds" that history, archaeology, and classics developed in the nineteenth century so extensively that the term "philology" that still appears in the American Philological Association (the professional association for classicists) is an archaic term referring to only a fraction of what contemporary classicists do; chap. 3 ("From Words to Worlds"), pp. 77–98.

9. The blend of exact translation and graceful paraphrase shows familiarity with John Dryden's precepts; e.g., "On the whole Matter, I thought fit to steer betwixt the two Extreams, of Paraphrase, and literal Translation: To keep as near my Author as I coul'd, without losing all his Graces, the most Eminent of which, are in the Beauty of his words: And those words, I must add, are always Figurative. Such of these as wou'd retain their Elegance in our Tongue, I have endeavour'd to graff on it; but most of them are of necessity to be lost, because they will not shine in any but their own. *Virgil* has sometimes two of them in a Line; but the scantiness of our Heroick Verse, is not capable of receiving more than one: And that too must expiate for many others which have none. Such is the difference of the Languages, or such my want of skill in chusing words. Yet I may presume to say, and I hope with as much reason as the *French* Translator, that making all the Materials of this divine Author, I have endeavoured to make *Virgil* speak such *English*, as he wou'd himself have spoken, if he had been born in *England*, and in this present age." "Dedication of the Aeneis" (1697), in *The Works of John Dryden*, Vol. 5, *Poems: The Works of Virgil in English*. Berkeley, Los Angeles: University of California Press (1987): 330–31.

10. Wendell Clausen, *A Commentary on Virgil, Eclogues* (Oxford: Clarendon Press, 1994), 32n15. Although they are known now as the *Eclogues*, Vergil's own term for the volume of poetry they appeared in was *Boucolica*, similar to his next book of poetry, the *Georgica* or *Georgics* (xx, n23).

11. Clausen, *Commentary*, 32n15.

12. The difference between them is underscored by the chiastic arrangement of words for "you" and "we" (*tu, nos*) in alliteration with Tityrus's name: *Tityre, tu . . . nos . . . nos . . . tu, Tityre*. This presentation follows Clausen, *Commentary*, 29n3: a small example of what he terms the "labyrinthine complexity" of words, lines, whole poems woven together in the structure of the *Eclogues* (xxii).

13. Michael C. J. Putnam, *Virgil's Pastoral Art: Studies in the 'Eclogues'* (Princeton: Princeton University Press, 1970), 20.

14. The historical Maecenas was more problematic and less talented than the Maecenas Wheatley creates here, but his friendship and support of Horace were real; for a narrative of his career based on ancient literary sources, see Kenneth J. Reckford, "Horace and Maecenas," *Transactions and Proceedings of the American Philological Association* 90 (1959): 195–208. He was criticized for an addiction to luxurious ways and was said to have an "effeminate" (or unRoman, unStoic) manner; this alleged failing may be a construction of Maecenas as an example for philosophical polemic rather than a serious account of his life and personal style. See Margaret Graver, "The Manhandling of Maecenas: Senecan Abstractions of Masculinity," *American Journal of Philology* 119 (1998): 607–32.

15. This is the same rhyme but gracefully alliterative and metrically more skillful than the example of bad versification she could see in Pope's *Essay on Criticism* (356–57), to which we will turn shortly: "A needless Alexandrine ends the Song, / That like a wounded Snake, drags its slow length along."

16. Pope's comment on the opening of book 16 is especially perceptive about the emotions of Patroclus and Achilles, and Wheatley follows his interpretation up to a point: "We have at the Entrance of this Book one of the most beautiful Parts of the Iliad. . . . We see *Patroclus* touch'd with the deepest Compassion for the Misfortune of the *Greeks* (whom the *Trojans* had forc'd to retreat to their Ships, and which Ships were on the Point of burning) prostrating himself before the Vessel of *Achilles*, and pouring out his Tears at his Feet. *Achilles*, struck with the Grief of his Friend, demands the Cause of it. . . . The *Pathetic* of *Patroclus*'s Speech is finely contrasted by the *Fierté* of that of Achilles. While the former is melting with Sorrow for his Countrymen, the utmost he can hope from the latter, is but to borrow his Armour and Troops; to obtain his personal Assistance he knows is impossible. At the very Instant that Achilles is mov'd to ask the Cause of his Friend's Concern, he seems to say that nothing could deserve it but the Death of their Fathers; and in the same Breath speaks of the total Destruction of the *Greeks* as of too slight a Cause for Tears"; Pope, *The Iliad of Homer: Books X–XXIV*, ed. Maynard Mack (New Haven: Yale University Press, 1967), 233–34.

17. Gregson Davis, *Polyhymnia: The Rhetoric of Horatian Lyric Discourse* (Berkeley: University of California Press, 1991), 11.

18. Ibid., 29. Since sincerity is never the issue, it is possible to confess one's inability to write many kinds of great poetry, not just epic. For an example of the Horatian *recusatio* or generic disavowal at work, see Christopher Smart's poetic version of the opening of *Odes* 4.2, "Any poet seeking to rival Pindar" (*Pindarum quisquis studet aemulari*):

> Whoever vies with Pindar's strain
> With waxen wings, my friend, would fly,
> Like him who nam'd the glassy main,
> But could not reach the sky.

The one who named the glassy main is the artisan Daedalus's son Icarus, whose fall gave his name to the Icarian Sea. The occasion of this poem was an invitation from Iullus Antonius, the son of Marc Antony, to celebrate a victory of Augustus over the Germanic Sygambri in 16 BCE. The epinician or victory odes of Pindar (518–446 BCE) would have been the inevitable model for Horace to follow, so he celebrates the art of Pindar in this brilliant late poem (13 BCE) about why he cannot be another Pindar. *Odes* 4.2 figures prominently in the reception of the early fifth-century BCE Greek poet Pindar and will be further discussed in chapter 6, below.

19. See Aldo Schiavone, *The End of the Past: Ancient Rome and the Modern West*, trans. Margery J. Schneider (Cambridge, Mass.: Harvard University Press, 2000), 108–31 ("Ancient and Modern Slavery"). For an argument for the existence of "proto-racism" in the ancient Mediterranean world, cf. Benjamin Isaac, *The Invention of Racism in Classical Antiquity* (Princeton: Princeton University Press, 2004). We are inclined to agree with David Wiesen, who argued in an article which deserves to be much better known, that modern students of racial difference and racism tend to project their own views back onto antiquity as they search for the origins of their present world; see David Wiesen, "Herodotus and the Modern Debate over Slavery," *Ancient World* 3 (1980): 3–16.

20. *The Classick Pages: Classical Reading in Eighteenth-Century America*, ed. Meyer Reinhold (State College: Pennsylvania State University Press, 1975), 143–47.

21. Terence, *The Comedies of Terence, Translated into Familiar Blank Verse*, 2 vols., trans. George Colman (London: Becket, De Hondt and Baldwin, 1768), 1:lxvii–lxx.

22. Horace ties his immortality not only to the landscape of Rome, but also to his native Apulia (modern Puglia, the southeastern heel of Italy). The Aufidus River (modern Ofanto) begins near his hometown of Venusia; the legendary king Daunus founded Apulia.

23. *Phillis Wheatley: Complete Writings*, ed. Vincent Carretta (New York: Penguin Books, 2001), ix–xx. For a sustained reading of the way Wheatley wrote her poetry for several audiences at the same time—free, enslaved, white, black, Christian or non-Christian, English or Colonial American—see Paula Bennett, "Phillis Wheatley's Vocation and the Paradox of the 'Afric Muse.'" *PMLA* 113 (1998): 64–76, esp. 74n11: "Like much of her other poetry, this poem (sc. "On Being Brought from Africa") is susceptible to different readings depending on the reader's perspective. Although Wheatley's audience was overwhelmingly white, she often seems, as here, to direct her poetry to more than one audience."

24. Henry Lewis Gates, Jr., *The Trials of Phillis Wheatley: America's First Black Poet and Her Encounters with the Founding Fathers* (New York: Basic Civitas Books, 2003).

25. W. E. B. Du Bois, "Phillis Wheatley and African American Culture," in *The Oxford W. E. B. Du Bois Reader*, ed. Eric J. Sundquist (New York: Oxford University Press, 1996), 328–42.

26. William H. Robinson, *Phillis Wheatley and Her Writings* (New York: Garland Publishing, 1984), 430–48, quotation p. 444.

27. Rev. Mr. Philip Frances, *The Satires of Horace, In Latin and English*, 7th ed. (Dublin: Leathley and Exshaw, 1764), 3:278.

28. In her study of Pope's poetry Wheatley had company in other women poets of her day. See Caroline Winterer, *The Mirror of Antiquity: American Women and the Classical Tradition, 1750–1900* (Ithaca: Cornell University Press, 2007), 12–39, esp. 31–34, on Phillis Wheatley, whom she credits with "one of the most sustained engagements with Alexander Pope" in eighteenth-century America.

29. Horace, *Ars Poetica* 24–37.

30. Robert Kuncio, "Some Unpublished Poems of Phillis Wheatley," *New England Quarterly* 43, no. 2 (1970): 287–297, esp. 290.

31. Julian A. Mason, *The Poems of Phillis Wheatley* (Chapel Hill: University of North Carolina Press, 1989), xxx.

32. Muktar Ali Isani, "Phillis Wheatley and the Elegiac Mode," in *Critical Essays on Phillis Wheatley*, ed. William H. Robinson (Boston: G. K. Hall, 1982), 42.

33. M. A. Richmond, *Bid the Vassal Soar: Interpretive Essays on the Life and Poetry of Phillis Wheatley (ca. 1753–1784) and George Moses Horton (ca. 1797–1883)* (Washington, D.C.: Howard University Press, 1974).

34. T. S. Eliot, *The Waste Land: A Facsimile and Transcript of the Original Drafts Including the Annotations of Ezra Pound*, ed. Valerie Eliot (New York: Harcourt Brace, 1971), 127.

35. Gregory Tillotson, *On the Poetry of Pope*, 2nd ed. (Oxford: Clarendon Press, 1950), 2.

36. Ibid., 85.

37. Paul Fussell, *Theory of Prosody in Eighteenth-Century England* (New London: Connecticut College, 1954), 43.

38. Ibid., 43.

39. Albert Raboteau, *Slave Religion: The Invisible Institution in the Antebellum South* (New York: Oxford University Press, 1983), 243–66 ("Religious Life in the Slave Community").

40. Maria Stewart, *America's First Black Woman Political Writer: Essays and Speeches*, ed. Marilyn Richardson (Bloomington: Indiana University Press, 1987).

41. Raboteau, *Slave Religion*, 231.

42. Richard P. Martin, *The Language of Heroes: Speech and Performance in the "Iliad"* (Ithaca: Cornell University Press, 1989).

43. D. T. Niane, *Sundiata: An Epic of Old Mali* (London: Longmans, 1964).

44. Ibid., 60–61.

45. Tillotson, *On the Poetry of Pope*, 72–73.

46. John Dryden, preface to *Ovid's Epistles* (1680), in *Theories of Translation: An Anthology of Essays from Dryden to Derrida*, ed. Rainer Schulte and John Biguenet (Chicago: University of Chicago Press, 1992), 17.

47. Vincent Carretta suggests that Wheatley saw an engraving of one of Wilson's paintings of Niobe (*Phillis Wheatley: Complete Writings*, 181). Whether she saw one of Wilson's paintings in London or only an engraving of it is a fair question not likely to be answered now. For our reading of the poem, the fact or the fiction of this claim is less important than the ekphrastic tradition she invokes by linking word and text: "from *Ovid's* Metamorphoses, Book VI. and from a view of the Painting of Mr. *Richard Wilson*."

48. For a modern edition of Sandys's 1632 edition, see *Ovid's* Metamorphosis [*sic*]: *Englished, Mythologized, and Represented in Figures by George Sandys*, ed. Karl K. Hulley and Stanley T. Vandersall (Lincoln: University of Nebraska Press, 1970). For Wheatley's consultation of Sandys, see Julian Mason, "Examples of Classical Myth in the Poems of Phillis Wheatley," in *American Women and Classical Myth*, ed. Gregory Staley (Waco: Baylor University Press, 2009), 23–33.

49. Leonard Barkan, *The Gods Made Flesh: Metamorphosis and the Pursuit of Paganism* (New Haven, Yale University Press, 1986), 10.

50. Sandys, *Ovid's* Metamorphosis, 9–10.

51. In contemporary classics the technical Greek term *epyllion* ("little epic") coined by nineteenth-century German classicists is now widely used to describe poems like Catullus 64 and its Hellenistic Greek predecessors such as Callimachus's *Hecale*, but of course is not one Wheatley would have known.

52. He also gives Niobe one more son and daughter than Homer does; it was noted in antiquity that there was disagreement about how many sons and daughters she did have. See Sir James George Frazer, *Apollodorus: The Library* (Cambridge, Mass.: Harvard University Press, 1921), 1:340–41.

53. Sandys, *Ovid's* Metamorphosis, 292.

54. Ibid., 293.

55. See Emily Greenwood, "Classics and the Atlantic Triangle: Caribbean Readings of Greece and Rome via Africa," *Forum of Modern Language Studies* 4 (2004): 365–76.

56. For the parallels between Greek tragedy and Morrison's *Beloved*, see Shelley P. Haley, "Self-Definition, Community, and Resistance: Euripides' *Medea* and Toni Morrison's *Beloved*," *Thamyris* 2 (1995): 177–206; for a more general discussion, Tracey L. Walters, *African American Literature and the Classicist Tradition: Black Women Writers from Wheatley to Morrison* (New York: Palgrave MacMillan, 2007).

Chapter Two

1. On the bilingualism of African Americans, see Geneva Smitherman, *Black Talk: Words and Phrases from the Hood to the Amen Corner* (Boston: Houghton Mifflin Company, 2000), 27–38.

2. Alice Walker, *The Color Purple* (New York: Washington Square Press, 1983), 182–83.

3. Henry Louis Gates, Jr., *The Signifying Monkey: A Theory of African-American Literary Criticism* (New York: Oxford University Press, 1988), 127–69.

4. Olaudah Equiano, *The Interesting Life and Other Writings*, ed. Vincent Carretta (New York: Penguin, 1998), 43–44.

5. Fredric Jameson, *The Political Unconscious* (Ithaca: Cornell University Press, 1981), 34.

6. William S. McFeely, *Frederick Douglass* (New York: Norton, 1990), 34.

7. *Journals of Ralph Waldo Emerson: 1841–1844*, ed. Edward Waldo Emerson and Waldo Emerson Forbes (Boston: Houghton Mifflin, 1911), 520–21.

8. Frederick Douglass, *Narrative of the Life of Frederick Douglass, an American Slave* (New York: Library of America, 1994), 45.

9. Caleb Bingham, *The Columbian Orator: Containing a Variety of Original and Selected Pieces; Together with Rules; Calculated to Improve Youth and Others in the Ornamental and Useful Art of Eloquence* (Boston: J. H. A. Frost, 1832), 3: "As no advantage could arise from a methodical arrangement, the Author has preferred variety to system. In his choice of materials, it has been his object to select such as should inspire the pupil with the ardour of eloquence, and the love of virtue."

10. Douglass, *Narrative of the Life*, 143.

11. Frederick Douglass, *My Bondage and My Freedom* (New York: Library of America, 1994), 216–17.

12. Charles Colcock Jones, *The Religious Instruction of the Negroes in the United States* (Savannah, Ga.: Thomas Purse, 1842), 206–20 ("Benefits Which Would Flow from the Faithful Religious Instruction of the Negroes").

13. *Narrative of the Life*, 242–43.

14. *My Bondage and My Freedom*, 217.

15. Ibid., 218.

16. Ibid., 222.

17. Ibid., 223.

18. It is "a profoundly relational type of thinking" created by the arbitrary relation that slavery establishes between description and meaning, an example of the way modern semiotic theory complements (and in this instance restates) ancient rhetorical theory; Henry Louis Gates, Jr., "Binary Oppositions in Chapter One of *Narrative of the Life of Frederick Douglass: An American Slave Written by Himself*," in *Afro-American Literature: The Reconstruction of Instruction*, ed. Dexter Fisher and Robert B. Stepto (New York: Modern Language Association, 1979), 212–32, esp. 222.

19. Morris W. Croll, "The Cadence of English Oratorical Prose," *Studies in Philology* 16 (1919): 1–55, esp. 22–23: "There is no better definition of the *period* than Hobbes' curt translation of Aristotle in his *Brief of the Art of Rhetorick* (1681; 3. 8) 'A period is such a part as is perfect in itself, and has such length as may easily be comprehended by the understanding.'"

20. Compare the system devised by Thomas Sheridan, whose importance for Thomas Jefferson's sense of style and speech Jay Fliegelman demonstrates in his analysis of the significance of pauses in Jefferson's writing. One slash (/) marks incomplete sense, and two (//) completion of sense. Jay Fliegelman, *Declaring Independence: Jefferson, Natural Language, and the Culture of Performance* (Stanford: Stanford University Press, 1993), 4–28 ("Jefferson's Pauses"). See also Thomas Sheridan, *Lectures on the Art of Reading* (London: Printed for C. Dilly, 1781), 107: "Nothing has contributed so much, and so universally, to the corruption of delivery, as the bad use which has been made of the modern art of punctuation,

by introducing artificial tones into all sentences, to the exclusion of the natural; for the teachers of the art of reading, in order to distinguish, with greatest accuracy, the stops from each other in utterance, annexed to them different notes of the voice, as well as different portions of time."

21. The main obstacle to seeing these kinds of structures, Sheridan argues, is modern punctuation, which is almost entirely grammatical: it marks off syntactical units in a sentence and often offers no aid at all to anyone who wants to learn how to read aloud, and effectively; Fliegelman, *Declaring Independence*, 12–13.

22. This is a point frequently stressed by historians of rhetoric and literacy, from earliest times to the high Roman Empire; e.g., G. W. Bowersock, *Greek Sophists in the Roman Empire* (Oxford: Oxford University Press, 1969); William V. Harris, *Ancient Literacy* (Cambridge: Harvard University Press, 1989).

23. Sandra M. Gustafson, *Eloquence Is Power: Oratory and Performance in Early America* (Chapel Hill: University of North Carolina Press, 2000), 267.

24. Douglass, *Narrative of the Life*, 97.

25. Ibid.

26. Ibid., 98.

27. Abolitionists quoted Matthew 23:27 to attack pious slave owners; there Jesus is scolding scribes, Pharisees, and hypocrites.

28. Douglass, *Narrative of the Life*, 99–100.

29. Ibid., 49: "Will not a righteous God visit for these things?"

30. Ibid., 100–101.

31. Ibid., 102.

32. Croll, "Cadence of English Oratorical Prose," 22.

33. The democratizing tendencies that Kenneth Cmiel describes in *Democratic Eloquence* eventually made likely that Americans would recognize only two levels of speech, the honest and sincere style in which a speaker said only what he or she truly felt, and the more flowery, "rhetorical" style in which the insincere and manipulative worked (hence the contemporary pejorative meaning of the word "rhetoric"). For Americans of the eighteenth and early part of the nineteenth century, however, the standard classical division of oratory was still clearly a familiar one that any competent orator was expected to know and work with; Fliegelman, *Declaring Independence*, 26–27: "The standard classical division of oratory, as Jefferson himself put it, had three styles: 'the elevated,' for which 'Orators and Poets will furnish subjects,' the 'middling,' the province of 'historians,' and the 'familiar,' appropriate to 'epistolary and comic writers.' . . . The 'familiar' would eventually present itself as normative in a fashion that stigmatized the other two as unnatural affectations. The orator, like Wordsworth's poet later in the century, must be 'a man speaking to men.'"

34. Bingham, *Columbian Orator*, 27.

35. Elsewhere Quintilian cites the Greek term *homoeideia* (a condition of "having the same form/shape"), an error that Perkins's sample seems prone to: "A worse fault . . . is *homoeideia*, or sameness, a term applied to a style which has no variety to relieve its tedium, and which presents a uniform monotony of hue. This is one of the surest signs of lack of art, and produces a uniquely unpleasing effect, not merely on the mind, but on the ear, on account of its sameness of thought, the uniformity of its figures, and the monotony of its structure" (8.3.52).

36. Douglass, *My Bondage and My Freedom*, 240.

37. Kenneth Cmiel, *Democratic Eloquence: The Fight over Popular Speech in Nineteenth-Century America* (New York: William Morrow, 1990), 94–122. The phrase for humble speech (*sermo humilis*) comes from a book originally published by Erich Auerbach in German in 1958, *Literary Language and Its Public in Late Latin Antiquity and in the Middle Ages* (Princeton: Princeton University Press, 1993).

38. As Granville Ganter observes, the *Orator* gave Douglass an invaluable education in Jeffersonian republicanism long after that comparatively liberal moment in the early years of the United States had faded from view; "The Active Virtue of *The Columbian Orator*," *New England Quarterly: A Historical Review of New England Life and Letters*, 40 (1997), 463–76.

39. George Kennedy, *Quintilian* (New York: Twayne, 1969); see also Kennedy, *The Art of Rhetoric in the Roman World* (Princeton: Princeton University Press, 1994), 487–514.

40. Lewis Hyde, *Trickster Makes This World: Mischief, Myth and Art* (New York: Farrar, Straus and Giroux, 1998), 226–51.

41. Douglass, *Life and Times of Frederick Douglass* (New York: Library of America, 1994), 533–34.

42. Douglass, *My Bondage and My Freedom*, 218.

43. McFeely, *Frederick Douglass*, 158–60. Douglass's grandmother was owned by a member of the Anthony family, not by Auld, and Auld himself had saved Douglass from being lynched by putting him in jail and refusing to sell him.

44. Douglass, *My Bondage and My Freedom*, 412–18: 418.

45. Bingham, *Columbian Orator*, 211.

46. Noting Douglass's words, "The slave was made to say some very smart things in reply to his master," Thad Ziolkowski picks up on the artificiality and ventriloquism—we would say, characterization—that is typical of dramatized dialectic; "Antitheses: The Dialectic of Violence and Literacy in Frederick Douglass's *Narrative* of 1843," in *Critical Essays on Frederick Douglass*, ed. William L. Andrews (Boston: G. K. Hall, 1991), 148–65, esp. 163.

47. John Blassingame's introduction to volume 1 of his edition of Douglass's speeches, debates, and interviews is an exceptionally good account of Douglass's evolving style as an orator; Frederick Douglass, *The Frederick Douglass Papers*, ser. 1, ed. John W. Blassingame (New Haven: Yale University Press, 1979–1992), 1:xxi–lxxii.

48. Douglass, "The Heroic Slave," in Julia Griffiths, ed., *Autographs for Freedom* (Boston: John P. Jewett, 1853), 174–239, quotation p. 307; reprinted in Frederick Douglass, *Frederick Douglass: The Narrative and Selected Writings*, ed. Michael Meyer (New York: Modern Library, 1984), 299–348.

49. The details of this historical account come from Howard Jones, "The Peculiar Institution and National Honor: The Case of the *Creole* Slave Revolt," *Civil War History* 21 (1975): 28–50.

50. Jones, "The Peculiar Institution," 34.

51. Douglass, *Frederick Douglass*, 344.

52. One of the best examples is the opening of Tacitus's biography of his father-in-law, the *Agricola*, part of which Douglass would already have known from the *Columbian Orator* (162–65, "The Speech of Galgachus to the Caldeonian Army"): "The ancient custom of transmitting to posterity the deeds and character of famous men" ("Clarorum virorum facta moresque posteris tradere antiquitus usitatum"). The speech of Calgacus (the preferred modern spelling, *Agricola* 30–32) has the famous phrase, "They make a desert and call it peace" ("ubi solitudinem faciunt pacem appellant").

53. Douglass, *Frederick Douglass*, 300.

54. Douglass, *Narrative of the Life*, 74.

55. Douglass, *Frederick Douglass*, 18.

56. Gates, "Binary Oppositions," 222.

57. Douglass, *Frederick Douglass*, 300.

58. Ibid., 302.

59. Douglass, *Narrative of the Life*, 59.

60. Ibid., 59–60.

61. Douglass, *Frederick Douglass*, 302.

62. E.g., Charles Rollin, *The Method of Teaching and Studying the Belles Lettres*, Translated from the French, 6th ed. (London, 1769), 2:56–65 ("Of the Sublime").

63. Douglass, *Frederick Douglass*, 303.

64. William Lloyd Garrison, Preface to the *Narrative* (*Narrative*, ed. Meyer, 5).

65. McFeely, *Frederick Douglass*, 213: "A reporter for *The Christian Recorder* left one of the richest accounts we have of 'the magnetism and melody of his wonderfully elastic voice.' The reporter allowed that the printed text gave a 'fair view of the *ideas*, but no printed sentences can convey any adequate idea of the manner, the tone of voice, the gesticulation, the action, the round soft, swelling pronunciation with which Frederick Douglass spoke, and which no orator we have ever heard can use with such grace, eloquence and effect as he.'" (*Christian Recorder*, January 18, 1862, quoted in a headnote to Douglass, "Fighting the Rebels with One Hand," in Blassingame, *Frederick Douglass Papers*, 3:473–88.)

66. *The Frederick Douglass Papers*, ser. 1, 1:15–17.

67. William Andrews, *The Oxford Frederick Douglass Reader* (New York: Oxford University Press, 1996), 199.

68. Andrews, *Douglass Reader*, 182.

69. Winifred B. Horner, *Rhetoric in the Classical Tradition* (New York: St. Martin's Press, 1988), 161: "A maxim is the statement of a general truth and can serve as either a premise or a conclusion of an enthymeme. Maxims are truths, such as proverbs, that are generally held to be true by certain cultures or groups within a culture. In order to use maxims successfully, the writer needs to be sensitive to the beliefs and values of the audience."

70. Andrews, *Douglass Reader*, 111, 118, 117.

71. Ibid., 110.

72. Ibid., 112.

73. Ibid.

74. Ibid., 110–12.

75. Ibid., 112.

76. *The Frederick Douglass Papers*, ser. 1, vol. 5 (1881–1895), 535–45: 534–35; 545.

77. See James Oakes, *The Radical and the Republican: Frederick Douglass, Abraham Lincoln, and the Triumph of Antislavery Politics* (New York: W. W. Norton, 2007). For Lincoln's changing views of the reasons for fighting the Civil War, see Henry Louis Gates, Jr., "Abraham Lincoln on Race and Slavery," in *Lincoln on Race and Slavery*, ed. Henry Louis Gates, Jr. and Donald Yacovonne (Princeton: Princeton University Press, 2009), xvii–lxviii.

78. Invisible Man's four speeches show how carefully Ellison worked out what Homeric scholars would term "type scenes," as he goes back over a scenario, changing the context and cast of characters so that each episode emerges as a variation on a recognizable theme. The first one sounds like nothing much more than a paraphrase of Booker T. Washington's

Atlanta Exposition speech—at points, even a direct quotation ("Cast down your bucket where you are!")—which Ellison's narrator delivers spitting blood as part of the entertainment for the white men who have awarded him a prize that will enable him to go off to college (Ralph Ellison, *Invisible Man* [New York: Vintage Books, 1995], 29–31). Next is a speech he improvises on a Harlem street in support of an old couple being evicted from their apartment, which attracts the notice of the Communist front organization, the Brotherhood (275–80); then a formal public address he gives after his adoption by Jack and the Brotherhood (341–46); and finally, his antimemorial speech about the murdered, ex-Brotherhood Brother Tod Clifton, who essentially commits suicide by provoking a policeman into shooting him down on a street in Midtown New York (454–59).

79. Ibid., 380–81.

Chapter Three

1. David Levering Lewis, *W. E. B. Du Bois: Biography of a Race, 1868–1919* (New York: Henry Holt & Co., 1993); Lewis, *W. E. B. Du Bois: The Fight for Equality and the American Century, 1919–1963* (New York: Henry Holt & Co., 2000; William Sanders Scarborough, *The Autobiography of William Saunders Scarborough: An American Journey from Slavery to Scholarship* (Detroit: Wayne State University Press, 2005); Scarborough, *The Works of William Sanders Scarborough: Black Classicist and Race Leader* (Oxford: Oxford University Press, 2006).

2. In addition to French, German, mathematics, and sciences, Fisk's extensive liberal arts course of study prescribed three years of selected readings in Cicero, Vergil, Horace, Livy, Tacitus, Homer, Demosthenes, Plato, Thucydides, and the Greek tragic poets; see Christine M. Kreyling, Wesley Paine, Charles W. Warterfield, and Susan Ford Wiltshire, *Classical Nashville: Athens of the South* (Nashville, Tenn.: Vanderbilt University Press, 1996).

3. W. E. B. Du Bois, *Writings* (New York: The Library of America, 1986), 372 ("Of the Dawn of Freedom," in *The Souls of Black Folk*).

4. Stepto, *From Behind the Veil*, 91: "*The Souls* is not a social scientific study or the verbal tracings of a muckraker; rather, it is a book of prophecy. In the narrative, data becomes metaphor, rough winds become melodious songs, swamps occasion meditations."

5. On the founding of Johns Hopkins, see Gildersleeve's memoir in *Soldier and Scholar: Basil Lanneau Gildersleeve and the Civil War*, ed. Ward W. Briggs, Jr. (Charlottesville: University Press of Virginia, 1998), 82–91. Writing in the last year of the Civil War (May 3, 1864), Gildersleeve was committed to the Confederate cause and the South's isolation from industrialization and modern commerce; he regarded its slave society's institutions as "great blessings" in an otherwise increasingly uncivilized world (304–7).

6. Lewis, *W. E. B. Du Bois: Biography of a Race*, 290.

7. Shelley P. Haley, "Black Feminist Thought and Classics: Re-membering, Re-claiming, Re-empowering," *Feminist Theory and the Classics*, ed. Nancy Sorkin Rabinowitz and Amy Richlin (New York: Routledge, 1993), 23–43.

8. Mary Church Terrell, *A Colored Woman in a White World* (1940), introd. Nellie Y. McKay (New York: G. K. Hall, 1996), introduction (n.p.).

9. Ibid., 1.

10. Ibid., 32.

11. Ibid., 40–41.

12. Ibid., 41; Haley, "Black Feminist Thought and Classics," 25.

13. Terrell, *A Colored Woman in a White World*, 45.

14. Frank M. Snowden, *Blacks in Antiquity: Ethiopians in the Greco-Roman Experience* (Cambridge, Mass.: Harvard University Press, 1970).

15. Terrell, *A Colored Woman in a White World*, 237: "Throughout my life, no matter what I was doing, I kept dreaming of the day I would have the leisure and the mental peace to write some of the things I have to say. But that day never came. In every diary that I have kept, the yearning to express my thoughts on the printed page and the poignant regret that I could not do so run like a Jeremiad from the first day of the year to the last. 'I am always getting ready to write something,' I lament in one place, 'but I am never prepared to begin. I am more like George Eliot's Casaubon than anybody either in fiction or out of it with whom I can be compared.'"

16. Scarborough, *Autobiography*, 57–58.

17. Ibid., 113.

18. Ibid., 199.

19. This point is brought out in both historical and personal terms, and with great frankness, by Patrice D. Rankine in his introduction to *Ulysses in Black: Ralph Ellison, Classicism, and African American Literature* (Madison: University of Wisconsin Press, 2006), 3–20.

20. E.g., his remarks in August 1915 to the National Negro Business League in Boston: "Why, don't you know that Greeks have come over here to this country and have taken the shoe-shining trade away from the colored man? Just think of it—the black boy is studying Greek and the Greek boy is blacking shoes!" in Michele Valerie Ronnick, "A Look at Booker T. Washington's Attitude toward the Study of Greek and Latin by People of African American Ancestry," *Negro Educational Review* 53 (2002): 59–70: 65, quoting *Selected Speeches of Booker T. Washington*, ed. E. Davidson Washington (Garden City, N.J.: Doubleday, Doran, 1932), 264.

21. Because of the huge range of Scarborough's work, much that he wrote was scattered and difficult to find until Michele Valerie Ronnick tracked it down; see Scarborough, *Works*, ed. Ronnick.

22. Scarborough, *Autobiography*, 116.

23. As Cmiel observes of classicists of Scarborough's generation, "They had no sense that scholarship was not a literary activity" (*Democratic Eloquence*, 170).

24. William S. Scarborough, *First Lessons in Greek* (New York: A. S. Barnes, 1881; Michelle V. Ronnick, "*First Lessons in Greek* (1881): William Sanders Scarborough's Date with Destiny," *AME Church Review* 118 (2002): 30–43.

25. Scarborough, *The Birds of Aristophanes*, 28–29.

26. Ibid., 14–16.

27. While at Dartmouth for the APA's annual meeting Scarborough learned how well he had made his reputation in white America through his introductory Greek textbook: "One of the students called me to his room to see his library. To my surprise and gratification he handed me my own Greek book, saying he had studied it with pleasure and profit at Kimball Union Academy" (*Autobiography*, 82).

28. Cmiel, *Democratic Eloquence*, 261: "Specialized language becomes celebrated as critical to the culture's health, and one becomes a star by writing for one's peers in professional journals, not by addressing the public in the newspapers. . . . Professional conversation too early became opaque and irrelevant to the uninitiated."

29. *Transactions and Proceedings of the American Philological Association* 16 (1884): vi.

30. Quoted in Cmiel, *Democratic Eloquence*, 261 and 327n10: "On Thursday last Prof. March performed a painful but necessary duty in unveiling the fallacies and intrigues of the

Neo-Grammarians. This band of philological heretics is now hard at work attacking the cardinal doctrines of orthodox philology. In the course of an article in the new edition of the Encyclopedia Britannica Prof. Sievers, the neogrammatical heresiarch has, according to Prof. March, had the recklessness to assert that 'glottogonic problems are insoluble,' and to pretend that inflections do not originate through agglutination. These shameless and brutal theories have been published, not in some obscure and disreputable newspaper, but in the great encyclopedia of the English-speaking races, and they are thus liable at any time to be brought to the knowledge of the young and innocent. No wonder that Prof. March's blood boiled at such an outrage, and that his scathing denunciations of the wretched Sievers were hailed with enthusiasm by all like-minded philologists."

31. He could as well have written and published his dissertation in German and taken his PhD from the University of Berlin, which at the time was the leading research university of the world, but the American foundation supporting his study in Germany refused to grant him any further support beyond the two years he had already won. With considerable disappointment he returned to Harvard and finished his dissertation there instead.

32. Scarborough, *Autobiography*, 311, 395n17, and 395n18.

33. Ibid., 320.

34. Ibid., 321.

35. This pedagogic use of Cicero is not alien to his own purposes, but as will be apparent, it almost demands that those using *Pro Archia* as a defense of literature overlook the ringing endorsement of Cicero and his heroic consulship, delivered by none other than Cicero himself. For the original circumstances of the oration, in which what was ostensibly delivered as a judicial argument but which was actually an epideictic oration turning legal argument into an eloquent testimony of the literary stature of the orator himself, see John Dugan, "How to Make (and Break) a Cicero: Epideixis, Textuality, and Self-fashioning in the *Pro Archia* and *In Pisonem*," *Classical Antiquity* 20 (2001): 35–77. For the reception of the *Pro Archia*, which was taken very seriously indeed as an apology for literature in spite of some difficulties, see William Malin Porter's rhetorical analysis in "Cicero's *Pro Archia* and the Responsibilities of Reading," *Rhetorica* 8 (1990): 137–52.

36. At Antony's order his head and hands were chopped off and then nailed to the Rostra in the Roman forum. For this mutilation as a defining act of Cicero's career as both an orator and a writer, see Amy Richlin, "Cicero's Head," in *Constructions of the Classical Body*, ed. James I. Porter (Ann Arbor: University of Michigan Press, 1999), 190; more generally, Shane Butler, *The Hand of Cicero* (London: Routledge, 2002).

37. Dugan, "How to Make (and Break) a Cicero," 52–53 and note 70.

38. Ibid., 61 and note 100.

39. Ibid., 44. Dugan's reference here and everywhere to Cicero's "self-fashioning" draws on Stephen Greenblatt's Foucauldian theory of a conscious construction of the self, first introduced in *Renaissance Self-Fashioning: From More to Shakespeare* (Chicago: University of Chicago Press, 1980).

40. Carrie Cowherd, "The Wings of Atalanta: Classical Influences in *The Souls of Black Folk*," in *The Souls of Black Folk: One Hundred Years Later*, ed. Dolan Hubbard (Columbia: University of Missouri Press, 2003), 284–97, esp. 295.

41. W. E. B. Du Bois, *The Souls of Black Folk*, ed. Henry Louis Gates, Jr., and Terri Hume Oliver (New York: W. W. Norton, 1999), 46 and note 1.

42. Ibid., 407–8.

43. Ibid., 408.

44. Ibid., 410.

45. Ibid., 414.

46. Lewis, *W. E. B. Du Bois: The Fight for Equality*, 220–28.

47. W. E. B. Du Bois, "So the Girl Marries," in *W. E. B. Du Bois: A Reader*, ed. David Levering Lewis (New York: Henry Holt, 1985), 128–33: 129.

48. *Ovid's Metamorphoses, Books 6–10*, ed. William S. Anderson (Norman: University of Oklahoma Press, 1972), 524 (on 10.591).

49. Du Bois, *Souls of Black Folk*, 416.

50. Anderson, *Ovid's Metamorphoses*, 524–25 (on 10.594–96).

51. Ovid, *The Metamorphoses of Ovid*, trans. Allen Mandelbaum (New York: Harcourt Brace, 1993).

52. Cowherd, "The Wings of Atalanta," 288, arguing against Arnold Rampersad's observation that "The Quest" "sends him back to his Bulfinch" (Rampersad, *The Art and Imagination of W. E. B. Du Bois* (Cambridge, MA: Harvard University Press, 1976), 77).

53. Du Bois, *Souls of Black Folk*, 415.

54. Ibid., 438.

55. Ibid., 415–16.

56. Ibid., 416.

57. In a striking illustration of why no single translation can be trusted at every step, for every purpose, Mandelbaum's oddly ignores all this strip-tease cleverness: Venus is made to say Atalanta's name when she doesn't (10.560) and then the god from the temple is made not to say the name, when he actually does (10.565).

58. Anderson's commentary is particularly sharp in pointing out how Ovid defangs and humanizes a far more feral version of Atalanta in Hesiod (*Catalogues of Women*, fragment 14) and the ancient mythographers Hyginus (1985) and Apollodorus (*The Library* 3.9.2.2); *Ovid's Metamorphoses*, ed. Anderson, 518, 523 (on 10.571–72), 528 (on 10.638–41 and 649–51), 630 (on 10.676–78). Atalanta's psychology, her hesitation as well as her attraction to Hippomenes, is finely drawn.

59. As Anderson observes, this is usually the case in folktales and other narratives that tell of motifs in threes (Goldilocks and the Three Bears, etc.); *Ovid's Metamorphoses*, 530 (on 10.672–75).

60. Du Bois, *Souls of Black Folk*, 416–17.

61. Andrew Carnegie, "Wealth," *North American Review* 148, no. 391 (June 1889): 653–57.

62. Du Bois, *Souls of Black Folk*, 417.

63. Ibid., 417–18.

64. Ibid., 419.

65. Ibid., 421–22.

66. Cf., however, one of *The Souls of Black Folk*'s otherwise most sympathetic critics, Stepto, *From Behind the Veil*, 59: "Bound rather tediously to the ancient myth of Atalanta, Hippomenes, and the golden apples, 'Of the Wings of Atalanta' expresses Du Bois' fear that the Mammonism of the new South, as symbolized by the postwar prosperity of Atlanta, will soon engulf and corrupt the black race."

67. Du Bois, *Souls of Black Folk*, 423.

68. Readers who find Du Bois's mythologizing not to their liking can flip forward to our discussion of Schuyler and *Black No More* in chapter 7, below.

69. Gould had "Atalanta" made for himself in 1888. Du Bois possibly even knew of this egregious symbol of capitalist wit. Gould was able to enjoy riding around the South looking for Hippomenes' golden apples for only four years before he died in 1892. Today the "Atalanta" can be visited in Jefferson, Texas, now a small town but once alleged to be a mighty river port whose town fathers refused to let the riffraff building Gould's Texas & Pacific Railroad come through. In 1872 on his visit there Gould wrote in the guest register his usual signature with a drawing of a jaybird, and the words "End of Jefferson, Texas." The railroad went through Marshall, Texas, 16 miles to the north, and Gould's curse more or less came true. Today visitors can enjoy that archival moment and then walk across the street, where the "Atalanta" is permanently parked and open for tours led by the women of the Jesse Allen Wise Garden Club.

Chapter Four

1. Veblen is a social critic who knows how to make serious arguments about economics and society in disarmingly amusing ways; good advice about how to read him can be found in, e.g., Stephen S. Conroy, "Thorstein Veblen's Prose," *American Quarterly* 20 (1968): 605–16; and Teresa Toulouse, "Veblen and His Reader: Rhetoric and Intention in *The Theory of the Leisure Class*," *Centennial Review* 29 (1985): 249–67. For a later economist inspired to follow the same path that Veblen took—and who suffered the same kind of opprobrium from his fellow professional economists—see the work of John Kenneth Galbraith; e.g., his history of the 1929 stock market crash and beginning of the Great Depression, *The Great Crash, 1929*, 3rd ed. (Boston: Houghton Mifflin, 1972).

2. Du Bois, "Of the Wings of Atalanta," 421–22: "The Wings of Atalanta are the coming universities of the South. They alone can bear the maiden past the temptation of golden fruit."

3. W. E. B. Du Bois, *Dusk of Dawn: An Essay toward an Autobiography of Race Concept* (New York: Oxford University Press, 2007), chap. 9, "Revolution," 750–93, quotation on 751.

4. Rampersad, "The Quest of the Silver Fleece," in *Art and Imagination of Du Bois*, 116–32, esp. 132; also Lewis, *W. E. B. Du Bois: Biography of a Race*, 443–50.

5. Rampersad, *Art and Imagination of Du Bois*, 39. Du Bois quotes himself from the paper he wrote for Wendell on October 3, 1890, in *Dusk of Dawn*, "Education," 582: "Barrett Wendell rather liked that last sentence. He read it out to the class."

6. Lewis, *W. E. B. Du Bois: Biography of a Race*, 445.

7. Rampersad, *Art and Imagination of Du Bois*, 127: "The novel vividly illustrates the conflict between realism and romance common in so much serious writing at the turn of the century, especially in such authors as Norris and Garland."

8. Lewis, *W. E. B. Du Bois: Biography of a Race*, 444–45: "Du Bois' final, slightly amended title was faithful to the economic *idée maîtresse* of the work, an idea that had become stronger as he reworked the numerous plots in his large narrative."

9. Rampersad, *Art and Imagination of Du Bois*, 131–32, citing Arthur P. Davis, *From the Dark Tower: Afro-American Writers, 1900 to 1960* (Washington, D.C.: Howard University Press, 1974), 22–23.

10. Du Bois, *Souls of Black Folk*, 547 ("THE AFTER THOUGHT. *Hear my cry, O God the Reader . . .*").

11. Rampersad, *Art and Imagination of Du Bois*, 126–27.

12. Ibid., 122.

13. Ibid., 124: "Du Bois criticizes white society, holding up only Miss Smith as a moral hero. But apart from the rehabilitated Zora, Bles, and some of the poor peasantry who appear in vignettes, the blacks are little better. This is especially true of those in the city, who should be providing the leadership for the black masses."

14. Ibid., 124–25.

15. For a more sympathetic reading of Fauset's fiction generally, see, e.g., Sharon L. Jones, *Rereading the Harlem Renaissance: Race, Class, and Gender in the Fiction of Jessie Fauset, Zora Neale Hurston, and Dorothy West* (Westport, Conn.: Greenwood Press, 2002). As should be apparent, we are more in accord with David Levering Lewis, *When Harlem Was in Vogue* (New York: Knopf, 1979), 124: "A few hundred families strong, living (like the author's own ancient Philadelphia family) on the margins of affluence in a style of worn, fustian gentility, clinging to color, pedigree and gracious manners, Fauset's characters have the straitened pretensions of aristocrats after a revolution. The sentiments of her figures—especially the women—are aristocratically farfetched or celestially elevated, but they are nonetheless authentic and saved from caricature because they reflect faithfully the attitudes of a class that was itself a caricature."

16. Jessie Fauset, *The Chinaberry Tree: A Novel of American Life* (Philadelphia: J. B. Lippincott, 1931), vii–viii. Gale's introduction is omitted without comment in the most recent reprint of the novel (Jessie Fauset, *The Chinaberry Tree: A Novel of American Life & Selected Writings*, with a new foreword by Marcy Jane Knopf (Boston: Northeastern University Press, 1995).

17. Susan Tomlinson, "'An Unwonted Coquetry': The Commercial Seductions of Jessie Fauset's *The Chinaberry Tree*," in *Middlebrow Moderns: Popular Women Writers of the 1920s*, ed. Lisa Boston and Meredith Goldsmith (Boston: Northeastern University Press, 2003), 227–43.

18. Ibid., 229, quoting Gale, introduction, vii.

19. Ibid., 101n7; Gale, introduction, viii.

20. Elizabeth Ammons, *Conflicting Stories: American Women Writers at the Turn into the Twentieth Century* (New York: Oxford University Press, 1992), 156: "Perhaps Fauset alone of the women novelists of the New Negro Renaissance had a classical tragic vision of life which pervades even her 'comedies.'"

21. Tomlinson ("'An Unwonted Coquetry,'" cited above) is particularly good in her careful analysis of the market strategy and potential readerships, to both of which Fauset gave a great deal of time and thought.

22. For the literary and historical phenomenon of "passing" and the stereotype of the Tragic Mulatto, see Werner Sollors, *Neither Black Nor White Yet Both: Thematic Explorations of Interracial Literature* (New York: Oxford University Press, 1997), 221–93; for a recent discussion of some of Fauset's most important models, cf. Eve Allegra Raimon, *The "Tragic Mulatta" Revisited: Race and Nationalism in Nineteenth-Century Antislavery Fiction* (New Brunswick: Rutgers University Press, 2004).

23. Lupton, "Bad Blood in Jersey," 385–86, quoting Hiroko Sato, "Under the Harlem Shadow: A Study of Jessie Fauset and Nella Larsen," in *The Harlem Renaissance Remembered*, ed. Arna Bontemps (New York: Dodd, Mead, 1972), 76.

24. Joseph J. Feeney, "Greek Tragic Patterns in a Black Novel: Jessie Fauset's *The Chinaberry Tree*." *College Language Association Journal* 18 (1974): 211–15.

25. James B. Twitchell, *Forbidden Partners: The Incest Taboo in Modern Culture* (New York: Columbia University Press, 1987), 172, "No gothic has ever allowed a known situation of

incest to develop to consummation. Only the pornographic novel can sustain that eventuality and, even there . . . it is accomplished in the service of wholesale social subversion."

26. Mark R. Anspach, introduction to René Girard, *Oedipus Unbound: Selected Writings on Rivalry and Desire*, ed. Mark R. Anspach (Stanford: Stanford University Press, 2004), xxv, quoting from Jean-Pierre Vernant, "Ambiguity and Reversal: On the Enigmatic Structure of *Oedipus Rex*," in Jean-Pierre Vernant and Pierre Vidal-Naquet, *Myth and Tragedy in Ancient Greece* (New York: Zone Books, 1990).

27. Anspach, introduction to Girard, *Oedipus Unbound*, xxvi; Northrop Frye, *The Anatomy of Criticism* (Princeton: Princeton University Press, 1971), 47.

28. Frye, *Anatomy of Criticism*, 41, quoted in Anspach, introduction to Girard, *Oedipus Unbound*, xxx.

29. For the cultural meaning of Jocasta's and Phaedra's suicides by hanging, as opposed to heroic male choices, see Nicole Loraux, *Tragic Ways of Killing a Woman*, trans. Anthony Forster (Cambridge: Harvard University Press, 1987), 23–24.

30. Twitchell, *Forbidden Partners*, 223, referring to John T. Irwin, *Doubling and Incest/ Repetition and Revenge: A Speculative Reading of Faulkner* (Baltimore: Johns Hopkins University Press, 1975); and Constance H. Hall, *Incest in Faulkner: A Metaphor for the Fall* (Ann Arbor, Mich.: UMI Research Press, 1985).

31. See the provocative argument of Twitchell, *Forbidden Partners*, 229 ff., that in American fiction in the nineteenth and early twentieth centuries "'bad girls' are not allowed to grow up."

32. David F. Dorsey, "Countee Cullen's Use of Greek Mythology," *College Language Association Journal* 13 (1969): 68–77, esp. 68–69.

33. Ibid., 77.

34. Thomas Bulfinch, *The Age of Fable; or, Beauties of Mythology* (Boston: S. W. Tilton, 1855), 214–16.

35. For a comprehensive study of the Daedalus myths in art, see Sarah P. Morris, *Daedalus and the Origins of Greek Art* (Princeton: Princeton University Press, 1992).

36. William W. Cook, "The New Negro Renaissance," *Blackwell's Companion to Twentieth Century Poetry*, ed. Neil Roberts (Oxford: Blackwell, 2001), 138–52.

37. Lewis, *When Harlem Was in Vogue*, 76: "Those who knew the poet personally insist that literary critics and doctoral drones have been unduly diverted by the dark aspects in his life. They remember Cullen as outgoing, bubbly, and too busy writing and teaching for eccentricity or despair. 'He was always a perfect gentleman,' is a refrain among the Harlem survivors of the period."

38. Bulfinch, *Age of Fable*, 279.

39. Countee Cullen, *On These I Stand: An Anthology of the Best Poems of Countee Cullen* (New York: Harper and Brothers, 1947), 71.

40. Harvey Curtis Webster, "A Difficult Career," *Poetry* 7 (1947). The "monstrosity" of "Dear Friends and Gentle Hearts" is a late poem published for the first time in *On These I Stand* (163). The second half of the poem leads to where Cullen's poems nearly always lead if given half a chance: to the death of the poet, and the sentiment, You will be sorry when I'm gone.

41. Ibid.

42. Lewis, *When Harlem Was in Vogue*, 76 ("A few nubile young ladies tittered that Cullen was uninterested in women and preferred the company of Harold Jackman, handsome West Indian man about town, and there were comrades who snickered about his adoration of

his adoptive father [rumored to be a menace to choirboys and oddly fond of Mrs. Cullen's cosmetics]") and 77 ("Like his lowly birth and orphanage, Cullen's homosexuality was to be a source of shame he never fully succeeded in turning into a creative strength"). See also Alden Reimonenq, "Countee Cullen's Uranian 'Soul Windows,'" in *Critical Essays: Gay and Lesbian Writers of Color*, ed. Emmanuel S. Nelson (New York: Haworth Press, 1993), 143–66; A. B. Christa Schwarz, "Countée Cullen: 'His virtues are many; his vices unheard of,'" in *Gay Voices of the Harlem Renaissance* (Bloomington: Indiana University Press, 2003), 48–67. A minor point of orthography: Cullen was a teacher of French and regularly used the *accent aigu* in his first name; e.g., his inscription of a copy of *The Ballad of the Brown Girl* (1927) for Arthur C. Schomburg is signed "Countée Cullen" (from Schomburg's copy now in the Schomburg Library of the New York Public Library). The published version of *On These I Stand* omits this affectation.

    43. Cullen, *On These I Stand*, 3.

    44. Countee Cullen, *Copper Sun* (New York: Harper & Brothers, 1927), 18–19. Dedicated to Yolande, "One Day We Played a Game" is understandably not included in *On These I Stand*, which is dedicated to Cullen's second wife, Ida.

    45. Rankine, *Ulysses in Black*, 95.

    46. Cullen, *On These I Stand*, 153.

    47. William P. McDonald, "The Blackness of Medea," *College Language Association Journal* 19 (1975): 20–37, esp. 22.

    48. For a recent and more sympathetic reading of Cullen that reads the *Medea* and "Byword for Evil," the additional prologue and epilogue that were later written to introduce and conclude the original drama, see Rankine, *Ulysses in Black*, 94–103.

    49. Philip Blair Rice, "Euripides in Harlem," *Nation* 141, (September 18, 1935).

    50. See, for instance, Helene P. Foley's discussion of Medea's masculine heroic role and her feminine maternal self, "Medea's Divided Self," *Classical Antiquity* 8 (1989): 61–85. In the first role she is the murderer of her own children, and in the second, the mother who mourns for their loss even before she kills them.

    51. Countee Cullen, *The Medea of Euripides and Some Poems* (New York: Harper and Brothers, 1935), 11.

    52. A. S. Way, translator, in *Four Famous Greek Plays*, ed. P. N. Landis (New York: Modern Library, 1929), 156–57.

    53. John Jay Chapman, *Two Greek Plays* (Boston: Houghton Mifflin, 1928), 64–65.

    54. Cullen, *The Medea*.

    55. Way, in Landis, ed., *Four Famous Greek Plays*, 65.

    56. Cullen, *The Medea*, 11.

    57. Rice, "Euripides in Harlem," 336: "The most serious omission, which seems without justification, is that of the two passages which are *loci classici* for Euripides' 'feminism'; these are not extraneous to the dramatic action, since they express part of the heroine's motivation."

    58. It is worth noting that literary criticism accompanying popular versions of the play could be as fully in denial about what Euripides had created as Cullen; e.g., Landis, who goes to some lengths to reassure his readers that *Medea* has nothing to do with the world *they* live in: "*Medea* is the story of a woman wronged. Her story is interesting because she is interesting, not as it is the story of mankind. It was the nature of Greek tragedy to present heroic but typical characters, in extraordinary but typical crises. Medea is a strange, exotic

woman in a trying situation, and her solution is entirely her own. Hers is perhaps the most terrible display of passion in literature, but it lacks the universality characteristic of Greek drama" (*Four Famous Greek Plays*, xvi).

59. Cullen, *The Medea*, 12, 14.

60. Dudley Fitts, *New York Times*, February 23, 1947.

61. Rankine, *Ulysses in Black*, 102.

62. Gerald Early, *My Soul's High Song: The Collected Writings of Countee Cullen, Voice of the Harlem Renaissance* (New York: Doubleday, 1991), 507.

63. Ibid., 599.

64. Ibid., 601.

Chapter Five

1. See Houston A. Baker, *Blues, Ideology and African-American Literature: A Vernacular Theory* (Chicago: University of Chicago Press, 1984); for connections through jazz in writers commonly seen as quite diverse (Ralph Ellison, James Baldwin, and LeRoi Jones/Amiri Baraka), see Walton M. Muyumba, *The Shadow and the Act: Black Intellectual Practice, Jazz Improvisation, and Philosophical Pragmatism* (Chicago: University of Chicago Press, 2009).

2. Arnold Rampersad, *Ralph Ellison: A Biography* (New York: Alfred A. Knopf, 2007).

3. Patrice Rankine, *Ulysses in Black: Ralph Ellison, Classicism, and African American Literature* (Madison: University of Wisconsin Press, 2006).

4. *The Collected Essays of Ralph Ellison*, ed. John F. Callahan (New York: Modern Library, 1995).

5. Rampersad, *Ralph Ellison*, 170, who quotes Herman Melville in 1851: "To produce a mighty book, you must choose a mighty theme."

6. Rampersad, *Ralph Ellison*, 194; Ellison, "The Art of Fiction," in *Shadow and Act* (New York: Random House, 1964), 176.

7. Ralph Ellison, *Juneteenth: A Novel*, ed. John F. Callahan (New York: Random House, 1999); Rankine, *Ulysses in Black*, 145–51.

8. Patrice Rankine, *Ulysses in Black*, 127, quoting Ellison, "Change the Joke and Slip the Yoke," in *Shadow and Act*, 61–73: 72.

9. Rankine, *Ulysses in Black*, 128, quoting Ellison, "Change the Joke and Slip the Yoke," 70.

10. The meaning of the epigraphs remains invisible unless we recall Melville's *Benito Cereno* and Eliot's *Family Reunion*. For the first epigraph ("'You are saved" cried Captain Delano, more and more astonished and pained; 'you are saved: what has cast such a shadow upon you?'"), the answer to Delano's question is "The Negro," Babo, who had led a slave revolt on Don Benito's ship in *Benito Cereno*. In *The Family Reunion*, the character Harry is enraged because no one really sees him, to the point that he might as well be dead, and their regard for him, nothing but the love of the dead, necrophilia: "I tell you, it is not me you are looking at, Not me you are grinning at, not me your confidential looks Incriminate, but that other person, if person, You thought I was: let your necrophily Feed upon that carcase."

11. Houston A. Baker, Jr., "A Forgotten Prototype: *The Autobiography of an Ex-Coloured Man* and *Invisible Man*," *Virginia Quarterly Review* 49 (1973): 433–49.

12. For Rankine's reading of the novel per se, see *Ulysses in Black*, 121–44. "Ulysses in Black" is an organizing trope for a study of the relationship between classical European myth and literature and African American literature (3–21).

13. Athena stops in its tracks a battle that is erupting between the kinsmen of the slain suitors of Penelope and Odysseus and his family with the simple injunction, Stop at once or Zeus will be angry (*Odyssey* 24, end).

14. James M. Harding, "Adorno, Ellison, and the Critique of Jazz," *Cultural Critique* 31 (1995): 129–58, esp. 144: "Armstrong's significance derives from an ability to create poetic meaning out of a situation with which the invisible man is only beginning to come to terms. . . . He begins to understand the revitalizing power of the vernacular amidst the dominant discourse which excludes him."

15. Lawrence Patrick Jackson, *Ralph Ellison: The Emergence of Genius* (New York: John Wiley & Sons, 2002), 430: "Among the changes—some minor and others not so minor—the technical decision to transfer most of the prologue into the epilogue was the most weighty. . . . He decided to split his efforts in the intellectually robust prologue in half and shuttle most of the insight to the end."

16. Rampersad, *Ralph Ellison*, 227: "Although *Invisible Man* is in many ways an epic, Ralph adopted the form mainly to improvise on it like a disciplined jazzman."

17. Leon Forrest, "Luminosity from the Lower Frequencies," in *Ralph Ellison's 'Invisible Man': A Casebook*, ed. John F. Callahan (Oxford: Oxford University Press, 2004), 267–86.

18. Leslie Fiedler, "Come Back to the Raft Ag'in, Huck Honey," *Partisan Review*, June 1948; *Invisible Man*, 187–88: "He leaned forward. 'Look,' he said, his face working violently, 'I was trying to tell you that I know many things about you—not you personally, but fellows like you. Not much, either, but still more than the average. With us it's Jim and Huck Finn . . . I'm afraid my father considers me one of the unspeakables . . . I'm Huckleberry, you see . . .' He laughed dryly as I tried to make sense of his ramblings. *Huckleberry?* Why did he keep talking about that kid's story?"

19. Forrest, "Luminosity from the Lower Frequencies," 276.

20. Rampersad, *Ralph Ellison*, 227.

21. Scarborough, *Works*, 302–4.

22. "How can he tell this to white men, I thought, when he knows they'll say that all Negroes do such things? I looked at the floor, a red mist of anguish before my eyes" (58). Note the cardinal colors white, black (Negroes), red.

23. See Robert M. Polhemus, *Lot's Daughters: Sex, Redemption, and Women's Quest for Authority* (Stanford: Stanford University Press, 2005), 217–52.

24. Lord Raglan, *The Hero: A Study in Tradition, Myth, and Drama* (New York: Oxford University Press, 1937), 3–4: "Only the smallest fraction of the human race has ever acquired the habit of taking an objective view of the past. . . . The events of our own past life are remembered, not as they seemed to us at the time, but merely as incidents leading up to our present situation. We cannot persuade ourselves, in fact we make no attempt to do so, that undertakings which ended in failure or fiasco were entered upon with just as much forethought and optimism as those which have profoundly affected our lives. We suppose our beliefs and mental processes to have been ever the same as they now are, and regard the story of our lives not as a cross-country walk upon which we are still engaged, but as a path, cut deliberately by fate and ourselves, to the positions which we now occupy."

25. Rankine, *Ulysses in Black*, 176.

26. See G. E. R. Lloyd, *Polarity and Analogy: Two Types of Argumentation in Early Greek Thought* (Cambridge: Cambridge University Press, 1966), 31–41. Lloyd also draws on

Lévi-Strauss for comparative evidence; Claude Lévi-Strauss, "Do Dual Organizations Exist?," in *Structural Anthropology* (New York: Basic Books, 1963), 1:132–63.

27. The *Odyssey* poet omits any mention of Agamemnon's sacrifice of his daughter Iphigenia at Aulis. This notorious event, much in evidence in Aeschylus and Euripides' treatment of the myths of Agamemnon, is almost but not perhaps entirely suppressed in the *Iliad* as well. There he immediately attacks the seer Calchas for "always" finding evil prophecies for Agamemnon to contend with (*Iliad* 1.106–8).

28. Ellison, "Living with Music," in *Shadow and Act*, 187–98.

29. Ellison, "The Art of Fiction," in *Shadow and Act*, 167–183, esp. 178.

30. Aristotle says the *Odyssey* is *anagnorêsis*, or recognition, from start to finish (*Poetics* 24.1459b15).

31. Ellison, "Living with Music," 194.

32. Robert J. Butler, "Dante's *Inferno* and Ellison's *Invisible Man*: A Study in Literary Continuity," *College Language Association Journal* 28 (1984): 54–77. Butler ends with the interesting speculation that the absence of such a clear model as Dante's may account for Ellison's failure to write another novel; without the structure and "transitions" he had developed by following Dante, the successor to *Invisible Man* could never materialize (75–77).

33. Ellison, "The Art of Fiction," 176–77.

34. The ultimate fate of the soul (its salvation) is the true purpose of the entire *Commedia*, which has scarcely begun to be realized by the time we leave *Inferno*, however regretfully, and start up the delicious mountain of *Purgatory*. This is a basic tenet of such Dante scholars as John Freccero; *Dante: The Poetics of Conversion*, ed. Rachel Jackoff (Cambridge, Mass.: Harvard University Press, 1986).

35. For a delightful taxonomy of this kind of complex literary relationship, see Gérard Genette, *Palimpsests: Literature in the Second Degree*, trans. Channa Newman and Claude Doubinsky (Lincoln: University of Nebraska Press, 1997), 294–303 and 367–75. In giving literature his own version of what might be termed the third degree, Genette deploys neologisms with great brio; e.g., 374: "*Friday and Robinson* is a transposition of a transposition, and thus typically a hyper-hypertext that is in some respects closer to its hypo-text, *Robinson Crusoe*, than was its own hypo-text, *Friday, or The Other Island*." Something like this is going on in *Invisible Man*—we think.

36. Richard Wright, "How 'Bigger' Was Born," in *Richard Wright: Early Works* (New York: The Library of America, 1991), 851–81, esp. 881. See Frederick T. Griffiths, "Copy Wright: What Is an (Invisible) Author?" *New Literary History* 33 (2002): 315–41, esp. 332.

37. Fyodor Dostoevsky, *Notes from Underground*, ed. and trans. Michael R. Katz (New York: W. W. Norton, 2001), 3. For a discussion of the challenge of translating these three sentences from the original Russian into English, see ibid., xi–xiv, "A Brief Note on the Translation."

38. Forrest, "Luminosity from the Lower Frequencies": "The grandfather is the oldest member of the tribe within the hero's family memory. And who is the *grandfather*'s authority? No doubt the oldest member of the tribe in his memory, perhaps *his* grandfather—and then we are back in slavery; so that in a highly oral culture the grandfather is the proper high priest to pass on mythical reality and survival wisdom from the battle zone."

39. A passage of time much noted by Odysseus (19.485) and then later mythologists; Apollodorus, *Gods and Heroes of the Greeks: The Library of Apollodorus*, trans. Michael

Simpson (Amherst: University of Massachusetts Press, 1976), 241 and note 8 (Apollodorus, *The Library* 3.18).

40. Steven D. Levitt and Stephen J. Dubner's comparison of black and white American practices in naming their children in *Freakonomics: A Rogue Economist Explores the Hidden Meaning of Everything* (New York: William Morrow, 2005), 204: "An overwhelming number of parents use a name to signal *their own expectations* of how successful their children will be. The name isn't likely to make a shard of difference. But the parents can at least feel better knowing that, from the very outset, they tried their best" (*italics original*).

41. Richard D. Alford, *Naming and Identity: A Cross-Cultural Study of Personal Naming Practices* (New Haven, Conn.: Human Relations Area Files Press, 1987), 145–47.

42. For a close reading of the scene, see Jenny Strauss Clay, *The Wrath of Athena: Gods and Men in the 'Odyssey'* (Princeton: Princeton University Press, 1983), 53–68.

43. Ibid., 59.

44. The *Odyssey* and Homeric verse generally seethe with this kind of play. Clay (*Wrath of Athena*, 56) points to a similar homophony in the verb *oïdzysas* ("having suffered woe") and *Odysseus* when Homer introduces Odysseus's recital of his adventures to Penelope after the two have finally reunited in book 23:

> But Zeus-born *Odysseus* told her all—all the troubles he set
> upon men, and all that he himself had suffered (*oïdzysas*) in misery. (306–8)

45. Alford, *Naming and Identity*, 29: "Just as naming objects and places in the natural world makes them socially significant by providing a common label, naming a child is a part of the process of bringing the child into the social order. A named child has, in a sense, a social identity. To know a child's name, in a sense, is to know who that child is. And when the child is old enough to know his own name, he, in a sense, knows who he is."

46. *Soon, One Morning: New Writing by American Negroes*, ed. Herbert Hill (New York: Alfred A. Knopf, 1963).

47. Ibid., 242–90.

48. Ellison, "Out of the Hospital and under the Bar," in *Soon, One Morning: New Writing by American Negroes, 1940–1962*, ed. Herbert Hill (New York: Alfred A. Knopf, 1963), 243: "For those who would care to fit it back into *Invisible Man* let them start at the point where the explosion occurs in the paint factory, substitute the following happenings, and leave them once the hero is living in Mary's home."

49. John Stark, "*Invisible Man*: Ellison's Black Odyssey," *Negro American Literature Forum* 7, no. 2 (1973): 60–63.

50. Robert N. List, *Daedalus in Harlem: The Joyce-Ellison Connection* (Washington, D.C.: University Press of America, 2003), 283.

51. We see the same phenomenon in the name of Odysseus's dog (17.292), where the adjective *argós*, "fleet," "swift" is turned into the proper name *Árgos* ("Swifty") by the same recessive accent; W. B. Stanford, *The Odyssey of Homer*, 2nd ed. (London: Macmillan, 1964), 1:359 (on 9.366) and 1:361 (on 9.408).

52. Homer, *The Odyssey*, trans. Robert Fagles (New York: Viking, 1996).

53. Marcel Detienne and Jean-Pierre Vernant, *Cunning Intelligence in Greek Culture and Society*, trans. Janet Lloyd (Atlantic Highlands, N.J.: Humanities Press, 1978).

54. Irving Howe, "Black Boys and Native Sons," in *A World More Attractive: A Voice of Modern Literature and Politics* (New York: Horizon Press, 1963; reprinted in Bloom's

Ralph Ellison, BioCritiques series, ed. Harold Bloom (Philadelphia: Chelsea House, 2003), 109–28.

55. Howe, "Black Boys and Native Sons," 110.

56. Ibid., 118.

57. Ralph Ellison, "The World and the Jug," in *Shadow and Act* (New York: Vintage Books, 1964), 107–43.

58. Ibid., 113.

59. Ibid., 115.

60. Important earlier readings in Ellison criticism along this line (though without reference to classical parallels) include Jonathan Baumbach, "Nightmare of a Native Son: Ralph Ellison's *Invisible Man*," *Critique* 6 (1963): 48–65; Jerry Wasserman, "Embracing the Negative: *Native Son* and *Invisible Man*," *Studies in American Fiction* 4 (1976): 93–104; and Michael Fabre, "From *Native Son* to *Invisible Man*: Some Notes on Ralph Ellison's Evolution in the 1950s," in *Speaking for You: The Vision of Ralph Ellison*, ed. Kimberly W. Benston (Washington, D.C.: Howard University Press, 1987), 199–216.

61. Hazel Rowley, *Richard Wright: The Life and Times* (New York: Henry Holt, 2001), 150–61.

62. Leonard Muellner, *The Anger of Achilles: Mênis in Greek Epic* (Ithaca: Cornell University Press, 1996). Muellner argues that the divine anger, or *mênis*, in Achilles links him to Hesiod's account of the generation of the gods and the rise to supreme power of Zeus in the *Theogony*. *Mênis* also describes the rage of Demeter over the rape of her daughter Persephone in the Homeric *Hymn to Demeter*. Homer's theme thus has cosmic dimensions that our conception of individual emotion does not convey.

63. Arnold Rampersad, introduction to Richard Wright, *Native Son* (New York: Harper Collins, 1998), ix.

64. For a reading of Ellison's Battle Royal as one of a series of scenes of ritualized violence, see Muyumba, *The Shadow and the Act*, 55–65.

65. George Lakoff and Zoltán Kövecses, "The Cognitive Model of Anger in American English," in *Cultural Models in Language & Thought*, ed. Dorothy Holland and Naomi Quinn (Cambridge: Cambridge University Press, 1987), 195–221. Muellner's *Anger of Achilles* cited above is an explicit application of this cognitive model to classical philology.

66. Lakoff and Kövecses, "The Cognitive Model of Anger," 206.

67. Daltonism is named after the British scientist John Dalton (1766–1844) who discovered colorblindness of red and green in himself and his brother, and it also signifies colorblindness in a general sense.

68. Wasserman, "Embracing the Negative," 99: "After listening to Max's political explanation, and 'trying to [compare] the picture Max was drawing . . . with what he had felt all his life,' Bigger arrives at the falsity of Max's vision and the essential uniqueness of his own life. He shatters Max's utopian dream by affirming, this time absolutely, the self he created by killing, the free and complete embrace of the only terms the white world would allow him."

Chapter Six

1. Jon Staunton Woodson, "A Critical Analysis of the Poetry of Melvin B. Tolson" (PhD diss., Brown University, 1978), 2–61, argues that "The Man from Halicarnassus" is the hermetic key to Tolson's mature poetics and devotes sixty pages of commentary to its seventy-three lines. A later distillation of his interpretation can be found in "Melvin Tolson and the

Art of Being Difficult," *Black American Poets between Worlds, 1940–1960*, ed. R. Baxter Miller (Knoxville: University of Tennessee Press, 1986), 19–42. Wilburn Williams, Jr., "The Desolate Servitude of Language: A Reading of the Poetry of Melvin B. Tolson" (PhD diss., Yale University, 1979), p. 187, found it a poem "so clogged with recondite Classical lore that it seems all paraphrase and quotation." Robert M. Farnsworth's summary in his biography of Tolson is more patient but also much clearer than the poem it explicates; *Melvin B. Tolson, 1898–1966: Plain Talk and Poetic Prophecy* (Columbia: University of Missouri Press, 1984), 191–94.

2. One correction for future explicators with a higher tolerance for this overstuffed poem than we have: *Pornilon* in the phrase *Pornilon telos* in line 18 is a misprint for *pornikon* (a Greek adjective derived from *pornê*, "whore"); the *pornikon telos* is the "prostitution tax" that King Cheops collected from his daughter's willing prostitution of herself to help build his great pyramid (Herodotus, 2.124).

3. Arnold Rampersad, *The Life of Langston Hughes*, vol. 2, *1941–1967: I Dream of a World* (Oxford: Oxford University Press, 2002), 234–35.

4. David C. Young, "Pindaric Criticism," in *Pindaros und Bakchylides*, ed. William Musgrave Calder III and Jacob Stern (Darmstadt: Wissenschaftliche Buchgesellschaft, 1970), 48.

5. Sarah Webster Fabio, "Who Speaks Negro?" in *Black Expression: Essays by and about Black Americans in the Creative Arts*, ed. Addison Gayle (New York: Weybright and Talley, 1969), 115–19, esp. 119: "Melvin Tolson's language is most certainly not 'Negro' to any significant degree. The weight of that vast, bizarre, pseudo-literary diction is to be placed back into the American mainstream where it rightfully and wrongmindedly belongs. Allen Tate recognized the distorted mirror image of the pseudo neo-classical Anglo-American diction and, I think, rightfully interpreted this language as a device of parody."

6. Young, "Pindaric Criticism," 3 and note 4.

7. Gregson Davis argues that Horace's famous ode is not really about Pindar at all, but that it uses Pindar's grandiose odes as a foil to Horace's small-scaled songs in the lyric meters of Sappho and Alcaeus; *Polyhymnia*, 133–44, esp. 134: "Horace did not believe for a moment that Pindar was emancipated from all metrical constraints!"

8. John T. Hamilton, *Soliciting Darkness: Pindar, Obscurity, and the Classical Tradition* (Cambridge: Harvard University Press, 2003), 101; 97–129.

9. Samuel Johnson, *Lives of the English Poets* (London: Oxford University Press, 1964), 1:39.

10. Hamilton's translation; *Soliciting Darkness*, 98: "Appended to practically every edition of Pindar's *epinicia* from the sixteenth century on, Horace's simile of the rushing river readily formulated what everyone expected of Pindar—an original genius, ungovernable and sublime: closer to nature than to art, less comprehensible than overwhelmingly effective."

11. Johnson, *Lives of the English Poets*, 2:462–63.

12. Paul H. Fry, *The Poet's Calling in the English Ode* (New Haven: Yale University Press, 1980).

13. Young, "Pindaric Criticism," 23.

14. *Pindar: The Olympian and Pythian Odes*, ed. Basil L. Gildersleeve (New York: Harper & Brothers, 1890); Young, "Pindaric Criticism," 28: "Gildersleeve was certainly the most independent of Pindar's scholars and in many ways the best."

15. *Basil Lanneau Gildersleeve: An American Classicist*, ed. Ward W. Briggs, Jr., and Herbert W. Benario (Baltimore: Johns Hopkins University Press, 1986).

16. See Hamilton's discussion of the absurd, Pindarizing bard who appears midway through Aristophanes' comedy *The Birds*, produced long after Pindar's death, in 414 BCE (*Soliciting Darkness*, 19–22).

17. *Pindar* (ed. Gildersleeve), xii: "It was no treason to Medize before there was a Greece, and the Greece that came out of the Persian war was a very different thing from the cantons that ranged themselves on this side and on that of a quarrel which, we may be sure, bore another aspect to those who stood aloof from it than it wears in the eyes of moderns, who have all learned to be Hellenic patriots. A little experience of a losing side might aid historical vision. That Pindar should have had an intense admiration of the New Greece, should have felt the impulse of the grand period that followed Salamis and Plateau, should have appreciated the woe that would have come on Greece had the Persians been successful, and should have seen the finger of God in the new evolution of Hellas—all this is not incompatible with an attitude during the Persian war that those who see the end and do not understand the beginning may not consider respectable."

18. *Pindar* (ed. Gildersleeve), xxv; cf. Gray, "The Progress of Poesy," 112–23:

> Oh! lyre divine, what daring spirit
> Wakes thee now? Though he inherit
> Nor the pride nor ample pinion,
> That the Theban eagle bear
> Sailing with supreme dominion
> Through the azure deep of air:
> Yet oft before his infant eyes would run
> Such forms as glitter in the Muses' ray
> With orient hues, unborrowed of the sun:
> Yet shall he mount and keep his distant way
> Beyond the limits of a vulgar fate,
> Beneath the Good how far—but far above the Great.

19. Rita Dove, "Telling It Like It I-S IS: Narrative Techniques in Melvin Tolson's *Harlem Gallery,*" *New England Review and Breadloaf Quarterly* 8 (1985): 89–117, quotation on 110.

20. Ibid., 112–13; Geneva Smitherman, *Toastin' and Signifyin': The Language of Black Americans* (Boston: Houghton Mifflin, 1977); and William W. Cook, "The Mouth's the Message: Language in Melvin Tolson's *Harlem Gallery*" (paper presented at the annual meeting of the College Language Association, Jackson, Miss., April 21–23, 1977).

21. Cf. Williams, "Desolate Servitude of Language," 166–67 (the forty-two lines of proverbs in "Sol" "needlessly repeats what has already been done") and especially 16: "The *Libretto* could very well end here [sc. with the ending of "La," line 254]. The 'official necessities of the occasion' have been observed with all due respect. The symbolic marriage of Europe, Africa, and America in the life of Ashmun restores the community sundered at Songhai. The remaining two-thirds of the poem is not concerned with Liberia as an historical entity." In our view, the Pindaric tradition would necessarily move beyond historic entities, just as Pindar himself moves far beyond anything his patrons and victorious athletes might have expected. On the contrary, the *Libretto* would have lost the most distinctive quality of an ode if it had been concerned only with Liberia as a historical entity.

22. E.g., Selden Rodman (*New York Times Book Review*, January 24, 1954), "It is by all odds the most considerable poem so far written by an American Negro, but a work of poetic synthesis in the symbolic vein altogether worthy to be discussed in the company of 'The Wasteland,' 'The Bridge,' and 'Paterson.' . . . By the same token the weaknesses one encounters in Tolson are the weaknesses one encounters in 'The Wasteland.' At Tolson's worst these

are magnified into balderdash. . . . This kind of writing becomes at its best academic and at its worst intellectual exhibitionism, throwing at the reader undigested scraps of everything from Bantu to Esperanto in unrelaxed cacophony. . . . One is reminded of Picasso's dictum: 'To search means nothing; to find is everything.' At his best, Tolson finds a great deal. His poem opens virtues undreamt of by the English-speaking poets of his race and by few poets of other races." Coralie M. Beyers, *Antioch Review* 14 (1954): 3: "Full of striking rhythmic patterns and trenchant language, his *Libretto* is marred nonetheless by the fact that nearly every brief stanza must be referred to in the copious Notes to be properly understood. . . . Such erudition is not democratically wide spread. Reading this volume is akin to the chore of going through Skeat's *Chaucer* and not quite as rewarding."

23. Melvin B. Tolson, *Libretto for the Republic of Liberia* (New York: Twayne, 1953). Just to make sure this twentieth-century version of an authenticating document wasn't missed, Allen Tate's endorsement is stamped on the front cover of the volume: "'There is a great gift for language, a profound historical sense, and a first-rate intelligence at work in this poem from first to last . . .' From the Preface by Allen Tate."

24. Tolson published an earlier draft of "Ti" without notes in *Poetry* 76 (1950): 208–15. He made a number of revisions before the final version was published, nearly all of them for the better—or at the very least, more difficult. Wilburn Williams adduces this publication as an instance of "a willful literariness" in the *Libretto*: "Alain Locke [1886–1954] who objected to language interlarding in the 1950 draft, would have been put off even more to discover that the final draft retained all the foreign expressions and added six new ones in Spanish alone, a language used not a single time in the 1950 version" ("Desolate Servitude of Language," 185).

25. Melvin B. Tolson, *Caviar and Cabbage: Selected Columns from the Washington Tribune, 1937–1944*, ed. Robert M. Farnsworth (Columbia: University of Missouri Press, 1982); Gary Lenhart, "Caviar and Cabbage: The Voracious Appetite of Melvin Tolson," *American Poetry Review* 29 (1989): 35–40.

26. Tuan Wreh, *The Love of Liberty: The Rule of President William V. S. Tubman in Liberia: 1944–1971* (London: C. Hurst, 1978), 11: "No President may be elected for two consecutive terms of eight years, but should a majority of the ballots cast at a second or any other succeeding election by all of the electors voting thereat elect him, his second or any other succeeding term of office shall be for four years."

27. Ibid., 39.

28. Fry, *The Poet's Calling in the English Ode*, 221.

29. Hamilton, *Soliciting Darkness*, 89, quoting William Fitzgerald, *Agonistic Poetry: The Pindaric Mode in Pindar, Horace, Hölderlin, and the English Ode* (Berkeley: University of California Press, 1987), 24: "Water is singled out and apparently rendered absolute, as the superlative epithet 'best' (*ariston*) would confirm. But no sooner is the notion of supremacy announced, than it is marred by the particle *men*, which, when coordinated with *de*, as here, is usually translated 'on the other hand.' In positing an absolute, Pindar immediately establishes a relation. As William Fitzgerald has noted, this entire priamel moves in a 'progression from the absolute to the contingent.' The appearance of this 'on the one hand,' which is inserted between the two elements of a simple nominal sentence, already undercuts the absolute value of water. The syntax, in other words, subverts the posited primacy of what is 'best'—'water is best on the one hand.'" The dependence of what is primary upon all that is not primary is made explicit in the *de* clause that follows. Here a further relativisation occurs by means of a simile: Not only is gold's preeminence dependent on the other sources of

wealth (from which it stands apart), but this brilliance is like fire. Strikingly, the superiority of gold, i.e. its distance from or dissimilarity to all other forms of wealth, is grounded in a similarity. Gold is unlike all other riches just like the brightness of fire is unlike the darkness of night. Gold and fire are similar, that is, in their dissimilarity."

30. *O My Land, My Friends: The Selected Letters of Hart Crane*. Langdon Hammer and Brom Weber, editors (New York: Four Walls Eight Windows, 1997), 137.

31. Melvin B. Tolson, *Harlem Gallery*, book 1, *The Curator* (New York: Twayne Publishers, 1965), 11.

32. Ibid., n.p.

33. Williams ("Desolate Servitude of Language," 193) argues that "these lines are a defensive reaction to the poet's anxiety about the possible unworthiness of his subject. To write a mighty poem one must have a mighty theme. But these lines speak to the poet's fears about the *Libretto*'s obscurity. . . . When he associates the *Libretto*'s obscurity with the work of a castrated pedant, he is voicing deep reservations about his art." This may be true at a literal level, if Tolson were simply speaking *in propria persona*, but strikes us as improbable.

34. Woodson, "A Critical Analysis," 118–19.

35. Robert G. O'Meally, *Romare Bearden: A Black Odyssey* (New York: DC Moore Gallery, 2007).

36. W. E. B. Du Bois, *The World and Africa: An Inquiry into the Part Which Africa Has Played in World History*, new enlarged ed. (New York: International Publishers, 1965), 211.

37. Tennyson's "Timbuctoo" was written before "Timbuktu" became the standard English spelling.

38. J. Gus Liebenow, *Liberia: The Quest for Identity* (Bloomington: Indiana University Press, 1987), 13.

39. Ralph Randolph Gurley, *Life of Jehudi Ashmun, Late Colonial Agent in Liberia* (New York: Leavitt, Lord, 1835), 111–12: "It was expected that the operations of this Society, would unfetter and invigorate the faculties, improve the circumstances, animate the hopes and enlarge the usefulness of the free people of colour; that by awakening thought, nullifying objections, presenting motives convincing to the judgment, and persuasive to the humanity of masters, they would encourage emancipation; that in Africa their results would be seen, in civilized and Christian communities; in the substitution of a lawful and beneficial commerce for the abominable slave trade; of peaceful agriculture for a predatory warfare; knowledge for ignorance; the arts that refine for vices that degrade; and for superstitions vile, cruel and bloodstained, the ennobling service and pure worship of the True God."

40. Woodson, "A Critical Analysis," 137–38.

41. Ibid., 139–40.

42. Gunnar Myrdal, *An American Dilemma: The Negro Problem in Modern Democracy* (New York: Harper & Row, 1944; 1962), lxxii: "The American Negro problem is a problem in the heart of the American. It is there that the interracial tension has its focus. It is there that the decisive struggle goes on. This is the central viewpoint of this treatise. Though our study includes economic, social, and political race relations, at bottom our problem is the moral dilemma of the American—the conflict between his moral valuations on various levels of consciousness and generality. The 'American Dilemma,' referred to in the title of this book, is the ever-raging conflict between, on the one hand, the valuations preserved on the general plane which we shall call the 'American Creed,' where the American thinks, talks, and acts under the influence of high national and Christian precepts, and, on the

other hand, the valuations on specific planes of individual and group living, where personal
and local interests; economic, social, and sexual jealousies; considerations of community
prestige and conformity; group prejudice against particular persons or types of people; and
all sorts of miscellaneous wants, impulses, and habits dominate his outlook."

43. Herbert Aptheker, *The Negro People in America: A Critique of Gunnar Myrdal's "An
American Dilemma"* (New York: International Publishers, 1946).

44. Ibid., 25–26.

45. Ibid., 27.

46. Ibid., 19: "Pertinent to the critique of the Myrdal work is the question: what is a dilemma? Webster tells us that a dilemma is 'a situation involving choice, especially in actions,
between equally unsatisfactory alternatives.' It is perhaps understandable how an adviser to
and an official of the government of Sweden, which treated the late war against fascism as a
dilemma and preferred neutrality (especially a neutrality made lucrative by 'necessary' trad-
ing with Nazi Germany) might decide to christen the fact of the exploitation and oppression of the American Negro people a dilemma—'a situation involving choice . . . between
equally unsatisfactory alternatives.'"

47. Woodson, "A Critical Analysis," 143.

48. Williams reads this entire section of the griots' proverbs as a miscalculation: "At
this juncture Tolson commits what can only be called an error. Tolson extends the bird
imagery rather neatly when he has the parrots of line 170 chatter the charge that Africa has
no history. The proverbs that Tolson offers as refutation are brilliant in their wit, but this
entire phase of the poem is a misconception. The accusation of the parrots was implicit in
the second line of 'Re': "The world is too large—that's why we do not hear everything." The
history of Songhai that followed was its refutation. The forty-two lines of proverbs in 'Sol'
needlessly repeat what has already been done. One suspects that Tolson was so taken with
the sheer genius of the proverbs that he worked them into the poem at the first opportunity without thinking of their place in the poem's larger design" ("Desolate Servitude of
Language," 166).

49. Ibid., 167–68.

50. Arthur Edward Waite, *The Pictorial Key to the Tarot: Being Fragments of a Secret
Tradition under the Veil of Divination* (N.p.: CreateSpace, 2008), 92; Woodson, "A Critical
Analysis," 144.

51. Dido's Semitic and African identities were often repressed in assessments of her role
in the *Aeneid* and in history; see Ralph Hexter, "Sidonian Dido," in *Innovations of Antiquity*,
ed. Ralph Hexter and Daniel Selden (New York: Routledge, 1992), 332–84.

52. Williams, "Desolate Servitude of Language," 168: "He will not be satisfied until he
can be assured that the saving pattern of Liberian history can furnish a paradigm for the
history of the rest of mankind."

53. William Smith, *Smith's Bible Dictionary: More than 6,000 Detailed Definitions, Articles,
and Illustrations* (Nashville, Tenn.: Thomas Nelson, 2004), 90.

54. Farnsworth, *Melvin B. Tolson*, 147.

55. Waite, *Pictorial Key to the Tarot*, 116; Sylvie Simon, *The Tarot: Art, Mysticism, and Divination* (London: Alpine Fine Arts Collection, 1986), 40: "The Hanged man sacrifices himself
for others in complete self-abnegation. His sacrifice is voluntary and in no way resembles
torture. He has the relaxed, smiling face of the Magician, but he is suspended by one blue

(spiritual) foot, and his legs, sheathed in red (therefore active), are crossed like those of the Emperor but in reverse, a sign of renunciation, that he may reach his development and perfect his inner knowledge. With his foot he makes a cross, an act of will."

56. Woodson, "A Critical Analysis," 170.

57. Williams, "Desolate Servitude of Language," 173.

58. Ibid., 180.

59. Karl Shapiro, introduction to Melvin B. Tolson, *Harlem Gallery* (New York: Twayne Publishers, 1965), 15.

60. Just to make things more complex, piling on one more bit of learning, Tolson adopts the ancient book divisions which Homer's Alexandrian critics devised for the books of both the *Iliad* and *Odyssey*, which are each divided into twenty-four books and labeled by the twenty-four letters of the Greek alphabet. If one is out-Pindaring Pindar—to say nothing of out-Pounding Pound—who else to invoke but Homer?

61. Raymond Nelson, "Notes and Commentary to *Harlem Gallery*," in *"Harlem Gallery" and Other Poems of Melvin B. Tolson*, ed. Raymond Nelson (Charlottesville: University of Virginia Press, 1999), 365–469: e.g., 450, on the lines "I was a kid . . . then . . . with the unbridled intelligence of Professor Marotelli's cat" at line 310 of *Phi*: "I can't tell you about Professor Marotelli's smart cat. I wish I could." So do we. A Google search turns up a Dr. G. Martorelli of Milan, who did extensive research on the pedigree of domestic cats, as reported by the naturalist Richard Lydekker (1849–1915) in *Mostly Mammals: Zoological Essays* (New York: Dodd Mead, 1903), 190. More often than we could wish, Tolson reminds us of the obsessed prospectors in Chaplin's *Gold Rush* or John Huston's *Treasure of the Sierra Madre*, panning for the most obscure allusion he can find.

62. Young, "Pindaric Criticism," 91: "The greatest obstacle to an increased understanding of the poems has been the unwillingness of the various critics to recognize and utilize the ideas of their fellows. Many a critic has proclaimed that he and he alone has found the secret for discovering the unity (or the disunity) of the odes. It has always been assumed that the odes must remain an unassailable mass unless some special insight into Pindar's method of composition or thought were discovered, a special theory of criticism that would work for Pindar and Pindar only. It is true that much—if not most—of what has been written about Pindar is worthless, usually misguided, and frequently ridiculous. But that should not prevent us from taking advantage of that small part of Pindaric criticism which is of value." Since the most salient characteristic of classical philology is its sometimes obsessive devotion to doxography, Young's criticism is all the more surprising. To judge from the work of such leading Pindarists as Most, Kurke, and Hamilton, it is no longer fashionable to ignore the work of one's predecessors in this difficult field.

63. Hamilton, *Soliciting Darkness*, 17.

64. Craig Werner, "Blues for T. S. Eliot and Langston Hughes: The Afro-Modernist Aesthetic of *Harlem Gallery*," *Black American Literature Forum* 24 (1990): 453–72: "Most readers of the Euro-American modernists simply ignore Tolson, while most members of the Afro-American audience prefer music to literature and, on the occasions when they turn to poetry, respond more readily to the relatively direct calls of Hughes or Gwendolyn Brooks. A blues irony, which Tolson would certainly have recognized, adheres to the situation. Public and private, racial and modern, Tolson's Afro-modernist blues suite remains ironically enmeshed in the dichotomies it so eloquently and thoroughly discredits" (471).

65. Nelson, "Notes to *Gallery*," 455.

66. Woodson, "A Critical Analysis," 244–45. How far to carry this reminiscence of Salome's performance is another question, especially when we recall how the dance is treated in Richard Strauss's setting of Oscar Wilde's *Salome*.

67. Woodson, "A Critical Analysis," 247.

68. Oswald Spengler, *The Decline of the West (Der Untergang des Abenlandes: Gestalt und Wirklichkeit)* (New York: Alfred A. Knopf, 1926), 1:124.

69. Nelson, "Notes to *Gallery*," 457.

70. Ibid., 460; Exodus 15:23–25 and 15:27.

Chapter Seven

1. Howard D. Weinbrot, *Menippean Satire Reconsidered: From Antiquity to the Eighteenth Century* (Baltimore: Johns Hopkins University Press, 2005), 6–7.

2. Ibid., on the influential theories of Northrop Frye (*The Anatomy of Criticism*) and Mikhail Bakhtin (*The Dialogic Imagination*), which Weinbrot regards as historically and factually impossible: "Current theories of Menippean satire based on Frye, and, largely, Bakhtin, allow too many texts at too many times to be Menippean" (296).

3. For an ancient Roman example of this connection between writing law and satire, see Frances Muecke's discussion of Horace's conversation with the jurist Trebatius in "Law, Rhetoric, and Genre in Horace, *Satires* 2.1," in *Homage to Horace: A Bimillenary Celebration*, ed. S. J. Harrison (New York: Oxford University Press, 1995), 203–18. To judge from the work of the professor of law Peter Goodrich, the affinities between legal practice and the literary phenomenon of satire are as strong as ever; Goodrich, "Satirical Legal Studies: From the Legists to the *Lizard*," *Michigan Law Review* 103 (2004): 397–517; and for a briefer introduction to the subject by the same author, "The Importance of Being Earnest: Satire and the Criticism of Law," *Social Semiotics* 15 (2005): 43–58.

4. See in general Susan Rubin Suleiman, *Authoritarian Fictions: The Ideological Novel as Literary Genre* (New York: Columbia University Press, 1983). The best example of this from surviving classical literature is Xenophon's *Education of Cyrus (Cyropaedia)*.

5. This observation comes from personal reminiscences of one of the authors (Cook), who frequently had to endure encomia of Philippa in the public schools of Trenton, New Jersey.

6. Obituary and notice "Philippa Schuyler, Pianist, Dies in Copter Crash in Vietnam," *New York Times*, May 9, 1967.

7. George S. Schuyler, *Black and Conservative: The Autobiography of George S. Schuyler* (New Rochelle, N.Y.: Arlington House, 1966).

8. *The Autobiography of Malcolm X*, with the assistance of Alex Haley (New York: Random House, 1964), chap. 3, 59–63, esp. 62–63: "I'm speaking from personal experience when I say of any black man who conks today, or any white-wigged black woman, that if they gave the brains in their heads just half as much attention as they do their hair, they would be a thousand times better off."

9. Jane Kuenz, "American Racial Discourse, 1900–1930: Schuyler's *Black No More*," *Novel: A Forum on Fiction* 30, no. 2 (1997): 170–92, esp. 177: "The effect of 'one-drop' ideology was to polarize the racial categories many people had until that time understood very well to be more fluid. It 'drove mulattoes toward blacks—or, in the case of those who were light enough to pass, toward a masked existence among whites'" (quoting Eric Sundquist, *To Wake*

the Nations: Race in the Making of American Literature [Cambridge, Mass.: Harvard University Press, 1993], 245).

10. Langston Hughes, "The Negro Artist and the Racial Mountain," *Nation*, June 23, 1926: "For racial culture the home of a self-styled 'high-class' Negro has nothing better to offer. Instead there will be perhaps more aping of things white than in a less cultured or less wealthy home. The father is perhaps a doctor, lawyer, landowner, or politician. The mother may be a social worker, or a teacher, or she may do nothing and have a maid. Father is often dark but he has usually married the lightest woman he could find. The family attend a fashionable church where few really colored faces are to be found. And they themselves draw a color line. In the North they go to white theaters and white movies. And in the South they have at least two cars and a house 'like white folks.' Nordic manners, Nordic faces, Nordic hair, Nordic art (if any), and an Episcopal heaven. A very high mountain indeed for the would-be racial artist to climb in order to discover himself and his people."

11. Kuenz, "American Racial Discourse," 176.

12. Weinbrot, *Menippean Satire Reconsidered*, 7.

13. Andrew Buni, *Robert L. Vann of the Pittsburgh Courier: Politics and Black Journalism* (Pittsburgh: University of Pittsburgh Press, 1974).

14. Schuyler, *Black and Conservative*, 330.

15. Ibid., 350.

16. Ishmael Reed, introduction to Schuyler, *Black No More*, ix.

17. Schuyler, *Black and Conservative*, 102.

18. Ibid., 121: "The people have to live and strive, and to do that they must have feelings of hope. . . . They need more optimism and less pessimism. Frederick Douglass saw that and so did Booker T. Washington."

19. Ibid., 154.

20. Frederick Law Olmsted, *The Cotton Kingdom: A Traveller's Observations on Cotton and Slavery in the American Slave States* (1861), ed. Arthur M. Schlesinger (New York: Alfred A. Knopf, 1953).

21. Schuyler, *Black and Conservative*, 173.

22. Ibid., 181.

23. George S. Schuyler, *Slaves Today: A Story of Liberia* (New York: Brewer, Warren and Putnam, 1931), 6: "All of the characters are taken from real life. . . . If this novel can help arouse enlightened world opinion against this brutalizing of the native population of a Negro republic, perhaps the conscience of civilized people will stop similar atrocities in native lands ruled by proud white nations that boast of their superior culture."

24. Schuyler, *Black No More*, xix–xx: in addition to "Kink-No-More," a hair-straightening compound allegedly invented in Asbury Park, N.J., Schuyler mentions one Dr. Yusaburo Noguchi in Japan who was reported to have changed a Negro into a white man by "glandular control and electrical nutrition."

25. In his reading of this scene Jason Haslam finds all this "a decidedly un-satirically presented instance of hatred," but we cannot agree. It is precisely the workings of hatred in both the author of the satire and the events within it that raise it to the kind of savagery familiar in Juvenal and Swift: everything is in the details, the more detailed, the better. See Jason Haslam, "'The Open Sesame of Pork-colored Skin': Whiteness and Privilege in *Black No More*," *Modern Language Studies* 32, no. 1 (2002): 15–30, esp. 27.

26. For Schuyler's signifying (classically speaking, satirizing) of the allegedly scientific bases for racism, see Stacey Morgan, "'The Strange and Wonderful Workings of Science': Race Science and Essentialism in George Schuyler's *Black No More*," *CLA Journal* 42 (1999): 331–51, esp. 337–47.

27. Kuenz, "American Racial Discourse," 188: "Certainly color is meaningless to Schuyler except as a social category, and though many of us might take that as a crucial exception, Schuyler's entire novel is devoted to mocking the notion that it could be anything else."

28. *Satires* 1.1.69: *quid rides? mutato nomine de te fabula narratur.*

29. See Ishmael Reed and Steve Cannon's interview with Schuyler originally published in *Yardbird* 2 (1973), later republished in "George S. Schuyler, Writer," in *Shrovetide in Old New Orleans*, ed. Ishmael Reed (Garden City, N.Y.: Doubleday, 1978), 195–218.

30. This revisionist move to an Afro-centric use of history can be traced back to classical antiquity; see Selden, "*Aithiopika* and Ethiopianism," 187–200.

31. "Atonist" is Reed's analogical formation from "atonal," suggesting something that does not harmonize with anything else.

32. Ishmael Reed, *The Free-Lance Pallbearers* (New York: Atheneum, 1988), 65. *Pallbearers* was written and published a year before King's assassination, at a time when he had many critics in black America both for his attempts to work within the American political world and for his opposition to black separatist movements.

33. Perhaps because of the outlandish role pepper sauce plays in his novel, Reed was constrained to use the generic "Louisiana Red" rather than the copyrighted brand name Tabasco. There are poetic considerations as well. The phrase is intriguing (Is it a person or a thing?) and has more jingle to it than a geographic name appropriated by copyright.

34. Hesiod, *Works and Days* 11–26.

35. *Conversations with Ishmael Reed*, ed. Bruce Dick and Amritjit Singh (Jackson: University of Mississippi Press, 1991), 52: "Gumbo is a metaphor for my writing. . . . The olden Creole cooks saw the possibility of exquisite and delicious combinations of making gumbo and hence we have many varieties until the occult science of a good gumbo à la Creole seems to find an inheritance of gastronomical lore to remain forever hidden away in the culture of this old southern metropolis. . . . You take the Knight Templars and any ideas from Western history and New Orleans jazz and painting and music and put all these things together into a gumbo."

36. See Gowers, *The Loaded Table*, 103–26, especially her culinary take on Roman satire as, literally, a humble fare: "Miscellaneous, and wallowing in the muddy and messy areas of life, satire drags itself straight down to the bottom of Roman literary hierarchy, which has room for epic, tragedy, and history, unified, important genres, at the top. From the earliest times, it was a rag-bag which held all the aspects of Roman life for which there was no room anywhere else: autobiography, jokes, daily conversation, miscellaneous lists. And food, a subject which provokes blushes and apologies, a subject which, however civilized, is inextricably linked to bodily functions, belongs there too. Satire is Rome's own humble pie, composed of the offal of every other genre" (124).

37. Ishmael Reed, *The Last Days of Louisiana Red* (New York: Atheneum, 1989).

38. Marian Musgrave, "Ishmael Reed's Black Oedipus Cycle," *Obsidian* 6 (1980): 60–67, quotation on 61–62.

39. George Steiner, *Antigones* (Oxford: Clarendon Press, 1986), 198.

40. Ishmael Reed, *New and Collected Poems* (New York: Atheneum, 1988), 107–8.

41. E.g., Jean Bethke Elstein, "Antigone's Daughters," in *Freedom, Feminism, and the State: An Overview of Individualist Feminism*, ed. Wendy McElroy (New York: Holmes and Meier, 1991), 61–75; cf. Winterer, *The Mirror of Antiquity*, 191–28 and 233n26.

42. Steiner, *Antigones*, 1: "Between c. 1790 and c. 1905, it was widely held by European poets, philosophers, scholars that Sophocles' *Antigone* was not only the finest of Greek tragedies, but a work of art nearer to perfection than any other produced by the human spirit."

43. Cf. R. Bracht Branham, *Unruly Eloquence: Lucian and the Comedy of Traditions* (Cambridge, Mass.: Harvard University Press, 1989), 130: "Given the centrality of literature and the memorization of texts to the classicizing ideology of Greeks in the empire, it is easy to see why satire might come to rely so heavily on parody as a means: in Lucian the parodied text or genre is as often the weapon as the target of satire."

44. Reed, *Louisiana Red*, 24.

45. Aristotle, *Poetics* 9.1452a1.

46. Steiner, *Antigones*, 198.

47. Ibid., 292–93: "This death (was A. S. more than seventeen?) lives for me in the play, and emphatically, in Haemon's impatience."

48. Sophocles' choruses in his other surviving tragedies are usually closer in identity and more in sympathy with his protagonists; Sophocles, *Antigone*, ed. Mark Griffith (Cambridge: Cambridge University Press, 1999), 11: "An especially crucial choice for the playwright, in determining mood, dynamics, and point(s) of view, is that of the identity and character of the Chorus. In this case, by making them elderly Theban citizens, who are by gender, age, status, and experience much closer to Creon than to Antigone, Sophocles has isolated his heroine to an unusual degree, and has also provided a subtly distorting filter or lens for the audience's reception of the stage action." For an appreciation of the largely unfamiliar conventions of choral performance with particular attention to later attempts to understand them, see also Steiner, *Antigones*, 166–77.

49. Musgrave, "Reed's Oedipus Cycle," 64.

50. Steiner, *Antigones*, 300–301.

51. Ishmael Reed, *Writin' Is Fightin': Thirty-Seven Years of Boxing on Paper* (New York: Atheneum, 1988).

52. Musgrave, "Reed's Oedipus Cycle," 66n1, citing the standard mythological handbook that Reed would have been likely to use: H. J. Rose, *A Handbook of Greek Mythology* (New York: E. P. Dutton, 1959), 193 and 222. For a more recent exposition of the variants in the Antigone myth, including this one, see Timothy Gantz, *Early Greek Myth: A Guide to Literary and Artistic Sources* (Baltimore: Johns Hopkins University Press, 1993), 519–22.

53. Musgrave, "Reed's Oedipus Cycle," 63.

54. Thus Steiner begins *Antigones* with a Montaigne reference and its explication: "We are 'only the interpreters of interpretations'; so Montaigne—who is himself echoing Plato's description of the rhapsode as *herméneôn hermênês* in the *Ion*."

55. Randall Kennedy, *Nigger: The Strange Career of a Troublesome Word* (New York: Vintage Books, 2003).

56. Jim Haskins, *Richard Pryor: A Man and His Madness* (New York: Beaufort Books, 1984), 142.

57. Kennedy, *Nigger*, 136–39.

58. Ibid., 155–56n86, quoting Richard Pryor, with Todd Gold, *Pryor Convictions and Other Life Sentences* (New York: Pantheon, 1995), 175.

59. E.g., the work of Claudia Mitchell-Kernan on Oakland, California, in *Language Behavior in a Black Urban Community* (Berkeley: Language-Behavior Research Laboratory, 1971).

60. Jim Haskins and Hugh F. Butts, M.D., *The Psychology of Black Language* (New York: Barnes and Noble Books, 1973), 19: "One of the psychological consequences of racial oppression is a lowering of self-esteem resulting from an identification with the aggressor and an incorporation of his values." In a blending of the analytical and the apologetic, they dedicate their work "to Black people everywhere because they and the rich and beautiful language they speak are responsible for this book" (v), with an epigraph from Lewis Carroll's *Through the Looking Glass*: "'But "glory" doesn't mean "a nice knock-down argument,"' Alice objected. 'When I use a word,' Humpty Dumpty said in rather a scornful tone, 'it means just what I choose it to mean—neither more nor less.' 'The question is,' said Alice, 'whether you can make words mean so many different things.' 'The question is,' said Humpty Dumpty, 'which is to be Master—that's all'" (xiii).

61. David Dalby, "Black through White: Patterns of Communication in Africa and the New World," in *Black-White Speech Relationships*, ed. Walt Wolfram and Nona H. Clarke (Washington, D.C.: Center for Applied Linguistics, 1971), 99–138, quotation on 100.

62. Ibid., 100–101.

63. For an anthropological scrutiny of classicists and their ways, see James M. Redfield, "Anthropology and the Classics," *Arion* 1.2 (Spring 1991): 5–23.

64. Jessie Fauset, *Plum Bun: A Novel without a Moral* (Boston: Beacon Press, 1990). The heroine is light-skinned and learns why passing as white is not desirable. As will become clear, Oreo has great philological and lexicographical acumen and wouldn't be caught dead in the clichés of a tragic mulatta story.

65. "Memorable Quotes from *Blazing Saddles*": http://www.imdb.com/title/tt0071230/ quotes.

66. "The Henny Youngman Definitive Collection" (http://www.funny2.com/henny.htm); see Henny Youngman, *Take My Wife . . . Please! My Life and Laughs* (New York, Putnam, 1973).

67. For a full philological account of the work, beginning with its title, see Seneca, *Apocolocyntosis*, ed. P. T. Eden (Cambridge: Cambridge University Press, 1984).

68. Like the names discussed in Levitt and Dubner's *Freakonomics*, the *redender Name* (German, a "speaking" or "signifying name") is a pervasive feature of archaic literature in many traditions; in addition to Nagy's work on Homer, see "Adam," the "earth creature," "made from earth" in Genesis, one of many etymologies discussed by Phyllis Trible in *God and the Rhetoric of Sexuality* (Philadelphia: Fortress Press, 1978).

69. A wordplay "impossible to reproduce in English"; *Plutarch: Lives*, vol. 1, trans. Bernadotte Perrin (Cambridge, Mass.: Harvard University Press, 1914), 9.

70. The only substantial biography of Fran Ross to date is in Harryette Mullen's foreword to her edition of *Oreo*: Fran Ross, *Oreo* (Boston: Northeastern University Press, 2000), xi–xxviii. See also Mullen's later critical essay, "'Apple Pie with Oreo Crust': Fran Ross's Recipe for an Idiosyncratic American Novel," *Melus* 27 (2002): 107–29.

71. Ross's key (209–12) enables readers to find out on their own all the parallels between Theseus's story and Oreo's. Like the lexicography and etymologies, this is a send-up as much as a demonstration that the author has done her homework, a typical move for learned Menippean satirists.

72. Anne G. Ward et al., *The Quest for Theseus* (New York: Praeger, 1970).

73. Joseph Campbell, *The Hero with a Thousand Faces*, 2nd ed. (Princeton: Princeton University Press, 1968), 30–31.

74. A black-figure vase painting of Theseus and Sciron's dangerous turtle appears in Ward et al., *Quest for Theseus*, 13.

75. For greater detail as well as genealogical charts and maps of Theseus's route and exploits, see Ruth B. Edwards, "The Story of Theseus," in Ward et al., *The Quest for Theseus*, 7–24.

76. Leo Rosten, *The Joys of Yiddish* (New York: McGraw Hill, 1968).

77. This is a much simplified version of the family tree adapted from Ward et al., *The Quest for Theseus*, 8.

78. There are abundant etymological studies of English surnames, including three published in a single year not so long before *Oreo* appeared; Percy H. Reaney, *The Origin of English Surnames* (New York: Barnes and Noble, 1967); C. M. Matthews, *English Surnames* (London: Weidenfeld & Nicolson, 1966; New York: Scribners, 1967); and Alfred J. Kolatch, *The Name Dictionary: Modern English and Hebrew Names* (New York: J. David, 1967).

79. *Nu* from Russian *nu*, "well," "well now," is cognate with English "now" and, per Rosten, "the word most frequently used in speaking Yiddish. And with good reason: *nu* is the verbal equivalent of a sigh, a frown, a grin, a grunt, a sneer." *The Joys of Yiddish*, 167–68. As the present note illustrates, philological commentary easily breeds more philological commentary.

80. The citation "*c*nt*" is slightly in error; see Eric Partridge, *Origins: A Short Etymological Dictionary of Modern English* (London: Routledge & Kegan Paul, 1958), 135, s.v. "c**t."

81. Eric Partridge, *A Dictionary of Clichés* (London: George Routledge & Sons, 1941), 2.

82. Partridge, *Dictionary of Clichés*, 7: "Is not the primary criterion of a cliché its commonplaceness, its too frequent employment, rather than its phrase-nature? In short, the extensive use, not the phrasal quality, determines the cliché. Moreover, the cliché is often uneconomical and nearly always unnecessary. *I do not wish to labor the point*; but is not 'to all intents and purposes' inferior to 'virtually,' '*bête noir*' to 'bugbear,' 'to have neither chick nor child' to 'to be childless'"?

83. Partridge, *Origins*, 239, s.v. f**k.

84. Oreo of course has no choice but to say "Scott" again, since both his surname and Christian name (French *prénom*) are the same.

85. Campbell, *Hero with a Thousand Faces*, 116.

86. Cf. Tru Leverette, "Traveling Identities: Mixed Race Quests and Fran Ross's *Oreo*," *African American Review* 40 (2006): 89: "She is a utopian character not limited by stereotypes of race or gender but one who, instead, offers new options for identity through an understanding of history and through broadened understandings of the present and future. She illustrates the problematic metaphors of mixed race identity that suggest such individuals are travelers to utopian spaces of racial harmony, pioneers who may lead society to a utopian future Indeed, Ross's character is a precursor for postmodern imaginings of racial mixture; she is representative of metaphors that acknowledge an Oreo as made of both cookie and cream, that depict the mixed-race individual as two together, no matter where that one (or two-in-one) may travel."

Chapter Eight

1. Ekaterini Georgoudaki sees the poem mainly as an attack on the scholar's misogyny in "Rita Dove: Crossing Boundaries," *Callaloo* 14, no. 2 (1991): 419–33, esp. 423; besides the sexism and racism of the scholar, Bonnie Costello observes the poet-teacher's care for her

students in "Scars and Wings: Rita Dove's *Grace Notes*," *Callaloo* 14, no. 2 (1991): 434–38, esp. 437; Helen Vendler, on the other hand, granting that "race is the central concern," finds the poem a failure "because it has no imaginative interest in the lecturer whom it accuses of racism"; "Rita Dove: Identity Markers," *Callaloo* 17, no. 2 (1994): 381–98; quotations at 393 and 398n21. See also the pioneering work of Deborah Roberts, "The Drunk and the Policeman: Arrowsmith, Convention, and the Changing Context of Twentieth-Century Translation" (paper delivered at the Postmodern Language Association annual meetings in 2000), 8–9 on *Arrow*; Elizabeth Scharffenberger, "Aristophanes' *Thesmophoriazousai* and the Challenges of Comic Translation: The Cast of William Arrowsmith's *Euripides Agonistes*," *American Journal of Philology* 123 (2002): 429–63, esp. 458–59 on "Arrow"; Edith Hall, "The Scythian Archer in Aristophanes' *Themophoriazusae*," in her *The Theatrical Case of Athens: Interactions between Ancient Greek Drama and Society* (Oxford: Oxford University Press, 2006), 225–54, esp. 253–54 and note 103.

2. Marjorie Garber and Nancy J. Vickers, eds., *The Medusa Reader* (New York: Routledge, 2003), 258. The excerpt from Jean-Pierre Vernant ("Frontality and Monstrosity," 210–31) explains the fascination of the Gorgon's face throughout Greek myth and the changing images of it that the Greeks themselves had: "Depending on the case, Gorgo's image [sc. Latin *Gorgon* from Greek *Gorgô*, the generic name for Medusa and her sister Gorgons] can lean toward either the horrible or the grotesque. It may appear terrifying or ridiculous, repulsive or attractive. Sometimes the charming traits of a monster who grimaces in a hideous smile. From the late fifth century, at the moment itself when the motif of the mirror arises, the turning point begins that will lead to representing Medusa as a young woman of marvelous beauty" (227).

3. Therese Steffen, *Crossing Color: Transcultural Space and Place in Rita Dove's Poetry, Fiction, and Drama* (Oxford: Oxford University Press, 2001), 82: "The laugh of the Medusa shatters any placid surface constituted by the petrifying gaze of a single hermeneutic decoding. Dove's 'Medusa' always remains one leap or one dive ahead of the pack."

4. In a reading of these and other poems at Dartmouth in 1982, Arrowsmith in fact finally declined to read more than a few lines from the Aristophanes translation, merely alluding to it as unperformable in the current climate of opinion.

5. Scharffenberger, "Aristophanes' *Thesmophoriazousai*," 459 and note 46.

6. Drawing on Deborah Roberts's 2000 paper "The Drunk and the Policeman," Elizabeth Scharffenberger provides a full account of Arrowsmith's and other translators' efforts to render ancient ethnic humor for modern audiences ("Aristophanes' *Thesmophoriazusai*," 459): "The subsequent verses of Dove's poem indicate that the translator publicly defended his rendering as an effort to 'celebrate our differences,' and, when I met him in 1991, Arrowsmith assured me that he did not intend his translation of *Thesmophoriazousa* to convey a racist message, and that the Soldier was meant neither to harm nor offend."

7. Tim Reynolds, *Peace*, in *The Tenth Muse: Classical Drama in Translation*, ed. Charles Doria (Chicago: Swallow; Athens: Ohio University Press, 1980), 315–420, quotation at 321.

8. Douglass Parker, "WAA: An Intruded Gloss," *Arion*, 3rd ser., 2.2 and 2.3 (1992–1993), 251–66.

9. Stokely Carmichael and Charles V. Hamilton, *Black Power: The Politics of Liberation in America* (New York: Random House, 1967), 44–56.

10. Vendler, "Rita Dove," 393.

11. A rare example of such a title is the Latin of Sutton Griggs's 1899 novel *Imperium in Imperio*, about a separatist black empire within the white American empire. But the title

amounts to not much more than a learned way of saying "The Empire within an Empire," with no classical connection beyond the title page; Sutton E. Griggs, *Imperium in Imperio* (New York: Modern Library, 2003).

12. Therese Steffen, *Crossing Color*, 112: "Any threshold is a space to move through daringly and judgingly, but as a puppeteer Virginia is familiar with the nature of illusion, that is, the proscenium as well as the shifting between imagination and reality."

13. Rita Dove, *Through the Ivory Gate* (New York: Pantheon, 1992), 154–55. The translation quoted is by Robert Fitzgerald, then and still now the best (or most poetic) of *Odyssey* translations.

14. Rita Dove, *Fifth Sunday: Stories* (Lexington: University of Kentucky Press, 1985), 59–68.

15. Aristotle, *Poetics* 16.1454b20–1455a15. The least artistic kind of discovery in tragedy is made by tokens, letters, etc., while the best arises from incidents like the shepherd's innocent appearance before Oedipus in Sophocles — or Amalia and Augustus's sudden discovery of their kinship in *The Darker Face of the Earth: A Play by Rita Dove*, 3rd ed. (Ashland, Ore.: Story Line Press, 2000).

16. Malin Pereira, "'When the pear blossoms / cast their pale faces on / the darker face of the earth': Miscegenation, the Primal Scene, and the Incest Motif in Rita Dove's Work," *African American Review* 36, no. 2 (2002): 195–211. This paper appears in a slightly more muted form in Pereira's book *Rita Dove's Cosmopolitanism* (Urbana: University of Illinois Press, 2002), 31–52, though it keeps the tendentious phrase "cultural mulatto" in spite of Dove's objection (50n1) to Trey Ellis's deliberate confusion of artistic and personal identities — an objection we agree with. See Trey Ellis, "The New Black Aesthetic," *Callaloo* 12 (1989): 233–43.

17. Dove's own account of the writing and revising of *Darker Face* is not the kind of confessional that psychoanalytic criticism inspires, but focuses instead on the work she had to do to think through and write a challenging work for the theater. By the end of it she had a script that succeeds in adapting Sophocles' *Oedipus* into a tragedy of American and African American character and fate; see her interview with Robert McDowell in *Darker Face of the Earth* (3rd ed., 2000), 153–63.

18. Therese Steffen, *Crossing Color: Transcultural space and place in Rita Dove's Poetry, Fiction, and Drama* (Oxford: Oxford University Press, 2001, 174.

19. John P. Jackson, Jr., *Social Scientists for Social Justice: Making the Case against Segregation* (New York: New York University Press, 2001).

20. Ibid., 135–45, 153–55, 220–22.

21. Ibid., 137.

22. Pereira, "When the pear blossoms," 205; Mike Hammer and Christina Daub, "Interview," *Plum Review* 9 (1996): 27–41.

23. See Asli Gocer's discussion of the Myth of the Cave and its connections to popular comic art and satire, "The Puppet Theater in Plato's Parable of the Cave," *Classical Journal* 95 (1999): 110–29, "Plato's famous worry is that the majority is childlike, because like children most people judge anything on basis of the immediate and primal pleasure it brings about. Certainly the common man thinks that puppet theater is good simply because it makes him laugh."

24. Scott Cutler Shershow, *Puppets and "Popular" Culture* (Ithaca: Cornell University Press, 1995), 222–23: "One puppeteer declared to me sadly that just as children's theater

seems doomed to remain a small and subordinate branch of theater, so adult puppetry seems doomed to remain an even smaller and correspondingly subordinate branch of puppetry. Not even the most relentless efforts of aesthetes and theorists to reclaim the performing object as an autonomous form of theatrical art seem likely soon to break the peculiar link between the puppet and the child that prevails in contemporary culture."

25. George Haley, "The Narrator in *Don Quixote*: Maestro Pedro's Puppet Show," *Modern Language Notes* 80, no. 2, Spanish issue (1965): 145–65, esp. 160.

26. Wayne Ude, "Having the Picture Coalesce in a Kind of Whoosh!," in Rita Dove, *Conversations with Rita Dove*, ed. Earl G. Ingersoll (Jackson: University Press of Mississippi, 2003), 91: "One thing that disturbs me sometimes about the form of a novel is its tendency to wrap everything up—the compulsion to bring the main character to a big realization so all the pieces fall into place, and the story can deliver its punch. Life just ain't like that. Life sometimes offers little revelations, and their consequence may never find any kind of dramatic fruition, or their drama may be played out so late in the characters' lives, after so many other events, that it would ruin the shape of your novel."

27. Steffen, *Crossing Color*, 120.

28. Shershow, *Puppets and "Popular" Culture*, 241.

29. Dove, *Darker Face of the Earth* (3rd ed., 2000), 158.

30. Ibid., 158–59.

31. Therese Steffen, "The Darker Face: A Conversation with Rita Dove," *Transition* 74 (1997): 172, "When the play was workshopped in Oregon in 1994, people complained about the death of Augustus, and their argument was that in the original, Oedipus lives. To me, that was no argument to change the ending. It wasn't until I began working through the play again that I realized that the tragedy of the original Oedipus is that he is a living dead man. So it doesn't really matter whether Augustus lives or dies; either he dies and that's it, or he lives, but in a nihilistic sense. Ultimately we know only what history tells us: this slave rebellion will fail, has failed. Since we know how slavery ended, we can also imagine the end of Augustus; though he is still alive at the end of the play, we know what the immediate future holds."

32. Ibid.

33. Pereira, "Interview with Rita Dove," 160–61.

34. Instead of cluttering the text with a forest of quotation marks, we here adapt a technique known in contemporary American collegial manuals of plagiarism as the "mosaic"; the arresting language in this paragraph that is not in quotation marks is a mosaic of phrases taken directly from Rita Dove, *Mother Love* (New York: W. W. Norton, 1995), xi–xii.

35. Charles Segal, *Orpheus: The Myth of the Poet* (Baltimore: Johns Hopkins University Press, 1989), 118–54, esp. 127: "Even as early as the fifth century B.C., Orpheus served as a symbol for the persuasive power of poetry over death. But Rilke abandons that one-dimensional meaning of the Orpheus myth for a more complex vision. His Orpheus is a symbol of process rather than fixity, a locus where irreconcilable, and therefore tragic, oppositions meet. The power of language that he symbolizes is not merely language as magical persuasion but language reaching toward transcendence while yet not denying its ground in the time, death and suffering of language users, mortals."

36. Helene P. Foley, ed., *The Homeric Hymn to Demeter: Translation, Commentary, and Interpretive Essays* (Princeton: Princeton University Press, 1994), 151–69.

37. Rainer Maria Rilke, *The Best of Rilke*, trans. Walter Arndt (Hanover: Dartmouth College, University Press of New England, 1989), 144–45.

38. Pat Righelato, *Understanding Rita Dove* (Columbia: University of South Carolina Press, 2006), 142–73, quotation at 169.

39. Foley, *The Homeric Hymn to Demeter*, 169.

40. Steffen, *Crossing Color*, 131.

41. Ibid., 138.

42. Timothy Gantz, *Early Greek Myth: A Guide to Literary and Artistic Sources* (Baltimore: Johns Hopkins University Press, 1993), 63–70.

43. James I. Porter, "What Is 'Classical' about Classical Antiquity?," in *Classical Pasts: The Classical Traditions of Greece and Rome*, ed. James I. Porter (Princeton: Princeton University Press, 2006), 1–68, esp. 50–53.

44. E.g., the argument that the *Odyssey* and Athenian cults developed at the same time and influenced each other; see Erwin Cook, *The Odyssey in Athens: Myths of Cultural Origins* (Ithaca: Cornell University Press, 1995), 128–79.

45. Foley, *Homeric Hymn to Demeter*, 30–31.

46. Ibid., 28–29.

47. Segal, *Orpheus*, 125: "The *Sonnets* are both multiple and unitary; they are fifty-five separate poems, each one complete in itself, and also compose a unified *Sonnet*-book. They may therefore be viewed on both a paradigmatic and a syntagmatic axis, both as symbol and as narrative. Each sonnet is a separate interpretation and realization of the meaning of Orpheus; yet the succession of individual sonnets also follows a quasi-narrative development or syntagmatic progression."

48. In her translation Helene Foley follows the widespread custom of Hellenists in transliterating the Greek names rather than laundering them through Latin. All subsequent translations of the Homeric *Hymn* are by her.

49. *The Annotated Mother Goose*, ed. William S. Baring-Gould and Celia Baring-Gould (New York: C. N. Potter, 1962), 20–21.

50. For a reading of the *Hymn to Demeter* that stresses divine (and mortal) political calculations, see Jenny Strauss Clay, *The Politics of Olympus: Form and Meaning in the Major Homeric Hymns* (Princeton: Princeton University Press, 1989).

51. The two female goddesses who merely hear the cries of Persephone are balanced by Helios, who actually sees her. Foley, *Homeric Hymn to Demeter*, 38: "The text emphasizes the isolation of Demeter and Hekate from the rest of the universe. . . . This passage (51–89) emphasizes the important theme of seeing and hearing in the poem. The narcissus is wonderful to *see* (10, 427). Hekate and Demeter alone of gods or mortals *hear* the cry (22–23, 39)."

52. John Ashbery, *Selected Poems* (New York: Penguin, 1986), 221.

53. Foley, *Homeric Hymn to Demeter*, 48.

54. Ibid., 50–51.

55. Norman Holmes Pearson, foreword to H.D., *Hermetic Definitions* (New York: New Directions, 1972), v–vi.

56. Pereira, *Rita Dove's Cosmopolitanism*, 146.

57. Rita Dove, "Motherhood," in *Thomas and Beulah: Poems* (Pittsburgh: Carnegie-Mellon University Press, 1986).

58. Foley, *Homeric Hymn to Demeter*, 92: "By bringing divinity closer to mortal suffering and mortals closer to divine power, the story pattern of wrath, withdrawal, and return as it is enacted in both the *Iliad* and the *Hymn* mixes worlds that the entire Greek cosmos is

designed to keep apart. When the world is reconstructed at the return, it can never be quite the same."

59. Righelato, *Understanding Rita Dove*, 165.

60. Foley, *Homeric Hymn to Demeter*, 60: "Demophoön is symbolically reincorporated into the world of mortals by a gesture and scenario reminiscent of the Amphidromia, rather than completing an initiation into immortality."

61. In Foley's translation, the names are in fact simply transliterated, as is often the custom in contemporary Hellenists' translations. While we do not ourselves care for this practice when it pronounces the puzzling "Akhilleus" for the Romanized "Achilles," the advantage in this particular passage is that the transliterated names give a fair idea of what it all sounds like in the original Greek. This is something that laundering the names through Latin of course obscures.

62. Righelato, *Understanding Rita Dove*, 167.

63. Foley, *Homeric Hymn to Demeter*, 63–64.

64. Steffen, *Crossing Color*, 139.

65. Pereira, *Rita Dove's Cosmopolitanism*, 151; similarly, Righelato, *Understanding Rita Dove*, 169.

Bibliography

Alford, Richard D. *Naming and Identity: A Cross-Cultural Study of Personal Naming Practices.* New Haven, Conn.: Human Relations Area Files Press, 1987.

Allen, Woody. "Notes from the Overfed." *New Yorker*, March 16, 1968.

Ammons, Elizabeth. *Conflicting Stories: American Women Writers at the Turn into the Twentieth Century.* New York: Oxford University Press, 1992.

Andrews, William. *The Oxford Frederick Douglass Reader.* New York: Oxford University Press, 1996.

Apollodorus. *Gods and Heroes of the Greeks: The Library of Apollodorus.* Translated with an introduction and notes by Michael Simpson. Amherst: University of Massachusetts Press, 1976.

Aptheker, Herbert. *The Negro People in America: A Critique of Gunnar Myrdal's "An American Dilemma."* New York: International Publishers, 1946.

Aristophanes. *Aristophanes: The Complete Plays.* Translated by Paul Roche. New York: New American Library, 2005.

Aristotle. *Aristotle: On the Art of Poetry.* Translated by Ingram Bywater. Oxford: Clarendon Press, 1959.

Asante, Molefi Kete. *The Afrocentric Idea.* Revised and expanded ed. Philadelphia: Temple University Press, 1997.

Ashbery, John. *Selected Poems.* New York: Penguin, 1986.

Bailey, Derek. *Musical Improvisation: Its Nature and Practice in Music.* New York: Da Capo Press, 1993.

Baker, Houston A., Jr. "A Forgotten Prototype: *The Autobiography of an Ex-Coloured Man* and *Invisible Man.*" *Virginia Quarterly Review* 49 (1973): 433–49.

Bakhtin, Mikhail. *The Dialogic Imagination: Four Essays.* Edited by Michael Holquist. Translated by Caryl Emerson and Michael Holquist. Austin: University of Texas Press, 1981.

Baring-Gould, William S., and Celia Baring-Gould. *The Annotated Mother Goose*. New York: C. N. Potter, 1962.

Barkan, Leonard. *The Gods Made Flesh: Metamorphosis and the Pursuit of Paganism*. New Haven: Yale University Press, 1986.

Bennett, Paula. "Phillis Wheatley's Vocation and the Paradox of the 'Afric Muse.'" Special issue, Ethnicity, *PMLA* 113, no. 1 (1998): 64–76.

Bercovitch, Sacvan. *The American Jeremiad*. Madison: University of Wisconsin Press, 1978.

Bernal, Martin. *Black Athena: The Afroasiatic Roots of Classical Civilization*. New Brunswick, N.J.: Rutgers University Press, 1987–2006.

Bérubé, Michael. *Marginal Forces/Cultural Centers: Tolson, Pynchon, and the Politics of the Canon*. Ithaca: Cornell University Press, 1992.

Beye, Charles Rowan. *Epic and Romance in the Argonautica of Apollonius*. Carbondale: Southern Illinois University Press, 1982.

Bingham, Caleb. *The Columbian Orator: Containing a Variety of Original and Selected Pieces; Together with Rules; Calculated to Improve Youth and Others in the Ornamental and Useful Art of Eloquence*. Boston: J. H. A. Frost, 1832.

Bloom, Harold. *Ralph Ellison*. Edited and with an introduction by Harold Bloom. Philadelphia: Chelsea House, 2003.

———. *Robert Hayden*. Philadelphia: Chelsea House, 2005.

Boime, Albert. *The Art of Exclusion: Representing Blacks in the Nineteenth Century*. Washington, D.C.: Smithsonian Institution Press, 1990.

Bowersock, G. W. *Greek Sophists in the Roman Empire*. Oxford: Oxford University Press, 1969.

Branham, R. Bracht. "Defacing the Currency: Diogenes' Rhetoric and the Invention of Cynicism." In *The Cynics: The Cynic Movement in Antiquity and Its Legacy*, ed. R. Bracht Branham and Mari-Odile Goulet-Cazé. Berkeley: University of California Press, 1996.

———. *Unruly Eloquence: Lucian and the Comedy of Traditions*. Cambridge, Mass.: Harvard University Press, 1989.

Breau, Elizabeth. "Identifying Satire: Our Nig." *Callaloo* 16, no. 2 (1993): 455–65.

Briggs, Ward W., Jr., and Herbert W. Benario, eds. *Basil Lanneau Gildersleeve: An American Classicist*. Baltimore: Johns Hopkins University Press, 1986.

Brown, William Wells. *My Southern Home, or, The South and Its People (1880): From Fugitive Slave to Free Man; The Autobiographies of William Wells Brown*. Edited with an introduction by William L. Andrews. Columbia: University of Missouri Press, 2003.

———. *Narrative of William A. Brown, A Fugitive Slave, Written by Himself*. In *From Fugitive Slave to Free Man: The Autobiographies of William Wells Brown*, edited and with an introduction by William L. Andrews. Columbia: University of Missouri Press, 2003.

Broyard, Bliss. *One Drop: My Father's Hidden Life: A Story of Race and Family Secrets*. New York: Little, Brown, 2007.

Bulfinch, Thomas. *The Age of Fable; or, Beauties of Mythology*. Boston: S. W. Tilton, 1855.

Buni, Andrew. *Robert L. Vann of the Pittsburgh Courier: Politics and Black Journalism*. Pittsburgh: University of Pittsburgh Press, 1974.

Burnell, Peter. "The Death of Turnus and Roman Morality." *Greece and Rome*, 2nd ser., 34, no. 2 (1987): 186–200.

Bury, Adrian. *Richard Wilson R.A.: The Grand Classic*. Leigh-on-Sea: F. Lewis, 1947.

Butler, Robert J. "Dante's *Inferno* and Ellison's *Invisible Man*: A Study in Literary Continuity." *College Language Association Journal* 28 (1984): 54–77.

Butler, Shane. "Cicero's Capita," *Litterae Caelestes* 4 (2009): 9–42.

———. *The Hand of Cicero*. London: Routledge, 2002.

Campbell, Joseph. *The Hero with a Thousand Faces*, 2nd ed. Princeton: Princeton University Press, 1968.

Camus, Marcel. *Orfeu Negro [1959]*. Lopert Films, Inc.; Co-Production Franco-Italienne, Dispatfilm, Gemma Cinematografica avec la participation de Tupan Filmes LTDA. Extended International Version. Irvington, N.Y.: Criterion Collection, 1999.

Carmichael, Stokely, and Charles V. Hamilton. *Black Power: The Politics of Liberation in America*. New York: Random House, 1967.

Carnegie, Andrew. "Wealth." *North American Review* 148, no. 391 (June 1889): 653–57.

Chapman, John Jay. *Two Greek Plays*. Boston: Houghton Mifflin, 1928.

Child, Julia et al. *Mastering the Art of French Cooking*. New York: Knopf, 1961–1970.

The Classick Pages: Classical Reading in Eighteenth-Century America. Edited by Meyer Reinhold. State College: Pennsylvania State University Press, 1975.

Clausen, Wendell. *A Commentary on Virgil, Eclogues*. Oxford: Clarendon Press, 1994.

Clay, Jenny Strauss. *The Politics of Olympus: Form and Meaning in the Major Homeric Hymns*. Princeton: Princeton University Press, 1989.

———. *The Wrath of Athena: Gods and Men in the "Odyssey."* Princeton: Princeton University Press, 1983.

Cmiel, Kenneth. *Democratic Eloquence: The Fight over Popular Speech in Nineteenth-Century America*. New York: William Morrow, 1990.

Coffey, Michael. *Roman Satire*. London: Methuen; New York: Barnes and Noble, 1976.

Cook, Erwin. *The Odyssey in Athens: Myths of Cultural Origins*. Ithaca: Cornell University Press, 1995.

Cook, William W. "The Mouth's the Message: Language in Melvin Tolson's *Harlem Gallery*." Paper presented at the annual meeting of the College Language Association, Jackson, Miss., April 21–23, 1977.

Costello, Bonnie. "Scars and Wings: Rita Dove's *Grace Notes*." *Callaloo* 14, no. 2 (1991): 434–38.

Cowherd, Carrie. "The Wings of Atalanta: Classical Influences in *The Souls of Black Folk*." In *The Souls of Black Folk: One Hundred Years Later*, edited and with an introduction by Dolan Hubbard, 284–97. Columbia: University of Missouri Press, 2003.

Crane, Hart. *O My Land, My Friends: The Selected Letters of Hart Crane*. Edited by Langdon Hammer and Brom Weber. New York: Four Walls Eight Windows, 1997.

Crane, Stephen. "In the Desert." In *The Black Riders and Other Lines*. Boston: Small, Maynard, 1905.

Croll, Morris W. "The Cadence of English Oratorical Prose." *Studies in Philology* 16 (1919): 1–55.

Cullen, Countee. *The Ballad of the Brown Girl, an Old Ballad Retold*. With illustrations and decorations by Charles Cullen. New York: Harper & Brothers, 1927.

———. *The Black Christ & Other Poems*. New York: Harper & Brothers, 1929.

———. *Copper Sun*. New York: Harper & Brothers, 1927.

———. *The Medea of Euripides and Some Poems*. New York: Harper & Brothers, 1935.

———. *On These I Stand: An Anthology of the Best Poems of Countee Cullen*. New York: Harper and Brothers, 1947.

Dalby, David. "Black through White: Patterns of Communication in Africa and the New World." In *Black-White Speech Relationships*, ed. Walt Wolfram and Nona H. Clarke. Washington, D.C.: Center for Applied Linguistics, 1971.

Davis, Arthur P. *From the Dark Tower: Afro-American Writers, 1900 to 1960*. Washington, D.C.: Howard University Press, 1974.

Davis, Gregson. *Polyhymnia: The Rhetoric of Horatian Lyric Discourse*. Berkeley: University of California Press, 1991.

Davis, Natalie Zemon. *Slaves on Screen: Film and Historical Vision*. Cambridge, Mass.: Harvard University Press, 2000.

Deren, Maya. *Divine Horsemen: Voodoo Gods of Haiti*. Preface by Joseph Campbell. New York: Dell, 1972.

Detienne, Marcel, and Jean-Pierre Vernant. *Cunning Intelligence in Greek Culture and Society*. Translated by Janet Lloyd. Atlantic Highlands, N.J.: Humanities Press, 1978.

Dorsey, David F. "Countee Cullen's Use of Greek Mythology." *College Language Association Journal* 13 (1969): 68–77.

Dostoevsky, Fyodor. *Notes from Underground*. Edited and translated by Michael R. Katz. New York: W. W. Norton, 2001.

Douglass, Frederick. *Autobiographies: Narrative of the Life of Frederick Douglass, an American Slave; My Bondage and My Freedom; Life and Times of Frederick Douglass*. Edited by Henry Louis Gates, Jr. New York: Library of America, 1994.

———. *Frederick Douglass: The Narrative and Selected Writings*. Edited by Michael Meyer. New York: Modern Library, 1984.

———. *The Frederick Douglass Papers*. Ser. 1. Edited by John W. Blassingame. New Haven: Yale University Press, 1979–1992.

Dove, Rita. *Conversations with Rita Dove*. Edited by Earl G. Ingersoll. Jackson: University Press of Mississippi, 2003.

———. *The Darker Face of the Earth: A Play by Rita Dove*. 3rd ed. Ashland, Ore.: Story Line Press, 2000.

———. *The Darker Face of the Earth: A Verse Play in Fourteen Scenes*. Brownsville, Ore.: Story Line Press, 1994.

———. *Fifth Sunday: Stories*. Lexington: University of Kentucky Press, 1985.

———. *Grace Notes*. New York: W. W. Norton, 1989.

———. *Mother Love*. New York: W. W. Norton, 1995.

———. "Telling It Like I-S IS: Narrative Techniques in Melvin Tolson's *Harlem Gallery*." *New England Review and Breadloaf Quarterly* 8 (1985): 89–117.

———. *Thomas and Beulah: Poems*. Pittsburgh: Carnegie-Mellon University Press, 1986.

———. *Through the Ivory Gate*. New York: Pantheon Books, 1992.

Dryden, John. "On Translation." In *Theories of Translation: An Anthology of Essays from Dryden to Derrida*, ed. Rainer Schulte and John Biguenet. Chicago: University of Chicago Press, 1992.

———. Preface to *Ovid's Epistles*. In *Theories of Translation: An Anthology of Essays from Dryden to Derrida*, ed. Rainer Schulte and John Biguenet. Chicago: University of Chicago Press, 1992.

———. *The Works of John Dryden*. Vol. 5. Illustrated with notes by Sir Walter Scott. Edinburgh: A. Constable, 1821.

———. *The Works of Virgil*. Berkeley: University of California Press, 1987.

Du Bois, W. E. B. *Dusk of Dawn: An Essay toward an Autobiography of Race Concept*. New York: Oxford University Press, 2007.

———. "Phillis Wheatley and African American Culture." In *The Oxford W. E. B. Du Bois Reader*, ed. Eric J. Sundquist. New York: Oxford University Press, 1996.

———. "So the Girl Marries." In *W. E. B. Du Bois: A Reader*, ed. David Levering Lewis. New York: Henry Holt, 1985.

———. *The Souls of Black Folk*. Edited by Henry Louis Gates, Jr. and Terri Hume Oliver. New York: W. W. Norton, 1999.

———. *The World and Africa: An Inquiry into the Part which Africa Has Played in World History*. New enlarged ed. New York: International Publishers, 1965.

Dugan, John. "How to Make (and Break) a Cicero: Epideixis, Textuality, and Self-fashioning in the *Pro Archia* and *In Pisonem*." *Classical Antiquity* 20 (2001): 35–77.

Early, Gerald. *My Soul's High Song: The Collected Writings of Countee Cullen, Voice of the Harlem Renaissance*. New York: Doubleday, 1991.

Ellis, Trey. "The New Black Aesthetic." *Callaloo* 12 (1989): 233–43.

Eliot, T. S. *The Waste Land: A Facsimile and Transcript of the Original Drafts Including the Annotations of Ezra Pound*. Edited by Valerie Eliot. New York: Harcourt Brace, 1971.

Ellison, Ralph. "The Art of Fiction." *Paris Review* 8 (1955). Also published in *Shadow and Act* (New York: Random House, 1964).

———. *Invisible Man*. New York: Vintage Books, 1995.

———. "Out of the Hospital and under the Bar." In *Soon, One Morning: New Writing by American Negroes, 1940–1962*, ed. Herbert Hill, 242–90. New York: Alfred A. Knopf, 1963.

———. *Shadow and Act*. New York: Random House, 1964.

Euripides. *Medea*. Translated by Rex Warner. New York: Dover, 1993.

Farnsworth, Robert M. *Melvin B. Tolson, 1898–1966: Plain Talk and Poetic Prophecy*. Columbia: University of Missouri Press, 1984.

Fauset, Jessie. *The Chinaberry Tree: A Novel of American Life*. Philadelphia: J. B. Lippincott, 1931.

———. *The Chinaberry Tree: A Novel of American Life & Selected Writings*. With a new foreword by Marcy Jane Knopf. Boston: Northeastern University Press, 1995.

———. *Plum Bun: A Novel without a Moral*. Boston: Beacon Press, 1990.

Feeney, Joseph J. "Greek Tragic Patterns in a Black Novel: Jessie Fauset's *The Chinaberry Tree*." *College Language Association Journal* 18 (1974): 211–15.

Fiedler, Leslie. "Come Back to the Raft Ag'in, Huck Honey." *Partisan Review*, June 1948.

Fitzgerald, William. *Agonistic Poetry: The Pindaric Mode in Pindar, Horace, Hölderlin, and the English Ode*. Berkeley: University of California Press, 1987.

Fliegelman, Jay. *Declaring Independence: Jefferson, Natural Language, and the Culture of Performance*. Stanford: Stanford University Press, 1993.

Foley, Helene P., ed. *The Homeric Hymn to Demeter: Translation, Commentary, and Interpretive Essays*. Princeton: Princeton University Press, 1994.

———. "Medea's Divided Self." *Classical Antiquity* 8 (1989): 61–85.

Forrest, Leon. "Luminosity from the Lower Frequencies." In *Ralph Ellison's "Invisible Man": A Casebook*, ed. John F. Callahan. Oxford: Oxford University Press, 2004.

Fowler, Alastair. *Kinds of Literature: An Introduction to the Theory of Genres and Modes*. Cambridge: Harvard University Press, 1982.

Freccero, John. *Dante: The Poetics of Conversion*. Edited and with an introduction by Rachel Jackoff. Cambridge, Mass.: Harvard University Press, 1986.

Freudenburg, Kirk. *Satires of Rome: Threatening Poses from Lucilius to Juvenal*. Cambridge: Cambridge University Press, 2001.

Fry, Paul H. *The Poet's Calling in the English Ode*. New Haven: Yale University Press, 1980.

Frye, Northrop. *The Anatomy of Criticism*. Princeton: Princeton University Press, 1971.

Furth, Leslie. "'The Modern Medea' and Race Matters: Thomas Satterwhite Noble's 'Margaret Garner.'" *American Art* 12, no. 2 (1998): 37–57.

Fussell, Paul. *Theory of Prosody in Eighteenth-Century England*. New London: Connecticut College, 1954.

Galinsky, Karl. "The Anger of Aeneas." *American Journal of Philology* 109, no. 3 (1988): 321–48.

Gantz, Timothy. *Early Greek Myth: A Guide to Literary and Artistic Sources*. Baltimore: Johns Hopkins University Press, 1993.

Garber, Marjorie, and Nancy J. Vickers, eds. *The Medusa Reader*. New York: Routledge, 2003.

Gates, Henry Louis, Jr. "Binary Oppositions in Chapter One of *Narrative of the Life of Frederick Douglass: An American Slave Written by Himself*." In *Afro-American Literature: The Reconstruction of Instruction*, ed. Dexter Fisher and Robert B. Stepto, 212–32. New York: Modern Language Association, 1979.

———. Introduction. In *The Autobiography of an Ex-Coloured Man*. New York: Vintage Books, 1989.

———. *Lincoln on Race and Slavery*. Princeton: Princeton University Press, 2009.

———. *The Signifying Monkey: A Theory of African-American Literary Criticism*. New York: Oxford University Press, 1988.

———. *The Trials of Phillis Wheatley: America's First Black Poet and Her Encounters with the Founding Fathers*. New York: Basic Civitas Books, 2003.

———. "The Trope of a New Negro and the Reconstruction of the Image of the Black." Special issue, America Reconstructed, 1840–1940, *Representations* 24 (1988).

Genette, Gérard. *Palimpsests: Literature in the Second Degree*. Lincoln: University of Nebraska Press, 1997.

Georgoudaki, Ekaterini. "Rita Dove: Crossing Boundaries." *Callaloo* 14, no. 2 (1991): 419–33.

Gide, André. *Two Legends: Oedipus and Theseus*. Translated by John Russell. New York: Vintage Books, 1950.

Girard, René. *Oedipus Unbound: Selected Writings on Rivalry and Desire*. Edited and with an introduction by Mark R. Anspach. Stanford: Stanford University Press, 2004.

Gocer, Asli. "The Puppet Theater in Plato's Parable of the Cave." *Classical Journal* 95, no. 2 (1999): 110–29.

Goldhill, Simon. *How To Stage Greek Tragedy Today*. Chicago: University of Chicago Press, 2007.

Goodrich, Peter. "The Importance of Being Earnest: Satire and the Criticism of Law." *Social Semiotics* 15 (2005): 43–58.

———. "Satirical Legal Studies: From the Legists to the *Lizard*." *Michigan Law Review* 103 (2004): 397–517.

Gould, Stephen J. *The Mismeasure of Man*. New York: W. W. Norton, 1981; revised and expanded ed., 1996.

Gowers, Emily. *The Loaded Table: Representations of Food in Roman Literature*. Oxford: Oxford University Press, 1993.

Graver, Margaret. "The Manhandling of Maecenas: Senecan Abstractions of Masculinity." *American Journal of Philology* 119, no. 4 (1998): 607–32.

Gray, Thomas. "The Progress of Poesy. A Pindaric Ode." In *Poems by Mr. Gray*. London: Printed for J. Dodsley, 1768.

Greenblatt, Stephen. *Renaissance Self-Fashioning: From More to Shakespeare*. Chicago: University of Chicago Press, 1980.

Griffiths, Frederick T. "Copy Wright: What Is an (Invisible) Author?" *New Literary History* 33 (2002): 315–41.

Griffiths, Julia, ed. *Autographs for Freedom*. Boston: John P. Jewett, 1853.

Griggs, Sutton E. *Imperium in Imperio*. Preface by A. J. Verdelle; introduction by Cornel West. New York: Modern Library, 2003.

Gurdjieff, G. I. *All and Everything: Ten Books, in Three Series, of Which This Is the First Series; Beelzebub's Tales to His Grandson*. New York: E. P. Dutton, 1950.

Gurley, Ralph Randolph. *Life of Jehudi Ashmun, Late Colonial Agent in Liberia*. New York: Leavitt, Lord; Boston: Crocker & Brewster, 1835.

Gustafson, Sandra M. *Eloquence Is Power: Oratory and Performance in Early America*. Chapel Hill: University of North Carolina Press, 2000.

Haley, George. "The Narrator in *Don Quixote*: Maestro Pedro's Puppet Show." Spanish issue, *Modern Language Notes* 80, no. 2 (1965): 145–65.

Haley, Shelley P. "Black Feminist Thought and Classics: Re-membering, Re-claiming, Re-empowering." In *Feminist Theory and the Classics*, ed. Nancy Sorkin Rabinowitz and Amy Richlin. New York: Routledge, 1993.

———. "Self-Definition, Community, and Resistance: Euripides' *Medea* and Toni Morrison's *Beloved*." *Thamyris* 2 (1995): 177–206.

Hall, Constance H. *Incest in Faulkner: A Metaphor for the Fall*. Ann Arbor, Mich.: UMI Research Press, 1985.

Hall, Edith. "The Scythian Archer in Aristophanes' *Themophoriazusae*." In *The Theatrical Cast of Athens: Interactions between Ancient Greek Drama and Society*. Oxford: Oxford University Press, 2006.

Hall, Kim F. *Things of Darkness: Economies of Race and Gender in Early Modern England*. Ithaca: Cornell University Press, 1995.

Hamilton, John T. *Soliciting Darkness: Pindar, Obscurity, and the Classical Tradition*. Cambridge, Mass.: Harvard University Press, 2004.

Hammer, Mike, and Christina Daub. "Interview." *Plum Review* 9 (1996): 27–41.

Hardwick, Lorna. *Reception Studies*. Greece & Rome, New Surveys in the Classics 33, "From Classical Tradition to Reception Studies," 1–12. Cambridge: Cambridge University Press, 2003.

Hardy, Thomas. *The Dynasts: A Drama of the Napoleonic Wars, in Three Parts, Nineteen Acts, and One-Hundred and Thirty Scenes*. New York: Macmillan, 1904.

Harris, Middleton A. et al. *The Black Book*. New York: Random House, 1974.

Harris, William V. *Ancient Literacy*. Cambridge: Harvard University Press, 1989.

Haskell, Francis, and Nicholas Penny. *Taste and the Antique: The Lure of Classical Sculpture 1500–1900*. New Haven: Yale University Press, 1981.

Haskins, Jim. *Richard Pryor: A Man and His Madness*. New York: Beaufort Books, 1984.

Haskins, Jim, and Hugh F. Butts, M.D. *The Psychology of Black Language*. New York: Barnes & Noble Books, 1973.

Haslam, Jason. "'The Open Sesame of Pork-Colored Skin': Whiteness and Privilege in *Black No More*." *Modern Language Studies* 32, no.1 (2002): 15–30.

Hatcher, John. *From the Auroral Darkness: The Life and Poetry of Robert Hayden.* Oxford: Oxford University Press, 1984.

Henderson, Jeffrey. "Women and the Athenian Dramatic Festivals." *Transactions and Proceedings of the American Philological Association* 121. (1991): 133–47.

Hershkowitz, Debra. *Valerius Flaccus' Argonautica: Abbreviated Voyages in Silver Latin Epic.* New York: Clarendon Press, 1998.

Hesiod. "Catalogue of Women, Fragment 14." In *Hesiod*, ed. and trans. Glenn W. Most. Cambridge, Mass.: Harvard University Press, 2006–2007.

Hexter, Ralph. "Sidonian Dido." In *Innovations of Antiquity*, ed. Ralph Hexter and Daniel Selden. New York: Routledge, 1992.

Highbarger, Ernest Leslie. *The Gates of Dreams: An Archaeological Examination of Vergil, Aeneid VI, 893–899.* Baltimore: Johns Hopkins University Press, 1940.

Hill, Herbert, ed. *Soon, One Morning: New Writing by American Negroes.* New York: Alfred A. Knopf: 1963.

Hirsch, Marianne. *The Mother/Daughter Plot: Narrative, Psychoanalysis, Feminism.* Bloomington: University of Indiana Press, 1989.

Hollander, Robert. *Dante: A Life in Works.* New Haven: Yale University Press, 2001.

Homer. *The Odyssey.* Translated by Robert Fitzgerald. New York: Farrar, Straus and Giroux, 1998.

Homer. *The Odyssey.* Translated by Stanley Lombardo. Introduction by Sheila Murnahan. Indianapolis: Hackett, 2000.

Horace. *The Works of Horace: Translations into Verse with a Prose Interpretation for the Help of Students and Occasional Notes.* By Christopher Smart. London: W. Flexney et al., 1767.

Horner, Winifred B. *Rhetoric in the Classical Tradition.* New York: St. Martin's Press, 1988.

Howard, Sydney. *Gone with the Wind: The Screenplay, by Sydney Howard.* Based on the novel by Margaret Mitchell. Edited and with an Introduction by Herb Bridges and Terryl C. Boodman. New York: Delta, 1989.

Howard-Pitney, David. *The African American Jeremiad: Appeals for Justice in America.* Philadelphia: Temple University Press, 2005.

Howat, Roy, ed. *Chopin: Pianist and Teacher as Seen by His Pupils.* Compiled by Jean-Jacques Eigeldinger. Translated by Naomi Shohet with Krysia Osostowicz and Roy Howat. Cambridge : Cambridge University Press, 1986.

Howe, Irving. "Black Boys and Native Sons." In *A World More Attractive: A Voice of Modern Literature and Politics.* New York: Horizon Press, 1963.

Hughes, Langston. "The Negro Artist and the Racial Mountain." *Nation*, June 23, 1926.

Hyde, Lewis. *Trickster Makes This World: Mischief, Myth and Art.* New York: Farrar, Straus and Giroux, 1998.

Irwin, John T. *Doubling and Incest/Repetition and Revenge: A Speculative Reading of Faulkner.* Baltimore: Johns Hopkins University Press, 1975.

Isaac, Benjamin. *The Invention of Racism in Classical Antiquity.* Princeton: Princeton University Press, 2004.

Isani, Muktar Ali. "Phillis Wheatley and the Elegiac Mode." In *Critical Essays on Phillis Wheatley*, ed. William H. Robinson. Boston: G. K. Hall, 1982.

Iser, Wolfgang. *The Act of Reading: A Theory of Aesthetic Response.* Baltimore: Johns Hopkins University Press, 1978.

Jackson, John P., Jr. *Social Scientists for Social Justice: Making the Case against Segregation*. New York: New York University Press, 2001.

Jackson, Lawrence Patrick. *Ralph Ellison: The Emergence of Genius*. New York: John Wiley & Sons, 2002.

Jahnn, Hans Henny. *Dramen I*. Edited by Ulrich Bitz. Hamburg: Hoffmann und Campe, 1988.

Jameson, Fredric. *The Political Unconscious*. Ithaca: Cornell University Press, 1981.

Johnson, James Weldon. *The Autobiography of an Ex-Coloured Man*. With an introduction by Arna Bontemps. New York: Hill and Wang, 1960.

Johnson, Samuel. *A Dictionary of the English Language*. London: P. Knapton, 1755.

———. *Lives of the English Poets*. Vols. 1–2. London: Oxford University Press, 1964.

Jones, Charles Colcock. *The Religious Instruction of the Negroes in the United States*. Savannah, Ga.: Thomas Purse, 1842.

Jones, Howard. "The Peculiar Institution and National Honor: The Case of the *Creole* Slave Revolt." *Civil War History* 21 (1975): 28–50.

Jones, Sharon L. *Rereading the Harlem Renaissance: Race, Class, and Gender in the Fiction of Jessie Fauset, Zora Neale Hurston, and Dorothy West*. Westport, Conn.: Greenwood Press, 2002.

Kasson, Joy S. *Marble Queens and Captives: Women in Nineteenth-Century American Sculpture*. New Haven: Yale University Press, 1990.

Keane, Catherine. *Figuring Genre in Roman Satire*. New York: Oxford University Press, 2006.

Kennedy, George. *The Art of Rhetoric in the Roman World*. Princeton: Princeton University Press, 1994.

———. *Quintilian*. New York: Twayne, 1969.

Kennedy, Randall. *Nigger: The Strange Career of a Troublesome Word*. New York: Vintage Books, 2003.

Kolatch, Alfred J. *The Name Dictionary: Modern English and Hebrew Names*. New York: J.David, 1967.

Kuenz, Jane. "American Racial Discourse, 1900–1930: Schuyler's *Black No More*." *Novel: A Forum on Fiction* 30, no. 2 (1997): 170–92.

Kuncio, Robert. "Some Unpublished Poems of Phillis Wheatley." *New England Quarterly* 43, no. 2 (1970): 287–97.

Lachelin, Gillian C. L. *Miscarriage: The Facts*. Oxford : Oxford University Press, 1985.

Lakoff, George, and Zoltán Kövecses, "The Cognitive Model of Anger in American English." In *Cultural Models in Language & Thought*, ed. Dorothy Holland and Naomi Quinn (Cambridge : Cambridge University Press, 1987).

Larsen, Nella. *Passing*. Edited and with an introduction and notes by Thadious M. Davis. New York: Penguin Books, 1997.

Latham, R. E. *Lucretius: On the Nature of the Universe*. Baltimore: Johns Hopkins University Press, 1951.

Lefkowitz, Mary R. *The Lives of the Greek Poets*. Baltimore: Johns Hopkins University Press, 1981.

———. *Not Out of Africa: How Afrocentrism Became an Excuse to Teach Myth as History*. New York: Basic Books, 1996.

Leverette, Tru. "Traveling Identities: Mixed Race Quests and Fran Ross's *Oreo*." *African American Review* 40 (2006): 79–91.

Lévi-Strauss, Claude. *Structural Anthropology*. New York: Basic Books, 1963.

Lewis, David Levering. *W. E. B. Du Bois: Biography of a Race: 1868–1919*. New York: Henry Holt, 1993.

——. *W. E. B. Du Bois: The Fight for Equality and the American Century, 1919–1963*. New York: Henry Holt, 2000.

——. *When Harlem Was in Vogue*. New York: Alfred A. Knopf, 1979.

Liebenow, J. Gus. *Liberia: The Quest for Identity*. Bloomington: Indiana University Press, 1987.

List, Robert N. *Daedalus in Harlem: The Joyce-Ellison Connection*. Washington, D.C.: University Press of America, 2003.

Little, Malcolm, or El-Hajj Malik El-Shabazz. *The Autobiography of Malcolm X*. With the assistance of Alex Haley. New York: Random House, 1964.

Llorens, David. "Writers Converge on Fisk University." *Negro Digest* 15 (1966) : 54–68.

Lloyd, G. E. R. *Polarity and Analogy: Two Types of Argumentation in Early Greek Thought*. Cambridge: Cambridge University Press, 1966.

Locke, Alain. *The New Negro: An Interpretation*. Edited by Alain Locke; book decorations and portraits by Winold Reiss. New York: A. & C. Boni, 1925.

Lupton, Mary Jane. "Bad Blood in Jersey: Jessie Fauset's *The Chinaberry Tree*." *College Language Association Journal* 27 (1984): 383–92.

Macaulay, Thomas Babington. *Lays of Ancient Rome*. London: Longman, Brown, Green and Longmans, 1842.

Martin, Richard P. *The Language of Heroes: Speech and Performance in the "Iliad."* Ithaca: Cornell University Press, 1989.

Martindale, Charles, and Richard F. Thomas. *Classics and the Uses of Reception*. Oxford: Blackwell, 2006.

Mason, Julian. "Examples of Classical Myth in the Poems of Phillis Wheatley." In *American Women and Classical Myth*, ed. Gregory Staley, 23–33. Waco: Baylor University Press, 2009.

Matthews, C. M. *English Surnames*. London: Weidenfeld & Nicolson, 1966; New York: Scribners, 1967.

McCarthy, Kathleen. *Slaves, Masters and the Art of Authority in Plautine Comedy*. Princeton: Princeton University Press, 2000.

McDonald, William P. "The Blackness of Medea." *College Language Association Journal* 19 (1975): 20–37.

McFeely, William S. *Frederick Douglass*. New York: Norton, 1990.

Mitchell-Kernan, Claudia. *Language Behavior in a Black Urban Community*. Berkeley: University of California, Language-Behavior Research Laboratory, 1971.

Morgan, Stacey. "'The Strange and Wonderful Workings of Science': Race Science and Essentialism in George Schuyler's *Black No More*." *CLA Journal* 42 (1999): 331–51.

Morris, Sarah P. *Daedalus and the Origins of Greek Art*. Princeton: Princeton University Press, 1992.

Morrison, Toni. *Beloved*. New York: Knopf, 1987.

——. *Song of Solomon*. New York: Knopf, 1977.

Muellner, Leonard. *The Anger of Achilles: Mênis in Greek Epic*. Ithaca: Cornell University Press, 1996.

Mugglestone, Lynda, ed. *Lexicography and the OED: Pioneers in the Untrodden Forrest*. Oxford : Oxford University Press, 2000.

Murray, James A. H., ed. *A New English Dictionary; Founded Mainly on the Materials Collected by the Philological Society*. Oxford: Clarendon Press, 1888–1928.

Musgrave, Marian. "Ishmael Reed's Black Oedipus Cycle." *Obsidian* 6 (1980): 60–67.

Muyumba, Walton M. *The Shadow and the Act: Black Intellectual Practice, Jazz Improvisation, and Philosophical Pragmatism*. Chicago: Universtiy of Chicago Press, 2009.

Myrdal, Gunnar. *An American Dilemma: The Negro Problem in Modern Democracy*. New York: Harper & Row, 1944; 1962.

NAACP. *Fighting a Vicious Film: Protest against "The Birth of a Nation."* Boston: Boston Branch of the National Association for the Advancement of Colored People, 1915.

Nagy, Gregory. *The Best of the Achaeans: Concepts of the Hero in Archaic Greek Poetry*. Rev. ed. Baltimore: Johns Hopkins University Press, 1999.

Nettl, Bruno, and Melinda Russell, eds. *In the Course of Performance: Studies in the World of Musical Improvisation*. Chicago: University of Chicago Press, 1998.

The New Encyclopaedia Britannica. 15th ed. Chicago: Encyclopaedia Britannica, 2007.

Niane, D. T. *Sundiata: An Epic of Old Mali*. London: Longmans, 1964.

Oakes, James. *The Radical and the Republican: Frederick Douglass, Abraham Lincoln, and the Triumph of Antislavery Politics*. New York: W. W. Norton, 2007.

Olmsted, Frederick Law. *The Cotton Kingdom: A Traveller's Observations on Cotton and Slavery in the American Slave States; Based upon Three Former Volumes of Journeys and Investigations by the Same Author*. (1861). Edited by Arthur M. Schlesinger. New York: Alfred A. Knopf, 1953.

O'Meally, Robert G. *Romaire Bearden: A Black Odyssey*. New York: DC Moore Gallery, 2007.

Ovid. *After Ovid: New Metamorphoses*. Edited by James Lasden and Michael Hofmann. New York: Farrar, Straus & Giroux, 1996.

———. *The Metamorphoses of Ovid*. Translated by Allen Mandelbaum. New York: Harcourt Brace, 1993.

———. *Ovid's Metamorphoses: Books 6–10*. Edited with introduction and commentary by William S. Anderson. Norman: University of Oklahoma Press, 1972.

———. *Ovid's* Metamorphosis [sic]*: Englished, Mythologized, and Represented in Figures by George Sandys*. Edited by Karl K. Hulley and Stanley T. Vandersall. Lincoln: University of Nebraska Press, 1970.

Parker, Douglass. "WAA: An Intruded Gloss." *Arion*, 3rd ser., 2.2 and 2.3 (1992–1993): 251–66.

Partridge, Eric. *A Dictionary of Clichés*. London: George Routledge & Sons, 1941.

———. *Origins: A Short Etymological Dictionary of Modern English*. London: Routledge & Kegan Paul, 1958.

Pearson, Norman Holmes. Foreword. In *Hermetic Definitions*, by H. Doolittle. New York: New Directions, 1972.

Pereira, Malin. "An Interview with Rita Dove." *Contemporary Literature* 40, no. 2 (1999): 183–213.

———. *Rita Dove's Cosmopolitanism*. Urbana: University of Illinois Press, 2002.

———. "'When the pear blossoms / cast their pale faces on / the darker face of the earth': Miscegenation, the Primal Scene, and the Incest Motif in Rita Dove's Work." *African American Review* 36, no. 2 (2002): 195–211.

Petronius. *Satyrica*. Edited and translated by R. Bracht Branham and Daniel Kinney. London: J. M. Dent, 1996.

Phillips, David Graham. *Golden Fleece: The American Adventures of a Fortune Hunting Earl*. New York: McClure, Phillips, 1903.

Pindar. *The Odes of Pindar*. Translated by Richmond Lattimore. Chicago: University of Chicago Press, 1947.

———. *Pindar: The Olympian and Pythian Odes*. Edited by Basil L. Gildersleeve. New York: Harper & Brothers, 1890.

———. *Pindar's Victory Songs*. Edited and translated by Frank J. Nisetich. Baltimore: Johns Hopkins University Press, 1980.

Plutarch. *Plutarch: Lives*. Vol. 1. Translated by Bernadotte Perrin. Cambridge, Mass.: Harvard University Press, 1914.

Polhemus, Robert M. *Lot's Daughters: Sex, Redemption, and Women's Quest for Authority*. Stanford: Stanford University Press, 2005.

Pope, Alexander. *The Iliad of Homer: Books X–XXIV*. Edited by Maynard Mack. New Haven: Yale University Press, 1967.

Porter, James I., ed. *Classical Pasts: The Classical Traditions of Greece and Rome*. Princeton: Princeton University Press, 2006.

Porter, William Malin. "Cicero's *Pro Archia* and the Responsibilities of Reading." *Rhetorica* 8, no. 2 (1990): 137–52.

Pryor, Richard, with Todd Gold. *Pryor Convictions and Other Life Sentences*. New York: Pantheon, 1995.

Pucci, Pietro. *The Violence of Pity in Euripides' "Medea."* Ithaca: Cornell University Press, 1980.

Putnam, Michael C. J. *Virgil's Pastoral Art: Studies in the "Eclogues."* Princeton: Princeton University Press, 1970.

Quintilian. *Institutio Oratoria of Quintilian*. Translated by H. E. Butler. London: W. Heinemann; New York: G. P. Putnam's sons, 1920–1922.

Raboteau, Albert. *Slave Religion: The Invisible Institution in the Antebellum South*. New York: Oxford University Press, 1983.

Raimon, Eve Allegra. *The "Tragic Mulatta" Revisited: Race and Nationalism in Nineteenth-Century Antislavery Fiction*. New Brunswick, N.J.: Rutgers University Press, 2004.

Rampersad, Arnold. *The Art and Imagination of W. E. B. Du Bois*. Cambridge, Mass.: Harvard University Press, 1976.

———. *Ralph Ellison: A Biography*. New York: Alfred A. Knopf, 2007.

Rankine, Patrice D. *Ulysses in Black: Ralph Ellison, Classicism, and African American Literature*. Madison: University of Wisconsin Press, 2006.

Reaney, Percy H. *The Origin of English Surnames*. New York: Barnes & Noble, 1967.

Reckford, Kenneth J. "Horace and Maecenas." In *Transactions and Proceedings of the American Philological Association* 90 (1959): 195–208.

Redfield, James M. "Anthropology and the Classics." *Arion* 1.2 (Spring 1991): 5–23.

Reed, Ishmael. *Conversations with Ishmael Reed*. Edited by Bruce Dick and Amritjit Singh. Jackson: University of Mississippi Press, 1991.

———. *The Free-Lance Pallbearers*. New York: Atheneum, 1967, 1988.

———. Introduction. In *Black No More* by George Schuyler. New York: Modern Library, 1999.

———. *The Last Days of Louisiana Red*. New York: Atheneum, 1989.

———. *New and Collected Poems*. New York: Atheneum, 1988.

———. *Writin' Is Fightin': Thirty-Seven Years of Boxing on Paper*. New York: Atheneum, 1988.

Reimonenq, Alden. "Countee Cullen's Uranian 'Soul Windows.'" In *Critical Essays: Gay and Lesbian Writers of Color*, ed. Emmanuel S. Nelson. New York: Haworth Press, 1993.

Reinhardt, Mark. "Who Speaks for Margaret Garner? Slavery, Silence, and the Politics of Ventriloquism." *Critical Inquiry* 29, no. 1. (2002): 1–19.

Reynolds, Tim. *Peace*. In *The Tenth Muse: Classical Drama in Translation*, ed. with an introduction by Charles Doria (Chicago: Swallow; Athens: Ohio University Press, 1980.

Rice, Philip Blair. "Euripides in Harlem." *Nation* 141 (September 18, 1935).

Richlin, Amy. "Cicero's Head." In *Constructions of the Classical Body*, ed. James I. Porter. Ann Arbor: University of Michigan Press, 1999.

———. *The Garden of Priapus: Sexuality and Aggression in Roman Humor*. Rev. ed. New York: Oxford University Press, 1992.

Richmond, M. A. *Bid the Vassal Soar: Interpretive Essays on the Life and Poetry of Phillis Wheatley (ca. 1753–1784) and George Moses Horton (ca. 1797–1883)*. Washington, D.C.: Howard University Press, 1974.

Rickford, John Russell, and Russell John Rickford. *Spoken Soul: The Story of Black English*. New York: John Wiley & Sons, 2000.

Riffaterre, Michael. *Fictional Truth*. Baltimore: Johns Hopkins University Press, 1990.

Righelato, Pat. *Understanding Rita Dove*. Columbia: University of South Carolina Press, 2006.

Rilke, Rainer Maria. *The Best of Rilke: 72 Form-True Verse Translations with Facing Originals, Commentary, and Compact Biography*. Translated by Walter Arndt; foreword by Cyrus Hamlin. Hanover: Dartmouth College, University Press of New England, 1989.

Ristori, Adelaide. *Studies and Memoirs: An Autobiography*. Boston: Roberts Brothers, 1888.

Roberts, Deborah. "The Drunk and the Policeman: Arrowsmith, Convention, and the Changing Context of Twentieth-Century Translation." Paper delivered at the annual meetings of the Postmodern Language Association, 2000.

Robinson, William H. *Phillis Wheatley and Her Writings*. New York: Garland Publishing, 1984.

Rollin, Charles. *The Method of Teaching and Studying the Belles Lettres*. 6th ed. Vol. 2. Translated from the French. London, 1769.

Ronnick, Michele Valerie. "*First Lessons in Greek* (1881): William Sanders Scarborough's Date with Destiny." *AME Church Review* 118 (2002): 30–43.

———. "William Sanders Scarborough: The First African American Member of the Modern Language Association." Special Millennium Issue, *PMLA* 115, no. 7 (2000): 1787–93.

Rose, H. J. *A Handbook of Greek Mythology*. New York: E. P. Dutton, 1959.

Ross, Fran. *Oreo*. With a new introduction by Harryette Mullen. Boston: Northeastern University Press, 2000.

Rosten, Leo. *The Joys of Yiddish: A Relaxed Lexicon of Yiddish, Hebrew and Yinglish Words Often Encountered in English . . . from the Days of the Bible to Those of the Beatnik*. New York: McGraw-Hill, 1968.

Rowley, Hazel. *Richard Wright: The Life and Times*. New York: Henry Holt, 2001.

Ruotolo, Cristina L., and James Weldon Johnson. "James Weldon Johnson and the Autobiography of an Ex-Coloured Musician." *American Literature* 72, no. 2 (2000): 249–74.

Sato, Hiroko. "Under the Harlem Shadow: A Study of Jessie Fauset and Nella Larsen." In *The Harlem Renaissance Remembered*, ed. Arna Bontemps. New York: Dodd, Mead, 1972.

Scarborough, William Sanders. *The Autobiography of William Sanders Scarborough: An American Journey from Slavery to Scholarship*. Edited by Michele Valerie Ronnick, with a foreword by Henry Louis Gates, Jr. Detroit: Wayne State University Press, 2005.

——. "Bellerophon's Letters, *Iliad* VI.168f." *Transactions and Proceedings of the American Philological Association* 22 (1891), l–liii.

——. *The Birds of Aristophanes: A Theory of Interpretation.* [Boston:] Cushing, 1886.

——. "Booker T. Washington and His Works." *Education* 20 (1900): 270–76.

——. "The Chronological Order of Plato's Dialogues." *Transactions and Proceedings of the American Philological Association* 23 (1892): 213–18.

——. *The Educated Negro and His Mission.* Washington, D.C.: American Negro Academy, 1903.

——. *First Lessons in Greek: Adapted to the Greek Grammar of Goodwin and Hadley and Designed as an Introduction to Xenophon's "Anabasis" and Similar Greek.* New York: A. S. Barnes, 1881.

——. "The Greeks and Suicide." *Transactions and Proceedings of the American Philological Association* 38 (1907): xxii–xxiii.

——. "Iphigenia in Euripides and Racine." *Transactions and Proceedings of the American Philological Association* 29 (1898): lviii–lx.

——. "Iphigenia in Euripides, Racine, and Goethe." *Transactions and Proceedings of the American Philological Association* 32 (1901): xxxvii–xxxviii.

——. "The Negro Element in Fiction." *Transactions and Proceedings of the American Philological Association* 21 (1890): xlii–xliv.

——. "Notes on the Function of Languages in Modern Africa." *Transactions and Proceedings of the American Philological Association* 27 (1896): xlvi–xlviii.

——. *The Works of William Sanders Scarborough: Black Classicist and Race Leader.* Edited by Michele Valerie Ronnick, with a foreword by Henry Louis Gates, Jr. Oxford: Oxford University Press, 2006.

Scharffenberger, Elizabeth. "Aristophanes' *Thesmophoriazousai* and the Challenges of Comic Translation: The Case of William Arrowsmith's *Euripides Agonistes.*" *American Journal of Philology* 123 (2002): 429–63.

Schiavone, Aldo. *The End of the Past: Ancient Rome and the Modern West.* Translated by Margery Schneider. Cambridge, Mass.: Harvard University Press, 2000.

Schneider, Steven. "Coming Home: An Interview with Rita Dove." *Iowa Review* 19.3 (November 1998): 112–23.

Schuyler, George S. *Black and Conservative: The Autobiography of George S. Schuyler.* New Rochelle, N.Y.: Arlington House, 1966.

——. *Black No More.* New York: Modern Library, 1999.

——. *Slaves Today: A Story of Liberia.* New York: Brewer, Warren and Putnam, 1931.

Schwarz, A. B. Christa. *Gay Voices of the Harlem Renaissance.* Bloomington: Indiana University Press, 2003.

Scott, James C. *Domination and the Arts of Resistance: Hidden Transcripts.* New Haven: Yale University Press, 1990.

Segal, Charles. *Orpheus: The Myth of the Poet.* Baltimore: Johns Hopkins University Press, 1989.

Selden, Daniel L. "*Aithiopika* and Ethiopianism." In *Studies in Heliodorus,* edited by Richard Hunter. Cambridge: Cambridge Philological Society, 1998.

Seneca. *Apocolocyntosis.* Edited by P. T. Eden. Cambridge: Cambridge University Press, 1984.

——. *Epistulae morales ad Lucilium.* Selected and edited by Anna Lydia Motto. Chico, California: Scholars Press, 1985.

Sheridan, Thomas. *A Course of Lectures on Elocution.* Providence, RI: Carter and Wilkinson, 1797.

——. *Lectures on the Art of Reading; in Two Parts*. London: Printed for C. Dilly, 1781.

Shershow, Scott Cutler. *Puppets and "Popular" Culture*. Ithaca: Cornell University Press, 1995.

Shields, John. "Phillis Wheatley's Subversion of Classical Stylistics." *Style* 27 (1993): 252–70.

Silva, Fred. *Focus on the Birth of a Nation*. Englewood Cliffs, N.J.: Prentice-Hall, 1971.

Simon, Sylvie. *The Tarot: Art, Mysticism, and Divination*. London: Alpine Fine Arts Collection, 1986.

Smethurst, James Edward. *The Black Arts Movement: Literary Nationalism in the 1960s and 1970s*. Chapel Hill: University of North Carolina Press, 2005.

Smith, William. *Smith's Bible Dictionary: More than 6,000 Detailed Definitions, Articles, and Illustrations*. Nashville, Tenn.: Thomas Nelson, 2004.

Smitherman, Geneva. *Black Talk: Words and Phrases from the Hood to the Amen Corner*. Boston: Houghton Mifflin, 2000.

——. *Toastin' and Signifyin': The Language of Black Americans*. Boston: Houghton Mifflin, 1977.

Sollors, Werner. *Neither Black Nor White Yet Both: Thematic Explorations of Interracial Literature*. New York: Oxford Univesity Press, 1997.

Sophocles. *Antigone*. Edited by Mark Griffith. Cambridge: Cambridge University Press, 1999.

Spengler, Oswald. *The Decline of the West*. New York: Alfred A. Knopf, 1926.

Stanford, W. B. *The Odyssey of Homer*. 2nd ed. Vol. 1. London: Macmillan, 1964.

Stark, John. "*Invisible Man*: Ellison's Black Odyssey." *Negro American Literature Forum* 7, no. 2 (1973): 60–63.

Steffen, Therese. *Crossing Color: Transcultural Space and Place in Rita Dove's Poetry, Fiction, and Drama*. Oxford : Oxford University Press, 2001.

——. "The Darker Face: A Conversation with Rita Dove." *Transition* 74 (1997): 104–23.

Steiner, George. *Antigones*. Oxford : Clarendon Press, 1986.

Stepto, Robert B. *From Behind the Veil: A Study of Afro-American Narrative*. 2nd ed. Urbana: University of Illinois Press, 1991.

Suleiman, Susan Rubin. *Authoritarian Fictions: The Ideological Novel as Literary Genre*. New York: Columbia University Press, 1983.

Sundquist, Eric. *To Wake the Nations: Race in the Making of American Literature*. Cambridge, Mass.: Harvard University Press, 1993.

Sypher, Wylie, ed. *Comedy: "An Essay on Comedy," by George Meredith, and "Laughter," by Henri Bergson*. Baltimore: Johns Hopkins University Press, 1980.

Terence. *The Comedies of Terence, Translated into Familiar Blank Verse*. Translated by George Colman, 2 vols. London: Becket, De Hondt and Baldwin, 1768.

——. *Publii Terenti Afri Comoediae*. Birmingham: John Baskerville, 1772.

Terrell, Mary Church. *A Colored Woman in a White World*. With an introduction by Nellie Y. McKay. New York: G. K. Hall, 1996.

Tillotson, Gregory. *On the Poetry of Pope*. 2nd ed. Oxford: Clarendon Press, 1950.

Tolson, Melvin B. *Caviar and Cabbage: Selected Columns from the Washington Tribune, 1937–1944*. Edited and with an introduction by Robert M. Farnsworth. Columbia: University of Missouri Press, 1982.

——. *Harlem Gallery*. Book 1, *The Curator*. Introduction by Karl Shapiro. New York: Twayne Publishers, 1965.

——. "*Harlem Gallery" and Other Poems of Melvin B. Tolson*. Edited by Raymond Nelson. Introduction by Rita Dove. Charlottesville: University Press of Virginia, 1999.

———. "The Odyssey of a Manuscript." Typescript. Library of Congress, N.d.

Tomlinson, Susan. "'An Unwonted Coquetry': The Commercial Seductions of Jessie Fauset's *The Chinaberry Tree*." In *Middlebrow Moderns: Popular Women Writers of the 1920s*, ed. Lisa Boston and Meredith Goldsmith. Boston: Northeastern University Press, 2003.

Trible, Phyllis. *God and the Rhetoric of Sexuality*. Philadelphia: Fortress Press, 1978.

Twitchell, James B. *Forbidden Partners: The Incest Taboo in Modern Culture*. New York: Columbia University Press, 1987.

Vendler, Helen. *The Given and the Made: Recent American Poets*. London: Faber and Faber, 1995.

———. "Rita Dove: Identity Markers." *Callaloo* 17, no. 2 (1994): 381–98.

Vernant, Jean-Pierre. "Ambiguity and Reversal: On the Enigmatic Structure of *Oedipus Rex*." In *Myth and Tragedy in Ancient Greece*, by Jean-Pierre Vernant and Pierre Vidal-Naquet. New York: Zone Books, 1990.

Waite, Arthur Edward. *The Pictorial Key to the Tarot: Being Fragments of a Secret Tradition under the Veil of Divination*. N.p.: CreateSpace, 2008.

Wald, Gayle. "The Satire of Race in James Weldon Johnson's Autobiography of an Ex-Coloured Man." In *Cross Addressing: Resistance, Literature and Cultural Borders*, ed. John C. Hawley. Albany: State University of New York Press, 1996.

Walker, Alice. *The Color Purple*. New York: Washington Square Press, 1983.

Walters, Tracey L. *African American Literature and the Classicist Tradition: Black Women Writers from Wheatley to Morrison*. New York: Palgrave Macmillan, 2007.

Ward, Anne G. et al. *The Quest for Theseus*. New York: Praeger Publishers, 1970.

Washington, Salim. "Of Black Bards, Known and Unknown: Music as Racial Metaphor in James Weldon Johnson's *The Autobiography of an Ex-Coloured Man*." Special issue, Jazz Poetics, *Callaloo* 25, no. 1 (2002): 233–56.

Wasserman, Jerry. "Embracing the Negative: *Native Son* and *Invisible Man*." *Studies in American Fiction* 4 (1976): 93–104.

Waterlow, Sidney. *The Medea & Hippolytus*. New York: G. P. Putnam's Sons, 1906.

Watkins, Mel. *On the Real Side: A History of African American Comedy*. Chicago: Lawrence Hill Books, 1994, 1999.

Watson, Alan. "Roman Slave Law and Romanist Ideology." *Phoenix* 37, no. 1 (1983): 53–65.

Way, A. S. *Four Famous Greek Plays*. Edited by P. N. Landis. New York: Modern Library, 1929.

Weber, Manfred. *Medea: Hans Henny Jahnn*. Hg. Schauspiel Köln, ein Theaterbuch von Manfred Weber. Berlin: Edition Hentrich, 1989.

Webster, Harvey Curtis. "A Difficult Career." *Poetry* 7 (1947): 224–25.

Weinbrot, Howard D. *Menippean Satire Reconsidered: From Antiquity to the Eighteenth Century*. Baltimore: Johns Hopkins University Press, 2005.

Weisenburger, Steven. *Modern Medea: A Family Story of Slavery and Child-Murder from the Old South*. New York: Hill and Wang, 1998.

Wells, H. G. *The Outline of History, Being a Plain History of Life and Mankind*. Vol. 1. London: George Newnes, 1919–1920.

Wheatley, Phillis. *The Collected Works of Phillis Wheatley*. Edited and with an essay by John Shields. New York: Oxford University Press, 1988.

———. *Phillis Wheatley: Complete Writings*. Edited by Vincent Carretta. New York: Penguin, 2001.

———. *The Poems of Phillis Wheatley*. Edited by Julian A. Mason, Jr. Chapel Hill: University of North Carolina Press, 1989.

Wiesen, David. "Herodotus and the Modern Debate over Slavery." *Ancient World* 3 (1980): 3–16.

Williams, Wilburn, Jr. "The Desolate Servitude of Language: A Reading of the Poetry of Melvin B. Tolson." PhD diss., Yale University, 1979.

Willinsky, John. *Empire of Words: The Reign of the OED*. Princeton: Princeton University Press, 1994.

Wilson, Harriet E. *Our Nig: Or, Sketches from the Life of a Free Black*. Edited by Gabrielle Foreman and Reginald H. Pitts. New York: Penguin, 2005.

———. *Our Nig: Or, Sketches from the Life of a Free Black, In a Two-Story White House, North; Showing that Slavery's Shadows Fall Even There*. Edited and with an introduction by Henry Louis Gates, Jr. New York: Vintage Books, 1983.

Winterer, Caroline. *The Culture of Classicism: Ancient Greece and Rome in American Intellectual Life, 1780–1910*. Baltimore: Johns Hopkins University Press, 2002.

———. *The Mirror of Antiquity. American Women and the Classical Tradition, 1750–1900*. Ithaca: Cornell University Press, 2007.

Woodson, Jon Staunton. "A Critical Analysis of the Poetry of Melvin B. Tolson." PhD diss., Brown University, 1978.

Wreh, Tuan. *The Love of Liberty: The Rule of President William V. S. Tubman in Liberia: 1944–1971*. London: C. Hurst, 1978.

Wright, Richard. "How 'Bigger' Was Born." In *Richard Wright: Early Works*, 851–91. New York: Library of America, 1991.

———. *Native Son*. With an introduction by Arnold Rampersad. Restored text established by the Library of America. New York: Harper Collins Publishers, 1998.

Yanuck, Julius. "The Garner Fugitive Slave Case." *Mississippi Valley Historical Review* 40 (1953): 47–66.

Young, David C. "Pindaric Criticism." In *Pindaros und Bakchylides*, ed. William Musgrave Calder III and Jacob Stern. Darmstadt: Wissenschaftliche Buchgesellschaft, 1970.

Youngman, Henny. *Take My Wife . . . Please! My Life and Laughs*. As confessed to Carroll Carroll. New York: Putnam, 1973.

Zetzel, James E. G. "Romane Memento: Justice and Judgment in *Aeneid* 6." *Transactions and Proceedings of the American Philological Association* 119 (1989): 263–84.

Index

Cullen, Countee, 4, 114, 126, 141–54; compared to Tolson, 225–26; contemporary criticisms of, 126, 143, 144, 148–49, 150–51; as "Uranian" (gay/homosexual/same-sex) person, 145, 393n42
Cullen, Rev. Frederick Asbury (Countee Cullen's adoptive father), 144
Cyclops. *See* Polyphemus, in *Odyssey* and *Invisible Man*

Daedalus and Icarus, in Ovid and Cullen, 142
Dalby, David, 293
Daltonism (color blindness), 203, 399n67
dance, in Greek and African public life, 217
Dante, *Inferno*, 173, 246; numerology in, 164; salvation of the soul in, 397n34
Darker Face of the Earth, The (Dove), 311; blindness of Augustus and Oedipus in, 334; compared to *The Chinaberry Tree* (Fauset), 136; as imitation of Sophocles' *Oedipus*, 330–40; incest in, 330–40; revisions of, 332–40, 414n31; title of, 331–32. *See also* Aristotle; incest; Oedipus; *Oedipus* (Sophocles); psychoanalytic criticism
Dartmouth College, 3, 61, 388n27
Davis, Gregson, 18–19, 400n7
"Dear Friends and Gentle Hearts" (Cullen), 144
Declaration of Independence, 65
Decline of the West, The (Spengler), 252
"Dedication" (Milosz), 313–14
Demeter: attempt to immortalize, 355–57; in Dove, 354–57, 368–69; rage (*mênis*) of: compared to Achilles'; rage (*mênis*) of: in *Homeric Hymn*, 367–68
Demeter and Persephone, 312, 341, 340–75 passim; replacing Orpheus and Eurydice in Rilke's *Sonnets to Orpheus*, 342
Demodocus (bard in the *Odyssey*), 166. *See also* Barber, Homer A., in *Invisible Man*
Demophoön, archaeology of the episode, 355–56, 416n60
deutero- or secondary learning, 3. *See also* Douglass, Frederick
dialectic: Frederick Douglass's study of, 51, 72–73. *See also Columbian Orator, The*; "Dialogue between a Master and a Slave"

"Dialogue between a Master and a Slave" (*The Columbian Orator*), 51, 72–73
Dido, in Vergil's *Aeneid*, 241, 404n51
difficult poetry: author's annotation of, in Thomas Gray, 212–13; Tolson, 212
Dilemma, The (Schuyler), parody of *The Crisis*, 274
Dindorf, Wilhelm, 104
Divine Comedy, numerology in, 164
dolls, and American racism, 325–28. *See also* Clark Doll Test; puppets and puppetry; *Through the Ivory Gate*
Don Quixote, 328
Dornseif, Franz, 210
Dorsey, David F., 141
Dostoevsky, Fyodor, 162, 164, 167, 176
double consciousness (Du Bois), 158–59
Douglass, Frederick, 3, 49–91; Christian ministry of, 62–65; compared to Phillis Wheatley, 2–3, 58, 61; as imagined by Ellison's Invisible Man, 89–91; naming of, 50; as orator, 386n65; parodies of pro-slavery Christians' hymns by, 82–83; as satirist, 263; self-education of, 49–50; self-portrait of, 73–82; in Tolson's *Libretto*, 233; as trickster, 70
Dove, Rita, 4, 5, 311–75; blending of ancient and modern worlds, 352 and passim; compared to Cullen and Robinson, 153–54; education of, in classics and German literature and language, 311–12; and Fauset, 136; love of puzzles and crosswords, 314; and Morrison, 47; as musician, 313; and satire, 263; as teacher, 312; on Tolson, 209, 215–16, 250; and Wheatley, 47. *See also Thomas and Beulah; Grace Notes; Through the Ivory Gate; The Darker Face of the Earth; Mother Love*
Dove-Viebahn, Aviva, 320; dramaturgic advice of, 335
Dozens, playing the. *See* "mother, your"
Dred Scott case (1857), 261, 263
Dr. Strangelove (Stanley Kubrick), 282–83
Dryden, John, 17, 35, 38, 379n9; Pindaric ode, conception of, 211; Tolson's allusion to, 223–24
Du Bois, W. E. B.: classical and sociological education of, 3–4, 94–95, 100, 105, 387n2; and Cicero, 107–24, 125–34, 258; feminism of, 129, 162, 189–91; literary

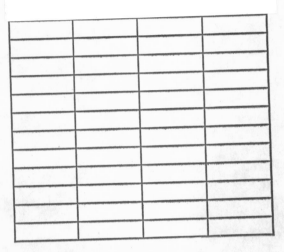

2019